P9-CQT-167

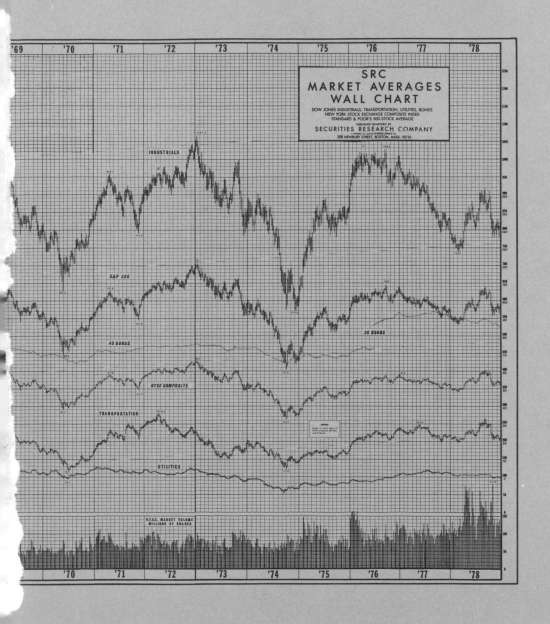

SRC
MARKET AVERAGES
WALL CHART

DOW JONES INDUSTRIALS, TRANSPORTATION, UTILITIES, BONDS
NEW YORK STOCK EXCHANGE COMPOSITE INDEX
STANDARD & POOR'S 500-STOCK AVERAGE

PUBLISHED QUARTERLY BY
SECURITIES RESEARCH COMPANY
208 NEWBURY STREET, BOSTON, MASS. 02116

PERSONAL INVESTING

The Irwin Series in Finance

Editors Myron J. Gordon   Robert W. Johnson
           University of Toronto   *Purdue University*

PERSONAL INVESTING

WILBUR W. WIDICUS
School of Business
Oregon State University

THOMAS E. STITZEL
School of Business
Boise State University

 1980   Third edition

RICHARD D. IRWIN, INC.   Homewood, Illinois   60430
Irwin-Dorsey Limited   Georgetown, Ontario   L7G 4B3

Endsheet illustrations courtesy of Securities Research Company,
208 Newbury Street, Boston, Massachusetts 02116

© RICHARD D. IRWIN, INC., 1971, 1976, and 1980

All rights reserved. No part of this publication may be
reproduced, stored in a retrieval system, or transmitted,
in any form or by any means, electronic, mechanical,
photocopying, recording, or otherwise, without the prior
written permission of the publisher.

ISBN 0-256-02341-7
Library of Congress Catalog Card No. 79–90536

Printed in the United States of America

1 2 3 4 5 6 7 8 9 0 A 7 6 5 4 3 2 1 0

LEARNING SYSTEMS COMPANY—
a division of Richard D. Irwin, Inc.—has developed a
PROGRAMMED LEARNING AID
to accompany texts in this subject area.
Copies can be purchased through your bookstore
or by writing PLAIDS.
1818 Ridge Road, Homewood, Illinois 60430.

TO ISABEL AND BONNIE

Preface

Much has happened in the world of investments since the last edition of *Personal Investing* was published. Security regulations have changed, security markets have greatly altered, and the importance of certain investments—options, commodities, and real property for example—has increased significantly. These and many other developments have been incorporated into the Third Edition of *Personal Investing,* but without altering the basic nature of the book. It remains true to its name by examining the world of investments from the viewpoint of the individual investor.

The authors' approach to investing assumes that investors must first learn about the environment in which they will operate. That is, they should know about the risks associated with different types of investments and the returns to be expected from them. They should be knowledgeable about the participants in the investment process—a group including organizations issuing and selling investment securities, firms which sell investment advice and information, and the regulators of the securities industry. After mastering these "basics" the investor may plan an investment program designed to use available financial resources to attain specific financial goals. This book provides information that allows investors to follow this approach to personal investing. Previous coursework in or knowledge of accounting, finance, or economics is not presumed. Pertinent topics from these areas are contained in *Personal Investing.*

The world of investments is complex. To understand its operation one must fluently speak its language. To this end, detailed definitions of investment terms are written as they occur during the logical presentation of the material. In addition, an expanded glossary provides brief definitions of all important investment terms. For the mathematically inclined, four end-of-chapter appendixes show how to calculate compound interest and growth rates, bond values, how to use a common stock valuation model, and how to value commercial real property investments. Numerous references and end-of-chapter reading lists enable students to pursue topics of special interest in greater depth. More than 150 illustrations of security certificates, tax forms, price charts, tables, and graphs are presented to add realism to the textual material. Of particular interest and uniqueness are chapters dealing with the tax aspects of investing, speculative investments, real property investments, and planning and managing an investment program. At the suggestion of our readers, increased coverage has been provided of options, investment in precious metals, investment timing, and economic analysis. Brief explanations of the concepts of random walk, efficient markets, and security alphas and betas are also included.

The world of investing is dynamic. New laws and regulations are passed and old ones are constantly being revised. Social conditions and national goals shift—witness the recent emphasis on increasing our sources of energy, containing inflation, and ecological planning. These and countless other changes affect investors' decisions. The investor's successful quest for wealth and security requires a continuous effort to up-date and reappraise information of all types. Change is not necessarily bad or harmful because it often provides the alert investor with opportunity for profit. This book points out ways by which investors may identify changing conditions and describes ways to use this knowledge to best advantage.

The *quintessence* of this book is embodied in its name—*Personal Investing*. As previously mentioned, it is designed for individuals. The word *investing* in the title points to the *action* emphasis of the book. The writing style can be described as providing useful information, "handles" on the concepts, and ways to relate the material to each person's circumstances.

Personal Investing has benefited greatly from the many valuable criticisms and suggestions of colleagues and friends. We are particularly grateful to the stock exchanges, regulatory agencies, investment information services, brokers, financial advisors, and reviewers for the time and effort they have expended on our behalf. Any errors or omissions which remain are our joint responsibility, of course, and in no way reflect upon the efforts of persons who have helped and advised us. We continue to welcome criticism of this book and suggestions for improving it.

January 1980   Wilbur W. Widicus
                                                                 Thomas E. Stitzel

Contents

vices: *Information and advisory services. Personal investment counsel. Stock market courses.* Other educational activities: *Investment literature. Investment clubs.*

part three
TYPES OF INVESTMENTS

ance. *Risk characteristics of new issues.* Turnaround situations: *Examples of a turnaround. Management as a factor. Risk characteristics of turnaround situations.* Trend buckers: *Examples of trend buckers. Risk characteristics of trend buckers.*

part four
INVESTMENT TIMING

part five
MANAGING YOUR INVESTMENTS

strategy for capital gains. Timing of investment income: *Taking losses or gains in a particular year. Tax treatment of debt securities sold at a discount.* Investments providing tax-free or reduced-tax income: *Municipal securities.* Investment in assets which receive preferential tax treatment: *Tax shelters. Retirement plans which defer taxes. Investments exempt from state income taxes.* Keeping records: *Keeping records for income taxes. Keeping records for investment purposes.*

part one

THE WHAT AND WHY OF INVESTING

1

Investment perspectives

INTRODUCTION

Stories of wealth accumulation are a part of history because they reflect a basic motivation of people to make their lives easier. *Anyone Can Still Make a Million* is one of a large group of books written to appeal to investors.[1] Many other writers describe ways to "get rich quick." *Personal Investing* does not follow this theme. This book's purpose is to provide a clear understanding of the investment environment. Opportunities and difficulties are discussed in a practical manner. Long established types of investments as well as the latest innovations are presented so that an individual can design a personalized investment plan. The reader will become a trained observer, aware of risks and returns, of the terminology of securities and procedures—or in other words the reader will become educated about the world of investments. A remark attributed to Frank Leahy, the outstanding Notre Dame football coach, expresses this sentiment in another way, "Luck seems to always go to the side having the heaviest tackles." Knowing the ins and outs of investing does not guarantee success, but very few people have been consistently successful without a thorough comprehension of the field of investments. *This book was written to provide a framework within which an individual can intelligently set investment goals and steer a course to achieve these desired results.*

---

[1] Morton Shulman, *Anyone Can Still Make a Million* (New York: McGraw-Hill, 1972).

SUCCESSES AND FAILURES

Countless instances of dramatic investment results have been recorded. Typical of the prosperous examples is the overnight wealth that befell many investors in oil and various mineral ventures. Florida land booms have been well publicized. Polaroid, Xerox, and IBM are companies that have rewarded their original investors with phenomenal gains in short time spans. This list could go on and on. However, there is another side to the coin, and a different group of experiences remains all too vivid in the minds of many.

Thousands of people have made financial commitments to enterprises which subsequently declined in value and often went bankrupt. Many of these cases involved fraudulent schemes, but vast numbers were honest ventures that for one reason or another just did not work. In a delightfully written book entitled *Wiped Out* the author relates how a fortune was lost by investing in the stock market during a period in which stock prices in general were rising to unprecedented levels.[2] This experience is not uncommon!

The purpose of this discussion has not been to dampen potential investors' spirits, but rather to emphasize the point that wealth is subject to both expansion and contraction. In other words, assets can grow or be depleted, and over a long period of time, both results will probably occur.

INVESTING DEFINED

Much confusion stems from lack of clear understanding of what is meant by various investment terms. Definitions will be stressed in each chapter to minimize this problem. The reader is advised to begin building an investment vocabulary immediately. Preparation of a glossary of terms similar to that appearing in the back of this book should prove to be most helpful.

At the end of a long day, a farmer announced to his wife that he ". . . was going to invest in the stock market because I would like to earn a dollar without having to sweat for it." An actor was sitting in an overstuffed chair in a thickly carpeted, air-conditioned Beverly Hills bro-

---

[2] Anonymous investor, *Wiped Out: How I Lost a Fortune in the Stock Market While the Averages Were Making New Highs* (New York: Simon & Schuster, 1966).

kerage office. In these plush surroundings he remarked as he watched the stock prices flash on the screen before him, "This investing sure beats going down to the race track." A secretary described her resources for investing as "mad money" and as funds with which she could "gamble." Between classes one college student told another ". . . this investment is just a hunch on my part—pure speculation. . . ." A husband and wife asked how "they could accumulate funds for the purpose of their children's education." Each of these quotes illustrates a different concept of what is loosely called *investing*.

It is highly desirable that reader and authors have similar thoughts triggered by this, the most important term used in this book. A framework for describing *investing* is presented in Table 1-1.

TABLE 1-1
Investing distinguished

Term	Research	Time span	Expected Loss or gain
Gambling..............	None	Short	Substantial
Speculating............	Substantial	Short	Substantial
Investing	Substantial	Long	Moderate

Each of these terms can be used appropriately to describe efforts designed to acquire and maintain wealth. Gambling is not limited to the Nevada or New Jersey casinos. It is a term that can be applied to actions based on tips, whims, or unexplained impulses. For example, a secretary repeats that her boss's golfing partner had said that a rival company was about to unveil an amazing new product. The purchase of that company's stock based solely on that information would indeed be a "gamble." The decision would be made without any attempt to accumulate and analyze other facts. Short-term or even overnight profits would be expected. Furthermore, the gains envisioned would occur rapidly so the annual return would be very high, even with a relatively small price rise.[3] Usually the gambler is aware that price declines could result. This is recognition of a potential risk, but no serious attempt is made to compare it with the anticipated gain.

---

[3] Suppose the price rises from $10 to $11 per share in one week. This is a 10 percent gain. However, returns are usually expressed on an annual basis. In this instance the conversion is made by multiplying the percentage increase by the number of weeks in a year, for example 10% × 52 = 520%, a healthy rise!

Speculators also seek fast action, but they are careful to appraise the situation. A rumor may create interest in a security, but a thorough study will be undertaken before a commitment is made. In his first rule of investing, Bernard Baruch cautioned against speculation unless it is made a full-time job.[4] As in gambling the potential risks and rewards are high and the time horizon is short.

The distinguishing characteristics of investing are the time span and risk and reward considerations. While an investor would not be upset by a quick profit, neither would such a person be disheartened by an immediate drop in stock price. Patience is a necessary virtue of the investor. True investing is a balancing of potential risks and rewards at a moderate level. In other words, investors are not trying to achieve wealth overnight by putting all their money on one horse.

It should be made perfectly clear that this presentation makes no value judgments regarding the activities of gambling, speculating, and investing. Such a decision is left entirely for each individual. It is interesting to observe, however, that any one person might undertake all of these activities at some time or other during a wealth-building career. This book focuses on investment processes, with occasional discussions of speculative techniques.

The preceding paragraphs provide a basis for distinguishing between investing and other types of activities. There remains, however, additional discussion necessary to present a refined definition. In the first place, what kinds of commitments are meant? While money is the most common form of a pledge, several other interpretations are used. For example, Mary is investing in her future by spending time and money to receive a college education. In this book *investing* means the commitment of money.

Another point needing clarification involves the use for which money is to be committed. Real estate, collectors' items, and animals are but a few of literally thousands of different assets which people in general consider to be investment media. This book is written primarily for those interested in acquiring securities, such as stocks or bonds. However, one chapter is devoted to real estate, and brief references are made to other investment opportunities outside the area of securities.

Investing then means *the committing of money for the purchase of*

---

[4] Bernard Baruch, *My Own Story* (New York: Henry Holt & Co., 1957), p. 254.

assets, primarily of the security type, based on a careful analysis of risks and rewards anticipated over a period of one year or more.[5]

INVESTING PURPOSES

On the surface it might seem that all persons who invest desire to accumulate wealth. While this is perhaps the most common goal, it is certainly not the only purpose. One motivation has been superbly described in a best selling book, *The Money Game.*[6] In a most convincing manner the author tells how various individuals invest for the sheer excitement of being involved in the stock market. The playing of the game is the real stimulus for these people. The actual dollar gains and losses are secondary matters—a way of keeping score.

This gaming desire is evidenced in another manner. A host of parlor games based on the stock market has appeared in the last few years. "Transaction," "Buy or Sell," "Broker," "Stock Market," "Walstrete," "Acquire," and "Stocks and Bonds" are representatives.

Even those investors who are primarily concerned about wealth accumulation have differences in their investment purposes. One group desires cash returns on a regular basis for current needs. These people are also concerned about the safety of their investment. This need to preserve capital, coupled with current income requirements, dictates the types of securities that will be held. Typical of this group of investors would be a retired couple that needs income for living expenses. They cannot afford to risk loss of principal, and they would be hesitant to consume any of the wealth they have previously accumulated.

Investors receive returns in two ways. *Income* is provided in the form of interest or dividends. The other source is known as a *capital gain.* This is achieved whenever a security is sold above its purchase price.[7] Gains occur sporadically and only when the price has advanced and when the investor *actually sells.* Income is normally received regularly. This difference in the time pattern of returns provides one way

---

[5] The terms *investing* and *speculating* will be used whenever it is important that they be distinguished. However, in the interest of writing brevity, investing should be understood to include speculative activity.

[6] Adam Smith, *The Money Game,* 2d ed. (New York: Random House, 1968).

[7] The opposite can and, of course, does occur, and is a capital loss. For income tax purposes a capital gain refers to net profits realized when the securities have been owned for at least one year. A discussion of tax aspects of investing is presented in Chapter 15.

of studying an investor's objectives. If this person relies on a definite amount of return from security holdings the returns are probably needed for current uses. Thus, income often provides for present consumption; capital gains are the normal means of acquiring wealth for future consumption. This describes what is essentially a "tradeoff" situation. Emphasis on capital gains usually dictates holding securities that do not provide much income. Investments that offer substantial income payments normally have relatively stable prices. A young couple might represent the group hopeful of capital gain. Salary income provides for their living expenses, but they wish to build an estate for future needs, such as their children's educations and their own retirement.

The income versus capital gain is not strictly an either-or situation. It is a matter of emphasis. Many securities offer a combination of moderate income and some potential for price appreciation. So, there is really a broad spectrum of purposes for investors seeking monetary returns.

TYPES OF INVESTMENTS

The purpose of this section is to call attention to the myriad of potential investment media. A detailed examination of the "world of investments" would fill a library. The discussion that follows is meant to be suggestive and to make the reader aware of the hosts of possibilities.

Securities

Securities are certificates evidencing debt or ownership.[8] They are available in an abundant variety of types but are usually grouped into two broad classes—stocks and bonds. Common stocks are the most popular versions of ownership, with a lesser role being played by preferred stocks. Each of these categories has numerous sets of subclassifications. For example, sophisticated investors are aware of Class B, nonvoting, common stock and of Series D, 7 percent, cumulative, participating convertible preference shares. A detailed discussion of pre-

---

[8] Several types of savings plans use a certificate. These and passbook savings accounts are discussed in Chapter 6.

ferred and common stock may be found in Chapters 8 and 9, respectively.

Evidences of debt include bonds. They are classified according to the type of entity that has borrowed money and issued bond certificates. Knowledgeable persons have learned about *corporates*, including convertibles, and *governments* which embrace Treasury, agency, and municipal obligations. These issues are covered in Chapters 7 and 8.

Another category of securities may be broadly termed partnership interests. This group consists of many innovations and deserves investor attention. Many city dwellers have become absentee farmers through this vehicle. Several companies offer programs in which they will buy, feed, and breed animals in return for the investor's dollar. The value of this investment grows as offspring are sold. Beavers and beef cattle are available in this type of animal management contract. Interest in land, to be planted in citrus trees, for example, is offered under a similar plan. This, incidentally, has been advertised for people near retirement. The commitment is made, the land purchased, trees planted, watered, sprayed, and so on and in a few years when the investor retires and his or her salary income drops, the harvest begins and profits hopefully materialize!

Housing condominiums resemble the lease-a-cow plans. The buyer acquires a primary residence or a vacation home and part interest in common facilities, such as a swimming pool and a restaurant. When the owner wishes, a management company will rent the property. Real Estate Investment Trusts stress investment in income-producing property, such as office buildings, apartments, and shopping centers.

Several billion dollars have been committed by investors in the past few years in oil drilling participations. Many of these are organized as limited partnerships and are designed mainly for wealthy individuals. Special tax laws that apply to the search for oil and gas make such investments especially attractive to persons having high incomes. The basic plan is again the same. For this and the other programs described, a syndication of investors is formed. Then a group of professionals, for example geologists, animal husbandmen, horticulturists, or real estate property managers, is employed to manage the assets for the interest of the investor.

Popularity of types of security investments waxes and wanes. Recently, stock options as described in Chapter 11, have been the most rapidly growing form.

Real estate

"Land is not nearly so exciting as the stock market. You'll miss those big surprises every morning." These statements were used in an advertisement by a firm seeking to dramatize a difference between securities and land investments. Security prices, in general, and common stocks, in particular, tend to move up and down with some rapidity. Property values also change, but in many areas this pattern is seen as an almost uninterrupted price rise. Most securities are priced continuously and have instantaneous marketability. Real estate values, on the other hand, are not known unless someone provides the time and expense required for appraisals. Even then accurate results are not guaranteed and will not be revealed until an actual sale is completed. In spite of uncertain valuation and a lack of ready marketability, thousands of investors are attracted to ventures in land. This interest is especially keen when people experience anxieties over inflation and/or declining stock prices, such as during 1974. In the long run, investors realize the supply of land is fixed while the demand continues to grow. Expressed somewhat differently, "Land, air, and water will never go out of style. Combine this fact with the tremendous population rise and the great demand for investment capital to develop our natural resources to meet the needs of this population...."[9]

There are several methods of classifying real estate investments, but perhaps the simplest division is between raw and developed land. Placed in the former grouping would be areas close to population centers—out-of-town, but in a path of probable development. Recreational property such as river frontage is another example. Farms would be a third. In general, undeveloped land offers the greatest appreciation potential, but it is also accompanied by the highest risk.

Developed property is most often sought by persons seeking current income. These ventures are somewhat less risky. They might involve shopping centers, residential additions, and office buildings. These and other land investment opportunities are discussed in Chapter 12.

Notwithstanding the attractiveness of real estate investing, there are many people who choose to exclude this vehicle from their commitments. These individuals might say:

---

[9] Walter Youngquist, *Our Natural Resources: How to Invest in Them* (New York: Frederick Fell, 1966), p. 13. This book has been updated and extensively revised in Walter Youngquist, *Investing in Natural Resources: Today's Guide to Tomorrow's Needs* (Homewood, Ill.: Dow Jones-Irwin, 1975). © 1975 by Dow Jones-Irwin.

Stocks have the advantage that they don't have to be mowed, picked clear of empty beer cans, and are not subject to curb, paving, and sewer assessments. If they don't produce current income, they aren't taxed. Higher and higher real estate taxes are becoming one of the best recommendations for stock ownership. Also if you don't like the weather in Mandan, North Dakota (35° below recently), you can put your stocks in your hat and move to Florida or Arizona. Try doing that with 160 acres, or six city lots.[10]

Commodities

Arthur W. Cutten, a Canadian bookkeeper, parlayed $90 into $300 million over a 30-year time span at the turn of the century. J. Ogden Armour, who headed his namesake meat packing firm familiar to most people, lost almost $150 million. These fortunes were made and lost in the same activity, and in a manner that is unknown or not understood by millions of investors. The efforts involved *trading commodity futures.* This term refers to the buying and selling of raw agricultural products, livestock, precious metals, foreign currencies, and most recently, interest rate futures. Beginning with apples and ending with zinc, the list includes cocoa and copper, gold and GNMA bonds, mercury and molasses, platinum and plywood, potatoes and pork bellies, oats and orange juice, and stud lumber and Swiss francs. A basic discussion of this type of investment is found in Chapter 11.

Collectors' items

Thousands of items are not particularly useful themselves, but they nevertheless have value because they offer pleasure to collectors. The goods they covet also provide a medium for investors. There is a limited supply of these items, whether there is only one, as an original painting, or only a limited number, as multiple copies of stamps. As more people become interested, the demand rises, forcing price increases. This situation provides the investor with the essential ingredient—an opportunity to buy low and sell high. So the connoisseurs are joined by others who want to profit by trading.

Paintings have long been a source of interest to both groups. Recent innovations have facilitated investor involvement. Several companies

---

[10] Walter Youngquist, "Fortnight Notes," a bimonthly publication of Craig-Hallum, Inc., February 9, 1970, p. 2.

buy and sell art for profit. Shares in these firms can be bought to give the individual an indirect interest in the business. This allows participation in lesser amounts than would be required to deal directly in art.

Thousands of people are numismatists and philatelists. These coin and stamp collectors also include investors in their groups. "I saw the market conditions and realized my money was dwindling ... I was fighting a losing cause in trying to set aside money for my children's educations. Stamps seemed the one way to assure me that the dollars wouldn't remain static or go downward."[11] This man and nine others put up $500,000 to establish a fund for stamp investing.

As the list of investment possibilities grows, it becomes more unusual. Collectors pay substantial sums for rare books, old bottles, and three-foot lengths of aged barbed wire. Returns from selected investment alternatives are presented in Table 1–2. Wherever the collector's interest appears, the investor will not be far behind!

TABLE 1–2
Returns from selected investment alternatives

Investment	1968–78 compound annual growth rate
Chinese ceramics	19.2%
Gold	16.3
Stamps	15.4
Old masters	13.0
Coins	13.0
Diamonds	12.6
Oil	11.5
Farmland	10.6
Housing	9.2
Silver	9.1
Foreign exchange	6.2
Consumer Price Index	6.1
Bonds	6.1
Stocks	2.8

Source: R. S. Salomon, Jr., "Stocks Are Still the Only Bargain Left," *Portfolio Planning*, Salomon Brothers Research Department, July 3, 1978.

It is hoped that this discussion has helped the reader become aware of a wide variety of potential investment media because this is a book about *personal* investing. Aroused interest can be pursued in the references cited.

---

[11] Melodie Bowsher, "As Other Investments Sour, More Americans Turn to Rare Stamps," *The Wall Street Journal*, February 4, 1970, p. 1.

PERSONALIZING THE INVESTMENT PROCESS

The personal emphasis of this text can be readily brought into focus by a relatively simple and yet highly important exercise—the preparation of an individual statement of net worth. This effort involves listing the market value of items owned (assets) and then subtracting amounts owed to others (liabilities) to arrive at an estimate of individual net worth. The concept is to imagine converting all one's assets into cash and then paying off debts just as might be done if a person wanted to sell everything, settle accounts, and move away with an amount of cash as the net result of efforts to date. The personal balance sheet, which is again discussed in Chapter 16, is shown in Table 1–3.

TABLE 1–3
Simplified statement of net worth

Assets	
Cash	$ 1,000
Investments	4,000
Savings deposits	3,000
Cash value of life insurance	500
Home and furnishings	55,000
Automobile	3,000
Other assets	6,000
Total assets	$72,500

Liabilities	
Consumer debt*	$ 300
Home Mortgage loan	36,000
Total liabilities	36,300
Net Worth	$36,200

* Unpaid bills, credit card debt, department store credit, and so on. This amount should be the average of this type of debt.

Readers are encouraged to prepare their own statement at this point and to update the information when finishing the book. Not only can comparisons be made over the time elapsed but also the learning process in the ensuing chapters will be enhanced by keeping in mind a means for measuring wealth accumulation.

OUTLINE FOR THE BOOK

This book is written in five parts. In the first part the "what" and "why" of investing are discussed. Basic concepts are presented for application. The perspectives just discussed, and the investment returns and risks attending them, are considered. This provides a framework for analyzing any type of investment.

Part Two examines the organization of security markets, sources of investment information, and financial statement interpretation. The impact of regulation on the people who participate in the investment process is discussed. These chapters provide the "where" and part of the "how" background which is essential to a full understanding of the investment world.

Part Three describes the many types of investments available to individuals. Characteristics of savings accounts at different financial institutions are discussed. A study of the major types of bonds follows. Preferred and common stock are examined, and a framework of analysis is given. Investment companies are treated in some detail. Speculative types of investments are presented next. In the last chapter, qualitative and quantitative factors for analyzing real estate investments are presented.

Part Four covers the timing or the "when" of investing. It features methods of relating security prices to economic conditions and to their historical price behavior.

Investing must be "personalized." That is to say, the individual is the key to any investment situation. Part Five, Managing Your Investments, emphasizes this belief. Tax considerations are presented so the reader can appreciate this aspect of the environment. The concluding chapter brings together the many factors that must be evaluated in establishing a personal investment program. Personal investment objectives, resources to meet them, and individual constraints are emphasized. Special effort has been made to offer the reader information that will be of lasting value in the quest for wealth accumulation.

SUMMARY

The objective of this book is to provide a framework within which an individual can set personal investment goals and steer a course to achieve the desired results. The path of wealth accumulation is not free from difficulties and disappointments.

Security buying and selling activities can be identified as *gambling* when a person tries for large gains in short periods of time without making an effort to analyze each situation before acting. *Speculators* nvestors prepare their personal statements of net

_INGS

tor. *Wiped Out: How I Lost a Fortune in the Stock Mar-_ _e Averages Were Making New Highs._ New York: Simon & _66.

d M. *My Own Story.* New York: Henry Holt & Co , 1957.

olburn. *Dun & Bradstreet's Guide to Your Investments,* New York: Crowell Publishing, 1978.

ert. *The Naked Investor.* New York: Delacorte, 1977.

, Claude. *The Common Sense Way to Stock Market Profits.* New . New American Library, 1978.

rg, Jerome R. *Managing Your Own Money.* New York: *Newsweek,* 9.

, Maury. *Land Investment.* Homewood, Ill.: Dow Jones-Irwin, 1975.

nan Morton. *Anyone Can Still Make a Million.* New York: Bantam Books, 1973.

ith, Adam. *The Money Game.* New York: Random House, 1968.

ith, Albert C. *The Individual Investor in Tomorrow's Stock Market.* New York: Vantage, 1977.

Van Caspel, Venita. *The New Money Dynamics.* Reston, Va.: Reston, 1978.

Williams, Darnell L. *A Guide to Stocks and Bonds for the Beginner.* New York: Vantage, 1979.

Wyckoff, Peter. *The Language of Wall Street.* New York: Hopkinson & Blake, 1973.

Youngquist, Walter. *Investing in Natural Resources: Today's Guide to To-morrow's Needs.* Homewood, Ill.: Dow Jones-Irwin, 1975.

QUESTIONS

1. Define investing.
2. Distinguish between investing...
   ample of each activity in the...
   What is the purpose of inves...
3. Briefly discuss opportunitie...
   and collectors' items.
4. Cite advantages and disa...
   media listed in Question...
5. Discuss what makes an...
6. Many books of the ty...
   Why do you suppose...
7. this book?
   Why do so many...
8. worth every year?...

a...
and...
items,...
open to...
unlimited....
wealth accum...

This is a basi...
and when" of pers...

PROBLEMS

1. Interview some people wh...
   what they do. Do you think t...
2. Look for the label or some ident...
   of clothing which you are wearing...
   lowing information about this comp...
   a. Location of its headquarters.
   b. Sales and earnings for the last year.
   c. Recent price of its stock.
3. Next time you go shopping make a list of eac...
   you have visited. Then look up the stock price...
   Why do you suppose this information is not avai...
   companies you listed?
4. Interview two or more persons who consider themselve...
   Determine what types of investments they make—stocks,...
   tate, commodities, and so on. Learn why they do or do not o...
   the alternative investment types mentioned in this chapter.
5. Prepare a statement of net worth for yourself.

SELECTED REA...

Anonymous inve...
ket While t...
Schuster, 1...
Baruch, C. C...
Hardy, 1978-79...

Heller, Rob...
Rosenberg...
York...
Rosenbe...
197...

Seldin...
Shul...

Sm...
S...

Risk and return

INTRODUCTION

Most investors are primarily concerned with deciding what is a good stock to buy. This is an extremely difficult problem. Part of this difficulty is simply because no one really knows which particular shares will increase in price. A further complication concerns the individual seeking an investment, for it is this person's unique circumstances that will largely determine the answer. An analogy may help to illustrate this thought. The question "Where is a good place to go fishing?" will bring a wide range of replies, most of which will be a series of questions prefaced by the phrase, "It all depends on...." How good a fisherman are you? What kind of tackle do you have? Are you patient? How far are you willing to drive? What kind of fish do you like to eat? The point is that whether one is trying to "gather" fish or dollars, the circumstances surrounding each individual situation must be carefully considered.

A suitable investment for one person may not be appropriate for another. Does this mean that all investors do not share a common desire to buy securities which will increase in price? Not at all, because a major reason for investing is wealth accumulation. The various ways of properly matching investors and investments are the result of how two factors relate to the individual. These factors are known in broad terms as *risk* and *return*. They are the most important characteristics of any security. Investment risks must be recognized and understood before they can be avoided or at least minimized. Returns offered to s should be appraised in the light of the risks that are incurred. e surface relationship between risk and return is really quite ightforward. A moment's reflection should illustrate the connection. A test pilot earns more than an airline pilot. A college football coach is paid more than a professor of business administration. Many people earn more by working for themselves than they would if they were employed by someone else. The reader can probably think of numerous additional examples of past wealth accumulation that involved substantial risks of health, job security, or business failure. As a general statement, then, risk and return *tend* to move in the same direction. This is illustrated in Figure 2-1. The graph shows that higher returns are achieved by accepting greater risks.[1] It should be emphasized that this is a general relationship and there are many exceptions. An individual does not acquire wealth simply by taking large risks. This is a tendency averaged over many cases and for long periods of time. In the short run and in particular instances, increasing risk may only lead to financial ruin.

The units of measurement are not given in Figure 2-1. This is because there are many ways to evaluate risk and return. Precise calculations and empirical evidence are best postponed until there is a clearer understanding of what is meant by the two factors. At the moment then, the case will rest on an intuitive logic that risk and return, in general, are commensurate.

FIGURE 2-1
Relationship of risk and return in investing

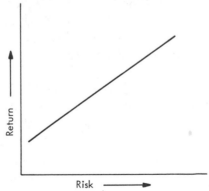

---

[1] For brevity the terms *return* and *risk* are used alone in this discussion. However, the reader should remember that the modifiers "expected" or "anticipated" are implied since it is the *future* that is of concern.

Risk is commonly defined as the chance or possibility of injury, damage, or loss. This exclusive emphasis on negative aspects is not necessary. The potential for gain is the attraction for most investments. Risk is involved here, too. This may sound odd, but it is really quite logical to consider change in either direction.[2] Note also that risk focuses on returns in the *future*. The words "chance," "possibility," and "potential" all refer to some event that is yet to happen. A determination of the degree of risk is based mainly on past records, but the purpose of the appraisal is definitely for application in the future.

The term *risk* shall be used in this book to mean the degree of the possibility of gain or loss occurring in investments.[3] A major objective of this book is to identify risks encountered in the investment process and to use this knowledge to maximize profits or minimize losses.

TYPES OF RISK

The previous definition presents a broad concept of risk. There is a need to be more precise because the term has many dimensions. The gain or loss from investments is the result of a number of different factors. Securities can be graded with respect to these factors or happenings. Grading is done by looking back and examining investment performance when certain events occur. The causative factors are identified with risk and referred to as *types of risk*.[4]

The investment process is basically concerned with putting money to work for the purpose of earning *future* returns. This involves risk because no one knows what actually will happen in the future. No investment is absolutely safe. All alternatives carry some risk. The following sections describe a framework for identifying risks and provide a means for classifying or grading securities with respect to the degree of each type of risk.

---

[2] The concept of risk that includes both upward and downward movements is presented in Harry Sauvain, *Investment Management*, 4th ed. (Englewood Cliffs, N.J.: Prentice-Hall, 1973), p. 13. Some of the following discussion is also based on Sauvain's presentation in his Chapters 4–7.

[3] Some writers distinguish between risk and uncertainty, using the former term to identify situations in which future events can be described in probability terms. For example, the probability of a "head" appearing with the toss of a coin is 0.5. Uncertainty is used where probabilities cannot readily be assigned to the occurrence of future events.

[4] Considerable research has been done in quantifying risk and relating it to returns. The efficient market hypothesis, random walk, and the capital asset pricing model are all concepts which are treated extensively in the more advanced investment textbooks listed at the end of this chapter.

Financial risk

The most obvious kind of risk is known as financial risk. This refers to *the uncertainty of future returns from a security because of changes in the financial capacity of the organization that issued the security.* There is a wide range of possible variation in financial ability. To facilitate analysis of this risk, securities are grouped into the broad categories of bonds, preferred stocks, and common stocks.

Bonds and preferred stock. Almost all bonds promise to pay interest and principal according to a preset plan. The financial capacity of the bond issuer determines whether or not these pledges will be honored. Bonds are evaluated by appraising past records, current financial health, and future prospects. The organization least likely to undergo drastic change in financial ability is the U.S. government. So long as it has the power to print money and levy taxes, it is hard to imagine that it could go "bankrupt." This means, then, that U.S. Treasury bonds are the safest form of security investment with respect to financial risk. By convention we say that these bonds are the highest grade.

Other governmental bodies also issue bonds—both foreign countries and domestic units such as state and local governments. These securities usually are considered to be slightly higher in financial risk. That is, they are assigned lower grades. Corporate bonds are also rated on the issuer's ability to make payments. Many companies that issue bonds have unquestioned credit. Others are not financially strong. Some have had wide variations in their profits. These particular securities may represent situations in which the future returns are uncertain. However, financial risk is a matter of degree. Some bonds are superbly secure and are thus high grade while others are of questionable value and thus are low grade.

In general, future returns from preferred stocks are less certain than those expected from corporate bonds. This is because failure to meet the bond obligations results in a default, whereas inability to pay preferred dividends has much less severe consequences. Firms are more hesitant to forego bond interest payments than they are to reduce preferred stock dividends.[5] Again, there is a wide range of grades of pre-

---

[5] An additional margin of safety is present for a firm's bondholders that is missing for the preferred stockholder. This is because the claims of the former group come first. If a company were liquidated, nothing would be paid to the owners of preferred stock until the claims of creditors, including bondholders, had been met. A further discussion of these priorities may be found in Chapter 7.

ferred stocks with each one being dependent upon the likelihood that dividends will be paid.

Common stock. Common stockholders are residual owners. This means they are entitled to payments *only* after the other security holders have had their claims satisfied. Future dividends may be quite uncertain in a company which has a large amount of bonds and/or preferred stock outstanding. This is especially true if the firm itself is not expected to enjoy uninterrupted prosperity. Being the last in line to receive company payments also means the owner of common stock will be the first to suffer when the firm experiences bad times. This event may be rather remote for some businesses, while in others a downturn must be considered a distinct possibility. With common stocks there is also a wide range of financial risks with grades being assigned accordingly.

Grading securities. The preceding discussion can be summarized by the illustration in Figure 2–2. This chart shows a general pattern of increasing grade of security with regard to financial risk of common stock, preferred stock and corporate bonds, and government bonds, respectively. This is a general trend, and many exceptions exist. Hence, the graph has been drawn to show overlap between the different security categories. A few common stocks are of higher grade than certain types of government bonds because the bonds carry a higher risk of future payments compared to those common stock issues. This ranking is in spite of the priorities which add a protective factor to the bondholder claims.

So far, no mention has been made about what is specifically meant by *financial ability*. This term refers to income generating power and to a lesser extent to the composition of assets and liabilities. The financial risk of securities is appraised by a careful review of these and other factors for each issuing government or firm. In the former organization, the most crucial measure is the source of revenues. For the business group, the key information is the earning power of the firm. But these figures are only a beginning. A thorough analysis requires much additional data, the evaluation of which is a complicated task. Fortunately, there are professional security rating agencies. Their methods and other techniques are discussed in Chapters 7, 8, and 9.

Financial risk can also be called *business risk*. This term is used because it draws attention to the operation or *business* of an organization. The concern is that although a company's present financial condition may be sound, there is a possibility that its products or ser-

FIGURE 2–2
Security grading and financial risk

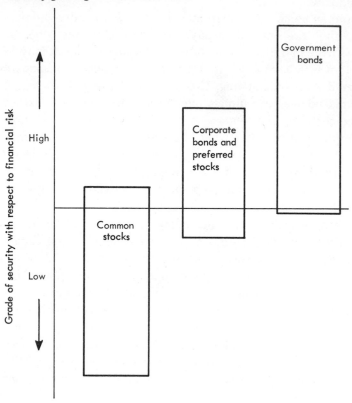

vices might become outmoded. Few people doubt that the communications industry, in general, and American Telephone and Telegraph Company, in particular, are in any serious danger of survival in the near or even distant future. However, there is concern about the "staying power" of some firms, especially new ones or those producing certain types of goods or a single product. Most people can readily recall several automobile makers who ceased to exist. Some railroads and movie producers have unstable pasts and rather uncertain futures. New York and Cleveland are examples of municipal bond issuers who experienced financial troubles in recent times. The term *financial risk* is used in preference to *business risk* because the concept is applicable to governmental bodies as well as corporations.

Market risk

Market risk is the uncertainty of future prices because of changes in investor attitudes. This dimension of risk can be identified by observing the price movements of securities while they are being traded. One may ask why these prices change. Literally millions of people have pondered this question. Many answers have been given but most of them express, in one way or another, the notion that it is investor expectations which cause prices to move. These expectations are directly related to feelings about financial ability. However, waves of optimism and pessimism sweep investors' minds. These shifts in attitudes sometimes occur without changes in financial capacity.[6] They may be termed broadly as *market psychology.*

It is usually very difficult to tell whether a price change has been caused by a change in financial ability or by a shift in investor attitudes or something else. Nonetheless, there can be no doubt that market psychology is a factor of influence on stock prices. Credence to this statement can be derived from a brief study of the severe decline on the New York Stock Exchange in 1974. Based on daily figures during the September 3–17 period, there were 4,108 instances of stock issues trading at new low prices for the year. This is a marked contrast to the ten cases during the same period in which issues reached record highs.[7] The extremely large number of record lows in proportion to new highs was not due just to changes in financial ability but was caused mainly by a widespread pessimistic feeling. Companies whose outlooks were not at all bleak were dragged down by the general fears that were then prevailing.

There are other times when the influence of market psychology can be identified rather easily. These situations arise when a crisis is created by the occurrence of some unforeseen event having widespread effects. Table 2–1 lists some surprise announcements which had marked effects on stock prices.

Grading securities. The concept of grading securities with respect to financial risk also applies to the analysis of market risk. In this case,

---

[6] One of the most widely adopted ways to measure investor attitudes toward a company is to examine the ratio of its stock market price to its earnings. A discussion of price-earnings ratios is presented in Chapters 9 and 13.

[7] Data taken from the Market Diary section of *The Wall Street Journal.* This period was selected because it covered the last weeks of the market downturn.

TABLE 2-1
Unpredictable news and stock market behavior

	Days of decline	Percent loss*
Battleship *Maine* sunk (1898)	32	16½
San Francisco earthquake (1906)	14	11
Lusitania sunk (1915)	32	11
Austrian crisis (1938)	31	25
Munich crisis (1938)	53	14
Czechoslovakian crisis (1939)	24	22
Poland invaded (1939)	17	7
Fall of France (1940)	26	25
Pearl Harbor (1941)	14	9
Berlin crisis (1948)	72	9
Korean crisis (1950)	13	12½
President Eisenhower's illness (1955)	12	10
Cuban crisis (1962)	6	5½
Kennedy assassination (1963)	1	6
Southeast Asia crisis (1964)	3	2
Czechoslovakian crisis (1968)	14	6

* Based on the Dow-Jones Industrial Average (DJIA)—a measure of average stock price movements on the New York Stock Exchange.
Source: "Rotnem Crisis Study," from *Market Interpretations* by Harris, Upham & Co., Inc., May 15, 1972.

the highest grade securities are those least susceptible to wide swings in investor favor. As a general rule, bonds, both government and corporate, are less affected by this factor than preferred stocks. In turn, these groups are less vulnerable than common stocks. In this latter category, the lowest grade securities are the so-called *glamor* companies. These are firms which at times are especially appealing to investors. Past examples of favorites are conglomerates and firms in the electronic, publishing, franchising, and health care industries.

Purchasing power risk

Once upon a time, a descendant of Rip Van Winkle became an investor by purchasing 100 shares of IBM and 200 shares of General Motors. Then, like the famous ancestor, this investor fell asleep for 20 years. Upon awakening, he called a stockbroker to ask how much his investments were worth. After some figuring, the broker reported these rather modest holdings now had a market value of $3 million. The man's feeling of excitement ceased abruptly when the telephone operator interrupted to say, "Your time is up, please deposit $1 million for your call!" The discovery of being a millionaire left this investor with very little to cheer about. He had become a victim of inflation.

One of the most widely recognized economic events is the rising level of prices. School children know their lunches, gum, movies, and so on, all cost more as time passes. Adults see these and countless other examples. The one cent parking meter, the five cent daily paper, the 19 cent hamburger, 30 cent per gallon gasoline, and the $25,000 home are all memories of a not-too-distant past. Similar rises in other costs are ample reasons for concern.

People invest mainly to accumulate wealth. Their records are usually kept in dollar terms. The Van Winkle experience illustrates a shortcoming of this measure. A more precise statement of investor aims would be a desire to build up *purchasing power.* Just having dollars is not enough. They must have the capability of being traded for goods and services which the consumer wants. Anyone in the past who "stuffed a mattress" with money to purchase items in the future was in for a big disappointment upon discovering the things wanted now cost two "mattresses of money."

Investors, then, are really concerned about purchasing power as opposed to dollars. The ability to buy goods and services is the critical factor. *Purchasing power risk is defined as the uncertainty of the purchasing power of future returns due to changes in the price level.*

Changes in the cost of living are usually measured by the *Consumer Price Index.*[8] Figure 2–3 traces the CPI for the post-World War II period. The Index shows a continual upward trend with the most rapid increases coming in 1973 and 1974. The long-run rise in the cost of living is a well-accepted fact which many people have adjusted to.[9] The problem is one of degree. Moderate increases can be accepted with relatively little inconvenience. But when the CPI rises at more than, say 3 percent per year, large groups of persons are affected. For example, an increase of 2 percent per year means the cost of living will double about every 36 years, which is a relatively long time. But if prices rise at an average rate of 12 percent per year, they will double in only

---

[8] This is a relatively elaborate measure of average retail prices of a broad range of consumer goods and services bought by moderate income groups within the U.S. urban population. It is compiled by the U.S. Bureau of Labor Statistics and is reported monthly.

[9] Although the long-run trend is definitely upward, price levels have declined in the past. This section has been written about inflation because it is widely held as being the most likely direction of future price level movements. Readers should be aware that *deflation* is possible and that fixed return securities are most desirable in those periods.

six years![10] This rapid deterioration of purchasing power would be felt by virtually everyone but would pose an extreme hardship on those people having fixed incomes, mainly the elderly. Any person planning for needs ten or more years hence will be considerably affected by any moderate, but persistent, price rise.

FIGURE 2–3
U.S. cost of living (1967 = 100)

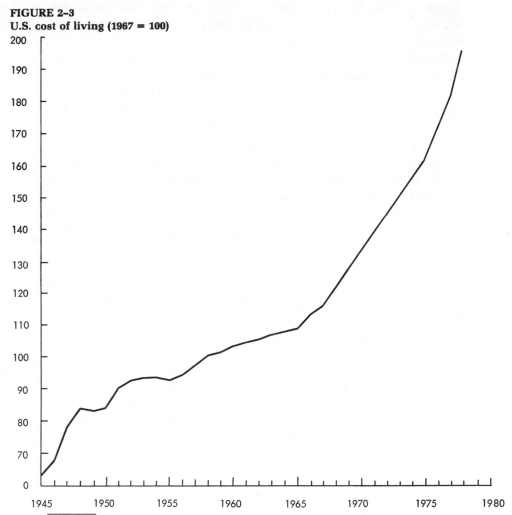

[10] An especially helpful "rule of thumb" to remember is called the *Rule of 72*. It states that the product of the growth rate and the time required to double will be approximately equal to 72. Thus, in the example above it was stated that a 2 percent growth rate would double the cost of living in 36 years (2 × 36 = 72). Often this relationship is used to approximate growth rates. If the earnings per share for a company doubled in nine years, the rule would indicate that the profits had grown at an 8 percent compound annual rate (72 ÷ 9 = 8).

The graph shows the United States has been fairly successful in preventing rampant inflation until recent times. In fact, the United States ranks high compared to the rest of the world. For example, in the 1975–78 period, consumer prices rose 21 percent in the United States. The International Monetary Fund reported increases in other countries during the same time as follows: Germany, 11; Netherlands, 21; Japan, 23; Canada, 27; United Kingdom, 46; Israel, 166; and Argentina, 4031.

It is the recent inflationary experience that is of utmost concern. In 1978 the cost of living rose 9 percent. Prices have been reflecting rising raw material costs and wage increases. The persistent high rates of inflation during the past decade have resulted in the purchasing power risk becoming the most critical type of risk for investors to recognize and react to.

Grading securities. Grading of securities with respect to purchasing power risk is a very complex matter although it might seem relatively easy at first glance. The idea is simply to assign higher grades to the issues which offer returns that compensate best for the erosion of purchasing power. Traditionally, common stocks have been graded higher than bonds in this respect. This is mainly due to the flexibility in the pattern of stock returns compared to the fixed nature of bond yields. In the former instance, the arrangement that gives common stockholders the opportunity of sharing in the firm's earnings has been translated into a belief that this would provide for increasing returns. This has certainly been the experience over long periods of time, as depicted in Figure 2–4.

This graph shows that during most of the 20th century common stocks have increased in price and paid dividends in sufficient amounts so as to more than offset the rises in the cost of living. However, when the time period is shortened, a very different picture emerges. Since 1965, inflation has continued at a high level while stock prices ended at about the same point as they began. In 1974 when the consumer price index rose 12 percent, prices on the New York Stock Exchange declined 30 percent! So instead of offsetting a rise in the cost of living, common stock investment compounded the problem. Many persons who were attracted to equity issues for their protection against inflation learned, in a very painful way, that a considerable time period might have to pass before their investments provided them with the results they desired. The bottom chart in Figure 2–4 shows returns from dividends afforded the investor better protection against

FIGURE 2–4
Common stocks as inflation hedges

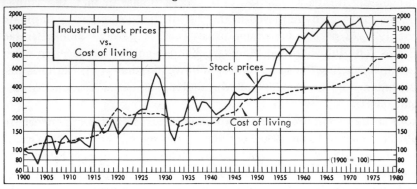

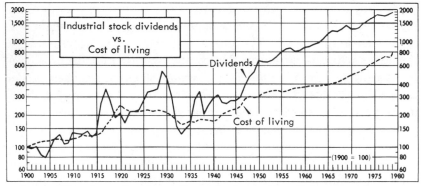

Source: *Wiesenberger Investment Companies Service*, New York, 1978, p. 57.

an erosion of purchasing power in recent times. The parallel pattern of the two lines since 1965 indicates that dividend increases offset the higher cost of living.

Returns to stockholders are expected to grow because of two main reasons. First, companies expand their business by selling more of improved and/or new products. This often leads to increased profits, higher dividends, and stock price rises. The same results may occur when increases in the costs of doing business are passed on to the consumer in the form of higher prices. Thus, growth in sales, earnings, dividends, and stock prices may be the result of inflation as well as efforts on the part of a firm to expand operations. The effect of inflation on returns to stockholders varies for each industry and for companies within an industry. Firms having large reserves of natural resources such as oil, minerals, and timber are often thought to provide investors with protection against declines of purchasing power. Other firms may be good investments in inflationary periods because they are able to expand sales and profits. The electronics and the food industries are examples. On balance however, common stocks have *not* benefited from inflation and investors are cautioned against relying on them as being a good hedge. Remember that this is especialy true for the short run.

Another concept will prove helpful in relating returns from bonds to the loss of purchasing power. Most financial data are expressed in dollars along with a particular time period. For example, Gross National Product (GNP) for the United States in 1977 and 1978 was reported as $1,887 and $2,107 billion, respectively. These numbers are known as current dollars. They indicate GNP rose almost 12 percent. However, it would not be proper to say that the economy expanded by that amount. The increase could have been caused in whole or in part by a *rise in the prices* which are used in valuing output. In order to determine what happened to the production of goods and services, the current dollar figures must be adjusted to account for a change in price levels. For GNP the base year is 1972. The reported figures, *after allowing for price increases,* were $1,333 and $1,385 billion in 1977 and 1978, respectively. This presents quite a different picture. It means that instead of expanding 12 percent, the country experienced a real growth of slightly less than 4 percent.

The adjusted figures are called *constant dollars.* In a similar manner adjustments can be made to returns from securities to show whether or not investors have gained purchasing power on balance. Data for returns from the bonds of the most credit-worthy corporations are plotted in Figure 2–5. The graph clearly shows that bonds have provided a long-run return sufficient to more than offset inflation. On average, the annual return from high grade corporate bonds exceeded the CPI by 2.7 percent in the 1959–78 period. However, care must be exercised in interpreting this statistic. In any one year bondholders may not have been protected against inflation. In 1974 for example, the

Figure 2-5
Aaa corporate bond yields: Current versus adjusted for purchasing power

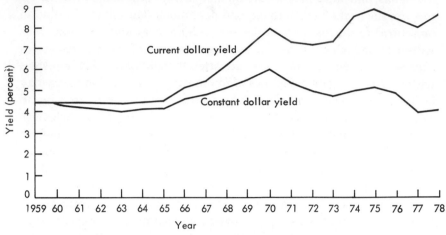

bond yield of 8.6 percent was reduced by the 12 percent rise in the cost of living index to leave the investor with not a gain but instead a net loss of over 3 percent in terms of purchasing power! While a negative yield occurred only twice in the past two decades, there have been numerous periods in which the purchasing power of returns from bonds has been quite low. People who own bonds paying low rates of interest are quite unhappy to see their returns wiped out by cost of living increases. Furthermore, when bonds are redeemed the principal is repaid in current dollars. These amounts will buy considerably less in comparison to the purchasing power of those dollars when the bonds were originally issued. This, of course, is the reason why fixed income securities have been avoided at times when investors are worried about inflation.

Where does this leave us? Bonds are low grade with respect to purchasing power risk. During the past twenty years, dividend increases on common stocks have offset inflation even though stock prices, in general, have not. Over longer periods shares have risen sufficiently to provide protection. The record would then indicate that common stocks are high grade with respect to purchasing power risks, especially in the long run.

There is no denying that rapid increases in the cost of living do present problems for investors. If "double digit" inflation becomes a regular pattern, most owners of securities will face difficult times. The keypoint to remember is that while there has been a persistent rise in prices, the rate of increase has *varied* considerably. Economists are in general agreement that the degree of inflation will continue to fluctuate in the future. This suggests that one solution would be to purchase investments currently offering and considered likely to continue to offer high returns. Regular receipts of these funds enable one to offset all or at least the majority of the erosion of purchasing power of the dollar. Methods of identifying these opportunities will be treated in later chapters.

Interest rate risk

Interest rate risk is defined as the uncertainty of future returns due to changes in market rates of interest.

In 1946, American Telephone and Telegraph Company sold bonds to investors with the promise of paying a "coupon" or interest of 2⅝ percent each year until they mature in 1986 when the original amount borrowed would be repaid to the bondholder. In April 1979, these bonds could be purchased for about 69.5 percent of their original price. What happened? Why had the price of these bonds fallen so drastically? There had not been any developments that spelled doom to the company. They had never missed any interest payments. No technological breakthrough had been announced that would make the telephone obsolete. AT&T was not facing bankruptcy. Their continued existence was in no way in jeopardy. In fact, these bonds were superbly secure. There was virtually no question that the firm would not be able to make payments as promised. These aforementioned troubles have fallen on numerous other corporations in the past and, in some cases, caused their bond prices to decline. AT&T had not suffered any traumatic setbacks, yet these bonds were being bought and sold at about two-thirds of their original value. The reason for this decline is the subject of this section—interest rate risk.

Previous discussions have outlined other causes of variation in security prices. These were identified as changes in financial capacity, in investor psychology, and in price levels. Attention is now drawn to a fourth reason—changes in interest rates.

Bond interest is fixed. That is, it does not change over the life of the bond. In the example previously mentioned, AT&T promised to pay no more or no less than 2⅝ percent each year for the entire 40 years that particular bond was to be outstanding. This rate is constant, but the market rate of interest, which is essentially rent paid for the use of money, changes over time. The current price for money will be reflected in the new bonds that are sold. This is illustrated by AT&T, which has a large appetite for money. It sells more and more bonds as time passes. Whenever it does, it enters into a new agreement with investors and it pays the going rate for money. A partial listing of AT&T bonds outstanding as of April 1979, is presented in Table 2–2. Interest rates paid varied from 2⅝ percent in 1946 to 8⅘ percent in 1974. They were set each time bonds were sold based on what investors then required.

TABLE 2–2
American Telephone and Telegraph Company (bonds outstanding as of April 1979)

Year issued	Percent interest	Year issued	Percent interest
1945	2 3/4	1966	5 5/8
1946	2 5/8	1966	5 1/8
1947	2 3/4	1967	5 1/2
1947	2 7/8	1967	6
1954	3 1/4	1970	8 3/4
1956	3 7/8	1971	7
1957	4 3/8	1972	7 1/8
1960	4 3/4	1972	6 1/2
1961	4 3/4	1974	8 4/5
1962	4 3/8	1975	8 5/8
1962	4 5/8	1975	7 3/4
1963	4 3/8		

Source: Standard & Poor's *Bond Guide*, April 1979, pp. 15, 16.

After bonds have been originally purchased, they may be resold many times in the open market. Other investors buy them, but the price they pay is determined by the going interest rate at that moment. People buying bonds have the alternative of buying either newly issued bonds or those which had been issued earlier. If the current interest rate is higher than that paid on outstanding bonds, investors will not buy the older bonds unless their price drops enough so that the return is made equivalent to that currently being offered. In other words, people will pay less for AT&T's 2⅝ percent issue than they will for the 8⅘ percent one.

Remember that the interest rate is quoted on the basis of par value, which is the same as or very close to the original purchase price. In the example just used, investors in 1979 would have the choice of receiving either $88.00 or $26.25 yearly interest for each $1,000 bond. Naturally they prefer the larger amount; so, if the 2⅝ percent bonds are going to find any buyers, their price must be lowered. In this case, the equilibrium point was about $695, which meant for this amount an investor could purchase a bond that would pay $26.25 per year until 1986, when AT&T would redeem the bond for $1,000.[11] Conversely, if the current level of interest rates happened to be below rates offered on outstanding bonds, investors would choose the old bonds. In so doing, they would bid up those prices above par to a point where the return was equivalent to the present rate.

This discussion identifies a very important relationship between prices of outstanding bonds and market rates of interest, which is shown in Figure 2–6. This graph indicates that bond prices vary inversely with interest rates. When interest rates increase, bond prices decrease, and vice versa. Note the dotted lines which show that when the market rate of interest is the same as the interest rate paid on the bond, the price will be $1,000.

Grading securities.   Securities having the highest grade in financial risk tend to be the lowest grade in interest rate risk because prices of these issues are determined almost entirely by the prevailing market rates of interest. This means that these bond prices will be very re-

FIGURE 2–6
Relationship of bond prices and interest rates

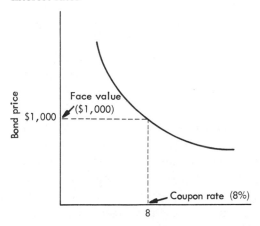

Market rate of interest

---

[11] The mathematics of determining the relationship of interest rates and bond prices is presented in Chapter 7.

sponsive to changes in the cost of money; they are, therefore, low grade with respect to interest rate risk. On the other hand, bonds sold by organizations having questionable financial capacity will be purchased by investors seeking returns based primarily on the prospects of improvement in financial ability of the issuer. These people are not so concerned with interest rates, and those particular bond prices will not be so sensitive to changing money rates. This means the lower the grade of bonds in financial risk, the higher the grade will be in interest rate risk.

Another refinement has to do with the length of maturity of the bonds. As a general rule, the longer a bond has before it expires, the greater the change in price will be due to a change in interest rates. Stated somewhat differently, a small price change in short-term bonds has a large effect on returns. This means that interest rate risk grade is inversely proportional to length of maturity, or the longer a bond has before redemption, the lower the grade.

Attention has been focused exclusively on bond price changes. There are also returns in the form of interest to consider. Uncertainty of future income from this source can be reduced by purchasing long-term bonds. This is so because the interest rate on any particular bond is fixed over its lifetime. If a 9 percent, 25-year bond is bought, the owner will receive 9 percent for the quarter of a century that the bond is outstanding, regardless of any later changes in interest rates. If, on the other hand, a 9 percent five-year bond were selected, the owner would have to reinvest at the going money rate five years hence when the bond has matured. Interest rates could be higher or lower then. The long-term bond provides more certainty simply because the investor is guaranteed a known amount for a longer period. The short-term bondholder might possibly reinvest in four other five-year bonds, and at the end of 25 years have earned more interest than the investor that held the long-term bond. But the returns are *uncertain,* which by definition means that short-term bonds are lower grade when interest income is concerned. This grading arrangement contradicts that used for price. It is resolved by again considering the individual investor's circumstances. If this person is primarily interested in receiving a known and regular amount, then the choice would be long-term issues. If the dominant concern were protection of principal from loss, then short-term bonds would be chosen.

The discussion of interest rate risk has thus far been limited to bonds. The basic relationship developed can also be applied to some preferred and common stocks. These would consist of those known as *income stocks*. They are issues which are sought mainly for dividends and not so much for the growth of price potential. Typical of this type would be some utility company stocks that traditionally have paid large dividends. If the general level of interest rates rises, income stock prices will fall just like bonds until their yields are equivalent to prevailing rates.

Political and social risks

There are at least two other identifiable causes of change in returns to holders of securities. One of these has to do with political developments. When a country devalues its currency, both good and bad effects will result to the financial capabilities of different organizations. A more serious development is the nationalization of facilities, which is usually quite damaging to companies whose assets were seized.

Social change is another factor to be recognized. This involves shifts in public attitudes. Examples may be found in the increasing concern about the quality of the environment. Pollution and population control movements will have substantial impacts on some lines of business. An increasing social awareness may cause shifts in consumption patterns. That is, people may use less and less of some types of goods. The horsepower mania of Detroit yielded to smaller and less polluting autos. For the most part, social changes are slow to evolve. This provides investors with sufficient time to react. Political change often takes place literally overnight. This latter risk, can be taken into account by investors, but both of these types affect a rather limited segment of investment alternatives.

RETURNS FROM INVESTMENTS

The initial section of this chapter presented the argument that risk and return are commensurate. The following pages expanded the concept of risk, breaking it down into four major categories. Documentation was provided to establish the risk-return relationship for (1) market, (2) purchasing power and (3) interest rate risk types. Evidence of the risk-return connection for the fourth category, financial risk, has been withheld for special treatment at this point because it is usually considered the most dominant type. Whenever the term risk is used alone without any modifying adjective, it most often means financial risk. This usage will be adopted here.

Bonds

Bonds are graded on the likelihood that pledges to pay interest and principal will be met. These grades are a measure of risk. The risk-return relationship for several classes of bonds since World War II is shown in Figure 2–7. U.S. government bonds are the most credit-worthy type issued. Aaa is the rating assigned to the safest corporate debt securities. Baa bonds are considered lower medium-grade obliga-tions. Note from the graph that while interest rates have varied consid-

FIGURE 2–7
Yields on different risk classes of bonds

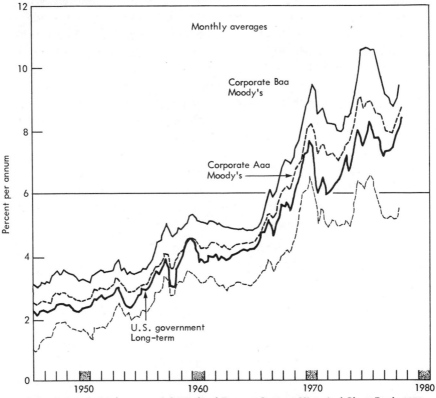

Source: Board of Governors of the Federal Reserve System, *Historical Chart Book*, 1978, p. 97.

erably over the past quarter century, at all times the yields were lowest for U.S. government bonds and highest for the Baa category. This substantiates the claim that risk and return are commensurate.

The reason why this is so consistent with bonds is that there is widespread acceptance of the rating system. Investors, in general, do not like to take higher risks unless they are compensated for doing so. Lower grade bonds must provide higher yields. It is somewhat like the structure of life insurance premiums. Individuals pay more as they grow older because the risk of dying soon increases. In addition, some jobs are hazardous, and insurance rates for those workers reflect it. Likewise, securities in different risk categories require different rates of return. Figure 2–7 provides clear support to the risk-return hypothesis applied to bonds.

Common stocks

Equity issues, in general, are more risky than bonds because claims of these securities are junior to those of debtholders. According to the rule, then, returns from stocks should be higher. Post-World War II stock and bond yields are plotted in Figure 2–8. Everything went according to form until 1958, when the curves crossed and bond yields rose above stock yields and remained higher. Something happened. Perhaps the risk-return hypothesis was no longer valid? A moment's reflection will show no need to discard this relationship.

First of all, the graph shows that the change in yield position was developing over a number of years. This means that investors were gradually turning their attention to common stocks because they offered returns not only from dividends but also through the opportunity for capital gain as stock prices rose. Remember that the interest rate paid on any particular bond will not change. As more investors became aware of the general rising trend in stock prices in the past, they anticipated a continuation of this trend. Thus, they were willing to pay higher prices in the present. The dividends on stock, while growing steadily, did not keep pace. Since the stock yields on the graph were calculated by dividing dividends by price, the ratio, or yield, declined. The comparison of stock and bond yields, then, is misleading. It only tells part of the story. For bonds, most of the return is indeed realized by the payment of interest. Returns from stock, on the other hand, are usually dominated by the changes in price, and in the long run by the trend toward increased dividend payments by most firms. The result is

FIGURE 2–8
Yields on high-grade debt securities, preferred and common stock

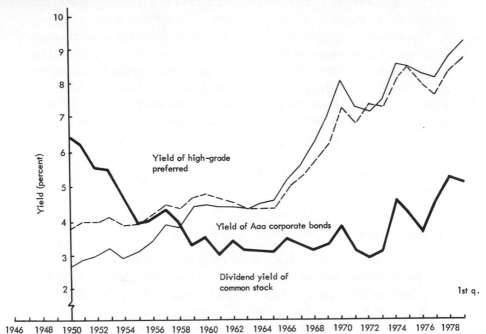

Source: Aaa Corporate Bond Interest series taken from *Federal Reserve Bulletins*; Dividend yield of Preferred from *Moody's Industrial Manual*; Common stock yields from Standard & Poor's 500 stock index.

that for stock the dividend yield is an inappropriate measure for this comparison. Notice that the discussion has always used risk and *return*. Yield was introduced with bonds because there it does measure return reasonably well. But with stock, the price change part of the return must be taken into account.

Risk-return studies.   Numerous research efforts have been directed toward answering the question "What is the risk-return relationship in investments?" A study covering the 1926–76 period found the compound annual rate of return for common stocks to be 9.2 percent compared to 4.1 percent for corporate bonds.[12] The variability of returns, as measured by the standard deviation, from these two investment vehicles was 22.4 percent and 5.6 percent. These results confirm the risk-

[12] R. G. Ibbotson and R. A. Sinquefield, *Stocks, Bonds, Bills, and Inflation: The Past (1926–1976) and the Future (1977–2000)*, (Chicago: Roger Ibbotson and Rex Sinquefield, 1977).

return hypothesis; common stocks, with significantly greater risks, have indeed provided higher returns than bonds.

In another research project, returns were calculated for investments of equal amounts in the stock of each corporation listed on the New York Stock Exchange.[13] Different time periods were used. For example, stocks were purchased at the beginning of 1926 and sold at the end of that year. Another "purchase" was made at the start of 1926 and sold two years later. This procedure was repeated over and over, increasing the holding period one year each time. Then investments were made in all the listed stocks at the beginning of 1927 and sold one year later, two years later, and so on. This represented all possible combinations of buying in and selling out after one year or multiples of one year had passed. A total of 820 time periods were involved between 1926 and 1965. While the entire study is much too lengthy to report here, the major findings are as follows:

1. The return over the longest time span covered was 9.3 percent. These returns are compound annual rates figured before taxes and with reinvestment of dividends. They can then be compared with interest rates paid by banks and published yields on most other investment media.

2. There is considerable variation of return, depending, of course, on dates of purchase and sale. During 1931 the return was a negative 48 percent. In 1933 a gain of 108 percent would have resulted. If someone had bought at the end of 1927, it would have been 14 years later before the securities could be sold out without having a loss. During the last 20 years covered by the study, the returns were consistently high with positive results in 95 percent of the 220 possible time periods. There was no ten-year time span in which the return was less than 11 percent.

These results present rather convincing evidence that common stocks have provided investors with substantial returns over the long run. But one might counter this remark by saying, "I'm an individual who can neither buy all listed stocks nor necessarily hold them for

---

[13] Most significant results have been published in these three articles: Lawrence Fisher and James H. Lorie, "Rates of Return on Investments in Common Stock, the Year-by-Year Record, 1926–1965," *Journal of Business*, July 1968, pp. 291–316; Lawrence Fisher, "Outcomes for 'Random' Investments in Common Stocks Listed on the New York Stock Exchange," *Journal of Business*, April 1965, pp. 149–61; Lawrence Fisher and James H. Lorie, "Some Studies of Variability of Returns on Investments in Common Stocks," *Journal of Business*, April 1970, pp. 99–134.

long periods." Is there any practical result supporting the case for common stock? Fisher and Lorie tackled this question with a gigantic computer program. They calculated results for every possible combination of month-end buy and sell dates for every stock during the 1926–60 period. This involved 87,900 different monthly buy-sell combinations for any one company. For all stocks listed, it meant tabulating results on 45,557,538 such possible transactions! Adjustments were made to allow for dividends and brokerage commissions.

The returns were then expressed in a frequency distribution, which in turn showed the probability of gains and losses. For example, if someone randomly selected a company, purchased shares at the end of a randomly chosen month, and then sold that stock at the end of a later randomly selected month, the investor would have made money about three out of every four times. The tables also indicated a 50 percent chance that the return would have been at least 10 percent per annum. Furthermore, of every 100 transactions, 19 provided at least a 20 percent annual increase compared to only 6 that would have yielded losses at the annual rate of 20 percent or more. Other tests indicated that the chance of loss would have been considerably reduced and the amount of gain substantially increased if the investor had randomly chosen several stocks instead of just one and if the minimum holding period had been one year or more instead of one month.

The risk-return relationship in common stocks can also be examined with the aid of Figure 2–9. This graph shows stock price performance in two different markets. The companies whose stock is traded in these markets have different characteristics. The New York Stock Exchange (NYSE) tends to list the older and larger firms with national reputations. Any securities not traded on a stock exchange are by definition in the over-the-counter (OTC) market.[14] The firms issuing these securities cover a very broad range from some that are old, well-established, and with worldwide operations to some that have been newly formed. The majority of this category are lesser known and have a smaller trading interest compared to those companies listed on the NYSE.

In general, the risks would be greatest in the OTC category and relatively less in the NYSE group. Figure 2–9 shows returns have been proportional to this classification of risk. The graph also shows wider

---

[14] A detailed discussion of the organization of security markets can be found in the next chapter.

price swings in the OTC stocks compared to those listed on the NYSE. Variation in price, it will be recalled, is another measure of risk.

A word of caution must be given before leaving the risk-return discussion. All the empirical results shown are averages. These can cover up important information.[15] Many individual experiences will be different from what the averages would indicate. For example, it would be folly to feel assurance of large profits by buying stock in a company that had a very shaky past and an even more precarious future. The risk-return hypothesis does not say this at all. Instead, the preceding discussion has shown that for large numbers of stocks and over long periods of time, there is a greater return for the more risky situations. Remember then that this is a *tendency* which would become more uncertain as the time period is shortened and if only a very few investments are made. In order to reap the benefits of a plan which emphasizes risky investments, the investor must be able to diversify holdings and be prepared to experience some losses, especially in the short run. The limitation as to how large returns are sought is determined by each individual's ability to sustain temporary setbacks. History has shown that the odds favor the risk-taker in the long run. To the extent that investors are able to expose themselves to greater risks, their wealth will tend to grow more rapidly.

SUMMARY

Risk is defined as the uncertainty of future returns from a security due to the occurrence of some causal event. These events can be grouped into four major categories. If the cause is the change in financial ability of the issuer, it is referred to as *financial risk*. Attitudes toward the value of securities vary over time. These are shifts in investor psychology and give rise to *market risk*. Inflation deteriorates the value of returns from securities. The uncertainty of what future dollars will buy due to this cause is known as *purchasing power risk*. Returns may also change as the result of a shift in market rates of interest and this particular cause is identified with the *interest rate* type of *risk*.

Securities can be rated according to their response to each of the different causes of change in returns. High grades are assigned to those

---

[15] One is reminded of the statistician who drowned while attempting to wade across a river which had an average depth of two feet.

FIGURE 2–9

Comparison of Dow Jones Industrial Average and National Quotation Bureau Industrial Average

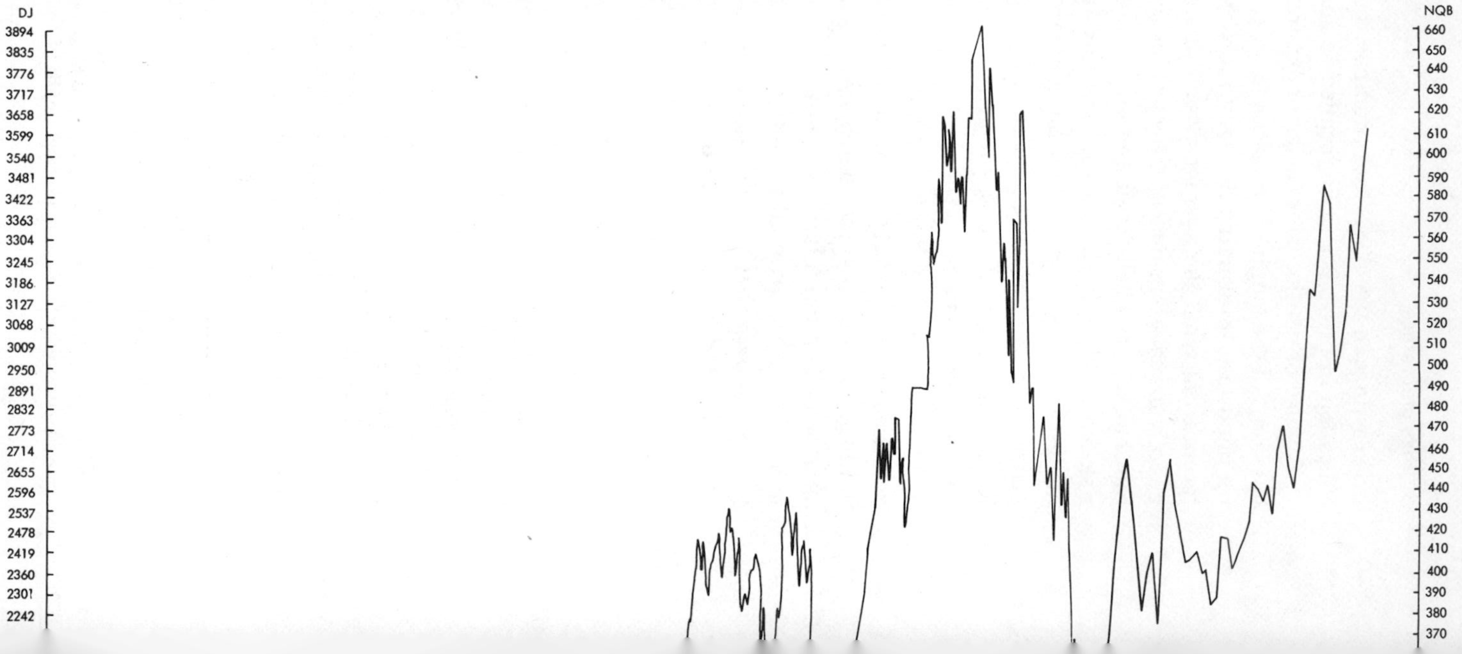

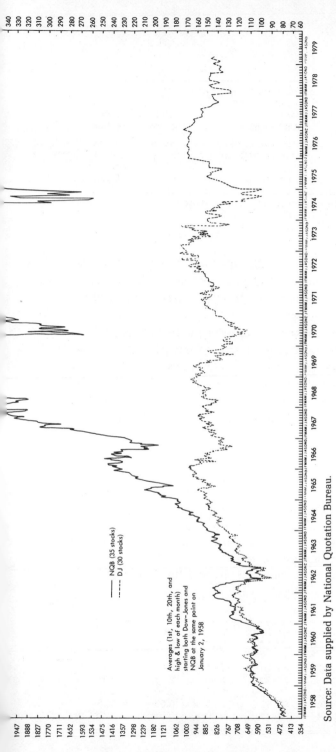

Source: Data supplied by National Quotation Bureau.

TABLE 2–3
Risks and security grades

Type of risk	Uncertainty of future returns due to changes in	High grade	Low grade
1. Financial......................	Financial capacity	Bonds	Stock
2. Market.........................	Investor psychology	Bonds	Stock
3. Purchasing power...........	Price level	Stock*	Bonds
4. Interest rate..................	Interest rates	Stock	Bonds

* This grading applies to the long run. In shorter periods common stock is lower grade.

issues which are relatively immune to the specific types of change, and low grades are given to securities that are quite sensitive to certain events. Table 2–3 shows how the major concepts of risk and security grading can be tabulated.

The grading system is established by appraising the history of what happened to returns when each type of change occurred. Numerous studies have indicated risk and return are commensurate. These results are tendencies averaged for groups of securities and over long periods of time. Individual investments can and sometimes do lead to financial ruin. However, the odds in the long run have favored the risk-taker.

PROBLEMS

1. Make a list of occupations which have varying degrees of risk, either of being injured, losing money, or losing the job. Determine about how much a person in each of the categories would make. See if the highest risk jobs tend to offer the highest returns.

2. The following data are for three companies listed on the New York Stock Exchange:

Year	Stock price range (rounded)			Earnings per share		
	AT&T	Natomas	Northrop	AT&T	Natomas	Northrop
1	71–60	12–08	35–20	3.41	1.62	2.10
2	64–50	16–10	32–20	3.69	2.18	2.51
3	63–50	24–11	46–27	3.79	1.60	2.86
4	58–48	40–16	54–31	3.75	0.58	3.28
5	58–49	131–34	54–33	4.00	(0.04)	3.80

Based on the above data, rank the companies according to risk. What measures do you feel are most appropriate?

3. Look through the headings in the yellow pages of a telephone book and develop a list of industries which you feel offer investments which will be good hedges against inflation in the future.

4. Choose an investment alternative from the list in Table 1–2 and determine the price performance over the most recent five-year period. Your answer can be approximate, but you may wish to visit such places as a coin or stamp shop, an art gallery, the library, a brokerage house, or a real estate office.

QUESTIONS

1. What is the general relationship between risk and return?
2. Does investing in the more risky situations assure high returns? Explain.
3. What is *financial risk*?
4. Are bonds higher grade with respect to financial risk compared to common stocks? Why?
5. Define *market risk*.
6. Explain how investor psychology affects security prices.
7. Give a definition of *purchasing power risk*.
8. Would bonds issued by the U.S. government be high or low grade with respect to purchasing power risk? Support your answer.
9. What is *interest rate risk*?
10. What is the relationship between interest rates and bond prices?
11. Which is the more important consideration to investors in the U.S. companies, *political* or *social risk*? Explain.
12. Cite studies which support the risk-return hypothesis.
13. Suppose someone told you they had invested in common stocks to "hedge against inflation" and that the stocks had fallen while the cost of living had risen. What would you say to this person?
14. "Securities which are high grade with respect to one type of risk may be low grade with respect to another type of risk." Explain, using examples.

SELECTED READINGS

Dreman, David N. *Psychology and the Stock Market.* New York: American Management Association, 1977.

Fischer, Donald E., and Jordan, Ronald J. *Security Analysis and Portfolio Management.* 2nd ed. Englewood Cliffs, N.J.: Prentice-Hall, 1979.

Fisher, Philip A. *Conservative Investors Sleep Well.* New York: Harper & Row, 1975.

Fogler, H. Russell. *Analyzing the Stock Market: Statistical Evidence and methodology.* 2nd ed. Columbus, Ohio: Grid, 1978.

Ibbotson, R. G., and Sinquefield, R. A. *Stocks, Bonds, Bills, and Inflation: The Past (1926–1976) and the Future (1977–2000).* Chicago: Roger Ibbotson and Rex Sinquefield, 1977.

Sharpe, William F. *Investments.* Englewood Cliffs, N.J.: Prentice-Hall, 1978.

Winkler, Paul. *New Discoveries in the Psychological Approach to the Stock Market.* Albuquerque: American Classical College Press, 1978.

part two

HOW AND WHERE TO INVEST

3

Security markets

INTRODUCTION

The first two chapters discussed the "what and why" of investing. They established a perspective for personal investing. Much of the material was conceptual. Attention is now turned to the considerations of "how and where" to invest. This chapter and the next are devoted to a description of the environment of the investing process—a changing and complex arrangement of people, customs, and regulations.

FUNCTIONS OF SECURITIES MARKETS

Millions of persons are reached by newspapers and newscasts which feature stock market reports. Most people are quite aware of stock exchanges, but they tend to view them simply as places to buy and sell. Security markets are much broader in scope. The exchanges and other investment markets play roles which are very basic to the free enterprise system.

The economic function

In the U.S. economy, consumers are "kings"; efforts to satisfy their wishes keep the system going. The production of goods and services requires a combination of land, labor, and *capital*. Funds are needed to develop new ideas and to replace and expand facilities which are producing goods that are in demand.

An important role of securities markets is to provide a channel through which money that is not presently needed by some can be used by others so that production can occur to satisfy consumer wishes. *Facilitating flows of funds from sources to uses is the economic function of securities markets.* The more efficiently this can be done, the higher will be the living standard of the population. This not only means more cars, houses, and toys, but also more roads, water systems, and schools. Securities markets are not required in a system where the state owns the production facilities. In a free enterprise economy it is necessary that the savings of individuals, both large and small, be made available to those organizations that will build and produce.

The continuous market function

An important characteristic of most securities is that they can readily be sold for cash. This feature attracts many individuals who might otherwise invest in other assets, for example, land or rental property. The ability to buy or sell quickly without driving the price up or down is provided by securities markets, and is known as *marketability*. The transaction speed is one dimension of this term. A house, for example, is not very marketable because to achieve a quick sale the price might first have to be lowered considerably. Most securities can be bought or sold quickly.

A second aspect of marketability involves the impact of an order on the price. Consumers can readily relate to this factor. Individuals filling their gasoline tanks don't cause the station operator to immediately raise the price. However, repeated heavy demand will inevitably result in higher prices. Security prices are also determined by supply and demand, but most securities markets are capable of filling individual orders without the occurrence of wide price movements. The price of any security will increase or decrease if the orders are predominantly either to buy or to sell, but the movement caused by each order will be very small if the particular security is highly marketable.

The third dimension of marketability is the constant availability of price information. Investors can rely on quotes to continuously calculate the precise value of their holdings if they own marketable securities.

Liquidity goes one step further in that it refers to the ability to convert assets into cash with little money loss in relation to the original purchase price. It is important to distinguish between these concepts. Securities can be marketable without being liquid, but they cannot be liquid unless they are marketable. Markets provide marketability but not necessarily liquidity because the latter depends on price movements of the security. Short-term U.S. government obligations—for example, Treasury Bills—are the most liquid type investments since their market values fluctuate very little. Common stocks, which typically have greater price volatility, are less liquid.

The fair price function

In addition to continuous pricing the market system provides quotes that are "fair." This means that prices should deviate as little as possible from "true" investment value.[1] The worth of any security is determined by the future returns that are *expected* to accrue to the owner. Note the emphasis on expected returns. These will, of course, vary depending on who is making the estimates. In fact, this is largely why so much security trading occurs. Investors who have a lower appraisal of the amount of future return than that indicated by the present price sell. Other persons figuring the future returns will be higher, buy. A "good" market will produce quotes that represent the consensus of investor opinion regarding value. If the price is too high, people wanting to sell will be unable to find buyers. If too low a price is established, orders for purchase will go unfilled. A proper price level will result in maximum satisfaction to both buying and selling groups. At this point, trading activity will be the greatest.

An example will help illustrate the concept of a fair price. Imagine a group of investors interested in the stock of XYZ Company. Each person independently estimates the value of this security, and the tabulation of their appraisals is presented in Table 3-1. The highest price anyone is willing to pay is $19¾ and the lowest is $18. On the sell side someone is willing to part with shares for $18¼, while another stockholder wants *at least* $20 per share. Notice the phrase "at least."

It means that the shares offered at $20 would also be available at any higher price. The person willing to pay $19¾ would be happier if

---
[1] This particular section has benefited from W. J. Eiteman, C. A. Dice, and D. K. Eiteman, *The Stock Market,* 4th ed. (New York: McGraw-Hill, 1966), pp. 8–11.

TABLE 3-1
Trading interest in XYZ stock

Price	Buy	Sell
20	0	100
19¾	100	300
19½	200	600
19¼	300	800
19	600	400
18¾	200	300
18½	300	300
18¼	200	200
18	100	0

the shares could be bought at a lower price. The investor appraisal information then can be retabulated on a basis that reflects this willingness to sell for "at least" or buy for "at most." This is done in Table 3-2.

The question arises, "What is a fair price?" If $19¾ per share were established as the fair price, 100 shares would be purchased from the 2,900 shares offered. If the price were set at $18, no shares would exchange hands, leaving unfilled buy orders for 2,000 shares. At a $19 price, 1,200 shares would be traded. This is the maximum activity that could occur given the wishes of investors as set forth in Table 3-1. The function of a securities market is to facilitate trading at fair prices. This means disclosing the price which maximizes turnover, which in this example is $19 per share. The information is depicted graphically in Figure 3-1. The two curves show supply and demand for XYZ shares. At prices above and below $19 there is excess supply or demand. The greatest number of shares trade hands at $19. This presumably means more people are happy with that price than any other.

TABLE 3-2
Cumulative trading interest in XYZ common stock

Shares wanted	Possible prices	Shares offered
0	20	3,000
100	19¾	2,900
300	19½	2,600
600	19¼	2,000
1,200	19	1,200
1,400	18¾	800
1,700	18½	500
1,900	18¼	200
2,000	18	0

FIGURE 3–1
Supply and demand for XYZ stock

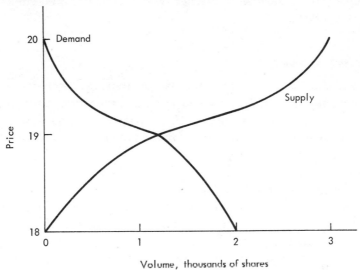

Much of the remaining chapter will be devoted to a study of just how markets are organized so that fair prices can be disclosed.

PRIMARY MARKETS

Recall that a major function of securities markets is economic and involves channeling savings into investments. This transfer or conversion is accomplished in many ways. Banks accept deposits and make loans. Savings and loan associations, credit unions, and insurance companies also turn savings into investments. Individuals sometimes bypass the institutional intermediaries and invest directly. Whenever funds are made available to a user regardless of whether they come directly or indirectly from the individual savers, new investment is said to be taking place. Securities of many types are sold by issuers to investors. This is different from the trading of securities *between* investors where no new investment takes place. This distinction is much like the new and used car markets. General Motors' sales are increased when automobiles are purchased by original owners, but there is no impact on the manufacturer when used cars are sold. The initial step of offering securities in exchange for cash involves what is known as *primary markets.* After securities are outstanding, they can be resold time and again in *secondary markets* which are somewhat similar to used car markets.

Investment banking

Investment banking is the business of assisting organizations in raising money. This aid is provided to both corporations and governmental units. It consists mainly of help in marketing new securities which are sold for the cash desired by the issuer. Investment bankers are middlemen who bring together those with funds to invest and those who have need for money. Their work is done in financial centers and small communities. Some of these firms in the United States have been in business for more than a century and help raise several billion dollars each year. Others are currently being formed and act on a very limited scale.

Functions of investment banking. Investment bankers fulfill two major roles. They act as *advisors* to the organization seeking funds and they sell securities. In the advisory capacity they offer counsel to the issuer on the *type, terms,* and *timing* of the fund raising. Types of offerings include several categories of bonds and stocks as well as the particular method that will be used to market the security. Numerous decisions must be made on such terms as interest rates and maturities for bonds and the price of common stock. In addition, consideration should be given to a host of other features known as "sweeteners" that can be used to make the offering more attractive to potential investors. Finally, the decision must be made on *when* to sell the issue. Some offerings are postponed in hopes that investors will be more receptive later.

Literally thousands of combinations of terms can be used. However, there are relatively few alternatives that can be put together in an offering that will be both advantageous to the issuer and still be attractive to the investor. This is true because many characteristics that are desired most by investors, such as high interest rates, are least desirable to the issuer. Investors are a fickle group, and their requirements are changing constantly. Because investment bankers are in constant contact with the sources of funds, which are the investors, they develop a sense of what characteristics are currently held as being important.

After most of the details of a security offering have been set, the investment bankers help assemble the relevant information required by various regulatory bodies. This activity will be discussed in the next chapter.

Advisory services are also provided by investment bankers to firms seeking to merge with or acquire other companies. Sometimes the investment banker actually initiates merger and acquisition activity.

The second major type of investment banking function is known as *underwriting*. This involves purchasing the securities to be sold from the issuer and then reselling them to the public. Underwriting means to assume liability in the event of loss or damage. The investment banker buys the securities at a stated price and then resells them immediately to the public at a higher price. At least this is the hope. But securities markets are constantly changing, and what appears attractive to investors one day will sometimes find less interest the next. Underwriters assume the risk of being unable to sell the securities at a profit, but the issuers receive their money no matter what happens. The issuers are thus insured against loss due to a change in investor attitudes, and they are guaranteed the receipt of a certain amount of money at a certain date.

When small or new companies need capital, the investment banker may not wish to underwrite the offering because of the high degree of risk involved in marketing the securities. In these cases, a *best efforts* offering may be used. The investment banker attempts to sell the issue but does not *guarantee* that the offering will be successful. Any securities remaining unsold after employing "best efforts" will be returned to the issuer. This arrangement is like selling goods on consignment.

In practice, most offerings are underwritten and sold to investors. The underwriter makes a profit by paying a certain price to the issuer and then reselling at a higher price to investors. The markup, or commission, as it is called, depends on (1) the type of security, (2) the issuer, and (3) the amount being sold. Commissions are lower on bonds than on stock because bonds are sold mainly to institutions and wealthy people. They buy in large amounts so the selling costs are lower. Common stock, on the other hand, is often sold to thousands of investors in smaller amounts. This requires more effort and results in higher costs.

Commissions are lower for the better known, financially sound issuers. Organizations having well-established reputations often have a following of investors who are willing to buy more of their securities.

The third major determinant of underwriting costs is the dollar amount of securities being sold. In general, the larger the offering, the smaller the percentage commission will be. This is because some parts of the fees charged are for items that require about the same expense whether half a million or half a billion dollars is being raised.

Documentation for the type of security and the effects of the size of the offering on the cost of selling securities is presented in Table 3–3. In almost every instance the data confirm the relationships just described.

TABLE 3–3
Costs of selling securities to the general public (expressed as a percent of gross proceeds)

Size of issue (millions of dollars)	Debt	Preferred stock	Common stock
Under 1.0	12.0	N.A.	22.2
1.0– 1.9	17.0	11.7	16.5
2.0– 4.9	6.2	N.A.	11.9
5.0– 9.9	3.1	2.5	8.7
10.0–19.9	1.9	1.8	6.6
20.0–49.9	1.4	1.7	5.0
50.0–99.9	1.2	1.6	4.2
100 and over	1.0	2.4	3.2
Average	1.6	1.9	12.4

Source: Securities and Exchange Commission, *Cost of Flotation of Corporate Securities, 1971–72* (Washington, D.C.: U.S. Government Printing Office, December 1974).

Negotiated sale or competitive bid.   Most new security offerings are made after the investment banker and the issuer decide on the type, terms, and timing of the issue. This procedure is known as a *negotiated sale* because the underwriter is directly involved in "putting together" the offering that will be sold. Federal, state, and local governments, railroads, and some public utilities use a different process for raising funds. They invite investment bankers to *bid* for their securities. This system is known as *competitive bidding*. Investment bankers may, in some instances, furnish advice to these organizations, but they must then bid along with others for the opportunity of selling the issue. Competitive bidding is required to prevent collusion between officials of the issuer and the investment banker.

Public offering versus private placements.   In many cases, funds are raised by selling an entire issue of securities to a small group of large investors such as insurance companies, mutual funds, pension funds, banks, and wealthy individuals. Sales of this type are known as *private placements* as opposed to the *public offerings* which occur when large numbers of investors are solicited. Private placements offer several advantages to the issuer. In the first place, the cost of selling is usually less. This is simply because the transaction often can be accomplished by a few telephone calls. Secondly, this procedure avoids legal requirements that are necessary for public offerings. Compliance with the regulations is a time-consuming and costly process. Finally, specific terms of the issue may be renegotiated with the small group of investors involved in a private placement. This provides flexibility that can be very helpful later if any difficulties arise.

The main disadvantage of private placements is that most investors are denied access to the issues. This may prevent the issuer from gaining an additional loyal group of customers, both for its products and for any of its subsequent security offerings.

An announcement of a private placement appears in Figure 3–2.

FIGURE 3–2
Example of a private placement announcement

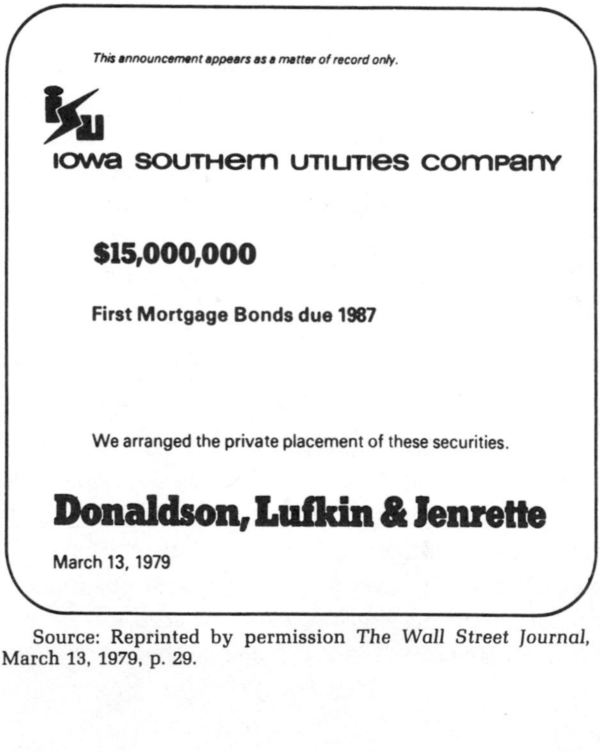

This announcement appears as a matter of record only.

IOWA SOUTHErn UTILITIES COMPANY

$15,000,000

First Mortgage Bonds due 1987

We arranged the private placement of these securities.

Donaldson, Lufkin & Jenrette

March 13, 1979

Source: Reprinted by permission *The Wall Street Journal,* March 13, 1979, p. 29.

The advertisement tells that Donaldson, Lufkin & Jenrette, acting as an investment banker, arranged for investors such as life insurance firms and pension funds, to purchase the bonds issued by Iowa Southern Utilities Company.

Marketing of new issues. In a typical public offering, the investment banker is faced with the task of selling an issue to raise many millions of dollars. To better accomplish the marketing job and spread the risk, one firm will usually combine with others to form an *underwriting syndicate*. This is a temporary association organized for the sole purpose of selling a specific security issue. It may involve 100 or more investment bankers who each buy a portion of the offering. If the issue is very large, an additional set of securities firms will be organized as a *selling group*. Each member of the set receives an allotment from the underwriting syndicate or purchasing group, which they in turn sell for a commission. Both groups retail the issue to their customers.

After sales begin, some investors immediately sell what they just bought. If substantial numbers did this, the security price might decline considerably. Then any unsold securities could not be sold at the original price. To help minimize risks due to immediate price declines, the underwriters may *stabilize* the security price by buying back securities offered. This is perfectly legal for a period up to 30 days. Hopefully, the entire issue will have been sold by then. If not, the investment bankers may lose considerable sums of money. If, on the other hand, trading in the new issue is accompanied by a price rise, the underwriters cannot raise their price above the original offering price. This means that their profits are limited to underwriting fees, but their losses have no such restriction. In practice, most securities are sold at the intended price.

SECONDARY MARKETS

Once securities have been sold for the first time, they may be traded again and again. Buying and selling activities after the "birth" of the new issue comprise *secondary markets*. They are divided into two categories—*organized exchanges* and the *over-the-counter* (OTC) market. The first type consists of a number of organizations located in a few major cities. OTC markets literally exist all around the world, wherever securities are traded without the use of stock exchanges.

Stock exchanges

The practice of trading securities at a specific place and with regulations governing activities is centuries old. The first exchange in America had its beginnings in New York City 16 years after the Declaration of Independence was signed. A listing of the 9 registered U.S. stock exchanges, together with sales volumes, appears in Table 3–4. Note that the New York and American exchanges account for almost 90 percent of the trading activity. Because of its dominant position the New York Stock Exchange (NYSE) will be discussed in detail.

TABLE 3–4
Total market value of stocks sold on stock exchanges in the United States (1978 year-end data)

Exchange	Millions of Dollars
American Stock Exchange	15,205.0
Boston Stock Exchange	1,535.8
Cincinnati Stock Exchange	433.2
Intermountain Stock Exchange	.8
Midwest Stock Exchange	10,461.2
New York Stock Exchange	210,426.4
Pacific Coast Stock Exchange	7,099.2
Philadelphia Stock Exchange	4,085.8
Spokane Stock Exchange	9.7
Total of all registered exchanges	249,257.1

Source: Securities and Exchange Commission, *Statistical Bulletin,* April 1979, p. 137.

The New York Stock Exchange

To most people, the stock market and the NYSE are synonymous. This is because it is the oldest and largest organized securities market in the United States. It began in 1792 with a gathering of those interested in selling stocks and bonds under a buttonwood tree on Wall Street. As the economy and business activity grew, security trading increased and the procedures became more formalized. Today, the NYSE is an association of members organized for the purpose of buying and selling securities for investors. The exchange itself only provides the facilities. The members, in effect, have a franchise to trade among themselves. There is a board of governors which establishes policies and regulations covering the activities of the membership.

Since 1953, there have been only 1,366 members, or "seats" as they are often called. Entry is gained by buying a seat from an existing member or from the estate of a deceased member. Costs of a seat are determined largely by trading volume and stock price levels on the exchange. The record membership price of $625,000 was set in 1929. The lowest price in this century was $17,000, paid in 1942. On March 12, 1979, a seat sold for $125,000.

Commission and floor brokers. The major types of memberships on the NYSE are shown in Table 3–5. The largest class is composed of *commission brokers*. These people execute orders for customers of their firms. Some brokerage houses have several seats to handle orders relayed to them by registered representatives in various cities throughout the world. Commission brokers act as agents for investors. When one of them has more orders than can be effectively handled, some of them may be given to a *floor broker* for execution. This type of member operates mainly on overflow business in heavy trading periods. Sometimes they assist commission brokers by handling large orders that require considerable time to be filled.

TABLE 3–5
Classification of New York Stock Exchange membership as of June 1978

Commission brokers	741
Specialists	385
Floor brokers	124
Others	116
Total membership	1,366

Source: Personal correspondence from the NYSE.

Specialists. One of the most important and yet least understood types of exchange members are the *specialists*. Their function is to maintain a fair and orderly market in one or more securities that have been assigned to them. They stay at a particular location or "post" on the floor of the exchange. Brokers come to them with their orders. Sometimes trades are effected right away. In other cases the broker leaves the order with the specialist, who records the information for later execution. Specialists constantly receive orders and quote prices based on them. Some of these buy and sell orders are matched and executed immediately. Specialists also maintain an inventory of shares which are used to fill other requests which in turn dampens wide price fluctuations that might result if they relied solely on bringing buyers and sellers together. The continual buying and selling action centering around the specialist is the reason for the frequent referrals to the NYSE as an *auction market.* Strict regulations and close surveillance are employed to help assure that specialists do not use their positions for personal gain at the expense of the public.

Other classes of members. The remaining categories of membership are less important in the sense that they perform roles that complement the major functions of the NYSE. Approximately 20 firms trade the almost 2,900 listed bond issues.[2] In 1978 a new type of member, the *Registered Competitive Marketmaker,* was instituted.[3] These individuals, who number about 50, typically trade for their own accounts in any of the listed stocks in ways that assist the Exchange's marketmaking function. Orders involving fractions of 100 share multiples are now handled by the particular specialist in the stock. These *odd-lot* transactions were formally handled by the now extinct category of *odd-lot dealers.* Odd-lot activity has continued to decline relative to round-lot orders and currently comprises less than 3 percent of the total trading volume.[4] The majority of the other memberships are held by 30 inactive individuals or their estates. In 1978 a new provision to promote more active use of memberships was established by allowing a seat to be leased.

Listing. Before securities can be traded on the NYSE, they must meet certain requirements for *listing.* These tests are designed to provide a group of stocks and bonds issued by larger, profitable firms in which there is a national interest.[5] From time to time, securities may be delisted due to a decline in trading interest, number of shareholders, profitability, mergers, and so on.

Types of orders. Investors use several methods to instruct their brokers to buy or sell securities.[6] The most common order used on the exchange is the *market order.* This requests the broker to buy or sell at the best price obtainable at the moment. Sometimes investors wish to buy or sell at a particular price, so they use a *limit order.* In this case, a price is specified that is different from the prevailing market. For example, if XYZ shares were selling at $20, a limit order might be placed

---

[2] New York Stock Exchange *1978 Annual Report,* p. 13.

[3] NYSE *1978 Annual Report,* p. 2.

[4] NYSE *1978 Fact Book,* p. 69.

[5] Specific requirements are given in the NYSE *1978 Fact Book,* pp. 31–33.

[6] The most common orders are described in this section. For a detailed description of 13 other types see Keith V. Smith and David K. Eiteman, *Essentials of Investing* (Homewood, Ill.; Richard D. Irwin, 1974), pp. 438–41.

to buy at $19. If the quote fell to that level or below, the order would be executed. A seller might give a limit order at $22, which would be filled if and when the price rose to at least this level.

A special type of limit order is known as the *stop* or *stop-loss order*. This is used in several ways, the most common being when an investor wants to "protect a profit." For example, suppose a stock, previously purchased at $10, is now quoted at $20. A stop order placed at some point below $20, say $18, assures the investor of a minimum profit of $18 minus $10 or $8 per share. If the stock does not drop but instead rises, the stop-order price can be increased.

In addition to specifying a price in all types of limit orders, a time period must be given to indicate how long the order is to be in effect. Usually the periods are for one day, one week, one month, or they may be "good till canceled" (GTC). If the stated price is not reached during the time period allowed, the order expires unfilled.

The difficulty with limit orders is that they may cause action or inaction which is not really best for the investor. When plain limit orders are used, execution may never take place. In the first example, an order was placed to buy at $19 when the market was $20. The price might only fall to $19⅛ and then rise to $30 or higher. The investor would have "missed the market." The same thing would happen with a sell order at $21 if the price rose to $20⅞ and then fell. Again profits would have been lost. In the case of stop orders, the price may drop just a little too far. In the example used, a decline from $20 to $18 would cause the shareholder to be sold out. If the price then reversed and started rising, an opportunity for profits would have been missed. The opponents of using limit orders as a technique are quick to point out the hazards of just barely missing the market. They argue that if someone wants to sell or buy, the stock should be closely watched. When a feeling develops that the time is right, action should be taken using a market order. Critics also say that use of limit orders which try to maximize profits just does not achieve that result very often, and in the long run the investor suffers losses because of them. Considerable care should be exercised in the use of limit orders.

Short selling and margin trading. Two techniques can be used in conjunction with security orders. *Short selling* involves selling borrowed securities, anticipating that the same issue can be bought back later at a lower price. Details of this procedure are discussed in Chapter 11. The other technique is known as *margin trading*. Margin is the amount of down payment required to purchase securities. The balance due is usually borrowed from the investor's broker or banker. Margin buying permits leverage, allowing more to be accomplished with a given amount of money. For example, if an investor purchased stock costing $10,000 and it increased 20 percent in value, the gain would be $2,000. With a 65 percent margin, $10,000 could be used in conjunction with a loan to purchase up to $15,385 in stock. If these shares rose the same 20 percent, the gross profit would be $15,385 × 1.2 − $10,000, or $8,462. The interest due on the $5,385 borrowed and commissions on the transaction would reduce this figure; however, the benefit of the margin technique in this example is obvious.

Of course, if the stock price had fallen instead of rising, leverage would have increased the loss just as it increased the gain. Furthermore, a decline in the price may result in a *margin call*. A NYSE regulation requires maintenance of a certain value in margin accounts in relation to the market value of the margined securities. If prices drop far enough, the investor will be called to put up more cash. Details of this procedure can be obtained at any brokerage office.

The painful reality of margin calls was dramatically illustrated in the speculative market boom of the late 1920s. Many investors had purchased stock on 10 percent margin. As stock prices declined, thousands were unable to put up the required cash. The stocks were sold, causing further price declines, more margin calls and so on.

After this debacle, margin activity has been more closely regulated. Since 1934 the Federal Reserve Board of Governors has set the margin requirement which has varied between 40 and 90 percent. In mid-1979, the margin requirement was 50 percent. The NYSE requires a minimum down payment of $2,000 for securities bought on margin. The Securities and Exchange Commission (SEC) can require temporary 100 percent margins (no credit) on individual securities in situations where unusual speculative activity has occurred. As with limit orders, margin trading should be used with considerable care.

Commissions. Buying and selling securities is the business of investment firms or brokerage houses, as they are often called. They act as an agent for the investor much like the realtor does in real estate transactions. They charge a commission for this service. Minimum fees were fixed by the NYSE during the first 183 years of the Exchange's operation. Since 1975, member firms have been permitted to charge whatever rates they choose. Investors now find different charges at each brokerage house.

Table 3–6 presents a partial commission schedule representative of

TABLE 3-6
Schedule of typical commission fees*

Total dollar cost:

Price per share	50 shares	100 shares	500 shares
$ 5	$23.38	$26.39	$ 98.62
10	26.31	33.21	129.70
20	33.27	50.24	193.55
30	42.02	64.94	254.57
50	59.83	86.07	356.49

Cost per share:

Price per share	50 shares	100 shares	500 shares
$ 5	$ 0.47	$ 0.26	$ 0.20
10	0.53	0.33	0.26
20	0.67	0.50	0.40
30	0.80	0.65	0.51
50	1.20	0.86	0.71

Cost as a percentage
of transaction amount:

Price per share	50 shares	100 shares	500 shares
$ 5	9.35%	5.28%	3.94%
10	5.26	3.32	2.59
20	3.33	2.51	1.94
30	2.80	2.16	1.70
50	2.39	1.72	1.43

* Average fees charged by a sample of NYSE member firms surveyed by the authors on March 23, 1979. The figures do not include payments by the seller of (1) the New York state transfer tax of up to five cents per share and (2) the SEC fee of one cent for each $500 of transaction value.

"full service" brokerage firms. The total commission appears in the top part of Table 3-6. Fees are expressed in dollars per share in the middle section and in the bottom part costs are figured as a percentage of the total value involved in the transaction. For example, an investor wishing to buy or sell 100 shares of a stock at $30 per share would pay a commission of $64.94. This amounts to 65 cents per share or 2.16 percent of the $3,000 (100 shares times $30 per share) order.

Notice that the commission cost per share declines as the number of shares in the order increases. Also, higher priced shares carry lower proportionate commissions. The two main variables in any transaction, the number of shares and the price per share, can be combined into a total value figure. The general observation then is *commission costs expressed as a percentage of the transaction decrease as order sizes become larger.*

It is not much harder to fill a 500-share order compared to a 100-

share request. This experience is reflected in the cost schedule. Indeed, if one studies the different commission charges in effect over the years, a long-term trend to set fees more in line with costs is revealed. This has resulted in charges on smaller orders being increased while fees on the larger deals have declined. Pressure by the SEC and large investors such as insurance companies and mutual funds hastened this shift to a cost-oriented commission schedule.

The unfixing of commissions stimulated brokerage firms to introduce a number of different plans designed to better meet needs of individual investors. Figure 3–3, showing parts of advertisements, illustrates this development. The old, uniform pricing system meant many investors were not using all the services that in effect were being paid for. Now, investors can better match their needs with a system of paying for these services. Details of these services and alternative plans are discussed in the next chapter.

The elimination of what was essentially price fixing of commissions means that investors can, in theory, negotiate fees with their brokers.

FIGURE 3–3
Special plans offered by brokers for investors

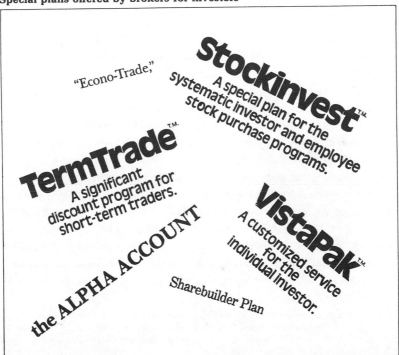

However, it is unlikely that brokers will bargain with very many investors. Negotiating commissions is typically limited to the larger trades involving amounts of about $50,000 or more.

In Table 3–6 the 100-share trade of the $30 stock had an average commission of $64.94. However, the NYSE member firms who were sampled when preparing the table charged between $58.75 and $72.90. While the typical fees are close to the averages presented, certain investors may wish to do business with a *discount broker* or "boutique" or "pipe rack" firm as they are sometimes called.[7] These organizations offer a no-frills order execution service for 10 to 40 percent (or more) below the fees levied by most full-service brokers. The discount firms offer no research or other costly programs. Their customers do not seek their advice on buying and selling or expect other aids provided by the major brokerage houses.

As previously indicated, odd-lot trading is decreasing. The proportionately higher commissions on these orders are the primary reason. In addition, the NYSE adds 12.5 cents per share (⅛ point) to the cost of these trades. This means an investor placing an order to buy 50 shares at $20 per share would pay $20.125 per share plus commission. An odd-lot seller would receive $19.875 per share less the commission.

The commissions on bond trades typically range from $7.50 to $25 per bond depending on the size of the order and the broker.

Investors are cautioned against devoting an undue amount of time and energy in shopping for the best net price on each order. However, they are advised to be aware of transaction costs and to make an effort to be sure that they are "paying for only what they need."

Illustration of an order. The operation of the New York Stock Exchange can perhaps be better understood by describing what happens when an order is placed. Suppose Mary Doe, an investor in Walla Walla, Washington, decides to invest in General Motors. She calls her broker or registered representative with instructions to buy 100 shares of GM common stock *at the market.* The broker, who is employed by a member firm of the NYSE, has this market order teletyped to the "floor" of the NYSE. This is a high-ceilinged, open room about half the size of a football field, located in a building near the southern tip of Manhattan Island. A photograph of the trading floor is shown in Fig-

---

[7] See "Discount Brokers Do What They Advertise," *Wall Street Journal,* April 5, 1977, p. 1; "Discount Broker Offers No Frills—and No Advice," *Chicago Tribune,* November 29, 1978, p. 18; and "Discount Brokers Gain Credibility," *Business Week,* March 26, 1979, p. 89.

ure 3–4. Around the edge of this room are message centers where trading information is received and transmitted by each of the member firms. A clerk, employed by the same firm as the Walla Walla broker, takes the order from the teletype and gives it to the firm's *commission broker*. If trading is especially active it might be given to a *floor broker* instead.

In either event, the clerk hands the order to a broker who then proceeds to the particular spot where GM is traded. This would be at one of 18 cogwheel-shaped counters called *trading posts*. A quote board above the post indicates that the last trade in GM was at $65, so the broker knows the price will be close to this figure. In the hope of buying for less, the broker asks the *specialist,* "How's GM?" The reply might be "three-quarters, one-quarter," meaning, I will pay $64¾ for GM, and I will sell it to you for $65¼. These are *bid* and *asked* prices; the bid is always given first. The difference between the two figures is the markup or spread on which the specialist makes a profit. The broker now knows that a market order can be executed by paying $65¼.

FIGURE 3–4
Trading floor of New York Stock Exchange

Courtesy of New York Stock Exchange

Note: By early 1980 a new trading floor arrangement will be installed. The new posts, in the shape of two adjoining cogwheels, will provide a highly automated trading environment.

However, he might say "65 for 100," which means he is offering to buy 100 shares at $65 per share. Somewhere between $65 and $65¼ a price will be agreed upon. Since this is a market order, the broker will not wait long before buying the shares. A *limit order* would have been left with the specialist to be filled when the price specified by Mary Doe was reached.

Perhaps some other brokers who also want to buy and sell GM arrive before the first broker leaves. They might also enter into the bidding. In any case the broker with a market order to fill will quickly purchase 100 shares of GM. Notes are made indicating who bought, who sold, the price, and the number of shares. Details of the transaction are electronically transmitted back to the registered representative in Walla Walla. Mary Doe is then informed of prices and commissions directly. The whole process usually takes only five minutes or less. In two or three days she will receive a written confirmation of the transaction. Investors have five business days after the order was filled in which to pay for the stock. The stock certificate will be sent to them in about a month if desired.

In busy periods, trading on the NYSE is a fascinating display of "orderly pandemonium." A glass-enclosed visitors gallery enables people to view the proceedings below.[8] Everything is at a rapid pace with people scurrying all over much like ants in a broken bag of sugar. "How's GM? GMthreequartersonequarterIgohundredsixty-five Takeit" rolls into an unintelligible mumble. In a typical day, almost 30 million shares, representing values of more than $800 million will change hands, all in a symphonic, orderly, six-hour period of seeming chaos.

Other stock exchanges

The other national exchange in the United States is the American Stock Exchange (AMEX). Though it is dwarfed by the NYSE, it represents a very active trading arena for investors.

The AMEX has had a colorful history since its birth during the California gold rush in 1849. Prior to 1953, it was called the New York Curb Exchange because trading activities over the first 72 years were carried

---

[8] In 1979 the Visitors Center was renovated. This attraction provides a highly educational opportunity.

out on the sidewalks of lower Manhattan under open skies. Brokers wore brightly colored hats and jackets so they could be identified in the street crowds by their message clerks who were perched on upper story windowsills in surrounding buildings. Finally, after succumbing to stifling heat, extreme cold, driving rain, snow, and sleet, the exchange moved indoors in 1921.

Today there are many similarities between the two major exchanges. Trading procedures are the same in principle, though some details are different. Other characteristics are alike but on a reduced scale. For example, it costs less to become a member of the AMEX. In general, the companies listed are smaller and lesser known firms compared to their NYSE counterparts. Some investors have a special interest in the AMEX because stock prices there have tended to fluctuate widely. In 1974, the AMEX introduced trading in call options. This type of investment, which is described in Chapter 11, has proven very popular and has helped stimulate interest in the AMEX.

Regional stock exchanges are located in various metropolitan centers throughout the country. Around 90 percent of the stocks traded on most of these exchanges are also bought and sold on either the New York or the American Stock Exchange. This practice is known as *dual listing*. It provides a marketplace for issues with national interest to brokerage firms with a regional clientele. Different trading hours and slight variations in commission schedules are among the reasons why some stocks are traded on more than one exchange. Prices of any dually listed stock are always closely in line with the New York quotes.

The Midwest Stock Exchange, located in Chicago, is the largest regional exchange. Perhaps the most unique is the *Pacific Coast Stock Exchange,* with its two trading floors 400 miles apart in San Francisco and in Los Angeles. The system is organized so that transactions can be carried out in either city.

Over-the-counter markets

Securities traded without the use of stock exchange facilities are by definition traded in the OTC market.

It has been called an amorphous market because of the wide array of locations, participants, and securities involved. The majority of issues traded are government bonds—both federal and municipal—

and corporate bonds and stocks in which there is too little investor interest for them to be listed on an exchange. By tradition, most banks and insurance companies, together with many nonfinancial corporations have chosen not to list their securities, even though many of these firms might well qualify for exchange trading. Because of the marketing techniques used to sell their shares, none of the mutual funds is listed. OTC trades are made in hundreds of cities and in thousands of different issues. It is easy to see why the market is usually defined in terms of what it is not.

The OTC dealer. The central figures in the OTC trading are the dealers.[9] They perform a function similar to that carried out by the specialist on the NYSE. To do this dealers maintain inventories of securities. When someone wants to buy or sell, they come to the dealer. On the stock exchange there is usually only one "dealer" for each security, but in the OTC market there is no limit to how many people may set themselves up as dealers in any particular issue. They compete for business in a stock primarily on the basis of the price which they will pay and the price at which they offer to sell. Bid and asked prices are continually being quoted to brokerage firms around the country on a vast automated network known as NASDAQ (pronounced NAZDAK). This computerized system (acronym for National Association of Securities Dealers Automated Quotations) was introduced in 1971. It replaced a cumbersome communications procedure over telephone and teletype lines. As a result the OTC market was transformed into a nationwide, visible marketplace with a trading "floor" over 3,000 miles long. NASDAQ offers instantaneous quotations from OTC dealers. This is accomplished by the marketmakers, around the country, entering their names and bid and asked prices for stocks into a computer terminal. The information is transmitted to a central computer where it becomes available to any other broker/dealer who is tied into the system. When an investor places an order, the broker pushes a few buttons on a keyboard to access all this data. In an instant a display appears showing the quotations from around the nation. The broker will then place the order with the dealer offering the highest bid price if the investor is selling; a buy order will

---

[9] Most securities firms are broker-dealer businesses. They act as agents or *brokers* in handling buy and sell orders for investors. They assume the role of principal or *dealer* when they make a market in securities, buying and selling for their own account.

be executed with the dealer quoting the lowest asked price. The powerful system enables brokers to become very efficient shoppers for their clients. It is much like having someone give you up-to-the-second information on the price of XYZ canned beans in every grocery store.

NASDAQ has greatly stimulated OTC trading activity. During 1978, the number of shares traded over this system was more than one-third of the NYSE volume and about double the number of shares traded on all other exchanges combined. The vast majority of bond trading occurs in the OTC.

OTC commissions.   OTC orders are filled in two different ways— on an *agency* or on a *principal* basis. In the former case, commissions are added to the price quoted for buy orders and subtracted from the price on sell orders. Most firms charge the same commissions on OTC trades as on listed security transactions. However, no odd-lot differential charges are levied in the OTC market.

In the other case the broker, acting as principal or dealer, fills the order from the firm's own account. The prices quoted to investors are on a net basis and no commissions per se are charged. Dealers hope to make money by buying at prices which are lower than their selling prices—just like any merchant.

The third market.   This involves OTC trading in stocks listed on the exchanges. In the early 1970s, commissions were based on the cost of trading in round lots. The charges for 300 shares were three times that for a 100-share order. For 3,000 shares, the multiple was 30. As trading by large institutional investors (such as mutual funds) increased, there arose considerable discontent over this type of proportionate charging. Brokerage firms that were not exchange members began seeking out large investors and arranging trades without the benefit of the exchanges. They charged lower commission rates for this service. Some nonmember firms also maintained inventories of listed stocks, and they often bought and sold these securities for their own accounts.

Another market has been developed for the large investors. It is known as the *fourth market* and involves trading of listed securities directly between institutions without the use of a broker. Bypassing of the agent, of course, saves commissions. Several services that use computers to match buy and sell orders have been organized and have stimulated the fourth market activity.

The OTC is a market place for virtually every investor, offering an abundant variety of security types and grades of risk. This variety should not discourage investor participation but should rather serve to open new investment opportunities.

The National Market System

During the 1960s the increasing ownership of securities by pension funds, insurance companies, mutual funds, and so on, led Congress to direct the SEC to study the impact of this trend on the public interest. The report, which was completed in 1971, stated:

> ... our objective is to see a strong central market system created to which all investors have access, in which, all qualified broker-dealers and existing market institutions may participate in accordance with their respective capabilities, and which is controlled not only by appropriate regulation but also by the forces of competition.[10]

Subsequent studies and discussions have supported this position which was written into a federal law passed in 1975. While critics contend the evolution toward the National Market System has moved with glacial speed, several highly significant developments had occurred before 1980.

The securities industry applied computer and other electronic technology to offer a medium for reporting in one place, the prices, volumes, and exchanges where trades had taken place. This *Consolidated Tape* keeps the investment community and the public accurately informed of listed stock transactions in all markets. In addition, a *Consolidated Quotation System* provides bid and asked prices and number of shares available or wanted for listed and major OTC stocks. These two innovations offer people the basic information necessary to obtain the best order execution. The *Intermarket Trading System* electronically links the six major U.S. stock exchanges in a nationwide trading and communications network. These developments make buying and selling stocks somewhat analogous to a person being able to determine prices of grocery items and the inventories at every store in town to be better able to decide where to shop.

Another facilitation of stock trading has been realized by clearance and settlement mechanisms to transfer necessary funds and securities

---

[10] *Institutional Investor Study of the Securities and Exchange Commission,* Letter of Transmittal (Washington, D.C.: U.S. Government Printing Office, March 10, 1971).

balances electronically after trades are completed. Work is progressing on a "central limit order file" which is intended to assure that investors receive their specified price when any market reaches that point and their order is first in line. The schematic diagram in Figure 3–5 shows how market and limit orders are handled in the National Market System.

FIGURE 3–5
Order flow in the National Market System

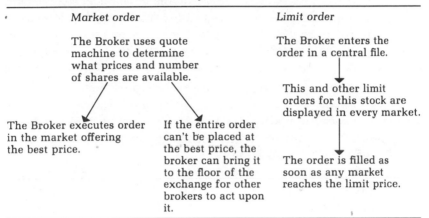

Market order		*Limit order*
The Broker uses quote machine to determine what prices and number of shares are available.		The Broker enters the order in a central file.
		This and other limit orders for this stock are displayed in every market.
The Broker executes order in the market offering the best price.	If the entire order can't be placed at the best price, the broker can bring it to the floor of the exchange for other brokers to act upon it.	The order is filled as soon as any market reaches the limit price.

REGULATION OF SECURITY MARKETS

Conduct of the financial community is overseen by many state, federal, and industry organizations. The purpose of this surveillance is to provide protection for the public from dishonest practices by members of the securities industry. Trust in transacting business is a cornerstone of this industry. This confidence has been fostered by the formation and operation of agencies to regulate the investment community. Statutes and regulatory operations that apply to the securities industry are discussed in this section.

Federal regulation

After the skyrocketing stock prices in the 1920s and the subsequent stock market crash, comprehensive federal legislation was enacted to regulate the securities industry. Excessive speculation and outright fraud influenced the writing of the statutes. Before the first federal law was passed in 1933, the concept of *caveat emptor* (let the buyer beware) prevailed in the investment business. The new legislation modified this principle by requiring disclosure of information about security issues, by banning fraudulent practices, and by providing surveillance of trading activities.

The Securities Act of 1933. This law, also called the truth-in-securities act, was passed to provide full and fair disclosure of information about companies selling securities to the public. The logic behind this act is not to prevent investors from losing money but instead to make it possible for them to evaluate new issues on an informed and realistic basis. The burden is on the investor to select securities, some of which certainly do become valueless. The law merely assures that investors have access to complete and accurate information on which to base decisions. The information is filed with the Securities and Exchange Commission in a *registration statement* and is made available to investors in a *prospectus*. This document contains relevant details about the offering and the issuer.

The cover page and the table of contents of a prospectus for an offering of Ingersoll-Rand, Inc., common stock are shown in Figure 3–6. A general statement about the role of the SEC in the offering always appears on the front page of the prospectus along with basic details of the issue and the name of the managing underwriter(s). The main purpose of the disclaimer for the SEC is to make certain that investors do not have the impression that the federal government has endorsed or passed on the merits of the securities being sold. The range of information indicated by the Table of Contents illustrates the full disclosure concept of the 1933 Act. The 28-page pamphlet includes a rather thorough description of the current state of company operations, management's plans for use of the money raised from the offering, and other details of the underwriting. Financial statements, attested to fairness and accuracy by an independent certified public accounting firm, appear at the end.

When a registration statement is filed with the SEC, a preliminary prospectus or *red herring* is usually prepared to inform potential buyers about a forthcoming offering. This unusual name is derived from the red lettering used for the following statement appearing on the cover:

> A registration statement relating to these securities has been filed with the Securities and Exchange Commission, but has not yet become

FIGURE 3–6
Illustration of a prospectus

PROSPECTUS

1,000,000 Shares

Ingersoll-Rand Company

COMMON STOCK

($2 par value)

The Company's Common Stock is listed on the New York Stock Exchange.

THESE SECURITIES HAVE NOT BEEN APPROVED OR DISAPPROVED BY THE SECURITIES AND EXCHANGE COMMISSION NOR HAS THE COMMISSION PASSED UPON THE ACCURACY OR ADEQUACY OF THIS PROSPECTUS. ANY REPRESENTATION TO THE CONTRARY IS A CRIMINAL OFFENSE.

PRICE $76 A SHARE

	Price to Public	Underwriting Discounts and Commissions	Proceeds to Company(1)
Per Share	$76.00	$2.85	$73.15
Total	$76,000,000	$2,850,000	$73,150,000

(1) Before deduction of expenses estimated at $185,500.

The Shares are offered by the several Underwriters named herein, subject to prior sale, when, as and if accepted by the Underwriters, and subject to approval of certain legal matters by Davis Polk & Wardwell, counsel for the Underwriters. It is expected that delivery of the Shares will be made on or about May 7, 1975 at the office of Morgan Stanley & Co. Incorporated, 140 Broadway, New York, N. Y., against payment therefor in New York funds.

MORGAN STANLEY & CO.
Incorporated

MERRILL LYNCH, PIERCE, FENNER & SMITH
Incorporated

SMITH, BARNEY & CO.
Incorporated

April 29, 1975

No person is authorized in connection with this offering to give any information or to make any representations not contained in this Prospectus, and any information or representation not contained herein must not be relied upon as having been authorized by the Company or any Underwriter.

TABLE OF CONTENTS

AVAILABLE INFORMATION

The Company is subject to the informational requirements of the Securities Exchange Act of 1934 and in accordance therewith files reports and other information with the Securities and Exchange Commission. Information, as of particular dates, concerning directors and officers, their remuneration, options granted to them, the principal holders of securities of the Company and any material interest of such persons in transactions with the Company is disclosed in proxy statements distributed to shareholders of the Company and filed with the Commission. Such reports, proxy statements and other information can be inspected at the principal office of the Commission at Room 6101, 1100 L Street, N. W., Washington, D. C. 20005, where copies of such material can be obtained at prescribed rates. Such material can also be inspected at the offices of the New York Stock Exchange, Inc., 11 Wall Street, New York, N. Y. 10005.

IN CONNECTION WITH THIS OFFERING, THE UNDERWRITERS MAY OVER-ALLOT OR EFFECT TRANSACTIONS WHICH STABILIZE OR MAINTAIN THE MARKET PRICE OF THE COMMON STOCK OF THE COMPANY AT A LEVEL ABOVE THAT WHICH MIGHT OTHERWISE PREVAIL IN THE OPEN MARKET. SUCH TRANSACTIONS MAY BE EFFECTED ON THE NEW YORK STOCK EXCHANGE OR IN THE OVER-THE-COUNTER MARKET. SUCH STABILIZING, IF COMMENCED, MAY BE DISCONTINUED AT ANY TIME.

2

effective. Information contained herein is subject to completion or amendment. These securities may not be sold nor may offers to buy be accepted prior to the time the registration statement becomes effective. This prospectus shall not constitute an offer to sell or the solicitation of an offer to buy nor shall there be any sale of these securities in any State in which such offer, solicitation or sale would be unlawful prior to registration or qualification under the securities laws of any such State.

The prospectus shown in Figure 3–6 is a final copy, so the above statement does not appear on it.

The SEC examines the registration statement for compliance with the full and fair disclosure provisions of the statutes. In this examination, errors of omission and commission are identified. An example of incomplete disclosure appeared in a proposed offering by Republic Cement Corporation.

> . . . the registrant had failed to disclose that its proposed output of gray cement combined with that of a presently producing plant in its market area would far exceed any past or present market demand and that the existing plant had not been operating at full capacity. It further found that the registrant's proposed output of white cement exceeded 25 percent of the annual consumption of that product in the entire United States. The company's plant construction cost figures were determined to be much lower than those of its competitors because certain installations which are normally part of a cement plant were to be eliminated, and the registrant had not provided for sufficient storage capacity for its finished product. The Commission also found that despite the representation in the prospectus that the registrant had on its properties 1,851,300,000 tons of limestone suitable for the production of cement, only the most rudimentary type of exploration had been performed on the properties, and no systematic core drilling or sampling was used to test the continuity, depth, and quality of the limestone.[11]

When the examination process is completed, the SEC notifies the underwriter that registration has become effective. A final prospectus is then printed, including any amendments, and used to offer the issue to the public.

Certain types and sizes of issues are exempted from the registration provisions of the Securities Act. For example, bonds of federal and

---

[11] Securities and Exchange Commission, *23rd Annual Report* (Washington, D.C.: U.S. Government Printing Office, 1957), p. 46.

municipal governments and nonprofit organizations need not be registered with the SEC. Issues sold entirely to residents of the state in which a company conducts the major part of its business are also exempted from federal registration. These are *intrastate offerings;* even secondary trading across state lines is prohibited until at least one year after the issue has been sold.

Issues of $1.5 million or less do not have to meet full registration requirements. These small issues are known as Regulation A, or Reg. A issues for short. The SEC still oversees this group of offerings, but it only requires the filing of an abbreviated disclosure report. This results in substantial savings to the company of both time and money. Reg. A offerings, like those using the full registration, may be sold in as many states as the issuer obtains clearance from the state authorities to do so.

The Securities Exchange Act of 1934. This law was passed to extend federal regulation of the securities industry to include security trading. The act empowered the SEC to regulate trading procedures and practices of most stock exchanges in the U.S.[12] A major accomplishment of the 1934 Act and the amendments added in 1964 was to require all corporations whose securities are listed on any stock exchange and other firms having at least 500 shareholders and $1 million in assets to periodically file up-to-date financial data with the SEC.

Another provision places restrictions on trading activities of corporate *insiders.* These are people who by virtue of their relationship with the company are privileged to know certain information which is not available to the public. Generally, insiders are usually defined as company officers, directors, and owners of 10 percent or more of the corporation's stock.[13] To discourage unfair use of confidential information, insiders must file monthly statements with the SEC, outlining their transactions in the company's securities.

---

[12] It also established the Securities and Exchange Commission to administer the federal security statutes. The 1933 Act had been administered by the Federal Trade Commission.

[13] The SEC has been quite active in regulating insider activities in the latter part of the 1960s. A landmark case involved stock purchases by officers and certain employees of Texas Gulf Sulfur Co. before the firm announced it had discovered a sizeable ore deposit in Canada. In another recent proceeding the SEC alleged that the brokerage firm of Merrill Lynch, Pierce, Fenner and Smith used "inside information" to warn some of their institutional clients that Douglas Aircraft was going to announce losses. These cases may serve to greatly extend the definition of insiders to include anyone who receives and acts upon inside information.

The 1934 Act also makes the SEC responsible for regulating broker-dealer activities and the procedures used in bringing company business to shareholders for their approval.

Other federal legislation. Abuses in many areas of investment activity led to additional remedial legislation. For example, the Public Utility Holding Company Act of 1935 was designed to correct improper practices in the public utility industry.

The *Maloney Act of 1938* made it possible to organize the National Association of Securities Dealers (NASD). This is a private organization which establishes fair trade practices and assures compliance to them by self-regulation. This industry group is discussed in a later section.

The *Bankruptcy Act of 1938* provides a procedure for reorganizing financially troubled firms. The SEC assists the courts to help assure soundness and fairness in the reorganization plans.

The *Trust Indenture Act of 1940* was passed to provide protection for bondholders by regulating the actions of the trustee as outlined in the bond indenture.

Congress enacted the *Investment Company Act of 1940* in an attempt to prevent improper practices of firms who invest in the securities of other organizations:

> ... it provides a comprehensive framework of regulation which, among other things, prohibits changes in the nature of an investment company's business or its investment policies without shareholder approval, protects against loss, outright theft or abuse of trust, and provides specific controls to eliminate or to mitigate inequitable capital structures. The Act also requires that an investment company disclose its financial condition and investment policies; requires management contracts to be submitted to shareholders for approval; prohibits underwriters, investment bankers, or brokers from constituting more than a minority of the investment company's board of directors; regulates the custody of its assets; and provides specific controls designed to protect against unfair transactions between investment companies and their affiliates.[14]

Further discussion of this legislation appears in Chapter 10.

The *Investment Advisors Act of 1940* was designed to protect the public from those who sell investment advice. This law calls for registration of advisors and stipulates against certain practices.

---

[14] Securities and Exchange Commission, *39th Annual Report* (Washington, D.C.: U.S. Government Printing Office, 1974), p. 124.

The *Securities Acts Amendments of 1975* mandated the National Market System and broadened the powers of the SEC. Linking all markets would, in the view of Congress, provide greater efficiency and cost effectiveness in serving investors.

In its role as the chief administrator of the federal securities statutes, the SEC becomes involved in a wide array of activities as illustrated in the clippings shown in Figure 3–7. The SEC's 1977 *Annual Report* discussed the central market, automated trading information systems, the structure and level of commission rates, option market

FIGURE 3–7
Activities of the SEC

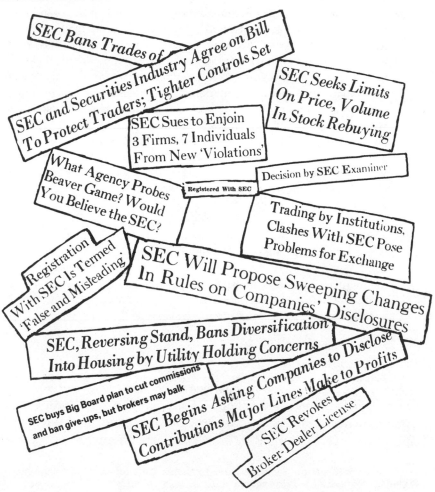

regulation, tax sheltered investments, and forecasts of company performance.

The function of the SEC is brought into perspective in a recent pamphlet:

> Securities are by their very nature much different from almost any other type of "merchandise" for which there are established public markets. A person who wishes to purchase a new car or household appliance—or for that matter, a peck of potatoes or a bag of beans—can pretty well determine from personal inspection the quality of the product and the reasonableness of the price in relation to other competing products. But this is not so with respect to a bond or a share of stock.
>
> An engraved certificate representing an interest in an abandoned mine or a defunct gadget manufacturer, for example, might look no less impressive than a "blue chip" security with a history of years of unbroken dividend payments. Beyond that all comparisons cease— and for the average investor to differentiate between the securities of little or no value and those offering at least reasonable prospect of a satisfactory return on his investment requires (1) a personal inspection of the properties and operations of the issuer (which for all practical purposes is generally impossible), or (2) that he place almost complete reliance on the oral and written representations and available literature about the company, its prospects, and the terms of its securities.
>
> . . . It should be understood that the securities laws were designed to facilitate informed investment analyses and prudent and discriminating investment decisions *by the investing public*. It is the investor, *not* the Commission who must make the ultimate judgment of the worth of securities offered for sale. The Commission is powerless to pass upon the merits of securities; and assuming proper disclosure of the financial and other information essential to informed investment analysis, the Commission cannot bar the sale of securities which such analysis may show to be of questionable value.[15]

State regulation

States enacted securities regulations more than two decades before comprehensive federal legislation was passed. The state statutes became known as *Blue Sky Laws* because they were designed to prevent sale of fraudulent securities by firms who were offering only a "piece

---

[15] "The Work of the Securities and Exchange Commission," (Washington, D.C.: U.S. Government Printing Office, April 1978), p. vii.

of the blue sky" to investors. The current laws cover, for the most part, registration of persons and firms who buy and sell securities, registration of information on securities to be offered for sale, and prevention of fraudulent activities. The philosophy of the act is to provide investor protection within each state, by requiring full disclosure of all pertinent facts surrounding securities offerings.

Some states have gone one step further and permit enforcing authorities to ban the sale of certain securities which they feel are objectionable. Usually the state administrators do not make economic judgments regarding the feasibility of a given project; rather they determine if the investors are receiving a "fair run" for their money. This, of course, requires a great deal of discretion and subjective judgment on the part of the administrators. Some states, notably New York, rely solely on antifraud provisions to deter any issuer from not giving the investor a "fair shake."

Industry regulation

In addition to federal and state regulation, there are several private organizations which seek to oversee activities of their memberships.

National Association of Securities Dealers. The NASD is a self-regulatory body composed of most of the broker-dealer firms in the securities industry. Its stated purposes are

1. To promote the investment banking and securities business.
2. To standardize its principles and practices.
3. To promote high standards of commercial honor and to promote among members observance of federal and state securities laws.
4. To provide a medium through which the membership may consult with governmental and other agencies.
5. To cooperate with governmental authority in the solution of problems affecting this business and investors.
6. To adopt and enforce rules of fair practice in the securities business.
7. To promote just and equitable principles of trade for the protection of investors.
8. To promote self-discipline among members.
9. To investigate and adjust grievances between members and between the public and members.[16]

---

[16] "1978 Report to Members," National Association of Securities Dealers, p. 33.

Regulation by the stock exchanges. Most of the exchanges carefully scrutinize the business of their memberships. They have rules to govern activities both on and off the trading floors. They fine or suspend members who are found guilty of infractions. This group has also contributed to minimizing dishonest practices in the securities industry.

Securities Investor Protection Corporation (SIPC). In 1970, Congress established a private, nonprofit corporation for the purpose of protecting customers of broker-dealer firms. The Act, which was amended in 1978, provided a safeguard by insuring investors against loss due to failure of a brokerage firm. SIPC will pay up to $100,000 of each investor's claim caused by bankruptcy of a broker-dealer. It is important to note that this protection is not against losses investors may sustain from fluctuating security prices. Thus SIPC offers some investor protection and thereby promotes confidence in securities markets. The financial base of SIPC is derived from assessments of less than one percent of the gross revenues of the members which include essentially all of the broker-dealer firms in the industry.

Other forms of investor protection. Most brokerage firms also maintain a vigilant watch over their individual operations. Many firms have a staff of lawyers, accountants, or former FBI men to guard against frauds.

Despite the massive efforts from many sources, improper practices in the investment community continue. Security price manipulations have all but disappeared, but other schemes and dishonest activities have developed and will continue to exist. Investors play a crucial role in the regulation process. They should carefully investigate situations before committing funds and report questionable practices. No one can protect an investor from making unwise decisions.

SUMMARY

Securities markets are a complex combination of people, customs, and regulations. These markets help make savings available to organizations so that they can use them to provide goods and services for the public. In addition to this economic function, securities markets provide a place where securities can be bought and sold at fair prices.

Governmental bodies and corporations often raise funds by exchanging stocks and bonds for money. These activities comprise *primary markets*. Assistance to the organizations seeking funds is provided by *investment bankers*. They offer advice on the type, terms, and timing of the issue. They buy new securities from the issuer and then sell them to investors. This is known as an *underwriting*. Usually groups of investment bankers are formed to buy the offering, and if it is large, an additional *selling group* may be organized to help market the issue. Sometimes the securities are offered only to a small number of investors through a *private placement*. Investment bankers enter *competitive bidding* to underwrite securities of railroads, utilities, and governmental bodies.

After the securities are sold initially, they are traded in *secondary markets*. These include organized *stock exchanges* and *over-the-counter* markets. The New York Stock Exchange dominates common stock trading. Its membership has an exclusive right to buy and sell securities through the NYSE facilities. Some members are *commission brokers* who execute orders for customers of their brokerage firms. *Floor brokers* assist commission brokers by handling orders in periods of heavy trading activity. *Specialists* are exchange members who are responsible for maintaining a fair and orderly market in one or more stocks. They set prices by buying and selling for their own account. Other classes of membership include *registered competitive market makers*, and *bond brokers*. Investors may trade stock using *market orders*, which are executed immediately, or they may place price and time restrictions on their requests by the use of *limit orders*. *Commissions* vary somewhat at different brokers but always are a declining percentage as the transaction size becomes larger.

The American Stock Exchange, which is the other national exchange, lists stocks not traded on the NYSE. *Regional exchanges* list mainly stocks that are also traded on the NYSE or the AMEX. Any securities not listed on the exchanges are traded *over-the-counter*. The OTC marketplace exists in communities throughout the United States. Security prices are set by dealers who buy and sell for their own accounts. An automated information system, *NASDAQ* has greatly improved the OTC market. The *National Market System* links all markets together via common quotation and trade reporting mechanisms. Many financial institutions bypass the exchanges and trade large blocks of listed stocks in the *third market*.

The *Securities Act of 1933* requires organizations seeking funds to disclose relevant information about the offering to potential investors. The other major piece of federal legislation was the *Securities Exchange Act of 1934* which provided regulation of trading in outstanding issues. Congress has passed several other acts to strengthen investor protection. States also regulate the securities industry by administering what are known as *Blue Sky Laws*. The industry itself engages in considerable self-policing activity through the *National Association of Securities Dealers*, the exchanges, and compliance efforts within each brokerage firm. The *Securities Investor Protection Corporation* offers limited financial protection to customers of broker-dealer firms. Despite all rules and regulations, protection from loss remains largely the responsibility of individual investors.

PROBLEMS

1. Obtain a prospectus from a brokerage office or an investor. Write a two or three paragraph summary of the offering, being sure to include the nature of the issuer's business, the intended use of the proceeds from the offering, and other details which you feel are especially important.
2. Visit a local government agency and find out how they sell bonds to raise funds. You might try the city, county, or school district offices.
3. Calculate the spread on ten OTC stock quotations, using the formula:

$$\text{Spread} = \frac{\text{Asked price} - \text{Bid price}}{\text{Bid price}} \times 100$$

Why do you suppose the spreads differ?

QUESTIONS

1. What are the functions of securities markets?
2. Distinguish between *marketability* and *liquidity*.
3. Give an example of an asset that is marketable but is not very liquid.
4. Explain how security prices are influenced by supply and demand.
5. Using an analogy of new and used car dealers, distinguish between *primary* and *secondary markets*.
6. What is *investment banking*?
7. Why are services provided by investment bankers needed by governmental and corporate bodies?
8. Define the following terms:
   a. Underwriting syndicate
   b. Competitive bid
   c. Dual listing
   d. Margin
   e. Best efforts offering
   f. Private placement
   g. Red herring
   h. Auction market
9. Briefly outline the major types of orders for securities listed on the New York Stock Exchange.

10. Describe the functions of each class of membership of the New York Stock Exchange.
11. Discuss the major features of the *National Market System*.
12. Explain the major provisions of the *Securities Act of 1933* and the *Securities Exchange Act of 1934*.
13. What is the purpose of a *prospectus*?
14. What restrictions are placed on *insider trading*?
15. What is the role of the NASD?
16. Commission rates as a percent of transaction value decline as the order size increases. Why?
17. Tell what the following letters stand for and identify the terms: NYSE, AMEX, NASDAQ, SEC.

SELECTED READINGS

Brooks, John. *Once in Golconda: A True Drama of Wall Street*, 1920–38. New York: Harper & Row, 1969.

Dirks, Raymond L., and Gross, Leonard. *The Great Wall Street Scandal*. New York: McGraw-Hill, 1974.

Ellis, Charles D. *The Second Crash*. Westminster, Md.: Ballantine Books, 1974.

Flumiani, C. M. *Stock Market and Wall Street: The Essential Knowledge Which Everybody, But Absolutely Everybody Ought to Have of the Stock Market and Wall Street*. Albuquerque: American Classical College Press, 1978.

Friend, Irwin. *Investment Banking and the New Issues Market, Summary Volume*. Philadelphia: Wharton School of Finance and Commerce, University of Pennsylvania, 1965.

Galbraith, John K. *The Great Crash*. Boston: Houghton Mifflin, 1954.

Levine, Sumner N., ed. *Financial Analysts Handbook*, vols. 1 ard 2. Homewood, Ill.: Dow Jones-Irwin, 1975.

Securities and Exchange Commission. *Annual Report*. Washington, D.C.: U.S. Government Printing Office, published yearly.

Sobel, Robert. *The Big Board—A History of the New York Stock Exchange*. New York: Free Press, 1965.

Sokoloff, Kiril. *The Thinking Investor's Guide to the Stock Market*. New York: McGraw-Hill, 1978.

4

Sources of information

GENERAL MARKET INFORMATION

Occasionally investors have told brokers to "never mind all the data, just plug me into the action!" This is a dangerous approach. Much is to be gained by investigating before investing. Careful consideration of available information does not guarantee profits, but there are few, if any, successful investors who have not studied each situation before they made commitments.

There are three major inputs to any investment decision process. The first pertains to the *capacity* and *limitations* of the individual investor. The second involves *characteristics* of different types of securities. The third area consists of *historical data* about particular securities and the markets in which they are bought and sold. The first two inputs refer to knowledge about the investor, the investment alternatives, and their accompanying risks. Most of this book is devoted to discussions of these topics. Information about particular securities and markets is presented in this chapter.

Measures of market levels

Comprehensive news sources include a report of security market activity. Even local newspapers carry some coverage of trading information. Mention is made in all these reports about what happened to stock and bond prices in general as well as quotations on some individual securities. Investors want to know whether "the market" was up, down, or unchanged. They also want to know how far the general price movement proceeded.

A wide variety of measures have been developed to indicate the price performance for groups of securities. They range from relatively simple averages of a sample of stocks from a large population to carefully constructed indexes comprised of the entire list of stocks in a particular market. Some measures are calculated for individual industries. Others are developed for specific types and grades of securities such as high-grade public utility bonds. Each measure attempts to portray what happened to prices in the class of securities it represents.

Dow Jones averages. The most widely known indicator of stock prices in this country is the *Dow Jones Industrial Average* (DJIA).[1] It dates back to 1885 when stocks of railroads dominated trading activity on the New York Stock Exchange. Over the years the sample has changed to reflect changes in trading activity of particular stocks. Since 1928 the list has included 30 firms which are, for the most part, widely known to investors. This group of stocks is listed in Table 4-1.

The DJIA is computed by adding the prices of each of the 30 stocks in the group and dividing by a number which reflects stock splits and stock dividends over the years. Adjustments to the divisor have been necessary to minimize distortions. For example, if a stock were split two for one, the price would fall about one half. If the divisor were not changed, the DJIA would decline just because the split had occurred.[2]

Dow Jones and Company also publishes a transportation average of 20 firms, a utility average of 15 companies, a composite average of the 65 stocks in the three individual averages, and a number of averages for different types of bonds.

Standard & Poor's indexes. Standard & Poor's Corporation publishes measures of stock price movements which are more refined than the Dow Jones Averages. These are *indexes* of stock prices. They have the advantage of indicating relative changes compared to a base period of the years 1941–43. Furthermore, the indexes are constructed so as to reflect the "importance" of each stock used. This is done by a weighting procedure which incorporates the number of shares outstanding

---

[1] Evidence of the widespread public acceptance of this measure may be found in several songs and the Broadway musical "How Now Dow Jones." Also, Get Well Dow Jones greeting cards have been offered in periods of market decline.

[2] These adjustments have caused a minor complication in interpreting the DJIA. The closing figure on April 10, 1979, was 873.70 which indicated the price level of the 30 stocks if no stock dividends or splits had ever occurred.

TABLE 4-1
Companies in the Dow Jones Industrial Average

Allied Chemical	General Foods	Owens-Illinois
Aluminum Company (Alcoa)	General Motors	Procter & Gamble
American Brands	Goodyear	Sears
American Can	IBM	Standard Oil of Calif.
American Tel. & Tel.	Inco (Int'l Nickel)	Texaco
Bethlehem Steel	International Harvester	Union Carbide
Du Pont	International Paper	United Technologies
Eastman Kodak	Johns-Manville	U.S. Steel
Exxon	Merck	Westinghouse Electric
General Electric	Minnesota Mining (3M)	Woolworth

Source: *The Wall Street Journal,* October 22, 1979, p. 47.

for each company. A price change in a firm with millions of shares has more impact on the index than an identical price change in a corporation having fewer shares. Standard & Poor's publishes four major common stock price indexes: the industrial with 400 stocks, the transportation with 50 stocks, the utility with 50 stocks, and a composite of all 500 stocks. In addition, it calculates indexes for numerous other groupings, such as airline stocks, preferred stocks, and a wide variety of bonds.

New York Stock Exchange indexes. The most comprehensive measure of stock price movement was begun in 1966 by the New York Stock Exchange. The NYSE Common Stock Index is a composite of all common stock issues traded on the exchange.[3] This can be compared to the samples of 65 stocks in the Dow Jones and 500 in the Standard & Poor's market indicators. The index is constructed in a manner similar to the Standard & Poor's indexes in that they both reflect changes in market values of outstanding shares. The base was set at 50.00 as of December 31, 1965. The index has been calculated back to 1939 so historical comparisons can be made. The NYSE also supplies finance, industrial, transportation, and utility indexes.

Other market measures. Several other organizations calculate their own market indicators. *Barron's,* a weekly publication of Dow Jones and Company, computes several measures, including a "Low Priced Stock Index" and a "Most Active Stock Average." *Moody's Investors Service* supplies indicators for broad groupings as well as for small categories, such as gas transmission firms, large life insurance companies, and savings and loan associations. The *American Stock*

---

[3] At the beginning of 1979, 1,581 companies were listed on the NYSE.

Exchange publishes its own market measure. Indexes for companies based in various geographical regions are calculated by some brokerage and advisory firms. Several organizations compute measures of OTC price movements. The most well-known indexes are supplied by NASDAQ. They include measures of groups such as banks, industrials, insurance, transportation, and utilities, as well as a composite index for all of the approximately 2,600 stocks listed in the NASDAQ system.

A comprehensive measure of stock price movements is prepared by *Value Line,* an investment advisory service. It is an average of 1,600 plus actively traded stocks selected from the New York Stock Exchange, the American Stock Exchange, regional stock exchanges, Canadian stock exchanges, and the OTC market. The broadest market measure of all is published by Wilshire Associates, Inc. It is an index computed weekly of the total market value of all stocks listed on the NYSE, the AMEX, and those actively traded OTC. The index was $973.557 billion on April 6, 1979.[4]

Comparisons of market measures. The preceding discussion identified many of the indicators of security price movements which are available. The question often arises as to which measure is the "best." The answer depends upon the purpose for which the indicator is to be used. If a measure is needed to serve as a benchmark for evaluating price performance in a particular portfolio, then the "best" indicator would probably be one that is composed of similar securities. For example, if an investor has been holding bonds, a measure of bond price performance would be chosen. Furthermore, if the investor owned mainly municipal bonds, an index of municipal bonds would be the logical yardstick for comparison purposes. If the major portion of investments were in unlisted securities, the OTC index would be used. A portfolio of the well-established firms listed on the New York Stock Exchange would best be measured against the Dow Jones Industrial Average or the Dow Jones Utility Average if this particular industry were the main one represented in the list of stocks. The point is to avoid comparing apples and oranges and to choose instead a measure which represents the securities similar to those whose performance is being evaluated.

Several indicators purport to measure price movements in the same group of securities. Historical data for three of the best-known barom-

---

[4] *Barron's,* April 9, 1979, p. 87.

FIGURE 4-1
Indicators of price movements on the New York Stock Exchange

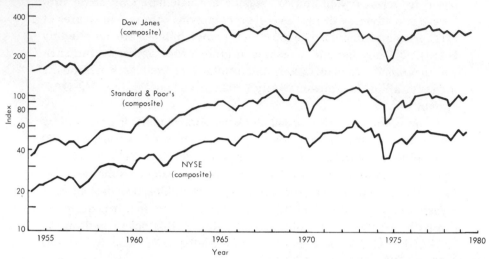

Source: Dow Jones Composite, taken from *Barron's*, various issues; Standard & Poor's Composite from *Standard & Poor's Trade & Securities Statistics*, 1978; and NYSE from *Federal Reserve Bulletin*, various issues.

eters of the New York Stock Exchange are plotted in Figure 4-1. Note that the price patterns are very similar in all cases. This means that, for many purposes, any one of the particular NYSE measures would be acceptable. However, there are times when the choice of a barometer is quite important. A careful examination of the historical changes in the indexes and averages will reveal differences in the patterns. Some measures indicate wider swings than others. Some may be slower to show a price change. These differences are due to the differences in the securities that are used in the measure and also to the various ways in which the prices are combined—the weighting. The composite indicators for Dow Jones, Standard & Poor's, and the NYSE registered gains during the first three months of 1979 of 7.4, 5.7 and 6.5 percent, respectively. These data illustrate that while the directions of price movements may all be similar, the amount of the change may vary, depending on which measure is used.

Another reason for choosing one measure over another is based on practical considerations rather than statistical grounds. This factor is the general availability of the measure. Some barometers have been calculated back into the late 1800s. Others have a much more limited history, such as the NYSE indexes, which only go back to 1939. Some measures are figured once a week. Others are figured daily, hourly, or by the minute. The Dow Jones Averages are quoted in most daily papers and over many broadcasts, whereas considerable effort might be required to stay current on the Moody's Averages.

The preceding discussion has described a variety of security price measures that are available, each having different characteristics and historical behavior patterns. The "best" barometer depends on the user and the purpose for using the yardstick. Several different market measures are cited throughout this book to help familiarize the reader with them and to indicate that, in most instances, they can be used interchangeably.

Price quotations

A major advantage of securities is that they are being continuously traded at prices which are made known to the investing public. A wide variety of methods are used to disseminate this information, and it is wise for investors to know about these sources.

Stock prices. Trading information is published in most daily newspapers. Some accounts are quite abbreviated. One of the most thorough reports appears in *The Wall Street Journal.* A partial listing of the New York Stock Exchange-Composite Transactions appears in Figure 4-2. This is an integrated record showing trading statistics gathered from the NYSE and the major regional exchanges. Data from the regionals are included to prepare a composite report of the NYSE listed stocks, no matter where the trades actually occurred.

The first two columns of numbers in Figure 4-2 represent the highest and lowest prices at which each share of stock has traded during the most recent 52-week period. The name of the company that issued the stock appears next, followed by the dividend information. Because there are many variations in the ways dividends are paid, footnotes, indicated by letters, are often used for further explanation. The next column indicates the yield which is calculated by dividing the dividends paid during the last 12 months by the closing price for the day. Entries under the P/E ratio are obtained by dividing the current earnings per share into the closing market price per share. The price/earnings ratio indicates how much investors are willing to pay for a dollar of earnings of a firm. The ratio is not computed if the company is cur-

FIGURE 4–2
Examples of stock price quotations

NYSE-Composite Transactions

Wednesday, April 11, 1979

Quotations include trades on the New York, Midwest, Pacific, Philadelphia, Boston and Cincinnati stock exchanges and reported by the National Association of Securities Dealers and Instinet.

52 Weeks High	52 Weeks Low	Stocks	Div.	Yld %	P-E Ratio	Sales 100s	High	Low	Close	Net Chg.
14½	12⅜	DelmP	1.38	11.	7	308	13	12¾	13	+ ¼
58	36½	DeltaAir	1	2.5	6	423	41½	40⅝	40½	− ⅜
12¼	5⅜	Deltec	5.50c	..	22	3	6½	6½	6½	.....
15¼	7⅛	Deltona		..	33	78	13½	13	13	+ ⅛
21¾	17¾	DenMf	s 1	4.7	9	56	21¾	21½	21½	− ⅛
35	20	Dennys	.88	3.9	8	188	22⅝	22½	22½	− ⅛
25½	13¾	Dentsply	.80	4.8	14	27	17	16¾	16¾	− ⅛
17¾	11	DeSoto	1	8.7	6	20	11½	11⅜	11½	+ ⅛
16¾	13⅜	DetEd	1.60	11.	8	181	15⅛	14⅞	14⅞	.....
86¼	69	DetE	pf7.68	10.	..	z360	73½	73½	73½	.....
83¾	67¼	DetE	pf7.45	10.	..	z800	72	72	72	+2½
80½	66¼	DetE	pf7.36	11.	..	z30	70	70	70	.....
28	24½	DetE	pf2.75	11.	..	8	25¼	25⅛	25⅛	− ¼
27⅞	24⅝	DE	pfB 2.75	11.	..	3	25	25	25	− ¼
24⅛	20	DetE	pr2.28	11.	..	14	21	20½	20½	− ¾
23¾	16	Dexter	.80	3.7	9	11	22	21¾	21⅞	− ⅜
14¼	8⅝	DiGior	.48	4.2	7	682	11⅜	11⅜	11⅜	+ ⅛
23¼	14⅝	DiGior	pf.88	4.8	..	z40	18½	18	18½	+ ½
40⅝	30	DialInt	2.20	5.9	8	229	38	37¼	37⅜	+ ⅛
29¾	19	DiamS	1.48	6.3	7	1008	23⅝	23¼	23⅝	− ⅛
29½	11⅜	Dictaph	.84	2.9	11	85	u29¾	29	29	− ½
24⅝	14⅛	Diebold	.60	2.6	14	486	u24½	23½	23½	− ⅛
58¼	38⅝	DigitalEq		..	15	964	56¼	54	55	−1¼
11½	7	Dillingm	.52	5.9	9	102	9⅛	8¾	8⅞	.....
26½	20½	Dillingm	pf2	9.1	..	1	22	22	22	.....
34¾	27½	Dillon	1.32b	4.5	10	9	29½	29¼	29¼	− ¼
47⅛	33½	Disney	.48	1.2	12	569	40⅝	39⅝	39¾	+ ⅝
4⅝	1⅛	DivrsIdIn		..	10	113	4¼	4	4¼	.....
6½	2⅝	DivrsMtg		..	..	128	5¾	5½	5½	− ⅛
20¼	13⅞	DrPeppr	.64	4.1	13	312	15⅝	15½	15½	.....
100½	62¾	DomeM	.80a	.9	10	173	88¼	83¾	84¼	−4½
6½	3	DonLJ	.14	3.2	15	81	4⅜	4¼	4⅜	+ ⅛
33¾	24½	Donnly	1	3.5	10	108	29⅛	28¾	28¾	− ⅛
26¾	15¾	DorOliv	.60	2.7	10	365	22⅝	22½	22½	− ⅛
22½	11	Dorsey	.60	4.5	5	30	13½	13¼	13¼	− ⅛
51¼	39½	Dover	1.40	2.8	10	5	50¾	50¼	50¾	+ ¾
30⅞	22⅜	DowCh	1.40	5.0	9	1370	28⅝	28¼	28¼	.....
39	31	DowJn	1.44	4.0	12	15	36⅜	36⅜	36⅜	.....
35⅛	24⅞	Dravo	1.28	4.6	8	19	28¼	28	28⅛	− ⅛
47¾	35	Dressr	1	2.2	8	390	45⅛	44½	44½	− ¼
16⅞	14½	DrexB	1.60	10.	..	14	15⅞	15⅝	15¾	+ ⅛
17¾	10	Dreyfs	.77e	5.3	7	12	14⅝	14½	14½	.....
144⅞	103¼	duPont	6	4.3	9	590	143¼	139⅛	139½	−3¼
49	42½	duPnt	pf3.50	8.1	..	2	43⅝	43⅝	43⅝	− ½
62¼	54½	duPnt	pf4.50	8.3	..	2	54½	54½	54½	− ½

52 Weeks High	52 Weeks Low	Stocks	Div.	Yld %	P-E Ratio	Sales 100s	High	Low	Close	Net Chg.
47¼	33	Getty	1.20	2.6	12	538	47¼	46⅝	46¾	− ¼
18½	17⅞	Getty	pf1.20	6.7	..	2	18	18	18	.....
10⅝	6¾	GiantPC	.60	6.2	12	83	9⅝	9	9⅝	+ ⅝
16½	10¼	GibrFn	.60	4.2	6	110	14½	14	14⅛	− ⅜
16¾	12¾	GidLew	.70	4.3	4	81	16¼	16	16¼	+ ¼
16⅝	13⅛	GiffHill	s .80	5.5	5	32	14⅝	14½	14⅝	.....
33	24	Gillette	1.60	6.3	8	116	25⅝	25⅛	25½	− ⅛
12¼	6¼	GinosInc	.20	2.5	6	38	8⅛	8	8⅛	.....
23⅝	14	GleasW	.80	3.5	8	41	22⅞	22½	22⅝	+ ⅜
20	10⅞	GlobMar		..	10	260	19⅝	18⅝	18⅝	− ½
14	10⅝	GldWFn	.50	3.7	6	120	13¾	13½	13½	− ¼
23⅝	16⅛	Gdrich	1.44	7.2	5	162	20⅛	19⅞	20	− ⅛
18⅞	15⅝	Goodyr	1.30	7.4	6	1256	17⅞	17⅜	17½	+ ⅛
22½	16⅝	GordJw	.60	2.9	6	59	20⅞	20⅜	20½	+ ⅛
34¼	25	Gould	1.60	6.2	8	195	26¼	25⅞	26	− ¼
33	25	Gould	pf1.35	5.4	..	2	25	25	25	.....
32⅝	25⅝	Grace	1.90	6.5	7	171	29⅝	29¼	29¼	− ⅛
38	28⅝	Graingr	.76	2.3	11	95	33	32⅝	32⅝	− ⅜
17¼	10⅞	Granitvl	1	8.9	375	14	11½	11¼	11¼	.....
19¾	12½	GrayDr	.80	5.6	6	9	14⅜	14¼	14⅜	.....
9¼	5	GtAtPc		..	57	106	7⅜	7¼	7⅜	+ ⅛
42½	24⅝	GtLkD	1a	2.5	5	28	39¾	39⅝	39⅝	.....
27⅝	21⅝	GNIrn	2.25e	8.7	9	43	26⅝	25⅝	25⅞	−1
38¼	26⅛	GtNoNk	1.40	3.7	9	617	38¼	37⅞	38	.....
19⅝	16¾	GtWFin	s.84	4.5	5	416	19	18⅝	18⅝	− ½
14⅞	11	Greyh	1.04	8.7	9	404	12¼	11⅞	12	− ¼
1⅛	5-16	Greyhnd	wt	..	..	47	½	½	½	.....
11⅞	7¾	GrowC	.44b	4.8	6	21	9⅛	9	9⅛	+ ⅛
6⅝	2⅞	GthRty		..	..	20	5⅜	5⅜	5⅜	+ ⅛
24⅞	14¾	Grumm	1.20	6.8	7	77	18⅝	17¾	17¾	− ¾
20⅞	14	Guardln	.36	2.3	6	67	15¾	15	15¾	+1
16¼	11¼	GlfWstn	.75	5.1	3	349	14⅞	14⅝	14⅝	− ¼
72½	67¾	GlfW	pf 5.75	8.5	..	1	67¾	67¾	67¾	.....
36⅛	28¼	GlfW	pf 2.50	7.6	..	1	33	33	33	.....
27⅝	22¼	GulfOil	1.90	7.1	7	1303	u27¾	26¾	26¾	− ¼
14	8½	GulfRes	.32	2.5	9	166	13	12¾	12¾	− ⅛
19⅝	15¼	GulfR	pf1.60	8.7	..	62	18½	18⅜	18⅜	.....
14⅛	11⅝	GlfStUt	1.36	10.	8	203	13⅜	12¼	13⅛	.....
16⅝	12⅛	GulfUtd	.92	6.1	7	553	15½	15	15⅛	− ¼
11⅞	6	Gulton	.40	3.5	9	198	11½	11⅛	11⅜	.....
		— H-H-H —								
4⅝	2¾	HMW		..	7	36	3⅜	3¼	3¼	− ¼
40½	32¾	HackW	3.60	9.0	8	1	39⅞	39⅞	39⅞	+ ⅛
7¾	4⅜	Hajoca		..	4	22	6⅛	6⅛	6⅛	.....
31	21¼	HallFB	1.24	4.8	10	246	25¾	25½	25¾	.....

EXPLANATORY NOTES

(For New York and American Exchange listed issues)

Sales figures are unofficial.

The 52-Week High and Low columns show the highest and the lowest price of the stock in consolidated trading during the preceding 52 weeks plus the current week, but not the current trading day.

u–Indicates a new 52-week high. d–Indicates a new 52-week low.

s–Stock split or stock dividend amounting to 25 per cent or more since January 1, 1979. The 52-week high-low range and dividend begin with the date of split or stock dividend, and do not cover the entire 52-week period.

n–New issue since January 1, 1979. The 52-week high-low range begins with the start of trading in the new issue and does not cover the entire 52-week period.

Unless otherwise noted, rates of dividends in the foregoing table are annual disbursements based on the last quarterly or semi-annual declaration. Special or extra dividends or payments not designated as regular are identified in the following footnotes.

a–Also extra or extras. b–Annual rate plus stock dividend. c–Liquidating dividend. e–Declared or paid in preceding 12 months. i–Declared or paid after stock dividend or split up. j-Paid this year, dividend omitted, deferred or no action taken at last dividend meeting. k–Declared or paid this year, an accumulative issue with dividends in arrears. r–Declared or paid in preceding 12 months plus stock dividend. t–Paid in stock in preceding 12 months, estimated cash value on ex-dividend or ex-distribution date.

x–Ex-dividend or ex-rights. y–Ex-dividend and sales in full. z–Sales in full

cld–Called. wd–When distributed. wi–When issued. ww–With warrants. xw–Without warrants. xdis–Ex-distribution.

vj–In bankruptcy or receivership or being reorganized under the Bankruptcy Act, or securities assumed by such companies.

Source: Reprinted by permission *The Wall Street Journal*, April 12, 1979, pp. 37–38.

rently losing money or if the particular issue is a preferred stock. Further discussion of the P/E ratio appears in Chapters 9 and 13.

The last five columns present information about trading that took place during the day preceding the publication of the paper. First, the volume of trades is shown. This is recorded in hundreds of shares. High and low prices achieved during the day and the price of the last trade are tabulated in the next three columns. The last entry is for the change from the closing price on the preceding day compared to the closing price on the day being recorded.

Note that fractions are used for prices rather than decimals. There is a long-standing practice for quotes to be in dollars or *points* and fractions thereof with the smallest increment usually being ⅛ of a point, or 12.5 cents. The row circled in Figure 4–2 serves as an example for this discussion. The information indicates that 569 hundred or 56,-900 shares of Walt Disney Productions common stock changed hands on Wednesday, April 11, 1979. The top price paid was $40⅜ and the lowest trade was at $39⅜. The stock closed at $39¾ which was up $⅝ from the close on Tuesday, April 10. Dividing the closing price by the last 12 months' earnings indicates that investors paid $12 for each dollar of Disney earnings. These shares have traded in the range from $33½ to $47⅛ during the last 52-week period. All this information presents a rather complete picture of daily transactions in each company's shares. Integrating sales of NYSE listed stocks with NYSE stocks traded on regional exchanges is a major feature of the previously discussed National Market System.

The Wall Street Journal reports prices of stocks on the American Stock Exchange, the regional exchanges, and two Canadian exchanges. Option trades on 5 exchanges are also published; discussion of these investments and their quotations is included in Chapter 11.

Over-the-counter markets are reported in a somewhat different manner compared to the listed stocks. The OTC price quotes do not represent actual transactions nor does the information cover one day of activity. Instead, the report shows only the bid and asked prices quoted by dealers as of a certain time. A sample of these records appears in Figure 4–3. Note the quotation that has been circled for Alaska International Industries. The asked price for this stock was $9¼ per share and the bid price was $8¼ as of 4:00 p.m. EST, April 17, 1979. The dots in the last column indicate that the bid price was unchanged compared to the quote at the same time on the preceding day.

More than 50,000 unlisted issues have some degree of trading activity. *The Wall Street Journal* publishes daily quotations for around 1,500 OTC securities. The majority of OTC prices must be found elsewhere. Many OTC firms are of regional interest only; prices of their stock are published in newspapers in those areas. Other quotes can be obtained from several financial publications.[5]

----

[5] See *Barron's, The Commercial and Financial Chronicle* and *The O-T-C Market Chronicle.*

FIGURE 4-3
Price quotations

Over-the-Counter Markets

4:00 p.m. Eastern Standard Time Prices, Tuesday, April 17, 1979

All over the counter prices printed on this page are representative quotations by the National Association of Securities Dealers through Nasdaq, its automated system for reporting quotes. Prices don't include retail markup, markdown or commission. Volume represents shares that changed ownership during the day. Figures include only those transactions effected by Nasdaq market makers but may include some duplication where Nasdaq market makers traded with each other.

Volume, All Issues, 12,766,200

SINCE JANUARY 1

	1979	1978	1977
Total sales	909,943,371	650,281,848	556,765,055

MARKET DIARY

	Tues	Mon	Thurs	Weds	Tues
Issues traded	2,555	2,554	2,554	2,556	2,554
Advances	333	244	408	323	490
Declines	508	692	413	628	348
Unchanged	1,714	1,618	1,733	1,605	1,716
xNew highs	74	71	113	124	164
xNew lows	46	39	19	20	19

x-Based on 4 p.m. Eastern time bid quote.

ACTIVE STOCKS

	Volume	4:00 Bid	Chg.
Credo Petroleum	411,700	3/16	.....
Tosco Corp	230,000	12⅞	....
Solar Technology	226,600	5/16	.....
Teleco Oilfield Svc	223,300	14	....
Penn Life Co	173,900	7⅛	+3/16
De Beers Cons ADR	139,600	6 3/16	+1/16
TONM Oil Gas	129,200	11/16	−1/16
Citzns Sth Nat Bk Ga	121,400	5⅞	....
Royster Co	117,000	8⅞	+ ⅛
Bio-Gas Colo	110,300	⅜	....

Stock & Div.	Sales 100s	Bid	Asked	Net Chg.
--A A--				
Academy Insu	39	2 13-16	3 1-16	−1-16
Accelrtn Corp	45	7½	8½	...
Aceto Ch 5.5k	5	14¾	15¼	...
Acme El .48g	8	6¼	7	− ¼
ADA Res .10d	22	5¾	6⅛	− ⅛
AddWesley .50	1	11½	12¼	...
Advan MicroD	138	23¾	24½	+ ½
Advanced Pat	129	5¾	6½	− ¼
Advent Corp	61	3¾	4¼	...
AEL Indu A 5i	78	8	8½	− ¼
Aero Syst Inc	137	2⅜	2¾	− ⅛
Aerosonic Cp	181	7¾	8¼	...
Affil Bksh 1.28	57	22¾	23¾	...
A E S Technlg	63	12	12¾	− ¾
AgMet Incorp	57	3⅞	4⅝	− ¼
Agnico Eagle	110	5½	5¾	...
Air Florida Sy	86	5⅛	5⅝	− ⅛
Airlift Intrnatl	199	1⅛	1 5-16	...
AlaBancp 1.24	11	22½	23½	...
AlaTennNG 2a	5	27½	28¼	...
Alamo Sv .50b	1	25¾	26¾	...
AlaskaIti .26h	15	8¼	9¼	...
AlexandA 1.40	269	28	28¾	...
Alex Bald 1.20	100	17½	18	+ ¼
AlicoIncp .25d	38	19	19½	...
AlleghBev .30	69	4½	4¾	...
AlliedBncshr 1	30	32⅜	32⅞	...
Allied Leisure	140	5¼	5⅝	− ⅛
Allied Tech	54	1 3-16	1 7-16	+1-16
Allied Tel .76g	106	16⅜	16⅞	− ½
Alpex Comptr	46	3½	3⅞	...
Alphanumric	43	1	1¼	...
Alphtype .35d	17	13	13¾	+ ½
Amarco Resrc	43	19-32	21-32	...
Amarex Incrp	69	19¼	19¾	+ ⅛
Amber Resour	165	1⅜	1⅝	...
Amcole Enrgy	310	15-16	1 3-16	...
Am Apprsl .30	1	7⅝	8	...

Stock & Div.	Sales 100s	Bid	Asked	Net Chg.
Chattem .36	22	7⅞	8⅜	+ ⅛
ChemNucl .05f	108	19½	20½	− ½
Chemd Cp 1.80	18	32	33	...
ChemLea 1.20	z50	24¼	25¼	...
Chemineer .24	2	7⅛	7⅝	...
Chemlawn Cp	50	25	28	+ 1
Cherry El .04b	13	10	10¾	...
Ch NW Trans	23	14	14¾	− ¾
Childrn World	31	3⅜	3¾	− ⅛
ChiltonCo 1g	z1	84	86	...
Chomerics Inc	23	27	28½	+ ½
ChubbCrp 2.20	146	36¼	36¾	+ ¼
Chur Dwt 1.40	10	31½	34½	...
Chyron Corpn	13	1¾	2¼	+ ⅛
CIC Fnc'l .50	2	9	10	...
CinnFncl 1.20g	1	27¼	27¾	...
Cindys Inc	93	4	4½	+ ⅛
Circle In .21b	30	12½	13	− ⅛
Citz FedSv .72	3	23½	24½	...
CitizenFid 1.40	26	22¾	23¾	− ¼
CitzSthnC 1.04	5	16½	17½	...
CitzSoNB Ga	1214	5⅞	6¼	...
CitzUtil A 6.8i	36	37¼	38	− ¾
Citz UtilB 2.56	1	33¼	34	− ¼
CityNatlCp .80	48	22	23	− 1¼
CitytrBncp .80	z30	12⅞	13⅜	...
Clark Mfg 1.10	z95	30	31½	...
Classfied Fncl	40	5½	6¼	...
ClevTrRlt .05b	93	7¼	7¾	− ⅛
Clevetrust 2.20	42	34¾	35¾	...
Clincl Science	42	3⅛	3⅜	+ ⅛
Clow Corp .40	85	8¼	8¾	+ ¼
Cobe Labrator	23	26¼	27	...
CoCBotCn .60a	48	19	20	− 1
CoCBtlMia .60	2	14	15½	...
Coherent Incp	171	22¾	23½	+ ¼
ColeConP .02d	15	4¼	5	...
College Un .25	3	33	39	...
Colon Bnc 1.80	8	18½	19½	...

Stock & Div.	Sales 100s	Bid	Asked	Net Chg.
1stCapital 1.85	5	33	34½	...
1stCml Bk 1.20	88	13	13½	− ¼
1stCtlRIE .53b	40	8¼	8¾	+ ¼
1stDenvr Mtg	73	3⅜	3¾	...
1st Empire St	70	11⅛	11⅝	+ ⅛
Fst Exectv Cp	28	5½	6	...
FstExec pf .50	12	11⅜	11⅞	...
1stFarwest .25	17	10½	11	...
1stFlaBnks .36	84	5⅜	5⅞	...
1stHawaiin 2	18	26	27	...
1stJersNtl 1.20	3	16¾	17½	...
FstKtyNtl 1.64	25	30	31	...
1stLincoln Fcl	32	8½	9	...
1stMarnBk .26	65	5¾	6⅛	...
1stMdBnc 1.40	26	20½	21¼	...
1st MerCp 1.46	20	21	21¾	...
FstMtge Invst	645	1⅞	2 1-16	−1-16
FstNtlBcp 1.04	z30	17¼	18¼	...
FstNatlCinci 2	5	29	30	− ½
1stNHldAtl .84	8	13¼	14	...
1stNatSup .02d	12	7	8	...
1stOklaBnc .30	1	14⅞	15⅜	...
FstSv & Ln .48	8	13½	14½	...
1st Sec Cp .86	18	19⅞	20⅜	...
1stSec Natl .76	2	18½	19½	...
1stTennNtl .72	31	12⅜	12⅞	− ⅛
Fst UnBncp 2	37	27	28	− ¼
1stUnionCp .92	18	14¾	15¼	...
FstUtdBc 1.16	17	23¾	24½	− ¼
First West Fin	237	5¼	5½	...
FstWisc MtgT	23	4	4⅜	...
FisonsLtd .26b	z14	6⅛	6⅜	...
FlagshpBk .40	254	12⅛	12⅝	+ ⅛
Flame Industr	33	15	17	...
Flexsteel .68	2	12	12¾	...
Flickinger .60	8	13⅝	14⅛	− ⅛
FloatPnt Syst	28	12	13	...
Florafax Intl	117	4½	5	...
FlaBnkshr .32	2	12	15	...

EXPLANATORY NOTES

z-Sales in full.

a-Annual rate plus cash extra or extras. b-Paid so far in 1979, no regular rate. c-Payment of accumulated dividends. d-Paid in 1978. e-Cash plus stock paid in 1978. f-Cash plus stock paid in 1979. g-Annual rate plus stock dividend. h-Paid in 1979, latest dividend omitted. i-Paid in stock in 1978. j-Percent in stock paid in 1979, latest dividend omitted. k-Percent paid in stock in 1979. ut-Units. wt-Warrants. x-Ex-dividend, ex-rights or ex-distribution. (z) No representative quote.

Source: Reprinted by permission *The Wall Street Journal,* April 18, 1979, p. 34.

Investors also ask brokers for stock price information. Their sources are mainly from a vast network of electronic communication systems which will be discussed in a later section.

Bond prices. All bonds are issued with a stated face amount, or par value. This is the amount the owner will receive if the bond is held until it matures. The most common denomination is $1,000, although bonds between $100 and $1,000,000 are also sold. To avoid confusion in quoting prices, a standard of 100 is used. This means at a price of 95, a

FIGURE 4-4
Bond price quotations

New York Exchange Bonds
Monday, February 5, 1979

Total Volume, $13,060,000

| | Domestic | | All Issues | |
	Mon	Fri	Mon	Fri
Issues traded	.778	741	795	752
Advances	.281	348	284	353
Declines	.314	224	324	226
Unchanged	.183	169	187	173
New highs	.5	9	5	9
New lows	.13	12	15	12

SALES SINCE JANUARY 1		
1979	1978	1977
$367,901,000	$426,963,000	$580,986,000

Dow Jones Bond Averages

	–1976–		–1977–		–1978-79–			–1979–			–1978–		–1977–	
High	Low	High	Low	High	Low					MONDAY				
93.20	85.70	93.87	90.69	90.86	84.09	20 Bonds	85.87	– .03	89.79 + .05	91.36 + .21
98.56	87.46	99.10	94.98	95.00	86.21	10 Utilities	88.47	– .13	94.17 + .05	97.05 + .24
87.85	78.58	89.18	85.31	86.79	81.61	10 Industrial	83.27 + .07	85.41 + .04	85.68 + .18

Corporate bond quotation table (left and center columns) and Treasury Issues table (right column) follow; detailed figures are a reproduction of newspaper listings.

Treasury Issues
* * *
Bonds, Notes & Bills

Monday, February 5, 1979
Over-the-Counter quotations; sources on request. Decimals in bid-and-asked and bid changes represent 32nds; 101.1 means 101 1/32. a-Plus 1/64. b-Yield to call date. d-Minus 1/64. n-Treasury notes.

EXPLANATORY NOTES
(For New York and American Bonds)
Yield is current yield. cv-Convertible bond.
ct-Certificates. f-Dealt in flat. m-Matured bonds, negotiability impaired by maturity. r-Registered. st-Stamped. wd-When distributed. ww-With warrants. x-Ex-interest. xw-Without warrants. vj-In bankruptcy or receivership or being reorganized under the Bankruptcy Act, or securities assumed by such companies.

Source: Reprinted by permission *The Wall Street Journal*, February 6, 1979, p. 31.

$1,000 bond would be $950 or $9,500 for a $10,000 par bond. Fractions rather than decimals are used in bond quotations; eighths for corporate bonds, and thirty-seconds or sixty-fourths for government issues. Examples of bond price information appearing in *The Wall Street Journal* are shown in Figure 4-4. The reporting treatment of listed corporate bonds is similar to that of listed stocks and includes price ranges during the year and data for the day's high, low, close, and change from the preceding day. The major difference lies in the description of the issue. Most firms have only one class of common stock and none or perhaps one issue of preferred stock. However, companies typically sell several bonds at different times, so it is important to distinguish between each issue. Particular features of each bond follow the name of the company. The interest rate and maturity date are given at this point in an abbreviated style. An issue of Shell Oil is circled in Figure 4–4. The phrase "8s 07" identifies this issue as bearing an interest rate of 8 percent with a maturity date of 2007. The current yield of 8.9 percent is computed by dividing the interest rate by the closing price.

Figure 4–4 shows that government bond price reports differ considerably from the corporate bond information. The first three columns of the Treasury Issues section list the amounts of yearly interest and maturity dates. Figures for the bid and asked prices and net change that follow are similar to any other OTC security except for the use of decimal points. This is somewhat misleading because the decimal is just used to separate the dollar figures from the fractions, which in this case are thirty-seconds. The last column in the report indicates the *yield to maturity* for the bond. This is a percentage figure which is computed to include the interest paid and an allowance for the fact that the bond will be redeemed at maturity for par value even though it was purchased for a different price.[6]

The government bond discussion may be summarized by referring to the row circled in the Treasury Issues section of Figure 4–4. The particular issue indicated is a bond bearing an interest rate of 7¼ percent and maturing in August, 1992. The bid and asked prices are reported as "87.8" and "87.16." This means a $1,000 par value bond is offered by dealers for purchase and sale for $872.50 and $875.00, respectively.[7] The next column indicates that the bid price fell that day by 6/32 or $1.875 for a $1,000 bond. The yield to maturity of 8.85 percent is the average annual return offered to investors who buy this bond for $875, receive interest of $72.50 each year, and receive $1,000 when the security matures in 1992.

Other price quotations. Many financial reports also include special sections for prices of foreign securities, commodities, mutual

---

[6] Details of the calculation procedure may be found in the appendix to Chapter 7.

[7] These prices were quoted in 32nds, so 24/32 is equal to $.75 on a $100 basis or $7.50 for a $1,000 bond.

funds, and stock options. Details of mutual fund and option quotations may be found in Chapters 10 and 11.

BROKERAGE SERVICES

Virtually all investors use professional assistance for their security transactions. This aid is available from thousands of stock brokerage offices located throughout the United States whose main function is to execute buy and sell orders for the investing public. The objective of this section is to describe a variety of other services offered by the brokerage firms and to discuss factors which are influential in the selection of a particular broker.

Portfolio planning and review

A service offered by many brokerage firms involves an analysis and appraisal of an investor's security holdings. This examination might include a rather detailed review of the client's financial capacity as well as a study of each security owned. The purpose of this service is to see that investors and their investments are properly matched.[8] If a person is just beginning to invest, this help involves mainly establishing goals for the investment program within the individual's financial constraints. If the investor already owns securities, an additional check will be made to see if the current holdings are properly aligned with the objectives and resources available to meet them.

Most of this type of work is done in the research office of the brokerage firm with the registered representative acting to bring the investor and the portfolio analyst together. Recommendations are made which the investor may accept or reject. This service is usually performed at no charge. Some investors ask that the firm actually manage their account, buying and selling when the firm feels it is proper to do so. A management fee is typically charged in this discretionary arrangement. Several firms offer computerized portfolio analyses for individual investors. These programs provide an objective measure of the risks associated with the securities owned.

---

[8] Recall the discussion in Chapter 2 which emphasized the need to consider the individual investor's situation before selecting securities; what is appropriate for one person may not be at all suitable for another.

Research

Brokerage firms, with the important exception of discount brokers, are busy investigating securities so as to identify what should be bought or sold. The larger, full-service firms employ a staff of security analysts to perform this function. These are highly trained people who specialize in a specific area of analysis. Many of them have technical backgrounds in the industry in which they concentrate. For example, engineers and scientists are often hired away from their technical jobs to analyze the investment prospects of companies in their areas of expertise.

Medium-size and small brokerage firms often buy research reports from a firm that specializes in security analysis. In addition to the "in-house" and external research, most individual brokers try to investigate situations which they feel may show promise for investors. The object of all these efforts is to provide a continuing stream of buy or sell recommendations. These reports lead to the lifeblood of the business. That is, they generate orders that mean commissions. Furthermore, brokerage firms want to keep their customers for repeat business. Hence, considerable efforts are made to uncover situations that will make money for clients.

Increasing importance of research in the securities business has been accompanied by the development of a new professional group known as the Chartered Financial Analysts (CFA). To become a member, a person must demonstrate a high degree of knowledge of security analysis similar to the accounting expertise required to become a Certified Public Accountant (CPA). About 5,000 CFAs work in research positions in the securities industry.

Research information is distributed in a variety of ways. Lengthy reports are prepared for investors on prospects for individual companies. Often booklets are written which discuss a specific industry and also the corporations within that grouping. Many brokerage houses distribute a *market letter* to their clients. These publications are usually one to three pages long and are issued at regular intervals: as daily, weekly, or monthly. Titles of these reports are indicative of their contents: *Research Review, Market Interpretations, Current Selections, the Market Review, Investments for a Changing Economy, Financial and Business Review, Market Communique, Analysts' Commentary,* to name but a few. The typical format includes a few paragraphs about each of a number of companies relating to their prospects for earnings and sales and to any new developments. Some firms publish several types of market reports. Research information is usually free for the asking.

Most brokers also make available financial data which are assembled by other firms. The Standard & Poor's *Stock Guide,* a monthly publication, is one of the broadest compilations of security information available. Figure 4–5 shows a sample page from this source. Standard & Poor's also publishes *Listed Stock Reports* and *O-T-C Reports.* These materials provide a summary of financial histories and current developments of thousands of firms. They are updated several times a year and are available in many brokerage offices. A sample of one of these reports is shown in Figures 4–6 and 4–7. Recall again that discount brokers charge drastically reduced commissions but do not offer the research and other services offered by the regular type firms.

Price quotations

Another important function of brokerage firms is to provide current price information. This service yields up-to-the-minute quotations by a variety of methods.

Stock ticker tapes.   Offices of firms who are members of one or more stock exchanges usually have a "ticker" to receive trading data which is shown on electronic display. A sample from the NYSE is reproduced in Figure 4–8. Abbreviations of the companies whose stock has been traded appear in the top row—AVT, WIX, N, BY, and USI are symbols for Avnet, Inc., The Wickes Corporation, International Nickel Company, Bucyrus-Erie Co., and U.S. Industries, respectively. One- to five-letter abbreviations are assigned to each issue listed. Usually the name of the company is obvious from the symbol used, but there are many exceptions, for instance X stands for U.S. Steel. The bottom row on the tape indicates the number of shares and the prices at which they were traded. For example, 4s31.31 means 400 shares of Avnet exchanged hands at $31 per share followed immediately by a 100-share trade also at $31 per share. The next activity in Avnet was 100 shares at $30⅞ followed by 200 shares at the same price. The second transaction recorded for International Nickel involved two round lots at prices of $35¼ and $35⅜, respectively. The largest trade shown in Figure 4–8 was 2,000 shares of U.S. Industries at $31½. By convention, only round-lot transactions (multiples of 100 shares) are shown on the tape.

FIGURE 4–5
Important data on stocks

130 Len-Lio — STANDARD & POOR'S CORPORATION

Index	Ticker Symbol	Stocks — Name of Issue (Call Price of Pfd. Stocks)	Market	Com Rank. & Pfd. Rating	Par Val.	Inst. Hold Cos	Inst. Hold Shs. (000)	Principal Business	Price Range 1960-77 High	1960-77 Low	1978 High	1978 Low	1979 High	1979 Low	Mar. Sales in 100s	March, 1979 Last Sale Or Bid High	Low	Last	% Div. Yield	P-E Ratio
1	LNX	Lenox, Inc	NY	A—	1¼	35	1397	Fine china,jewelry,candles	45⅝	3¼	32¾	23¾	30	24¼	768	30	24¼	29¼	4.4	9
2	LES	Leslie Fay	NY	B+	1	10	368	Women's dresses, sportswear	17½	1½	10¼	6⅜	9	7¼	527	8	7¼	7¾	6.2	5
3	LFB	Leverage Fd Boston Cap	NY,Ph	...	1	12	149	Diversified closed-end,Cap:	15	3½	18⅛	10⅝	17⅝	15⅜	411	17⅜	15⅝	17	...	..
4	Pr	$0.75 cm Inc Shrs (13.725 in '82)	NY	NR	1	...	....	cap gains: Inc: inv income	15	9⅞	14¾	13⅛	14⅛	13¼	70	14⅛	13¾	14⅛	†10.1	..
5	LVI	Levi Strauss & Co	NY,M,P	A	1	55	3683	Apparel: jeans, slacks, shorts	31 11/16	6 1/16	38⅝	27¼	47⅝	34⅜	6577	47⅝	41¼	47	3.8	7
6	LEV	Levitz Furniture	NY,B,M,Ph,P	B	40¢	17	569	Retail home furniture chain	242	5	26⅝	17⅛	23	17⅞	2085	20⅞	17⅞	20⅝	†3.9	5
7	LWIS	Lewis (Palmer G)	N	B+	1	2	33	Building material distributor	9⅝	2¾	16⅞	8½	13¾	12¼	195	13½	13	13¼B	s1.8	8
8	LFE	LFE Corp	NY,B,Ph	B—	1	3	149	Process,fluid,traffic controls	64⅛	1⅞	13¼	5⅝	8⅞	5⅞	545	8⅞	6½	8⅞	1.1	8
9	Pr	$0.50 cm Cv A Pfd (10)vtg	NY	NR	No	1	.2	pumps,electro-mech devices	9⅞	4	8½	6½	6¼	5¾	12	6¼	5¾	6B	8.3	..
10	LOF	Libbey-Owens-Ford	NY,B,M,Ph,P	B+	5	54	669	Auto glass for GM: bldg glass	70½	12½	29½	23	25¾	23⅞	1269	25¼	24⅜	25⅛	†9.2	5
11	Pr	$4.75 cm CvAPfd(100)vtg	NY	A	No	8	17	hose fluid-carrying applic	107¾	46	61¼	51½	55	51	83	55	54¼	54½	8.7	..
12	LIBRF	Liberian Iron Ore Ltd	N,Tc	...	No	2	16	Hldg co: jt w/Liberian gvt	21	8½	10	5⅜	7⅜	5¾	36	7⅜	6⅝	7¼B	...	d
13	LC	Liberty Corp	NY	...	2	31	1857	Insurance hldg: TV: R.E.	28¼	7	34¼	20¾	34½	29½	585	33½	30⅜	33½	2.6	7
14	LBY	Liberty Fabrics of NY	AS	B	1	...	....	Knitted lace: nettings	25¾	1	12	5⅛	8¾	6	432	8¾	6¼	6⅞	s...	4
15	LIBH	Liberty Homes	N	B—	1	...	....	Mfr of mobile homes	25¾	¾	6⅝	2⅞	4½	3¼	313	4¼	4	4⅛B	4.8	4
16	LLC	Liberty Loan	NY	C	1	4	173	Personal loan:insur subsids	41⅝	1⅜	5⅞	2½	3⅜	2½	620	3	2½	2¾	...	5
17	Pr	$1.25 cm Pref(25)1/5 vote	NY	C	25	2	9	financ'g install loans	26⅛	2	13¾	9½	10	9½	73	10	9¾	10	...	..
18	LNBK	Liberty Nat'l Bk & Tr	N	...	8⅓	8	348	Gen'l bank'g,Louisville,Ky	40	12¾	32	23	32	31	53	32	31½	31½B	4.2	7
19	LIBN	Liberty Nat'l Corp	N	...	5	7	588	Bank hldg: Oklahoma City	23	9⅜	27¼	21¾	26	23	45	23½	23	23¼B	5.6	6
20	LNAT	Liberty Natl Life Ins	N	...	2	69	4131	Ordinary & industrial life	38⅛	11⅛	26	20	24¾	21¾	8255	24½	22¾	23⅜B	4.3	8
21	LIGA	Life Insur Co Ga[60]	N	...	2½	18	1294	Life,accident,health insur	42	9	37¼	23½	56⅝	31	4323	56⅝	46	56⅝B	2.5	14
22	LINV	Life Investors	N	...	1	9	281	Life,health,title insurance	31⅝	3¼	16	8⅜	12⅞	10¼	2717	12⅞	10¾	12⅝B	1.6	6
23	LICO	Lifesurance Corp	N	...	1½	1	.1	Life and health insurance	10	1	8⅜	6¼	8½	7	246	8½	7¾	8¼B	...	16
24	LGT	Liggett Group[61]	NY,B,C,M,Ph	B+	1	39	596	Liquor,pet food,tobacco	74¼	24⅛	37⅞	26¼	41¾	34⅛	5879	41¾	36⅝	37	6.8	8
25	Pr	7% cm Pfd (NC) vtg	NY(10)	A	100	2	.4	cereals,watch bands,clean-	164½	72	90	79	79	75	5	79	75	75¼B	9.3	..
26	Pr A	$5.25 cm Cv Pref ([64]105)vtg	NY	BBB	1	...	....	ing products: sport eq	165	58½	84¼	65	90¼	79	2	90¼	90¼	86B	6.1	..
27	LOL	Lightolier, Inc	AS	B	1	3	75	Light'g fixtures,port lamps	27¾	1⅞	9⅛	5¾	9⅝	6½	198	9⅝	8⅝	9½	2.5	6
28	LCFS	Lil'Champ Food Stores	N	NR	10¢	...	....	Convenience stores,Florida	11⅛	4⅛	10¾	5½	9¾	8¾	266	9¾	9¼	9½B	s2.5	7
29	LLA	Lilli Ann	AS,P	B	No	3	121	Women's high-fashion apparel	23¼	3½	8¼	5⅛	7⅝	6	71	7⅝	6⅛	7¼	3.3	14
30	LLY	Lilly (Eli) & Co	NY,B,C,M	A+	62½¢	308	27051	Ethical drugs:agri chem,cosm	92½	7⅜	54	36⅝	54½	47⅛	13224	54½	49⅞	53⅜	3.4	14
31	LIMT	Limited Stores	N	B+	No	4	280	Women's apparel stores	18⅛	⅛	21¾	7½	10¼	6½	3604	8½	6½	8½B	0.9	19
32	LINB	LIN Broadcasting	N	B+	2	35	769	Radio & TV stations	32½	2	43¼	21⅝	38¾	35¾	1850	37¾	35¾	36½B	...	9
33	LAC	Lincoln American	AS	...	1	7	511	Insurance-life,prop-liab	31⅜	1⅛	6¼	3½	7⅛	4½	1570	7⅛	5½	6⅞	...	10
34	LFIN	Lincoln Fin'l	N	...	10	5	296	Bank hldg:Fort Wayne, Ind	35⅝	15⅜	34½	26½	29½	24½	61	29	28	28B	5.7	5
35	LFBK	Lincoln First Banks	N	...	10	15	188	Multiple bank hldg:Roch,NY	51½	14½	28	21¾	28½	23¼	762	28½	25½	28½B	6.6	6
36	LINC	Lincoln Income Life Ins	N	...	1	2	18	Life & disability insurance	17⅞	4⅞	20½	11¾	15¾	11⅞	69	14¾	13⅞	14B	‡4.9	5
37	LNMG	Lincoln Mtge Inv SBI	N	...	No	...	....	Real estate investment trust	10⅜	⅛	3	1 1/16	2½	1⅞	251	2½	2⅜	2⅜B	...	10
38	LNC	Lincoln Nat'l	NY,M	...	2½	108	5919	Insur hldg:life, accident	48¾	19	43	33⅜	39	35½	2082	39	35⅞	39	7.2	6
39	Pr	$3.00 cm Cv A Pfd (80)vtg	NY,M	NR	No	8	84	& health: title insurance	97½	38½	86	66¾	77½	71	40	77½	71½	76½B	3.9	..
40	LND	Lincoln Nat'l Dir P Fd	NY	...	1	5	4	Closed end non-div mgt inv	25⅜	12¾	19¼	15½	17¾	16¼	327	17½	16¼	17⅛	†10.6	..
41	LTEL	Lincoln Tel & Tel	N	A—	6¼	12	153	Telephone serv, Nebraska	49	15⅞	35	30¼	46¼	33½	1540	46¼	37¼	45½B	5.7	9
42	LNDL	Lindal Cedar Homes	N	B—	1	...	....	Pre-cut cedar homes	42	⅝	4	2	3¼	2¼	130	2½	2¼	2¼B	8.9	3
43	LIND	Lindberg Corp	N	B+	2½	1	8	Heat treating of metals	6¾	⅞	12⅞	6⅛	10¾	9⅝	528	10⅜	9⅝	10¼B	4.5	9
44	GRRR	Lion Country Safari	N	NR	1¢	2	11	African wildlife/amuse park	24½	⅛	2⅛	⅝	1¾	1⅛	3452	1¾	1⅛	1⅝B	...	d
45	LIO	Lionel Corp	NY,B,M,Ph,P	B+	10¢	2	31	Retail toys,leisure gds:mfg	35⅞	1	8⅜	3	6	4⅝	3653	6	4⅝	5½	2.2	8

Uniform Footnote Explanations—See Page 1. Other: [51]⊙$1.22,'78. [52]△$1.07,□$0.53,'78. [53]⊙$2.16,'74. [54]⊙$2.35,'75. [55]⊙$2.94,'76. [56]⊙$3.47,'77. [57]Accum on Pfd. [58]Fiscal Dec'76 & prior. [59]⊙$3.50,'78. [60]Dutch concern plans tender, $60. [61]Co to sell Liggett&Myers Tobacco Co,$122M. [62]□$3.33,'77. [63]□$1.96,△,$3.43,'78. [64]To 1-24-80, scale to $100 in'85. [65]⊙$0.89,'78. [66]⊙$4.10,'78. [67]⊙$4.55,'78. [68]⊙$4.75,'78. [69]□$1.20,'76. [70]△$3.01,'77. [71]⊙$0.69,'78.

COMMON AND PREFERRED STOCKS — Len—Lio 131

Index	Cash Divs. Ea. Yr. Since	Dividends — Latest Payment Per $	Date	Ex. Div.	$ So Far 1979	Total Ind. Rate	$ Paid 1978	Financial Position Mil-$ Cash & Equiv.	Curr. Assets	Curr. Liabs.	Balance Sheet Date	Capitalization Long Term Debt Mil-$	Shs. 000 Pfd.	Com.	Ended	Earnings $ Per Shr — Years 1974	1975	1976	1977	1978	Last 12 Mos.	Interim Earnings or Remarks Period	$ Per Share 1977	1978	Index
1	1958	Q0.32½	3-23-79	2-26	0.32½	1.30	1.12	2.61	79.7	21.8	9-30-78	7.69	...	3962	Dc	1.84	2.02	2.51	2.94	P3.39	3.39				1
2◆	1962	Q0.12	4-6-79	3-14	0.24	0.48	0.46	2.24	62.1	22.4	1-27-79	10.2	...	3600	Ap	0.99	0.87	1.27	0.64	ʃ[51]1.23	1.54	9 Mo Jan△	0.88	1.19	2
3	.....	None Paid			....	Nil	....	Net Asset Val $21.27			3-23-79	....	1978	1978	Dc	§5.40	§10.96	§17.53	§16.51	§18.99	....				3
4	1967	†0.85¾	4-30-79	4-5	†1.04½	1.42	†1.35½	...	...	...		....	1978	...	Dc	1.13	1.02	1.09	1.35	1.42	....				4
5◆	1935	Q0.45	4-2-79	3-2	0.85	1.80	1.50	255.	824.	302.	11-26-78	83.3	...	p19888	Nv	1.60	2.95	4.71	5.87	6.56	6.80	3 Mo Feb△	1.48	1.72	5
6◆	1977	†0.35	4-27-79	4-5	†0.50	0.80	0.50	11.9	128.	11.9	10-31-78	133.	...	4244	Ja	0.92	d0.03	1.47	2.81	P3.84	3.84				6
7◆	1961	Q0.06	2-14-79	1-18	0.06	0.24	s0.184	0.29	21.7	13.1	1-26-79	8.79	...	1475	Ja	0.65	0.73	0.91	1.23	P1.58	1.58				7
8◆	1978	0.09	7-17-78	6-27	....	0.10	0.09	0.24	42.0	11.4	1-26-79	22.4	166	1522	Ap	•0.45	•0.55	•0.19	•0.46	•0.89	1.18	9 Mo Jan△	•0.56	0.85	8
9	1970	S 0.25	4-1-79	3-9	0.25	0.50	0.50	Conv into 0.55 shrs common				....	166	...	Ap	6.40	7.73	2.95	6.48	9.78	....				9
10	1933	Q0.50	3-15-79	2-13	0.50	2.30	†2.30	49.4	427.	145.	12-31-78	98.1	1014	11080	Dc	2.40	△2.05	4.92	4.88	△[52]□4.96	4.96				10
11	1968	Q1.18¾	3-10-79	2-13	1.18¾	4.75	4.75	Conv into 1.5 shrs common				....	1014	...	Dc	28.92	25.63	57.86	58.12	58.13	....				11
12	1965	t0.10	11-30-78	11-8	....	Nil	t0.70	4.40	4.51	0.49	9-30-78	....	...	3955	Dc	3.35	6.28	4.54	1.43	Pd1.79	d1.79				12
13	1941	Q0.22	3-30-79	3-14	0.22	0.88	0.83	Equity per shr $27.49			9-30-78	27.8	...	6648	Dc	[53]□2.24	[54]□2.43	[55]□3.00	△[56]3.47	P△4.60	4.60				13
14◆	.....	5%Stk	8-31-78	8-8	....	Stk	5%Stk	0.11	11.1	3.29	9-30-78	2.79	19	p832	Dc	•0.94	•0.91	1.53	1.54	P1.61	1.61				14
15	1978	0.05	2-16-79	1-19	0.05	0.20	0.15	9.90	19.1	8.53	9-30-78	....	...	4528	Dc	0.11	d0.13	0.38	0.78	P1.06	1.06				15
16	.....	0.10	1-1-74	12-7	....	[57]Nil	....	Equity per sh $3.38			12-31-78	114.	947	2672	Je	d5.90	□△d3.36	[58]d9.13	•△0.40	△•0.78	0.58	6 Mo Dec	•△0.32	•0.12	16
17	.....	0.312	4-1-74	3-8	....	Nil	....	...	...	...		....	610	...	Je	d19.67	d10.65	[58]d31.14	2.69	4.10	....	Accum $5.93¾ to 1-1-79			17
18◆	1941	Q0.33	2-1-79	1-16	0.33	1.32	1.20	Book Value $35.54			12-31-78	5.00	...	1224	Dc	□3.68	□3.36	△3.44	△3.61	P□4.74	4.74				18
19◆	1935	Q0.32½	4-20-79	3-29	0.65	1.30	1.15	Book Value $29.29			12-31-78	23.2	400	1655	Dc	△2.55	△2.74	△2.95	□3.25	□[59]3.61	3.61				19
20	1933	Q0.25	5-4-79	4-19	0.50	1.00	0.91	Equity per shr $24.76			12-31-78	....	...	18967	Dc	2.03	2.06	2.42	□2.67	□2.99	2.99				20
21	1934	Q0.36	3-14-79	2-26	0.36	1.44	1.26	Equity per shr $31.73			9-30-78	....	...	6000	Dc	□2.89	□3.02	□3.31	△3.59	P△4.00	4.00				21
22	1974	S 0.10	4-27-79	4-6	0.10	0.20	0.16	Equity per shr $12.08			12-31-78	17.9	75	6149	Dc	□1.00	□0.52	△0.91	□1.55	□2.05	2.05				22
23	.....	None Paid			....	Nil	....	Equity per shr $12.25			12-31-77	....	...	761	Dc	△•0.50	□0.72	△•0.21	□d0.08	P•△0.50	0.50				23
24	1912	Q0.62½	3-1-79	2-8	0.62½	2.50	2.50	109.	533.	179.	12-31-78	174.	230	8373	Dc	3.30	▲4.25	4.17	[62]3.45	□△[63]4.97	4.79				24
25	1912	Q1.75	4-2-79	3-9	3.50	7.00	7.00	...	...	...		....	103	...	Dc	247.7	315.7	340.2	278.2	417.2	....				25
26	1969	Q1.31¼	5-1-79	4-6	2.62½	5.25	5.25	Conv into 2.3 shrs com,$43.50				....	127	...	Dc	232.6	303.2	272.3	237.9	339.1	....				26
27	1976	Q0.06	4-16-79	3-16	0.12	0.24	0.20	0.09	36.9	12.0	9-1-78	10.9	...	1349	My	1.06	0.90	0.94	0.90	1.14	1.60	9 Mo Feb△	0.69	1.15	27
28◆	1975	Q0.06	6-1-79	5-1	0.12	0.24	s0.228	0.65	3.04	2.39	1-27-79	1.29	...	671	Ap	0.79	0.92	0.88	0.96	1.16	1.30	39 Wk Jan△	0.77	0.91	28
29	1973	A0.24	7-15-78	6-21	....	0.24	0.24	3.88	10.5	2.44	9-30-78	0.87	13	597	Dc	0.70	□0.76	0.87	0.36	....	0.52	9 Mo Sep	0.45	0.61	29
30	1885	Q0.45	3-10-79	2-5	0.45	1.80	1.65	387.	1305	594.	12-31-78	4.72	...	72891	Dc	2.59	2.66	2.87	3.07	3.81	3.81				30
31◆	1970	Q0.02	3-19-79	3-5	0.02	0.08	0.073	4.16	37.3	20.0	1-27-79	35.9	...	13167	Jl	0.12	0.18	0.39	0.75	[65]0.90	0.45	6 Mo Jan△	0.66	0.21	31
32	.....	h....	1-7-69	12-23	....	Nil	....	16.8	26.5	16.4	9-30-78	21.7	...	2654	Dc	0.95	•1.66	2.36	3.01	P[66]4.14	4.14				32
33	.....	0.07½	2-24-70	2-2	....	Nil	....	Equity per shr $7.37			2-28-78	6.40	15	5169	Fb	•△0.32	△0.12	△0.11	□0.47	....	0.68	9 Mo Nov	□0.16	•△0.37	33
34◆	1941	Q0.40	4-2-79	3-9	0.80	1.60	1.543	Book Value $41.24			12-31-78	....	....	1104	Dc	□2.93	△4.06	△4.77	□5.52	□5.67	5.67				34
35	1963	Q0.47	2-1-79	1-16	0.47	1.88	1.88	Book Value $47.31			9-30-78	106.	2007	3217	Dc	□3.26	△3.19	□△3.20	□3.60	P□[67]5.16	5.16				35
36◆	1956	5%Stk	4-17-79	3-19	‡0.219	0.68	‡0.56	Equity per shr $17.03			12-31-77	....	...	1326	Dc	△1.79	△1.89	△2.07	□△2.18	P□2.90	2.90				36
37	.....	0.07	2-21-74	1-29	....	Nil	....	Equity per shr $1.17			12-31-78	10.8	...	1155	Mr	d2.69	d2.26	d0.72	d0.53	....	0.24	9 Mo Dec	d0.47	•0.30	37
38	1920	Q0.70	5-1-79	4-4	1.30	2.80	2.20	Equity per shr $48.34			9-30-78	58.2	848	22444	Dc	□3.19	□2.38	□3.92	□5.68	P□6.49	6.49				38
39	1965	Q0.75	6-5-79	5-9	1.50	3.00	3.00	Conv into 2 shrs common				....	848	...	Dc	46.26	37.95	71.66	150.2	....	....				39
40	1973	†0.49	3-6-79	2-13	†0.49	1.81	†1.79	Net Asset Val $19.13			2-28-79	....	...	2450	Dc	§17.92	§18.73	§20.08	§19.80	§19.37	....				40
41◆	1937	Q0.65	4-10-79	3-26	1.25	2.60	2.30	1.58	10.6	14.1	12-31-78	80.2	118	1865	Dc	3.38	3.81	4.03	4.03	[68]4.91	4.91				41
42	1978	0.20	1-4-79	12-15	0.20	0.20	0.10	1.12	4.23	2.65	12-31-78	2.49	...	605	Dc	d4.08	d0.81	•0.54	•0.51	•0.79	0.79				42
43◆	1956	Q0.11½	3-1-79	2-5	0.11½	0.46	0.43	2.55	12.3	4.71	9-30-78	7.09	...	3476	Dc	0.68	0.77	0.70	0.86	P1.19	1.19				43
44	.....	None Since Public			....	Nil	....	0.33	0.41	0.90	9-30-78	0.92	...	1760	Dc	d4.46	d0.69	□[69]0.03	△[70]d0.13	....	d0.20	9 Mo Sep	△0.01	d0.06	44
45	1977	Q0.03	3-5-79	2-1	0.03	0.12	0.11	2.27	73.5	67.7	9-30-78	★33.9	...	4874	Dc	0.17	0.30	■0.39	ʃ0.67	P[71]0.70	0.70				45

◆ Stock Splits & Divs By Line Reference Index [2]Adj to 5%,'77. [5]2-for-1,'76. [6]1-for-4 reverse,'77. [7]2-for-1,'76:5-for-4,'78:Adj to 4%,'78. [8]10%,'78. [14]Adj to 5%,'78. [18]3-for-2,'78. [19]2-for-1,'77. [28]Adj to 5%,'78. [31]2-for-1,'75,'77:3-for-2,'76,'78. [34]5-for-4,'75:10%,'76:7-for-6,'78. [36]Adj to 5%,'79. [41]Vote Apr 2? on 2-for-1. [43]2-for-1,'75,'77:3-for-2,'78.

Source: Standard & Poor's *Stock Guide,* April 1979, pp. 130–31.

FIGURE 4–6

Standard & Poor's listed stock report—page 1

Levi Strauss 1347

NYSE Symbol LVI   Options on Pac

Price	Range	P-E Ratio	Dividend	Yield	S&P Ranking
Feb. 28'79	1978-9				
41½	42⅝-27¼	6	1.80	4.3%	A

Summary

The world's largest apparel manufacturer, this company is BEST known for its "Levi's" jeans and slacks. After several years of above-average progress, jeans now appear to be entering a period of more stable growth. With this in mind, management has embarked on programs aimed at development and expansion of new product categories. These moves, combined with the company's established position in domestic markets, bode well for the long term.

Current Outlook

Earnings for fiscal 1979 are estimated at $7.75–$7.80 a share, up from the prior year's $6.56 (about $7 pro forma on fewer shares).

Dividends, recently raised to $0.45 quarterly, may be increased again this year.

Sales for fiscal 1979 are expected to rise roughly 12% from fiscal 1978's $1.68 billion. Demand for womenswear should remain strong, and moderate progress in sportswear and youthwear should temper the effects of further disappointing jeanswear comparisons in the U.S. Margins should be reasonably well maintained, as possible improvement in returns overseas offsets continued high marketing expenses domestically.

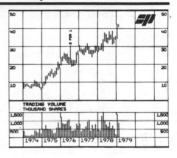

Net Sales (Million $)

Quarter:	1977-8	1976-7	1975-6	1974-5
Feb.	371	311	259	202
May	381	393	299	258
Aug.	472	433	332	275
Nov.	458	423	330	281
	1,682	1,560	1,220	1,016

Sales for the fiscal year ended November 26, 1978 rose 7.9% from those of fiscal 1977. Pretax income was up 3.9%. After taxes (48.3% versus 51.9%), net income advanced 12%.

Common Share Earnings ($)

Quarter:	1977-8	1976-7	1975-6	1974-5
Feb.	1.48	1.17	1.00	0.24
May	1.39	1.51	1.20	0.84
Aug.	1.87	1.64	1.30	0.99
Nov.	1.82	1.55	1.22	0.87
	6.56	5.87	4.72	2.94

Important Developments

Feb. '79—The company completed its tender offer to repurchase 2,000,000 of its common shares at $43.50 a share. The shares will be placed in the treasury.

Feb. '79—LVI is taking the first step towards a separate tops division to further develop and expand its sizable shirt business. A new men's tops marketing division is being formed within the jeanswear division to provide marketing specialization and concentration in sales, merchandising, and advertising for shirts and other tops.

Dec. '78—The company announced the sale of its 212,000 sq. ft. distribution center on 20 acres in San Jose, Calif. for $3,500,000.

Next earnings report due in early March.

Per Share Data ($)

Yr. End Nov. 30	1978	1977	1976	1975	1974	1973	¹1972	1971
Book Value	26.28	21.32	16.51	12.16	9.39	7.91	7.68	6.76
Earnings	6.56	5.87	4.71	2.95	1.60	0.54	1.15	0.92
Dividends	1.50	0.82½	0.40½	0.26	0.18	0.24	0.23	0.08
Payout Ratio	23%	14%	8%	9%	11%	44%	20%	9%
Prices²—High	38⅝	31⅝	27⅝	21⅜	11⅛	24¾	29⅞	30¾
Low	27¼	24¼	18⅞	6½	6	6¼	20⅛	16⅝
P/E Ratio—	6-4	5-4	6-4	7-2	7-4	46-11	26-18	33-18

Data as orig. reptd. Adj. for stk. div(s). of 100% Aug. 1976, 100% Jan. 1971. 1. Reflects merger or acquisition and accounting change. 2. Cal. yr.

Standard NYSE Stock Reports
Vol. 46/No. 46/Sec. 17

March 7, 1979

Standard & Poor's Corp.
345 Hudson St., NY, NY 10014

FIGURE 4–7

Standard & Poor's listed stock report—page 2

Background

Levi Strauss & Co.

Income Data (Million $)

Year Ended Nov. 30	Revs.	Oper. Inc.	% Oper. Inc. of Revs.	Cap. Exp.	Depr.	Int. Exp.	Net Bef. Taxes	Eff. Tax Rate	Net Inc.	% Net Inc. of Revs.
1977	1,559	290	18.6%	31.4	13.7	20.1	270	51.9%	130	8.3%
1976	1,220	217	17.8%	18.5	9.8	10.9	207	49.5%	105	8.6%
1975	1,015	149	14.7%	10.4	9.3	13.1	137	52.6%	65	6.4%
1974	898	99	11.0%	24.3	9.7	13.7	73	52.1%	35	3.9%
1973	653	54	8.2%	28.9	8.3	10.1	34	64.9%	12	1.8%
¹1972	504	60	11.8%	18.2	6.5	4.3	48	47.7%	25	5.0%
1971	405	42	10.5%	15.9	4.9	4.2	² 34	42.7%	19	4.8%

Balance Sheet Data (Million $)

Nov. 30	Cash	Current Assets	Current Liab.	Ratio	Total Assets	Ret. on Assets	Long Term Debt	Common Equity	Total Cap.	% LT Debt of Cap.	Ret. on Equity
1977	161	694	264	2.6	824	17.5%	80.7	464	555	14.5%	31.5%
1976	137	570	225	2.5	664	18.0%	66.6	363	434	15.3%	33.3%
1975	77	408	155	2.6	496	13.4%	68.7	265	337	20.4%	27.5%
1974	24	383	188	2.0	470	8.2%	72.2	206	278	26.0%	18.2%
1973	16	306	156	2.0	383	3.4%	48.1	176	224	21.4%	6.9%
¹1972	15	252	98	2.6	307	9.1%	37.6	170	207	18.1%	15.7%
1971	14	190	66	2.9	242	NA	28.2	148	176	16.0%	NA

Data as orig. reptd. 1. Reflects merger or acquisition and accounting change. 2. Incl. equity in earns. of nonconsol. subs. NA-Not Available.

Business Summary

Levi Strauss, the world's largest apparel manufacturer, is currently undergoing a change from its traditional western "blue jeans" orientation to a broadly based apparel firm serving worldwide markets. Sales by operating groups were as follows in fiscal 1978:

	Sales%
Jeanswear	50%
Sportswear	13%
International	35%

The Jeanswear Group includes the Jeanswear division (39% of total sales), the leading manufacturer of jeans in the U.S. and a marketer of shirts and jackets for men; and Youthwear (11%), a manufacturer of jeans, casual pants, and other clothing for kids and teens.

The Sportswear Group includes a division (7% of sales) under the same name marketing men's and young men's casual and dress slacks, coordinated and sports jackets, sweaters, and outerwear under the Panatela, David Hunter, and Wildfire brands; and the Womenswear division (6%), which handles a line of sportswear for both juniors and misses.

Accessories include belts, wallets, briefcases, and other items. The Activewear line began national distribution in late 1978 and includes men's and women's ski overalls and down parkas and vests.

The International Group is structured along geographic lines rather than product categories and comprises four divisions: Europe (19% of total sales), Canada (7%), Latin America (6%), and Asia/Pacific (4%). Sales consist primarily of basic lines of pants, shirts, and jackets.

Employees: 35,100.

Dividend Data

A dividend reinvestment plan is available.

Amt. of Divd. $	Date Decl.	Ex-divd. Date	Stock of Record	Payment Date
0.40	Apr. 5	Jun. 2	Jun. 8	Jul. 3'78
0.40	Jul. 28	Aug. 31	Sep. 7	Oct. 2'78
0.40	Nov. 10	Dec. 1	Dec. 7	Jan. 2'79
0.45	Jan. 19	Mar. 2	Mar. 8	Apr. 2'78

Next dividend meeting: early Apr. '79.

Capitalization

Long Term Debt: $83,292,000.

Common Stock: 19,887,783 shares ($1 par). The Haas family and associates own about 50%. Institutions own about 20%. Shareholders: 19,208 (of record).

Office—Two Embarcadero Center, San Francisco, Calif. 94106. Tel—(415) 544-6000. Pres & CEO—P. E. Haas. VP-Secy-Treas—R. B. Kern. Investor Contact—T. K. Michel. Dirs—W. A. Haas, Jr. (Chrmn), R. F Anderson, M. L. Bacharach, D. W. Baran, M. L. Bundy, H. H. Cohn, J. R. Cullman III, G. J. Daly, R. T. Grohman, P. E. Haas, W. A. Haas, R. W. Heyns, R. B. Kern, W. R. Kimball, D. E. Koshland, A. Miller, L. G. Nogales, A. V. Sanguinetti, F. A. Thomas. Transfer Agent & Registrar—Crocker National Bank, NYC & San Francisco. Reincorporated in Delaware in 1970.

Information has been obtained from sources believed to be reliable, but its accuracy and completeness are not guaranteed.

FIGURE 4–8
New York Stock Exchange ticker quotations

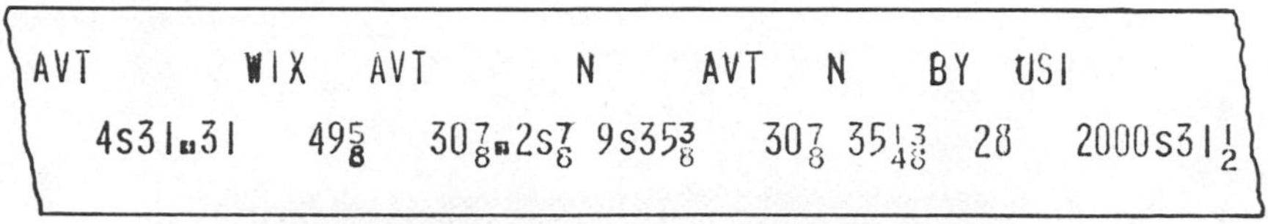

With the advent of the *Composite Tape,* trades of NYSE listed stocks occurring on the regional exchanges are incorporated on the ticker display. The non-NYSE transactions are indicated by a letter following the stock symbol, that identifies the particular regional exchange.

Many brokerage offices have equipment which projects the ticker tape data onto a large screen that can then be seen by many people simultaneously. Brokers and some investors watch this data so they can be current on trading activity.

Quotation devices. Several electronics firms offer equipment to provide trading information at the fingertips of brokers around the country. An example of one device is shown in Figure 4–9. This desktop machine makes available on a TV-like screen up-to-the-second market information on thousands of different bond and stock issues, both listed and OTC. Brokers press letter keys for the stock symbol and one of several other buttons for information on security price, volume, earnings, and dividends. They can also get market averages and other statistics such as the ten stocks which have advanced, declined, or traded most actively up to the time when the inquiry is made. Most brokerage offices have even greater capacity information retrieval systems. These systems provide, in addition to all the features described above, capability to supply material from an extensive statistical data base containing most of the facts and figures influencing the value of all types of securities. The user can access news from leading financial publications. Detailed records on options and commodities are also available instantly. Some securities firms have gone a step further by integrating client records into the system. A broker so equipped has a tremendous potential for matching investment alternatives with investor needs.

Within a few years many persons will have their own computers. Price quotes and other investment information can be stored in these computers, allowing individuals to easily and quickly review price and other data and perform at-home analyses of securities.

FIGURE 4–9
Electronic quotation machine

Courtesy of GTE Information Systems

Other services

In addition to research reports, most brokerage offices have a library of data sources and space where the investor can do analysis work. Many financial publications are much too expensive for the average investor to purchase. Access to them and a vast array of other data can be highly beneficial to individuals who like to do their own research.

Full service firms will store securities for their clients if this is desired. Some brokers offer free aid in transferring stock in the settlement of estates. They will also arrange to collect dividends and interest and redistribute them to an investor upon request. Loans for buying securities can by arranged through brokerage firms.[9] Interest is

---

[9] The procedures involved in borrowing money for the *margin* accounts are discussed in Chapter 3.

charged on the money borrowed, but until recently this was just about the only service outside of buying and selling securities for which a fee was collected.

Choosing a broker

In many ways the task of choosing a broker is more difficult than selecting a personal physician. Doctors usually practice individually or they join with several others in a local clinic. Brokers are almost always a part of an organization which may be nationwide and have thousands of employees. The problem of choosing a broker is really twofold. First, a firm must be selected and then a particular registered representative with the firm's office is chosen.[10]

Selecting a brokerage firm.   There are around 3,000 different brokerage firms in the United States.[11] These vary considerably in their organization, clientele, and services offered. For example, some firms concentrate on OTC issues. They are usually not members of any exchange, although they can buy and sell listed securities through correspondent relationships with member brokerage firms. The OTC houses may do considerable research into small companies located within their areas. Some firms, both those having exchange memberships and those who do not, do a relatively large amount of underwriting. This means investors interested in new issues would be likely to do business with them. A few firms avoid underwriting activities because they feel they can better serve their clients if they act strictly as agents and do not try to sell issues that they own themselves.

Some firms do a substantial business in mutual funds and in buying and selling commodities futures. Others do not handle these forms of investments. Some firms will not place orders for low-priced, speculative issues, while others make this an important part of their business. The discount brokers are in reality order takers who serve only those

---

[10] In many cases brokers "find" investors rather than the reverse. This often happens when a broker is aggressively seeking new customers and is out soliciting their business. This selection describes the situation of an investor searching for a broker.

[11] The National Association of Security Dealers had 2,813 member firms at the beginning of 1979. Recall that the NASD is the self-regulatory body of the securities industry. Its membership includes the vast majority of the industry. Only a few, usually local and newly formed firms, are not NASD members. The NASD includes all members of the New York Stock Exchange, which had 498 member organizations as of the end of 1978.

investors who have already decided what and when to buy or sell. A few firms discourage small investors, while others actively solicit accounts of all sizes. Policies of brokerage firms can be learned by talking to an office manager or to one of the brokers.

In addition to types of securities that are handled, the services offered by the firms and the amounts and ways of charging for them vary considerably. A complete line of services like those described in this chapter would require a central office staff of several hundred people. A few firms employ the required personnel and have a hundred or more offices with thousands of brokers scattered throughout the world. Many investors do not need all of the services offered by a large firm and choose to do business with a small brokerage house. For example, a library of financial information is a must for some investors but is rarely used by others. The do-it-yourself trend has led to a rising number of discount brokers.

Perhaps a factor of dominant influence in the selection of a brokerage firm is its accessibility to the investor. It is often desirable to be able to personally visit the office, so one that is conveniently located may be of major importance. However, many individuals do all of their business by phone, and proximity to the office is not necessary. In fact, some investors deal with firms hundreds or thousands of miles away. Virtually every section of the United States is served from about 7,000 brokerage offices staffed with almost 190,000 registered representatives.

Finding a broker. After a securities firm has been selected, the investor must decide on a particular broker in that office. Personalities often play a large role in this decision. The investor should have the same kind of confidence in a broker as in other professional people such as a doctor, dentist, or lawyer. Age of the professional is important to some individuals. Some like older brokers who have lived through many market ups and downs. Others prefer youthful vigor, especially when it represents the new ideas and thoughts of "Wall Street." A conservative investor might seek a broker who has similar views.

The training of brokers varies considerably among different firms and to a much lesser extent within the same firm. Some brokerage houses require their representatives to take part in a formal training program that lasts for six months or longer. Other firms have a much less ambitious program and rely heavily on the individual to develop the required background independently. All securities sales personnel must be licensed by the state and also by the federal authorities if the firm does interstate business. The licensing procedure usually involves demonstration of good character and passing an examination covering the securities business.

After a firm and a particular registered representative have been selected, the investor may become dissatisfied for one reason or another, such as losing money. A common solution is to switch brokers, but this may not solve the problem.[12] No securities firm or broker can consistently advise when to buy securities at their lowest points and to sell them at their highest prices, just as no baseball player can hit a home run every time at bat. Much of the anxiety and unhappiness caused by making poor investments can be avoided by realizing that brokers, for the most part, are trying to do the best possible job they can. They want nothing more than to help their clients make money.

Brokers with full-service firms earn commissions whenever securities are bought or sold. They have an incentive to urge greater investment activity than might be the case if they were paid on some other basis, such as a straight salary as are the brokers with the discount houses. This is one of the reasons why many organizations sell advice to investors but do not engage in any brokerage business. These firms point out that by separating the advising and brokerage functions their recommendation will never be influenced by the amount of commissions which might be forthcoming. Advisory services are discussed in the next section.

After repeated experiences of buying and selling too soon or too late, or if it appears that a broker is applying undue pressure to urge greater trading activity, it may be wise to seek another broker. However, the investor is cautioned that frequent switching will not insure success. Displeasure because of personality clashes can be minimized by interviewing several registered representatives before a choice is made.

To be sure, some investors may be well served by simply looking for a firm in the yellow pages, walking into an office, and choosing the broker with the loudest clothing. However, most investors will be better

---

[12] A reportedly true and definitely sad story tells how one investor tried unsuccessfully to reverse his losses by seeking new investment ideas. Perhaps the major reason for the continual drop in his portfolio value was his frequent hopping from one broker to another. See Anonymous Investor, *Wiped Out: How I Lost a Fortune in the Stock Market while the Averages Were Making New Highs* (New York: Simon and Schuster, 1966).

off by considering carefully what they want from a firm and its employees before they make a commitment.

INVESTMENT SERVICES

Most brokerage firms still make their money by offering free advice and then charging commissions on security transactions. Hundreds of other organizations do not buy and sell securities but instead provide information, advice, and other investment services for a fee.

Information and advisory services

Information offered by such firms as Standard & Poor's and Moody's has been discussed. These and many other companies sell advisory services by subscription.[13] Figure 4–10 illustrates the nameplates from a number of these firms. Some of them concentrate on providing data—such as charts of stock prices—leaving interpretation of the graphs to the investor. Most of the services assemble the information, analyze it, and make recommendations to buy or sell. Often these selections are made in a relative manner, with stocks classified into groups according to their likely performance in the future. The wide variety of approaches and objectives used by the advisors usually can be identified as *fundamental* or *technical* services.

Fundamental advisory services. These firms rely on selecting securities based on a corporation's present financial status and likely future developments. Emphasis is placed on company sales, earnings, dividends, and stock price. An example of this type of report is prepared by Arnold Bernhard & Company and is depicted in Figure 4–11. The page shown includes a considerable amount of information about Levi Strauss & Co. Historical data on financial characteristics and a brief discussion of current news and expected developments are presented. The company is rated on several criteria, and by following instructions provided, readers can form judgments as to how suitable an investment this stock would be for them.[14]

---

[13] One publication gives brief descriptions of about 500 investment advisory services. See Select Information Exchange, *1978 Investor* (New York: George H. Wein, 1978).

[14] Details of this procedure are found at the beginning of each report. They are not reproduced here because this example is used for illustration purposes only. The *Value Line Investment Survey* is published weekly. This service evaluates 1,400 of the best-known common stocks, and the report for each company is updated and distributed four times a year.

FIGURE 4–10
Investment advisory services

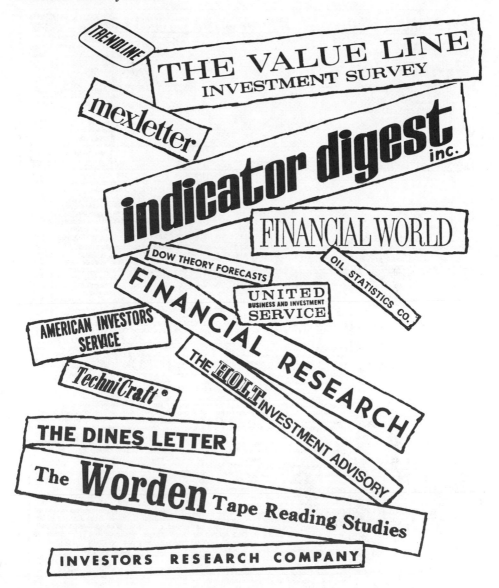

FIGURE 4–11
Value Line stock report

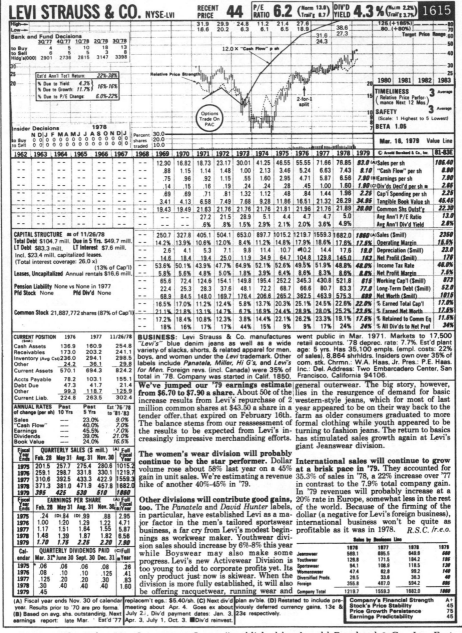

Source: "The Value Line Investment Survey" published by Arnold Bernhard & Co., Inc. Factual material is obtained from sources believed to be reliable but cannot be guaranteed.

Value Line offers a regular review of essentially the same group of better known companies. They also write up "Special Situations" which arise on an intermittent basis. This type of recommendation is used by many investment services offices. That is, the advisor follows a large group of stocks but reports only on those which warrant buy or sell action. These publications are quite similar to market letters issued by brokerage firms.

Advisory services using technical analysis. Another approach to recommending security purchases or sales is used by a group called *technical analysts*. They believe that the key to profitable investing can be found by the analysis of stock price and volume data. They graph this information, which is discussed in Chapter 14, to provide them with buy or sell signals. Their interpretations of these charts are published in newsletters. Again, investors need only to read recommendations on particular issues which the advisor feels have displayed buy or sell signals and then place their orders.

A number of services are based on computerized programs to analyze stocks from technical and/or fundamental approaches.

Other categories of advisory services. Sometimes advice is sold on investments in particular geographic areas. Market letters for Australia, the Bahamas, or California are examples. Some reports are written for certain clients only, such as the institutional investors (banks, insurance companies, mutual funds). Subscriptions to reports on a specific type of investment can be bought. Examples of these include recommendations on commodities, options, bonds, convertible securities, life insurance stocks, growth stocks, low-priced stocks, income stocks, and mutual funds.

Costs of the service. The wide variety in advisory services is matched by the broad range of their costs. Some offer occasional reports for as low as $1 each. Others sell service by the year at prices up to $5,000 or more. Many offer special inducements to begin a subscription, such as free trials or books as a bonus. No one has attempted a thorough appraisal of the predictive abilities of a significant number of advisors because of the vast array offered and for many other reasons. People can be found who swear by and swear at most of the services.

Personal investment counsel

Another type of assistance is offered by organizations that will completely handle an individual's investments. These groups usually do no brokerage business and receive their income solely from fees charged to manage money for investors. Like the advisory services, they feel it is best to separate the influence of commissions from the investment decision. Another point cited in their behalf is that the investment counselor is a trained professional who is studying and managing investments full time, whereas most individuals are part-time investors.

Some managers offer a special philosophy and approach to investing, but most of the services do not make a commitment to any specific technique. They all begin by establishing goals of the program that they feel are appropriate to the specific situation of each investor.

People who turn their accounts over to investment managers may simply be too busy to personally invest their own funds. Others are untrained in investment analysis. Some have no inclination to learn or desire to be bothered with the tasks of investing. Most of them share a common quality, namely, wealth. Substantial efforts are required just to set up and supervise a managed account. These efforts are in part independent of the size of the fund being established. In other words, fixed costs are involved that would necessitate prohibitive charges on small portfolios. In fact, many management firms establish minimums of $10,000 or more for accounts that they will accept. Fees are based on a percentage of the fund size. Typical annual charges are 2 percent for the first $50,000 with the percentage declining to 0.1 percent on amounts over $1 million.

Many large banks, in addition to their trust and regular investment management services, will invest small amounts by combining the funds with other small accounts. These are called *common trust funds, or comingled accounts.* They are somewhat similar to mutual funds that are described in Chapter 10 in that individual attention is not paid to each account. In the process of pooling accounts the identity of the investor is lost. Each investor owns a share of the fund assets.

Many people are do-it-yourself types and wish to handle their own investments. Others feel full-time professional management and freedom from the investment activity are worth the fees charged as long as the portfolio returns are high.

Stock market courses

Numerous organizations offer programs designed to educate investors so they can better invest on their own. These efforts include sessions sponsored by brokerage houses, investment courses at colleges and universities, and correspondence instruction offered by firms similar to or as a part of advisory services. Some of these courses are free and others cost several hundred dollars.

Programs that are free are usually short and often cover introductory material only. Home-study courses may be quite rigorous and include lessons at advanced levels. Most of them teach "How to Invest" according to the "XYZ Institute." That is, the organization has developed techniques which it feels will enable students to achieve financial success in their personal investments. The following statements illustrate these approaches. "The stock market is talking to you. Are you listening? We can help you understand what it is saying." Another course is based on "The Laws of Supply and Demand and Cause and Effect."

The study of investments is a rewarding one, both in terms of personal satisfaction and in potential financial gain. If it were otherwise, this book would never have been written. The stock market courses offer a comprehensive learning experience as opposed to self-taught approaches that tend to be disorganized and as a result often leave out important parts of a well-rounded education. Costs of instruction are in most instances well spent, although investors should be aware that some courses concentrate on very specialized techiques. In those instances, an outside effort should be made to supplement the training received to achieve a broad background in addition to knowledge in a specific area.

OTHER EDUCATIONAL ACTIVITIES

One quality common to most investors who have been successful over a long period is their quest for knowledge. This educational process is accomplished in ways which have been previously outlined and by other possibilities yet to be discussed.

Investment literature

In addition to sources of data, hundreds of books have been written on investment topics. Some of them are nothing more than get-rich-quick techniques which have allegedly worked well for the author. Many millionaires have shared their secrets, but one wonders (1) if they have written *everything* which led to their success and (2) if the environment has changed since their fortunes were accumulated, making a repetition of their experience difficult. The stories are interesting reading, but investors are cautioned against feeling that they can follow in the author's exact footsteps.

Certain books are held in high regard throughout the investment community. Many of these sources are listed at the end of each chapter. Investors are encouraged to read in them as much as possible. The value of *The Wall Street Journal* or *Barron's* for data is illustrated in this and other chapters. Much can be gained by reading other parts of these publications, such as the feature articles on companies, managements, and product developments. Other sections include dividend and earnings reports, examples of which are shown in Figure 4–12. Financial sections of newspapers and many magazines such as *Business Week, Forbes, Fortune,* and *Money* publish articles relevant to investors. Publications such as the *Financial Analysts Journal* and the *Institutional Investor* are read by experienced individuals.

Investment clubs

Several million people have been introduced to and/or educated about securities through investment clubs. In 1979, there were an estimated 22,000 of these organizations in the U.S. They consist of a group of people who meet regularly to invest small sums that are contributed by each member. The purpose of these clubs is to learn by doing, or in other words, to become educated about investing by investing.

Typical clubs have 10 to 20 members who each contribute $20 to $25 monthly. Everyone participates in security selections. They each analyze companies and present reports to the membership. The studies are discussed and votes are taken to buy or sell. Most clubs have tended to outperform the market averages in bull markets and in periods of moderate declines. However, in severe down markets, such as 1973 and 1974, the clubs, as a group, fall more than the averages. These associations offer a good educational opportunity for investors. Information about starting an investment club can be obtained from the National Association of Investment Clubs at 1515 East Eleven Mile Road, Royal Oak, Michigan 48067.

SUMMARY

Considerable amounts of information are available to investors. Study of this data does not guarantee profits, but few investors have

FIGURE 4–12
Reports of earnings and dividends

Digest of Earnings Reports

VANCE SANDERS SPEC FD (O)		
	Mar 31, '79	Mar 31, '78
Net assets	$52,733,926	$46,344,220
Shares	4,159,454	4,854,811
Asset shr	12.69	9.55

VEECO INSTRUMENTS INC. (N)		
Quar Mar 31:	1979	1978
Sales	$21,629,316	$14,496,519
Net income	2,361,030	1,646,435
Shr earns:		
Net income	.80	a.56
6 months:		
Sales	38,806,182	27,136,259
Net income	4,162,124	3,066,262
Shr earns:		
Net income	1.41	a1.05
a-Adjusted to reflect three-for-two stock split in December 1978.		

VENDO CO. (N)		
Quar Mar 31:	1979	1978
Sales	$29,170,000	$26,925,000
Net income	503,000	355,000
Shr earns:		
Net income	.19	.14

VIRGINIA RL EST INV TR (N)		
Quar Mar 31:	1979	1978
Income	$134,867	$93,933
Extr charge	....	30,050
Net income	134,867	63,883
Avg shares	1,205,187	1,250,828
Shr earns:		
Income	.11	.08
Net income	.11	.05

WEBB CO. (O)		
Quar Mar 31:	1979	1978
Sales	$21,805,100	$18,696,100
Net income	1,029,900	949,000
Avg shares	1,461,169	1,437,884
Shr earns:		
Net income	.70	.66
Corrected from earlier edition.		

WARNACO INC. (N)		
Quar Mar 31:	1979	1978
Sales	$101,831,000	$87,532,000
Income	1,929,000	1,510,000
aExtr credit	713,000	355,000
Net income	2,642,000	1,865,000
bCom shares	4,138,023	4,122,378
Shr earns (primary):		
bIncome	.44	.34
bNet income	.62	.43
Shr earns (fully diluted):		
bIncome	.41	.32
bNet income	.56	.40
a-Tax-loss carry-forward. b-Adjusted for a 5% stock dividend payable in May 1979.		

WASHINGTON GAS LIGHT CO. (N)		
Quar Mar 31:	1979	1978
Revenues	$160,767,000	$159,707,000
Income	16,515,000	19,216,000
Acctg adj	a4,410,000	....
Net income	20,925,000	19,216,000
Shr earns:		
Income	3.62	4.25
Net income	4.63	4.25
12 months:		
Revenues	354,022,000	348,528,000
Income	11,143,000	15,825,000
Acctg adj	a4,410,000	....
Net income	15,553,000	15,825,000
Shr earns:		
Income	1.89	2.95
Net income	2.90	2.95
a-Credit; cumulative effect of change in accounting.		

WELDWOOD OF CANADA (T)		
Quar Mar 31:	1979	1978
Revenues	$126,500,000	$104,800,000
Net income	10,600,000	4,500,000
Shr earns:		
Net income	2.15	.90
Amounts in Canadian dollars.		

WEST CO. (O)		
Quar Apr 1:	1979	1978
Sales	$31,632,000	$27,460,000
Net income	2,428,000	2,041,000
Shr earns:		
Net income	.63	.53
Corrected from earlier edition.		

WESTERN AIR LINES (N)		
Quar Mar 31:	1979	a1978
Revenues	$210,601,000	$192,200,000
Income	12,652,000	b10,486,000
Acctg adj	....	c16,201,000
Net income	12,652,000	b26,687,000
Shr earns:		
Income	.93	.79
Net income	.93	2.06
Shr earns (fully diluted):		
Income	.71	.59
Net income	.71	1.49
a-Restated. b-Includes gain of $8,700,000 from settlement with vendor. c-Credit; cumulative effect of accounting change.		

WISCONSIN CENTRIFUGAL (O)		
Year Mar 31:	a1979	1978
Sales	$68,535,000	$59,654,000
Net income	3,688,000	3,342,000
Shr earns:		
Net income	2.11	b1.92
a-Reflects LIFO accounting. b-Adjusted for a 10% stock dividend paid in July 1978.		

WISCONSIN GAS CO. (N)		
Quar Mar 31:	1979	1978
Oper revs	$141,707,000	$123,012,000
Net income	13,262,000	10,629,000
Shr earns:		
Net income	3.15	2.50
12 months:		
Oper revs	335,053,000	301,153,000
Net income	17,303,000	15,211,000
Shr earns:		
Net income	3.83	3.35

Dividend News

Stewart-Warner Split Set, Cash Payout Is Boosted

CHICAGO — Stewart-Warner Corp. declared a five-for-four stock split and a 47-cent-a-share quarterly dividend on the increased shares. The cash dividend is equal to about a 12% increase from the preceding 52½-cent-a-share quarterly rate.

Both the additional shares and the cash dividend will be paid June 9 to stock of record May 18, the mechanical and electronic systems concern said.

* * *

RLC Corp. declared a three-for-two stock split, payable June 1 to stock of record May 14. The company also declared a 10-cent-a-share dividend on the post-split shares, payable June 15 to stock of record May 15. The company had been paying 14 cents a share. The new 10-cent rate on post-split shares equals a 15-cent rate on the presplit shares, or an increase of one cent from the previous 14 cent-a-share quarterly. RLC is a trucking and automobile leasing firm.

Nicholas Fund Inc. said a two-for-one stock split will be presented for shareholder approval at the mutual fund's annual meeting June 6.

* * *

Dividends Reported April 27

Company		Period	Amt.	Payable date	Record date
REGULAR					
Adobe Oil & Gas		Q	.05	6–29–79	6– 1
AffiliatedHospitalProd		Q	.07	5–30–79	5–16
Amer National Fin'l		Q	.13	6–28–79	6–15
Amer Precision Indust		Q	.10	7–16–79	6–29
Armco Inc		Q	.34	6– 4–79	5–11
Armco $2.10pf		Q	.52½	6–29–79	6– 1
Bethlehem Copper		Q	b.15	6–15–79	6– 1
Bluefield Supply Co		Q	.30	6–29–79	6–15
Brown & Sharpe Inc		Q	.20	6–15–79	5–25
Carter-Wallace Inc		Q	.10	5–30–79	5– 9
Coachmen Industries		Q	.15	6– 8–79	5–18
Community Public Svc		Q	.47	6–15–79	5–15
Consol-Bathurst		Q	b.20	6–18–79	5–25
Dillingham Corp		Q	.13	6–12–79	5–14
Dillingham Corp$2pf		Q	.50	6–12–79	5–14
Dinner Bell Foods Inc		Q	.12½	5–25–79	5–11
Duke Power 8.70%pf		Q	2.17½	6–16–79	5–18
Duke Power 8.20%pf		Q	2.05	6–16–79	5–18
Duke Power 7.80%pf		Q	1.95	6–16–79	5–18
Duke Power 8.28%pf		Q	2.07	6–16–79	5–18
Duke Power 8.84%pf		Q	2.21	6–16–79	5–18
Duke Power 6.75%pf		Q	1.68¾	6–16–79	5–18
Duke Power 10.76%pf		Q	.67¼	6–16–79	5–18
Equitable of Iowa Cos		Q	.30	6– 4–79	5–18

Source: Reprinted by permission *The Wall Street Journal*, April 30, 1979, pp. 22, 26.

been successful without analyzing relevant information before making commitments.

Numerous indicators are published to tell what has happened to stock market prices. The *Dow Jones Averages* are the oldest and most widely quoted yardsticks, but other more comprehensive measures have been developed. There is no one best indicator, and the choice of a particular barometer depends on the user and his or her purpose.

Security prices are quoted in most newspapers. *The Wall Street Journal* offers a detailed listing, including price ranges and dividend and interest data, in addition to the daily trading results. Up-to-the-second prices and a host of other investment information are available at brokerage offices on their electronic quotation machines.

Brokers offer many other services to clients at little or no charge. For example, through portfolio planning and review efforts, they attempt to match characteristics of investments with the needs of the investor. They also distribute research reports on industries and particular companies. Discount brokers offer order taking services only. This separation has presented investors with an opportunity to choose from a range of plans and fees for brokerage services. Choosing a broker involves looking at the firm for such factors as reputation, specialization in types of securities and services offered, commissions, and accessibility. In selecting an individual registered representative, characteristics such as training, age, and personality all play a part. Investors who become dissatisfied with a broker should remember that rapid switching from one to another will not guarantee improvement.

Brokers are paid by commissions related to the amount of security trades they execute for their customers. Because of this type of remuneration plan, many services sell only information and advice to investors. They argue that separating the commission incentive from recommendations permits them to give unbiased counsel. Some of the services concentrate on providing data only; others make specific buy and sell recommendations. The advice may be based on *fundamental* or *technical* analysis and is sometimes offered for particular types of securities.

Complete investment management services are available as opposed to do-it-yourself investing. In the latter approach investors can take home-study courses, and read from a wide variety of books, magazines, and journals which concentrate on investment matters. An especially popular way of education has been through membership in investment clubs, which are located in most communities.

PROBLEMS

1. Suppose you wanted to compile detailed information about a company. Prepare an outline of headings which you would use. (Hint: Read reports of Moody's, Standard & Poor's, or a brokerage firm to see what kinds of information they consider to be relevant.)
2. Look up several measures of stock market activity and compare the percentage change in each measure over a period of several months or years. Why do the indicators not all show the same price changes?
3. Visit a brokerage office and see how they receive security price information.
4. Attend a meeting of a local investment club. (You may be able to find out when and where the meetings are held by asking a broker.)

QUESTIONS

1. Why are there so many measures of stock market activity?
2. What would cause someone to prefer one measure over another?
3. How do the price quotations for listed stocks differ from the OTC reports?
4. Outline briefly the major services provided by brokerage firms.
5. Why might an investor first choose a brokerage firm before selecting an individual broker?
6. Why do you suppose some investors do business with several brokerage firms?
7. Cite an argument used by advisory services as an advantage for using their recommendations as opposed to those given by brokerage firms.
8. In Figure 4–4, the 7¼s of August 1992 Treasury Bond (see the circled row) has bid and asked prices of 87.8 and 87.16, respectively. Is the asked price higher than the bid? Explain your answer.
9. Investors should seek to do business with the broker charging the lowest commissions. Do you agree or disagree?
10. Give reasons why some people use personal investment counselors.
11. What are the advantages and disadvantages of joining an investment club?
12. Why do you suppose there are so many more advisory services, investment counselors, and so on, offering assistance in security investments as compared to those involved in real estate investments?

SELECTED READINGS

Cohen, Jerome B.; Zinbarg, Edward D.; and Ziekel, Arthur. *Investment Analysis and Portfolio Management,* 3d ed. Homewood, Ill.: Richard D. Irwin, 1977.

The Dow Jones Investor's Handbook. New York: Dow Jones, published yearly.

Financial Analysts Journal, published bimonthly.

Guide to Business and Investment Services. New York: George H. Wein, published periodically.

Industry Surveys. New York: Standard & Poor's, published periodically.

Investment Facts. New York: New York Stock Exchange, published periodically.

Levine, Sumner N., ed. *Financial Analysts Handbook,* vols. 1 and 2 Homewood, Ill.: Dow Jones-Irwin, 1975.

Money. Published monthly.

Moody's Handbook of Common Stocks. New York: Moody's Investors Service, published four times each year.

Moody's Manuals in Banking and Finance, Industrials, Municipal and Governments, Public Utilities, and Transportation. New York: Moody's Investor Services, published yearly.

New York Stock Exchange Fact Book. New York: New York Stock Exchange, published yearly.

Spencer, Robert L. *The Performance of the Best Investment Advisory Services.* New York: Odd John, 1977.

5

Analysis of financial statements

INTRODUCTION

Financial statements are issued periodically by all American and foreign corporations which have publicly traded securities. Annual statements are prepared by the company's management and are usually audited by an independent public accounting firm. Semiannual and quarterly statements are usually not audited. Financial information is available from the company itself or from firms which gather corporate financial data and condense them into standard format reports. All large companies must file a Form 10–K or equivalent report with the Securities and Exchange Commission. This document is usually more detailed than the annual report and must carry information not required in the annual report. The 10–K report is available from the company upon request.

Through the financial statements interested parties may analyze the past operations of the company and make projections of future profits, sales, and other accounting measures which affect the value of the company's securities. This chapter has been designed to provide a basic understanding of financial statements, their construction, and their analysis. The meaning of the balance sheet and income statement is explained in the first part of the chapter. Each account of a "representative" company is examined and defined in this process. Persons who have taken a previous course in accounting may omit this portion, as they should be familiar with its contents.

The second part of the chapter examines financial statements by using some of the basic tools of financial analysis. The goal of this analysis is to discover weak or strong areas in a company's operations, and to rate its performance against certain norms. Readers who have had a second accounting course, or a course in corporation or business finance, will probably be familiar with these techniques and may prefer to skip this chapter entirely. It should be emphasized that this chapter is *basic* in its scope. It will not turn readers into accountants or security analysts, but it should provide a basic understanding of corporate financial statements.

UNDERSTANDING CORPORATE FINANCIAL STATEMENTS

There are a variety of financial statements, the most common being balance sheets and income statements. Since every company prepares these two, our efforts will be directed to understanding them.

Financial statements of Levi Strauss & Co. have been chosen as the central illustration for this chapter because (1) its financial statements are relatively straightforward and easy to read, (2) the business (clothing manufacturing) is easily understood and visualized, (3) the capital structure of the company is uncomplicated. This analysis is not undertaken to indicate that Levi Strauss is a "good" or a "bad" company, or that the stock of the company is a "good" or a "bad" buy. The company was chosen as an illustration entirely because of the usefulness of its financial statements.

Levi Strauss manufactures and markets apparel throughout the United States and much of the world. Company operations are organized into three major groups: the Jeanswear Group, the Sportswear Group, and the International Group. The Jeanswear and Sportswear Groups represent the domestic operations of the company. They are subdivided into divisions that serve various product markets: Womenswear, Youthwear, and so on. The International Group is organized geographically with four major divisions: Europe, Canada, Latin America, and Asia/Pacific.

The company is incorporated in Delaware; its executive offices are in San Francisco. Manufacturing plants are located in California and most of the southern states as well as in Canada, South and Central America, Europe, Australia, and the Philippines. Levi Strauss stock was first sold publicly in 1971. The stock is listed on the NYSE and its symbol is LSI.

Later in this chapter Levi Strauss' financial ratios will be compared to those of similar manufacturing companies to learn how well this firm has done relative to its competitors.

The balance sheet

Levi Strauss' 1978 balance sheet is presented as Figure 5-1. As is conventional, prior year figures are included to provide a basis for comparison. Notes which accompany the financial statements are presented as Figure 5-2. The company's income statement is presented later as Figure 5-3. The balance sheet gives the bookkeeping value of the company's assets, liabilities, and capital *as of* November 26, 1978. It is as if the operation of the company had momentarily stopped at that date, and management had taken an inventory of the historical cost of all things owned by the company (its assets), all things the company owed to others (its liabilities), and the ownership interest of its shareholders (stockholders' equity). The Notes to Consolidated Financial Statements provide additional information important to the understanding of the balance sheet and income statement. Levi Strauss prepares its annual report at the end of each November because for accounting purposes its "year" ends then.[1] Quarterly and semiannual statements are also prepared, but these are in briefer form.

Consolidated and unconsolidated statements

The Figure 5-1 balance sheet tells us (top left-hand corner) that it covers Levi Strauss and *subsidiary companies,* and that it is prepared on a consolidated basis. This means that Levi Strauss owns other companies, known as subsidiaries, and that the financial statements of these companies are combined with that of the Levi Strauss company itself. This procedure is called *consolidation.*[2] Assets, sales, and net income from foreign operations are presented separately in a section

---

[1] Any yearly period (January 1 to December 31, May 5 to May 4 of the next year, July 1 to June 30, and so on) may be specified as the yearly accounting period. Many businesses adopt a period which ends shortly after a seasonal peak in their business activity. Inventories then are probably low and more easily counted, and the business will at that time have completed a full yearly cycle of operation. For example, many retail trade companies use either February 1 or March 1 as the beginning date of their accounting period because this is a slack period in their activities.

[2] Most companies, including Levi Strauss, do not report earnings or expenses of subsidiaries separately although separate reporting for different, broadly defined, product lines is required.

FIGURE 5–1

Consolidated Balance Sheets
Levi Strauss & Co. and Subsidiaries
(Dollar Amounts in Thousands)

		November 26, 1978	November 27, 1977
Assets:	Current Assets:		
	Cash	$ 34,866	$ 31,063
	Temporary investments of cash	219,955	129,878
	Trade receivables (less allowances for doubtful accounts: 1978 — $5,489; 1977 — $4,154)	241,125	203,239
	Inventories		
	Raw materials and work-in-process	135,146	135,836
	Finished goods	163,348	158,267
	Other current assets	29,787	35,975
	Total current assets	$824,227	$694,258
	Property, Plant and Equipment (less accumulated depreciation: 1978 — $88,707; 1977 — $76,026)	141,319	119,255
	Other Assets	8,328	10,640
		$973,874	$824,153
Liabilities and Stockholders' Equity:	Current Liabilities:		
	Current maturities of long-term debt	$ 9,741	$ 6,310
	Short-term borrowings	11,623	35,344
	Accounts payable	89,102	46,118
	Accrued liabilities	65,962	56,963
	Salaries, wages and employee benefits	57,558	51,089
	Taxes based on income	59,662	61,173
	Dividends payable	8,757	6,529
	Total current liabilities	$302,405	$263,526
	Long-Term Debt — Less current maturities	$ 83,292	$ 80,647
	Deferred Liabilities	$ 12,859	$ 16,125
	Stockholders' Equity:		
	Common stock — $1.00 par value: authorized 30,000,000 shares; issued 21,999,404 shares	$ 21,999	$ 21,999
	Additional paid-in capital	71,895	73,178
	Retained earnings	484,947	374,950
		$578,841	$470,127
	Less treasury stock, at cost: 1978 — 111,621 shares; 1977 — 238,938 shares	3,523	6,272
	Total stockholders' equity	$575,318	$463,855
		$973,874	$824,153

The accompanying accounting policies and notes to consolidated financial statements are an integral part of these balance sheets.

Source: Levi Strauss & Co. *1978 Annual Report.*

of the annual report titled Notes to Consolidated Financial Statements.

To classify a company as a subsidiary the "parent" company must own controlling interest (normally 51 percent or more) in the subsidiary company's common stock. If consolidation is chosen, the financial statements of parent and subsidiary are joined into a single set of statements. The owning company's balance sheet could contain an asset called *Investments in Unconsolidated Subsidiaries* if a controlling but not consolidated interest in the subsidiary firm were owned. If the parent company owned less than a controlling interest, the cost of the partially-owned company would be contained in an asset account known simply as *Investments*. Since Levi Strauss' balance sheet contains neither of these accounts, it can be presumed that all subsidiaries are wholly owned.

Assets

This balance sheet classification lists all things of value owned by the company. Quite commonly, the assets category is broken into two parts: current assets, and long-term or fixed assets. Levi Strauss has chosen to use three asset subclassifications: current assets; property, plant, and equipment; and other assets.

Current assets include cash and other assets which are expected to be converted into cash within one year after they are acquired in the normal course of the business. Examples of these are cash, securities, inventory, accounts receivable, and notes receivable. *Long-term or fixed assets* are those which are expected to be held permanently in the business, and which are not readily converted into cash. Property, plant, and equipment are without question fixed assets (see Figure 5–1).

The *cash* account is mainly checking account balances held in commercial banks. These funds are available for immediate use. This business, like most others, uses very little cash in the form of coins and bills.

Temporary investments of cash are investments of a short-term, highly liquid nature. These investments are often Treasury bills and commercial paper but may be in any security which can be turned into cash quickly and with little loss of value.

Trade receivables are amounts *owed* to the company. For a firm of this type these assets would be mainly uncollected sales. As of November 26, 1978, Levi Strauss was owed $241,125,000 of trade receivables.

The company expects to be unable to collect $5,489,000 of its sales and has made allowance for this anticipated loss by deducting this amount from trade receivables. This $5,489,000 "loss" is an expense of doing business and has been charged against (deducted from) the revenue of the company on the income statement.

Inventories are assets that the company had for resale to customers on the date of the balance sheet. These are listed "at lower of cost or market," which means that if the market price of inventory is for some reason less than its cost to the company, it is valued at this more conservative figure. Loss of value might be caused by deterioration, a decline in market price, obsolescence, style changes or any of several other events.

Inventory cost normally includes the price of raw materials and amounts spent to make raw materials into finished products. Manufacturing companies commonly record inventories as being either *raw materials, goods in process of manufacture,* or *finished goods.* These classifications describe how close to being marketable the inventory is. Natural resource companies usually classify undeveloped resources—standing timber, oil, or minerals in the ground—as long-term assets. Once these resources have been "harvested," they become part of inventory, a current asset.

Other current assets are those that do not fit into any of the clearly defined current asset categories. This account is usually of an insignificant amount relative to other accounts.

Property, plant and equipment are the fixed assets of this company. These assets are a permanent part of the business and are used in manufacturing, shipping, storing, and selling the company's products. For a manufacturing company these assets might be machinery, buildings, trucks, and other equipment; they would probably make up a large portion of the company's total assets. Levi Strauss, like many other companies, chooses to *lease* some of its assets. These leases are classified as *operating* or *capital* leases. Operating lease payments are charged against income as are other expenses. Capital leases are recorded differently. Because these lease agreements more nearly resemble the purchase of an asset, the amount of the lease is entered as both a long-term asset and a long-term liability. The notes to financial statements, Figure 5–2, carry more information about lease agreements.

Depreciation, amortization, and *depletion* are three ways in which an asset may be used up, or otherwise reduced in value. A company typically pays for a fixed asset when it is purchased, but uses it for many years. To charge this total payment as an expense of doing business *when it is incurred* is unrealistic and misleading. It violates the principle of matching income and expenses to each other when they occur. For example, assume that a company purchased an asset that cost $3,000 and had an expected useful life of three years. If the company charged the entire $3,000 against the income of the period in which the purchase took place, that period's income would be *reduced* by the full $3,000. In the following two periods income would be *increased* from the use of the asset (presuming that it was a profitable investment of funds), but there would be no cost associated with this increased income. Stated income would be "too low" in the first period and "too high" in the next two.

Depreciation charges are a method of spreading the cost of a fixed asset over its productive life. In the above example, when the asset was purchased it would be entered on the books of the company as a fixed asset having a value (its original cost) of $3,000. At the end of the first year of ownership the value of the asset would be lowered by $1,000, the amount (one-third of the price) that had been consumed during this year of use. A corresponding charge (the depreciation charge) would be levied against the income of the company for that period. The asset would then be valued at $2,000 after the first year of use, and the company's income for that period would be reduced by $1,000 rather than the full $3,000.

Table 5-1 shows how the value of the asset would be reduced and depreciation charges levied. This is an example of *straight-line depreciation*. Under this type schedule it is assumed that the asset wears out or loses value by an equal amount each year.

Accelerated depreciation schedules are often used to charge off more of an asset's cost during its early life because this is the way some assets are consumed or used up.[3] Levi Strauss has chosen to use straight-line depreciation on most assets, but many other companies use a combination of straight-line and accelerated schedules.

Assets may lose value to the firm for reasons having nothing to do with their use. Improvements made on leased property belong to the owner of the property when the lease period ends—regardless of the

---

[3] For example, an automobile loses more of its value the first year after purchase than the second, and more the second than the third, and so on. To depreciate such an asset an equal amount each year would not record the true loss of value.

TABLE 5–1
Asset values and depreciation charges

Beginning asset value	$ 3,000
Less first-year depreciation charge	−1,000
Beginning second-year asset value	$ 2,000
Less second-year depreciation charge.........................	−1,000
Beginning third-year asset value..................................	$ 1,000
Less third-year depreciation charge	−1,000
Ending asset value	−0−

duration of their useful life. The usual method of recording the eventual loss of leasehold improvement value is to reduce the original cost of the improvement on a piece of property by whatever fraction of its value is "lost" each year. For example, a $10,000 leasehold improvement on a piece of property that was leased for five years should be reduced in value by an average of $2,000 per year because at the end of five years the asset will cease to be owned by the purchaser. This charge, and other similar ones, are called *amortization charges* and have the same effects as depreciation charges on a company's balance sheet and income statement.[4]

Depletion is used to record the actual physical consumption of what are known as *wasting assets*. These are such things as oil deposits, standing timber, gravel in a gravel pit, coal in a mine, or other assets of this type. The recording procedure is exactly the same as in the above two examples. Neither amortization nor depletion charges are listed on the financial statements of Levi Strauss.

Normal accounting procedure is to list the cost of all assets that are to be depreciated, amortized, or depleted, and to deduct from this figure the appropriate charges. The 1978 balance sheet illustration records Levi Strauss as having property, plant and equipment valued at $141,319,000 net of depreciation. The Property, Plant and Equipment note in Figure 5–2 contains a more complete statement of depreciation amounts and values of owned and leased assets. A total of $88,707,000 in depreciation charges have been written off against assets in use in the business. In 1978, $16,126,000 in depreciation charges were counted

---

[4] Amortization charges may be levied against any assets which suffer a periodic loss of value but are not depreciated. Such assets are patents, copyrights, certain purchase or sale options, and so on. The amortization schedule may, like depreciation schedules, be accelerated.

FIGURE 5–2

Accounting Policies
(Dollar Amount in Thousands)

Principles of Consolidation	The consolidated financial statements include the accounts of the Company and all subsidiaries.
Inventory Valuation	Inventories are valued substantially at the lower of average cost or market. Market is based on anticipated selling price less allowances to maintain the Company's normal gross margin for each product line.
Leases	Capital leases are recorded in the accounts as assets and related obligations. Operating leases are recorded as charges to income in the period when rentals are due.
Depreciation Methods	Provision for depreciation is generally computed on a straight line basis over the estimated useful lives of the related assets.
Retirement Plans	Pension costs include the cost of current services and the amortization of unfunded past service liabilities over periods of up to sixteen years. Pension costs normally are funded as accrued.
Income Taxes	Deferred income taxes are provided on timing differences in the recognition of income and expense for tax and for financial statement purposes. The Company does not provide for taxes which would be payable if the net cumulative undistributed earnings ($115,710) at November 26, 1978 of its foreign subsidiaries were remitted to the Company. Normally such earnings are reinvested in the subsidiary operations unless it is advantageous for tax or foreign exchange reasons to remit a subsidiary's earnings.
Net Income Per Share	Earnings per share are calculated on the basis of the average number of common shares outstanding for the period including a minor dilutive effect of stock options granted and outstanding.

Source: Levi Strauss & Co. *1978 Annual Report.*

FIGURE 5-2 (continued)

Notes To Consolidated Financial Statements
(Dollar Amounts in Thousands Except Per Share Data)

Operations	Information concerning the Company's domestic and foreign operating groups (all in the apparel industry) may be found on page 23. Those results include the effect of exchange losses of $2,263 in 1978 and gains of $48 in 1977. Also, as a result of currency devaluations, inventory values, as expressed in U.S. dollars, were reduced by $7,438 in 1978 and $8,502 in 1977 to maintain normal gross margins. Substantially all of these amounts, which totaled $9,701 in 1978 and $8,454 in 1977, affect the profit contribution from the international group.

Property, Plant and Equipment

The components of property, plant and equipment, including both leased and owned assets stated at cost, are shown in the table below:

	1978		1977	
	Owned	Leased	Owned	Leased
Land	$ 5,444	$ 715	$ 4,490	$ 715
Buildings and leasehold improvements	81,363	24,506	60,525	24,802
Machinery and equipment	109,262	7,108	89,028	9,209
Construction in progress	1,628	—	6,512	—
	$197,697	$32,329	$160,555	$34,726
Less accumulated depreciation	79,321	9,386	67,352	8,674
	$118,376	$22,943	$ 93,203	$26,052

Depreciation expense for 1978 and 1977 amounted to $16,126 and $13,666, respectively.

Income Taxes

The provision for taxes on income consists of:

	Federal	State	Foreign	Total
1978				
Current	$ 85,870	$ 8,118	$42,322	$136,310
Deferred	(1,476)	(45)	611	(910)
	$ 84,394	$ 8,073	$42,933	$135,400
1977				
Current	$101,162	$11,467	$25,724	$138,353
Deferred	440	47	1,333	1,820
	$101,602	$11,514	$27,057	$140,173

The Company's effective income tax rate was 48.3% in 1978 and 51.9% in 1977. The difference between the effective rates and the U.S. Federal income tax rate of 48% is due primarily to the effect of foreign currency fluctuations, state income taxes, the incurrence and utilization of foreign operating losses and various differences in tax regulations between foreign countries and the United States.

At November 26, 1978, foreign operations had cumulative losses of about $12,098 which are available to reduce their future taxable income. These tax losses expire as follows: $1,629 in 1979, $3,799 in 1980, $2,102 in 1981, $3,763 in 1982 and the remainder in 1983.

FIGURE 5-2 (continued)

Short-Term Borrowings and Lines of Credit	Short-term borrowings, all foreign, and unused lines of credit are summarized below:		

During the Year:	1978	1977
Average borrowings	$ 23,023	$ 53,586
Average interest rate	14.5%	23.6%
Maximum borrowings based on month-end balances	$ 43,419	$ 72,078

At November 26, 1978 and November 27, 1977:		
Total borrowings	$ 11,623	$ 35,344
Average interest rate	8.2%	20.6%
Unused lines of credit:		
Domestic	$ 70,000	$ 71,000
Foreign	$180,000	$223,000

The domestic lines provide for borrowings on renewable short-term notes at bank prime interest rates. The foreign lines provide for borrowings on both renewable short-term notes and on an overdraft basis at varying rates. The most common terms of the credit lines with domestic banks include an average annual compensating balance requirement of 10% of the line of credit or 20% of the amount borrowed, whichever is greater. These compensating balances, which are not legally restricted, are available to the Company for operating purposes and are compensation to the banks for other services. Credit arrangements with foreign lenders generally have no compensating balance requirements.

Long-Term Debt

Long-term debt is summarized below:

	1978	1977
Secured by Properties:		
Notes payable, 4% to 21%, due in installments through 1998	$18,719	$17,114
Capital leases due through 1997	23,430	26,835
	$42,149	$43,949
Unsecured:		
Notes payable to an insurance company, 8¾%, due in annual installments of $2,960 through 1991	38,160	41,120
Other unsecured indebtedness	12,724	1,888
Total long-term debt	$93,033	$86,957
Less current maturities	9,741	6,310
	$83,292	$80,647

At November 26, 1978 and November 27, 1977, the original cost of properties pledged to secure indebtedness was $55,298 and $55,725, respectively.

The Company's principal debt agreement, among other things, limits the declaration of dividends (other than stock dividends) and the redemption of its capital stock. Under this agreement, the amount of retained earnings so restricted and the minimum amount of working capital which must also be maintained, are substantially below current levels.

The aggregate long-term debt maturities for the next five years are:

Year	Principal Payments
1979	$ 9,741
1980	10,271
1981	6,943
1982	5,614
1983	5,505

FIGURE 5-2 (continued)

Incentive and Award Plans	The Company's Management Incentive Plan is based on achieving specified levels of profit and return on investment and on individual employee performance. Under the Plan, aggregate incentive awards in any year may not exceed 6% of the excess income before taxes over 15% of beginning stockholders' equity. The awards for 1978 and 1977 were $2,893 and $3,503, respectively, which were significantly below the maximum amounts allowable.
Retirement and Savings Plans	The Company and certain of its subsidiaries have noncontributory profit sharing, pension and employee retirement plans which provide retirement benefits for their employees except those covered by union plans. At November 26, 1978, unfunded past service costs of such plans approximated $28,509. The Pension Plan and Employee Retirement Plan provide for contributions to actuarially fund defined employee retirement benefits. Subject to certain limitations, the Profit Sharing Plan requires a minimum annual contribution of approximately 3% of income before taxes and contributions to the plan. The Company also has a Stock Purchase and Investment Plan to which participating employees may make voluntary contributions of up to 10% of their earnings and may designate up to one-half of their contributions to be invested in Company stock. Unless there is a loss, the Company makes an additional contribution of 50% of the voluntary employee contributions designated for purchase of Company stock. The aggregate cost of these plans for 1978 and 1977 totaled $23,432 and $20,119, respectively.

Common Stock

Changes in shares of common stock are summarized below:

	Issued	Treasury Stock	Outstanding
Balance November 28, 1976	21,957,374	—	21,957,374
Purchases of treasury stock	—	(326,318)	(326,318)
Shares issued to employees	42,030	87,380	129,410
Balance November 27, 1977	21,999,404	(238,938)	21,760,466
Purchases of treasury stock	—	(110,889)	(110,889)
Shares issued to employees	—	238,206	238,206
Balance November 26, 1978	21,999,404	(111,621)	21,887,783

The treasury stock is available for issuance under the Company's Stock Option Plans and Stock Incentive Plan (Stock Service Award Program).

Stock Options

The stockholders have approved two stock option plans — the 1971 Plan and the 1976 Plan — under which qualified and non-qualified options have been granted to eligible employees at the fair market value on the date of grant. These Plans allow the option holders to purchase up to 2,000,000 shares of the Company's common stock. The options become exercisable in installments with the qualified options expiring in five years and non-qualified expiring in ten years.

The Plans also permit the granting of stock appreciation rights in connection with the granting of non-qualified options. Subject to certain limitations, such rights permit grantees to surrender a portion of their shares under option and receive cash or shares in the amount of the excess of the then market value over the option price of the shares surrendered.

FIGURE 5-2 (continued)

The following summary sets forth activity under the Plans for the year ended November 26, 1978:

| | Shares Available Under | | |
	Stock Options	Stock Appreciation Rights	Option Price
Outstanding November 27, 1977	706,311	43,500	$ 8.00-30.06
Granted	236,250	81,500	$28.56-34.06
Exercised	(168,792)	—	$ 8.00-26.94
Cancelled	(24,950)	—	$ 8.38-26.94
Outstanding November 26, 1978	748,819	125,000	$ 8.38-34.06

At November 26, 1978, the total options outstanding on 748,819 shares include those granted with stock appreciation rights. Options on 274,764 shares were exercisable and 800,391 shares were available for subsequent grant.

Leases

The Company and its subsidiaries are obligated under both long-term capital and operating leases for real estate (office space, warehouses, plants and other facilities) and equipment, primarily vehicles and computers.

At November 26, 1978, the Company was obligated as follows:

| | Type of Lease | |
	Capital	Operating
Minimum Lease Payments:		
Year Ended November		
1979	$ 3,388	$13,242
1980	2,977	10,063
1981	2,696	8,224
1982	2,189	7,337
1983	1,905	6,228
Remaining years	15,487	31,493
Total minimum lease payments	$28,642	$76,587
For Capital Leases:		
Less estimated executory costs	176	
Net minimum lease payments	$28,466	
Less amount representing interest	5,036	
Present value of net minimum lease payments—see note on Long-Term Debt	$23,430	

In general, leases relating to real estate include renewal options up to twenty years. Some leases contain escalation clauses relating to increases in executory costs. Total rental expense for operating leases was $23,224 and $16,952 for 1978 and 1977, respectively.

Commitments

The Company has agreed to purchase, if so requested, its unregistered common stock held in trust under the Employee Retirement Plan. Such shares would be acquired at the market price. At November 26, 1978, 89,793 such shares were held in trust.

Quarterly Data—Unaudited

Summarized unaudited quarterly data for 1978 and 1977 may be found on page 21.

FIGURE 5-2 (concluded)

Replacement Cost Information
– Unaudited

The Securities and Exchange Commission requires the Company to estimate and report information as to the replacement cost of its plant, equipment and inventory and the related impact on cost of sales and depreciation. The information was developed based on broad guidelines and the basic hypothetical assumption that the Company would replace virtually all its worldwide productive capacity and inventory as of November 26, 1978.

The results indicate that the estimated replacement cost exceeds the actual historical cost due to various factors which include general and specific price level changes, the economic life of the fixed assets and the turnover and costing system in the case of inventory. Historically, however, the Company has been able to successfully react to cost increases in maintaining a high level of profitability on sales. Detailed quantitative information relating to the estimated replacement cost amounts and the basis on which they have been calculated is included in the Company's annual report on Form 10-K, a copy of which is available on request.

Subsequent Event

On January 31, 1979, the Company made an offer to repurchase up to 2,000,000 shares of its common stock at $43.50 per share.

Report of Independent Public Accountants

To the Stockholders
and Board of Directors
of Levi Strauss & Co.:

We have examined the consolidated balance sheets of Levi Strauss & Co. (a Delware corporation) and subsidiaries as of November 26, 1978 and November 27, 1977, and the consolidated statements of income, stockholders' equity and changes in financial position for the years then ended. Our examination was made in accordance with generally accepted auditing standards, and accordingly included such tests of the accounting records and such other auditing procedures as we considered necessary in the circumstances.

In our opinion, the accompanying financial statements present fairly the financial position of Levi Strauss & Co. and subsidiaries as of November 26, 1978 and November 27, 1977, and the results of their operations and the changes in their financial position for the years then ended, in conformity with generally accepted accounting principles consistently applied during the periods.

ARTHUR ANDERSEN & CO.

San Francisco, California,
January 4, 1979, except for the
Subsequent Event Note as to
which the date is January 31, 1979.

as an expense of doing business. Land cannot be used up and is not generally depreciated. As the previous discussion indicated, resources above and below ground may be *depleted* if they are actually being consumed.

The final asset account, *other assets,* includes trademarks, copyrights, patents, and assets that don't fit logically into any other asset accounts. The amount of this account is usually insignificant.

Liabilities

A company's liabilities—what it owes to others—are usually classified as current and long-term liabilities. *Current liabilities* are those which are to be paid within the next accounting period, while *long-term liabilities* are expected to remain on the company's books for at least one year. Bonded debt might remain as a liability for 30 or more years. Levi Strauss' liability accounts (Figure 5–1) are representative of liability accounts in general.

Current maturities of long-term debt is the portion of the company's long-term debt (largely notes payable) which was outstanding on November 26, 1978, and which is expected to be repaid during the next year. A fuller explanation of this account is contained in Figure 5–2 under the heading Long-Term Debt.

Short-term borrowings are the amounts of short-term credit that were outstanding at year end 1978, and which are expected to be repaid during the 1979 year. Information contained under the heading Short-Term Borrowings and Lines of Credit, in Figure 5–2, reveals that the entire liability of $11,623,000 is debt owed to foreign lenders.

Accounts payable are amounts owed to other businesses. Levi Strauss grants credit to its customers and is granted credit by the companies from which it buys things. Accounts payable are often large liabilities for merchandising companies because they purchase on credit nearly everything that they sell. A typical manufacturing company purchases less from others, and as a consequence accounts payable are relatively less important for these firms.

Accrued liabilities are amounts owed by the company which are not listed in other liabilities accounts. These liabilities are mainly rent and lease expenses which have not yet been paid.

Salaries, wages, and *employee benefits* are amounts owed employees. Since companies commonly pay twice or even once per month, earned but unpaid salaries are a liability of the company until paid.

Employee benefit liabilities for insurance, retirement, and so on are a part of this account.

Taxes based on income are taxes which are *currently owed* to the federal government and are expected to be paid within the coming year. Corporations pay these taxes four times during the year; the current year taxes have been mostly paid by the time the balance sheet is constructed. This company's tax position is complicated by its overseas operations. In the Notes presented as Figure 5–2 the company's income tax liabilities and method of calculation are discussed.

Dividends payable are dividends to common or preferred shareholders which have been declared but which are not yet paid. This and the previous six accounts constitute the current liabilities of the company.

Long-term debt less current maturities is made up of $59,862,000 of notes payable and other unsecured indebtedness and $23,430,000 of capital lease liabilities. Figure 5–2 provides information on the payment schedule on this debt and certain of its other characteristics.

Deferred liabilities is an account set up to provide for future income tax and other liabilities which the company will eventually incur. The deferred items account usually arises because a company has lowered current income taxes by using accelerated depreciation for purposes of calculating tax liabilities, but straight-line depreciation on its annual report. At a later time, when the benefit from accelerated depreciation has been exhausted, tax payments will increase. The liability of these increased future tax payments is recorded as a deferred credit. Almost all companies presently have such an account because they use accelerated depreciation.

Stockholders' equity

The *stockholders' equity* accounts identify the interest that shareholders have in the company. These are probably the most difficult accounts to understand because there is a natural tendency to try to equate the dollar values of the various accounts to the market price of the stock or to the amount available for stockholders in the event that the corporation is liquidated. These accounts have practically no relationship to either value except in very unusual situations. A stock's market price is largely determined by the profitability of the company; the liquidated value of a common share is dependent upon the sale price of a company's assets and the amount of its liabilities.

The typical corporation's capital account contains at least three different subaccounts. These are the *common stock account,* the *paid in capital account,* and the *retained earnings account.* Companies issuing preferred shares (discussed in Chapter 8) have a *preferred stock account.* Some corporations have separate capital accounts for treasury stock, partially paid stock, and other accounts. Any standard financial accounting text will detail the meaning of these accounts.

Common stock may have a par or stated value or be true no par stock. A company having *no par stock* usually has only one capital stock account. The amount of this account is the total received from the sale of common stock. The common stock account usually states how many of the *authorized shares* have been sold (usually listed as outstanding or issued shares). No more than the authorized number may be sold. A company which has common stock with a par or stated value will normally have two stock accounts: the common stock account and an account titled *additional paid in-capital* or *premium on sale of common stock.* Regardless of what the account is called, it represents the amount paid to the company in excess of the par or stated value of the stock.[5]

An example may clarify this procedure. A hypothetical company is organized with 3,000 authorized shares of $10 par common stock. Only 2,000 of these shares are sold, but they are sold at a price of $15 each. The capital stock account would list the par value of total shares sold (2,000 shares × $10 = $20,000). The premium of $5 per share would be recorded as additional paid-in capital (2,000 shares × $5 = $10,000). The capital section of this company's balance sheet would appear as below, assuming the company had just begun operations and had no other capital accounts.

Capital stock:

3,000 shares authorized, 2,000 issued. Par value $10	$20,000
Additional paid-in capital...	10,000
Total	$30,000

Retained earnings are the amounts that the company has reinvested in the business over the years. This is a cumulative figure. A newly or-

---

[5]Shares are seldom sold below their par value because shareholders become liable for the difference between what they paid for the stock and its par value in case the company goes bankrupt.

ganized company would usually have no retained earnings. If during its first year of operation after-tax profits were $100,000 and no dividends were paid, the retained earnings account would contain $100,000. Assume now that in the second year of operation, profits were again $100,000, but $25,000 of dividends were paid to stockholders. The retained earnings account would contain $175,000 calculated as follows:

Retained earnings at end of first year		$100,000
Net income for second year	$100,000	
Less dividends paid	25,000	
Addition to retained earnings....................		75,000
Retained earnings at end of second year		$175,000

Losses would be *deducted* from retained earnings.

The Levi Strauss shareholders' equity account states that of the 30 million shares of common that are authorized, 21,999,404 have been issued. The statement further reveals that the stock has a par value of $1 per share. Under the accounting procedures previously outlined, the common stock account should contain $21,999,404 ($1 par times 21,999,404 shares issued) which it does.

An additional accounting statement, a statement of shareholders' equity, is presented as part of Figure 5–3. This statement presents a more detailed look at recent changes in the shareholders' equity account, in particular the purchase and reissuance of treasury stock. *Treasury stock* is stock that has once been issued, and later reacquired by the company. Such stock is often reissued to employees under stock option compensation plans. These plans are briefly explained in the notes to the financial statements, Figure 5–2.

The income statement

The *consolidated statement of income*, which is also called *statement of profit and loss* or *earnings report*, presents the revenues and costs obtained and incurred by the business *over a certain period of time*. This statement is related to the company's balance sheet in that the balance sheet lists the assets, liabilities, and capital of the company as of the *end* of a revenue period, and the income statement tells how much profit the company made *during this period*. Levi Strauss' balance sheet described the financial condition of that company as of No-

FIGURE 5-3

Consolidated Statement of Income
Levi Strauss & Co. and Subsidiaries
(Dollar Amounts in Thousands Except Per Share Data)

	Year (52 weeks) Ended	
	November 26, 1978	November 27, 1977
Net sales	$1,682,019	$1,559,341
Cost of goods sold	1,058,439	996,767
Gross profit	$ 623,580	$ 562,574
Marketing, general and administrative expenses	344,536	286,473
Operating income	$ 279,044	$ 276,101
Interest expense	11,178	20,048
Interest and other income, net	(12,503)	(13,913)
Income before taxes	$ 280,369	$ 269,966
Provision for taxes on income	135,400	140,173
Net income	$ 144,969	$ 129,793
Net income per share	$ 6.56	$ 5.87
Average common and common equivalent shares outstanding	22,114,936	22,128,673

Consolidated Statement of Stockholders' Equity
Levi Strauss & Co. and Subsidiaries
(Dollar Amounts in Thousands Except Per Share Data)

	Common Stock	Additional Paid-In Capital	Retained Earnings	Treasury Stock
Balance November 28, 1976	$21,957	$73,480	$266,948	$ —
Net income			129,793	
Purchases of treasury stock				(8,566)
Shares issued to employees	42	(302)		2,294
Cash dividends declared ($1.00 per share)			(21,791)	
Balance November 27, 1977	$21,999	$73,178	$374,950	$(6,272)
Net income			144,969	
Purchases of treasury stock				(3,611)
Shares issued to employees		(1,283)		6,360
Cash dividends declared ($1.60 per share)			(34,972)	
Balance November 26, 1978	$21,999	$71,895	$484,947	$(3,523)

The accompanying accounting policies and notes to consolidated financial statements are an integral part of these statements.

Source: Levi Strauss & Co. *1978 Annual Report.*

vember 26, 1978; their income statement covers the period from No-vember 28, 1977 to November 26, 1978.

The title of Levi Strauss' income statement notifies readers that in-come and expenses of subsidiary companies are presented together in this statement. If this company had unconsolidated subsidiary com-panies, the income from these companies would be stated separately.

All income statements follow the same general format. Revenue is listed first, and expenses are deducted from revenues to produce in-come or profits. Most companies arrange their statements to produce an "income before taxes" computation and then deduct taxes from this amount. Dividend and interest payments are usually stated as separate expenditures to make it easier to use these figures in analyzing the fi-nancial position of the company. This point will become clearer as the company's operations are evaluated by using the tools of financial analysis.

Sales. The title of this account reflects the company's main source of revenue. It would be called *operating revenue* for a utility, railroad, or bank; an insurance company would call it *premium income;* for most manufacturing and merchandising companies it is titled *sales.* *Net sales* are total sales made during the income period less customer returns. This is the revenue generated through the normal operation of the business. Interest and other income is also revenue; it is listed sepa-rately because it is not produced from the normal operation of the business. Companies sometimes receive large amounts of revenue from the sale of assets or from another nonrecurring source. These amounts are identified separately as *extraordinary items* so that per-sons reading the income statement will recognize that they were not produced from the regular operation of the business and that they are not likely to be repeated.

Costs and expenses. These are the costs directly associated with the production of revenue. *Cost of goods sold* represents wages, raw material, and other direct costs of production. *Marketing, general, and administrative expenses* are those incurred in operating the business: sales commissions, salaries, rent, electricity, depreciation, and other costs of this type. Some individual expenses, depreciation, for exam-ple, are often listed separately if the account has particular importance.

Operating income is net sales less cost of goods sold and other major expenses of doing business. This equation typically excludes in-terest income and expense and other income and expense.

Interest expense is the interest paid on the company's debt.

Interest and other income, net, represents income unrelated to the normal operation of the business. Levi Strauss has a large portion of its assets in the form of cash and near cash investments. The $12,503,000 of income in this account is mainly interest received from these investments.

Income before taxes is a preliminary profit figure obtained by subtracting costs and expenses of obtaining revenue from the revenue obtained.

Provision for taxes on income lists the amount of income taxes paid or incurred by a firm during the entire accounting period under examination. Total federal income taxes are expected to be $135,400,000 for the income period that ended November 26, 1978. The liability for income taxes of $59,662,000 which appears on the balance sheet is the amount not yet paid.

Net income is the final computation on some income statements. It represents the amount of revenues remaining after all expenses have been paid. Levi Strauss had $144,969,000 of net income in 1978, up from $129,793,000 in 1977.

Net income per share. Income as well as dividends are usually recorded on a per share basis. Stating these amounts in this way is accomplished by dividing the total amount of each item by the average number of shares outstanding for the year.

$$\text{Net income per share in 1978} = \frac{\text{Total net income}}{\substack{\text{Average number} \\ \text{of common shares}}}$$
$$= \$144,969,000/22,114,936$$
$$= \$6.56.$$

Dividends per share are usually stated as the total amount paid on each share during the year. Dividends are normally paid quarterly. Levi Strauss paid dividends of $1.00 per share in 1977 and $1.60 per share in 1978.

Fully diluted earnings per share is the preferred way of stating earnings. Companies having securities which are convertible into the common stock of the company and companies having stock option plans which may result in an addition to outstanding common stock both prepare earnings per share figures on a "fully diluted basis." This figure is often presented separately and tells what earnings per share would be if all convertible securities were converted and all stock options were exercised. Because additional common shares are presumed outstanding in this calculation, amounts stated in *per share* terms are lowered. Such computations serve to notify shareholders of the potential for lower per share earnings if conversion does take place. Stock option plans usually add so few shares of stock that dilution from this source is minor. Use of the term *common equivalent shares outstanding* when calculating earnings per share indicates that Levi Strauss' earnings per share amounts are fully diluted.

The auditor's report

All companies whose stock is listed on the American or the New York Stock Exchange, and all unlisted companies having $1 million or more of assets and 500 or more shareholders, must supply audited financial statements. An independent accounting firm is employed by the company to prepare audited financial statements.

The auditor's report appears as a part of the financial statement. If the report is *unqualified*, the company's statements have satisfied the auditors of their reasonableness. The company's accounting procedures have also met the standards of the American Institute of Certified Public Accountants and the Financial Accounting Standards Board. If the statements do not meet these standards, the auditor's report is *qualified*. The reasons for qualification are stated as part of the report. Levi Strauss' 1978 financial statements were audited by Arthur Anderson & Co., whose statement appears as a part of Figure 5–2. The report is unqualified.

ANALYZING FINANCIAL STATEMENTS

This part of the chapter presents several commonly used methods of examining financial statements. Levi Strauss' statements are used as examples, but the techniques are generally applicable to other companies. Many firms present a *performance record* or *summary of operations* as a regular part of their annual report. These statements provide much financial information. Financial reporting companies and brokerage houses often prepare more detailed analyses of company operations. Investors seldom have to make these computations on their own, but they should know how they are made and how to interpret their meaning.

Ratios are used almost exclusively in this type of analysis so that the performance of one company can be compared directly to that of another. The measures may be divided into three general classifications:

1. *Liquidity ratios,* which measure the firm's ability to pay short-term obligations, and thereby to remain in business.
2. *Profitability ratios,* which attempt to measure the relative profitability of the firm.
3. *Financial ratios,* which measure the equity and debt contributions to the financing of the firm, and the return to investors.

A ratio is created whenever one quantity is divided into another to create either a percentage or a magnitude relationship. If quantity A is 30 and B is 100, the relationship of one to another may be stated in one of two generally accepted ways: B is 3.33 times as large as A ($B/A = 100/30 = 3.33:1$) or A is 30 percent of B ($A/B = 30/100 = 0.30$ or 30 percent). To be useful in financial analysis, ratios must be constructed of variables that are related to each other in such a way that the ratios produced have meaning.

Banks and other businesses construct and use ratios largely to predict the creditworthiness of potential customers. Several companies provide average ratios—called composite ratios—of firms in various identifiable industries. These ratios may be used as benchmarks against which ratios of similar companies being analyzed can be compared. Figure 5–4 is a portion of a list of manufacturing industry ratios prepared by Dun & Bradstreet, a company which provides credit information on companies and individuals.[6] It should be noted that the average ratios of different types of manufacturing firms differ greatly—even though all firms are in the general category of manufacturing. Ratios vary even more between firms in different industries. For example, electric utilities (because they cannot store electricity) have practically no inventory. Consequently, when inventory is used

---

[6] The Robert Morris Associates (also known as The National Association of Bank Loan and Credit Officers) presents a great deal of industry ratio information in its publication *Annual Statement Studies* (Robert Morris Associates, Research Department, Philadelphia National Bank Building, Philadelphia, Pennsylvania). Trade associations often publish financial ratios of member companies, and many banks prepare their own norms for ratio analysis. A publication which presents financial ratios taken from federal income tax statements is *Almanac of Business and Industrial Financial Ratios* (Englewood Cliffs, N.J.: Prentice-Hall, published annually). The Federal Trade Commission and the Securities and Exchange Commission jointly publish quarterly ratio studies of different industry groups of U.S. corporations.

142

FIGURE 5–4
Dun & Bradstreet's key business ratios

Manufacturing

Line of Business (and number of concerns reporting)	Current assets to current debt	Net profits on net sales	Net profits on tangible net worth	Net profits on net working capital	Net sales to tangible net worth	Net sales to net working capital	Collection period	Net sales to inventory	Fixed assets to tangible net worth	Current debt to tangible net worth	Total debt to tangible net worth	Inventory to net working capital	Current debt to inventory	Funded debts to net working capital
	Times	Per cent	Per cent	Per cent	Times	Times	Days	Times	Per cent	Per cent	Per cent	Per cent	Per cent	Per cent
2337 Suits & Coats, Women's & Misses' (69)	2.70	3.61	22.37	23.07	12.48	13.82	37	20.5	4.6	62.1	97.0	41.1	82.9	4.0
	1.89	1.85	12.04	15.45	8.57	9.39	46	11.1	10.9	131.4	178.3	77.0	141.4	17.8
	1.38	1.06	1.80	9.13	6.24	6.42	69	7.0	23.2	245.4	266.7	148.4	251.7	48.3
2311 Suits, Coats & Overcoats, Men's & Boys' (87)	2.91	4.35	17.39	21.88	9.79	11.19	18	8.8	5.1	40.2	65.3	67.5	61.8	9.2
	2.15	1.61	6.54	9.03	5.68	6.76	45	7.0	16.8	100.0	167.0	97.1	85.8	30.7
	1.48	0.46	0.69	2.69	2.99	3.98	62	4.7	53.2	200.0	300.0	146.8	154.1	77.8
3841-42-43 Surgical, Medical & Dental Instruments (62)	5.13	5.97	17.61	26.53	3.85	4.41	48	6.3	15.1	19.1	51.8	57.4	35.2	10.9
	3.03	4.24	10.93	16.60	2.93	3.45	59	4.9	32.8	42.0	68.7	69.8	69.5	27.1
	2.25	1.33	3.12	5.98	1.71	2.47	72	3.5	54.4	73.5	136.8	90.2	99.5	48.7
3942-44-49 Toys, Amusement & Sporting Goods (69)	2.98	5.91	18.44	26.84	5.54	7.74	44	7.7	13.4	40.9	87.0	60.4	61.0	16.2
	2.32	3.15	13.03	15.72	3.77	4.43	62	5.5	41.1	72.2	130.4	87.1	99.4	47.1
	1.53	1.40	3.83	9.05	2.46	2.93	86	3.6	68.8	122.5	227.6	125.5	157.9	83.7
2327 Trousers, Men's & Boys' (54)	2.91	3.92	18.86	21.08	8.00	8.50	26	13.9	11.8	44.9	60.1	51.4	72.2	8.1
	2.17	2.20	9.02	11.11	6.30	6.74	42	7.0	26.8	70.9	99.2	88.7	91.7	23.1
	1.82	1.04	2.56	5.90	3.36	4.41	66	4.6	44.2	139.6	189.2	118.8	143.4	48.7
2341 Underwear & Nightwear, Women's & Children's (48)	2.79	3.05	17.21	18.08	9.68	11.09	35	12.9	6.1	53.5	55.6	57.2	59.8	7.3
	2.11	1.47	7.71	7.87	6.18	6.23	49	6.7	14.4	110.4	148.2	99.7	131.5	17.9
	1.48	0.63	1.77	2.14	3.84	4.00	63	4.4	26.0	195.9	201.8	164.4	194.0	30.5
2511-12 Wood Household Furniture & Upholstered (116)	4.78	5.42	15.76	24.18	5.83	7.03	37	9.2	20.0	19.2	40.2	54.4	46.6	14.2
	2.88	2.36	7.91	12.46	3.20	4.68	46	6.9	32.9	40.9	86.7	73.6	68.5	35.2
	2.00	0.43	1.29	3.39	2.11	3.34	57	4.4	62.0	80.3	151.0	106.4	106.7	75.2
2328 Work Clothing, Men's & Boys' (42)	3.97	6.17	21.58	29.13	8.94	13.23	31	11.5	9.5	32.1	67.7	55.6	38.4	11.6
	2.12	3.32	12.55	17.25	5.97	6.17	41	4.9	36.2	81.6	124.0	69.6	69.4	37.0
	1.48	1.76	6.95	8.25	3.48	3.68	55	3.9	74.7	164.5	185.3	135.8	141.5	62.2

Note: See Figure 5–5 for a discussion of how the ratios are constructed.
Source: Reprinted with the special permission of Dun & Bradstreet, Inc.

as a part of a financial ratio, the utility's ratio will probably be very different in value from that of a firm which holds inventory. Some companies—grocery stores, liquor stores—sell only for cash. Their accounts receivable ratios will be very different from those of department stores, which grant credit freely to customers.

When comparing financial ratios of one company to those of another or to a group of companies, the analyst must make certain that the companies are similar enough in their operation to be compared. Comparing the financial ratios of Levi Strauss to those of U.S. Steel will produce little meaningful information. Levi Strauss, because of its emphasis upon the manufacturing of trousers probably most closely resembles the classification presented as category 2327 in Figure 5–4. A statement prepared by Dun & Bradstreet to explain how the ratios are computed, and what they indicate, is included as Figure 5–5.

These ratios have been constructed primarily for use in determining whether certain companies are good credit risks, not necessarily whether they are good investments. Some of the ratios are useful in both capacities, however. Levi Strauss will now be "analyzed" by constructing and comparing several of its more relevant ratios to those of the trouser manufacturing industry.

Liquidity ratios

The current ratio. This is sometimes referred to as the working capital ratio. It is a good one to begin with because it shows clearly how data may become more meaningful when presented as a ratio.

Net working capital is computed by subtracting current liabilities from current assets; this measure is always presented as a certain number of dollars. *Working capital* is considered to be that available for use in the day-to-day conduct of the business, as opposed to the fixed capital represented by fixed assets.[7] Levi Strauss' net working capital at the end of 1978 was as follows:

Current assets	$824,227,000
Less current liabilities...................	302,405,000
Equals net working capital	$521,822,000

This amount can be compared to net working capital for previous years—$430.7 million in 1977, $343.5 million in 1976, and so on as calculated in Figure 5–6—but it cannot be compared meaningfully to working capital of other firms, unless the other firms happen to be of the same size as Levi Strauss. Stating the same figures as a *ratio* of current assets to current liabilities makes similarly derived ratios of other companies more readily comparable.

$$\text{The current ratio} = \text{Current assets/Current liabilities}$$
$$= \$824,227,000/\$302,405,000$$
$$= 2.73 : 1.$$

To determine whether this ratio of $2.73 of current assets to each dollar of current liabilities is "good," the ratio must be compared to

---

[7] The term *working capital* refers to the firm's current assets. *Net working capital* means current assets net of (less) current liabilities. Many accountants and others have adopted the term working capital to mean net working capital. Levi Strauss uses this term while Dun & Bradstreet uses net working capital; they mean the same thing.

FIGURE 3-5
Explanation of Dun & Bradstreet's ratio computations

How the Ratios are Figured

Although terms like "median" and "quartile" are everyday working language to statisticians, their precise meaning may be vague to some businessmen.

In the various ratio tables, three figures appear under each ratio heading. The center figure in bold type is the **median**; the figures immediately above and below the median are, respectively, the **upper** and **lower quartiles.** To understand their use, the reader should also know how they are calculated.

First, year-end financial statements from concerns in the survey (almost exclusively corporations with a tangible net worth over $100,000) are analyzed by Dun & Bradstreet statisticians. Then each of 14 ratios is calculated individually for every concern in the sample.

These individual ratio figures, entered on data-processing cards, are segregated by line of business, and then arranged in order of size—the best ratio at the top, the weakest at the bottom. The figure that falls in the middle of this series becomes the **median** for that ratio in that line of business. The figure halfway between the median and the top of the series is the **upper quartile**; the number halfway between the median and the bottom of the series is the **lower quartile.**

In a statistical sense, each median then is the **typical ratio figure** for all concerns studied in a given line. The upper and lower quartile figures typically the experience of firms in the top and bottom halves of the sample.

Current Assets to Current Debt Current Assets are divided by total Current Debt. Current Assets are the sum of cash, notes and accounts receivable (less reserves for bad debt), advances on merchandise, merchandise inventories, and Listed, Federal, State and Municipal securities not in excess of market value. Current Debt is the total of all liabilities falling due within one year. This is one test of solvency.

Net Profits on Net Sales Obtained by dividing net earnings of the business, after taxes, by net sales (the dollar volume less returns, allowances, and cash discounts). This important yardstick in measuring profitability should be related to the ratio which follows.

Net Profits on Tangible Net Worth Tangible Net Worth is the equity of stockholders in the business, as obtained by subtracting total liabilities from total assets, and then deducting intangibles. The ratio is obtained by dividing Net Profits after taxes by Tangible Net Worth. Tendency is to look increasingly to this ratio as a final criterion of profitability. Generally, a relationship of at least 10 percent is regarded as a desirable objective for providing dividends plus funds for future growth.

Net Profits on Net Working Capital Net Working Capital represents the excess of Current Assets over Current Debt. This margin represents the cushion available to the business for carrying inventories and receivables, and for financing day-to-day operations. The ratio is obtained by dividing Net Profits, after taxes, by Net Working Capital.

Net Sales to Tangible Net Worth Net Sales are divided by Tangible Net Worth. This gives a measure of relative turnover of invested capital.

Net Sales to Net Working Capital Net Sales are divided by Net Working Capital. This provides a guide as to the extent the concern is turning its working capital and the margin of operating funds.

Collection Period Annual net sales are divided by 365 days to obtain average daily credit sales and then the average daily credit sales are divided into notes and accounts receivable, including any discounted. This ratio is helpful in analyzing the collectibility of receivables. Many feel the collection period should not exceed the net maturity indicated by selling terms by more than 10 to 15 days. When comparing the collection period of one concern with that of another, allowances should be made for possible variations in selling terms.

Net Sales to Inventory Obtained by dividing annual Net Sales by Merchandise Inventory as carried on the balance sheet. This quotient does not yield an actual physical turnover. It provides a yardstick for comparing stock-to-sales ratios of one concern with another or with those for the industry.

Fixed Assets to Tangible Net Worth Fixed Assets are divided by Tangible Net Worth. Fixed Assets represent depreciated book values of building, leasehold improvements, machinery, furniture, fixtures, tools, and other physical equipment, plus land, if any, and valued at cost or appraised market value. Ordinarily, this relationship should not exceed 100 percent for a manufacturer, and 75 percent for a wholesaler or retailer.

Current Debt to Tangible Net Worth Derived by dividing Current Debt by Tangible Net Worth. Ordinarily, a business begins to pile up trouble when this relationship exceeds 80 percent.

Total Debt to Tangible Net Worth Obtained by dividing total current plus long term debts by Tangible Net Worth. When this relationship exceeds 100 percent, the equity of creditors in the assets of the business exceeds that of owners.

Inventory to Net Working Capital Merchandise Inventory is divided by Net Working Capital. This is an additional measure of inventory balance. Ordinarily, the relationship should not exceed 80 percent.

Current Debt to Inventory Dividing the Current Debt by Inventory yields yet another indication of the extent to which the business relies on funds from disposal of unsold inventories to meet its debts.

Funded Debts to Net Working Capital Funded Debts are all long term obligations, as represented by mortgages, bonds, debentures, term loans, serial notes, and other types of liabilities maturing more than one year from statement date. This ratio is obtained by dividing Funded Debt by Net Working Capital. Analysts tend to compare Funded Debts with Net Working Capital in determining whether or not long term debts are in proper proportion. Ordinarily, this relationship should not exceed 100 percent.

those of other firms in a similar line of business. Looking down the column titled current assets to current debt (Figure 5–4) to the Trousers,
Men's and Boy's classification reveals three average ratios. The center
number, 2.17, indicates that half the 54 firms examined had current
ratios greater than this number and half had lower ratios. The top
number, 2.91, is the lower limit of the upper quartile: 25 percent of the
firms examined had ratios greater than this. The lower number identifies the upper limit of the lower quartile. Comparing Levi Strauss' current ratio to that of the other trouser manufacturers reveals that its
current ratio is slightly better than average.

Inventory to net working capital.   This is another liquidity ratio
which indicates the proportion of net working capital that is tied up in
inventory. A low ratio is desirable in this case. Levi Strauss' 1978 ratio
is

$$\text{Inventory to net working capital} = \text{Inventory/Net working capital}$$
$$= \$298{,}494{,}000/\$521{,}822{,}000$$
$$= .57 \text{ or } 57\%.$$

Column 12 of Figure 5–4 reveals that this ratio is bettered by slightly
over one-fourth of the companies under examination. There are other
liquidity ratios that might be computed (current debt to net worth,
current debt to inventory, the "acid-test ratio," which is currrent
assets less inventories divided by current liabilities), but these ratios
are more relevant to short-term lending decisions than to investment
decisions and are omitted from this discussion.

Profitability ratios

These ratios attempt to measure the relative profitability of the firm.

Net income to sales.   Often called the net operating margin, this
ratio is derived by dividing net sales into net income (called net profits
by some companies including Dun & Bradstreet). In 1978 Levi Strauss
had the following ratio:

$$\text{Net income to sales} = \text{Net income/Net sales}$$
$$= \$144{,}969{,}000/\$1{,}682{,}019{,}000$$
$$= .0861 \text{ or } 8.6\%.$$

Compared to the Dun & Bradstreet averages this is an excellent
showing.

Net income on net worth. This measures the company's profitability on net worth. Net worth is assets less liabilities, which is the company's stockholder equity of $575,318,000.[8]

$$\text{Net income on net worth} = \text{Net income/Net worth}$$
$$= \$144,969,000/\$575,318,000$$
$$= .2519 \text{ or } 25.2\%.$$

Levi Strauss' performance is far above average in this category.

Net income on working capital. This measure relates income to working capital.

$$\text{Net income on working capital} = \text{Net income/Working capital}$$
$$= \$144,969,000/\$521,822,000$$
$$= .2778 \text{ or } 27.8\%.$$

This figure is also much above average.

Productivity of assets. The ratio of net income after taxes plus interest payments to total assets measures the rate of return on assets. It is often called the *return-on-investment* ratio. Interest expense is added to net income to compensate for the effect of borrowed funds (the more borrowed, the higher the interest payments) and makes this ratio more applicable to all companies. Levi Strauss' ratio is computed as follows:

Levi Strauss' 1978 net income	$144,969,000
Plus interest payments	11,178,000
Equals adjusted income	$156,147,000

$$\text{Net income to assets} = \text{Adjusted income/Assets}$$
$$= \$156,147,000/\$973,874,000$$
$$= .1603 \text{ or } 16.0\%.$$

This ratio is also prepared on a before-taxes basis. Dun & Bradstreet does not present this ratio as one of its "key ratios."

Gross operating margin. This widely used ratio relates net sales to

---

[8] *Tangible net worth* means that assets have been reduced by the amount of intangible assets (goodwill, trademarks, copyrights, patents, and the like) before calculating net worth. This is a more conservative way of making this calculation, but because most companies have small amounts of intangible assets the change in net worth is usually insignificant.

gross profit from sales. Gross profit from sales is net sales less cost of goods sold.

Levi Strauss' 1978 net sales...........................	$1,682,019,000
Less cost of goods sold..............................	1,058,439,000
Equals gross profit	$ 623,580,000

$$\text{Gross operating margin} = \text{Gross profit/Net sales}$$
$$= \$623,580,000/\$1,682,019,000$$
$$= .3707 \text{ or } 37.1\%.$$

This ratio indicates that Levi Strauss' average price markup is about 37 percent above what it cost to produce this merchandise. Gross margin varies greatly between different kinds of businesses. Those having large, slow-moving inventories (furniture stores, hardware stores) usually have high gross margins. Grocery stores and service stations have smaller, more rapidly sold inventories, but lower price markups. Dun & Bradstreet does not list this ratio as one of its "key ratios." Standard & Poor's does provide industry ratios of gross operating margin in its *Industry Surveys: Basic Analysis.*

There are many profitability ratios which are unique to certain industries. Net profits per ton-mile is a common measure of the profitability of a railroad; net profits per seat-mile is commonly used in the airline industry.[9] An advertising firm might use profits to gross billings.

Financial ratios

These are of more importance to the investor because their emphasis is on the financial position of the company. Many of these measures are concerned with the company's capitalization, and they relate debt to net worth or some other measure. As debt increases, financial risk increases because interest payments must be made or the company becomes insolvent. However, debt is not automatically "bad." A company which can earn more on borrowed funds than it costs to borrow them can increase common stockholders' earnings and make the company more profitable by borrowing some of its capital. Stability of income is the main factor which controls a company's ability to

---

[9] A ton-mile is one ton shipped one mile. It is the product of total tonnage shipped times total miles traveled by the trains.

go into debt safely. Utilities have very constant income and can borrow large proportions of their funds. The income of most manufacturing companies is variable, and as a consequence they can borrow less. A well-managed company will borrow as much as it can, with safety, to increase the company's profitability. This amount varies greatly between individual firms and between firms in different industries.

Debt to net worth. Several ratios equate debt to net worth or to total assets. Debt to net worth is the most common of these ratios. Levi Strauss' ratio for 1978 is

$$Debt \ to \ net \ worth = Total \ debt/Net \ worth$$
$$= \$398,556,000/\$575,318,000$$
$$= .6927 \ or \ 69.3\%.$$

Column 11 of Figure 5–4 shows that in relation to other trouser manufacturers, Levi Strauss' ratio is low. This type financing is conservative, but income to equity owners might be increased if more funds were borrowed.

Current debt to net worth. This ratio (or its complement, the ratio of long-term debt to net worth) measures the importance of current (or long-term) debt in the company's capital structure. Dun & Bradstreet considers a ratio of 0.8:1, or 80 percent to indicate financial difficulties, but this figure differs greatly with the industry. Levi Strauss' 1978 ratio is 52.6 percent, somewhat lower than the industry average.

$$Current \ debt \ to \ net \ worth = \$302,405,000/\$575,318,000$$
$$= .5256 \ or \ 52.6\%.$$

Horizontal and vertical analysis. Examining ratios or other data over time is sometimes called *horizontal analysis*. Another type is *vertical*, or *common size*, analysis. In this kind of computation, all balance sheet items are stated as a percent of total assets, and all income statement items are presented as a percent of total sales or revenue. The value from this form of presentation is the same as that from using other ratios: It allows the financial statements of different firms to more easily be compared one to another. A slightly abbreviated form of the Levi Strauss 1978 income statement is presented in this fashion in Table 5–2. Such data can be prepared "horizontally" for several years. Presented in this way it sometimes reveals *trends* that have taken place over time.

Many firms prepare summaries of their operations as part of their

TABLE 5–2
Percentage distribution of Levi Strauss' 1978 income statement
(dollars in thousands)

Net sales	$1,682,019	100.0%
Cost of goods sold	1,058,439	62.9
Gross profit	$ 623,580	37.1%
Marketing, general and		
administrative expenses	344,536	20.5
Operating income.....................	$ 279,044	16.6%
Interest expense.........................	11,178	0.7
Interest and other income, net	(12,503)	(0.7)
Income before taxes..................	$ 280,369	16.7%
Provision for taxes		
on income	135,400	8.0
Net income............................	$ 144,969	8.6%

annual report. Figure 5–6 is Levi Strauss' ten-year summary. Several of the ratios constructed earlier are a part of this statement and several measures not previously explained are also used.

Most data in Figure 5–6 except book value and stock dividends should be self-explanatory. Book value is simply the company's assets less its liabilities, or in other words, its net worth. Book value per share is this amount divided by the number of shares outstanding at the time book value was computed. Analysts regard book value as a rough indication of the worth of some firms. Book value is re-examined in Chapter 9.

The *summary of operations* shows that sales have increased greatly since 1969. Profitability took a big jump (net income as a percent of sales) in 1976 and has remained high through 1978, even though sales did not increase greatly (7.9 percent) during that year. Earnings per share and dividends per share have also increased markedly since 1973, a rather poor year for the company. A big advantage of the ten-year financial summary is that it allows one to examine changes in important financial data as they have occurred. A shortcoming of this type of analysis is that it does not provide a basis for comparison with other companies.

Levi Strauss' ratios are shown to compare extremely favorably with those of the industry in Table 5–3. They are near the top quartile ratios in every category. The profit on sales ratio is much higher than the industry average and much higher than practically any other industry classification presented by Dun & Bradstreet.

FIGURE 5–6

10-Year Financial Summary
Levi Strauss & Co. and Subsidiaries
(Dollar Amounts in Millions Except Per Share Data)

Year Ended November:		1978	1977
	Net Sales	$1,682.0	$1,559.3
	Gross Profit	$ 623.6	$ 562.6
	Interest Expense	11.2	20.0
	Income Before Taxes	280.4	270.0
	Provision for Taxes on Income	135.4	140.2
	Net Income	$ 145.0	$ 129.8
	Earnings Retained in the Business	$ 110.0	$ 108.0
	Cash Flow Retained in the Business[2]	125.5	128.7
	Income Before Taxes as % of Sales	16.7%	17.3%
	Net Income as % of Sales	8.6%	8.3%
	Net Income as % of Beginning Stockholders' Equity	31.3%	35.8%
	Current Assets	$ 824.2	$ 694.2
	Current Liabilities	302.4	263.5
	Working Capital	521.8	430.7
	Ratio of Current Assets to Current Liabilities	2.73/1	2.63/1
	Long-Term Debt — Less Current Maturities	$ 83.3	$ 80.6
	Stockholders' Equity	575.3	463.9
	Capital Expenditures	$ 42.9	$ 31.4
	Depreciation	16.1	13.7
	Property, Plant & Equipment — Net	141.3	119.3
	Number of Employees	35,100	37,200
Per Share Data:	Net Income	$ 6.56	$ 5.87
	Cash Dividends Declared	1.60	1.00
	Book Value (on Shares Outstanding at Year End)	26.28	21.32
	Market Price Range	38⅝-27¼	31⅝-24¼
	Average Common and Common Equivalent Shares Outstanding	22,114,936	22,128,673

[1] Restated in accordance with the requirements of the Financial Accounting Standards Board Statement on Accounting for Leases.
[2] Working capital provided by operations minus dividends declared.

Source: Levi Strauss & Co. *1978 Annual Report.*

Earnings per share and cash flow

These two measures differ from the ratios cited earlier in two important ways. First of all, these ratios cannot be interpreted in the same way that the current ratio, for instance, can. A current ratio of 2:1 is "better" than one of 1.5:1, all other things being equal. Earnings or cash flow of $10 per share is a practically meaningless ratio because unless the price of the stock is known, it is impossible to tell whether $10 of earnings per share is "good."

The previously studied ratios have some meaning of and by themselves. Earnings or cash flow per share almost always must be exam-

FIGURE 5–6 (*continued*)

1976[1]	1975	1974	1973	1972	1971	1970	1969
$1,219.7	$1,015.2	$ 897.7	$ 653.0	$ 504.1	$ 432.0	$ 349.5	$ 269.0
$ 439.9	$ 347.4	$ 275.5	$ 184.4	$ 160.3	$ 129.6	$ 112.0	$ 86.0
12.2	13.1	13.7	10.1	4.3	4.4	4.4	2.0
206.8	136.7	72.7	33.8	48.1	35.7	37.7	31.7
102.1	71.9	37.9	22.0	23.0	16.0	19.1	17.1
$ 104.7	$ 64.7	$ 34.9	$ 11.9	$ 25.0	$ 19.7	$ 18.6	$ 14.7
$ 94.8	$ 58.6	$ 29.6	$ 6.6	$ 20.9	$ 16.3	$ 15.7	$ 12.0
110.6	71.7	45.7	17.7	28.6	22.5	20.6	15.3
17.0%	13.5%	8.1%	5.2%	9.5%	8.3%	10.8%	11.8%
8.6%	6.4%	3.9%	1.8%	5.0%	4.6%	5.3%	5.5%
39.5%	31.4%	19.8%	7.0%	16.8%	23.2%	26.8%	25.6%
$ 570.1	$ 407.6	$ 383.5	$ 305.5	$ 252.4	$ 202.8	$ 169.0	$ 131.0
226.6	155.4	188.1	155.7	98.2	67.9	87.9	57.5
343.5	252.2	195.3	149.8	154.2	134.9	81.1	73.5
2.52/1	2.62/1	2.04/1	1.96/1	2.57/1	2.99/1	1.92/1	2.28/1
$ 79.2	$ 68.7	$ 72.2	$ 48.1	$ 37.6	$ 28.4	$ 25.4	$ 22.6
362.4	265.2	206.0	176.4	169.7	148.8	85.0	69.3
$ 19.5	$ 10.4	$ 24.3	$ 28.8	$ 17.6	$ 15.6	$ 14.5	$ 6.9
11.6	9.3	9.7	8.3	6.4	5.1	4.3	2.8
102.4	82.1	82.3	68.0	48.0	39.6	29.2	19.4
32,500	29,700	30,100	29,100	25,100	21,400	18,900	16,500
$ 4.71	$ 2.95	$ 1.60	$ .54	$ 1.15	$ .93	$ .96	$ .75
.45	.28	.24	.24	.19	.16	.15	.14
16.50	12.16	9.47	8.10	7.80	6.84	4.33	3.54
26⅝-17⅞	21½-6⅛	11¼-6¼	24⅞-8⅜	29⅞-20¼	32⅛-16⅝	—	—
22,238,374	21,949,514	21,760,160	21,760,160	21,760,160	21,172,000	19,322,000	19,508,000

ined over time and in the context of ratios of other similar companies to be interpreted meaningfully. For these reasons these two ratios have been treated separately. There are no "industry average ratios" of these two measures.

Earnings per share. This is unquestionably the most widely used measure of equity investment performance. It was calculated earlier so nothing more will be done with it at this time. Chapters 9 and 13 present thorough treatments of the use of this ratio.

Cash flow and cash flow per share. The term *cash flow* refers to the cash available for use of a business during a period of time. Most analysts define cash flow as net income after taxes plus any noncash–

TABLE 5–3

Key ratios of Levi Strauss compared to those calculated by Dun & Bradstreet

Ratio and calculation	Levi Strauss' 1978 ratio	Dun & Bradstreet's Industry Ratios		
		Top quartile	Median	Low quartile
Current ratio = Current assets + Current liabilities	2.73:1	2.91:1	2.17:1	1.82:1
Inventory to working capital = Inventory + working capital	57.2%	51.4%	88.7%	118.8%
Sales to inventory = Total sales + Ending inventory	8.71:1	13.9:1	7.0:1	4.6:1
Net profit to sales = Net profit + sales	8.6%	3.92%	2.2%	1.04%
Net profit to Net worth = Net profit + Net worth	25.2%	18.86%	9.02%	2.56%
Net profits on working capital = Net profit + working capital	27.8%	21.08%	11.11%	5.90%
Gross operating margin = Gross profit + Net sales	37.1%	NA	NA	NA
Debt to Net worth = Total debt + Net worth	68.9%	60.1%	99.2%	189.2%
Current debt to Net worth = Current debt + Net worth	52.24%	44.9%	70.9%	139.6%
Productivity of assets = Net income + Total assets	14.89%	NA	NA	NA

NA = not available.

using expenses such as depreciation, depletion, and amortization. It will be remembered that these expenses were deductions from sales in determining net income, but they are "noncash expenses" in that no money was actually paid out to cover them. A simple bookkeeping entry reduces income by the amount of the yearly charges, but the cash that would have paid these expenses, if they were the regular kind, remains in the business to be used by management for expansion, to repay debt, or even to pay dividends. Cash flow for Levi Strauss during 1978 would be computed as follows:

Net income	$144,969,000
Plus depreciation, amortization, and other items (from Notes to Consolidated Financial Statements)	16,126,000
Equals cash flow during 1978	$161,095,000

Cash flow per share=Total cash flow/Number of shares outstanding
$$=\$161,095,000/22,114,936$$
$$=\$7.28.$$

MAKING FINANCIAL STATEMENTS MORE USEFUL AND MORE REVEALING

Without a great deal of training, one can compute the various measures of financial analysis previously discussed. This is a necessary first step in the investment decision-making process. But before final inferences and conclusions can be drawn an intermediate step must be taken. This involves adjusting the financial statements so that they are consistent with the statements of other companies. One can assume that audited financial statements are accurate and that they meet the standards of the accounting profession. But these standards allow for fairly wide differences in the treatment of several categories of income and expense. Professional security analysts always examine a company's financial statements to identify how the company has accounted for certain critical items. The result of such examination is often the restatement of the company's earnings and financial ratios.

Inventory accounting

Gross profits are measured by the difference between net sales and the cost of the items being sold. For firms offering tangible items such as soft drinks, clothing, and so on, this profit calculation involves keeping track of the direct costs of preparing the items for the inventory.[10] Accounting procedures for this task are fairly straightforward and are not of concern in this discussion. However a problem of cost calculation develops when the costs of the items being sold are changing, as in a period of rapid inflation. As an example, imagine that after the items to be sold are produced, they are stacked in a large room. Suppose that the goods made most recently cost more than the earlier production. The shipping clerk who receives an order from the sales department will select one of the units from the inventory in the room. If the first one stored was chosen, the gross profit would be higher compared to the amount that would be calculated if the order had been filled with one of the recently produced items. This happens because the difference between the cost of this item and its sale price is greater than it would be if a new, higher-cost item were sold.

For the most part, accounting systems are not set up to identify which item was actually sold out of the inventory. Instead, the typical convention is to keep track of production costs and then to assume, for reporting purposes, that sales are either taken off the "top" or from the "bottom." These systems are referred to as *Fifo* (first in, first out) and *Lifo* (last in, first out). During a period of cost stability, both methods result in the same gross profits. However, when costs are rising rapidly, the choice of Lifo rather than Fifo will lower reported profits. Particularly affected will be companies which have large inventories that are relatively slow to turn over. Lack of uniform inventory accounting can cause difficulty for the analyst who is attempting to (1) compare one firm with another and/or (2) appraise a trend in profits over time. While firms always specify the basis for inventory accounting in the footnotes to the financial statements, it is perfectly acceptable to change the basis after obtaining permission from the Internal Revenue Service. In the 1970s when costs increased rapidly, many firms switched their accounting practice from Fifo to Lifo.[11]

Shifts in inventory accounting procedures can present a problem to the analyst. Much of the effort in appraising share values depends on comparing one firm with others. If all companies are not reporting in-

---

[10] The following discussion is written for a manufacturing type firm. The situation for retailing and wholesaling firms is quite similar.

[11] If prices were to decline substantially, a shift back to Fifo reporting might be justified because the company would have the older and higher cost inventory on the books. Continuance of Lifo reporting would result in overstating the current market value of the inventory and understating profits.

come and costs on the same basis, meaningful comparative analysis is made more difficult. Changing inventory accounting procedures causes distortions in year-to-year profit calculations of individual firms. Profits may be abnormally high or low in years when such shifts are made. Recognition of the distortions and educated guesses as to their magnitudes are the only practical solutions to these problems. A careful reading of annual report footnotes will provide the analyst with a better grasp of the firm's "true" profitability.

The 1978 annual report of Royal Dutch Shell company announced a 21 percent drop in net income on a 0.9 percent increase in sales. Over half of this reduction ($369.5 million) was attributed to the use of Fifo accounting for inventories, a system which had "helped profits" during the 1977 year.

Nonoperating income and expense

Firms often have income and expense items which are not directly related to their normal experience in doing business. For instance, a company may invest in securities of other corporations or of the U.S. government. Such investments may result in gains or losses; but, in either case, they have nothing to do with the company's main business. Accounting practice calls for identifying any of these items so that a clearer picture of past operations may be developed. Typically, income and expenses not classified as operating income or expense are identified as *other income* or *expense* or as *extraordinary* or *nonrecurring gains or losses*.

Extraordinary or nonrecurring gains or losses by definition are not expected to be repeated. Analysts almost always deduct them from the company's financial statements before calculating financial ratios.

Other types of financial statement adjustments

The list of items in the financial statements needing careful interpretation is a lengthy one. Depreciation and depletion accounting policies vary among firms and require close scrutiny. Taxation provisions are another troublesome area.

Whenever taxes paid are much less than 46 percent of taxable income, the investor should find out why. Losses incurred in prior years may be lowering taxes or accelerated depreciation of assets may be doing so. The annual report, and if necessary the SEC Form 10-K report, should be examined to see why taxes are not being paid at the normal rate. Higher earnings from lowered taxes may be temporary indeed.

Most large U.S. corporations obtain at least some income from overseas operations. Profits from these areas are often high, but additional risks are also involved. Companies having investments in underdeveloped or so called "third-world countries" face the risk that inhospitable governments will nationalize portions of their operation or otherwise take over productive resources. Companies so affected have little choice but to accept whatever payment the foreign government chooses to make.

New governments may cancel or change contracts made with private firms. In 1975 the government of Iran awarded Textron, a large U.S. corporation, a multi-million dollar contract to develop a new helicopter and to build a facility in Iran to produce 400 of these helicopters. In 1979 the new rulers of Iran decided to cancel the project. It is likely that Textron's losses from this decision will be great.

Investment in other than third-world countries is not without risk, but the risk is usually of a different type. Many U.S. firms have experienced currency exchange losses caused by the fact that the U.S. dollar has declined in value relative to most other currencies.

A 1977 suit against Ford Motor Company resulted in a damage award of over $100 million to relatives of a person killed in an accident involving a Ford automobile. This suit is still in court under appeal by the company and damages so large may never be paid. However, legal actions against corporations are an item of increasing importance to investors. Information about legal suits is presented in annual and quarterly corporate reports. The financial press publicizes the larger suits.

SUMMARY

Every investor should be familiar with the use and interpretation of at least the most common techniques of financial analysis. *Ratio analysis* is the relating of various accounting data by dividing one measure into another. In this way common performance measures from different companies can be compared more easily. Ratios may be divided into three general classifications: *liquidity ratios*, which measure the firm's ability to pay short-term obligations and thereby to remain in business; *profitability ratios*, which measure the relative profitability of the firm; and *financial ratios*, which measure the equity and debt contributions to the financing of the firm and the return to investors. These ratios are often compared to those of other similar companies or to ratios of groups of similar companies. Industry average ratios vary widely because of the way different industries operate. A high debt ratio may be normal in one industry but abnormal in another.

Financial data and ratios are often presented in sequence for a period of years. This so-called *horizontal analysis* makes it easier to identify trends and temporary fluctuations. *Vertical analysis* refers to the use of percentage distributions of balance sheet and income statement items to show the relative importance of each component of these accounts. Data presented in this form allow easy comparison between different firms.

Earnings per share and *cash flow per share* are two ratios commonly used as measures of present and future profitability. Such ratios must be interpreted differently than other financial ratios because it is impossible to determine whether a given earnings per share or cash flow per share ratio is good without obtaining additional information about the company involved.

Professional security analysts look deeply into a company's financial statements to identify accounts or accounting practices which might provide misleading information. They generally look to the method of accounting for inventory. They may adjust stated income by the amount of extraordinary gains or losses experienced. Tax liabilities are also examined as are depreciation, amortization, and depletion policies. The final result of this analysis is a more accurate estimate of the financial performance of the company.

PROBLEMS

1. Hypothetical financial statements of the ABC Company are presented below.
    a. Construct the ratios listed below from data in these statements.
        1. Working capital.
        2. Sales to working capital.
        3. Current assets to current liabilities.
        4. Net income to total assets.
        5. Current debt to net worth.
        6. Net income to sales.
        7. Debt to net worth.
        8. Earnings per share.

b. This firm sells underwear & nightwear, women's and children's (line No. 2341 of Dun and Bradstreet's "Key Ratios in 125 Lines," Figure 5–4). Compare the ratios of ABC Company with those of the average firm to answer these questions:

1. Is the company financially sound?
2. Is the company profitable?

ABC CORPORATION
Balance Sheet 12/31/19xx

Assets			Liabilities		
Cash	$ 7,000		Accounts payable	$ 11,000	
Accounts receivable	21,000		Notes payable	5,000	
Inventory	50,000		Other current liabilties	6,000	
Total current assets		$ 78,000	Total current liabili-ties		$ 22,000
Building and land (net of depreciation)		100,000	Mortgage		20,000
			Total liabilities		$ 42,000
			Capital		
			10,000 shares of no par stock authorized, 5,000 issued		$ 34,000
			Retained earnings		102,000
Total assets		$178,000	Liabilities and capital		$178,000

ABC CORPORATION
Income Statement for Year Ended 12/31/19xx

Net sales		$230,000
Cost of goods sold	$170,000	
Other expenses	53,100	
Total expenses		223,100
Income before taxes		6,900
Taxes		2,300
Income after taxes		$ 4,600

2. This question requires consultation with either the annual reports of a company, Moody's *Industrials Manual* or the Standard & Poor's *Industrial Manual*. Choose any large, well-known industrial company (to assure that data are available). Construct the following ratios from its financial statements for each of the past five years.

a. The current ratio.
b. Debt to net worth.
c. Sales to net worth.
d. Sales to assets.
e. Income to sales.
f. Income to net worth.
g. Earnings per share.

Use these ratios (and any others you feel are important) to determine whether the company is performing better or worse than it was five years ago.

QUESTIONS

1. Are composite industry ratios always a good basis of comparison when using ratio analysis to determine the performance of a firm?
2. Which of the ratios presented in Figure 5–4 are useful to the investor and which are useful to the banker or other lender? Justify your choices.
3. What advantage does trend analysis (horizontal analysis) have over simple one-year ratio analysis?
4. Would it be possible for a company to have a high current ratio and still go bankrupt?
5. What is *cash flow*? What does it indicate?
6. Why are there no composite earnings per share ratios for different industries?
7. Is it possible for the debt to net worth ratio of a company to be "too good"?
8. Why is depreciation called a "noncash expense"?
9. What does a balance sheet show?
10. What does an income statement show?
11. What determines whether an asset is recorded as a current or a long-term asset? Can long-term assets ever become current assets?
12. Levi Strauss' balance sheet does not list one particular asset which is of very great value to the company. What is this asset and why is it valuable?
13. In a time of rising prices, how does Lifo accounting for inventory affect current-year income?

SELECTED READINGS

Bernstein, Leopold A.   *Financial Statement Analysis: Theory, Application and Interpretation.* Rev. ed. Homewood, Ill.: Richard D. Irwin, 1978.

Christy, George A., and Clendenin, John C.   *Introduction to Investments.* 7th ed. New York: McGraw-Hill, 1978.

Cohen, Jerome B.; Zinbarg, Edward D.; and Zeikel, Arthur.   *Investment Analysis and Portfolio Management.* 3rd ed. Homewood, Ill.: Richard D. Irwin, 1976.

Gibson, Charles H., and Boyer, Patricia A.   *Financial Statement Analysis.* Boston: CBI Publishing Company, 1979.

Graham, Benjamin; Dodd, David L.; and Cottle, Sidney. *Security Analysis: Principles and Technique*. New York: McGraw-Hill, 1962.

Graham, Benjamin, and McGolrick, Charles. *The Interpretation of Financial Statements*. 3rd rev. ed. New York: Harper & Row, 1975.

"How to Read a Financial Report." New York: Merrill Lynch, Pierce, Fenner, and Smith. Published periodically.

Smith, Jack L., and Keith, Robert M. *Accounting for Financial Statement Presentation*. New York: McGraw-Hill, 1979.

part three

TYPES OF INVESTMENTS

6

Investing in savings

INTRODUCTION TO PART THREE

This chapter is the first of a series devoted to the characteristics of various investments.[1] The order of coverage roughly follows the plan of Table 6-1. This table illustrates not only the dollar amounts of various classes of financial assets, but it also shows how different types of assets have changed in importance over a period of time. Each of the assets listed is examined in the remaining chapters of this book. Demand deposits and currency, while comprising 6.5 percent of the financial assets of individuals in 1978, are not covered because very few people hold cash or its equivalent as an *investment*.

Life insurance and pension fund reserves are discussed in Chapter 16 which emphasizes investment goals and strategies. These assets are not investments as the term is defined in this book. Insurance or pension reserves may not be sold or used like any of the more conventional investments. In fact, from a technical viewpoint they are not directly owned by the policyholder or the owner of pension fund rights. Life insurance and retirement plans do have a bearing on an individual's investment policy because upon death or retirement they will provide the owner or the owner's heirs with money. Real property investments are not listed in Table 6-1 because these are not financial

---

[1] The chapters of Part Three have been written so that each stands on its own; they may be read in any order. The exception to this statement is that persons not familiar with the meaning of yield and compound interest should read the next two parts of this chapter before going to the later chapters.

TABLE 6–1
Financial assets of individuals (dollar amounts in billions)

Type of asset	1958 $ Amount	1958 Percent	1968 $ Amount	1968 Percent	1978 $ Amount	1978 Percent
Demand deposits and currency	68.8	7.8	111.6	5.8	218.9	6.5
Savings accounts	141.1	16.1	373.9	19.5	1,103.9	32.7
at commercial banks	56.6	6.5	167.6	8.7	479.0	14.2
at savings institutions	84.5	9.6	206.3	10.8	624.8	18.5
U.S. government securities.........	68.4	7.8	97.6	5.1	172.9	5.1
State and local bonds	24.0	2.7	37.6	2.0	89.4	2.7
Corporate and foreign debt instruments	9.0	1.0	19.2	1.0	63.2	1.9
Corporate stock (market value).........	360.0	41.0	806.4	42.1	748.1	22.2
Investment company shares (market value)	13.2	1.5	52.7	2.8	54.6	1.6
Mortgages	28.6	3.3	48.7	2.5	106.0	3.1
Life insurance reserves	78.5	8.9	120.0	6.3	188.6	5.6
Pension fund reserves	72.7	8.3	208.1	10.9	530.1	15.7
Miscellaneous assets	14.4	1.6	38.5	2.0	98.6	2.9
Total	878.8	100.0	1,914.2	100.0	3,374.3	100.0

Note: Details may not equal totals due to rounding error. 1978 data are preliminary.
Source: Flow of Funds Section, Board of Governors of the Federal Reserve System.

assets. However, they are an important form of investment for most persons. Such investments are examined in Chapter 12.

This chapter begins with a discussion of the general investment characteristics of savings accounts and the meaning of yield as it relates to savings-type investments. The operation of compound interest and its computation is described briefly. Savings investments in commercial banks, savings banks, savings and loan companies, and credit unions are next examined with the goal of describing the risk and return characteristics associated with savings investments in these *deposit financial institutions*.

INTRODUCTION TO SAVINGS ACCOUNTS

Savings accounts are by far the most common form of personal investment. Many children receive their first gifts in the form of a savings deposit at the local bank or savings and loan company. They often keep these accounts for many years, perhaps for an entire lifetime. By studying savings accounts first, one may look at debt contracts and yields in their simplest forms. Understanding the more complex types of investments should be easier after one has a good grasp of the basic concepts of interest and contractual debt obligations.

Each type of savings institution offers savers slightly different rates of return, withdrawal privileges, and degrees of safety and convenience. However, the main features of the agreement between the saver and the company accepting the savings are very similar. In all cases, the financial institution is obligated to pay upon request the amount deposited in a savings account plus any interest that has accumulated. Under certain conditions the company may refuse to make immediate withdrawal privileges available, but ultimately it must stand ready to repay these funds. This statement holds true even though the saver's legal position varies from that of a *creditor* in banks offering deposits to that of being an *owner* of savings shares in other institutions.

A second characteristic of all savings accounts is that the depositor must make application to withdraw money from an account. Checking accounts are *demand* accounts, not savings accounts. The institution offering this type of account must pay any part or the total amount of a demand account immediately upon request. By federal law no interest may be paid on these accounts. But recent legislation does allow financial institutions to pay interest on negotiable order of withdrawal accounts and to transfer funds automatically from interest bearing savings accounts to checking accounts. The effect is nearly that of paying interest on demand deposits. More about these accounts later.

The contract between the saver and the institution holding the savings is usually contained in a passbook or upon a certificate which evidences the deposit or savings share purchases. This contract will state the conditions under which withdrawals may be made. Rule 6 of the passbook presented in Figure 6–1 is a typical statement on withdrawal procedure.

State and federal laws force financial institutions that accept savings deposits to provide themselves with the *option* of not paying out deposits on demand. But as a practical matter savers can usually consider their regular savings accounts as payable upon demand. No savings institution will willingly fail to honor a deposit withdrawal request, unless a specified delay is required under the savings account contract.

A final characteristic of savings accounts is that interest or savings dividends (both terms are used for technical reasons discussed later) of a specified amount are paid on all *principal* which is on deposit. These payments are legal liabilities of the company; they must be paid when due.

YIELD CHARACTERISTICS OF SAVINGS ACCOUNTS

Chapter 2 examined the nature of the several types of risk encountered in almost all investments and how these characteristics are related to expected returns. The key to understanding investments lies in one's ability to *classify* the many different types of investments by their risk and return characteristics. Unless this approach to selecting investments is used, it is nearly impossible to choose those most suitable to the individual investment situation. Yield, which is often used synonymously with return, is one of the most important attributes of all investments.

Measuring yield

The yield of an investment refers to the amount received during a certain period of time over and above the amount originally placed into the investment. The simplest way to explain yield is by looking at the accumulation of money in a savings account. Yields from bonds,

FIGURE 6–1

A typical passbook of a commercial bank

RULES AND REGULATIONS GOVERNING
SAVINGS ACCOUNTS

DEPOSITOR AND BANK AGREE:

Rule 1. All savings deposits are received by
United States National Bank of Oregon subject
to rules and regulations as printed herein; as
shown on Bank's deposit and other forms; and
as changed from time to time by posting of
notice in Bank's lobby. Acceptance of this passbook, and inscription of name by depositor or
agent on signature card required by the Bank,
shall be deemed and held to be a valid assent
thereto.

(THE SAVINGS PASSBOOK)

Rule 2. A pre-numbered passbook shall be
issued for each savings account. All deposits
made by or for the account of the depositor
will be entered in the passbook at the time
they are made; or as soon thereafter as the
passbook shall be presented for such purpose.
The balance shown in the passbook to the
credit of depositor is subject to correction to
accord with the Bank's records.

Should the savings passbook be lost, destroyed or fraudulently obtained from any
depositor, immediate notice must be given
the office of the Bank at which the account is
carried. After such notice, if satisfactory explanation be made and bond of indemnity be
given in a form approved by the Bank's officers, the amount to the credit of the depositor
will be paid to such depositor, or a new book
will be issued therefor.

(ASSIGNMENT OF ACCOUNT)

Rule 3. No assignment of the depositor's
passbook or account, or any part thereof, shall
be valid unless made in writing, and shall not
bind the Bank until it has been filed with the
Bank in writing.

(DEPOSITS)

Rule 4. Deposits will be received of any sum
from one dollar to such maximum amount as
may from time to time be designated by the
Bank.

Items are credited conditionally at time of
deposit and may be forwarded on next business date after receipt. Bank may charge back
any item before ultimate payment, including
losses in transit; and it is not liable for
items drawn on this Bank; it is not liable for
losses in transit; and it may decline to honor
withdrawals against conditional credits. Depositor is bound by all clearing house and/or
Federal Reserve collection rules and practices.

The Bank may decline to receive any deposit
and at any time may require depositor to withdraw all or part of the funds on deposit. Notice
thereof will be mailed to the depositor by first-
class mail at his last address on file with the
Bank. Interest shall cease on such deposit or
part of deposit for which withdrawal is required after thirty days from date of such
notice.

(DEPOSITS OF MINORS)

Rule 5. Deposits made by any person or persons for or in the name of any minor shall be
made and received upon the express condition

that the Bank may pay out such deposit or part
thereof only upon the written order of the
minor.

Deposits made by any person or persons in
trust for any minor shall be made and received
upon the express condition that the Bank during the lifetime of the depositor may pay out
such deposit or part thereof only upon the
written order of the person or persons who
made the deposit in trust for the minor.

(WITHDRAWALS)

Rule 6. The passbook must be presented to
the Bank when a withdrawal is made.

Withdrawals may be made personally, the
depositor being required to sign a receipt for
the amount of the withdrawal, or by order
in writing satisfactorily authenticated, or by
power of attorney, duly authenticated.

It is understood and agreed that the Bank
may require, whenever in the opinion of any
of the officers it may be deemed advisable,
written notices of the intention of any depositor to withdraw as follows:

Thirty days' notice to withdraw any sum
up to $100; sixty days' notice to withdraw
any sum from $100 to $500; ninety days'
notice to withdraw any sum from $500 to
$1,000; four months' notice to withdraw
any sum from $1,000 to $3,000; six months'
notice to withdraw any sum over $3,000.

A second notice of withdrawal will not be
accepted until the first notice has expired or
been cancelled. Failure to demand payment at
the Bank within five days after the expiration
of the notice shall be constituted a waiver of
such notice and a new notice may be required.

(INTEREST)

Rule 7. Interest will be allowed and paid on
savings accounts on such terms and conditions
and at such rates and on such balances as may,
from time to time be designated by the Bank
or as limited by the Federal Reserve Board or
other legally constituted authority.

(SERVICE CHARGES)

Rule 8. All savings accounts, whether active
or inactive, shall be subject to service charges
now or hereafter in effect.

(AMENDMENTS)

Rule 9. These rules, conditions and regulations may be altered or amended, and new
ones made by the Bank at any time, but no
alterations or amendments of new rules, regulations or conditions shall be in force until
notice thereof shall have been posted in the
Bank lobby for at least thirty days. Such posting shall be held to be a personal notice to
each depositor.

Source: U.S. National Bank of Oregon, Portland, Oregon. (This statement was
in effect in early 1979.)

common stocks, and preferred stocks are computed somewhat differently. These methods will be discussed in the chapters devoted to each specific type of investment.

Computation of savings account yields. The *yield* of a savings account is the amount of interest that the institution will pay for the use of deposited money. Yield is usually presented as a percentage rate—5 percent for example. This means that interest will accumulate at a rate of 5 percent of principal, the amount on deposit. Yields are stated on an annual basis, which means that principal must remain in the account for one year to receive the full promised yield. Money left on deposit for half a year would receive interest at half the annual rate. A deposit left for one month would receive one-twelfth of the annual rate, and so on.

What happens to interest as it accumulates is of vital importance. If interest is withdrawn from an account as it is paid, the principal amount will never increase. But if interest is left on deposit, interest is then paid on this amount, as well as on the original principal. The term *simple interest* means that interest is paid on an unvarying amount of principal. *Compound interest* refers to the situation where interest is paid on principal and on the interest that has accumulated to the account.

If $100 were deposited at the beginning of the year in an account that paid a 5 percent yield, at the end of the year this account would have earned $5 of interest.

$$\text{Dollar amount of interest} = \text{Principal} \times \text{Interest rate}$$
$$= \$100 \times .05$$
$$= \$5.$$

This is an example of a simple interest calculation. If the $5 of interest were not withdrawn from the account it would increase the principal to $105. The next year, interest would be calculated at the same rate of 5 percent, but the amount of interest earned would be larger because interest would also be paid on the interest left on deposit. This is an example of compound interest.

Financial institutions commonly calculate interest on a quarterly, monthly, daily, or even continuous basis. The more often interest is calculated and credited to an account the more rapidly the account will grow. For example, an account paying 5 percent per year using quarterly compounding would pay $5.09 interest on $100 of principal left on deposit for one year. Daily compounding would create $5.13 of interest. There is much room for confusion over how interest rates are calculated and what yields mean in terms of how much money one can expect to earn on a savings account.[2] By convention and by law, savings institutions are required to disclose both the *nominal* and *effective* rates paid on savings deposits. The nominal rate is the annual rate which is the basis for single period interest calculations. The effective rate is the true rate earned on a deposit held for one year. Nominal and effective rates are identical if annual compounding is used. If interest is calculated more than once per year, the effective rate will be higher. The effective rate is calculated by dividing the total interest received over one year by the amount of principal on deposit at the beginning of the year. In the previous example using a 5 percent nominal rate and daily compounding, the effective rate would be 5.13 percent.

$$\text{Effective rate} = \frac{\text{Interest paid}}{\text{Beginning principal}}$$

$$= \frac{\$5.13}{\$100}$$

$$= .0513 \text{ or } 5.13\%.$$

A discussion of the mathematics of interest calculations is contained in the Appendix at the end of this chapter.

The power of compound interest. Over a short period of time, modest differences in the effective rates of interest on savings investments are not very important. This is particularly true when the amount of principal is small; then dollars of yield are often insignificant. But over many years of compounding, differences in interest rates have very important effects upon the amount of accumulated savings, even when the principal is small. Table 6–2 shows how much $100 would accumulate to in 10, 20, and 30 years under four different interest rates. Interest is compounded annually and allowed to remain in the account.

At 6 percent compounded annually, money doubles in amount in slightly less than twelve years; at 8 percent it doubles in slightly over nine years; at 10 percent doubling occurs in just over seven years, and

---

[2] A study by the American Bankers Association recorded over 100 different ways of calculating interest. See American Bankers Association, *Methods and Procedures in Computing Interest on Savings Deposits.* Also see "How to Pick the Best Saving Account," *Consumer Reports,* February 1975, pp. 90–97.

TABLE 6–2
Accumulation of interest and principal at various rates of compound interest

Original principal	Rate of interest	Principal and accumulated interest after		
		10 Years	20 Years	30 Years
$100..................	3%	$134.39	$180.61	$ 242.73
100..................	6	179.08	320.71	574.35
100..................	9	236.72	518.61	1,265.20
100..................	12	310.58	964.63	2,995.99

at 12 percent it doubles in just over six years. Over very long periods of time, the increase in principal due to compound interest is truly staggering.

In 1626, Peter Minuit, an official of the Dutch West Indies Company, purchased Manhattan Island for about $24 in trinkets. This purchase is widely acclaimed as one of the best real estate investments on record because of the tremendous increase in the value of the island. However, the original $24 if left at annual compound interest at 6 percent for the 354 years between 1626 and 1980 would have shown a rather large increase on its own. It would have been worth about $21.8 billion at the end of 1980!

Grace days and other savings account features. Over the long run the account offering the highest rate of interest with the highest number of compounding periods will produce the highest yield. Persons having relatively inactive savings accounts should seek such accounts. Those who expect to make frequent deposits or withdrawals from their savings accounts must consider grace days and other features of savings accounts because they may materially affect the yield from a given savings account.

Deposit grace days refer to the practice of many savings institutions of crediting interest from the first of the month on deposits received before a given date. The 10th and 15th of the month are common grace dates. *Withdrawal grace dates* are the number of days before the end of a month or other accounting period within which depositors are allowed to make withdrawals and still have interest on the deposit credited to the end of the period. In general, withdrawal grace dates are fewer in number than deposit grace dates; three days of withdrawal grace being common.

Some savings institutions levy *maintenance fees* on accounts which have been inactive for a given period of time. Some institutions levy charges for withdrawals of over a certain number during a given time period. Some institutions only pay interest on accounts of a minimum size. Often the minimum size is calculated as the smallest amount on deposit during the interest computation period. Under such a rule, no interest would be paid on an account, no matter how large the amount deposited, if the account were drawn down to a zero balance before the end of the interest computation period.

In a series of articles dealing with savings, four hypothetical savings accounts were compared to determine which gave the highest interest. The same amounts were deposited and withdrawn on the same dates in each account. Each account paid the same rate of interest, credited deposits, and compounded interest in the same manner. The only difference in the accounts was in the way interest was computed.[3] Figure 6-2 presents these calculations in the form of passbook savings account statements. The "best" account paid 68 percent more interest than the "worst."

Yields on savings accounts vary with general interest rate conditions. When credit becomes tight and interest rates rise, so do savings account yields. When interest rates decline, savings yields follow suit. Figure 6-3 clearly shows this relationship. Aaa corporate bond yields are used to measure changes in general interest levels. Note that as these bond yields decline, so do all types of savings rates. But savings rate changes tend to *follow* changes in other interest rates. When interest rates become very high, as they have in recent years, bond yields far exceed those paid on savings accounts.

Maximum rates that may be paid by savings institutions are regulated by federal and state agencies. Public policy has favored mutual savings banks and savings and loan companies by allowing them to pay slightly higher savings account yields. Historically, as Figure 6-3 shows, S&Ls have paid the highest averge yields and commercial banks the lowest. But even public policy changes: In recent years more competition has been allowed between financial institutions. S&Ls and MSBs may still pay higher savings account interest than commercial banks, but average yields have narrowed greatly since 1967.

DEPOSIT INSURANCE

Most of the companies engaged in the business of holding the savings of others are tightly regulated by federal or state laws, or both.

---

[3] "How to Pick the Best Savings Account," *Consumer Reports*, February 1975, pp. 90–97.

FIGURE 6–2

Example of saving account interest calculations

These four banks all pay the same interest rate—
yet interest payments range from $44.93 to $75.30.

There are many ways of computing interest, as the text of our report indicates. Here are four passbooks showing the identical deposits and withdrawals (made on the same days), with explanations of how the interest has been computed under four common methods. All four assume a six per cent interest rate and quarterly crediting and compounding.

LOW BALANCE
Under this method, interest is paid only on the smallest amount of money that was in the account during the interest period. Despite a balance that reached $4000 during the first quarter, this account earned interest only on $1000— the lowest balance during that period. (There are no withdrawals during the second quarter, so the low-balance formula is not important there.) This method, which tends to discourage deposits, is the most punitive to savers. Yet 30 per cent of commercial banks still use it, according to a study last year by the American Bankers Association.
Interest: $44.93

FIRST-IN, FIRST-OUT (FIFO)
With this method, withdrawals are deducted first from the starting balance of the interest period and then, if the balance isn't sufficient, from later deposits. This erodes the base on which your interest is figured and means you automatically lose interest on withdrawals from the start of the interest period rather than from the dates on which the withdrawals were actually made. Another variation of this method is to apply the first withdrawal to the first deposit, rather than to the beginning balance; this would earn $53.93. About 16 per cent of commercial banks use the FIFO methods, according to the ABA.
Interest: $52.44

LAST-IN, FIRST-OUT (LIFO)
Under this plan, withdrawals are deducted from the most recent deposits in the quarter and then from the next most recent ones. This method, which does not penalize savers as much as the two FIFO methods, is used by about 5 per cent of commercial banks.
Interest: $58.44

DAY-OF-DEPOSIT TO DAY-OF-WITHDRAWAL
Under this arrangement, the bank pays you interest for the actual number of days the money remains in the account. This method, which is sometimes called daily interest, instant interest, or day-in day-out, is the fairest to consumers. It is used by almost 50 per cent of commercial banks and 60 per cent of insured S&Ls (there are no industry figures for savings banks). It yields the greatest return.
Interest: $75.30

Source: Excerpted by permission from *Consumer Reports*, February 1975.

FIGURE 6-3
Average yields on savings accounts and Aaa corporate bonds

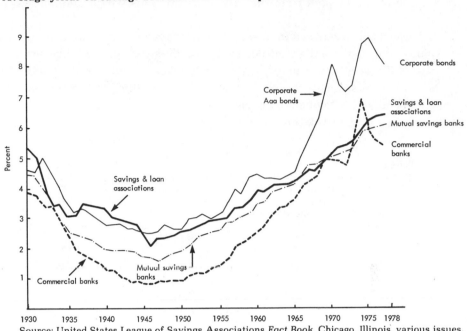

Source: United States League of Savings Associations *Fact Book,* Chicago, Illinois, various issues.

These institutions are forced to meet certain financial tests in order to remain in business. Most of the institutions have chosen to have their deposits insured by either the Federal Deposit Insurance Corporation (FDIC), The Federal Savings and Loan Insurance Corporation (FSLIC), the National Credit Union Association (NCUA), or one of several state-operated insurance plans.

The importance of deposit insurance cannot be overestimated. In late 1979, deposits of most financial institutions were insured to a maximum of $40,000 per deposit.[4] This means that if an insured institution has financial difficulties, depositors will receive the amount of their account, to a maximum $40,000 per account, from insurance. This

---

[4] Exceptions are credit unions, of which only about 77 percent are insured, and a very small number of other financial institutions which are uninsured because they either cannot qualify for insurance or for some other reason have chosen not to be insured.

would be paid immediately. The amount of the account in excess of $40,000 would be paid from the sale of assets. This would take more time.

Large-scale savers can increase their insurance coverage by placing deposits of no more than $40,000 each in *different* insured savings accounts. These accounts may be in separate insured banks, or they may be held in the same institution, but under different titles.[5] For example, a husband and wife might increase the insurance coverage of bank deposits in a single bank this way:

	Maximum
Type of account	*insurance*
Individual account of John Doe	$ 40,000
Individual account of Mary Doe	40,000
Joint account of John and Mary Doe	40,000
Revocable trust account with John and Mary Doe as trustees for son Thomas	40,000
Irrevocable trust account established by John Doe with Mary Doe as beneficiary	40,000
Total insured deposits..	$200,000

Any imaginative lawyer or bank trust officer could increase the total deposit insurance coverage of this couple to a very large amount, at least to $400,000 in a single bank. Other insured accounts could be placed in different banks practically without limit.

RELATIVE IMPORTANCE OF DIFFERENT TYPES OF SAVINGS

Table 6–3 lists the dollar amount of savings of various types for selected years. In 1978 these savings amounted to about 35 percent of the total financial assets of households. The largest amount of savings were held in commercial banks, followed by those held in savings and loan institutions. Table 6–3 shows that over the years shifts have occurred in the way that people save. Prior to 1960 more savings were held in mutual savings banks than in savings and loans. During that year savings and loans held nearly the same dollar amount of deposits as commercial banks. In recent years commercial banks have again become the largest holders of savings.

---

[5] To qualify for separate insurance, ownership of each savings account in the same bank must be *legally different*. A single saver having $40,000 in a checking account and another $40,000 in a savings account at the same bank would only have $40,000 of insurance because both accounts have the same legal owner.

ACCOUNTS IN COMMERCIAL BANKS

Banks have traditionally offered two types of accounts—demand deposits and time deposits. *Demand deposits* are those which can be obtained immediately. Most of us know them as checking accounts. Banks traditionally charge depositors for providing demand deposit services. By law they may not pay interest on any demand deposit.

Time deposits are savings deposits of various types. Banks may pay interest on time deposits. Although they are not required to do so, most do. Recent legislation has made it possible for commercial banks to offer what is known as an *automatic transfer account*. This is really two accounts, a checking account and a savings account. By special agreement the bank offers to transfer funds from the savings account to the checking account whenever the checking account is drawn down below an agreed upon amount. The effect of this is to allow interest to be paid on money that would normally be kept in a checking account.

Banks which are members of the Federal Reserve System are governed so far as savings deposits are concerned by the System's Regulation Q, titled "Payment of Interest on Deposits." State chartered banks which are not members of the Federal Reserve System are governed by the laws of the state in which the bank is chartered, and if they are insured banks, by the Federal Deposit Insurance Corporation. Most state laws closely follow rules of the Federal Reserve System in regard to the type of deposit accounts which may be offered and the amount of interest payable on these accounts.

Table 6–4 shows recent maximum interest rates that commercial banks and other financial institutions could pay on different types of deposits. *Negotiable order of withdrawal* accounts are really checking accounts. They are discussed later in this chapter.

Savings deposits refer to deposits which are left in the bank on an indefinite basis. These deposits are usually evidenced by a passbook, but some banks merely keep records (statements) of the deposits in the bank. In either case, the depositor usually looks at these deposits as "ready cash" which earns a modest amount of interest. The maximum rate of interest which may be paid on these accounts is the lowest of any savings deposit account, 5¼ percent as this book is being written. Remember, however, this is the *maximum* rate which may be paid. Individual banks may pay less than this, and all banks may change the

TABLE 6-3

Financial savings in the United States (dollar amounts in billions)

Method	1940		1960		1978	
	Amount	Percent	Amount	Percent	Amount	Percent
Commercial bank time and savings deposits	15.4	42.0	62.8	29.4	479.0	40.4
Mutual savings banks	10.7	29.2	36.3	17.0	142.9	12.0
Savings and loans.............	4.3	11.7	62.1	29.1	431.1	36.3
Credit unions...................	0.2	0.5	5.0	2.3	53.0	4.5
U.S. savings bonds	6.1	16.6	47.2	22.2	80.9	6.8
Total	36.7	100.0	213.4	100.0	1,186.9	100.0

Source: National Association of Mutual Savings Banks, United States League of Savings Associations, The Institute of Life Insurance, and Flow of Funds Section of the Federal Reserve System.

TABLE 6–4
Maximum rates payable on time and savings deposits at federally insured institutions (percent per annum)

Type and maturity of deposit	Commercial banks	Mutual savings banks and savings and loans
Negotiable order of withdrawal	5¼	5¼
Savings deposits.............................	5¼	5½
Variable-rate deposits	*	*
Other time deposits (multiple and single maturity):		
30–89 days..................................	5¼	†
90 days to 1 year	5½	5¾
1 to 2½ years	6	6½
2½ to 4 years	6½	6¾
4 to 6 years.................................	7¼	7½
6 to 8 years.................................	7½	7¾
8 years or more	7¾	8
Individual retirement accounts and Keogh (HR-10) plans, three-year minimum maturity...	8	8

Note: Maximum rates that may be paid by member banks are established by the Board of Governors under provisions of Regulation Q; however, a member bank may not pay a rate in excess of the maximum rate payable by state banks or trust companies on like deposits under the laws of the state in which the member bank is located. Beginning February 1, 1936, maximum rates that may be paid by nonmember insured commercial banks, as established by the FDIC, have been the same as those in effect for member banks.

* There are two types of variable-rate deposits, 26-week maturity time deposits and 4-year deposits. Commercial banks may pay yields equal to the discount rate on the most recently issued 6-month U.S. Treasury bills on 26-week deposits. MSBs and S&Ls may pay ¼ percentage point more than commercial banks to a maximum rate of 9 percent. Maximum rates of all institutions are equal above this rate. The 4-year deposits have a minimum maturity of this length. The maximum rate paid on these certificate accounts by MSBs, S&Ls, and other thrift institutions is one percent below the average yield of 4-year Treasury securities when the certificate is issued. Commercial banks may pay up to ¼ of a percentage point less than this rate. Both types of certificates are nonnegotiable.

† No separate account category.

Source: *Federal Reserve Bulletin,* August 1979, Table 1.16.

interest paid on this type of deposit at their option, with suitable notice to the depositor.

Variable-rate deposits are the newest type of savings accounts. These six-month and four-year maturity accounts may be offered by all commercial banks and savings institutions. Maximum rates of the shorter certificate accounts are tied to the Treasury bill discount rate. The longer account's maximum rates are at least one percentage point less than the average yield on four-year maturity Treasury securities. The top rate paid by commercial banks is typically ¼ of a percentage point less than the top rate paid by other savings institutions. The minimum amount of these accounts is $10,000. See the footnote accompanying Table 6–4 for a detailed description of how ceiling rates are set on these *money market certificate accounts.*

Multiple maturity time deposits take many forms and carry different names at different banks. The characteristic which most clearly distinguishes them from regular savings deposits is the limited withdrawal privilege and the potential for higher interest payments.

Single maturity time deposits, as the name implies, are those which mature on a specified date. These are often called *certificate accounts* because the deposit is evidenced by a certificate which lists its conditions: amount, interest rate, and rules for redemption. In most cases certificate accounts may be redeemed prior to the stated redemption date, but only by forfeiting interest. A typical penalty for early withdrawal reduces interest to the rate paid on passbook accounts.

The *time certificate of deposit* is a special type of single maturity certificate account. CDs, as they are called, may be negotiable or nonnegotiable. Those which are negotiable are usually of large denomination ($100,000 and above) and are not redeemable prior to their expiration date. Holders of negotiable CDs may sell them prior to maturity, a feature which provides for great liquidity.

Individual retirement accounts are special savings accounts into which retirement fund contributions are deposited. These savings receive special deferred income tax treatment, a topic which will be examined in later chapters. Once funds have been identified as individual retirement account payments and deposited, they are very difficult to obtain. If they are withdrawn at any time before retirement, income taxes are levied against the withdrawal, and interest is paid at a lower rate.

As Table 6–4 clearly indicates, regulatory authorities allow payment of higher interest on savings accounts that are of longer minimum duration and therefore less liquid. The saver sacrifices liquidity for higher yield; the bank pays higher interest on accounts that cannot be quickly withdrawn. Since the funds cannot be immediately withdrawn, the bank is protected from the possibility of large unanticipated losses of deposits. This allows the institution to invest these deposits in longer-term, and usually more profitable, assets.

Bank services

Commercial banks are rightly called full-service financial institutions. Banks or banking offices are located in almost every city and town in the country. Banking by mail makes banking services available to everyone. In addition to savings deposits, most banks offer checking accounts, business loans, personal loans, real estate loans, safe deposit boxes, credit cards, money order services, and personal trust services. Many banks have convenient drive-through teller stations and automated-teller facilities where deposits can be made and cash obtained during times when the main bank is closed. An increasing number of banks offer bill-paying services and point-of-sale payment procedures. The average commercial bank offers the widest variety of financial services of any financial institution, and for this reason practically everyone has some sort of account with a commercial bank. Even though the average commercial bank savings account pays less interest than is available elsewhere, the convenience of "one-stop banking" causes many persons to rely totally on their commercial bank for all financial transactions.

Insurance of bank deposits

As of August 1979, there were over 14,900 commercial banks in the United States. Over 98 percent of these banks were "insured banks," which means their depositors were insured against loss up to a maximum of $40,000 for each legally separate account. All banks which are members of the Federal Reserve System are *required* by law to be insured. Nonmember banks *may be* insured if they meet the requirements of the insuring agency, the Federal Deposit Insurance Corporation. The FDIC, as it is usually called, estimates that in recent years about 99 percent of all accounts in insured banks were completely covered by deposit insurance.

SAVINGS ACCOUNTS IN MUTUAL SAVINGS BANKS AND SAVINGS AND LOANS

From the viewpoint of the saver, mutual savings banks (MSBs) and savings and loan companies (S&Ls) have more similarities than differences. For this reason they can be discussed at the same time.

Types of savings accounts

Savings accounts offered by these institutions are of two general types—regular (passbook) accounts and special accounts. The first type closely resembles the commercial bank savings account. Each account is evidenced by a passbook, and deposits and withdrawals may be made upon presentation of the passbook. As is the case with commercial banks, these institutions have the right to hold up withdrawals for at least 30 days; like commercial banks, they seldom avail themselves of this privilege.

Special accounts may be classified as *notice, certificate,* or *bonus accounts.* Notice accounts most nearly resemble commercial bank open account time deposits. This account differs from the regular account in that the saver *must* give notice of intent to withdraw funds and then must wait a specified period before receiving the withdrawal. These accounts pay higher returns than regular accounts.

Certificate accounts most nearly resemble commercial bank certificates of deposit. These accounts are issued in fixed minimum amounts—usually $1,000—and have fixed maturities of six months to eight years. Many of the large commercial bank CDs are negotiable, but few of those issued by MSBs or S&Ls are. The liquidity for this type of account lies in the willingness of the issuing institution to redeem it before maturity. Some companies allow early redemption but only at a lowered rate of return. Often certificates may be used as collateral for loans and in this way can provide owners with some liquidity.

Figure 6–4 is a certificate which evidences a single payment certificate account at Cascade Federal Savings and Loan Association. The terms are clear enough so that they require no further explanation. Note the penalties associated with early withdrawal. Large denomination commercial bank CDs are usually "bearer instruments," which means that the person who has possession of them is presumed to be the legal owner. This type is more easily negotiable.

Bonus plans are systematic savings plans under which the participant agrees to save a certain amount of money periodically until a savings program goal is reached. If the savings program is completed as planned, the account is paid a bonus yield. If the plan is not completed, savings are rewarded at the lower rate of regular accounts.

Maximum interest rates payable by MSBs are set by the FDIC and state banking commissions and are fairly uniform from state to state. S&L rates are set by the Federal Home Loan Bank Board, which allows different maximum rates to prevail in different parts of the country. Higher rates are usually allowed where demand for housing is high so

FIGURE 6-4
Savings and loan certificate of deposit

CERTIFICATE OF DEPOSIT

1. Account Summary Section

Accountholder_____

Account No. _____   Initial Maturity Date _____

Date of Issuance_____   Extended Maturity Date—See Section 2

Opening Balance_____   Renewal Term_____ months

Rate of Earnings_____ % per annum.   Minimum Addition _____

Frequency of Compounding **Daily**   Earnings Distribution Dates Beginning_____

Minimum Balance Requirement _____,   _____ and _____thereafter,
with the last distribution on the final maturity date.

2. General Section
This certifies that the Accountholder holds a savings account with the Opening Balance and for the initial term expiring on the Initial Maturity Date shown hereon in Cascade Federal Savings and Loan Association.
The Accountholder may, from time to time, make additions to the balance in this account in any amount not less than the Minimum Addition provided for in Section 1. In the event of any such addition, the term of this account shall be extended so that the period from the date of such addition to the Extended Maturity Date (which shall be recorded with the entry as to such addition) shall not be less than the initial term (or Renewal Term, if the addition is made during a Renewal Term).

3. Earnings Section
This account shall receive earnings at the rate and with the Frequency of Compounding as the above set forth. Such earnings shall be payable on the Earnings Distribution Dates above set forth, provided the balance in the account is not reduced below the Minimum Balance Requirement. If such balance is reduced below the Minimum Balance Requirement, the Rate of Earnings on the remaining balance shall thereafter be reduced to the rate then paid on regular savings accounts (See also Section 5).

4. Renewal Section
This account shall be automatically renewed at the close of business on the maturity date or the maturity date of any renewal or extended term unless (1) withdrawn within the 10-day period referred to in Section 5 hereof or (2) at least 15 days prior to any such date, the Association gives written notice to the Accountholder that this account will not be renewed at the Rate of Earnings and/or the Renewal Term set forth above. In such event, the account will either be extended for such additional term and at such rate of earnings as set forth in said notice or the account will be converted to a regular savings account and receive earnings at the rate then paid on regular savings accounts.

5. Penalty Clause Section
Except as otherwise provided herein, in the event of any withdrawal from this account during the first three months (90 days) of the initial term or any renewal term, no earnings shall be paid on the amount withdrawn. In the event of any withdrawal thereafter, prior to a maturity date, earnings on the amount withdrawn shall be paid to the date of such withdrawal at the then current rate on regular savings accounts for the period since issuance or renewal (whichever is later) of the account, but which period shall not exceed the term of the account to the date of such withdrawal, less three months.
In computing earnings on the amount withdrawn, to the extent possible, such amount shall be considered as coming first from the addition, if any, last added to the account.
Any withdrawal which reduced the account balance below the Minimum Balance Requirement, or any change in the term or Rate of Earnings, shall be considered as a withdrawal of the entire account balance and shall be subject to the penalty prescribed herein.
Earnings credited to this account may be withdrawn at any time without penalty.
If the account or any portion thereof is withdrawn not more than 10 days after a maturity date, earnings shall be paid thereon at the rate then applicable to this account to the date of withdrawal without reduction of any penalty.
To the extent necessary to comply with these requirements, deductions shall be made from the amount withdrawn or the remaining account balance.

CASCADE FEDERAL SAVINGS AND LOAN ASSOCIATION

Date _____   BY_____
Authorized Signature

Courtesy of Cascade Federal Savings and Loan Association, Corvallis, Oregon

that more capital is attracted into these areas. Maximum rate settings are also based upon the competing rates of other savings institutions. Although the regulation of maximum interest rates of all financial institutions is accomplished by several agencies (the Federal Reserve Board, the Federal Home Loan Bank Board, and various state banking commissions), the effect has been to set a fairly uniform structure of maximum interest rates. This regulation has traditionally allowed S&Ls and MSBs to pay slightly higher rates than commercial banks. Table 6-4 lists recent maximum allowable rates on the most common types of savings accounts. It should be emphasized that these are *maximum* rates.

Organization, regulation, and insurance of savings and loan companies and mutual savings banks

Virtually all commercial banks are corporations. About 15 percent of the nearly 5,000 S&Ls are publicly owned stock corporations. The remainder of this group, and all of the 475 or so MSBs, take the mutual form of organization. Under the corporate form, shareholders own the company and elect its directors on the basis of one vote for each share owned. Directors are responsible for setting policy and hiring managers who actually operate the company. In mutual institutions, members own the organization. They too elect directors, but each member has one vote regardless of the proportion of the organization that is owned. Regulatory agencies in several states may by law appoint one or more persons to the boards of MSBs. Savers are little affected by the form of organization except that a saver in a corporate institution is legally a *creditor* while savers in mutual organizations may be legally defined as *owners*. The difference is largely meaningless so long as savings are insured.

Over 90 percent of all MSBs are located in the Middle Atlantic or New England states. About 60 percent are concentrated in the states of Massachusetts and New York. All are chartered and regulated by the states in which they do business and by insuring agencies. State regulation is less uniform and sometimes less strict than federal regulation, but MSBs have an enviable record so far as safety is concerned. In several states no MSB depositor has lost any money (principal or interest) since the beginning of the 20th century. Deposit insurance of up to $40,000 per account is provided by the Federal Deposit Insurance Corporation, the Federal Savings and Loan Insurance Corporation, or through state-sponsored insurance plans. Some state plans insure accounts for more than $40,000.

Savings and loans may be organized as mutuals, like MSBs, or as corporations, like commercial banks. They may be organized under federal or state charters. Deposit insurance equal to that offered by commercial banks and MSBs is provided for nearly all S&L accounts by the same insurers—the FDIC, FSLIC, or state agencies. Only a very few small state chartered institutions remain uninsured.

Services. Historically, both MSBs and S&Ls have invested most of their deposits in home mortgage loans. They have offered fewer services than other financial institutions, but generally have provided savers with higher savings rates than were available elsewhere. Times are changing, however. Federal and state regulations which rigidly controlled the actions of S&Ls, MSBs, and other financial institutions have been relaxed, allowing these institutions to compete more directly with the many services provided by commercial banks. MSBs have been very aggressive in their campaign to offer more financial services. Their efforts have met with success in the eastern states, where they have strong political representation, to the point that the larger MSBs now offer many of the services offered by commercial banks. Included among these services are traveler's checks, money orders, credit cards, retirement accounts, loan repayment through payroll deductions, personal trust services, safe deposit boxes, drive-through facilities, negotiable order of withdrawal accounts, checking accounts, and so on. They do not provide the wide variety of business and personal loans available at commercial banks, but their consumer loan services are expanding. Home mortgage loans continue to be the single most important type of loan made by MSBs.

Well over 80 percent of the assets of S&Ls are also invested in home mortgage loans. Like MSBs, these institutions have authority to broaden their services, but they have not been as aggressive in doing so. Some S&Ls offer education loans, home improvement loans, and other types of consumer loans. A few offer checking accounts and NOW accounts. However, for the most part, services offered to customers and depositors are not nearly so varied or extensive as those offered by MSBs or commercial banks.

SAVINGS IN CREDIT UNIONS

By number, credit unions are the largest single type of financial institution. At the start of 1979 there were approximately 22,300 credit unions in the United States; membership was about 39.6 million persons.[6] These institutions are mutuals, like mutual savings banks and most savings and loan companies. They have been formed as cooperative associations to accept savings from and make loans to their members only.

Savers at credit unions do not have a creditor position since they are technically the owners of the company. Membership in these organizations is limited to persons who belong to whatever group has formed

---

[6] Personal correspondence with the Credit Union National Association, Inc., Madison, Wisconsin.

the association. In theory, the membership can be made up of practically any grouping of people; in practice most credit unions are organized by groups of workers who are members of the same trade union or who are employees of the same company. The numbers of credit unions are very impressive, but because these institutions are so small, they hold a nearly insignificant proportion of the savings of persons in the United States. This proportion is increasing slowly, but in 1978 only about 4½ percent of U.S. personal savings were held in credit unions.

Regulation of credit unions

These institutions may have either state or federal charters, neither of which is difficult to obtain if the low minimum requirements for organization can be met. Once the association is operating, state and federal laws require that reserve or guarantee funds be established and annual audits be conducted. Aside from these restrictions, credit unions have wide discretion in the investment policies they pursue and in the rates of interest they pay savers.

Accounts may be insured to $40,000 through the National Credit Union Association. In early 1979 about 77 percent of all credit unions were insured. Safety also comes from the fact that all key employees are heavily bonded (in effect this insures the credit union against loss due to theft or misappropriation of funds by these persons), and the boards of directors are required to oversee periodic audits of the companies.

Services at credit unions

There is little variety in credit union savings accounts. Most CUs offer only passbook accounts although some of the larger institutions are beginning to sell certificate accounts which pay somewhat greater interest. Passbook interest may be as high as 7 percent, but there are great differences in the rates paid among institutions. Share account drafts, which are equivalent to the NOW accounts discussed in the next section, may also be offered by credit unions. In early 1979 few CUs offered this type of account. Like other financial institutions, credit unions may legally delay withdrawals, but they seldom do so.

The vast majority of credit union loans finance the purchase of automobiles and other consumer durables. These institutions may make longer term loans for home improvements or for home purchase. At the present time only a few of the larger CUs make such loans.

Most credit unions are equipped to accept savings through payroll deduction procedures. If this is not done, there is no great loss in convenience since the credit union itself is usually conveniently located for the members. However, payroll deduction is a feature nearly unique to these institutions.

Many credit unions provide free life insurance for owners of savings accounts. Usually there is an upper limit on the amount of insurance available, but some companies provide insurance equal to each saver's total account. Credit unions must be considered less safe, on the average, than other savings institutions. The fact that substantial numbers of these institutions have no insurance, and because most credit unions are organized around an occupation or a company, contributes to this lack of safety. When adverse economic conditions strike a particular occupation or company, the entire membership of the credit union is affected. Savers turn into borrowers rapidly and often strain the capacity of the organization.

The probable reasons why credit unions have continued to grow so rapidly is that they are convenient places to do business and they pay reasonably high yields. Saving there may be attractive to people who want their savings to be used to provide loans for fellow members. Many people probably purchase shares in these associations in anticipation of borrowing at a later time because loans are made only to members. Although cooperative businesses have never been particularly popular in America, it is anticipated that these mutual institutions will continue to increase in size and importance.

OTHER SAVINGS ALTERNATIVES

Many states allow businesses other than those just described to accept savings accounts. These companies are usually engaged in the consumer loan business and accept savings accounts from borrowers and others. Common names for these firms are "Thrift and Loan," "Consumer Thrift," "Credit Thrift," "Industrial Bank," and "Morris Plan Bank." From the standpoint of total dollars of deposits these institutions have very little importance. They are usually small in size and local in operation.

These organizations are state chartered and state regulated, usually by the state banking commissioner. Regulation and supervision vary with the state, but it is usually less intense than that imposed upon commercial banks. Industrial banks are eligible to join the FDIC and thereby obtain share insurance if they can meet the standards of membership. Insured banks would provide the depositor with the same safety as any other insured savings organization. Uninsured savings institutions are to be avoided in favor of those which are.

In recent years a substantial number of investment companies have developed investment programs which make ownership of their shares attractive to savers. These funds invest in bonds, money market instruments, and mortgages to provide the saver with returns potentially higher than could be obtained through savings deposits. These investments are discussed in Chapter 10.

Government securities have many characteristics that cause them to have appeal for savers. These investments will be examined in the next chapter.

Negotiable order of withdrawal (NOW) accounts. A *negotiable order of withdrawal* is a document which looks and acts much like a check in that it enables a person to make payment from an account to a third party. Legal differences between a checking and a NOW account are small. The practical difference is that interest may be paid on NOW accounts, while it cannot be paid on checking accounts. MSBs in Massachusetts and New Hampshire first received the right to offer these accounts in the early 1970s. The commercial banking community objected strenuously to NOW accounts and brought suits in state and federal courts to outlaw them. But MSBs are state chartered, and almost totally state regulated. These institutions are extremely important in many of the New England states where they have great political "clout." State regulations were changed or reinterpreted to allow NOW accounts in these states. In 1973 Congress passed legislation which gave federal sanction to NOW accounts issued by MSBs, S&Ls, and cooperative banks located in New Hampshire and Massachusetts.[7]

But commercial banks have not been idle. They have successfully petitioned the regulating authorities for the right to offer NOW accounts. More recently S&Ls and MSBs have been granted the right to offer checking accounts. And in 1978 commercial banks were granted the power to offer the automatic transfer accounts mentioned earlier.

---

[7] The Federal Reserve Bank of Boston monitors institutions offering NOW accounts. Information on these accounts is available by request from the Research Department of this bank.

These new services are not necessarily free. But the right to offer them has caused much more competition for savers' dollars among all financial institutions. It is expected that the trend toward less regulation of financial institutions will continue, and that competition will benefit savers in terms of more and better services and higher returns.

INVESTMENT CHARACTERISTICS OF SAVINGS ACCOUNTS

Low financial risk is the overriding characteristic of savings accounts. Safety comes both from insurance of accounts and from prudent reinvestment of savers' money. It is easy to determine whether a particular savings or banking institution offers insured savings accounts; it is difficult to tell how well savings are being reinvested. Because of the wide availability of insurance, and because uninsured accounts pay little if any additional interest, there is usually no reason to save except at an insured institution. Because of their low financial risk, savings account balances make excellent collateral. They may be easily "borrowed against" to provide ready cash.

Liquidity characteristics vary from the immediate liquidity offered by NOW accounts to the relative illiquidity of long-term certificate accounts. Certificate accounts usually may be redeemed before maturity, if one is willing to pay for this option by accepting a lowered interest return. Negotiable certificates of deposit are one of the most liquid of savings investments because they can be sold at a moment's notice. Liquidity of savings accounts is seldom a problem except when a savings institution suffers financial difficulties. If this occurs it is common for regulating authorities to "freeze" the assets and liabilities of the company until an audit can be performed. If the institution is insured, accounts will be made available in a short time. An uninsured institution might have to go through some sort of receivership proceeding before savings accounts or portions of accounts could be withdrawn. However, few banking or savings institutions fail.[8]

Purchasing power risk affects savings most adversely. Since interest returns are limited to whatever the institution pays, there is little pro-

---

[8] Liquidation or failure of a financial institution which holds savings does not necessarily mean that savers will lose money. A few of these institutions go out of business each year, are liquidated, and every creditor or owner of saving shares receives every dollar that is owed. In contrast to this, when a corporation is liquidated, it is usually liquidated because of bankruptcy. Creditors' claims may be satisfied, but common shareholders usually lose money.

tection against loss of purchasing power when inflation strikes. For example, during the ten-year period of 1968–1978 the consumer price index increased from 104.2 to 197.5. Over this time, $100 of savings placed in an account earning interest at six percent per annum would have increased in value to $179.08. The purchasing power of this amount in terms of 1968 prices was only $94.50 in 1978.

Savings accounts have little interest rate risk. Interest rates paid on savings accounts change as interest rates in general change, but more slowly. Changes in the market rate of interest do not affect the principal value of savings accounts, except those certificate accounts which are of fixed term and are negotiable. A negotiable CD which was issued to yield 7 percent would sell at a *discount* from its redemption value if market rates of interest on similar securities rose above this rate. It would sell at a *premium* if interest rates declined. The mechanics of the relationship between price and yield are discussed in the next chapter.

Market risk, or the uncertainty of future prices because of changes in investor attitudes, has little effect upon savings accounts because of their well-known safety. There is also very low political and social risk connected with these accounts. Savings accounts provide investors with a nearly ideal place to keep funds that might be needed on short notice—a personal liquidity reserve. Other investments, such as bonds, common stocks, real estate, and so on pay higher average yields. Most of the investor's funds will be used to purchase such assets.

SUMMARY

This chapter was an introduction to the most popular types of saving account investments. Yield and methods of computing yields were discussed first since these computations are common to all debt securities. The relationship of risk and return, first developed in Chapter 2, was applied to debt investments.

Savings investments in different financial institutions were next examined and compared one to another. The main thrust of this comparison was that (1) all insured accounts are nearly identically safe; (2) yield can be increased by investing in less liquid accounts—certificate or notice accounts; (3) the difference in yields between uninsured and insured institutions is not great enough to cause an investor to save at an uninsured institution; and (4) some savings institutions provide more services to depositors than others.

Investment characteristics of all savings accounts are low financial risk, low interest rate risk, good liquidity, and high purchasing power risk. Yields are lower than those available on nearly any other investment.

APPENDIX

Compound interest

The effects of compound interest are considerations which are of prime importance to most financial decisions. The compound interest formula is the basis for future value as well as present value calculations of all types. This formula is simple to derive and to use.

Assume that interest is paid at 6 percent per year on a $100 bank account. Interest is computed once at the end of the year, and the original principal and interest remain on deposits for two years.

Let

P = Principal, the amount on deposit.

i = Interest rate stated on a per annum basis.

n = Number of periods over which the principal is on deposit receiving interest.

$P_1, P_2, \ldots, P_n$ = Principal at end of 1st, 2d, . . . , nth periods.

$I_1, I_2, \ldots, I_n$ = Interest for 1st, 2nd, . . . , nth periods, respectively.

Then,

$$I_1 = P \times i = Pi \qquad\qquad \$100(0.06) \quad = \$6$$
$$P_1 = P + I_1 = P + Pi = P(1 + i) \qquad \$100 + \$6 \quad = \$106$$
$$I_2 = P_1 \times i = P(1 + i)i \qquad\qquad \$106(0.06) \quad = \$6.36$$
$$P_2 = P_1 + I_2 = P(1 + i) + P(1 + i)i \qquad \$106 + \$6.36 = \$112.36$$

Factoring $P(1 + i)$ from this equation,

$$P_2 = P(1 + i)\,(1 + i)$$
$$P_2 = P(1 + i)^2$$

The future value of P, for n periods of compounding interest at i interest rate is given by the general formula

$$P_n = P(1 + i)^n$$

Interest rates are usually stated as nominal annual rates, but interest is more often compounded semiannually, quarterly, daily, or continuously. An annual 6 percent rate of interest compounded semiannually would be compounded twice as many times per year at half the yearly interest rate.

$$P_n = P(1 + i/2)^{n \times 2}$$

This formula may be generalized. If t is the number of times per year that interest is compounded, then

$$P_n = P(1 + i/t)^{n \times t}$$

Compound interest tables have been published which give values of $(1 + i)^n$ for various rates of interest and compounding periods. Table 6–5 is a page from one of these tables. To solve the problem of what will be the value of $100 in two years if 6 percent annual interest is compounded semiannually, first determine i and n values. In this case $i = 0.06/2 = 0.03$, and $n = 2 \times 2 = 4$.

The table gives factors of $(1 + i)^n$ for values of $i = 1$ through $i = 20$ percent and n from 1 to 50 periods. Other tables cover different interest rates and time periods. To use this table to determine the value of $100 which has been compounded semiannually at an interest rate of 6 percent, simply locate the intersection of the n row and the i column. In this case the factor for $(1 + 0.03)^4$ is 1.1255.

The value of P_2 under the above conditions of compounding is

$$P_2 = \$100 \times 1.1255$$
$$= \$112.55$$

This amount is slightly larger than that obtained in the initial example due to the fact that the number of compounding periods has been doubled. The interest rate has been halved, from 6 to 3 percent, but the effect of the additional compounding periods outweighs the reduction in the compounding rate and results in a very slight increase in the true annual rate of interest over what it would have been under conditions of less compounding periods.

Many, perhaps most, financial institutions now calculate savings interest on a daily basis. The mathematics necessary for these calculations are no longer difficult because sophisticated calculators can easily handle the computations. Tables similar to Table 6–5 may also be used to calculate interest and principal amounts.

TABLE 6-5
Compound sum of $1.

Value of $1.00 n Periods Hence with Interest Rate i per Period

$$S(i, n) = (1 + i)^n$$

n	1%	2%	3%	4%	5%	6%	8%	10%	15%	20%
1	1.0100	1.0200	1.0300	1.0400	1.0500	1.0600	1.0800	1.100	1.150	1.200
2	1.0201	1.0404	1.0609	1.0816	1.1025	1.1236	1.166	1.210	1.322	1.440
3	1.0303	1.0612	1.0927	1.1249	1.1576	1.1910	1.260	1.331	1.521	1.728
4	1.0406	1.0824	1.1255	1.1699	1.2155	1.2625	1.360	1.464	1.749	2.074
5	1.0510	1.1041	1.1593	1.2167	1.2763	1.3382	1.469	1.611	2.011	2.488
6	1.0615	1.1262	1.1941	1.2653	1.3401	1.4185	1.587	1.772	2.313	2.986
7	1.0721	1.1487	1.2299	1.3159	1.4071	1.5036	1.714	1.949	2.660	3.583
8	1.0829	1.1717	1.2668	1.3686	1.4775	1.5938	1.851	2.144	3.059	4.300
9	1.0937	1.1951	1.3048	1.4233	1.5513	1.6895	1.999	2.358	3.518	5.160
10	1.1046	1.2190	1.3439	1.4802	1.6289	1.7908	2.159	2.594	4.046	6.192
11	1.1157	1.2434	1.3842	1.5395	1.7103	1.8983	2.332	2.853	4.652	7.430
12	1.1268	1.2682	1.4258	1.6010	1.7959	2.0122	2.518	3.138	5.350	8.916
13	1.1381	1.2936	1.4685	1.6651	1.8856	2.1329	2.720	3.452	6.153	10.699
14	1.1495	1.3195	1.5126	1.7317	1.9799	2.2609	2.937	3.797	7.076	12.839
15	1.1610	1.3459	1.5580	1.8009	2.0789	2.3966	3.172	4.177	8.137	15.407
16	1.1726	1.3728	1.6047	1.8730	2.1829	2.5404	3.426	4.595	9.358	18.488
17	1.1843	1.4002	1.6528	1.9479	2.2920	2.6928	3.700	5.054	10.761	22.186
18	1.1961	1.4282	1.7024	2.0258	2.4066	2.8543	3.996	5.560	12.375	26.623
19	1.2081	1.4568	1.7535	2.1068	2.5270	3.0256	4.316	6.116	14.232	31.948
20	1.2202	1.4859	1.8061	2.1911	2.6533	3.2071	4.661	6.727	16.367	38.338
21	1.2324	1.5157	1.8603	2.2788	2.7860	3.3996	5.034	7.400	18.821	46.005
22	1.2447	1.5460	1.9161	2.3699	2.9253	3.6035	5.437	8.140	21.645	55.206
23	1.2572	1.5769	1.9736	2.4647	3.0715	3.8197	5.871	8.954	24.891	66.247
24	1.2697	1.6084	2.0328	2.5633	3.2251	4.0489	6.341	9.850	28.625	79.497
25	1.2824	1.6406	2.0938	2.6658	3.3864	4.2919	6.848	10.835	32.919	95.396
26	1.2953	1.6734	2.1566	2.7725	3.5557	4.5494	7.396	11.918	37.857	114.475
27	1.3082	1.7069	2.2213	2.8834	3.7335	4.8223	7.988	13.110	43.535	137.370
28	1.3213	1.7410	2.2879	2.9987	3.9201	5.1117	8.627	14.421	50.065	164.845
29	1.3345	1.7758	2.3566	3.1187	4.1161	5.4184	9.317	15.863	57.575	197.813
30	1.3478	1.8114	2.4273	3.2434	4.3219	5.7435	10.063	17.449	66.212	237.376
35	1.4166	1.9999	2.8139	3.9461	5.5160	7.6861	14.785	28.102	133.175	590.668
40	1.4889	2.2080	3.2620	4.8010	7.0400	10.2857	21.725	45.259	267.862	1469.771
45	1.5648	2.4379	3.7816	5.8412	8.9850	13.7646	31.920	72.890	538.767	3657.258
50	1.6446	2.6916	4.3839	7.1067	11.4674	18.4202	46.902	117.391	1083.652	9100.427

Assuming the same nominal interest rate, increasing the number of compounding periods increases the *effective* yearly interest rate. The effective rate is determined by dividing the amount of interest received over one year by the amount of principal available at the first of the year. Most financial institutions include the nominal rate, the compounding period, and the effective rate in their advertisements. "Five percent annual interest compounded daily, for an effective savings rate of 5.127 percent per year."

Continuous compounding results in the highest effective yield. This form of compounding assumes that interest is being added to principal continuously—an infinite number of calculations. It is beyond the scope of this text to derive the continuous compounding formula, which is

$$P_t = P \, e^{i \times t}$$

P and *i* mean the same as before. The symbol *t* refers to the number of years over which compounding takes place. The symbol *e* is the irrational number which provides the basis for our system of natural logarithms. This number is 2.71828 calculated to six places, which provides sufficient accuracy for most financial problems. Continuous compounding of $100 at a nominal interest rate of 6 percent for two years would be calculated as follows:

$$P_2 = \$100 \times 2.71828^{.06 \times 2}$$
$$= \$112.75$$

This is an amount slightly greater than that produced in the prior example. Other things being equal, continuous compounding always produces the highest effective interest rate. Table 6–6 lists the future values of $100 of principal placed on interest at a nominal rate of 6

TABLE 6–6
Future values of $100 at different points in time, calculated at 6 percent nominal interest by different methods

Years	Annual compounding	Semiannual compounding	Daily compounding	Continuous compounding
0	$ 100.00	$ 100.00	$ 100.00	$ 100.00
1	106.00	106.09	106.18	106.18
5	133.82	134.39	134.98	134.99
10	179.08	180.61	182.20	182.21
20	320.71	326.20	331.98	332.01
50	1,842.02	1,921.86	2,008.07	2,008.55

percent for various periods of time under several compounding methods.

PROBLEMS

1. What are the current rates of interest being paid on savings deposits of various types? (Obtain this information from local savings institutions.) Considering all investment characteristics, which account offers the best combination of risk and return?
2. How much interest would be received over a one-year period on a $1,000 deposit under the following conditions?
    a. Interest is paid once at the end of the year at a rate of 6 percent.
    b. Interest is compounded semiannually and paid at the end of the year at a rate of 6 percent.
3. What is the future value of $100 invested as follows?
    a. $100 invested at 10 percent, interest compounded annually for ten years.
    b. $100 invested at 20 percent per annum compounded semiannually for six years.
4. You have the choice of saving $100 at a bank which offers interest of 4 percent compounded annually, or at a savings and loan company which pays interest at a rate of 4 percent compounded quarterly. How much interest will accumulate on these deposits in five years if no interest or principal is withdrawn?
5. A bank that originally paid 6 percent interest compounded annually on all savings accounts is considering daily compounding of interest. How much *additional interest* would be paid during the first year on each $100 of savings deposits if the 6 percent nominal rate is continued but interest is compounded daily? (Use a 365-day year.)

QUESTIONS

1. What are the main differences between *time deposits* and *demand deposits*?
2. How do savings and loan companies differ from commercial banks so far as safety, liquidity, and convenience are concerned? Adopt the viewpoint of a depositor.
3. What are the most important investment characteristics of savings accounts?
4. As a saver, which of the institutions described in this chapter has the most appeal to you? Why?
5. Credit unions are usually seen as being less safe places to save than commercial banks. Is this a justified criticism?

6. From the viewpoint of a saver, what are the advantages to be obtained from saving in a stock S&L rather than a mutual one?

7. Your rich uncle has given you $3,000 toward the purchase of a car under this agreement: The money may not be spent before your graduation from college in two years, and it must be placed in a savings account until spent. Which type of account in which savings institution would you choose? Why?

8. What are NOW accounts? How do they aid savers?

9. What are *grace days*? How do they aid savers?

10. "All banks pay the same time deposit rates. It does no good to shop around for the best deal." True or false? Discuss.

11. What is the difference between the *nominal* and the *effective* interest rate?

SELECTED READINGS

"Early History and Initial Impact of NOW ACCOUNTS." *New England Economic Review.* Published by the Federal Reserve Bank of Boston, January–February 1975.

"Finance Facts Yearbook." Washington, D.C.: National Consumer Finance Association, published yearly, free upon request.

"International Credit Union Yearbook." Madison, Wis.: CUNA International, published yearly, free upon request.

Meyer, Martin J., and McDaniel, Joseph M., Jr. *Don't Bank on It.* Lynbrook, N.Y.: Farnsworth Publishing, 1970.

"National Fact Book of Mutual Saving Banking." New York: National Association of Mutual Savings Banks, published yearly, free upon request.

"Savings and Loan Fact Book." Chicago: U.S. Savings and Loan League, published yearly, free upon request.

Investing in debt securities

INTRODUCTION

Debt security investments make up about $1 out of each $8 which individuals hold in the form of financial assets. These investments are of less importance than savings accounts or corporate stock but are more important than any other type of financial asset.

The nature of debt contracts

Debt contracts take many forms—bonds, notes, and bills being the principal types of debt contracts. These contracts differ in many ways, but they have several common characteristics. In all cases, one party lends money to another and is compensated for the loan by payment of interest from the borrower. Usually the principal of the loan (the par value of debt securities) must be repaid in total at a certain time.

Debt security investments are much more formal than the savings deposit agreement one has with a bank or other financial institution. Additional formality is necessary because the agreement is usually expected to last for many years. While savings may be left with a single financial institution for an equally long period of time, the agreement between the institution and the depositor can usually be changed at the option of either party upon suitable notice. Owners of debt contracts are usually prohibited from redeeming these securities before they mature or before the issuer wishes to retire them. Liquidity is provided by selling the security to another party. Very few bonds, except privately placed issues and U. S. savings bonds, are held until maturity by the person who originally acquired them.

Because of the long-term nature of bond contracts, and because the final owners of these investments may not have purchased them originally, every aspect of the debt agreement is set down in a carefully worded statement which is legally binding on the borrower. This statement, the bond *indenture,* lists each and every thing that the issuer promises to do. The indenture remains in effect until the bonds are matured, retired, or modified. Anyone purchasing a bond, whether it be purchased from the issuer or from another party, receives all the protection and benefits that are described in the indenture. Some bond indentures carry provisions which allow certain parts of the indenture to be changed if a minimum proportion of the bondholders—commonly two-thirds or three-fourths—agree to the change.

Federal, state, and local statutes exist to outline the types of bond agreements that these governments and other issuing agencies can enter into. Statutes serve the same purpose for these instruments as indentures do for privately issued bonds—they outline the liability of the issuer. Government issued securities have fairly uniform characteristics, although there are many different instruments. Corporations are not nearly so restricted in the types of debt agreements they may make. Corporate bond indentures are very complex, written in legal terminology, and difficult for the average person to interpret. The typical owner of a corporate bond cannot read the bond indenture with enough understanding to tell whether or not the corporation is meeting its obligations as they are stated in the indenture. For this reason the corporation appoints a *trustee* (usually a bank or other large financial institution) to oversee that the corporation is meeting the conditions set forth in the indenture. Should the corporation fail to live up to the indenture agreement, the trustee will bring legal action to protect the interests of bondholders. The trustee may also handle the payment of bond interest and the recording of ownership of the securities, but the *transfer agent* often does this.

Bond owners may obtain a copy of the indenture if they desire one. However, the main features of the bond issue are contained in the *prospectus,* which is provided to all original purchasers of securities. People buying bonds in secondary markets usually obtain information of the type contained in the indenture from financial reporting services such as Moody's or Standard & Poor's.

Ownership—registered and bearer securities

Names and addresses of the current owners of *registered securities* are recorded by the trustee or transfer agent. The owner's name is written on the face of the security and interest payments are mailed to the registered owner.[1] When these securities are sold they must be returned to the appropriate office so that the new owner's name and address can be recorded.

Bearer securities are not registered. The issuer has no record of who owns them, and the rightful owner is presumed to be the person holding them. Interest may be discounted, as it is for U.S. Treasury bills and Series E and EE savings bonds, or it may be paid by coupon. Debt securities paying discounted interest sell for less than their maturity values. The difference between the two amounts is interest. Securities paying coupon interest have attached coupons which entitle owners to receive an interest payment each time one of the coupons becomes due and payable.

Corporate securities are almost all registered. Most government issued securities are bearer securities. A few issues are registered as to principal but pay interest through coupons.

CLASSIFICATION AND IDENTIFICATION OF DEBT SECURITIES

There are a bewildering variety of debt securities. They may be classified and identified in several ways. The most usual method of doing this is on the basis of *issuer* and *security*. The issuer, of course, is the organization which originally sold the security. Security refers to either the collateral behind the bond or the source of payment of interest and repayment of principal. The outline presented below is designed to classify debt securities by these characteristics, but it should be understood that classification by other characteristics (maturity, legal standing, grade, taxability of interest, and so on) is both proper and common.

Classification of Debt Securities

I. By issuer
    A. Securities issued by governments
        1. Treasury securities

---

[1] Bonds and other securities left at a brokerage house are usually registered in the name of the brokerage company. Interest payments are sent to the broker who credits the payment to its true owner.

      2. Agency securities

      3. Municipals

          a. Full faith and credit bonds

          b. Revenue bonds

          c. Assessment bonds

  B. Securities issued by corporations

      1. Utilities

      2. Railroads

      3. Industrials

II. By security or source of repayment

  A. Mortgage bonds

  B. Collateral trust bonds

  C. Debenture bonds

  D. Equipment trust certificates

  E. Guaranteed bonds (including joint bonds)

  F. Income bonds

Classification by issuer

Government issued debt securities have three major subclassifications: *Governments* or *treasuries* are those issued directly by the U.S. Treasury; agency securities, usually referred to as *agencies*, are issued by such federal organizations as the Federal Home Loan Bank, the Federal National Mortgage Association, the Federal Land Bank, and other federal agencies. State and local government bonds are called *municipals* whether they are issued by a state, a city, a sewer district, or some other taxing district or agency. The general term *corporates* refers to any bond issued by a private corporation. *Utilities, railroads,* and *industrials* are easily identified sub-classifications.

Classification by security or source of repayment

Governments. The security behind the debt of governments is the willingness and ability of the issuer to pay interest and principal when due. Specific assets are almost never pledged as collateral for federal securities. Interest payments and repayment of principal on this type debt are usually made from general tax revenues.

Municipals. State and municipal bonds are usually classified as being *full faith and credit bonds, revenue bonds, assessment bonds,* or combinations of these three. Full faith and credit bonds are those which are unconditionally backed by the full taxing power of the issuer. These securities are usually the most highly regarded of the municipals because payment for these bonds may come from many different tax sources. Full faith and credit bonds seldom go into default.

Payments for revenue bonds come from the income generated by the facility which was paid for by the issuance of the bonds. Examples of such facilities are toll roads, toll bridges, municipal waterworks, transit systems, electric power departments, pollution control facilities, and other state and municipally owned enterprises. The usual procedure is for the issuing agency to build the facility and to charge fees for its use. The fees provide the revenue for the agency to pay off the debt incurred in financing it. Often the borrowing agency is granted a monopoly in offering this particular service, such as a toll bridge, transit system, or a utility distribution system. Occasionally the revenue from one of these projects is not adequate to satisfy the claims of the bondholders, but on the whole these securities have very little financial risk.

Assessment bonds are issued to finance the costs of improvements such as sewers, streets and sidewalks. Voters direct the assessment district to make the designated improvements. Charges—assessments—are then levied against the property owners of the district to pay for this debt. Of the three types of municipal bonds discussed in this chapter, these are the most risky. Even here the risk of nonpayment of interest or principal is very low.

Corporates. Interest and principal payments on corporate debt normally come from the income of the company . Corporate bonds are commonly identified by the security that is pledged against the bond, even though bondholders seldom anticipate that they will have cause to take over the security.

Mortgage bonds are securities which are backed by real property— land or buildings or both. Mortgage bonds were once thought to be the safest of all corporate securities because in case of default one could always obtain the real assets which were pledged as collateral for the bonds. In theory this was correct. However, in some instances bondholders who took over the collateral of defaulted issues found that the property which they received did not have as much value as it had when it was being used by the company which issued the bonds.

On the other hand, while the mortgaged property may have little value for the bondholder, it often is necessary to the operation of the business. Consequently, corporations usually do everything possible to keep mortgage bonds from going into default because the bondholders may then claim a specific piece of property which the company must control in order to operate.

Collateral trust bonds are backed by collateral—bonds or other securities. Collateral is often the bonds or common stock of subsidiary corporations, or sometimes it is the security investments of the company issuing the bonds. The market value of the collateral is of importance because this asset can easily be taken over by bondholders in case of default. It is usually more marketable than real estate or other fixed assets, and its market value is usually more easily determined.

Debenture bonds have no specific assets pledged as collateral. Bond owners are classified as general creditors of the company and have as collateral for their debt all the assets of the company not already pledged. All Treasury, agency, and most municipal bonds are debentures. The largest and most financially sound corporations often issue these bonds because their debt is so secure that there is no reason to pledge specific assets against it. Weaker companies may sell debentures because they have no assets which they can pledge. It is impossible to judge whether a bond is secure solely on the basis of whether it is a debenture.

Subordinated debentures are debenture bonds which hold a creditor position *beneath* that of general and other specified senior creditors. Many of the subordinated debentures currently issued are convertible into the common stock of the issuing company. Subordinated debentures are sometimes issued by companies which have recapitalized due to bankruptcy. These securities may contain substantial amounts of financial risk.

Equipment trust certificates are unique securities which are designed to allow companies having poor credit ratings to borrow at low rates of interest. Security for this obligation is personal property—a piece of equipment of some type. Railroads and airlines make heavy use of these securities. The unique ingredient of this financing device is that the collateral has a known value and a wide market. These debt instruments usually have low financial risk.

Guaranteed bonds, as their name implies, are debt securities which are backed by another party. All agency securities are implicitly guaranteed by the federal government in that the federal government would probably never allow an agency issue to default. Strong corporations often guarantee the securities of their lesser known subsidiaries so that the credit rating of the second company is higher. Such securities are becoming more common as larger companies acquire control over smaller firms.

Joint bonds are issued and guaranteed by two or more companies. They are often used to finance construction of commonly used facilities—railroad terminals, docks, and so on.

Interest on *income bonds* is paid only if the company has income sufficient to make the payment. Such securities are usually created when a company is reorganized. Holders of senior debt securities are then given income bonds, which have a lower claim on the company's income, so that the reorganized company can issue new senior debt securities. Interest payments that are passed do not usually become liabilities of the company.

Figure 7–1 is a picture of a bond issued by Bell Telephone Company of Pennsylvania. It is a debenture bond, paying semiannual interest of 8⅝ percent per annum. The bond is registered in the name of the owner, and interest payments are mailed by the company to this person. In case of loss or destruction, registered securities are much easier to replace than bearer securities since the company has no knowledge of who the bearer (owner) is. This bond was issued July 1, 1970, and matures in 36 years.

Notes and bills

Notes and bills are not bonds. They have many of the characteristics of bonds, but their maturities are usually shorter. The traditional definition of a bond is a debt security having an original maturity of at least five years.

The largest classification of nonbond debt is notes of one type or another. Businesses and individuals issue notes, which are simply promises to pay a stated sum of money at a specified future date. Few of these ever come into the possession of the average investor, however, because they are usually payable to banks or other businesses. The U.S. Treasury had outstanding nearly $266 billion of notes at the beginning of 1979. Maturities of these securities ranged from one to nine years. Notes having the longest maturities might well be confused with bonds since the main difference between them and bonds is their name. These securities pay interest periodically and are freely negotiable. They may be registered at the option of the owner. Individuals hold substantial amounts of them.

FIGURE 7-1
Bell Telephone Company of Pennsylvania bond

DOLLARS 1,000

No.

THE BELL TELEPHONE COMPANY OF PENNSYLVANIA

THIRTY-SIX YEAR 8⅝% DEBENTURE, DUE JULY 1, 2006

8⅝%
2006

The Bell Telephone Company of Pennsylvania,
a Pennsylvania corporation (herein referred to as the Company), for value received, hereby promises to pay to

SPECIMEN

registered assigns, at the office or agency of the Company in the Borough of Manhattan, The City of New York, State of New York,
the principal sum of

ONE THOUSAND DOLLARS

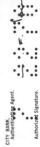

SEE REVERSE AS TO
ABBREVIATIONS

8⅝%
2006

CUSIP 078167 AK 9

on July 1, 2006, in such coin or currency of the United States of America as at the time of payment shall be legal tender for the payment of public and private debts, and to pay interest, semi-annually on January 1 and July 1, on said principal sum at the rate per annum specified in the title of this Debenture, at said office or agency, in like coin or currency, from the first day of January or July, as the case may be, to which interest on Debentures has been paid preceding the date hereof (unless the date hereof is a January 1 or July 1 to which interest has been paid, in which case from the date hereof, or unless the date hereof is prior to the first payment of interest, in which case from July 1, 1970) until payment of said principal sum has been made or duly provided for. Notwithstanding the foregoing, unless this Debenture shall be authenticated at a time when there is an existing default in the payment of interest on the Debentures, if the date hereof is after December 15 and before the next following January 1 or is after June 15 and before the next following July 1, this Debenture shall bear interest from such January 1 or July 1 provided, however, that if the Company shall default in the payment of interest due on such January 1 or July 1, then this Debenture shall bear interest from the next preceding July 1 or January 1, as the case may be. The interest so payable on any January 1 or July 1 will, subject to certain exceptions provided in the Indenture referred to on the reverse hereof, be paid to the person in whose name this Debenture shall be registered at the close of business on the December 15 prior to such January 1 or the June 15 prior to such July 1, whether or not such December 15 or June 15 shall be a business day.

This Debenture shall not be valid or become obligatory for any purpose until the appropriate certificate of authentication hereon shall have been executed by or on behalf of the Trustee under the Indenture referred to on the reverse hereof.

This Debenture is one of a duly authorized issue of Debentures of the Company and is subject to all of the provisions of this Indenture and such further provisions set forth on the reverse hereof, all of which provisions have the same effect as though fully set forth at this place.

In Witness Whereof, The Bell Telephone Company of Pennsylvania has caused this Debenture to be signed by its President or one of its Vice Presidents and by its Treasurer or an Assistant Treasurer, each by a facsimile of his signature, and has caused a facsimile of its corporate seal to be affixed hereunto or imprinted hereon.

The Bell Telephone Company of Pennsylvania,

By R.W. Wise
President.

By ....
Treasurer.

DATED

CERTIFICATE OF AUTHENTICATION
This is one of the Debentures described in the within-mentioned Indenture.
THE UNION NATIONAL BANK OF PITTSBURGH,
as Trustee.

By ....
Authorized Officer.

ALTERNATE CERTIFICATE OF AUTHENTICATION
This is one of the Debentures described within.
THE UNION NATIONAL BANK OF PITTSBURGH,
as Trustee.

By ....
FIRST NATIONAL CITY BANK,
Authenticating Agent.

By ....
Authorized Signature.

FIRST NATIONAL CITY BANK (NEW YORK, N. Y.) HAS BEEN DESIGNATED AS THE AGENCY FOR TRANSFER, EXCHANGE AND PAYMENT

FEDERATED-BARNETT COMPANY

Treasury bills are discount securities having maturities of one year or less. Almost $162 billion of these securities were outstanding at the beginning of 1979. Treasury bills are auctioned each week through the Federal Reserve banks and are purchased by investors seeking the ultimate in financial safety and liquidity. The minimum purchase of these securities is $10,000, and all are bearer instruments. The most popular maturities are three and six months, although there are occasional issues of shorter or longer maturity. Some businesses issue securities with very short maturities (commercial paper), but these are usually sold only in very large dollar amounts. They are seldom purchased by individuals. Price quotes of corporate bonds and Treasury securities appear as Figure 4–4 in Chapter 4.

Savings bonds

Since 1941 the U.S. Treasury has offered two series of bonds for sale to U.S. citizens and U.S. residents. Series E was a discount security which like a Treasury bill matured at a higher price than its purchase price. The difference between the two values represented interest earned on the security. Series H bonds were more conventional. They paid interest semiannually at a fixed rate. At the beginning of 1979, $72.537 billion of Series E and $8.322 billion of Series H bonds were outstanding.

The Treasury ceased selling these bonds at year-end 1979, replacing them with two similar issues designated as Series EE and HH. Series EE bonds are sold in face value (maturity value) amounts of $50, $75, $100, $200, $500, $1,000, $5,000, and $10,000. Their issue cost is one-half the maturity value: $25 for the $50 bond, $37.50 for the $75 bond, and so on. Securities mature in 11 years and 9 months from date of issue. They provide low yields in early years which increase to 6 percent if held for 5 or more years. These bonds are not eligible for redemption until 6 months after their purchase. They may be traded for Series HH bonds in multiples of $500 face value.

Series HH bonds pay interest semiannually at a rate of 6 percent of face value if held to maturity. Interest payments are made by check. Series HH bonds have 10-year maturities with no promise of extension at this time. However, series E and H bonds continued to draw interest at 6 percent after maturity, and it is possible that this privilege will later be extended to the new series of these securities. Denominations of Series HH bonds are $500, $1,000, $5,000, and $10,000. Up to $20,000 face amount of Series HH bonds and $15,000 of issue price of Series EE bonds may be purchased by any single investor in any one year.

Savings bonds are sold only in fully registered form and cannot be sold to a third party or used as collateral for a loan. Their market value is always the current redemption value. Regardless of what happens to market rates of interest, these securities always have a known value. Investment characteristics of savings bonds closely resemble those of certificate accounts of savings institutions.

The investor has a choice of when taxes are paid on Series E and Series EE bond interest. The total tax may be paid when the security is redeemed, or taxes may be paid annually on the amount of interest which accrues each year. Taxes on the income of these securities may be deferred for many years, as described in Chapter 15.

GRADING DEBT SECURITIES

The *grade* of a debt security refers to the likelihood that the issuer will be able to make the interest and principal payments called for in the bond indenture or other debt financing agreement. It is a measure of financial risk. U.S. Treasury securities are rated highest of any securities because of the ability of the federal government to print money and levy taxes to make payments. Other borrowers, whether they be states, local governments, or corporations, do not have the same authorizations. There is usually some risk, however small, that the issuer of these bonds will not be able to live up to the contract which was made with the purchasers. Financial analysts measure this risk. They indicate their assessment of its amount by assigning a grade to each individual issue of the publicly traded bonds of better known corporations and state and local governments.

The degree of risk is seen as being determined mainly by the amount and constancy of the issuer's income or tax revenue. The key relationship in this analysis is the ratio of the amount of funds available to pay interest to the amount which is required. This measure is called the *times interest earned* ratio or the *interest coverage* ratio.

Although there are several ways to calculate this ratio, in the case of corporate securities the preferred method is to divide the company's earnings before taxes and interest by the amount of interest payments.[2] A company having earnings before taxes of $25 million and $5 million of interest payments would have an interest coverage ratio of six-to-one calculated as follows:

$$\text{Interest coverage ratio} = \frac{\text{Earnings before taxes} + \text{Interest cost}}{\text{Interest cost}}$$

$$= \frac{\$25,000,000 + \$5,000,000}{\$5,000,000}$$

$$= 6$$

When interpreting coverage ratios, analysts examine the issuer's past earnings patterns and attempt to forecast future earnings. Companies with consistent earnings and taxing authorities with reliable tax revenue may have lower coverage ratios than other debt issuers but still have high-graded bonds. For example, an electric utility with stable income could have high-rated bonds with a coverage ratio as low as two or three to one. Another company, one having more variability in its earnings, might need a coverage ratio of five- or six-to-one to attain the same rating. Rating of bonds is done by the companies which publish financial information for the investment community. Moody's, Standard & Poor's, and Fitch Investors Service ratings are probably the most widely used, although several other companies publish their own bond ratings.[3] The descriptions of ratings in Figure 7-2 are indicative of what the rating services look to when devising a specific rating for a bond issue.

Treasury bonds are not graded. They are the standard against which all corporate and municipal bonds are measured. The grade of corporate and municipal bonds may change after the security has been

---

[2] The situation is complicated when more than one issue of bonds is outstanding. If all issues have the same security and are equal in other legal aspects all interest costs are added together and a ratio is calculated on this basis. This is known as the *overall method*. If one issue is clearly superior it is common practice to calculate a separate coverage ratio for this issue first. The interest on junior issues is then added to that of the senior issue and a new ratio is calculated. This ratio will always be smaller than the first ratio, of course, and will indicate that junior issues are less well covered. This is known as the *cumulative deductions method*.

[3] Moody's uses the symbols Aaa, Baa, and so on, for their ratings; Standard & Poor's and Fitch use AAA, BBB, and the like. The grades identified by the three companies are for all practical purposes identical within classes.

FIGURE 7–2
Standard & Poor's bond rating system

STANDARD & POOR'S Corporate and Municipal Bond Rating Definitions

A Standard & Poor's corporate or municipal bond rating is a current assessment of the creditworthiness of an obligor with respect to a specific debt obligation. This assessment may take into consideration obligors such as guarantors, insurers, or lessees.

The bond rating is not a recommendation to purchase, sell or hold a security, inasmuch as it does not comment as to market price or suitability for a particular investor.

The ratings are based on current information furnished by the issuer or obtained by Standard & Poor's from other sources it considers reliable. Standard & Poor's does not perform any audit in connection with any rating and may, on occasion, rely on unaudited financial information. The ratings may be changed, suspended or withdrawn as a result of changes in, or unavailability of, such information, or for other circumstances.

The ratings are based, in varying degrees, on the following considerations:

I. Likelihood of default–capacity and willingness of the obligor as to the timely payment of interest and repayment of principal in accordance with the terms of the obligation;

II. Nature of and provisions of the obligation;

III. Protection afforded by, and relative position of, the obligation in the event of bankruptcy, reorganization or other arrangement under the laws of bankruptcy and other laws affecting creditors' rights.

AAA Bonds rated AAA have the highest rating assigned by Standard & Poor's to a debt obligation. Capacity to pay interest and repay principal is extremely strong.

AA Bonds rated AA have a very strong capacity to pay interest and repay principal and differ from the highest rated issues only in small degree.

A Bonds rated A have a strong capacity to pay interest and repay principal although they are somewhat more susceptible to the adverse effects of changes in circumstances and economic conditions than bonds in higher rated categories.

BBB Bonds rated BBB are regarded as having an adequate capacity to pay interest and repay principal. Whereas they normally exhibit adequate protection parameters, adverse economic conditions or changing circumstances are more likely to lead to a weakened capacity to pay interest and repay principal for bonds in this category than for bonds in higher rated categories.

BB, B, CCC, CC Bonds rated BB, B, CCC and CC are regarded, on balance, as predominantly speculative with respect to capacity to pay interest and repay principal in accordance with the terms of the obligation. BB indicates the lowest degree of speculation and CC the highest degree of speculation. While such bonds will likely have some quality and protective characteristics, these are outweighed by large uncertainties or major risk exposures to adverse conditions.

C The rating C is reserved for income bonds on which no interest is being paid.

D Bonds rated D are in default, and payment of interest and/or repayment of principal is in arrears.

Plus (+) or Minus (–): The ratings from "AA" to "BB" may be modified by the addition of a plus or minus sign to show relative standing within the major rating categories.

Provisional Ratings: The letter "p" indicates that the rating is provisional. A provisional rating assumes the successful completion of the project being financed by the bonds being rated and indicates that payment of debt service requirements is largely or entirely dependent upon the successful and timely completion of the project. This rating, however, while addressing credit quality subsequent to completion of the project, makes no comment on the likelihood of, or the risk of default upon failure of, such completion. The investor should exercise his own judgment with respect to such likelihood and risk.

NR indicates that no rating has been requested, that there is insufficient information on which to base a rating, or that S&P does not rate a particular type of obligation as a matter of policy.

Debt Obligations of issuers outside the United States and its territories are rated on the same basis as domestic corporate and municipal issues. The ratings measure the creditworthiness of the obligor but do not take into account currency exchange and other uncertainties.

Bond Investment Quality Standards: Under present commercial bank regulations issued by the Comptroller of the Currency, bonds rated in the top four categories (AAA, AA, A, BBB, commonly known as "Investment Grade" ratings) are generally regarded as eligible for bank investment. In addition, the Legal Investment Laws of various states impose certain rating or other standards for obligations eligible for investment by savings banks, trust companies, insurance companies and fiduciaries generally.

Standard & Poor's does not act as a financial advisor to any issuer in connection with any corporate or municipal debt financing. Standard & Poor's receives compensation for rating debt obligations. Such compensation is based on the time and effort to determine the rating and is normally paid either by the issuers of such securities or by the underwriters participating in the distribution thereof. The fees generally vary from $1,000 to $10,000 for municipal securities, and from $500 to $15,000 for corporate securities. While Standard & Poor's reserves the right to disseminate the rating, it receives no payment for doing so, except for subscriptions to its publications.

Source: Standard & Poor's *Bond Guide,* New York. (This statement and additional information about ratings is contained in each monthly issue of the *Bond Guide.*)

sold, due to changes in the financial condition of the issuer. Changes in grade are important to investors because there is a definite relationship between the grade of a bond and its yield.

The relationship between bond rating and yield

As financial risk rises, it is logical that a purchaser of a fixed income security would demand a higher return from the investment to offset the additional risk. This is in fact what happens. At any point in time, the yield of a Baa rated security will be higher than the yield of an Aaa security of similar maturity. As the market rate of interest moves up and down over time in response to the supply of and demand for credit, the yields of the different grades of securities will *all* move up and down. Figure 7–3 shows this relationship clearly.

A somewhat closer viewing of Figure 7–3 indicates that at certain times the relationship between the different grades of securities changes. For example, the spread between long-term Treasury bonds

FIGURE 7–3 Long-term bond yields (quarterly averages)

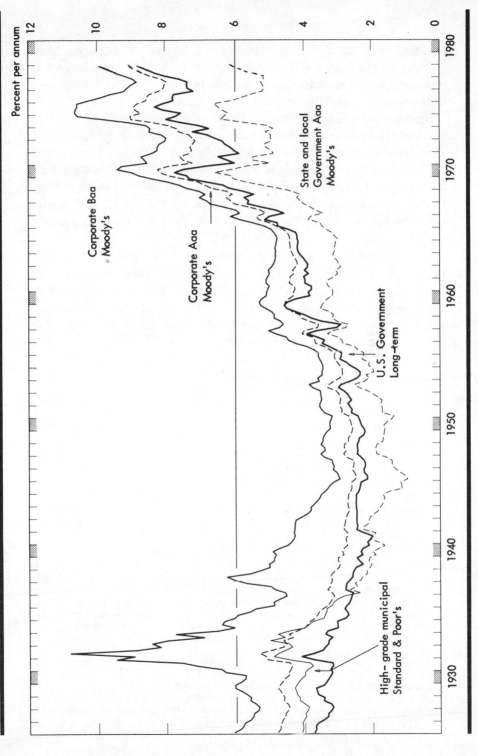

Source: Board of Governors of the Federal Reserve System, *Historical Chart Book*, 1978, p. 97.

and Baa rated corporate bonds averaged 107 basis points during 1962. During 1965, this spread declined to about 66 basis points. In 1975 it averaged an exceptional 270 basis points.[4] By 1979 the spread was more normal at slightly over 100 basis points.

Historically, the spread in yield between different grades of bonds is greatest when interest rates are rising rapidly and least when interest rates have been constant for some time. Persons who make their living by managing large portfolios of bonds are aware of these relationships and often follow an investment strategy which calls for them to shift from one grade of bonds to another when the basis point differential between the two issues becomes more than or less than a predetermined amount.

Characteristics other than grade which influence the yield of a given debt security include coupon rate, maturity date, call provisions, sinking fund provisions, convertibility, legality for investment, and amount outstanding. However, it is the grade that most strongly determines yield because financial risk is the most important consideration for most persons investing in debt securities.

REPAYMENT OF BONDS

A unique feature of debt is that it must someday be repaid.[5] When bonds are to be repaid and how the repayment is to be financed are of importance to the owner of debt securities.

Callable bonds

Most corporate bonds and some Treasury and state and local bonds have a feature which allows the issuer to redeem the bond before the

---

[4] A basis point is one one-hundredth of a percentage point. The difference between a yield of 3 percent and a yield of 4 percent is therefore 100 basis points.

[5] This statement is not completely true. There are several examples of debt securities which have been issued with no maturity date. It is expected that these securities will remain outstanding indefinitely. The British government has issued these bonds, called perpetuals, and several private corporations have also issued them. Other bonds have maturity dates so far in the future that they certainly must have seemed to be perpetual bonds to their original purchasers. The New York Central 4½s series A of 2007, issued in 1913; the Missouri Pacific General Income B 4¾s of 2030, issued in 1956; and the Duquesne Light Company Debenture 5s of 2010, issued in 1960 are examples of bonds with extremely long maturities. The dollar amount of bonds having maturities of 50 years and over is much larger than the dollar amount of perpetual bonds which have been issued. The amounts of both are small when compared to the amounts of shorter term bonds.

stated maturity date of the security. This feature is known as *callability*, and it means that the issuer may redeem the bond at any time after a certain date, up to the maturity date of the security. It can be assumed that the bond will not be called unless it is advantageous for the issuer to do so. And if it is advantageous to the issuer, it is usually not desirable for the security owner. Inclusion of a call feature in a debt contract tends to raise the interest rate buyers require because these securities are less attractive as investments.

Call protection and a *call premium* are granted to make callable bonds more salable at lower yields. Call protection simply means that the company issuing the securities agrees not to call them until a certain time period has elapsed *after* their issue. Most nonconvertible bonds have five to ten years of call protection.

The call premium provides the owner of a called bond with extra

TABLE 7–1

Call premium schedule of The Southland Corporation 9¾ percent Sinking Fund Debentures due 2003

Redemption
The Debentures may be redeemed, at the option of the Company, as a whole or in part at any time on at least 30 days' notice at the following redemption prices if redeemed during the twelve months' period beginning December 15, in each of the following years:

Year	Percentage of principal amount	Year	Percentage of principal amount
1978	109.125%	1990	103.650%
1979	108.669	1991	103.194
1980	108.213	1992	102.738
1981	107.756	1993	102.281
1982	107.300	1994	101.825
1983	106.844	1995	101.369
1984	106.388	1996	100.913
1985	105.931	1997	100.456
1986	105.475	1998	100.000
1987	105.019	1999	100.000
1988	104.563	2000	100.000
1989	104.106	2001	100.000
		2002	100.000

together in each case with interest accrued to the date fixed for redemption. Notwithstanding the foregoing provisions, the Company may not exercise its option to redeem any of the Debentures prior to December 15, 1988, directly or indirectly, from or in anticipation of moneys borrowed on indebtedness which shall have an interest cost to the Company of less than 9.40% per annum. If less than all the Debentures are redeemed, the Trustee shall select, in such manner as it shall deem appropriate and fair in its discretion, the particular Debentures to be redeemed. (Sections 3.01 and 3.02.)

Source: The Southland Corporation, *Prospectus*, December 13, 1978, p. 7.

compensation for having had the security called. The premium typically begins at one year's interest, declining in amount each year until it disappears altogether. Table 7–1 is the call premium schedule of an issue of The Southland Corporation bonds.

An innovation in the area of call protection is seen in the 10¾ percent Pacific Power and Light bond issue which was sold in 1975. These securities provide *owners* with the option of cashing in the bonds at par during 1985 or holding them until 1990. The advantage to this feature lies totally with the holder. If market interest rates on similar securities are higher than 10¾ in 1985, the bonds will be surrendered for their par value. If market interest rates are lower, the bonds will be held until 1990. Pacific Power and Light made this agreement because they believed that it would allow the issue to be sold at a higher price than could be obtained if a typical call contract agreement were used.

Sinking funds

An agreement which has as its purpose the gradual reduction of the outstanding amount of a debt issue is called a *sinking fund*. Such an agreement is seen as being advantageous to bondholders because it forces the corporation to begin making arrangements to repay the issue before it matures. If the terms of the sinking fund are not met, the bond issue is in default, and the bondholders may take legal action against the company. Over half of the bonds issued recently have had

FIGURE 7–4
Sinking fund provisions of The Southland Corporation 9¾ percent Sinking Fund Debentures due 2003

Sinking fund
As a Sinking Fund the Company must provide for the retirement of a minimum of $2,500,000 principal amount of Debentures on December 15 in each of the years 1984 to and including 2002. At the Company's option, it may pay into the Sinking Fund each year an additional amount not exceeding $2,500,000 for such year. The right to make such optional Sinking Fund payments is not cumulative. For the purpose of the Sinking Fund, Debentures are redeemable on at least 30 days' notice at the Sinking Fund redemption price, which amount is payable, prior to the redemption date, to the Trustee. The Sinking Fund redemption price is 100% of the principal amount together with accrued interest to the date fixed for redemption. The Company may, at its option, receive credit against Sinking Fund payments for the principal amount of (a) Debentures acquired by the Company and surrendered for cancellation and (b) Debentures redeemed or called for redemption, otherwise than through the operation of the Sinking Fund. (Sections 3.04 and 3.05.)

Source: The Southland Corporation, *Prospectus*, December 13, 1978, p. 7.

some form of sinking fund agreement in their indentures. Figure 7-4 presents a part of the sinking fund agreement for the debenture bonds of The Southland Corporation. Such information is presented in complete form in the indenture and prospectus. Briefer summaries of this information are compiled by Moody's, Standard & Poor's, and other such companies.

Serial repayment provisions

Sinking funds are used almost exclusively with corporate bonds. Treasury and federal agency bonds are usually refunded with a new issue when they mature. State and municipal securities and equipment trust certificates are usually retired *serially*. When an issue of serial bonds is sold, it is divided into portions having different yields which mature in various amounts at various times. Figure 7-5 is an announcement of a large issue of municipal bonds.

TAXABILITY

Interest from securities issued by state and municipal governments is not taxed by the federal government as ordinary income. Federal interest payments are not taxed as ordinary income by state governments. But because state income tax rates are so much lower than federal rates, this is not such an important consideration. Nontaxability is a definite advantage to the investor because all of the interest can be spent: none goes for taxes. Implications of this feature so far as the investor is concerned are covered in Chapter 15, Tax Aspects of Investments.

Lack of taxability is also important to the issuer because it allows the sale of debt securities at a lower yield cost. Investors appraise bonds primarily on factors of grade, maturity, and yield. If two bonds have identical grade and maturity characteristics, yield becomes the factor which determines the security to buy. Investors relate the *after-tax* yield of the taxable bond to that of the untaxed security. Obviously, taxable securities will have to yield more in order to have comparable yields—when the yield is computed after taxes. In March, 1979 high-grade tax exempt bonds of about 20-year maturity were sold at an interest cost of about 6.7 percent. At the same time, Texas Power and Light paid about 9.6 percent interest on its Aaa rated issue of bonds that matures in 2009.

FIGURE 7–5
Announcement of a new serial bond issue

New Issue

$125,000,000
State of California

VETERANS SERIES ZZ AND SERIES AB BONDS

Dated April 1, 1979   ($5,000 Denominations)

AMOUNTS, RATES, MATURITIES AND YIELDS OR PRICES

Amount	Due Aug. 1	Coupon Rate	Price to Yield	Amount	Due Aug. 1	Coupon Rate	Yield or Price
$4,000,000	1980	5.60%	5.10%	$5,000,000	1993	5.70%	5.50%
4,000,000	1981	5.60	5.10	5,000,000	1994	5.70	5.55
4,000,000	1982	5.60	5.15	5,500,000	1995	5.70	5.60
4,000,000	1983	5.60	5.15	5,500,000	1996	5.70	5.65
4,000,000	1984	5.60	5.20	5,500,000	1997	5.70	100
4,500,000	1985	5.70	5.20	5,500,000	1998	5¾	100
4,500,000	1986	5.70	5.20	5,500,000	1999	5¾	5.80
4,500,000	1987	5.70	5.25	6,000,000	2000*	5¾	5.85
4,500,000	1988	5.70	5.25	6,000,000	2001*	5¾	5.90
4,500,000	1989	5.70	5.25	6,000,000	2002*	5¾	5.95
5,000,000	1990	5.70	5.30	6,000,000	2003*	5¾	6.00
5,000,000	1991	5.70	5.40	6,000,000	2004*	5¾	6.00
5,000,000	1992	5.70	5.45				

*Callable on or after August 1, 1999

(Accrued interest to be added)

TAX EXEMPTION
In the opinion of counsel, interest payable by the State upon its bonds is exempt from all present Federal and State of California personal income taxes under existing statutes, regulations and court decisions.

Bank of America NT & SA   Merrill Lynch White Weld Capital Markets Group   Salomon Brothers
Merrill Lynch, Pierce, Fenner & Smith Incorporated

Blyth Eastman Dillon & Co.   Dean Witter Reynolds Inc.   Wells Fargo Bank, N.A.   Continental Bank
Incorporated   Continental Illinois National Bank and Trust Company of Chicago

The Northern Trust Company   Goldman, Sachs & Co.   E. F. Hutton & Company Inc.

Kidder, Peabody & Co.   Loeb Rhoades, Hornblower & Co.   Wertheim & Co., Inc.   BancNorthwest   Union Bank
Incorporated

Pittsburgh National Bank   The Bank of California, N.A.   R. H. Moulton & Company   Wm. E. Pollock & Co., Inc.

Stone & Youngberg   Sutro & Co.   Crowell, Weedon & Co.   Eldredge & Co.   Southern California Corporation
Incorporated   Incorporated

Stern, Brenner & Company   J. A. Overton & Co.

March 22, 1979

Source: *The Wall Street Journal*, March 22, 1979, p. 28.

CONVERTIBLE BONDS

In recent years between 1.5 and 22 percent of the new corporate bonds sold in the United States have been *convertible*. These debt securities have all the characteristics of other bonds—callability, par value, coupon rate of interest, maturity date, and so on—and the ability to be exchanged for common stock of the company which issued them. Because of this feature, these bonds lie somewhere between debt and equity securities so far as their investment characteristics are concerned. For this reason they are discussed along with convertible preferred stock in Chapter 8.

PRICES AND YIELDS OF BONDS

Par value is the face amount—the maturity value—of a bond. By far the most common par value is $1,000, although there are bonds of $500 par and even less. (These securities arc known as *baby bonds*.) The quoted price of a bond includes payment of principal only. In addition to this amount the buyer must usually pay the seller for all interest accrued from the last interest payment date to the day prior to when payment for the bond is made. When the next interest payment date arrives, the new owner receives the full interest payment.

As an example of how this works, assume that the 8⅝ percent Bell Telephone bond pictured earlier was purchased on January 20, payment to be made on January 26. Interest payment dates are January 1 and July 1 of each year. In addition to the cost of the bond itself, the purchaser must compensate the seller for the 24 days of interest accrued from the last interest payment date, January 1, to the day prior to the payment date, January 26. In this case, the buyer would pay $86.25 × 24/360 = $5.75 for accrued interest in addition to the bond's price and brokerage commission.[6]

Bonds are also sold with *flat quotes*. This term means that no accrued interest is assumed. Such securities carry an "f" or other designation near their price quote to alert buyers to this condition.

---

[6] Accrued interest on corporate bonds has traditionally been calculated using a 360-day year and 30-day months (called the 30/360 basis). Governments have traditionally been traded on an *actual* or *calendar* basis. The calendar method is more accurate, of course.

Yields of bonds

Purchase of a bond gives its owner the right to receive interest payments of a certain amount over a known period of time.[7] The owner also is entitled to receive the par value of the security when it matures. The current market price of a given bond is determined mainly by: (1) its par value, (2) the rate of interest paid, (3) the grade of the security, (4) the time remaining to maturity, (5) the current rate of interest paid on bonds having similar characteristics as the one being examined, and (6) the tax status of the interest payments.

Three assumptions will make it possible to reduce the number of variables which must be considered: (1) all par values are $1,000, (2) all bonds are of the highest possible grade, and (3) all bond interest is taxed as income for the purpose of computing income taxes. The maturity date of the security, the coupon rate of interest paid on the bond, and the current rate of interest being paid on similar bonds are now the only important variables which determine the market price of the security. Even with this simplification, there are several types of yield.

Coupon yield. The *coupon* or *nominal* yield of a bond is the yearly dollar amount of interest paid, divided by the bond's par value. It is the stated rate of interest paid annually over the life of a bond. This yield definition does not take into consideration time to maturity, the yield on similar bonds, or the fact that interest is paid twice each year.

Current yield. The *current yield* is the dollar amount of interest paid each year divided by the current market price of the security. A bond paying $70 interest each year would have a *coupon yield* of 7 percent regardless of the market price of the security. If this bond had a market price of 88 ($880), it would have a current yield of

$$\frac{\text{Yearly interest}}{\text{Market price}} = \frac{\$70}{\$880} = 0.07955 \text{ or } 8.0\%.$$

Coupon yield tells how much, in dollars or percents, one can expect to receive from a bond investment each year; current yield tells the

---

[7] This and the following statements are directed to interest bearing, freely marketable debt securities. Excepted from this discussion are noninterest-bearing debt securities—Treasury bills and other discount securities—and nonmarketable securities such as U.S. savings bonds. Yield on discount securities is the difference between the market price and the redemption price computed as a percent of the current market price of the security and adjusted for the time to maturity. Changes in the market rate of interest have a direct effect on the market prices of such securities. Since relatively few small-scale investors hold these securities, and since we hope to keep this book to a readable length, computation of yields on these securities will not be discussed.

yearly percent return *on the purchase price* of the bond. This computation will be the same as the bond's yield to maturity only if the bond
were purchased at par or if it were a perpetual bond. In all other cases
this formula does not consider the fact that if the market price of the
security is either more or less than the par value of the bond, the person holding the security to maturity will have either a capital loss or
gain when the bond is redeemed at par.

For example, the purchaser of the Reynolds 7s of 89 (quoted at 88 in
Figure 4–4) will have a $120 capital gain if the bonds are held until re-
demption. The Rochester Gas and Electric 10¾s of 83 (quoted at 102 in
Figure 4–4) would provide a capital loss of $20, the amount of the pre-
mium on the bond. The gain or loss on this transaction either adds to,
or subtracts from, the investment's current yield.

Yield to maturity.   The *yield to maturity* calculation takes into account the relationship between the maturity value, the time to maturity, the current price, and the coupon yield of a bond. This yield
calculation allocates the bond premium or discount over the life of the
security. For example, if a bond were purchased for $100 less than its
par value and if this security had ten years remaining until it matured,
the yield to maturity calculation would allocate approximately $10 of
this capital gain to each of the remaining years to maturity. If a bond
were purchased at a price greater than par, the capital loss would likewise be spread equally over the remaining life of the security. The
yield to maturity is the true annual yield that an investor would receive on a bond if it were held to maturity. An approximate form of
this calculation is the following:

Let

Y = Yield to maturity
C = Coupon yield in dollars per year
P = Par value of the bond
M = Market value of the bond
N = Number of years to maturity

Then

$$Y = \frac{C + \dfrac{P - M}{N}}{\dfrac{P + M}{2}}$$

In the case of the Reynolds Industries 7s, the yield to maturity would be computed as follows. (As of 1979, 9 years remain to maturity.)

$$Y = \frac{\$70 + \dfrac{\$1{,}000 - \$880}{9}}{\dfrac{\$1{,}000 + \$880}{2}}$$

$$= \frac{\$70 + \dfrac{\$120}{9}}{\dfrac{\$1{,}880}{2}}$$

$$= \frac{\$83.33}{\$940}$$

$$= 0.08865 \text{ or } 8.9\%.$$

This formula provides an approximate yield figure only. A more accurate and far quicker way to calculate yield to maturity is to use a book of bond value tables. These tables provide yield calculations which consider all the factors mentioned earlier except the grade of the security. A portion of a page from one of the tables is reproduced in Figure 7–6.

The 7 percent figure at the top of the page indicates that this part of the book is devoted to bonds having coupon rates of this amount. This particular page covers the price and yield relationships for bonds having a 7 percent coupon maturing from 6½ to 10 years into the future. The yield to maturity for the Reynolds bond is determined by looking down the 9 year maturity column until one comes to the amount closest to the bond's current market price. In this example the market price was $880, so $87.84 is the closest price. Look now to the yield column and read out the yield to maturity figure—between 8.9 and 9.0 percent in this case because the true price falls between those associated with these two yields. This figure is slightly different from that derived by using the approximate formula listed earlier. It is more accurate, because of the way the yield is computed, and it is far quicker to use the tables than to work through the formula.

The importance of the yield to maturity calculation cannot be overemphasized. All Treasury bonds are sold on the basis of yield to maturity. High-grade corporate and municipal securities are also sold on this basis, but their yield to maturity is not normally stated in the financial press. Persons buying or selling such securities make these

FIGURE 7–6
Page from a bond value table

7%			YEARS and MONTHS					7%
Yield	6-6	7	7-6	8	8-6	9	9-6	10
4.50	113.95	114.87	115.77	116.64	117.50	118.33	119.15	119.95
4.60	113.35	114.23	115.08	115.91	116.73	117.52	118.30	119.07
4.70	112.75	113.59	114.40	115.19	115.96	116.72	117.46	118.18
4.80	112.16	112.95	113.72	114.47	115.21	115.93	116.63	117.31
4.90	111.57	112.32	113.05	113.76	114.46	115.14	115.80	116.45
5.00	110.98	111.69	112.38	113.06	113.71	114.35	114.98	115.59
5.10	110.40	111.07	111.72	112.35	112.97	113.58	114.17	114.74
5.20	109.82	110.45	111.06	111.66	112.24	112.81	113.36	113.90
5.30	109.25	109.83	110.41	110.97	111.51	112.04	112.56	113.06
5.40	108.67	109.22	109.76	110.28	110.79	111.29	111.77	112.24
5.50	108.11	108.62	109.12	109.60	110.08	110.54	110.98	111.42
5.60	107.54	108.02	108.48	108.93	109.37	109.79	110.21	110.61
5.70	106.98	107.42	107.84	108.26	108.66	109.05	109.44	109.81
5.80	106.42	106.82	107.21	107.59	107.96	108.32	108.67	109.01
5.90	105.87	106.23	106.59	106.94	107.27	107.60	107.91	108.22
6.00	105.32	105.65	105.97	106.28	106.58	106.88	107.16	107.44
6.10	104.77	105.07	105.35	105.63	105.90	106.16	106.42	106.66
6.20	104.23	104.49	104.74	104.99	105.22	105.46	105.68	105.90
6.30	103.69	103.91	104.13	104.35	104.55	104.75	104.95	105.14
6.40	103.15	103.34	103.53	103.71	103.89	104.06	104.22	104.38
6.50	102.62	102.78	102.93	103.08	103.23	103.37	103.50	103.63
6.60	102.09	102.21	102.34	102.46	102.57	102.68	102.79	102.89
6.70	101.56	101.65	101.75	101.83	101.92	102.00	102.08	102.16
6.80	101.04	101.10	101.16	101.22	101.28	101.33	101.38	101.43
6.90	100.52	100.55	100.58	100.61	100.64	100.66	100.69	100.71
7.00	100.00	100.00	100.00	100.00	100.00	100.00	100.00	100.00
7.10	99.49	99.46	99.43	99.40	99.37	99.34	99.32	99.29
7.20	98.98	98.92	98.86	98.80	98.74	98.69	98.64	98.59
7.30	98.47	98.38	98.29	98.21	98.12	98.05	97.97	97.90
7.40	97.97	97.84	97.73	97.62	97.51	97.41	97.30	97.21
7.50	97.46	97.32	97.17	97.03	96.90	96.77	96.65	96.53
7.60	96.97	96.79	96.62	96.45	96.29	96.14	95.99	95.85
7.70	96.47	96.27	96.07	95.88	95.69	95.51	95.34	95.18
7.80	95.98	95.75	95.52	95.30	95.10	94.89	94.70	94.52
7.90	95.49	95.23	94.98	94.74	94.50	94.28	94.06	93.86
8.00	95.01	94.72	94.44	94.17	93.92	93.67	93.43	93.20
8.10	94.52	94.21	93.91	93.61	93.33	93.07	92.81	92.56
8.20	94.05	93.70	93.38	93.06	92.76	92.47	92.19	91.92
8.30	93.57	93.20	92.85	92.51	92.18	91.87	91.57	91.28
8.40	93.10	92.70	92.32	91.96	91.61	91.28	90.96	90.65
8.50	92.63	92.21	91.81	91.42	91.05	90.70	90.36	90.03
8.60	92.16	91.71	91.29	90.88	90.49	90.12	89.76	89.41
8.70	91.69	91.23	90.78	90.35	89.93	89.54	89.16	88.80
8.80	91.23	90.74	90.27	89.82	89.38	88.97	88.57	88.19
8.90	90.77	90.26	89.76	89.29	88.84	88.40	87.99	87.59
9.00	90.32	89.78	89.26	88.77	88.29	87.84	87.41	86.99
9.10	89.86	89.30	88.76	88.25	87.75	87.28	86.83	86.40
9.20	89.41	88.83	88.27	87.73	87.22	86.73	86.26	85.81
9.30	88.97	88.36	87.78	87.22	86.69	86.18	85.70	85.23
9.40	88.52	87.89	87.29	86.71	86.16	85.64	85.14	84.66
9.50	88.08	87.43	86.80	86.21	85.64	85.10	84.58	84.09
9.60	87.64	86.97	86.32	85.71	85.12	84.56	84.03	83.52
9.70	87.20	86.51	85.84	85.21	84.61	84.03	83.48	82.96
9.80	86.77	86.05	85.37	84.72	84.10	83.51	82.94	82.40
9.90	86.34	85.60	84.90	84.23	83.59	82.98	82.40	81.85

Source: *Supplementary High Rate Bond Values.* (Boston: Financial Publishing Co., 1958), p. 86.

calculations on their own, however, and it is yield to maturity which is the most important determinant in deciding which bond or bonds to purchase.

Yield to call. When it is logical to assume that a bond will be called rather than allowed to mature, *yield to call* is used. This yield calculation uses the call date as the maturity date and adds the call premium to the par value. The Reynolds Industry bond discussed earlier carries a call premium of 3.11 percent if redeemed between June 1, 1979, and May 30, 1980. A person anticipating a call during this period would calculate yield to maturity on the basis of the $1,031.10 call price.

Qualitative factors. Grade, taxability, legality for investment, and other qualitative characteristics of bonds are also important. As the grade of a bond declines, the yield on the security must increase because lenders require a higher return to induce them to accept additional financial risk. Bonds having interest payments which are fully or partially tax exempt yield less than taxable bonds, because tax exemption is an advantage which makes the bonds worth more to some investors. Bond which qualify as *legal investments*—for savings banks, trusts, and other financial institutions—yield less than those not qualifying because the demand for these bonds is greater. Small size bond issues of the less well-known companies may provide higher yields than bonds of other companies which have outstanding securities that are identical in every respect, except for the size of the company or bond issue. These companies usually pay a premium for being small and unknown, because their bonds are not as marketable as others. The important point of this discussion is that while bond yields are determined mostly by quantitative factors, qualitative factors also play a role.

RELATIONSHIP BETWEEN BOND PRICES, INTEREST RATES, AND MATURITY

When the market rate of interest rises, the market price of outstanding bonds declines. When the market rate of interest declines, prices of outstanding bonds rise. This relationship was initially discussed in Chapter 2, but because it is so confusing to many persons it bears repeating here.

Imagine yourself to be a potential purchaser of one bond. To simplify things, assume that your choice is between the outstanding 7 percent bond previously examined and another one which is to be issued today to mature in 9 years and which carries a coupon rate of 8 percent. The only difference in these securities is their coupon rates, and this difference can be traced to the fact that the cost of borrowing has risen since the 7 percent bonds were first sold. Would anyone buy the 7 percent bond if they could instead buy the one yielding 8 percent? Certainly not! Persons wishing to sell these 7 percent bonds will find that they must price them at a *discount,* below par, or no one will purchase them. The market price of the 7 percent bond will decline in a competitive market until the yield to maturity of both issues of bonds is close to 8 percent. To accomplish this, its price would be about $936.70. (Figure it out on your own using the bond value table.)

What would happen to the price of the 8 percent bond if in the future the market rate of interest *declined?* Its market price would *increase* above par because this security would then pay *more interest* than was being paid on new bonds of the same type and grade. Remember: When market rates of interest increase, prices of outstanding bonds decrease; when market rates of interest decrease, prices of outstanding bonds increase.

How much prices increase or decrease is determined by the time remaining to maturity or to the expected call date if a call is anticipated. The mathematics of yield calculations allocate premiums and discounts over the expected life of the security. Therefore, the longer a bond has until maturity, the greater the price discount or premium necessary to cause it to attain the same yield as is available in the market. The longest term bond is, of course, a perpetual bond since this security has no maturity. Figure 7–7 presents prices of a perpetual bond, a twenty-year bond, and a bond having a three-year maturity under changing market interest conditions. The only differences in these securities are their maturities. Each pays a 6 percent coupon rate and all are of the same grade. When the market rate of interest is 6 percent—the same as the coupon rates—all three securities should be priced at par. When market interest rates increase above 6 percent, each of the bonds will be priced at a discount. The 20-year bond declines less than the perpetual issue, but more than the short-term bond. When market interest rates decline, price changes are even more pronounced. At a market rate of 3 percent the perpetual bond would be worth $2,000 and the 20-year bond about $1,450. The three-year security would be priced at about $1,085.

It is the long-term high-grade bonds that are most affected by changes in market rates of interest. The same mathematical relationships apply to long-term low-grade bonds, but the yield premium levied because of their high financial risk acts to lower price movements caused by changing market interest rates. Yield on these bonds is set more by the financial risk characteristics than by any other factor.

FIGURE 7–7

Market prices of a perpetual, twenty-year, and a three-year bond at different rates of interest (coupon rates of all bonds are 6 percent)

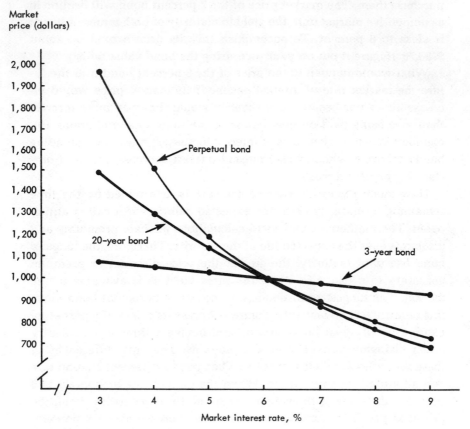

INVESTING AND SPECULATING IN DEBT

Debt securities can be used for both investment and speculation. To understand how they can be used in two seemingly contradictory ways, it is first necessary to look to their investment characteristics.

Investment characteristics of debt

High-grade bonds and other debt contracts have great financial safety and marketability, but they perform poorly so far as purchasing power risk and interest rate risk are concerned.

Financial risk. Payment of principal and interest on high-grade debt issues will be made as specified. It is true that many bond issues went into default in the 1930s and several have recently defaulted, but these were not high-grade issues.

Investors sometimes "reach" for yield by purchasing low-grade bonds. They reason that the difference in yield between high-grade and low-grade bonds, although it is seldom more than 2.5 percent, is "worth the risk." Such a strategy can only be pursued effectively if the investor is able to purchase so many different low-grade bonds that they are not all affected by the same economic events. Losses may result on a few securities, but they will be more than covered by the increased yield from the other bonds. Individuals who purchase just a few bonds cannot hope to obtain this average experience and therefore should forego the premium yields of low-grade securities.

Marketability and liquidity.   All high-grade bonds are easily *marketable,* but they are not necessarily *liquid.* Marketability refers to the ability to sell or buy large amounts of a given security in a short period of time without causing fluctuations in current market prices. All high-grade bonds have this characteristic.

To be *liquid* a security must be marketable, but it must also be marketable at a price near to its purchase price or par value. All short-term high-grade debt instruments—Treasury bills and notes, commercial paper, bonds soon to mature—are marketable and liquid. Because maturity is never far in the future, and because par value will be paid at maturity, market values of these securities stay near to par value. Lower grade debt securities may be neither marketable nor liquid, even though they are short term in duration.

Purchasing power risk.   One of the greatest disadvantages of debt securities is the loss of purchasing power experienced by owners during times of price inflation. Interest may be paid and securities may be redeemed as specified in the contract, but each dollar received purchases less goods and services.

Inflation strikes at all types of return. Common stock dividends, the market price appreciation of art objects, the appreciation of land values—all lose purchasing power through price inflation. However, the returns to these investments are not *limited* by contract. They may rise in value at a faster rate than that at which inflation occurs. Debt contracts do not have such protection.[8]

---

[8] There are two possible exceptions to this statement: floating rate notes and bonds denominated in foreign currencies. Interest payments on floating rate

In a time of price *deflation,* high-quality debt contracts become excellent investments. Not only is the income from these securities relatively secure, but it will purchase more during each period in which deflation continues. The United States has not experienced a period of deflation since the depression years of the 1930s. This was almost one-half century ago. During the ensuing period we have had years of relatively stable prices and a decade of great price inflation. In short, moderate or high price inflation is likely to continue. Every investor should consider this important fact when formulating a personal investment strategy.

Interest rate risk. One of the often-cited strengths of high-grade debt instruments used to be their great market price stability. Rapidly rising market interest rates have caused all outstanding marketable, long-term debt securities to decrease in price greatly and have caused investors to reappraise the value of bonds in this regard.

The Reynolds 7s of 1989 were issued in 1969 at approximately par. Eleven years later they are quoted at 88; a loss in market value of about 12 percent. The grade of the bond has not changed (it is still A grade), and it is no more or less marketable than before. Market rates of interest have simply risen, forcing these bonds to lose much market value. So long as interest rates remain high, holders of debt securities who purchased them when rates were lower are "locked in." They cannot sell their securities without taking a capital loss.

The individual who cannot afford to accept interest rate risk but who wishes to invest in long-term securities should give consideration to either U.S. savings bonds or long-term certificate accounts at financial institutions. These investments provide less yield than some bonds, but redemption values are known at all times.

Collateral for loans. High-grade marketable debt investments make good loan collateral. Treasury securities are such excellent collateral that during periods of easy credit many banks will lend up to 95 percent of their market value. Under this arrangement, if you had $100,000 of Treasury bonds you could borrow $95,000 against them.

---

notes are defined in terms of an interest rate series or index which is supposed to rise and fall with inflationary pressures. Theoretically, lenders are thus protected against purchasing power losses. Bonds denominated in foreign currencies which are expected to increase in value relative to the U.S. dollar may provide the same type of protection.

Banks cannot now lend more than $50,000 on listed common stocks having the same market value.[9]

Summary of investment characteristics. High-grade bonds have many obvious disadvantages during a period of rising prices and interest rates. However, many individuals (and some professional investors) have such a natural aversion to financial risk that they willingly accept all these disadvantages to obtain what they believe to be safety in their investments. High-grade debt securities do have a place in many investors' portfolios, but it must be realized that financial safety is acquired at a high cost in terms of purchasing power and interest rate risk. Convertible securities have helped to overcome some of the deficiencies of straight debt. These securities are discussed in the next chapter.

Speculating in debt

Speculation may be defined as the act of taking on more investment risk in the hope of higher than normal returns. This can be done in any of several ways using bonds or other debt contracts as the vehicle for speculation.

Low-grade securities. One may purchase the debt contracts of financially embarrassed companies or individuals. When one makes such a speculative investment, the security behind the contract becomes of extreme importance, for the issuer of the security is often facing bankruptcy. However, even bankruptcy need not always be feared, for if the claims of the debt security holders are strong enough, they may be paid quickly and in full. During periods of economic recession the grades of many debt securities are lowered. Companies do not have sufficient earnings to maintain the required coverage ratios to keep their high ratings. Lowering of the grade of a security will almost always cause its market price to decline, and as institutions and individuals sell these securities, market prices are driven down even further. At some point such bonds become very reasonable investments for persons who can accept this kind of investment risk. Studies have

---

[9] Legal lending limits on stock and securities convertible into stock are set by the Federal Reserve Board. Limits fluctuate with economic conditions. In early 1979, margin requirements were 50 percent for stocks and convertible bonds. Treasury securities do not come under Federal Reserve Board margin requirements. A bank could theoretically lend 100 percent of their market value.

shown that nearly all bonds are eventually redeemed at par by their issuers. In many instances it is just a matter of being able and willing to wait until this happens.

Speculation through financial leverage. It is also possible to speculate in "money rate bonds." These are the high-grade securities whose market prices are almost completely determined by the current market rate of interest. Speculation in these securities becomes possible when interest rates are relatively high and are expected to decrease. One may simply purchase long-term Treasury bonds and wait for their prices to rise as interest rates decline. There is not very much speculative risk, or profit, involved in this kind of investment because it would take a very large change in the market rate of interest to cause a substantial change in the price of these very high-grade securities. Such changes usually take much time.

To maximize the potential return from this type speculation the maximum amount of money should be borrowed at the lowest possible rate. The collateral for the loan would be the debt securities purchased. Depending upon capital market conditions, the speculator may be required to pay cash for between 5 and 25 percent of the total amount of securities purchased. Interest costs of the loan will also be determined by the availability of credit. The cost of holding this investment is the interest paid on the loan, plus the amount of return that is lost by not placing the cash portion of the investment in another investment (this cost is known as *opportunity cost*), plus brokerage and other fees. From this total the amount of interest received from holding the securities is deducted. The net figure represents the cost associated with holding the investment.

The investor will always incur a cost to hold this investment because interest received will be less than interest paid out and other costs. Each period that passes without a decline in the market rate of interest adds to these costs. If interest rates decline as expected, the increase in the market price of the bonds provides the speculator with a trading profit which can be used to pay these costs and provide a profit on the speculation.

There are two main problems associated with this type of speculation. One is obtaining the necessary financing on advantageous terms; the other is accurately predicting interest rate movements. It should be obvious that if interest rates rise rather than decline, the speculator incurs a paper loss on the transaction. The lender will probably ask for more cash to be placed against the declining market value of the bonds. This, of course, results in a most unfavorable situation. Even when interest rates do not rise the speculator is harmed. Costs of holding this investment accrue so long as the securities are owned. If interest rates do not decline within a reasonable period of time the costs of holding the securities may be larger than the profits, even though declining interest rates eventually cause security prices to rise. For the above reasons these speculations are short-term in nature.

SUMMARY

All debt contracts are similar in that the borrower receives the use of funds belonging to others and pays interest for their use. This agreement is formalized in the bond indenture or in federal or state laws.

Bonds may be classified by their security or the source from which their repayment is expected, in the following manner.

Classification of Debt Securities

I. By issuer
    A. Securities issued by governments
        1. Treasury securities
        2. Agency securities
        3. Municipals
            a. Full faith and credit bonds
            b. Revenue bonds
            c. Assessment bonds
    B. Securities issued by corporations
        1. Utilities
        2. Railroads
        3. Industrials
II. By security or source of repayment
    A. Mortgage bonds
    B. Collateral trust bonds
    C. Debenture bonds
    D. Equipment trust certificates
    E. Guaranteed bonds (including joint bonds)
    F. Income bonds

Notes and *bills* resemble bonds except that they are of short maturity and may be sold with discounted interest.

U.S. savings bonds are of two types: Series E and EE which have discounted interest, and Series H and HH which pay interest semiannually. These securities are not marketable, but may be redeemed at a prestated value prior to maturity. They may not be used as loan collateral.

U.S. Treasury securities are the most secure of all debt issues. They are issued in large denominations and are the standard against which other bonds are compared.

Corporate and *municipal bonds* are graded on the basis of financial risk. Yields and grades of all debt securities are related in that the highest graded securities have the lowest yields, and lower graded securities offer higher yields. Exceptions to this rule are *municipal bonds*. Interest on these securities is not taxed as income to its recipients. Consequently, they have lower market yields, per given grade, than any other bond.

Coupon yield, current yield, yield to maturity, and *yield to call* are different ways of computing yields. Only the yield to maturity or yield to call calculations provide mathematically correct statements of true yield.

Debt securities of high grade have general investment qualities of (1) negligible financial risk, (2) very high marketability, and (3) a high degree of purchasing power and interest rate risk. Most debt securities are good loan collateral.

High-grade debt instruments are usually purchased as investments to provide financial safety. Such securities may become vehicles for speculation if financial leverage is used to increase the profits (or losses) from holding these securities. Low-grade debt issues also offer speculative opportunities.

APPENDIX

Computation of bond values

The basic formula behind all bond value tables, present value tables, future value tables, and special tables which make use of a variant of these calculations is the compound interest formula $P_n = P(1 + i)^n$, which is derived in the appendix to Chapter 6.

A bond obtains its value from the two promises of the company issuing the security: (1) the promise to redeem the security at some time in the future for its par value, and (2) the promise to pay periodic interest of a known amount to the owner of the bond. Other determinants of the value of a bond are the grade of the security, and the current yield that is obtainable from bonds having similar grade and maturity characteristics to the one under analysis. To simplify the problem of valuation, assume that the bond to be analyzed is riskless or that other alternate investments have identical risk characteristics.

The first step in developing a *current* or *present theoretical market value* for a bond—the terms mean the same thing—is to break the promises of the bond issuer into two separate problems. These are the problems of arriving at present values for (1) a sum of money (the par value) which will be paid at a future date, and (2) the periodic payments of interest received over the remaining life of the bond.

The present value of a sum of money to be paid at some time in the future is dependent upon how much an investor could earn on money owned *now* on the next best alternative investment having similar risk characteristics. For purposes of this example assume that the bond to be valued matures in exactly ten years and that it pays $50 in interest each year at the end of the year. Its par value is the customary $1,000. Assume further that a current annual return of 4 percent can be obtained from other bonds of like grade and maturity.

The first part of the valuation problem, that of determining how much one should pay *now* for a contract which promises $1,000 in ten years, can be stated simply as how much money would one need to invest now, at 4 percent compounded annually, to have $1,000 of principal and accumulated compound interest at the end of ten years. The value P_n of the compound interest formula, $P_n = P(1 + i)^n$, is a *future value*. This is the amount that a present sum of money, P, would accumulate to at a given rate of compound interest. Solving this formula for P tells what amount would be necessary to invest now so that the amount P_n would result in n time periods through the working of compound interest.

$$P_n = (1 + i)^n$$

$$P = P_n \left[\frac{1}{(1 + i)^n} \right]$$

Inserting appropriate numbers in the problem, we get

$$P = \$1,000 \left[\frac{1}{(1 + 0.04)^{10}} \right]$$

$$P = \$1,000(0.67556)$$

$$P = \$675.56.$$

If $675.56 were invested now for ten years at 4 percent interest compounded annually, its value would be $1,000 in ten years. Therefore, the present value of the $1,000 par value of the bond is $675.56. Tables of present value factors for various interest rates and time periods are readily available, although no examples of these tables are presented in this text.[10]

The valuation of interest payments is more complex because these payments will be received $50 at a time at the end of each year for ten years.[11] However, the valuation of their present worth is done exactly as above. The $50 interest payment to be received at the end of the first year is equal to an amount now which if invested at 4 percent compound interest would increase to $50 at year end,

$$P = \$50 \left[\frac{1}{(1 + 0.04)^1} \right]$$
$$= \$50(0.96153)$$
$$= \$48.08$$

The present value of the first year's interest payment is $48.08 because if this amount were invested at 4 percent per annum it would be worth $50 at the end of one year, when the interest payment is to be received. Another way of stating this is that an investor who has alternative investments which will yield 4 percent should be willing to pay $48.08 *now* for the right to receive $50 in one year. This is logical because no more than this amount could be earned on any other investment having similar risk chracteristics. To value the ten-year stream of interest payments it is necessary to sum the ten present–value amounts derived from ten separate calculations which differ only in the n values of each term. Written mathematically, the equation for the present value of future interest payments would be:

$$P = \$50 \left[\frac{1}{(1+ 0.04)^1} + \frac{1}{(1+ 0.04)^2} + \frac{1}{(1+ 0.04)^3} + \cdots + \frac{1}{(1+ 0.04)^{10}} \right]$$
$$= \$50(8.11089)$$
$$= \$405.55$$

---

[10] Robert Cissell and Helen Cissell, *Mathematics of Finance*, 4th ed. (Boston: Houghton Mifflin, 1973) and Paul M. Hummel and Charles L. Seebeck, Jr., *Mathematics of Finance*, 3d ed. (New York: McGraw-Hill, 1971) present good coverage of financial calculations.

[11] In actuality bond interest is usually paid semiannually or quarterly. Annual interest payments have been asumed at this time to keep the problem as simple as possible. Semiannual compounding is covered later.

Total interest payments have a present value of $405.55 because if one had this amount accumulating interest at 4 percent per annum, one could remove $50 from this fund at the end of each year for ten years. The last $50 withdrawal would exhaust the fund.

Tables of present values of annuities of I amount received for n periods are available and were used to solve the above problem. They are not widely used in investments because these tables give only the present value of a series of interest payments. Of concern is the total present value of both parts of the bond contract: the promised par value payment and the promised interest payments. Stated mathematically, using the following abbreviations, we find the formula is as follows:

Let

P = Present value of the total contract

i = Current yield obtained from investments having similar risk and maturity characteristics

n = Number of time periods to maturity

I = Interest in dollars per period

M = Maturity value of the bond

$$P = I\left[\frac{1}{(1 + i)^1} + \frac{1}{(1 + i)^2} + \frac{1}{(1 + i)^3} + \cdots + \frac{1}{(1 + i)^n}\right] + M\left[\frac{1}{(1 + i)^n}\right].$$

Bond value tables, a sample page of which was presented previously, are no more than completed problems of the above form which have been worked out for a variety of values of P, I, n, and i. M, the par value of the security, is assumed to be $1,000. The values given in these tables are accurate only if the purchase of the bond is made on a day which begins an interest payment period. In practice it is rare for the date of purchase to occur on this date, so extrapolation is used to obtain an approximate value for the bond. Computer programs and calculators now figure prices more accurately than the bond value tables.

The market price of the above bond, from the bond value tables, is $1,081.80. Summing the present values of interest and principal as they were computed ($675.56 + $405.55) produces a value of $1,081.11. The difference in calculations of $0.69 is caused by rounding error and because interest was assumed to be paid once each year in the problem, while the formula used to construct the bond value table assumed that interest was paid twice per year.

When semiannual payment of interest is assumed, the formula is changed by dividing the annual interest payment and current yield by two and increasing the number of payments by a factor of two. The formula becomes

$$P = I/2 \left[\frac{1}{(1 + i/2)^1} + \frac{1}{(1 + i/2)^2} + \frac{1}{(1 + i/2)^3} + \ldots + \frac{1}{(1 + i/2)^{n \times 2}} \right]$$

$$+ M \left[\frac{1}{(1 + i/2)^{n \times 2}} \right]$$

PROBLEMS

1. From Moody's, Standard & Poor's, the *Federal Reserve Bulletin,* or any other source, obtain current yields of Aaa municipals, Treasury long-term bonds, and corporate Aaa and Baa bonds.
   a. Determine the basis point yield difference between each security using the bonds with the lowest yield as the standard against which the others are measured.
   b. Explain why the differences are what they are.
2. Compute the approximate yield to maturity of bonds having the following characteristics.
   a. Par value $1,000, coupon yield 9 percent, current market price 94, ten years to maturity.
   b. Par value $1,000, coupon yield 6 percent, current market price 106, seven years to maturity.
3. Record the yearly market price of a soon-to-mature Treasury bond each year for the past ten years. (Be certain you choose a bond that had at least a ten-year maturity when issued.) Explain why these market prices have differed from par and why they are now near par.
4. A bond with a maturity of ten years first becomes callable in 4 years. The $1,000 par bond has a coupon rate of 10 percent, but interest rates have lowered greatly since this security was issued.
   a. What is the bond's yield to maturity if it is purchased today at 109, and held for ten years?
   b. Assume that the bond will be called when it is first eligible for call and that the call premium is one year's interest. If the price is currently 109, what is the yield to call?
5. A 6 percent coupon bond having 20 years to maturity now sells to yield 8 percent if held to maturity. It is a $1,000 par bond. What is its current market price?

QUESTIONS

1. Bonds are identified as very *formal* financing agreements. Why are they formal and how is this formality accomplished?
2. Bonds issued by municipalities, federal agencies, or the U.S. Treasury seldom, if ever, have indentures. Why is this true?
3. How are debt securities usually classified? Is this a reasonable method of classification?
4. "Debenture bonds are often of the highest grade, even though there is no collateral pledged for the bond." Explain this statement.
5. Why is it that collateral trust bonds can be sold by companies of poor credit rating at such a low interest cost?
6. How do Series EE savings bonds differ from corporate bonds? To what kind of investor do they have the most appeal?
7. What is meant by *yield to maturity*? Why is this yield calculation more accurate and meaningful than *current yield*?
8. "Bond investing is not for me. I'm always looking for capital gains." Agree or disagree with this statement, basing your answer on your knowledge of bond price movements.
9. What is *yield to call*? Under what conditions is this the appropriate yield calculation to use.
10. What are the most important investment characteristics of debt contracts?
11. What is *call protection* for a bond purchaser?
12. What is a *call premium*?
13. How is it possible to speculate in bonds?

SELECTED READINGS

"Annual Review of the Bond Market." New York: Salomon Brothers, published annually.

Ascher, Leonard W. "Selecting Bonds for Capital Gains." *Financial Analysts Journal,* March–April, 1971.

Cohen, Jerome B.; Zinbarg, Edward D.; and Zeikel, Arthur. *Investment Analysis and Portfolio Management.* 3rd ed. Homewood, Ill.: Richard D. Irwin, 1977.

Comprehensive Bond Values Tables. 4th desk ed. Boston: Financial Publishing Co., 1958.

Graham, Benjamin; Dodd, David L.; and Cottle, Sidney. *Security Analysis: Principles and Techniques.* 4th ed. New York: McGraw-Hill, 1962.

"Handbook of the Securities of the United States Government." New York: First Boston Corp., published annually.

232

Hickman, W. Braddock. *Corporate Bond Quality and Investor Experience.* New York: National Bureau of Economic Research, 1958.

Homer, Sidney, and Leibowitz, Martin. *Inside the Yield Book: New Tools for Bond Market Strategy.* Englewood Cliffs, N.J.: Prentice-Hall, 1972.

Sherwood, Hugh C. *How Corporate and Municipal Debt is Rated.* New York: John Wiley & Sons, 1976.

Sherwood, Hugh C. *How to Invest in Bonds.* New York: McGraw-Hill, 1976.

8

Investing in preferred stock and convertible bonds

INTRODUCTION TO PREFERRED STOCK

All corporations issue common stock, most issue debt securities, and a much smaller proportion issue preferred stocks. As Table 8-1 indicates, new preferred issues are always less in amount than either bonds or common stock. Their importance varies greatly year to year, however, and at times has amounted to over half the dollar volume of new common issues.

The New York Stock Exchange lists 642 preferred issues for trading, and the American Stock Exchange lists 101.[1] At the end of 1978, the market value of preferred shares on the NYSE was about $24 billion; those on the AMEX were valued at about $2.1 billion. While this is a large amount of money, it is a small percentage of the total market value of the equity securities listed on the exchanges: about 2.9 percent of those on the NYSE and 5.5 percent of those on the AMEX. Preferred shares are also sold OTC. No accurate figures are available on the amount of preferred stock traded in this market or on the regional exchanges, but there is no reason to presume that it would be more or less important than it is on the two largest exchanges.

Before the days of high corporate income taxes, preferred stock was sold by a large proportion of American corporations. It was an important part of their financial structure, and it was widely held by individual investors. Most of these securities were not convertible into

---

[1] Data obtained from the New York and American Stock Exchanges.

233

TABLE 8–1
New issues of corporate securities sold in recent years (millions of dollars)

Year	Preferred stock	Common stock	Bonds
1978*	3,104	7,166	37,538
1977	3,878	8,135	42,193
1976	2,803	8,305	42,380
1975	3,458	7,405	42,756
1974	2,254	4,050	31,567
1973	3,375	7,655	21,022
1972	3,340	10,723	25,825
1971	3,670	9,291	32,123
1970	1,390	7,240	30,315
1969	682	7,714	18,347
1968	637	3,946	17,383
1967	885	1,959	21,954
1966	574	1,939	15,561
1965	725	1,547	13,720
1964	412	2,679	10,865
1963	343	1,011	10,856
1962	422	1,314	8,969
1961	450	3,294	9,420

* Annual estimate based on monthly data through September.
Source: *The Federal Reserve Bulletin* (various issues) and the Securities and Exchange Commission.

common stock. From the early 1900s until the present, straight (non-convertible) preferred shares have become less important as a financing device, except for utilities. The explanation for this decline in use appears in the next section of this chapter. Corporations own most of the high-grade straight preferred stock; lower grade preferreds and convertible preferreds are mostly held by individual investors. The face of a preferred stock issued by Pacific Power and Light Corporation appears as Figure 8–1.

LEGAL CHARACTERISTICS OF PREFERRED STOCK

Rights of preferred stockholders

Preferred stock is an *equity* security, which differs from the *common stock* of the corporation in that it receives some sort of preferential treatment. The rights and privileges of all preferred stock issues are described in the articles of incorporation of the company and often on the reverse side of the stock certificate. The most important of these

FIGURE 8-1
Preferred stock of the Pacific Power and Light Corporation

Courtesy of Pacific Power and Light, Inc., Portland, Oregon

rights and privileges are listed by several financial reporting services.[2]

Most preferred stocks receive preference in the sense that their dividends are paid before any dividends may be paid on the common. They also receive preferential treatment if the corporation is liquidated. In return for this, preferred shareholders receive a limited dividend return. Under normal conditions they may not vote to elect the board of directors of the corporation. However, some firms allow preferred shareholders to elect a small proportion of the board if preferred dividends have not been paid for some stated time period. In a still smaller number of cases, preferred shareholders have full voting rights.

Perhaps more importantly, preferred shareholders may have the right to veto certain actions of the corporation which could prove harmful to their interests. For example, they are often given veto

[2] Moody's and Standard & Poor's publish information of this type for most corporations having preferred stock issues.

TABLE 8–2
Earnings available to common shareholders under two types of financing

	Company A bond financing $100 of interest	Company B preferred stock financing $100 of dividends
Operating income	$300	$300
Less bond interest	100	-0-
Taxable income	200	300
Income tax @ 50% rate	100	150
After-tax income	100	150
Less preferred dividend	-0-	100
Available to common shareholders	$100	$ 50

power over the issuance of more preferred, or preferred having a superior legal position. They may have veto power over issuance of bonds, or of a merger. These rights are usually contained in the company's articles of incorporation, but some states provide such protection by statute. These protections are not nearly so well established in law as are the rights of common stockholders.

Preferred dividends are often confused with bond interest. Like bond interest, they are paid periodically and are usually a stated amount. The resemblance ends there, however. Legally, bonds are debt, and bondholders are creditors of the company. Bond interest payments are a cost of doing business and are therefore deductible from income when computing income taxes. Preferred stock is ownership capital, and preferred dividends are therefore not a cost of doing business. These dividend payments are paid "after taxes" and are more expensive than an equal dollar amount of bond interest. The effect of this different tax treatment can be seen in Table 8–2, which presents a situation where one company has financed with bonds while another has financed with preferred stock. Operating income and financing expenses are the same for each company, but there is a large difference in the earnings available to common shareholders.

When corporate income tax rates are low it makes little difference whether a company pays interest or dividends as its cost of obtaining financing. But when income tax rates are high, as they have been for many years, the method of financing has an important impact on profits. The natural result of this "tax disadvantage" has been an increase in the use of bonded debt and a decrease in the use of preferred stock. But there are exceptions to this statement: (1) Utility companies have continued to issue preferred stock because preferred stock dividends are classified as an allowable expense for the purpose of setting their rates. It is not surprising that a large proportion of the straight preferred shares listed on the exchanges is utility shares. (2) Convertible preferred stock has been issued in substantial amounts in years when common stock prices are relatively high. The securities are often issued by companies who might have had difficulty in selling convertible debt securities because of low or fluctuating earnings. (3) Preferred stock—usually convertible—is often issued when companies merge. The merger can then be completed by an exchange of shares, which has certain tax advantages over a cash purchase. The "bought out" shareholders receive securities which pay a known dividend, thus maintaining their income. If convertible, the securities offer an additional opportunity to share in the growth prospects of the merged company.

Types of preferred stock

There are not nearly as many types of preferred stock issues as bond issues. Most preferreds can be classified under one of the following headings, which identify them by the different claims they hold on dividends.

1. Straight preferred.
2. Cumulative preferred.
3. Participating preferred.
4. Convertible preferred.

Straight preferred stock has a fixed annual dividend payment. If the corporate directors declare this dividend, it is paid; if they do not make this declaration, it is not paid. The decision of whether or not to pay a dividend rests entirely with the board of directors. A dividend not paid in any year is not carried over to the next year as an obligation of the company. The only advantage that this security has over the common shares is that no dividends may be paid on the common until the *current* preferred dividend has been paid. This may be very small advantage indeed! A company could pass the dividends on both the preferred and common stock for one year and in the next year pay the regular preferred dividend and a "double" common dividend. Because of this possibility most preferred stocks have dividends which are cumulative.

Cumulative preferred stock is identical to the straight preferred except that when a preferred dividend payment is not made, the company continues to owe this amount to the preferred shareholder. This *dividend arrearage*, as it is called, is not a *liability* of the company in the same sense that interest payments are a liability. However, since no dividends may be paid to the common stock until all preferred dividend arrearages have been paid, the cumulative shareholder is in a somewhat stronger position than is the owner of straight preferred stock. If the corporation wishes to pay dividends on common shares, it must either pay the entire amount of preferred dividends in arrears or in some way dispose of the claims of this class of owners.

Some preferred stocks have large accumulated dividend arrearages. One might expect these stocks to be valued at the amount of the dividend arrearage plus the investment value of the security, but in fact this is seldom the case. The usual solution to a problem of large dividend arrearages is for the corporation to reach an agreement with the preferred shareholders whereby it either purchases the preferred stock from them or satisfies the arrearage claims with a payment of something less than the total amount of the claim.

Participating preferred shares receive a stated dividend before any dividend may be paid on common stock. If this and the common stock dividend are paid, and if earnings are high enough that further common dividends are justified, the participating feature allows the preferred shares to also receive additional dividends. Such an arrangement gives the preferred shareholders the best of two worlds. They receive preferential treatment on dividend payments, and they also may share in any large profits that the company obtains. Moody's lists fewer than 90 participating preferred issues.

An even rarer type is the ten issues of *cumulative participating* preferred stock. *Prior preferred* is a term which identifies a preferred stock having some sort of priority—in dividends or distribution of assets—over another preferred issue of the same company.

The outstanding characteristic of *convertible preferred stock* is the fact that it may be converted into the common stock of the company that issued it. Convertible preferred stock may have any of the features described above, but in practice most convertible preferred is cumulative. All the pertinent information on the convertibility features of these stocks is stated in the records of the corporation and usually on the stock certificates. Summaries of this information are prepared by several of the financial reporting services.

The investment characteristics of convertible stocks and convertible bonds are very similar. A discussion of both securities is presented at the end of this chapter.

nking fund features

While most corporate bond issues have sinking fund agreements, few preferred stocks do. It is believed that this device is used so infrequently because (1) for most corporations the preferred stock is a very small proportion of the total capitalization of the company. There is no need for the corporation to guarantee repayment of the issue by some certain date or over a certain time period because the financial obligation of the issue is relatively unimportant. (2) It is assumed that convertible preferred stocks will be converted into common, rather than being redeemed or retired in some other way.

Some preferred issues (most of these are issued by utilities) do have sinking fund agreements. This agreement might have some slight value to the owners of these securities because purchases of the securities for the sinking fund provide demand for these shares that might not otherwise exist. Such an advantage is probably very small. Yields on sinking fund preferreds are very close to yields of other preferreds of like grade.

Callability features

Callability for preferred stockholders has the same meaning that it does for bondholders. That is, under conditions stated in the corporation's articles, and usually on the stock certificate itself, the corporation may redeem its preferred stock. Although a call premium is associated with most callable preferred issues, it is seldom that a call will not cause financial harm to the owner of affected shares. When purchasing shares for sinking fund purposes companies usually have the choice of buying shares in the market or calling them and paying the call premium. Naturally, they will obtain the shares in the least costly way. Unless shares are needed to meet sinking fund requirements, most corporations will not consider redeeming them unless they can obtain new financing at a lower cost. Such a condition could come about if market interest and dividend rates lowered, or if the financial risk of the company declined. In any event, either cause should act to push the preferred stock already outstanding above its par or stated value. But this does not happen to callable shares. They seldom appreciate much above their call value because of the possibility of a call at a known price.

Some newly issued preferred stock, like some bonds, has a period during which the security cannot be called. This is known as *call pro-*

tection. The length of this period or whether call protection exists is determined by competitive forces in the capital markets when the issue is sold. Investors are often willing to accept a lower yield on a security having longer call protection, and vice versa.[3]

TAXATION OF PREFERRED STOCK DIVIDENDS

Corporations normally are taxed on only 15 percent of their dividend income. For example, if $100 of dividends are received, only $15 of this income is taxed. Stated another way, a corporation paying taxes at a rate of 46 percent on regular income would pay only 15 percent of this rate, or 6.9 percent, on dividend income.[4]

Because of this tax feature, preferred stock holds a yield advantage over bonds for corporate holders, and most high-grade preferred stock is held by corporations. Table 8–3 shows what before-tax yields are necessary on various types of securities to equal the after-tax yield on preferred stock entitled to the full 85 percent corporate tax exemption. A preferred stock yielding 7 percent before taxes has the same after-tax yield as a fully taxable bond yielding 12.04 percent or a tax-exempt bond having a 6.5 percent yield. Because of the yield advantages of preferred stock and tax-exempt bonds, strong corporate demand for these securities causes their market yields to be below those on high-grade corporate bonds.

Convertible and lower grade preferred shares are another matter entirely. While some corporations own these issues, most are held by individuals. These securities are somewhat speculative. The issues are

---

[3] Of the approximately 900 preferred issues listed in the 1977 issue of Salomon Brothers, *Preferred Stock Guide* (New York, 1978), only 15 were not callable. Issues listed in this guide are higher grade securities. However, there is no evidence to indicate that lower grade securities are less likely to be callable. All convertible securities are callable so that the corporation can force conversion.

[4] The dividend offset is designed to reduce what would be triple taxation. Without it taxes would be levied as follows: Corporation A would be taxed on its earnings, a portion of which were paid to Corporation B as dividends on the stock of A held by B. Corporation B would then be taxed on these dividends because they are income to it. When B declares dividends, B's shareholders will next be taxed.

The companies which can most easily and advantageously make use of the dividend offset are companies which hold large amounts of high-grade equity securities as investments. In practice these companies are property and casualty insurance companies, life insurance companies, and to a lesser extent other financial corporations. With the exception of a small dividend exclusion that is discussed in Chapter 15, individuals are fully taxed on their dividend income.

TABLE 8–3
Table of equivalent market yields necessary to provide the same after-tax yield as an 85 percent exempt preferred issue, assuming corporate taxes levied at 46 percent

Before-tax yield on preferred entitled to 85% exemption	Before-tax yield on fully-taxable debt security	Yield on tax-exempt debt security
7.0%	12.04%	6.50%
7.5	12.93	6.98
8.0	13.80	7.45
8.5	14.65	7.91
9.0	15.52	8.38
9.5	16.39	8.85
10.0	17.24	9.31
10.5	18.11	9.78
11.0	18.96	10.24
11.5	19.83	10.71

often fairly small in amount and may be illiquid. These are not the investment characteristics desired by corporations which generally seek securities having low financial risk and good liquidity. But such securities, convertibles in particular, are suitable for many individuals. This argument is examined further in the following sections of this chapter.

ANALYSIS OF PREFERRED STOCK

Grading preferred securities

Formal grading of preferred stocks is provided by Standard & Poor's, Moody's, Fitch Investors Service, and several other firms. Figure 8–2 is taken from the Fitch Investors Service *Corporate Bond Rating Guide,* which also includes ratings on preferred stock and commercial paper. It shows how this company assigns preferred stock ratings.

Grading of preferred stock—like the grading of bonds—is based upon the probability that future earnings will be sufficient to pay dividends. The most widely used analytical measure is the ratio of funds available to pay dividends to preferred dividend requirements. But this calculation is not so simple or straightforward as the interest coverage ratio (earnings before interest and taxes ÷ interest charges) discussed in the previous chapter. Dividends must be paid out of *after-tax* earnings, while interest is paid before taxes are calculated. Most analysts

242

FIGURE 8–2
Description of preferred stock ratings

"IT'S DEPENDABLE"

FITCH INVESTORS SERVICE

CORPORATE BOND RATING BOOK
TWELVE BARCLAY STREET
NEW YORK, N.Y. 10007
ESTABLISHED 1913

KEY TO FITCH PREFERRED STOCK RATING SYMBOLS   1978

AAA

The "AAA" rating represents the maximum safety in the realm of preferred stocks. It applies where asset protection is strong, the debt-and-preferred stock ratio to total capitalization is moderate, and there are positive indications that the maintenance of good coverages of fixed charges and preferred dividend requirements is assured. Sinking funds and redemption provisions could affect this rating, which would apply only to a senior preferred issue.

AA

The "AA" rating category is regarded as very high grade. It has characteristics only slightly below those of the "AAA" classification. The protective elements are less strikingly broad. There is reasonable assurance that they can be maintained.

A

The "A" preferred issues are not so heavily protected as the two upper classes. However, they are regarded as high grade. Asset protection and coverages of fixed charges and preferred dividend requirements are adequate and are expected to be maintained.

BBB

The "BBB" category is described as good grade. It lacks the more protective assurances of the preceding three rating categories. Dependence on current earnings is more manifest. While preferred stocks so rated may be held with reasonable assurance, current results should be watched closely for possible signs of reversal.

BB

The investment element of this category is not so well established as in the "BBB" category. The margin of protection is light or widely fluctuating. The future of the enterprise may not seem fully assured.

B

Preferred stocks so rated are lightly protected. While, as a rule, earnings will be sufficient to pay dividends, sharply unfavorable changes may cause threatened or actual default.

CCC

This rating indicates that the preferred stock is clearly hazardous and should be assessed on its chances in a possible reorganization of the company.

Source: *Corporate Bond Rating Guide* (New York: Fitch Investors Service, 1978), p. 197.

calculate the amount of before-tax income necessary to meet preferred dividend requirements and then add this amount directly to the firm's interest charges to produce a measure of dividend coverage. An example is perhaps in order.

The general formula for calculating how much pre-tax income is necessary to provide a given after-tax amount is

$$\text{Before-tax income} = \frac{\text{After-tax amount}}{1 - \text{Tax rate}}$$

The dividend requirement of an issue of 25,000 shares of preferred stock paying a $7 annual dividend is $175,000. If this company pays taxes at a 40 percent rate, it would have to earn $291,667 of before-tax income to have this amount available after taxes for the dividend payment.

$$\text{Before-tax income} = \frac{\$175,000}{1 - .4}$$
$$= \$291,667$$

This amount would then be added to any interest charges that the company had, and a measure, *times dividends earned—overall method*, is calculated.[5]

Proceeding with this example, if the company were obligated to pay $2 million of interest and had earnings before interest and taxes of $12 million, its preferred dividend coverage ratio would be 5.24 to 1.

$$\text{Coverage ratio} = \frac{\text{Earnings before interest and taxes}}{\text{Interest requirements} + \text{Dividend requirements}}$$
$$= \frac{\$12,000,000}{\$2,000,000 + \$291,667}$$
$$= 5.24$$

Whether this ratio is adequate to reasonably insure future payment of preferred dividends depends upon the variability of the company's earnings. Analysts usually calculate the ratio over enough years to include periods of low earnings to see how well the coverage ratio holds

---

[5] Another common way of computing the dividend coverage ratio is to divide earnings after interest and taxes by preferred dividend requirements. This method produces the same ratio as the overall method only if there are no interest charges—an unlikely situation for most companies. This calculation would indicate a dividend coverage ratio of over 34 to 1 for the preferred issue used in our example. But such a result is totally illogical! A senior issue of bonds cannot be less safe (as measured by the coverage ratio) than a junior issue of preferred. The overall method of measuring coverage ratios makes this fact obvious.

up under adverse circumstances. The dividend coverage ratio provides less assurance of dividend payments than the interest coverage ratio does of interest payments because dividends are never a legal liability of the company. The value of convertible preferred stock, like convertible bonds, is based more upon the current and expected future prices of the company's common stock than upon coverage ratios, as will be explained shortly.

Price and yield considerations

Preferred stocks are considered to be equity securities, but they more closely resemble bonds because of their fixed dividend payments and lack of voting power. Companies issuing preferred stocks often designate this stock as Class A common stock and the regular common stock as Class B common, or vice versa. In normal usage these securities are referred to as simply the "preferred" and "common" of the company.

For some corporations, utilities in particular, preferred stock is an important source of financing. These companies often have several series of preferred stock outstanding at the same time. Different series are usually designated by letters—Series A, Series B—or numbers—First Preferred, Second Preferred, and so on. Since these different issues will probably have been sold at different times and under different interest rate conditions, it is normal for the dividend rates of each issue to be different. For example, Long Island Lighting has outstanding four separate issues of $100 par preferred stock. All are listed on the NYSE, all are callable, none has sinking fund protection, and all are rated A by Standard & Poor's. Table 8–4 lists the important investment characteristics of these securities.

Note several important things in Table 8–4: Dividend rates are

TABLE 8–4
Yield and dividend rate on four Long Island Lighting preferred stock issues

Issues	First issued	Currently callable at	Dividend rate	Par value	Price 1/8/79	Yield 1/8/79
LIL Series "B"............	1952	101	5.00%	100	49	10.2
LIL Series "E"............	1954	102	4.35	100	43	10.1
LIL Series "J"............	1971	110	8.12	100	78	10.4
LIL Series "K"	1971	115	8.30	100	83	10.0

Source: Standard & Poor's *Stock Guide*, February 1979. Price quotes as of January 8, 1979.

low—4.35 and 5 percent—on the first two issues because they were sold when money rates in general were low. The dividend rates for the "J" and "K" issues are much higher because these securities were sold when market rates of interest were high. Preferred stock dividend rates and interest rates move up and down together because they are both determined by the supply of and demand for credit.

At any one time, dividend rates tend to be made uniform by the action of the market. This does not mean that every preferred stock of a given grade will yield exactly the same rate. These investments have other characteristics which make one issue more or less desirable than another, and yields mirror these differences. Markets for many preferred shares are relatively inactive, and the number of shares in each issue is often small. Market participants are often corporations, who buy and sell in large quantities. Trades of specific issues will often knock these yields temporarily "out of line."

Computation of preferred yields.   The yield on preferred stock is computed somewhat differently from that on bonds. Most bonds have a maturity date and a stated par value because it is expected that they will be redeemed sometime in the future. While most preferred stocks are callable, the time at which they will be called is unknown; the securities may remain outstanding indefinitely. Because of this, the yield to maturity calculation used in Chapter 7 is inappropriate.

The usual yield calculation is simply one of dividing the annual dividend by the current market price. For example, a preferred stock paying $5 per year in dividends, having a market price of $65 would yield 7.69 percent.

$$\frac{\$\,5}{\$65} = 0.0769, \text{ or } 7.69\%.$$

So long as this security continues to pay $5 per year in dividends, it will yield 7.69 percent to the person who purchased it at $65.

The yield calculation for preferred stock is certainly simple enough to perform, but even so, tables have been prepared which provide investors with approximate yields "at a glance." Figure 8–3 is a portion of such a table. The market price and dividend are "lined up" by looking down the appropriate dividend row and across the appropriate price column to determine the yield.

While the par value of bonds is nearly always $1,000, the par or stated amount of a preferred share may be practically any amount. The most common value is $100, followed by $50, $25, and $20. Par

FIGURE 8-3

Portion of a preferred stock yield table

DIVIDEND

Price	3.50	3.60	3.70	3.80	3.90	4.00	4.10	4.20	4.30	4.40	4.50	4.60	4.70	4.80	4.90	5.00	5.10	5.20	5.30	5.40	Price
																Yield					
50	7.00	7.20	7.40	7.60	7.80	8.00	8.20	8.40	8.60	8.80	9.00	9.20	9.40	9.60	9.80						50
52	6.73	6.92	7.12	7.31	7.50	7.69	7.88	8.08	8.27	8.46	8.65	8.85	9.04	9.23	9.42	9.62	9.81				52
54	6.48	6.67	6.85	7.04	7.22	7.41	7.59	7.78	7.96	8.15	8.33	8.52	8.70	8.89	9.07	9.26	9.44	9.63	9.81		54
55	6.36	6.55	6.73	6.91	7.09	7.27	7.45	7.64	7.82	8.00	8.18	8.36	8.55	8.73	8.91	9.09	9.27	9.45	9.64	9.82	55
56	6.25	6.43	6.61	6.79	6.96	7.14	7.32	7.50	7.68	7.86	8.04	8.21	8.39	8.57	8.75	8.93	9.11	9.29	9.46	9.64	56
57	6.14	6.32	6.49	6.67	6.84	7.02	7.19	7.37	7.54	7.72	7.89	8.07	8.25	8.42	8.60	8.77	8.95	9.12	9.30	9.47	57
58	6.03	6.21	6.38	6.55	6.72	6.90	7.07	7.24	7.41	7.59	7.76	7.93	8.10	8.28	8.45	8.62	8.79	8.97	9.14	9.31	58
59	5.93	6.10	6.27	6.44	6.61	6.78	6.95	7.12	7.29	7.46	7.63	7.80	7.97	8.14	8.31	8.47	8.64	8.81	8.98	9.15	59
60	5.83	6.00	6.17	6.33	6.50	6.67	6.83	7.00	7.17	7.33	7.50	7.67	7.83	8.00	8.17	8.33	8.50	8.67	8.83	9.00	60
61	5.74	5.90	6.07	6.23	6.39	6.56	6.72	6.89	7.05	7.21	7.38	7.54	7.70	7.87	8.03	8.20	8.36	8.52	8.69	8.85	61
62	5.65	5.81	5.97	6.13	6.29	6.45	6.61	6.77	6.94	7.10	7.26	7.42	7.58	7.74	7.90	8.06	8.23	8.39	8.55	8.71	62
63	5.56	5.71	5.87	6.03	6.19	6.35	6.51	6.67	6.83	6.98	7.14	7.30	7.46	7.62	7.78	7.94	8.10	8.25	8.41	8.57	63
64	5.47	5.63	5.78	5.94	6.09	6.25	6.41	6.56	6.72	6.88	7.03	7.19	7.34	7.50	7.66	7.81	7.97	8.13	8.28	8.44	64
65	5.38	5.54	5.69	5.85	6.00	6.15	6.31	6.46	6.62	6.77	6.92	7.08	7.23	7.38	7.54	7.69	7.85	8.00	8.15	8.31	65
66	5.30	5.45	5.61	5.76	5.91	6.06	6.21	6.36	6.52	6.67	6.82	6.97	7.12	7.27	7.42	7.58	7.73	7.88	8.03	8.18	66
67	5.22	5.37	5.52	5.67	5.82	5.97	6.12	6.27	6.42	6.57	6.72	6.87	7.01	7.16	7.31	7.46	7.61	7.76	7.91	8.06	67
68	5.15	5.29	5.44	5.59	5.74	5.88	6.03	6.18	6.32	6.47	6.62	6.76	6.91	7.06	7.21	7.35	7.50	7.65	7.79	7.94	68
69	5.07	5.22	5.36	5.51	5.65	5.80	5.94	6.09	6.23	6.38	6.52	6.67	6.81	6.96	7.10	7.25	7.39	7.54	7.68	7.83	69
70	5.00	5.14	5.29	5.43	5.57	5.71	5.86	6.00	6.14	6.29	6.43	6.57	6.71	6.86	7.00	7.14	7.29	7.43	7.57	7.71	70
71	4.93	5.07	5.21	5.35	5.49	5.63	5.77	5.92	6.06	6.20	6.34	6.48	6.62	6.76	6.90	7.04	7.18	7.32	7.46	7.61	71
72	4.86	5.00	5.14	5.28	5.42	5.56	5.69	5.83	5.97	6.11	6.25	6.39	6.53	6.67	6.81	6.94	7.08	7.22	7.36	7.50	72
73	4.79	4.93	5.07	5.21	5.34	5.48	5.62	5.75	5.89	6.03	6.16	6.30	6.44	6.58	6.71	6.85	6.99	7.12	7.26	7.40	73
74	4.73	4.86	5.00	5.14	5.27	5.41	5.54	5.68	5.81	5.95	6.08	6.22	6.35	6.49	6.62	6.76	6.89	7.03	7.16	7.30	74
75	4.67	4.80	4.93	5.07	5.20	5.33	5.47	5.60	5.73	5.87	6.00	6.13	6.27	6.40	6.53	6.67	6.80	6.93	7.07	7.20	75
76	4.61	4.74	4.87	5.00	5.13	5.26	5.39	5.53	5.66	5.79	5.92	6.05	6.18	6.32	6.45	6.58	6.71	6.84	6.97	7.11	76
77	4.55	4.68	4.81	4.94	5.06	5.19	5.32	5.45	5.58	5.71	5.84	5.97	6.10	6.23	6.36	6.49	6.62	6.75	6.88	7.01	77
78	4.49	4.62	4.74	4.87	5.00	5.13	5.26	5.38	5.51	5.64	5.77	5.90	6.03	6.15	6.28	6.41	6.54	6.67	6.79	6.92	78
79	4.43	4.56	4.68	4.81	4.94	5.06	5.19	5.32	5.44	5.57	5.70	5.82	5.95	6.08	6.20	6.33	6.46	6.58	6.71	6.84	79
80	4.38	4.50	4.63	4.75	4.88	5.00	5.13	5.25	5.38	5.50	5.63	5.75	5.88	6.00	6.13	6.25	6.38	6.50	6.63	6.75	80
81	4.32	4.44	4.57	4.69	4.81	4.94	5.06	5.19	5.31	5.43	5.56	5.68	5.80	5.93	6.05	6.17	6.30	6.42	6.54	6.67	81
82	4.27	4.39	4.51	4.63	4.76	4.88	5.00	5.12	5.24	5.37	5.49	5.61	5.73	5.85	5.98	6.10	6.22	6.34	6.46	6.59	82
83	4.22	4.34	4.46	4.58	4.70	4.82	4.94	5.06	5.18	5.30	5.42	5.54	5.66	5.78	5.90	6.02	6.14	6.27	6.39	6.51	83
84	4.17	4.29	4.40	4.52	4.64	4.76	4.88	5.00	5.12	5.24	5.36	5.48	5.60	5.71	5.83	5.95	6.07	6.19	6.31	6.43	84
85	4.12	4.24	4.35	4.47	4.59	4.71	4.82	4.94	5.06	5.18	5.29	5.41	5.53	5.65	5.76	5.88	6.00	6.12	6.24	6.35	85
86	4.07	4.19	4.30	4.42	4.53	4.65	4.77	4.88	5.00	5.12	5.23	5.35	5.47	5.58	5.70	5.81	5.93	6.05	6.16	6.28	86
87	4.02	4.14	4.25	4.37	4.48	4.60	4.71	4.83	4.94	5.06	5.17	5.29	5.40	5.52	5.63	5.75	5.86	5.98	6.09	6.21	87
88	3.98	4.09	4.20	4.32	4.43	4.55	4.66	4.77	4.89	5.00	5.11	5.23	5.34	5.45	5.57	5.68	5.80	5.91	6.02	6.14	88
89	3.93	4.04	4.16	4.27	4.38	4.49	4.61	4.72	4.83	4.94	5.06	5.17	5.28	5.39	5.51	5.62	5.73	5.84	5.96	6.07	89
90	3.89	4.00	4.11	4.22	4.33	4.44	4.56	4.67	4.78	4.89	5.00	5.11	5.22	5.33	5.44	5.56	5.67	5.78	5.89	6.00	90
92	3.80	3.91	4.02	4.13	4.24	4.35	4.46	4.57	4.67	4.78	4.89	5.00	5.11	5.22	5.33	5.43	5.54	5.65	5.76	5.87	92
94	3.72	3.83	3.94	4.04	4.15	4.26	4.36	4.47	4.57	4.68	4.79	4.89	5.00	5.11	5.21	5.32	5.43	5.53	5.64	5.74	94
96	3.65	3.75	3.85	3.96	4.06	4.17	4.27	4.38	4.48	4.58	4.69	4.79	4.90	5.00	5.10	5.21	5.31	5.42	5.52	5.63	96
98	3.57	3.67	3.78	3.88	3.98	4.08	4.18	4.29	4.39	4.49	4.59	4.69	4.80	4.90	5.00	5.10	5.20	5.31	5.41	5.51	98
102	3.43	3.53	3.63	3.73	3.82	3.92	4.02	4.12	4.22	4.31	4.41	4.51	4.61	4.71	4.80	4.90	5.00	5.10	5.20	5.29	102
104	3.37	3.46	3.56	3.65	3.75	3.85	3.94	4.04	4.13	4.23	4.33	4.42	4.52	4.62	4.71	4.81	4.90	5.00	5.10	5.19	104

Source: *Preferred Stock Guide, 1970 ed.* (New York: Salomon Brothers, 1970), p. 43.

value carries the same meaning for preferred shareholders as it does for bondholders. If either security is redeemed, the owner will receive this amount, plus any call premium for early redemption. When a company is dissolved, preferred shareholders and bondholders receive only the par value of their securities. Yield calculations are somewhat complicated by the fact that preferred dividends are sometimes stated as a percent of par and sometimes as a flat dollar amount. In the above example, the par value of the security can be *assumed* to be $100 since its yield is then reasonable in light of historical market conditions.

Financial risk

Straight preferred stocks closely resemble bonds so far as financial risk characteristics are concerned. There is practically no doubt that dividends on the higher graded securities will be paid for the foreseeable future. Lower graded or nongraded securities have more financial risk, as would be expected, and yields reflect the difference in risk. Table 8–5 shows this relationship by listing price and yield data of several utility preferred issues. All investment characteristics other than grade are nearly identical.

TABLE 8–5
Grade and yield of selected utility preferred stocks

Issue	Standard & Poors' rating	Dividend	Yield 2/28/79
Northern States Power "G"	AA	$ 4.56	9.4%
Central Illinois Light 4.50%	A	4.50	9.8
Niagara Mohawk Power "G"	BBB	5.25	10.6
Portland General Electric 11.50%	BB	11.50	11.1

Note: No AAA or B ranked public utility preferred stocks having investment characteristics similar to those above could be identified in March 1979.
Source: Standard & Poor's *Stock Guide*, March 1979.

Purchasing power risk

Dividends on outstanding preferred shares do not increase, so in a period of price inflation each dividend purchases less goods and services. Thus purchasing power risk affects straight preferred issues exactly like it affects straight bonds. Everything previously stated about how debt investments are affected by inflation pertains to these securities.

Interest rate risk

Preferred shares are seldom redeemed and therefore resemble perpetual bonds as far as interest rate risk is concerned. In practical terms this means that prices of these securities vary *even more* than those of bonds. Most bonds will be redeemed at some time in the future, at par, and market prices will return to near par as this time approaches. Preferred shares do not have this characteristic. As long as market dividend rates remain above coupon rates of outstanding preferred shares, prices of these securities will be below par.

Table 8–6 shows the effects of interest rate risk on straight preferred stocks of different grades. All these securities are listed on the NYSE. Two are industrial companies and three are utilities, but the investment characteristics of all securities are similar except for grade. On average these securities sold 40 percent *below* their 1967 prices in 1979. Over the same period of time, long-term Treasury bonds declined only 15 percent in price.

TABLE 8–6
Prices of selected stocks at three different dates

Security	Standard & Poor's rating	Dividend	Close or bid 1/31/79	Close or bid 1/30/70	Close or bid 1/31/67
General Motors $5.00 cumulative preferred .	AAA	$5.00	$61⅝	$72½	$99¼
Northern Indiana Public Service 4.25% cumulative preferred	AA	4.25	44¼	58¾	79¼
Kansas City Power & Light 4.5% cumulative preferred	A	4.50	47	59	84⅜
Long Island Lighting 4.35% cumulative preferred "E"	BBB	4.35	48	55½	82
Armour & Co. $4.75 cumulative preferred	BB	4.75	53½	57½	79½

Source: Standard & Poor's *Stock Guide*, February 1967, 1970, and 1979.

Currently, yield rates on high-grade preferred stocks are far more closely related to the movements in interest rates of long-term bonds than to the dividend rates on common shares. Figure 8–4 shows this re-

FIGURE 8–4
Yields on high-grade debt securities, preferred and common stock

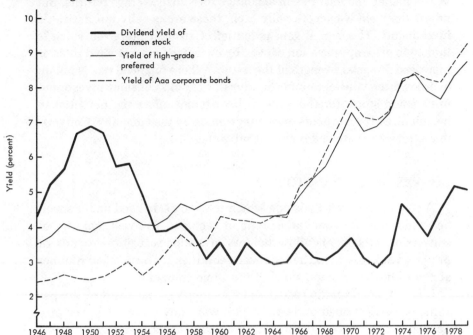

Source: Yield of Aaa Corporate Bonds taken from *Federal Reserve Bulletin*; Yield of High-Grade Preferred from *Moody's Industrial Manual*; Dividend Yield of Common Stock from *Standard & Poor's Basic Statistics.*

lationship clearly. This figure also shows that, in the eyes of recent investors, high-grade preferred stocks *appear* to have lower risk characteristics than do the highest grade debt securities—because they have had lower yields than bonds in most years since 1963. The explanation for this illogical relationship lies in the fact that the dividends on preferred stocks, so far as most corporations are concerned, are taxed at only 15 percent of the amount of the dividend, while all interest income is taxable.

INVESTING IN PREFERRED STOCK

With rare exception, high-grade straight preferred stocks are not attractive investments for the average individual. Their yields are lower than can be obtained on bonds, and bonds usually offer less financial and interest rate risk. Lower grade straight preferred stocks offer higher yields. These securities may be purchased by persons willing to accept higher financial risk in exchange for above average returns. But unless the yield is exceptionally high, these are usually not desirable investments. The capital gain potential of straight preferred stock is limited to price appreciation caused by decreased market yield rates or increased financial strength of the issuer. Where financial risk is not an overpowering consideration, the investor should consider investment in common stock, for this type of investment offers the potential to benefit directly from gains in earnings made by the company. Convertible preferred shares offer similar advantages.

CONVERTIBLE SECURITIES

A convertible security is one which may be exchanged under specified conditions for some other type of security. The vast majority of conversion agreements allow holders of senior securities—bonds or preferred stocks—to exchange these securities for a specified number of shares of the common stock of the same company.

It is estimated that in recent years as much as one-third of the par value of newly issued preferred stock was convertible. A lower proportion (from 1.5 to 22.0 percent) of newly issued bonds carried this feature. But because so many more debt securities are issued each year, a much larger dollar amount of convertible bonds are available to investors. For this reason, and because the investment characteristics of convertible preferred and convertible bonds are very similar, the following discussion will emphasize convertible bonds.

The conversion agreement

Convertible bonds closely resemble other corporate bonds in that they usually have a $1,000 par value, they pay a fixed amount of interest per annum, they have a fixed maturity date, and they are almost always callable. Most are debenture bonds, and their interest payments and other claims are often subordinated to those of other debt holders. The most important feature of these securities is that they can be exchanged for a certain number of shares of common stock in the company which issued them. This conversion agreement takes various forms. In one case a bond may be convertible until its maturity into a fixed number of shares of common stock. Another bond may be convertible into a fixed number of shares of stock of the company for some period after it is issued, and then convertible into a lesser number of shares after that date. The agreement might be written so that the bond cannot be converted until some time period has passed after the issue date. Like all other covenants of a bond issue, the description of the convertibility agreement will appear in the bond indenture and prospectus. For preferred shares, the conversion agreement is stated in the prospectus and usually on the face of the security. Moody's, Standard & Poor's, and other financial reporting companies summarize conversion agreements in their handbooks.

The actual conversion agreement may be written in two ways. The bond indenture may state that each bond is convertible into a certain number of shares of common stock, or it might say that the bond is convertible into common stock at a certain dollar value per share. The meaning of both statements is identical.

The conversion statement from the prospectus of American Hospital Supply Corporation is presented as Figure 8-5. In this example the statement describes the convertibility as being at a conversion price of $29.50 per share of common stock. The statement might have read

FIGURE 8-5
Conversion statement

$75,000,000

AMERICAN HOSPITAL SUPPLY CORPORATION
5¾% Convertible Subordinated Debentures Due 1999

The Debentures are convertible, unless previously redeemed, into Common Stock of American Hospital Supply Corporation at a conversion price of $29.50 per share, subject to adjustment in certain events. On November 25, 1974, the reported closing sales price of the Common Stock on the New York Stock Exchange was $26.125 per share.

Beginning on December 1, 1985, the Debentures are entitled to an annual sinking fund in installments of $4,125,000, which is calculated to retire at least 77 percent of the issue prior to maturity. AHSC also has the noncumulative option to increase any sinking fund payment by an amount not exceeding the mandatory payment. The sinking fund redemption price is 100 percent of the principal amount plus accrued interest. Interest is payable June 1 and December 1.

The Debentures are redeemable at AHSC's option, in while or in part, at any time on 30 days' notice, at 105.75 percent of the principal amount, plus accrued interest, if redeemed prior to December 1, 1975, at decreasing premiums thereafter, and without premium on and after December 1, 1994.

Source: American Hospital Supply Corporation, Prospectus, November 26, 1974, p. 1.

"convertible into 33.8983 shares of common," because dividing the par value of the bond by this number of shares gives a conversion price of $29.50 per share.

$$\frac{\text{Par value of bond}}{\substack{\text{Number of shares of stock} \\ \text{into which bond is convertible}}} = \text{Conversion price}$$

$$\frac{\$1{,}000}{33.8983} = \$29.50$$

Conversion agreements are normally protected against *dilution*. This term means that if the company changes its equity capitalization, the conversion ratio will automatically be altered so that holders of convertible securities will not be harmed. Dilution most commonly occurs through stock splits, stock dividends, exercise of rights or warrants, and mergers—topics which are covered in later chapters.

The aforementioned American Hospital Supply Corporation convertible bond is protected against dilution. If the company declared a two-for-one stock split, it would increase its authorized and outstanding common stock by a factor of two. Each shareholder would then own twice the shares held prior to the split. But because the company is no more profitable because of the split, it will have no additional value. As a consequence, the market price of the common stock should decrease to one-half of its before-the-split value. In this example, protection against dilution would take the form of halving the conversion price from $29.50 per share to $14.75. Or in terms of the conversion ratio, this ratio would be increased to 67.7966 shares of common for each bond. The result of these changes is to keep the conversion value of the bond the same as it was before the stock split. Most convertible securities are protected against dilution, but investors should satisfy themselves of this fact before purchasing any of them.

The value of convertibility

Convertible securities offer advantages to both buyers and issuers. These securities are expected to provide purchasers with interest or dividend income up to the time they are converted. Returns will probably be at a lower rate than is available from a similar conventional nonconvertible security. However, the advantage of possible price appreciation far in excess of that found in nonconvertible securities works to offset the lower returns. This potential results from the fact that the price of the common stock of the company may increase an unlimited amount.

As long as the market price of the common stock of American Hospital Supply is less than $29.50, the bond will *theoretically* be valued on the basis of its yield, grade, and maturity—just like conventional bonds. But as the price of the common stock increases toward the bond conversion price, the market price of the bond will increase. A convertible bond which has any potential for profitable conversion will almost always sell at a premium over nonconvertible securities, even when the price of the common stock is far below the conversion price of the bond. Figure 8–6 shows the theoretical relationship of stock and convertible bond prices of American Hospital Supply Corporation.

The situation pictured in Figure 8–6 is somewhat idealized in that it is assumed that interest rates have not changed from the time when this security was issued, and that the grade of the bond has also remained constant. When the market price of the common stock is low, from zero to $5 for example, the conversion privilege has little value. The bond will probably sell slightly above par because of the possibility that the common stock may rise in value. If the price of the common rises toward the point where the bond can be converted with a profit, the bond will begin to sell at a premium above par. This premium will usually reach a maximum above the "theoretical value" line when the price of the common stock is the same as the conversion value of the bond. In this example this value is $29.50 per share for the common stock.

As the stock exceeds $29.50 per share, the premium over conversion value will eventually disappear. For example, if this stock became worth $40 per share, the market price of the bond would probably be very near to its conversion value of $1,355.93. This happens because investors have ceased to look at the security as a bond; it becomes in their minds 33.8983 shares of common stock. While the bond continues to have value because it pays interest, the yield to maturity is lower than yields on other securities of equal grade and maturity. Furthermore, if common stock dividends have risen, they may be greater than the interest payment. When this occurs, the bond should probably be converted or sold. Prices of convertible preferred stocks are influenced by the same factors.

FIGURE 8-6
Theoretical value of a convertible bond of American Hospital Supply Corporation corresponding to different market prices of the common stock of the company

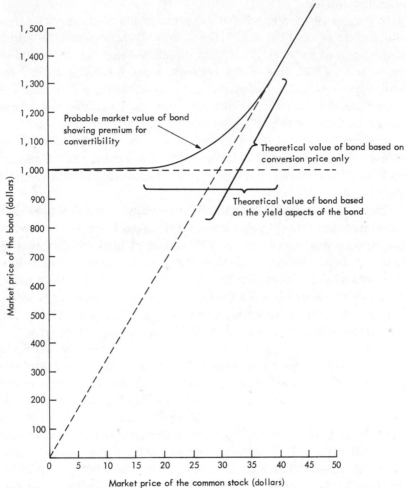

Note: Par value of the bond is $1,000; bond is convertible into common stock at $29.50 per share.

Investment characteristics of convertibles

Convertibility usually allows a company to sell securities at a lower than normal interest or dividend cost. In some cases, because of the risk characteristics of the company issuing them, securities which could probably be sold only at very high yield rates, if at all, may find a willing market if they are convertible. A further advantage of issuing convertibles is that the company is really selling common stock in disguise. Almost all convertible securities are callable so that the management of the company can force the owners to trade their senior securities for common stock or the call price if this action is desired.

Convertible securities are usually at least mildly speculative. A person buying such securities usually accepts a lower yield payment and a less firm creditor position in exchange for the possibility of above average profits. In 1973–74 there was a great decline in the amount of convertible securities issued. This decline was the result of the relatively low market prices of common stocks during these years. Most corporations do not sell convertible securities when this condition prevails, but investors have a wide selection of previously issued securities.

Potential for conversion.   When analyzing a convertible security, one always asks whether the price of the common can be expected to rise. If price appreciation cannot be anticipated with a reasonable degree of certainty, then the convertible security is probably not a good investment. Even if market conditions indicate an increase in stock prices, there are other things which must be examined before putting in a buy order. Is the market price of the common stock so far below the conversion price that it is unlikely that the conversion feature will ever have any value? A bond convertible into 20 shares of common will have little convertibility value until the price of the common is near $50 per share. If the market price of the common stock is $25, an investor might have to wait many years before reaping any benefit from the convertibility feature of the bond. In this case one might be better off to purchase the common stock if its price is expected to rise.

Many securities have conversion ratios which decline over time. Initially the bond might be convertible into 30 shares of common. After five years the conversion might be into 25 shares, and after another five years into 20. Under such a situation the market price of the common must not only rise, it must rise relatively soon because the conversion privilege becomes less valuable as time passes. It is possible to pay more in reduced yield and increased financial risk than the conversion privilege is worth.

Risk characteristics of convertibles. At various times there has been such a demand for convertible securities that many companies of really poor financial character have been able to sell them. Persons buying convertibles apparently believe that because these securities are not common stock they are relatively safe investments. This is not true. Persons purchasing convertible securities should examine them carefully to see that interest payments will be made while they wait for the convertibility feature of the security to have some value. Convertibles are probably more speculative in character than most investors realize, and yet these securities do provide the potential for sharing in the profits of the company, in a way which is impossible with a straight debt or preferred stock investment.

Convertibles and the small investor. Convertible securities should have special interest for the small investor who is willing to spend some time looking for bargains. Many preferred issues are small in size and therefore likely to escape the attention of the large security houses. With no one to place them on a "recommended list," they may often sell at less than their intrinsic, or true, value.

SUMMARY

This chapter examined the investment characteristics of *straight preferred stock* and *convertible securities.* Straight preferred stock has investment characteristics which make it resemble debt more than equity. Dividend payments are usually fixed and are paid before common dividends. If the corporation is dissolved, creditors are paid off first, then preferred shareholders. Preferred stock is classified as equity capital for purposes of computing a company's earnings, but preferred shareholders may not be allowed to vote for directors.

Most straight preferred stock is owned by corporations because they pay income taxes on only 15 percent of income they receive as dividends. For this reason yields on high-grade straight preferred stocks are lower than yields on bonds of similar grade.

Investment characteristics of straight preferred stock are low financial risk (depending upon grade), fair liquidity, high purchasing power risk, and extremely high interest rate risk. In this last respect they are more risky than bonds. Straight preferred stock is not considered a suitable investment alternative for most individuals because these securities have all the worst investment characteristics of bonds, along with more financial risk and less yield.

Convertible preferred stock and convertible bonds bear close resemblance to each other. Their most distinguishing feature is that these securities may be converted into a certain number of shares of the common stock of the company which has issued them. This feature makes possible a large rise in the market price of these senior securities—if the price of the common rises above the conversion price. When common prices are lower than this amount, the convertible securities are priced upon the basis of yield and grade, the determinants of price for nonconvertible bonds and preferred stocks.

Investment characteristics of convertible securities are (1) fairly high financial risk, (2) low interest rate and purchasing power risk because of their potential for vastly increasing prices, and (3) possible low liquidity, depending upon the individual issue.

PROBLEMS

1. An issue of preferred stock has a par value of $50 per share, a coupon dividend of 8 percent, and a current market price of $44 per share. This security has no call or maturity date. What is the current dividend in dollars, and the current yield?
2. If the security described in Problem 1 were convertible into two shares of common stock, and the common had a current market price of $26.50 per share, what would be the approximate theoretical market price of each preferred share? What if the common sold for $19.25 per share; what would be the market price of the preferred then?
3. A bond is convertible into 40 shares of common stock. What price will the stock have to attain before it becomes profitable to convert the bond? (Assume a $1,000 par, which is the price at which the bond is selling.)
4. You have the choice of purchasing either the convertible bonds of a company or its common stock. The bonds are priced at $1,100 and pay a coupon of 8 percent; each bond is convertible into 40 shares of common stock. The common sells fo $27.50 per share and pays a dividend of $2 per share. Would you purchase the common directly or the bonds? Give reasons for your choice.
5. A company has outstanding an issue of 6 percent bonds having a par value of $10,000,000 and a 7 percent preferred issue having a $5,000,000 par value. If the company has earnings before taxes of $2.5 million, what is the dividend coverage ratio for the preferred? (Assume the company pays 40 percent of earnings in taxes.)

6. A convertible bond issue is fully protected against dilution. The company has a three-for-one stock split. The original conversion ratio was 50 shares of common for each bond. What is the new conversion ratio and conversion price?

QUESTIONS

1. List the advantages and disadvantages of owning straight preferred stock.
2. What are the different types of preferred stocks and their legal characteristics?
3. What investment advantage does a cumulative preferred stock offer investors over common stock? What disadvantages?
4. What advantages do convertible securities offer investors and the companies which issue them?
5. Most straight preferred stock is owned by corporations. Why is this?
6. Convertible bonds are sometimes described as "equity investments with the risk removed." Explain the meaning of this statement.
7. Changes in market rates of interest affect which security most—noncallable high-grade straight preferred stock, or a typical high-grade corporate bond which is also noncallable?
8. Look through a stock guide and note the market prices, coupon (stated) yields, and current yields of preferred issues of any large utility. The market prices and coupon yields of securities of different issues will usually differ, perhaps greatly, but the current yields of all issues will be nearly identical. Why is this true?
9. Most convertible securities are protected against dilution. What does this statement mean? Is such protection desirable?
10. Check recent prices of the American Hospital Supply Corporation convertible bond and the company's common stock. Are these prices what you would expect? If not, why not?

SELECTED READINGS

Ahern, Daniel S. "The Strategic Role of Fixed Income Securities." *The Journal of Portfolio Management.* Spring, 1975.

"Annual Review of the Bond Market." New York: Salomon Brothers, published annually.

Christy, George A. and Clendenin, John C. *Introduction to Investments.* 7th ed. New York: McGraw-Hill, 1978.

Cohen, Jerome B.; Zinbarg, Edward D.; and Zeikel, Arthur. *Investment Analysis and Portfolio Management.* 3rd ed. Homewood, Ill.: Richard D. Irwin, 1977.

Darst, David D. *The Complete Bond Book.* New York: McGraw-Hill, 1975.

Liebowitz, Martin L. "Analysis of Convertible Bonds." *Financial Analysts Handbook.* Vol. 1. Homewood, Ill.: Dow Jones-Irwin, 1975, ch. 10.

Sharpe, William F. *Investments.* Englewood Cliffs, N.J.: Prentice-Hall, 1978.

Walter, James E. and Que, Agustin V. "The Valuation of Convertible Bonds." *Journal of Finance,* June, 1973.

9

Investing in common stock

INTRODUCTION

Every five years the New York Stock Exchange conducts an extensive survey of the number of persons owning common stocks. The most recent results of this investigation appear as Table 9-1. Survey methodology is such that shareholders owning common stock in more than one company or stocks traded in different markets are not counted twice. For example, a person owning NYSE-listed stock and stock listed on the AMEX would be counted as only one of the 25,206,000 persons owning stock in mid-1975. While the number of shareholders has increased about 25 percent during the period covered in the table, 1975 totals are approximately 5 million shareholders less than in 1970.

A 1978 NYSE study, *Public Attitudes Toward Investing,* attempted to learn why so many persons had abandoned direct ownership of common stocks. Among the reasons given were inflation, the perceived high risks of equity ownership, losses taken in market downturns, and the desire to invest in other "safer, less risky" investments. Savings deposits and real property were assets often identified as "more desirable." But at the same time, more people became indirect shareholders. Ownership of life insurance, a share in a pension fund, or investments in certain other financial institutions makes one an indirect owner of common stocks because the assets of these organizations are made up at least partially of common stocks. The NYSE estimates that from 1970 to 1975 the number of indirect shareholders increased by 15 mil-

TABLE 9–1
Total shareholders of public corporations (by types of issues owned)

Types of issues owned	1965		Mid-1975	
	Number of shareholders	Percent of total	Number of shareholders	Percent of total
New York Stock Exchange*	12,430,000	62.0%	17,910,000	71.4%
Other stock exchanges†	1,285,000	6.4	1,000,000	4.0
Over-the-counter‡	3,130,000	15.6	3,292,000	13.1
Investment companies only	3,205,000	16.0	2,890,000	11.5
Subtotal	20,050,000	100.0%	25,092,000	100.0%
Shareholdings in nominee names only (not classified by type of issue)...	70,000		114,000	
Total	20,120,000		25,206,000	

* Includes some persons who also own issues other than those listed on the New York Stock Exchange.
† Includes some persons who also own over-the-counter issues, investment company shares, or both.
‡ Includes some persons who also own investment company shares.
Source: New York Stock Exchange, *Shareownership U.S.A. 1975 Census of Shareowners.*

lion to 115 million persons. This is a trend that is expected to continue. A completely accurate tally of shareholders can't be made because the appropriate information does not exist. There is no doubt, however, that a substantial proportion of the adult American population owns common stock—directly, indirectly, or both ways. An understanding of the legal and other characteristics of this investment is extremely important to everyone.

LEGAL CHARACTERISTICS OF COMMON STOCK

The ownership in a corporation is vested in the common stock shareholders. While many corporations issue bonds, and a lesser number issue preferred stock, all corporations must issue common stock. Stock ownership is evidenced by the stock certificate. A copy of a stock certificate of Levi Strauss & Company is presented as Figure 9–1. This document is representative of most common stock certificates. On its face it contains an identifying serial number, a space to record the number of shares it evidences, the name of the registrar and transfer agent (if both are used), the par value of the stock (if a par value is stated), and usually a statement indicating that the shares are fully

FIGURE 9–1
Share of common stock

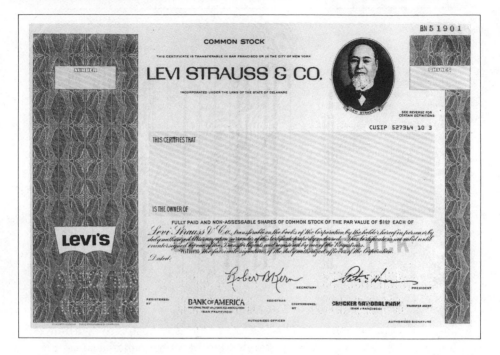

paid and nonassessable. This statement means that regardless of what happens to the company the purchaser has no legal liability to provide more money to it.

This is a very important advantage of common stock ownership. It means that if Levi Strauss & Company went bankrupt or was merged into another company which went bankrupt, Levi Strauss shareholders could not be called upon to provide more capital. The most that shareholders could lose is the purchase price of their shares.

The back of the certificate is usually an assignment statement which the shareholder fills out to transfer ownership of all or a portion of the certificates. Transfer may be made to another individual directly (no brokerage commissions on this kind of transaction), or the certificate may be sold through a broker to an unknown party. In the first case, if John Doe were selling these securities to Richard Roe, Richard Roe's name would be entered in the blank space after the statement, . . . "hereby sell, assign and transfer unto." John Doe would sign and date the security in the appropriate places, and give the certificate to

FIGURE 9–1 (continued)

LEVI STRAUSS & CO.

The Corporation will furnish to any shareholder upon request and without charge a full statement of the designations, relative rights, preferences and limitations of the shares of each class and series authorized to be issued so far as the same have been fixed, and the authority of the Board of Directors to designate and fix the relative rights, preferences and limitations of other series. Such request may be made to the Corporation or to the Transfer Agent.

The following abbreviations, when used in the inscription on the face of this certificate, shall be construed as though they were written out in full according to applicable laws or regulations:

TEN COM—as tenants in common
TEN ENT—as tenants by the entireties
JT TEN —as joint tenants with right of survivorship and not as tenants in common

UNIF GIFT MIN ACT—............Custodian............
(Cust)   (Minor)
under Uniform Gifts to Minors
Act...........
(State)

Additional abbreviations may also be used though not in the above list.

For value received,_____ hereby sell, assign and transfer unto

PLEASE INSERT SOCIAL SECURITY OR OTHER
IDENTIFYING NUMBER OF ASSIGNEE

(PLEASE PRINT OR TYPEWRITE NAME AND ADDRESS, INCLUDING ZIP CODE, OF ASSIGNEE)

_____ shares
of the capital stock represented by the within Certificate, and do hereby irrevocably constitute and appoint
_____ Attorney
to transfer the said stock on the books of the within named Corporation with full power of substitution in the premises.
Dated_____

NOTICE: THE SIGNATURE TO THIS ASSIGNMENT MUST CORRESPOND WITH THE NAME AS WRITTEN UPON THE FACE OF
THE CERTIFICATE IN EVERY PARTICULAR, WITHOUT ALTERATION OR ENLARGEMENT OR ANY CHANGE WHATEVER.

Courtesy of Levi Strauss & Company

Richard Roe. Roe would send the document to the transfer agent; in a few weeks a new certificate would be mailed to him. Mr. Roe would then be recorded as the owner of these shares on the books of the corporation. The only charge for this transaction is a very small transfer fee.

If the sale is through a broker, the securities are usually transferred by naming the broker's firm as the "attorney," and dating and signing the certificate as above. These securities are surrendered to the broker, who will sell them to a third party, Jane Poe for example, by inserting Ms. Poe's name in the "assign and transfer unto" space, and then sending the shares to the transfer agent. The same end may be accomplished by preparing a separate legal document, a *stock assignment*, and mailing this to the broker separately. The stock assignment method is a safe way to transfer securities because the certificates need not be signed. The assignment and the certificates may be mailed in separate envelopes, making theft of the securities even more difficult.

The corporate bylaws and charter contain detailed statements of the rights of shareholders. Because these statements appear there, rather than on the stock certificate, the certificate remains simple and uncluttered. Corporate bonds and preferred shares usually contain much "fine print" which attempts to set down the main contractual obligations of the company. These obligations usually vary from issue to issue and are not recorded in the charter or bylaws except in the most general terms.

The ownership of all common shares is recorded at the offices of the registrar and the corporation. In this sense these securities are registered. However, if they are lost or destroyed, the procedure for obtaining replacement certificates is involved, time-consuming, and somewhat expensive. Shareholders should keep all securities in a place safe from theft or fire; they should never be endorsed until just before they are sold. Most people use registered mail when mailing certificates. Many people leave their securities with their broker for safekeeping and for ease of transfer if they decide to sell.

Rights of common stockholders

The legal characteristics of common shares are more uniform than they are for other types of securities because, under common law, all equity owners receive several important rights. Certain of these rights may be canceled, but only through the agreement of the shareholders.

The right to vote.   Common shareholders elect corporate directors and vote upon other proposals of interest. These include choice of the corporate auditor (independent accountant), employee stock option plans, reorganizations, recapitalizations, mergers, and other important decisions. Under a procedure known as *statutory voting* each shareholder has the right to vote each share held for or against (or to refrain from voting at all) each proposal. This type voting procedure virtually guarantees that shareholders owning a majority of the common stock will elect all directors and will totally control voting on other issues. *Cumulative voting* is designed to give minority shareholders more opportunity to have a voice in management by making it easier to elect at least some corporate directors.

Assume this situation: Five directors are to be elected. Five candidates are supported by a group owning 101 common shares; five other candidates are supported by shareholders owning 100 shares. Under statutory voting the majority shareholders will elect all the directors because they can vote one more share for each of their five candidates. Under cumulative voting shareholders may place their total number of votes on a single candidate or split them up in any manner they choose. In this way minority shareholders may be able to elect one or more persons to represent their interests.

Most shareholders never vote their shares directly. Unless they attend the annual meeting in person, they vote through a *proxy* or not at all. A proxy is a legal document which allows a person to select someone, also called a proxy, to vote the shares. By law, shareholders must be allowed to vote by proxy, but many shareholders never avail themselves of this right.

Figure 9–2 is a *proxy card,* which if signed and returned, allows the shareholder to vote for or against several proposals presented by the company's management. A *proxy statement* accompanied this proxy card and explained management's proposals for the election of directors. Shareholders may vote by proxy and also attend the meeting. At the meeting, previously submitted proxy votes may be canceled and different votes cast on one or all of the issues.

Some corporations issue two classes of common stock—voting and nonvoting shares. This practice is far less common than it once was. In 1957 the New York Stock Exchange stopped listing shares of com-

266

FIGURE 9-2
Proxy card of Evans Products Company

MANAGEMENT PROXY

EVANS PRODUCTS COMPANY

ANNUAL MEETING OF SHAREHOLDERS, MAY 16, 1979

The undersigned hereby appoints Monford A. Orloff, J. Kenneth Brody, and Samuel J. Robinson, and each of them, with power of substitution to each, proxies of the undersigned, to vote or act with respect to all the shares of stock of Evans Products Company standing in the name of the undersigned at the close of business on March 30, 1979, at the Annual Meeting of Shareholders of Evans Products Company to be held on the 16th day of May, 1979, and at all adjournments thereof, with all the powers the undersigned would possess if personally present, (1) including or excluding the authority to vote for the election of persons nominated in the Proxy Statement as directors; (2) the proposal to adopt the Stock Option Plan—1979, described in the Proxy Statement; and (3) to vote in their discretion upon such other matters as may properly come before the meeting.

A majority of such proxies who shall be present and shall act at said meeting (or if only one shall be present and act, then that one) shall have and exercise all the powers of said proxies hereunder. The undersigned hereby revokes any proxy or proxies heretofore given to vote or act with respect to the shares held by the undersigned and hereby ratifies and confirms all that said proxies, their substitutes or any of them may lawfully do by virtue hereof.

This proxy may be revoked at any time prior to said meeting and the undersigned reserves the right to attend such meeting and vote said stock in person.

The undersigned hereby acknowledges receipt of the Notice of Annual Meeting of Shareholders dated April 12, 1979, the Proxy Statement furnished therewith, and the Annual Report of the Company for 1978 heretofore furnished.

PLEASE SIGN, DATE, AND MAIL THIS PROXY IN THE ENCLOSED ENVELOPE, WHICH REQUIRES NO POSTAGE IF MAILED IN THE UNITED STATES.

(Continued, and to be signed, on reverse side)

The Management recommends a vote FOR the following Management Proposals:

No. 1 Election of Directors	No. 2 Proposed 1979 Stock Option Plan
FOR WITHHELD	FOR AGAINST
☐ ☐	☐ ☐

PLEASE MARK VOTES ■ or ☒

DATED _____ , 1979

SIGNATURE(S) OF SHAREHOLDER(S)

P
R
O
X
Y

This proxy will be voted FOR Proposals 1 and 2 unless instructions to the contrary are indicated.

THIS PROXY IS SOLICITED ON BEHALF OF THE MANAGEMENT

Courtesy of Evans Products Company

panies having more than one class of common stock when the voting rights differed from one class to another. Some such shares are listed on the American Stock Exchange or traded over the counter. The usual intent behind the issuance of two classes of stock is to maintain control over a company with a minimum amount of investment.

Receive dividends on a prorata basis. The board of directors is under no legal obligation to declare dividends to common shareholders. However, if a dividend is declared, each shareholder by law receives an equal amount per share. Under normal circumstances a shareholder who is unhappy with the dividend policy of a corporation has two alternatives: the securities can be sold or an attempt can be made to elect a new board of directors. While it is difficult to replace directors, it should be noted that few things will unite shareholders into a powerful cohesive force more rapidly than omitted or lowered dividends. Directors know this and usually declare dividends if earnings are sufficient for them to do so.

Buy new shares of stock when issued. Under common law shareholders are allowed to maintain their proportion of ownership in a company. This means that if a company offers new common stock for sale, shareholders are entitled to purchase enough of it so that their proportionate interest in the company is not diminished. As an example, if a company were selling 10 percent more stock than it presently had outstanding, a person owning 200 shares would be entitled to purchase 20 additional shares.

This right is known as the *preemptive right,* and it extends to the sale of common stock as well as any bonds or preferred stock which are convertible into the company's common stock. In its strictest form it gives shareholders great protection against dilution of their interests through issuance of more common stock. However, the preemptive right may be denied in the corporate charter or bylaws. A person purchasing securities of such a company loses this right partially or entirely. Normally, the preemptive right is of less importance to the shareholder in the large corporation than to persons owning shares in a corporation that is small and closely held. Maintaining a proportionate ownership in General Motors, a company with over 287 million common shares outstanding and nearly 1.3 million stockholders, is certainly unnecessary so far as control is concerned. The largest shareholder probably owns less than 1 percent of the stock.

A very few corporations follow a policy of selling new common stocks through a *rights offering* to existing shareholders whether or not they have the preemptive right. These offerings and stock warrants are examined in Chapter 11.

Receive a prorata share of the business if it is dissolved. Common shareholders are often called residual owners. This term reflects the fact that they can receive no dividends until bond interest, preferred dividends, and other expenses have been paid. The term also reflects their legal position in the event that the firm ceases operation. When this happens all the creditors are paid, the preferred shareholders receive the par or stated value of their shares, and then, if anything remains from the sale of the corporation's assets, each common shareholder receives a prorata share of what is left. Corporations may cease operations for a reason other than bankruptcy, and when this happens there is often a residual amount, *a liquidating dividend,* paid to shareholders. Bankrupt firms may also pay this type of dividend. However, there is seldom anything of value left for the common shareholder because the firm will normally have used up all its assets or pledged them as collateral for loans in an attempt to continue operating.

Common shareholders have other rights which are of lesser importance for the average small investor. They may, through relatively costly legal procedures, obtain the list of stockholders of the company, examine the books of the company, and bring suit against the directors of the company when it can be proved that the directors have knowingly acted against the best interests of the corporation.

Maturity of common shares

Most bonds have a definite maturity date, a time at which the corporation agrees to redeem these securities. With the exception of *treasury stock,* common stock is seldom redeemed.[1] Since most modern corporations operate under perpetual charters, for all practical purposes the life of common shares is indefinite, ending only when the corporation is dissolved or otherwise ceases to exist.

Stated par and no par stock

Unsophisticated investors often attach the same meaning to the par value of a stock as they do to that of a bond. But there is absolutely no similarity in these two values. Bond owners can rightly expect their securities to be redeemed at the par value, but common shares are not expected to be redeemed. If the company is liquidated and the common shareholders are compensated in this liquidation, the amount of the liquidating dividend will be a prorata share of whatever remains after all liabilities are paid and all assets sold. This amount has nothing to do with the par value of the security.

---

[1] Treasury stock is stock that has been issued and then reacquired by the company. These shares may be resold, issued as stock dividends, used in mergers, or otherwise returned to general ownership. While they are held as treasury stock, they recieve no dividends, nor can they be voted.

Many years ago stocks were assigned high par values (often $100 per share) to indicate to investors that these shares were "valuable." However, investors who purchase securities at less than par value may be assessed the difference between what they paid for the stock and its par value if the company becomes financially insolvent. This is a type of liability which most investors do not wish to assume. Today, about half of the newly incorporated firms issue no par stock, and the other half issues shares having a nominal value. The debate over the desirability of no par versus low par is largely a legal one, best excluded from a book of this nature. Older corporations have lowered the par value of their shares through stock splits (explained later in this chapter) to the point that the par value has no relationship to the normal market value of their stock. For example, the present par value of Du Pont is $5.00, Ford Motor Company is $2.50, Ford Motor Company of Canada is no par, Capehart Corporation is $0.10, and Levi Strauss is $1.00. The recent market prices of these firms are many times greater than the par value of their shares.

INVESTMENT CHARACTERISTICS OF COMMON STOCK

The most important investment characteristics of fixed income securities were found to be yield, grade, and maturity. Measurement of grade and yield for common stocks is much more difficult than for either debt securities or preferred stocks because stock earnings, dividends, and prices change more rapidly and by greater amounts. Dividends play a key role in valuing equity securities so discussion of investment characteristics will begin with this topic.

Common stock dividends

The board of directors is responsible for deciding when dividends will be paid, and the amount of each dividend. In practice most companies pay dividends quarterly although some firms, particularly those having large swings in earnings, may declare special *year-end* or *extra* dividends. The directors have nearly complete discretion over dividend payments except that they may not pay dividends if their payment would result in the insolvency of the corporation. In some cases directors' actions may be controlled by loan agreements which limit dividends as a protection to debt holders.

Dividends are always the same amount for each share of stock.

They may be in cash, in the stock of the company, or in products of the company. However, the last type of dividend is most unusual.

Payment of dividends

Dividends on common and preferred stocks are always paid to persons owning the securities at the time the dividend payment becomes effective. The dividend payment procedure is usually spread over many weeks and follows this sequence: the directors meet and *declare* a dividend of a stated amount which is to be paid at a certain time in the future. This dividend is payable to persons listed as *holders of record* on a certain date. The holder of record is the person recorded by the corporation as owning its stock.

There is some difficulty in knowing exactly who owns shares in a company as of a certain date. A person could have sold shares just before the holder of record date, and the company might not have received notice of this transaction until after the holder of record date had passed. To simplify the ownership problem this rule is followed: Dividends remain with the stock until four business days *before* the date of record. On the fourth day preceding the date of record, the stock begins selling *ex-dividend*. This means that the dividend will be received by persons owning the stock on the fifth business day preceding the dividend record date. Persons purchasing the stock on the ex-dividend date or later will not receive the current dividend but will receive future dividends if they continue to own the stock. The dividend payment is announced publicly in many financially oriented periodicals.

Figure 9–3 is such an announcement. In this example, Anta Corporation declared a regular quarterly dividend of 9¢ per share to persons owning the stock on February 23, 1979. The stock went ex-dividend on February 19, 1979, which was four business days before the February 23 record date. The financial press notifies investors of the fact that a stock has gone ex-dividend by placing an "x" or some other notation near the dividend listing in the stock quote section of the newspaper.

Stock dividends. While the majority of stock dividends are in cash, some companies declare dividends of additional shares of common stock. The procedure for declaring these dividends is the same as for cash dividends except that the dividend is stated as a percent; 2 percent, 10 percent, and so on. This means that each shareholder will

FIGURE 9-3
Dividend report

Dividend News

* * *

Dividends Reported Feb. 9,10

Company	Period	Amt.	Payable date	Record date
REGULAR				
Anta Corp	Q	.09	3-9-79	2-23
Caldor Inc	Q	.10	3-16-79	3-2
Candian Tire	Q	b.14	3-1-79	2-20
Courier Corp	Q	.12	4-2-79	3-12
Deluxe Check Printers	Q	.30	3-5-79	2-19
Dixico Inc	Q	.07½	3-1-79	2-20
Equitable of Iowa Cos	Q	.30	3-15-79	2-27
First Exective1stSrpf	Q	.12½	2-28-79	2-16
Forest Oil Corp	Q	.20	3-9-79	2-26
Garan Inc	Q	.15	3-7-79	2-23
Gelco Corp	Q	.25	4-20-79	3-28
Homestake Mining Co	Q	.27½	3-12-79	2-26
Hudson Bay Oil&Gas	Q	.50	4-27-79	3-31
Imperial Oil Ltd	Q	b.25	3-30-79	3-1
Kansas-Neb Nat Gas	Q	.37	3-31-79	3-9
Malone & Hyde Inc	Q	.24	4-16-79	3-22
Maryland Cup Corp	Q	.14	5-15-79	4-18
Murray Ohio Mfg Co	Q	.25	4-1-79	3-15
Nat'l Aviation Underwr	Q	.17	3-15-79	3-1
Nat'l Presto Ind	Q	.37½	3-30-79	3-2
Pulaski Furniture	Q	.12½	3-15-79	3-1
Star Supermarkets	Q	.20	3-15-79	3-1
Starrett Housing	Q	.07½	3-16-79	2-23
Union Electric Co	Q	.36	3-30-79	3-9
Union Elec $2.125pf	Q	.53125	5-15-79	4-20
Union Elec $2.72pf	Q	.68	5-15-79	4-20
Union Elec $3.50pf	Q	.87½	5-15-79	4-20
Union Elec $4pf	Q	1.00	5-15-79	4-20
Union Elec $4.50pf	Q	1.12½	5-15-79	4-20
Union Elec $4.56pf	Q	1.14	5-15-79	4-20
Union Elec $6.40pf	Q	1.60	5-15-79	4-20
Union Elec $7.44pf	Q	1.86	5-15-79	4-20
Union Elec $8pf'71	Q	2.00	5-15-79	4-20
IRREGULAR				
Nationwide Real Estate		.12	3-9-79	2-23
Ozark Air Lines		.05	3-23-79	3-1
STOCK				
T-Bar Inc		25%	4-20-79	3-16
INCREASED				
Cabot Corp	Q	.35	3-9-79	2-21
Denison Mines new	Q	b.25	3-13-79	3-1
First Maryland Banc	Q	.35	4-2-79	3-16
Investors Group Ltd	Q	b.15	5-1-79	4-12
Kentucky Utilities	Q	.51	3-15-79	n2-23
n-Company corrected record date.				
Park Chemical Co	Q	.15	3-15-79	3-1
Progressive Corp	Q	.08	2-26-79	2-19
Santa Fe Internat'l	Q	.18	3-15-79	2-23
OMITTED				
Allied Van Lines Inc				

A-annual; Ac-accumulation; b-Payable in Canadian funds; F-final; G-interim; h-from income; k-from capital gains; M-monthly; Q-quarterly; S-semi-annual.

Source: Reprinted by permission *The Wall Street Journal,* February 12, 1979, p. 14.

be issued a percentage more stock than was owned when the dividend was declared.

There is much misunderstanding over the value of a stock dividend. Most investors see it as being favorable to their individual position, but a close examination of what takes place when this type of dividend is declared shows that this is not true. A straight stock dividend can have no value to any single shareholder because every shareholder has received a proportional increase in the number of shares owned. The value or earning power of the corporation has not changed; simply stated, each shareholder just has more pieces of paper which evidence ownership in the company. No one owns *proportionately* more of the company.

The following example illustrates this point. Assume a corporation which has outstanding 100 shares of common stock held by ten people each owning 10 shares. The corporation earns $50 per year, all of which it pays out in dividends, $0.50 per share. The company declares a 20 percent stock dividend so that each of the shareholders now owns 12 shares; the corporation then has a total of 120 shares outstanding. Total dividend payments remain at $50, which lowers the dividend per share to $50/120 shares = $0.4167 per share. Dividends paid to each share are lower, but each shareholder has 20 percent more shares. The dividend return to each investor remains the same as it was before the stock dividend, $0.4167 × 12 shares = $5. If the market price of the stock is related to the dividend per share, as we shall assume it to be, then the market price of each share must also have declined. However, the total value of each shareholder's securities remains constant. Studies have shown that stock dividends neither lower nor raise the total value of shareholders' investments.

Corporations may issue stock dividends and at the same time change the cash dividend. Boeing Company, off to a very profitable 1979 year, declared a 50 percent stock dividend and an increased cash dividend payment payable March 12, 1979. Before the stock dividend the company paid a quarterly cash dividend of 30¢ per share. After the stock dividend the cash dividend was reduced to 25¢ per share. But because each shareholder then owned 1.5 new shares for each single share previously held, dividends in terms of old shares were actually 37.5¢ per share.

$$1.5 \text{ shares} \times 25¢ \text{ per share} = 37.5¢ \text{ per share}$$

In this situation the market price of Boeing stock will probably not be reduced by the full proportion of the increase in shares outstanding. Increased dividends per share will act to make the shares more valuable. Had there been no increased dividend, share prices should have decreased by about one-third, a reflection of the increased number of shares outstanding.

Stock splits.   The major difference between a stock split and a stock dividend stems from the way that the dividend or split is accounted for on the books of the corporation. If the newly issued stock amounts to a small proportion of the total outstanding stock, the dividend is paid in stock of the company. This stock will have been authorized in the corporate charter but is as yet unissued; most corporations have this type of stock in generous amounts. If the dividend is to be a substantial proportion of the total amount of outstanding stock, this event is seen as being a recapitalization of the company.[2] This recapitalization is recorded by reducing the par value

---

[2] The American Institute of Certified Public Accountants states that a company should recapitalize (use a stock split) when the transaction promises to "materially affect" the market price of the stock. They suggest that this event is likely to happen when the dividend is over 25 percent, and unlikely to happen when the dividend is less than 20 percent. However, many corporations continue to declare large stock dividends (stock dividends of over 25 percent) and to record these distributions as dividends rather than stock splits. Doing so removes the amount of the stock dividend from the firm's retained earnings account, a desirable outcome from the viewpoint of many corporation managers.

of the stock by the same proportion that the stock dividend had to the total stock outstanding.

A company having a two-for-one stock split would give each shareholder twice the number of shares held before the split, and on the books of the corporation the par value of each share would be halved. Dividend payments would possibly be halved, and so would the market price of each share. Corporations usually split their stock to put its market price into what the company considers to be its "best" trading range. Many companies believe this to be between $20 and $50 per share. When the market price of the stock of such a company climbs above $50 the company may declare a two-for-one or three-for-one stock split. The shareholders all have more stock, but the market price of each share will be back into the "best" trading range. In May 1979 IBM shareholders approved a four-for-one stock split. The desired action being to reduce the market price of IBM common to a price range that would make it easier for investors to buy round lots of the stock.

A less common type of stock split is one where the number of outstanding shares is reduced. This usually occurs when the market price of a corporation's stock has dropped to the point where the directors believe it is "too low." In a reverse split, or "split up" as it is sometimes called, shareholders exchange their shares for a proportionately lesser number. Par value and market price are adjusted upward by a proportionate amount.

Perhaps the most compelling argument that one could use to prove that neither stock dividends nor splits have any value or cost for the individual shareholder is this: the Internal Revenue Service does not tax either stock dividends or splits as income, while any other type of dividend is so taxed. A company paying a cash and a stock dividend, as some do, would cause each shareholder to assume a tax liability on only the cash portion of the dividend.

The following companies are a few of the many having stock dividends during 1978. A complete listing of stock dividends and splits can be obtained from Standard & Poor's *Annual Dividend Record* or *Moody's Dividend Record*.

Merchants Bank of New York	5%
United Aircraft Products	10%
Bohemia, Inc.	13%
Rochester and Pittsburgh Coal	10%
Standard Container Company	10%
Sterling Precision, Inc.	5%

Dividend reinvestment plans

In early 1979 more than 1,000 American corporations offered their common shareholders some sort of dividend reinvestment program. Several types of programs exist, but all have the common feature of making it possible for shareholders to automatically reinvest dividends in additional shares of the company's common stock. Reinvestment of dividends has always been possible, of course. Shareholders could simply use their dividends to buy additional common stock. But for many investors this was not practical. Dividends were too small to buy more than a few shares of stock each quarter or year, and brokerage charges on these purchases were high.

Dividend reinvestment programs greatly lower the costs of purchasing new shares. Some plans require participants to pay brokerage fees and/or service fees, but these charges are much lower than the costs of buying new shares directly. In many cases the company pays all investment costs; each dollar of dividends purchases a dollar of new common stock. A majority of plans allow shareholders to make cash contributions in addition to their reinvested dividends. Shareholders are usually allowed to purchase fractional shares. Such securities are generally held by the company until additional dividends or contributions have provided funds sufficient to obtain whole shares. Shares may be held by the company for the shareholder, or distributed as they are acquired.

Participation in these plans is voluntary but open to all common stockholders of companies offering such plans. Participation is usually arranged by signing and returning an enrollment form to the company. Cancellation of the program is equally simple. Although participants do not receive dividend checks, they must pay taxes on dividends declared during each tax year. These reinvestment plans offer investors a low-cost way of automatically and inexpensively increasing their investment in the common stock of companies offering such plans.

Grading of common stocks

Most investment advisory services publish ratings of common stocks. Some of the ratings look much like those assigned to bonds, but they don't have the same clear and definite meanings. Bond ratings are more nearly *absolute* measures of financial risk. So long as a debt security has a high rating it is extremely unlikely that the company will default on its financial obligations. A deep recession would probably cause many bonds to be graded lower, because of their reduced ability to pay fixed charges. Under conditions of an extreme depression, few bonds might receive the highest rating because they could not meet absolute standards of financial risk.

Stock ratings are *relative*. Interpret these ratings to mean that higher ranked stocks are expected to perform better than those ranked lower. In a market downturn, high-ranked stocks might decline in price, but they would not be expected to decline as much as those of lower grade.

TABLE 9–2
Standard & Poor's common stock rating system

Symbol	Symbol Meaning
A+	Highest
A	High
A−	Above average
B+	Average
B	Below average
B−	Lower
C	Lowest
D	In reorganization

Source: Standard & Poor's *Stock Guide*.

Table 9–2 presents the Standard & Poor's stock ranking system. This system employs a single ranking measure, from A+ to D, for all stocks. The following words of caution are supplied by the Standard & Poor's Corporation along with a description of how they compile their common stock earning and dividend rankings.

> A ranking is not a forecast of future market price performance, but is basically an appraisal of past performance of earnings and dividends, and relative current standing. These rankings must not be used as market recommendations; a high-score stock may at times be so overpriced as to justify its sale, while a low-score stock may be attractively priced for purchase. Rankings based upon earnings and dividend records are no substitute for complete analysis. They cannot take into account potential effects of management changes, internal company policies not yet fully reflected in the earnings and dividend record, public relations standing, recent competitive shifts, and a host of other factors that may be relevant to investment status and decision.[3]

---

[3] Standard & Poor's *Stock Guide*, January 1979, p. 4.

Value Line creates rankings of several stock investment characteristics, but makes no overall ranking. The most important are financial strength, safety, timeliness for investment, and price performance during the next 12 months. All are relative measures. Other investment advisory services provide similar information.

Portfolio managers make heavy use of two other relative measures of stock performance to calculate expected returns from their portfolios. These are known as *alpha* and *beta*. Both are statistical measures of relative performance.

A stock's beta is a number which compares how it performed relative to all stocks. Monthly, weekly, or quarterly stock price data are used to make these comparisons. Price changes only may be compared, although in some cases dividends and other ingredients are included.

The market for stocks is assigned a beta value of one; this number never changes.[4] A stock having a beta of 1.2 would be expected to perform 20 percent better than the market when the market rises, and 20 percent worse when the market declines. A stock having a beta of less than one would be expected to increase and decrease its performance by smaller percentage amounts than the market.

Over the long run a stock may perform better or worse than the market. Alpha measures the relationship of long-run average market performance to long-run average stock performance. Because market performance is simply the average of the performance of all stocks making up the average, about half the common stocks have an alpha greater than zero and half have negative alphas. Betas are almost never negative because few stocks move opposite to the market.

Alpha and beta measures are used by many investment portfolio managers. These statistics provide estimates of portfolio risk that enable analysts to determine in advance the expected returns from a portfolio having known alpha and beta characteristics. Unfortunately, the measures are much less useful to persons buying individual securities or persons having portfolios containing but a few different securities. Over time, both alpha and beta measures change. Because these measures are taken from historical market and security perform-

---

[4] The Standard & Poor's common stock index and the NYSE common stock index are the most widely used measures of the total market for common stocks. While neither index contains all stocks, they both contain a large enough grouping of securities so that for purposes of statistical calculations they are effective as measures of the total market.

ance data they may be very different from current measures. Betas in particular have proved to be quite unstable. The average beta of a well-diversified investment portfolio will remain fairly constant because changes in the betas of individual securities tend to cancel out. But this canceling effect does not work for small portfolios or single securities. Investors are cautioned against the use of alpha and beta measures in these situations.

ANALYSIS OF COMMON STOCK

Common stock analysis has as its goal the identification of securities having market values different from their intrinsic values. Profits may be made by purchasing undervalued securities and holding them. Overvalued securities may be sold short to produce profits. Since short selling is not covered until Chapter 11, this discussion of stock analysis will emphasize the search for securities selling *below* their intrinsic values. The most often quoted statement defining the relationship between intrinsic value and market value follows.

> A general definition of intrinsic value would be "that value which is justified by the facts, e.g., assets, earnings, dividends, definite prospects, including the factor of management." The primary objective in using the adjective "intrinsic" is to emphasize the distinction between value and current market price, but not to invest this "value" with an aura of permanence. In truth, the computed intrinsic value is likely to change at least from year to year, as the various factors governing that value are modified. But in most cases intrinsic value changes less rapidly and drastically than market price, and the investor usually has an opportunity to profit from any wide discrepancy between the current price and the intrinsic value as determined at the same time.[5]

To be successful at this type of analysis one must be aware of the things that give value to a share of common stock. Although there are nearly as many theories of security analysis as there are security analysts, almost all valuation theories are ultimately based upon future earnings and dividends expected to be obtained by the common shareholders. Without dividends, which are made possible by earnings, it is seldom that common stock can have more than a speculative value.

Valuing common stocks is not only a quantitative procedure, but

---

[5] Benjamin Graham, David L. Dodd, and Sidney Cottle, *Security Analysis: Principles and Techniques*, 4th ed. (New York: McGraw-Hill), 1962.

one that also requires many qualitative judgments on the part of the security analyst or the person who uses the analyst's computations. Several things make common stock valuation most difficult: (1) common stock earnings and dividends are a residual, and because of this they may vary greatly in amount from year to year; (2) the corporation is under no legal obligation to pay common stock dividends; (3) investor psychology can cause common stock prices to fluctuate wildly, particularly in the short run.

As a practical matter, the average investor seldom makes intensive analyses of securities. However, all the major brokerage firms and investment advisors publish such studies. It is necessary that each investor understand the basis upon which these analyses are made because they will probably provide the background for many investment decisions.

Book value. Logically, the things that determine the value of a common stock are its expected future earnings and dividends. With certain exceptions, the book value of a company has little direct relationship to these measures. However, book value per share is such a common measure of value that an examination of its meaning is appropriate.

The *book value*, or *net asset value*, of a company is determined by subtracting its liabilities from its assets. The remainder is book value. The balance sheet provides information for this calculation, but most annual reports and stock fact sheets present the dollar amount directly. Usually the information is presented as *book value per share*, which means that the total book value has been divided by the number of shares of common stock outstanding.

This amount is not very useful in determining the intrinsic value of a share of common stock for several reasons: (1) It has little or no direct effect on future earnings or dividends; if book value per share doubled, earnings might increase or they might decrease; (2) It does not usually give a realistic market value of the business because most assets are carried on the books at their original cost less accumulated depreciation, not their present market value; (3) Some of the productive resources and liabilities of the business may not appear on the balance sheet.

There are some instances where book value does have meaning. The shares of mutual funds and other trust type investments are usually sold and redeemed on the basis of net asset value (book value) per share. In this case, book value and market value are identical except for sales or redemption charges.[6]

Book value may also have meaning when a company's earnings are exceptionally low or high. Valuing stock on the basis of earnings under either of these conditions is likely to result in an erroneous assessment of worth. It might be better to look at book value as the base from which profits flow and to reason that if similar firms earned 10 percent on book value over the long run, this firm should do the same. The stock could then be valued on the basis of these assumed long-run earnings.

Book value should have special meaning for natural resource companies because profits are tied directly to assets held in the form of oil, timber, copper ore, and so on. The difficulty in using book value to value them is that for these companies this value is invariably too low. Assets are recorded at *cost*, and balance sheet valuations of natural resource assets are usually far below the present or future market value of the assets. Security analysts often attempt to assign market values to natural resource type assets, "to see what the company is really worth." This approach has some merit, but huge reserves of oil, timber, or copper ore do not necessarily guarantee future profits. Costs of drilling, mining, logging, transporting or otherwise preparing the asset for sale may be so high that exploitation is uneconomical. A more explicit example of the difficulty of translating book values into future profits is found in the Weyerhaeuser Company annual reports. Weyerhaeuser's 1978 annual report valued its timber lands at less than $600 million. Responsible estimates of the current market value of this timber are over $8 billion. However, it will take many years to turn this timber into profits. How much is it really worth to a Weyerhaeuser shareholder today?

In 1978 Westinghouse Electric common sold at an average price of 20½; its book value per share was $28.41. General Electric's 1978 average common price was 50⅝ and its book value per share was $28.94. During the same year Dow Chemical common prices averaged about 26½; its book value per share was $18.27. Reichold Chemical had an average stock price of about 13⅝; its book value was $22.49. Obviously, book values and stock prices vary widely even among firms in the same industries.

---

[6] Chapter 10 examines these investments and computes the net asset value of a mutual fund share.

Liquidating value refers to the amount that would remain if a company ceased operations, paid off all creditors, sold its assets, and divided whatever was left among the common stockholders. The calculations for book value and liquidating value are identical except that in computing liquidating value, assets are priced at market value rather than at their balance sheet amounts. Some companies, especially those owning large amounts of real estate which is carried on their books at its original cost, may have a liquidation value per share far greater than either book value or current market value per share. These companies may be worth more "dead than alive." Book value may be looked at as the amount *put into* a company by common shareholders, while liquidating value is the amount that may be *taken out* if the company is liquidated.

Valuation on the basis of earnings and dividends

It will be remembered from the discussion of preferred stock valuation in the previous chapter that the most important elements were the grade of the security, the amount of the dividend, and the rate of return or yield required by investors. The grade of the stock and its rate of return were related in that investors required higher yields to compensate for lower graded (more risky) securities.

These relationships were presented in the formula used to calculate the current yield on a preferred stock.

$$\text{Yield} = \frac{\text{Yearly dividend}}{\text{Market price}}$$

Common stockholders judge equity securities in a similar manner. A high-grade common stock is one that pays dividends through bad years and good. Increasing uncertainty of future dividend payments causes investors to demand higher yields. Uncertainty causes investors to "discount" dividends at a higher rate. The result of such a procedure is lowered prices as yield requirements rise. Table 9–3 shows

TABLE 9–3
Discounting of dividends

Estimated average dividends	Discount rate	Computed market price of stock
$2	6%	$33.33
2	8	25.00
2	10	20.00

how stock prices are affected by increased dividend discount rates.

The computations in Table 9–3 and the logic of this kind of analysis are based upon the assumption of constant future dividends. If dividends are expected to increase over time, the discount rate is lowered below the "normal" rate. Market prices that investors are willing to pay for these "growth" securities then increase. From a mathematical standpoint this reasoning is incorrect because it does not consider the timing of increased or decreased dividend payments. However, this is in fact one of the methods used to determine the intrinsic value of common stock. For many years the rule of thumb was that "a good stock yields 6 percent." Or in our terms, dividends on good common stocks were discounted at a 6 percent rate. Figure 9–4 presents average common stock dividend/price ratios, average earnings/price ratios, and average bond yields from 1926 to 1979.

Logically, common stock yields should exceed high-grade bond yields. Common stocks have more risk so their dividends should be discounted at a higher rate. However, this line of reasoning does not take account of the possibility of dividend growth or growth in the market price of common shares.

During the years following World War II, America was expanding at an unparalleled rate. Businesses prospered and grew, dividends and stock prices increased. Taking this into account, investors discounted dividends at lower and lower rates, until, in 1958, dividend yields became less than the yields on high-grade bonds. The potential for growth was clearly of value to investors.

The yield formula presented earlier can be altered to take growth into account by adding the percent of price growth to the dividend yield.

$$\text{Yield} = \frac{\text{Yearly dividend}}{\text{Price}} + \frac{\text{Yearly growth in price}}{\text{Price}}$$

The yield on a common stock having a market price of $25, a yearly dividend of $1.25, and an expected yearly increase in market price of $1 per share would be 9 percent.

$$\begin{aligned}
\text{Yield} &= \frac{\$1.25}{\$25} + \frac{\$1}{\$25} \\
&= .05 + .04 \\
&= .09 \text{ or } 9\%.
\end{aligned}$$

FIGURE 9–4 Stock and bond yields
Earnings/Price Ratio: Annually, 1926–35; End of Quarter, 1936; All Others, Quarterly, 1926–1979

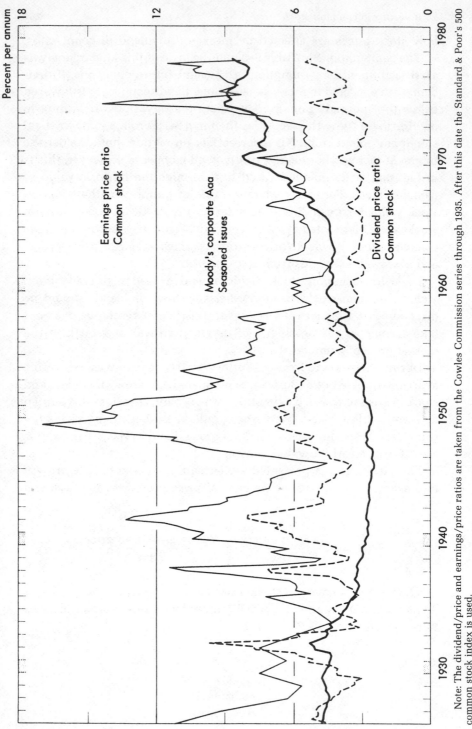

Note: The dividend/price and earnings/price ratios are taken from the Cowles Commission series through 1935. After this date the Standard & Poor's 500 common stock index is used.

Source: *Federal Reserve Historical Chart Book*, Board of Governors of the Federal Reserve System, Washington, D.C., 1978, p. 97.

One most often sees this formula in the modified form presented below, where it may be used to determine the intrinsic value of a stock.

$$\text{Intrinsic value} = \frac{\text{Dividend}}{\text{Yield} - \text{Yearly growth rate}}$$

The yearly dividend is, of course, the company's anticipated common stock dividend during the coming year. Intrinsic value is the value that the stock should have because of its dividend and growth expectations and required yield. In practice, the yield figure is often an *expected* or *necessary* percentage. A given investor may require a total yield on common stock of 15 percent, so this figure would be put into the equation. Another investor may use an industry average yield. Since this formula is a restatement of the previous one, it indicates an intrinsic value (a price) of $25 per share.

$$\$25 = \frac{\$1.25}{.09 - .04}$$

Valuation based entirely on earnings.   Many investors look to earnings, and particularly increasing earnings, as the primary source of security values. The argument for this measure is easily understood. Companies which have good growth prospects *should* pay low dividends or no dividends; capital which would normally go to shareholders is thus retained in the business. Shareholders benefit from this action because the earnings of the company increase over time, and may increase future dividends. Since the company is financing its expansion through retained earnings rather than new stock issues, the number of common shares remains constant. Increased company earnings are evidenced by increased earnings per share (EPS), and as EPS increases, so should the stock's market price.

Investors still arrive at an intrinsic value approximation through the process of discounting, but what they discount is earnings. This is done through the use of the earnings/price, or E/P ratio, which is computed by dividing quarterly or annual earnings per share by the average or end-of-period stock price.[7] Figure 9–4 shows average quarterly earnings/price ratios for common stocks in general. Such ratios are used to value individual securities.

A more common way of using the earnings/price relationship is by

---

[7] This ratio becomes meaningless when there are no earnings because the resulting ratio is infinitely small. It is not calculated for firms which are losing money.

FIGURE 9–5
Average yearly P/E ratios of IBM and the Standard & Poor's 400 industrial stock price index

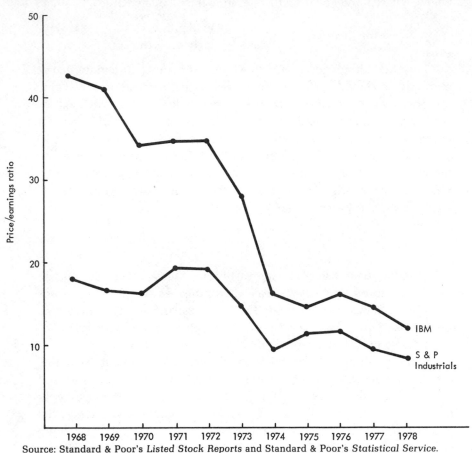

Source: Standard & Poor's *Listed Stock Reports* and Standard & Poor's *Statistical Service.*

reversing it. The price/earnings ratio tells how much investors are willing to pay for a dollar of earnings. Growth in earnings is not identified directly in the P/E ratio but companies that are expected to experience rapid growth in earnings are usually awarded higher P/E ratios. This is consistent with our earlier discussion of discount rates.

Analysts often compare P/E ratios of a single company to those of one of the stock market indexes. This has been done in Figure 9–5, which presents P/E ratios of IBM and the S&P 400 industrial stock price index. These comparisons have value because they provide perspective on current P/E ratios. Historical trends in the company's ratios are clearly shown, and they may be compared directly to those of the "average" company.

In 1968 and 1969 investors were willing to pay over twice as much for a dollar of IBM earnings as they were for securities making up the S&P industrial index. During the stock market decline of 1973–74 all P/E ratios declined, but IBM's declined far more. Since changes in either IBM's earnings or stock prices could have caused its P/E ratios to decline, one must look into the composition of the ratio (earnings per share and share prices) to obtain a clearer understanding of what has happened.

This information is presented in Figure 9–6 which shows that IBM's earnings per share have increased steadily at about a 13 percent annual rate over the entire period. Except for the years 1973 and 1974 prices of IBM stock have been near to or below the 1968 average price. Constant or declining stock prices, coupled with rising EPS, have caused the pronounced decline in the P/E ratios presented in Figure 9–5.

The analyst must now attempt to determine why IBM's stock price has declined in the face of rising EPS. The answer is obvious: the market has revalued earnings for IBM and other companies downward from their earlier high values. There are many theories to explain this change. Some analysts believe that tight money and high interest rates have lowered earnings multiples. Others lay the blame on inflation. Still others believe there is a fundamental change in investors' expectations of the economic future of the country. While no one knows for certain what has caused the lowered P/E ratios, every investor must decide whether the change is permanent or whether historically higher ratios will again be experienced, and then act upon this decision. In the case of IBM, an investor believing that the current P/E ratio is abnormally low (and of course it is far below the ten-year average) will expect an upward adjustment to cause a rise in stock prices. This person might see IBM or stocks in general as a good buy. Those who predict that low P/E ratios will remain for many years may wish to forego common stocks entirely, buying instead higher yielding debt securities or some other investment.

However, there is something to be said in favor of stocks selling at historically low P/E ratios. Assuming that they have reasonably good earnings prospects, they are not as likely to show large market price declines as are securities selling at very high P/E ratios. Investors award high P/E ratios to securities that are expected to perform in an

FIGURE 9–6
Earnings per share and average stock price of IBM (1968 through 1978)

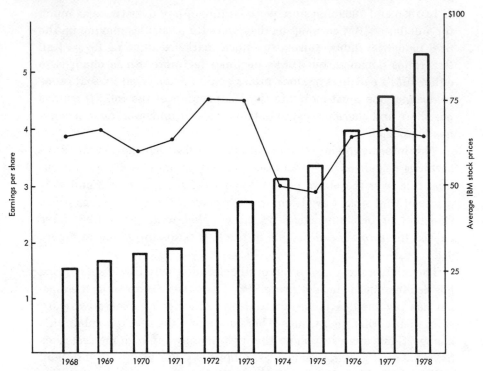

Note: The bar graph shows earnings per share (left-hand scale); the line graph shows average common stock prices (right-hand scale). Average stock prices are calculated as the midpoint of the yearly high and low prices.
Source: Standard & Poor's *Listed Stock Reports* and *The Wall Street Journal*.

exceptional manner. If these expectations are not realized there is often a rapid downward adjustment in the stock price, which creates a more normal P/E ratio for the company. Low P/E ratio stocks are just not as likely to suffer such large price declines because prices are already relatively low. In accord with this line of reasoning many investors place an upward limit on the P/E ratios of stocks they consider for purchase.

A growth oriented intrinsic value model. Since the computer has come into general use as a stock valuation tool, complex stock valuation models have become widely used. In most of these models, historical earnings growth and anticipated future growth have important roles in determining intrinsic values. As an example of how one simple model may be used to assess such values—but not to recommend it above all others—the following is presented.

$$\text{Intrinsic value} = \text{Normal EPS} \times \frac{37.5 + 8.8 \text{ (growth in EPS)}}{\text{Aaa bond interest rate}}$$

In nonmathematical terms, this equation states that the intrinsic value of a common stock is determined by its normal EPS, by growth in EPS, and by the Aaa corporate bond rate. The two numbers, 37.5 and 8.8, are statistically derived constants which have proved to be reasonably accurate over the years. IBM's 1978 EPS was $5.32; growth in EPS over the last ten years was at an annual rate of about 13 percent. The Aaa bond rate was about 9 percent. Inserting these values into the equation results in the following intrinsic value for IBM common shares:

$$\text{Intrinsic value} = \$5.32 \times \frac{37.5 + 8.8 \text{ (13)}}{9}$$

$$= \$5.32 \times \frac{37.5 + 114.4}{9}$$

$$= \$5.32 \times \frac{151.9}{9}$$

$$= \$5.32 \times 16.9$$

$$= \$89.90.$$

IBM shares sold well below this amount in early 1979 and would have been considered a possible bargain by analysts using this intrinsic value model.

But in early 1979 a large number of securities were identified as bargains by this and similar valuation models. Certainly few persons could have purchased even a single share of stock in all the companies identified as selling below their intrinsic values. Further analysis is therefore in order.

The person responsible for the previous model recommends great caution in its use. He suggests that the number of possible selections be reduced by considering for purchase only stocks which have financial strength (modest use of debt, fairly steady earnings, a minimum asset size, and other such characteristics). Additionally, he suggests that it is prudent to require that a stock sell at three-fourths, two-thirds, or even one-half its intrinsic value as a condition of purchase.[8]

---

[8] Benjamin Graham, "The Decade 1965–1974: Its Significance for Financial Analysts," from *The Renaissance of Value* (Charlottesville, Va: Financial Analysts Research Foundation, 1974), p. 11.

This will result in fewer stocks that meet the conditions for purchase, but those which do will hopefully be more profitable.

This example is designed to indicate in only the most general terms how analysts use models to value stocks. Many of these stock value models are more complex, incorporating additional factors in the analysis. Complexity does not necessarily mean that the derived intrinsic values are accurate, however. Many of these models are based upon *assumed* future growth rates and security prices. They are only as reliable as the predicted values that go into them. Investors must use caution when using or interpreting these models because it is easy to accept them as being scientific and therefore infallible. Security valuation always has been, is, and will probably continue to be an art rather than a science. Analytical tools are valuable aids to analysis, but investors must recognize their limitations.

SUMMARY

Common shareholders own the corporation. They elect directors to represent their interests and to oversee the management of the company. Stock ownership is evidenced by shares of stock, which may have a par or no par value. Shares may be voted on the basis of one vote per share for each proposal, *statutory voting,* or shares may be voted *cumulatively* if this method is followed. Since these shares are not redeemed in the normal course of business, par value of common stock does not have the same meaning as does the par value of a bond or a preferred share. Management is under no legal obligation to pay common dividends, nor may shareholders force payment of dividends under normal circumstances. But if dividends are declared, each share receives the same amount.

Under common law, shareholders have the right to maintain their prorata share in the company by being allowed first chance to purchase new shares of common stock or senior securities convertible into common stock. In practice many companies have abridged this *preemptive right* by denying it in the corporate charter. When a corporation is dissolved, common shareholders receive what remains after the claims of creditors and senior security owners are satisfied.

Common dividends may be in cash, or practically anything else. Companies may pay *stock dividends,* which result in each shareholder owning a larger *number* of the company's shares, but each shareholder continues to own the same proportion of the company as before. Unless cash dividends per share remain the same or are increased, a stock dividend has no value to the shareholder.

Common stocks are graded by several firms, but the grading is not as accurate or as meaningful as it is for bonds. Grading is based mainly upon the amount and consistency of dividend payments. Rankings are relative rather than absolute.

Analysis of common stock is directed toward determining what is the *intrinsic value* of a share. This value is that justified by the "facts"—earnings, assets, dividends, and future prospects. At one time or another *book value* or *liquidation value* may be a good indicator of intrinsic value. Analysts often use sophisticated *stock value models* and other analytical techniques to determine a stock's intrinsic value. A stock selling for more than this amount is overpriced; one selling for less in underpriced.

Investors often try to evaluate a security's *relative price* through the use of the earnings-per-share/price-per-share ratio. This ratio varies with changes in either earnings or price, of course, but it provides a benchmark to use in identifying which of a group of similar securities are relatively overpriced and which are relatively underpriced. Many analysts assign *basic price multipliers* to stocks on the basis of factors they believe to be most important in determining stock prices. An example of a simple valuation model is included in the chapter. A more sophisticated present-value stock value model is presented in the appendix which follows.

APPENDIX

The present value approach to common stock valuation

The logic of common stock valuation follows that for bonds. A share of stock is worth the present value of future dividend payments plus the present value of whatever the stock can be sold for at some future date. This is exactly the same reasoning presented in the Appendix to Chapter 7. However, in using the present value formula

$$P = I\left[\frac{1}{(1+i)^1} + \frac{1}{(1+i)^2} + \cdots + \frac{1}{(1+i)^n}\right] + M\left[\frac{1}{(1+i)^n}\right]$$

to value common stocks, we have the problem of assigning values to fluctuating yearly dividends and an unknown future market price.

These are formidable problems, and there are different ways of handling them.[9] The following example has been prepared to illustrate one way that the present value technique may be used to value common stock, and to clarify the concept of this type valuation. It will not provide the reader with a general formula into which data can be inserted to derive investment decisions.

The example carries the following assumptions:

1. Dividends are currently $2 per share. They are paid annually and are expected to increase by 5 percent per year.
2. The present market price of the stock is $40 per share. It is assumed to increase by 8 percent per year.
3. If the stock is purchased it will be purchased at the beginning of the year, after it has gone ex-dividend. It will be sold at the end of three years, receiving the third-year dividend.
4. Other securities of equal risk characteristics are currently discounted at a rate of 4 percent.

The first task is to determine yearly dividends over the three-year holding period:
Let

$$D_0 = \text{Beginning dividend of \$2.}$$
$$D_1, D_2, \text{ and } D_3 = \text{Dividends received for years 1, 2, and 3.}$$
$$r = \text{Yearly increase in dividends.}$$

The formula for determining the future dividends is

$$D_n = D_0(1 + r)^n$$

Time	Cash Dividend
Year before purchase	$2
1st year	$D_1 = \$2(1 + 0.05)^1 = \$2.10.$
2nd year	$D_2 = \$2(1 + 0.05)^2 = \$2.20.$
3rd year	$D_3 = \$2(1 + 0.05)^3 = \$2.32.$

Next is computed the future value of the security based upon an expected increase in its market price of 8 percent per year for three years. The same formula is used except that D_0 is now $40 and r becomes 8 percent.

$$P_n = \$40(1 + 0.08)^3 = \$50.40$$

[9] See W. Scott Bauman, "Investment Returns and Present Values," *Financial Analysts Journal*, 25, no. 6 (November–December 1969): 107 ff., or R. A. Bing, "Survey of Practitioners' Stock Evaluation Methods," *Financial Analysts Journal*, V 27 (May–June 1971), pp. 55–60.

It is but a simple matter to determine that the intrinsic value of this security is the present value of future dividends plus the future value of the security. These values are discounted at 4 percent.

$$P = \frac{D_1}{(1+i)^1} + \frac{D_2}{(1+i)^2} + \frac{D_3}{(1+i)^3} + \frac{P_3}{(1+i)^3}$$

$$P = \frac{\$2.10}{(1+0.04)^1} + \frac{\$2.20}{(1+0.04)^2} + \frac{\$2.32}{(1+0.04)^3} + \frac{\$50.40}{(1+0.04)^3}$$

$$= \$2.02 + \$2.04 + \$2.06 + \$44.80$$

$$= \$50.92.$$

This amount, $50.92, represents the current intrinsic value of this stock under the conditions defined above. Since the current market value is $40, it is a good buy. This example is oversimplified so that the analogy between common stock valuation and bond valuation can be seen more easily. The obvious difficulties in using this approach are not the mathematics (computers can solve these problems with ease) but rather those of determining future dividend payments and a future sale price. There is naturally some error in making these judgments. However, most all investment decisions are of necessity based upon judgments.

The above present value model can be used in several different ways. One could assume that the market price of the stock was expected to advance only 6 percent per year, or that dividends would remain constant at $2, or that they would decline. One could assume a longer holding period. As the basic assumptions change, the intrinsic or present value will change. These models are often used by assuming the worst possible future events and the best possible future events; this results in a low and high present value for the stock and gives the investor a somewhat better idea of the relative current price of the stock based upon different future expectations.

PROBLEMS

1. As a project, consult Standard & Poor's *Annual Dividend Record* and obtain names of several firms which paid stock dividends during the preceding year. Devise a test to determine whether the stock dividends had an effect on the market price of the securities chosen.
2. What would be the intrinsic value of a common stock that promised to pay a dividend of $2 per year for the foreseeable future if the next best investment alternative yielded 10 percent per year?
3. In 1979, the XYZ Company earned $6 per share. Stocks of similar com-

panies are selling at P/E ratios of 14:1. What is the maximum amount per share you would pay for this security on the basis of the above facts? What other important things would you wish to consider?

4. Choose two companies in different industries. From newspapers or investment manuals compute the P/E ratios for these companies over the past several years. Try to relate changes and absolute differences in these P/E ratios to such things as the degree of risk (grade) of each security, the growth in profits of each company, and any other factors considered important. Is one security a "better buy" than the other? If so, why?

5. Use one of the valuation formulas contained in this chapter to derive an intrinsic value for a common stock under the following conditions. The normal earnings per share are $4 per year. Earnings have increased at a rate of 3 percent and are expected to increase at that rate into the foreseeable future. The current Aaa bond interest rate is 8 percent. The company traditionally pays dividends of 20 cents per quarter.

6. Calculate the intrinsic value of a common stock having the following characteristics: Present market price is $44. Common stock dividends of similar companies are discounted at 8 percent per annum. The current dividend is $1.80 per share. This annual dividend is expected to increase by 10 percent per year. The stock will be sold in three years, after increasing in price by 7 percent per year. The third-year dividend will be received prior to sale. Use the present value approach discussed in the appendix to calculate the intrinsic value of this security.

7. A common stock is expected to pay a dividend of $2 per share over the coming year. Earnings and dividends of this company are expected to grow at a 6 percent annual rate. The investor requires a yield on equity investments of 12 percent per annum. Given this information what is the maximum amount the investor should pay for a share of this stock?

QUESTIONS

1. Compare the important characteristics of bonds and common stock.
2. What legal rights do most states grant owners of common stock?
3. What is the meaning of *par value* as it relates to common stock?
4. What is the usual dividend payment procedure?
5. What value does a stock dividend have for shareholders?
6. What is *statutory voting*? *Cumulative voting*?
7. What are the main differences between *stock dividends* and *splits*?
8. Why cannot common stocks be graded as accurately as bonds?
9. What is the difference between *market value* and *intrinsic value*?
10. Under what conditions would book value be a good approximation of market value?

11. How is the capitalization rate related to the grade of a stock?
12. "Stocks selling at above average P/E ratios should never be purchased by the cautious investor." Discuss this statement.
13. How do *market factors* cause stock prices to change?
14. Why is the present value approach to stock valuation an improvement over any other method?
15. What cautions are in order when using any stock valuation model?
16. Using information contained in Figure 9–3, when did the stock of Maryland Cup Corp. go to ex–dividend? What should have happened to the market price of the security on this date? When was the dividend actually paid out?

SELECTED READINGS

Christy, George A., and Clendenin, John C. *Introduction to Investments.* 7th ed. New York: McGraw-Hill, 1978.

Cohen, Jerome B.; Zinbarg, Edward D.; and Zeikel, Arthur. *Investment Analysis and Portfolio Management.* 3rd ed. Homewood, Ill.: Richard D. Irwin, 1977.

Davey, Patrick J. *Dividend Reinvestment Plans.* New York: The Conference Board, 1976.

Fisher, Lawrence, and Lorie, James H. *Rates of Return on Investments in Common Stocks.* Chicago: University of Chicago, Graduate School of Business, Center for Research in Security Prices.

Francis, Jack C. *Investments: Analysis and Management.* 2nd ed. New York: McGraw-Hill, 1976.

Graham, Benjamin. *The Intelligent Investor: A Book of Practical Counsel.* 4th rev. ed. New York: Harper & Row, 1973.

Graham, Benjamin; Dodd, David L.; and Cottle, Sidney. *Security Analysis: Principles and Techniques.* 4th ed. New York: McGraw-Hill, 1962.

Johnson, Timothy E. *Investment Principles.* Englewood Cliffs, N.J.: Prentice-Hall, 1978.

"New York Stock Exchange, 1978 Census of Share Owners." New York Stock Exchange, 1979.

Sharpe, William F. *Investments.* Englewood Cliffs, N.J.: Prentice-Hall, 1978.

Wendt, Paul F. "Current Growth Stock Valuation Methods." *Financial Analysts Journal,* March–April 1965.

10

Investing in investment companies

INTRODUCTION

An *investment company* is any of several types of companies which are formed for the purpose of acquiring and managing a portfolio of investment securities. Owners of the investment companies provide the capital to purchase these securities and receive the benefit of their ownership. There are two main types of investment companies in the United States. By any measure, the more important of these is the *open-end investment company*, or *mutual fund* as they are usually called. Developed earlier, but a distant second in size since World War II, are the *closed-end investment companies*. These more nearly resemble the standard business corporation and for this reason will be examined first. Other kinds of investment companies exist, but compared to these two they are relatively unimportant. Figure 10–1 shows the growth in assets of investment companies since 1940.

CLOSED-END INVESTMENT COMPANIES

Closed-end investment companies first appeared on the American investment scene in the 1920s. They differed from mutual funds and from the modern closed-end investment companies in that their capital structures often contained bonds and preferred stock. Use of these senior securities provided great financial leverage and created an investment that was potentially very risky.

The term *closed-end* refers to the fact that, like a regular corpora-

FIGURE 10–1
Growth in investment company assets

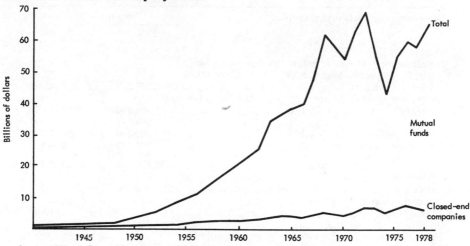

Source: Wiesenberger Investment Companies Service, New York, 1979.

tion, once the capital structure of the company was set, it could only be changed by issuing or retiring securities, or retaining earnings. While it was legal to change the size of these companies through these methods, in practice this was rarely done. Consequently, these funds were closed-ended in that they were not expected to increase the amount of their capital stock from what it was when the company was organized. Figure 10–2 presents the 1978 statement of assets and liabilities of Lehman Corporation, a large closed-end investment company representative of the type first organized in this country.

In a conventional company, profits come from the difference between sales revenue and the costs incurred to obtain these revenues. Investment company profits are generated in a somewhat different manner. Revenue takes the form of interest and dividends received and capital gains obtained on the securities owned by the company. Expenses are the costs of buying and selling the company's investment securities and the costs of administering the company. Nearly all of the assets of investment companies are investments in other companies. Management consists of buying securities which will, hopefully, give owners of investment company shares a higher return for a given amount of risk than they could obtain by investing an equal amount of money on their own.

One notices immediately that Figure 10–2 is arranged differently

FIGURE 10–2
Lehman corporation statement of assets and liabilities

Statement of assets and liabilities	December 31,	
	1978	1977
Assets		
Investments in stocks at market or fair value (average cost 1978—$295,023,745; 1977—$294,931,930)	$409,980,259	$401,214,665
Corporate short-term notes at cost plus discount earned	41,359,044	29,126,156
Cash	186,011	1,594,599
Receivable for securities sold	1,000,240	2,485,582
Dividends receivable	751,112	704,251
Total assets	453,276,666	435,125,253
Liabilities		
Payable for securities purchased	589,680	3,212,181
Deposits on securities loaned	—	4,054,000
Management fee payable	406,550	381,388
Accrued expenses and taxes	230,738	84,460
Provision for state and city taxes on unrealized appreciation	801,000	731,000
Total liabilities	2,027,968	8,463,029
Net assets	$451,248,698	$426,662,224
Shares of capital stock, $1.00 par value: authorized	40,000,000	40,000,000
Issued	33,377,184	32,604,547
Held in treasury	708,293	90,798
Issued and outstanding	32,668,891	32,513,749
Net asset value per share	$13.81	$13.12

Source: Lehman Corporation 1978 Annual Report, p. 17.

from the conventional balance sheet studied earlier. The emphasis of this accounting statement is on *net asset value per share*, which is the amount of assets "owned" by each share of outstanding capital stock. To obtain net asset value per share, the company's liabilities are deducted from the current market or fair value of its assets. The difference is *net assets*, a term which has the same meaning as *liquidating value*. Dividing net assets by the number of shares outstanding provides the measure net asset value per share.

Valuing closed-end shares

The market price of a closed-end investment company share (like that of any other corporation) is set by supply and demand. Supply and demand is in turn influenced by several factors. Expected future earnings and dividends are of great importance, but net asset value per share is also a determinant of market price.

Since closed-end investment company shares are not continuously redeemed, shareholders cannot obtain the net asset value of their shares from the company. Nevertheless increases and decreases in this value have an effect upon the market prices of all closed-end shares. Over the long run, market prices tend to increase when net asset value increases, and vice versa. At any given time, market prices may be above or below net asset value. These premiums and discounts are caused by current security market conditions, including investor favor or disfavor with respect to the major industries represented in the portfolio, expected future earnings of the company, and many other things which affect stock values.

The number of closed-end funds has increased in recent years. Most of the older funds invested in diversified portfolios of common stocks. The majority of the newer companies invest in bonds and specialized investments of one type or another. Over 40 closed-end bond funds have been started during the 1970–79 period.

OPEN-END INVESTMENT COMPANIES

While open-end companies closely resemble closed-end funds, there are definite differences which readily explain why the open-end type has become so much more important. Figure 10–3 shows the statement of assets and liabilities of Eaton and Howard Balanced Fund, a large, well-known open-end investment company. One can see that this statement looks much like that of the Lehman Corporation.

The most important difference in these companies is identified by the statement appearing as a footnote to Figure 10–3: "The Fund under its indenture of trust is authorized to issue unlimited shares of $0.50 par value." The closed-end investment company is essentially restricted in the amount of its capital stock to the initial amount authorized and sold. The open-end company may increase its capitalization at any time simply by selling more shares of its capital stock. This is the key difference because it enables the company to become larger as more persons purchase shares.

Valuing mutual fund shares

The net asset value of a share of stock in a mutual fund is of far more importance to the investor than is the net asset value of a share

FIGURE 10–3

Eaton and Howard Balanced Fund statement of assets and liabilities

---

Statement of assets and liabilities
(December 31, 1978)
Assets

Investments, at market value (identified cost $69,750,-727)		$82,669,415
Investments in short-term securities, at cost, which approximates market		1,397,326
Cash..		233,343
Receivables:		
Interest and dividends..		869,724
Fund shares sold		84,759
Miscellaneous		4,593
Total assets		85,259,160
Liabilities:		
Payables:		
Fund shares reacquired	$171,408	
Miscellaneous	103,185	
Total liabilities		274,593
Net assets applicable to outstanding shares		$84,984,567
Shares outstanding ($0.50 par value)*		11,019,232
Net asset value and redemption price per share (net assets divided by shares outstanding)		$ 7.71
Offering price per share—100/92.75 of net asset value per share†		$ 8.31

* The Fund under its indenture of trust is authorized to issue unlimited shares of $0.50 par value.

† Based upon a purchase of less than $10,000. Reduced sales charges are applicable to larger purchases.

Source: Eaton and Howard Balanced Fund 47th *Annual Report,* December 31, 1978.

---

in a closed-end company. This is because these companies offer to sell or buy their shares on the basis of current net asset values.

On the date of the Eaton and Howard statement, this company offered to sell its shares on the basis of the net asset value per share— $7.71 plus commissions—or to buy its shares at $7.71.

It is *net asset value* rather than supply and demand factors which determines the market price of mutual fund shares. In fact, shares of mutual funds are not traded on the securities exchanges. These firms sell new shares through underwriters and brokers or directly to investors. They repurchase all shares offered for sale.

Investment policies, even the individual investments, of a closed-end and open-end company might be identical. However, the open-end company has the ability to continuously sell and redeem its shares.

These companies often provide shareowners with a wide variety of services and accounts not provided by the closed-end companies. This is one reason for the rapid growth of these funds. Another very important reason is that there is incentive for these companies to continue to market their securities in a most aggressive fashion. As will be explained later, the managers of mutual funds, like those of closed-end funds, receive management fees based on the dollar volume of the company's assets. Larger assets mean larger fees.

Regulation of investment companies

Investment companies which have chosen to be regulated under the terms of the Investment Company Act of 1940 and the Investment Company Amendments Act of 1970 are known as *regulated investment companies*. These firms are also regulated under the Securities Act of 1933 and the Securities Exchange Act of 1934, as are all corporations which sell securities publicly to residents of at least two states. These laws affect investment companies mainly in that they require them to register issues of their stock with the SEC. Registration of these securities may be blocked by the SEC if it is determined that the company has made erroneous, misleading, or incomplete statements about itself. Investment companies, like other corporations, must provide prospectuses to persons interested in purchasing new issues of their shares.

The Investment Company Act of 1940 was designed specifically to cause changes in the way investment companies were managed. Companies were required to include outside (presumably independent) persons on their boards of directors. Each board was then required to pass upon contracts which the company made with certain other businesses or individuals. The purpose of this legislation was to keep the investment companies from giving management, brokerage, or other contracts to persons or firms which did not fully warrant receiving the contracts. The regulation also forced companies to provide a certain minimum amount of diversification of assets. At least 75 percent of a company's total assets must be invested in such a way that no more than 5 percent of this amount is in the securities of one company. No more than 10 percent of the outstanding voting securities of any company may be owned.

Finally, the act restricted the maximum amount of leverage that a regulated investment company could have in its capital structure. Open-end companies could have no financial leverage. Closed-end companies were allowed to issue only limited amounts of bonds or preferred stock.

Most investment companies choose to become regulated under the 1940 Act because of the special tax advantages offered to regulated companies. While the law is complex, the theory it follows is simple. Regulated investment companies are seen as being *conduits* through which income passes to their shareholders. So long as the investment company meets certain minimum tests as stated in the act, it pays no income taxes. However, dividends and interest received by investment company shareholders are taxed as income.[1]

The Investment Company Amendments Act of 1970 imposed a "fiduciary duty" standard upon investment company managers, directors, and officers. The result of this act has been to make it easier for shareholders to protest excessive management fees, sales charges, or other expenses.

An investment company that is regulated is not necessarily a "safe" or a "good" company. The regulation, like other security laws, is designed to provide investors with enough facts to make intelligent decisions and to protect them from fraud. Managers of investment companies can still make poor investment decisions; shareholders can and do lose money on these investments. There is no doubt, however, that investment company shares are much safer now than they were before federal regulation was passed.

Figure 10–4 is a copy of a mutual fund share. Note how closely it resembles a regular common stock certificate.

HOW MUTUAL FUNDS OPERATE

Figure 10–5 is a diagram which pictures all the participants of a mutual fund organization. It attempts to show how these groups are related and how mutual fund shares are sold. This is an illustration of a large company which sells its securities through an underwriter and other selling groups. There is always a sales commission when shares are sold this way. Smaller companies may sell directly to investors, performing the underwriting function themselves and bypassing the selling groups. These companies may require no sales commission.

---

[1] Tax treatment of mutual fund dividends is examined later in this chapter.

FIGURE 10–4

A share of mutual fund stock

Courtesy of Columbia Growth Fund, Inc.

FIGURE 10–5
Organization of a typical large mutual fund

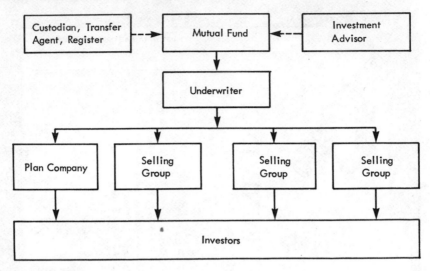

The mutual fund

The fund itself is the corporation in which the purchaser of mutual fund shares invests money.[2] This corporation is the legal owner of the investment securities and other assets which are purchased through the sale of its shares to the public. Managers of mutual funds spend much time marketing their company's securities. This effort includes preparation of promotional literature, hiring and instructing sales personnel, making sales agreements with brokerage companies, and devising mutual fund plans which have appeal for large numbers of investors. These companies must also handle the many details of share reinvestment, dividend payments, and investment policies. They are responsible for all the record keeping involved in operating this kind of business. The investment advisor also has great importance. The success or failure of the company rests largely on its profitability, which is determined by its investing decisions. The fund also receives a great amount of aid from accountants, the registrar, the custodian, and other related parties.

---

[2] Some mutual funds are organized in the legal form known as a Massachusetts trust. From the investor's viewpoint there is no significant difference between this and the corporate form.

Custodian, transfer agent, and registrar

These institutions perform the same services for the mutual fund (or the closed-end investment company) as they do for other corporations. The *custodian* holds the assets of the company, which are mainly in the form of investment securities, and guards them against physical loss.

The *transfer agent* accounts for the changes of ownership in the company's shares and makes certain that the shares it transfers are genuine. The transfer agent's certification appears on the face of all shares. (See Figure 10–4.)

The *registrar* is an officer of a trust company or commercial bank which is independent of the investment company and the transfer agent. This person's job is to make certain that the transfer agent's efforts have been diligent and that no unauthorized stock is issued by the investment company.

Investment advisor

For an investment company to be successful over the long run, it must be able to invest its owners' money in a more productive fashion than they themselves could do. Excellent investment management can do this, or so we are told by the managements of all mutual funds. Mutual fund managers set investment policy. The investment advisor provides the advice which determines which securities the mutual fund will purchase and sell to carry out this policy. The advisor is paid a fee for this service.

Often the advisor company (usually another corporation) is controlled by the same persons who manage or control the mutual fund. It is sometimes difficult to determine where a given person's responsibilities end as a fund manager and where they begin as an investment advisor. The investment advisor company is employed by contract, a contract which has been passed upon by the stockholder owners of the mutual fund. This contract can be terminated if the management of the mutual fund is sufficiently unhappy with the advice it has been receiving.

Underwriter

Underwriters of mutual fund shares perform the same service for those companies as underwriters perform for other corporations. That is, they purchase securities from the issuing company for resale to brokers or other selling groups or for direct sale to investors. But since mutual fund shares are continuously issued and repurchased, the underwriter of these securities has a continuous relationship with the mutual fund company. From earlier discussions of the underwriting of corporate securities, it will be remembered that the agreement between underwriter and issuer lasted only as long as necessary to sell the securities that were being issued.

In some cases the underwriter sells directly to investors, taking the entire commission from the sale. At other times the underwriter acts as a wholesaler, purchasing securities from the mutual fund for resale to brokers and others who in turn sell them to investors. Under this arrangement the wholesaler and other sellers share the commissions.

Selling groups

A substantial number of underwriters employ *selling groups* of brokers to give wider sales distribution to their products. These persons serve as agents of the underwriter. In some cases they have exclusive sales agreements with a single company. Under other arrangements a selling group may market securities of several different mutual funds.

Plan companies

Most large mutual funds sell their securities under a variety of sales plans. Some programs obligate customers to buy securities periodically, others require the mutual fund to sell securities and make periodic payments to account holders. When mutual fund shares are sold this way some group must be responsible for holding contributions, making certain that the correct number of securities are credited to each account, and performing the accounting for plan investors. A normal way of providing these services is by organizing a separate *plan company*.

This group markets the same securities that would be sold by the underwriter or by other selling groups. In fact, they typically obtain the securities from the underwriter as needed to meet sales demand. The plan company employs its own sales force and, like the other selling groups, splits commissions with the underwriter. No commissions go to the mutual fund itself. This company receives only the net asset value of the shares sold.

PURCHASES AND SALES OF INVESTMENT COMPANY SHARES

Closed-end companies

Recall that closed-end shares are publicly traded. Their prices are set by supply and demand, with some regard to the net asset value of the stock. *The Wall Street Journal* reports the weekly closing price of these securities each Monday in the format shown in Figure 10–6; on Wednesday, prices of closed-end bond funds are reported. Other financial news services carry the same information.

The *net asset value* of these companies is always published (N.A. Value), but the price at which stock is traded is listed in the third column under the abbreviation "Stk Price." Commission charges would be added to this amount if you were buying these securities; if you were selling, the commission would be deducted from the price. Commissions are computed in exactly the same way that they are computed for any other common stock because these securities are sold through brokers like any other stock. The percent-difference column tells the percentage that the stock price differs from the stock's net asset value.

Mutual funds

Mutual fund shares are not sold like other securities. The mutual fund company agrees to redeem shares in the company on any business day. At least twice each business day the net asset value of the

FIGURE 10–6
Closed-end fund prices

Publicly Traded Funds

January 12, 1979

Following is a weekly listing of unaudited net asset values of publicly traded investment fund shares, reported by the companies as of Friday's close. Also shown is the closing listed market price or a dealer-to-dealer asked price of each fund's shares, with the percentage of difference.

	N.A. Value	Stk Price	% Diff
Diversified Funds	**Common**		**Stock**
AdmExp	14.01	12⅜	−11.7
BakerFen	64.78	47	−27.4
aGenAlnv	13.93	10⅛	−27.3
Lehman	14.47	10¾	−25.7
Madison	19.21	14⅜	−25.2
NiagaraSh	13.96	10½	−24.8
OseasSec	4.49	3⅛	−30.5
Tri-Conti	23.46	19⅛	−18.5
US&For	22.25	16⅝	−25.3
Specialized Equity and Convertible Funds			
aAmGnCv	24.76	16⅝	−32.9
bASA	24.63	23½	− 4.6
BancrftCv	23.48	16⅜	−30.3
Castle	24.03	20⅜	−15.2
CentSec	8.18	6⅛	−25.1
ChaseCvB	11.55	8⅜	−27.5
Claremont	13.42	8¾	−34.8
CLAS	(−7.87)	..⅜	.....
DrexelUt	21.02	18⅝	−11.4
Japan	16.44	12⅞	−21.7
NatlAvia	32.47	29	−10.7
NewAmFd	24.06	18	−25.1
Pete&Res	23.17	24⅜	+ 5.2
RETIncC	2.45	1⅞	−23.5
S-GSecInc	1.48	1⅞	+26.7
Source	20.29	16¾	−17.4
ValueLn	4.07	2½	−38.6

a-Ex-Dividend. b-As of Thursday's close. z-Not quoted.

Source: Reprinted by permission *The Wall Street Journal*, January 15, 1979, p. 31.

FIGURE 10–7
Mutual fund prices

Mutual Funds

Tuesday, January 16, 1979
Price ranges for investment companies, as quoted by the National Association of Securities Dealers. NAV stands for net asset value per share; the offering includes net asset value plus maximum sales charge, if any.

	Offer NAV Price Chg.			Offer NAV Price Chg.	
Acorn Fnd	19.66 N.L.—	.18	**First Investors Fund:**		
Adv Invest	(z) (z)	...	Bond Ap	14.23 15.34+	.02
Afuture Fd	12.44 N.L.—	.09	Discovr	6.69 7.31—	.08
AGE Fund	4.41 4.50+	.02	Growth	8.34 9.11—	.09
Allstate	9.44 N.L.—	.09	Income	7.92 8.66+	.02
Alpha Fnd	12.22 N.L.—	.16	Stock Fd	7.89 8.62—	.02
Am Birthrt	9.90 10.82—	.09	1st MultiA	8.41 N.L.—	.02
American Funds Group:			1stMult Inc	.94 N.L.	...
Am Bal	8.23 8.99—	.05	Fst VRate	10.00 N.L.	...
Amcap F	8.39 9.17—	.09	44 Wall St	13.91 N.L.—	.34
Am Muti	10.05 10.98—	.13	Fnd Grwth	3.93 4.30+	.05
An Gwth	7.12 7.78—	.12	**Founders Group Funds:**		
Bnd FdA	13.66 14.92+	.01	Growth	4.94 5.40—	.04
Cash Mt	1.00 N.L.	...	Income	12.01 13.13—	.07
Fund Inv	6.88 7.52—	.09	Mutual	8.14 8.90—	.10
Gth FdA	7.47 8.14—	.34	Special	10.75 11.75—	.12
Inc FdA	7.78 8.50—	.03	**Franklin Group:**		
I C A	15.68 17.14—	.23	Brwn Fd	3.63 3.91—	.02
Nw Prsp	6.31 6.90—	.09	D N T C	8.45 9.11—	.12
Wash Mt	6.79 7.42—	.05	Growth	6.51 7.02—	.08
American General Group:			Income	1.77 1.91+	.01
A GnCBd	8.29 9.06+	.02	Liqd Ast	1.00 N.L.	...
A GC Gr	4.35 4.75—	.03	US GvSc	8.66 9.34+	.01
AG Entp	6.32 6.91—	.14	Utilities	4.72 5.09	...
High Yld	11.59 12.43+	.02	Res Capt	3.15 3.40+	.06
A Gn Inc	6.04 6.60—	.02	Res Eqty	3.91 4.22—	.05
AG Legl	6.78 7.41—	.09	Fundpack	6.33 6.43—	.07
A G Mun	22.97 24.12—	.02	**Funds Inco Group:**		
A GnVen	15.73 17.19+	.02	Impact	7.88 8.08—	.04
Comstk	7.63 8.34—	.01	Cm IncS	8.00 N.L.—	.02
Eqty Gth	7.60 8.31—	.03	Indus Tr	9.97 10.28—	.03
Fd Amer	6.77 7.40—	.08	Pilot Fd	8.24 N.L.—	.07
Harbor	8.95 9.78—	.04	GT Pac Fd	16.91 N.L.+	.03
Pace Fd	16.58 18.12—	.07	Gatewy Op	15.68 N.L.—	.10
Prov Inc	3.69 3.98—	.02	GE S&S Pr	26.05 (z) —	.33
Am Grwth	6.21 6.70+	.01	Genl Secur	10.85 N.L.—	.17
Am Heritg	1.71 (z) —	.01	Grth IndSh	22.28 N.L.—	.26

z-Quote not available. NL-No load. x-Ex-dividend. r-Ex-rights. d Ex-distribution. a-funds redemption price.

Source: Reprinted by permission *The Wall Street Journal*, January 17, 1979, p. 31.

company's shares is computed. It is at this net asset value that the shares are redeemed. Some mutual funds charge a modest amount for the privilege of redemption, but this is unusual.

Mutual fund share prices are quoted by nearly every newspaper in the United States because so many people own these investments. The list in Figure 10–7 contains only a part of the several hundred funds which are reported on a daily basis in *The Wall Street Journal*.

Mutual fund commissions. The *net asset value* (NAV) listed in Figure 10–7 is the value per share at the close of trading. The *offering price* is the price at which the company offers shares for sale. The difference between the NAV and the offering price is the amount of the maximum commission. It is usually between 7½ and 8½ percent of the NAV.

The mutual fund industry has come under criticism for these seemingly high commissions. While most funds have a scale of commission charges which is graduated down from the maximum rates, the graduation usually begins with purchases of $10,000 or $15,000.

Some mutual funds charge lower commissions to persons who sign a letter of intent to buy a substantial dollar amount of securities over a specified period of time. These purchasers pay commissions at the rate that they would have paid if they had purchased the total amount of securities all at one time. This way, the total commission on the purchase may be lower than it would have been if the securities had been purchased piecemeal. These and other features of mutual fund purchase plans may serve to lower the commission charge for some purchasers, but on the whole these charges remain substantial.

For several years the Securities and Exchange Commission has sponsored legislation which would lower mutual fund commissions. Suggestions have been made for a maximum commission of 5 percent, with lower rates on larger purchases. While no legislation has been passed which limits mutual fund commissions, more funds are being sold which charge no commissions. Recent changes in the commission structure of common stock purchases and sales have generally acted to increase the commissions on small trades. For example, the typical major brokerage house now charges about $40 or 4 percent to buy or sell $1,000 of common stock. The narrowing of the commission charges between mutual fund shares and small purchases of common stock will probably cause some persons to shift from direct stock investments to mutual funds.

No-load funds

Some mutual funds charge no sales commission—Acorn and Afuture, for example (see Figure 10–7). These are *no-load funds,* and the bid and ask prices of these securities are identical. No-load funds are usually sold directly to the purchaser by the fund. The sales effort of these companies is not at all aggressive, and for this reason these funds have not expanded in size nearly so rapidly as those which sell through underwriters and brokers and charge commissions on all securities sold. To purchase no-load securities, the investor must usually use some personal initiative. The best sources of information on these companies are *Investment Companies, Forbes,* and the financial press.

Few no-load funds offer the wide variety of purchase options and accounts commonly available at other funds. They all allow an investor to start off with 100 percent of his or her money invested, which should result in a larger return on the total amount invested—all other things being equal. A very few no-load funds charge a small fee to redeem shares.

ADVANTAGES AND DISADVANTAGES OF PURCHASING INVESTMENT COMPANY SHARES

Professional investment management

At the time of this writing there are in operation about 600 mutual funds and about 50 actively traded closed-end funds. All these companies are supposedly operated so as to attain a specific goal or goals for their owners, and all companies list professional management as one of their strengths.

Professional management usually implies that the investment company can manage the investor's money better than the individual, assuming that the goals of each are similar. Making any sort of scientific test of whether investment companies are in fact more successful investors than individuals is very difficult. An investment company having very successful investment performance in the past will not necessarily have the same success in the future, and one which has done poorly in the past may have great success in future years. The topic of measuring performance will be examined in detail later in this chapter. At this point it is sufficient to state that for the person who knows little about investments, or has limited time or little inclination to manage them, the professional management offered by the investment company is probably valuable.

Diversification

A diversified investment company is one which spreads the risk associated with the purchase of investments among many different holdings. It is difficult for an individual to do this unless substantial money is available to invest. If a person had $10,000, and wanted to invest it in such a way as to obtain the same amount of diversification as would be provided through purchase of shares in a regulated investment company, nearly 20 different securities would have to be purchased. A maximum dollar amount of $500 could be invested in each security, as no more than 5 percent of the total investment could be in any one form. These purchases would probably be of odd lots of securities, and commission charges would be high. Perhaps of more importance is the problem of managing 20 different investments. This large number of different securities would take a great deal of time—if they were adequately managed. Few people have or want to devote the necessary time to this task.

Diversification may take many forms. Bonds, preferred stocks, and common stocks may be purchased to provide different types of securities. Diversification may be by industry, or it may be geographical. It may be performed by purchasing securities of many different companies which are in the same type of business.

The purpose of diversification is to spread risk over a large number of different investments so that it becomes nearly impossible for the investor to have exceptionally poor investment results. But while it protects against loss, it also "protects" the investor against better-than-average profits. Because of this, a well-diversified investment company has great difficulty in performing much better than the stock market averages, even though the company has professional investment management.

In the late 1960s a new concept of investment company appeared. These companies were formed to provide investment *performance*, not diversification and safety. The strategy was to not diversify, but rather to concentrate investments in relatively few companies which have great growth potential. The professional management of these companies supposedly offsets the risk that one takes when investments are not diversified. More will be said about this type of fund when we discuss some of the different types of investment policies followed by various investment companies.

Low cost shifting of investments

All the larger mutual fund companies offer *families of funds*. These are simply funds that have different investment goals which are organized and sold by the same company. For example, in 1979 the Eaton and Howard group of investment companies included seven different funds. Shareholders may transfer the net asset value of their investment from one fund to another at a cost of $5. Since the objectives of all seven funds are different, the thrust of an investment program may be changed at practically no cost.

How valuable is this privilege? An investor wishing to shift from $10,000 market value of common stock to an equal amount of bonds would pay a commission of 2 or 3 percent to sell the stock and a smaller commission to buy the bonds. The shift would probably cost at least $400, an expense which would be repeated if the investment were shifted back to common stock. The usual $5 or $10 charge for shifting within a family of funds provides a significant cost saving.[3]

---

[3] John C. Boland, "Switch in Time: Holders of Mutual Funds Try to Profit by Swapping," *Barrons*, December 18, 1978, p. 11 ff.

Many funds allow accounts to be shifted over the phone—the ultimate in convenience. Others shift only after written notification, and some restrict switching privileges to a maximum number of changes per period. Shifting between unrelated no-load funds can of course be accomplished easily and at little or no cost by selling out of one fund and buying into another. However, all shifts, even those between securities in a family of funds where no cash changes hands, are recorded as sales and purchases of new securities for income tax purposes. This feature may be important to the investor's income tax position so far as capital gains or losses are concerned. This topic is examined in Chapter 15.

INCOME FROM MUTUAL FUND SHARES

Mutual funds usually do not pay taxes on their income. They pass it through the company to the fund's owners in the form of dividends. Shareholders pay taxes on these dividends in the year they are declared, even if all dividend payments are retained in the fund and used to purchase additional shares.

Dividends are usually paid quarterly. At the end of the year, the mutual fund is required to present each shareholder with a statement, such as that presented in Figure 10–8, which tells the amount and type of dividends the investor has received during the year. This is a valu-

FIGURE 10–8
Income tax form for reporting mutual fund dividends

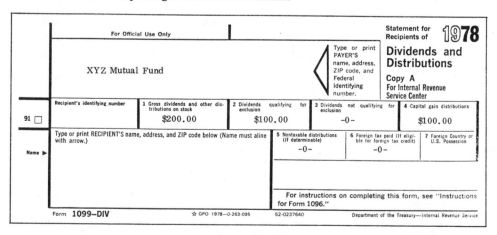

able service. Persons investing directly in securities must prepare this type of information themselves or hire someone to do it for them.

Gross dividends are the total dividends that have been paid to the shareholder. *Dividends qualifying for exclusion* are those paid from income that came to the investment company in the form of dividends from other corporations. Taxpayers should list these dividends along with other dividend income on their tax returns. The "qualifying for exclusion" phrase refers to the fact that $100 of dividend income is currently exempted from federal income taxes. This amount may be as high as $200 for married persons filing joint returns.[4]

Dividends not qualifying for exclusion are dividends on income that is taxable at ordinary rates. Income from interest payments and short-term capital gains are examples of this form of income. As the name indicates, these dividends are not eligible for exclusion under the dividend exemption.

Capital gain distributions are dividends from income generated by the sale of capital assets held for more than 12 months. This type of income is taxed at a lower rate than other income and is reported on a special schedule in the federal tax form.

Nontaxable distributions are dividends paid to the mutual fund from income that was not taxable; municipal bond interest for example. No one pays any tax on this income, but it must be reported.

The *foreign tax paid* column records the share of foreign taxes paid that are allocated to each shareholder.

Because of the several types of dividend distributions, it may seem that ownership of mutual fund shares has somehow complicated the tax position of the investor. This is not true. Ownership of these shares does not cause the investor to pay more or less taxes or have more or fewer types of income than would be the case if money had been invested directly in the same investments as were held by the fund. In fact, the records provided by all mutual funds actually simplify income tax preparation for most investors.

Taxation of closed-end investment company dividends usually follows the procedure outlined above. However, special benefits through ownership of shares of certain funds may be available to persons in the highest income tax brackets. For example, municipal bond funds provide tax advantages for these people.

---

[4] See Chapter 15, Tax Aspects of Investments, for a fuller explanation of the taxation of dividend income. Dividends entered in Figure 10–8 are carried through the tax recording procedure to the final income tax form in this chapter.

TYPES OF MUTUAL FUND ACCOUNTS

In marketing their products, managers of mutual funds have followed the examples set by the life insurance industry. They offer prospective buyers many different payment plans and several choices of dividend distributions. In sharp contrast to this, purchasers of closed-end investment company shares normally pay cash for their shares and have no option on dividend distributions. Table 10–1 shows the importance of the different type accounts.

TABLE 10–1
Types of shareholder accounts (mutual fund accounts, 000 omitted)

	1975		1976		1977	
	Number	Percent	Number	Percent	Number	Percent
Withdrawal accounts...............	211	2.1	191	2.1	176	2.0
Accumulation plans	1,155	11.8	1,042	11.6	945	10.9
Accounts with automatic dividend reinvestment..................	5,901	60.0	5,449	60.3	5,511	63.7
Regular accounts	2,564	26.1	2,352	26.0	2,024	23.4
Total............	9,831	100.0	9,034	100.0	8,656	100.0

Source: Wiesenberger Investment Companies Service, New York, 1978.

The regular account

This is the least complicated account sold by the mutual fund industry. Purchasers of these shares invest a certain amount of money (some funds have a minimum dollar amount of shares that they will sell) and receive a certain number of shares of stock in the fund. Investors make no agreement to purchase more shares of the fund, and dividends are disbursed periodically as they are realized. Income dividends are usually paid quarterly, and capital gains dividends annually.

Accumulation plans

These plans are of two types—voluntary and contractual. Under a *voluntary accumulation plan* the investor begins by purchasing some modest dollar amount of investment company shares. This may be as low as $100; the minimum amount varies among mutual funds. At the time of this purchase the investor declares an intent to make future periodic purchases of a minimum amount. The regular commission is charged on each future purchase and the number of shares purchased is credited to the investor's account. These are known as *level-loaded plans* because sales commissions are a constant percentage of each payment. Such plans allow persons to acquire shares in small amounts as money becomes available. Many plans allow the purchase of fractional shares. The investor has no legal liability to continue to make the agreed upon purchases and the account may be canceled and shares may be redeemed at their net asset value at any time.

The *contractual plan* differs from the voluntary in that the agreement between the buyer and the fund is much more formalized. When opening one of these plans, the purchaser agrees to buy a certain dollar amount of mutual fund securities over a given period of time. Most of these plans run at least two years, often much longer. Purchasers are allowed to miss payments or to make larger than agreed upon payments. Most plans allow early withdrawal of funds and reinvestment at no additional cost. This feature allows investors to use fund proceeds to meet temporary financial needs. Most of the plans allow the purchaser to have all dividends reinvested in additional shares of stock in the fund.

These investments are usually sold through the plan companies discussed earlier. Commissions are commonly at the highest rate allowed under law and would typically be close to nine percent of the total invested. But the commission is not usually deducted evenly as shares are purchased. Rather, most of the commission is deducted from early payments, a practice known as a *front-end load*.

The 1970 amendments to the Investment Company Act of 1940 created protections for contractual plan purchasers. Front-end loading of commissions is allowed, but maximum charges are specified. Investors may cancel out of a contractual plan within 45 days of its inception and receive back the current net asset value of their shares plus all commissions and other charges. Investors canceling within 18 months receive the net asset value of their shares and may receive a portion of sales charges. The 18-month cancellation privilege may or may not be available, depending upon how the commissions have been assessed. Information about commission payments and refunds is contained in the offering prospectus. This document should be carefully studied by all persons buying mutual fund securities, but it is especially important for those entering into contractual purchase plans.

Some companies sell insurance which is used to complete a plan if the plan owner dies prior to this time. This is simply term insurance which declines in amount as the investment plan is paid off. A medical examination to prove insurability is often required if the amount of insurance is over $10,000. Insurance premiums are usually paid monthly along with plan contributions.

Accounts with automatic dividend reinvestment

Automatic dividend reinvestment means that the income or capital gain dividends of the fund, or both, are reinvested immediately in additional shares of stock of the mutual fund. No dividends are received currently, but the new shares that are purchased with the reinvested dividends in turn receive dividends; the effect is similar to interest compounding.

Reinvestment of dividends may allow the investor to acquire more shares without paying the normal commissions. Reinvested income dividends are applied to the purchase of additional shares at the current *offering price*. This price includes commission charges. Capital gains dividends are often reinvested at the current *net asset value* of the company's shares. This price includes no commission. The procedure varies from fund to fund. Even though all dividends are reinvested, they are taxed as income in the period in which they are declared. Later, when the investor redeems the account and takes possession of these securities, no tax is levied on the amount that was reinvested.

Withdrawal accounts

These plans appeal to persons who wish to receive a certain sum of cash regularly from their investments. Savings accounts which pay interest directly to the account holder and annuities sold by life insurance companies most nearly resemble this investment.

The usual withdrawal plan begins when an investor purchases a minimum dollar amount (usually $10,000) of mutual fund shares. These are normally purchased in a single transaction, although most mutual funds allow other types of accounts to be changed into withdrawal plans if they are of sufficient size. The mutual fund agrees to make periodic payments from the account to its owner or to other designated persons.

Payments will be made as long as the account has value. If the beginning amount of the account was large and the withdrawals small, or if the investment experience of the fund were exceptional, payments could be made indefinitely. This is usually not the case. Withdrawal payments are first made from dividend income, and if the dividends do not cover the withdrawal, the additional amount is obtained by redeeming fund shares. If a mutual fund has very poor investment experience, and if withdrawal payments are large relative to the size of the investment, the principal of the investment might be rapidly used up.

INVESTMENT POLICIES OF INVESTMENT COMPANIES

Investment company shares are purchased for a variety of reasons. Convenience of purchase, ability to sell shares immediately, diversificaton of investments, and professional management are some of them. It is probably professional management which attracts most people to these investments. There is widespread belief that management of money by a professional will produce greater returns than could be obtained if the investor had invested directly in securities.

Whether or not professional management does provide greater profits is a topic for later discussion. The important thing now is to realize that investment companies, like individual investors, have different goals. The investor should first determine his or her own investment objectives. Then, if the purchase of investment company shares is desired, the shares of a company having an investment goal which parallels that of the investor may be purchased.

There were about 450 open-end companies selling 600 different mutual funds and about 50 actively traded closed-end funds being sold in the United States as of year end 1978. Every firm makes a statement of its policies and goals in its offering prospectus, a document easily obtained from the company or a broker. Most all investment companies may be classified as one of the following types, although many of them have unique features. Table 10–2 shows the importance of these different types of funds.

Balanced funds

The investment objective of these funds is long-term growth of both capital and income through purchase of bonds, preferred stocks, and common stocks. The term "balanced" comes from the policy followed by some of these companies of trying to "balance" portions of their investment portfolios among these different securities in some fairly constant proportions. While there is wide diversity in the performance of these funds, they are usually managed so that they offer sharehold-

TABLE 10-2
Investment companies classified by investment objective (as of December 31, 1978)

Type of fund	Number of funds	Combined assets ($000)	Percent of total
Balanced..	25	3,811,400	6.6
Bond and preferred stock	11	1,119,600	2.0
Money market	59	10,462,700	18.0
Income	119	8,904,400	15.3
Tax-exempt mutual bond	37	2,634,900	4.5
Common stock:			
Specialized..	23	732,800	1.2
Growth..	143	12,649,500	21.8
Growth and income..............................	80	13,209,800	22.7
Maximum capital gain	103	4,619,300	7.9
Total...	600	58,144,400	100.0

Source: *Investment Companies,* 1979 edition (New York: Wiesenberger Investment Companies Service), Table 5.

ers both capital gains and dividend income. Price fluctuations of the net asset values, or market values in the case of closed-end companies, are usually less than most other types of funds.

Bond and preferred stock funds

As the name implies, investments of such funds are all senior securities. The specific investment objective of these companies varies mainly in its emphasis upon income and price stability. One could not reasonably expect anything but very modest capital gains distributions from this type fund. Share value should be fairly constant, except when changes in market interest rates cause changes in prices of senior securities.

Money market funds

Money market or *liquidity* funds have greatly increased in number during recent years. These funds invest in short-term liquid debt securities—Treasury bills, bankers acceptances, commercial paper, and other such securities. They provide investors with a return that may be very high in periods when short-term interest rates are high. During such times these investments are much more attractive than savings accounts because they pay higher yields. Of course, as short-term interest rates decline, returns to these funds will also decline. Many of these investments are more liquid than savings accounts in that they allow owners to write checks against their accounts, or in other ways to quickly obtain funds. Money market fund securities cannot be expected to pay even modest capital gains dividends. Share value price fluctuations are typically least of all investment companies.

Income funds

These funds emphasize liberal current income. This objective may be realized through purchase of bonds, preferred stock, or common stock. Most of these companies hold a variety of investments. They offer greater than average price stability, high yearly income dividends, and low capital gains distributions. Many withdrawal plans are income funds.

Municipal bond funds

The earliest of these companies were organized as *unit trusts*, and some still are. Under this arrangement a portfolio of municipal securities is purchased and "units" or interests in the portfolio are sold. Units are not redeemed until the trust is wound up, but periodic distributions of tax-free interest are made to unit owners based upon the number of units owned. There is no continuous offering of these securities, but units may be sold to other investors.

Since 1976 mutual fund municipal bond funds have been offered. These resemble other mutual funds in that offering and redemption of securities is continuous. Management of the funds is provided by the mutual fund company, and income is passed through to shareholders in the usual manner. Both load and no-load funds are available. Growth of these funds has been rapid. Their appeal is tax-exempt income, safety of principal, and a fairly high yield for persons in the high-income tax brackets.

Common stock funds

These funds invest only in common stocks or securities which are convertible into common stocks. This general classification includes the largest number of funds in existence today. The objectives of these firms vary in the degree to which they seek dividend income or capital gains growth and in the way they go about attaining their investment objectives. Their shares would typically have less price stability than the shares of balanced funds, income funds, money market funds, or those holding senior securities.

Specialized common stock funds. These funds were organized with the objective of purchasing common stocks of firms engaged in a certain industry. They are offered as a way for investors to participate in the growth and profits of such industries as electronics, air travel, oceanography, and chemicals. What diversification there is in the investment company's portfolio comes from purchasing the shares of different companies in a given industry.

Several funds invest only in the shares of companies located in certain countries, for example the Japan Fund. They diversify investments among different types of companies, but all companies are located in the same country. The philosophy of this type investment is to participate in the economic growth of a certain country. Investments may be in bonds or stock, although stock investments are emphasized.

Growth, growth income, and capital gains funds

These titles serve to indicate that the investment objective of the fund is capital growth. The usual vehicle for this growth is investment in common stocks of smaller, less well-known companies. Some of these companies seek modest financial leverage by borrowing money to increase the fund's ability to purchase securities. Some of the funds diversify their investments, and some do not. It is very difficult to draw a line between this class of funds and the even more speculative ones next discussed. One should not expect much price stability in the shares of these companies or hardly any income dividends. Some of these funds have performed very well in rising markets; most of them have suffered substantial losses in share values in declining markets.

Hedge funds, special situations funds, and others

Many of these companies were first organized as private investment trusts and were unregulated by the SEC or the 1940 Investments Company Act as amended. Some are regulated investment companies but they have chosen to be nondiversified companies.[5] They vary greatly in their investment objectives and in the way they are operated.

One thing that these companies have in common is that the invest-

---

[5] Nondiversified companies must register as such and notify potential shareholders of their status. Nondiversified means that the company may have as few as 50 percent of its assets in diversified investments. No more than 25 percent of its assets may be invested in securities of a single company.

ment manager has very wide discretion over the type of investments that the company purchases. Borrowing is often used to obtain financial leverage. Put and call options may be sold or purchased and securities may be sold short. (See Chapter 11 for a discussion of these kinds of investments.) Normally this type of company would have very little diversification in its investment portfolio. Investors in these funds could expect to receive income dividends only by accident, as the company will not invest in securities of companies which emphasize payment of dividends or interest. The company may do a great amount of short-term trading of securities. Sometimes the fund's investment management contract specifies that the compensation of the manager is to be based upon the performance of the fund. Low performance, low management fee; high performance, high management fee. Persons investing in these companies must be willing to accept a great amount of price variability in their shares.

Dual purpose funds

Another type of investment company is the *dual purpose fund* (see Figure 10–9). The purpose of this closed-end fund is to provide a single investment opportunity for two different types of investors. To do this the fund sells two types of investment shares—income shares and capital shares. Income shares, or preference shares as they are often called, are purchased by persons seeking current investment income. Owners of these shares receive *all* the income from the entire investment portfolio. They are guaranteed a certain minimum annual dividend payment. Holders of capital shares receive no dividends of any type. As the company realizes capital gains in its investment portfolio, these gains are reinvested in more assets.

The leverage in this investment comes from the fact that income and growth shares were initially sold in *equal dollar amounts,* but one class of shareholders obtains *all* the capital gains and the other *all* the income. As the asset value of the fund increases, the market price of both classes of stock should increase, although not necessarily at the same rate. However, the shares of capital stock are not redeemable at their net asset value until after the income shares have been called in. These funds began operations with stated lives of between 12 and 18 years. The market price of both classes of shares will be set by supply and demand over these years. Market prices may be above or below net asset values, depending upon how investors assess future prospects for the shares of the investment company.

FIGURE 10–9
Prices of dual purpose fund
shares

Dual Purpose Funds

Friday, January 12, 1979
Following is a weekly listing of the unaudited net asset values of dual-purpose, closed-end investment funds'
capital shares as reported by the companies as of Friday's close. Also shown is the closing listed market price
or the dealer-to-dealer asked price of each fund's capital
shares, with the percentage of difference.

	Cap. Shs. Price	N.A. Val Cap. Shs.	% Diff.
Am DualVest	9¾	10.78	− 9.6
Gemini	22¼	26.48	−16.0
Hemisphere	1½	0.18	+733.3
Income and Cap	6¾	8.15	−18.17
Leverage	16⅞	20.74	−18.6
Pegasos Inco&Cap	7	7.34	− 4.6
Putnam Duo Fund	8⅞	10.32	−14.0
Scudder Duo-Vest	8½	10.22	−16.8
Scudder D-V Exch	20	27.26	−26.6
Lipper Analytical Distributors.			

Source: Reprinted by per-
mission *The Wall Street Journal*, January 15, 1979, p. 31.

Seven of the nine dual purpose funds listed in Figure 10–9 were started in 1967. Both classes of securities are callable, a feature which is necessary so that the funds can be liquidated and all the shareholders paid off at one time. The usual procedure will be to call both classes of stock and sell the assets of the fund at the same time. A specified amount (usually the par value) will next be paid to the owners of income shares—if there are sufficient assets to do this. Money remaining after this payment will be divided up and distributed to the owners of capital shares. The fund will cease to exist after this distribution because all its assets will have been paid out. Since practically all of these securities have traditionally sold at discounts from their net asset values, these may be good investments to buy and hold until the shares are called.

ANALYSIS OF INVESTMENT COMPANY SHARES: MEASURING PERFORMANCE

Performance of a given investment company should be measured against the stated objectives of the company. If the fund's goal is to produce maximum current income, then this is the main factor to be measured. If the objective is to obtain capital gains with little or no emphasis on dividend income, then this is the important thing to measure. Unfortunately, mutual fund sales representatives often emphasize the growth performance of their funds to the exclusion of other investment characteristics which may be more important to the investor in the long run.

Performance of a mutual fund—and most closed-end funds—has traditionally been measured by summing the effect of three different things: (1) changes in the net asset value of mutual fund shares, or the market value of shares of closed-end companies, (2) the amount of income dividends paid, and (3) the amount of capital gains dividends paid. This information is often presented by yearly periods as an index of performance. This index may be compared to the Dow Jones or other stock averages, or to an index of performance of other investment companies.

Several companies present investment company performance information in varying degrees of detail. Figure 10–10 is a portion of the information of the Eaton and Howard Balanced Fund presented in *Investment Companies*. The data are given in a form that makes it easy to see how this company has performed over a ten-year period. This is but a part of the information that *Investment Companies* provides on this and other funds. Investment company annual reports and prospectuses present similar information.

The recent trend in the measurement of mutual fund performance is toward *risk adjusted performance*. In general, average investment returns increase as risk increases: Average yields on common stocks are higher than yields on bonds because stocks are riskier. A mutual fund portfolio of common stocks should outperform (yield more than) one of bonds for the same reason.

Portfolio risk may be measured by the average beta and alpha of the portfolio. Remember (from Chapter 9) that beta measures how much the price of a given security is expected to rise and decline when security markets rise and decline. Alpha measures whether the returns on the security are expected to be better or worse than the average security. Portfolio beta and alpha values are calculated by all portfolio managers who seek to measure portfolio performance on a risk adjusted basis. Then, a theoretical portfolio having beta and alpha characteristics close to those of the real portfolio is created. The performance of the real portfolio is compared to the theoretical portfolio. Risk characteristics of both are the same, so if the real portfolio returns exceed those of the theoretical portfolio, it can be said that the fund achieved superior performance relative to its risk level.

Quite a number of risk adjusted performance studies of mutual funds have been done over the past decade. They indicate that bond funds are indeed less risky than common stock funds, and that funds with aggressive investment policies are more risky than others. This

FIGURE 10–10
Performance information

THE EATON & HOWARD GROUP OF FUNDS

This group is composed of seven open-end investment companies under the sponsorship and management of the Boston-based investment counsel firm of Eaton & Howard, Inc. Making up the group are Eaton & Howard Stock Fund, organized in 1931; the Balanced fund, which came out a year later; the Income fund (the former General Investors Trust), which joined the group in 1966; the Growth and Special funds, launched in 1968; the Cash Management fund, added in 1975; and Foursquare Fund, whose management was assumed in 1974.

On April 30, 1979 Vance, Sanders & Company, Inc. acquired substantially all of the assets of Eaton & Howard, Incorporated. The combined firm, Eaton & Howard, Vance Sanders Inc., has been approved by shareholders of the Eaton & Howard Funds as the investment manager and principal underwriter for each of those Funds.

Special Services: Voluntary accumulation plans also serve for automatic dividend reinvestment. There is a $20 minimum or subsequent investment requirement, except for Cash Management Fund which has a minimum of $1,000 initially, and Foursquare Fund which has a minimum of $50 initially. Income dividends are invested at offering price, except that dividends on Income Fund are invested at asset value less a 30-cent service charge, and dividends on Foursquare Fund, at asset value. Arrangements may be made for plan payments to be made through bank drafts on the investor's checking account. A periodic withdrawal plan is available without charge; annual withdrawals may not exceed 10% of the total amount deposited. Shares may be exchanged at asset value for those of other Eaton & Howard funds for a $5 service charge. A Keogh Plan custody agreement, master corporate profit-sharing and pension plans and Individual Retirement Account plans are available.

EATON & HOWARD BALANCED FUND

Eaton & Howard Balanced Fund is managed as if it were "the entire investment program of a prudent investor." Current income is an important objective, as well as reasonable growth of both principal and income. Balance among bonds, perferred stocks and common stocks is maintained at all times, with a maximum limitation of 75% for any single type of security.

At the end of 1978, the fund had 60.7% of its assets in common stocks, 28.2% in bonds and preferred stocks, and 11.1% in net cash and equivalent. About 39% of assets was in common stocks in five industry groups: oil, gas & oil systems (14.5% of assets); consumer goods & services (9%); banking & finance (5.8%); utilities (5.3%), and transportation & resource development (4.8%). The five largest individual common stock investments were Exxon (7.5% of assets), Southern California Edison (3%), Royal Dutch Petroleum (2.9%), Raytheon Co. (2.7%), and IBM (2.6%). The rate of portfolio turnover during the year was 24.5% of average assets. Unrealized appreciation was 15.3% of year-end assets.

was to be expected, of course. The studies also indicate that on the basis of risk adjusted performance the average mutual fund performs no better than an unmanaged (securities chosen randomly) portfolio having the same risk characteristics.

Similar conclusions can be drawn by looking at the performance records of funds having the same investment objectives. Reports of performance, current as well as historical, are published in *Investment Companies, Forbes, Barrons*, and a number of other financial services. There are very few examples of companies that consistently outperform others having similar investment objectives.

The task of choosing a mutual fund can be made easier by: (1) First and foremost purchasing shares in companies having investment goals that are the same as yours. Don't try to increase returns by buying into

FIGURE 10-10 (continued)

Statistical History

					AT YEAR-ENDS						ANNUAL DATA			
	Total Net Assets ($)	Number of Share-holders	Net Asset Value Per Share ($)	Offer-ing Price ($)	Yield (%)	— % of Assets in —			Income Div-idends ($)	Capital Gains Distribu-tion ($)	Expense Ratio (%)	Offering Price ($)	
Year						Cash & Equiv-alent	Bonds & Pre-ferreds	Com-mon Stocks				High	Low
1978	84,984,567	14,143	7.71	8.31	5.5	11	28	61	0.465	0.13	0.68	8.97	7.89
1977	94,718,244	15,225	7.94	8.56	5.2	1	40	59	0.453	0.15	0.69	9.70	8.27
1976	114,985,493	16,346	9.01	9.71	4.4	2	34	64	0.428	0.09	0.64	9.71	8.98
1975	111,903,341	17,707	7.98	8.72	4.8	3	36	61	0.42	—	0.66	9.15	7.57
1974	102,846,793	18,464	6.96	7.61	5.2	6	37	57	0.417	0.35	0.66	10.05	6.72
1973	142,448,003	18,960	9.50	10.38	3.8	5	34	61	0.414	0.652	0.64	11.29	9.91
1972	166,555,144	19,834	10.99	12.01	3.3	3	30	67	0.416	0.45	0.62	12.03	10.72
1971	159,267,777	20,769	10.40	11.37	3.9	6	32	62	0.458	0.36	0.63	11.38	10.38
1970	158,596,884	21,298	10.10	11.04	4.1	9	33	58	0.47	0.50	0.64	10.92	8.86
1969	166,898,244	21,747	10.51	11.49	2.5	9	29	62	0.30	0.60	0.59	13.57	11.25
1968	197,906,114	22,860	12.52	13.54	3.4	4	32	64	0.455	—	0.57	14.17	11.71

An assumed investment of $10,000 in this fund, with capital gains accepted in shares and income dividends reinvested, is illustrated below. The explanation on Page 162 must be read in conjunction with this illustration.

EATON & HOWARD BALANCED FUND

Cost of Investment January 1, 1969 $10,000

(Initial Net Asset Value $9,275)

Year end Dec. 31

December 31, 1978

*Includes Value of Shares Accepted as Capital Gains $2,248; Reinvested Income Dividends $4,072.

$12,315 Total Value of Investment*

'$5,995 Value of Original Shares

	1969	1970	1971	1972	1973	1974	1975	1976	1977	1978		Dollar amounts of distributions reinvested:	
												Capital Gains	Income Dividends
Value of Shares Initially Acquired Through Investment of $10,000	$8,173	$7,854	$8,087	$8,546	$7,387	$5,412	$6,205	$7,006	$6,174	$5,995	1969	$ —	$ 235
											1970	399	394
											1971	316	419
Value of Shares Resulting From Reinvestment of Capital Gains and Income Dividends (Cumulative)											1972	427	414
											1973	672	452
	207	999	1,780	2,777	3,432	3,237	4,236	5,494	5,614	6,320	1974	399	496
											1975	—	532
											1976	118	575
											1977	211	648
Total Return	8,380	8,853	9,867	11,323	10,819	8,649	10,441	12,500	11,788	12,315	1978	196	713
											Total	$2,738	$4,878

Results Taking Capital Gains in SHARES and Income Dividends in CASH		**Results Taking All Dividends and Distributions in CASH**	
Initial Investment At Offering Price, January 1, 1969	$10,000	Initial Investment At Offering Price, January 1, 1969	$10,000
Value as of 12/31/78 of Shares Initially Acquired	$ 5,995	Total Value, December 31, 1978	$ 5,995
Value of Shares Accepted as Capital Gains Distributions	$ 1,907#	Distributions From Capital Gains	$ 2,086
Total Value, December 31, 1978	$ 7,902	Dividends From Investment Income	$ 3,296
Total Dividends PAID From Investment Income	$ 3,909		
# Dollar Amount of these distributions at the time shares were acquired: $2,340			

Source: *Wiesenberger Investment Companies Service*, New York, 1979.

excessively risky funds. (2) Whenever possible, buying no-load funds. Historically there has been little difference in the performance of load and no-load funds. Investing in no-load funds puts your entire investment to work immediately. (3) Selecting funds that have relatively low operating costs. A study by the SEC concluded that on average, the higher costs associated with "aggressive" portfolio management and with large management fees did not increase portfolio returns.[6] (4) Avoiding funds that have poor performance records.

---

[6] United States Securities and Exchange Commission, *Institutional Investors Study* Report (March 10, 1971), Washington, D.C.: U.S. Government Printing Office. Also see Irwin Friend et al., A Study of Mutual Funds. Prepared for the SEC by the Wharton School of Finance and Commerce. (Washington, D.C.: U.S. Government Printing Office, 1962).

Investment characteristics of investment companies

The wide variety of investment companies offer something for everyone. Those with investment goals of "above average profits" or "capital gains through special situations," and so on, have great amounts of financial risk. Potential for high profits is matched by potential for large losses. The more conservatively managed funds have less financial risk, but they are sometimes (depending upon the proportion of fixed-income securities in their investment portfolios) subject to interest rate risk. Purchasing power risk is not nearly so much of a problem as it is for fixed-income securities, although "bond funds" typically suffer losses in purchasing power during inflationary periods.

Marketability has not been a problem for mutual funds, to date. Marketability for closed-end companies is provided by the security markets, and for most of these firms it is fairly good. Marketability for open-end fund shares comes from the fund's ability and willingness to repurchase any shares offered to it for redemption. There are no known recent examples of mutual funds which have had to resort to panic selling of portfolio securities to meet redemption requests. Consequently, marketability of shares in these companies may also be seen as good.

Mutual fund insurance

Since 1970, it has been possible for mutual fund investors to *insure* their accounts against loss. Persons investing in funds which offer the insurance feature (usually the more stable, income oriented funds) purchase a policy which guarantees that at the end of the policy period they will receive *at least* what was paid for the mutual fund. Policy periods are from 10 to 15 years. The total insurance premium, which is paid in advance, is about 6 percent of the amount insured.

SUMMARY

An *investment company* is a company formed for the purpose of purchasing and managing a portfolio of investment securities for its shareholders. These companies are of two main types: *open-end*, or *mutual funds*, and *closed-end* funds. Shares of open-end companies are sold and redeemed by the mutual fund on a continuous basis. Shares of closed-end companies are sold like those of any other corporation. Except in the case of dual purpose funds, shares of closed-end companies remain outstanding indefinitely. Mutual funds are of far more importance than closed-end funds.

Mutual fund shares are sold on the basis of *net asset value per share.* Commissions vary from nothing on no-load funds, to 8.5 percent on certain other shares.

Most investment companies are regulated under the Investment Company Act of 1940 as amended, and various rules of the SEC and certain state agencies. Regulation has been directed toward (1) providing investors with information which they may use to make informed decisions, and (2) controlling certain of management's actions. Investment companies regulated under the 1940 Act pay no taxes themselves, passing income through to their shareholders.

Investment companies offer shareholders two important things—*diversification* of investments and *professional investment management.* Diversification is the spreading out of investment risks by purchasing a large number of different kinds of investments. Diversification is "good" in that it reduces investment risk; a well-diversified investment portfolio should not experience exceptionally large losses. However, diversification also keeps the portfolio from experiencing above average profits. Really aggressive investment portfolios are seldom diversified. Studies of mutual fund performance indicate that the average mutual fund performs about as well as a randomly chosen selection of securities having the same risk characteristics.

Balanced funds invest in both common stock and fixed-income securities. These funds do not usually show great changes in market value over time.

Bond, preferred stock, and income funds are similar in that they seek high current returns and offer relative price stability.

Money-market funds invest in short-term highly liquid debt securities. These investments allow the small investor to obtain the high interest returns that are normally available only to persons or companies able to purchase large amounts of Treasury bills, commercial paper, and other high-yield debt instruments.

Municipal bond funds provide investors with the opportunity for tax-free income from a diversified portfolio of debt securities.

Common stock funds having growth and income objectives are probably the least risky, so far as financial risk is concerned, while those emphasizing maximum capital gains are probably most risky.

Investment characteristics vary greatly from fund to fund. As a general statement, the performance-oriented funds usually offer the most financial risk, while those invested in fixed income securities offer the least. Marketability of all fund shares has remained good.

PROBLEMS

1. Go to the latest copy of *Investment Companies* and outline the investment objectives of the Diversified Fund of State Bond & Mortgage Company and the Research Equity Fund. These funds would appeal to what kinds of investors? (Any two funds having different objectives may be used.)

2. In *Investment Companies,* or any of the other information sources on mutual funds, look up and record the investment performance of the above two funds over the last year. Have these companies performed as you would expect them to have performed given their stated investment goals?

3. The Kemp Fund has $150,400,000 of assets, $1,200,000 of liabilities, and 11,200,000 shares of stock outstanding.
    a. What is the net asset value of this company?
    b. What is the net asset value per share?
    c. If this company charged an 8 percent commission over NAV on all securities sold, what would be the offering price of 100 shares of Kemp Fund?

4. From an investment company's annual report, or from any of the financial services, obtain the performance data for a common stock fund over the past ten years. Compare this information to that of one of the stock market indexes. Rate the company's performance as good, average, or poor on the basis of this comparison and the company's stated investment policy (assume no reinvestment of dividends).

5. Double Vest, Inc. is a closed-end dual purpose fund. It was organized 15 years ago with 10,000 shares of $20 par value preferred stock and an equal number of shares of $20 common stock. The preferred stock has received all the income from the fund over the 15 years of its life. The common has received nothing, but when the fund is wound up and its assets are distributed, an event which will take place today, the common shareholders will receive the assets of the company after liabilities and the preferred shareholders have been paid off.

    The company has $700,000 of assets and $12,500 of liabilities. Assuming that the assets can be sold at their book value and that there are no costs associated with the distribution of the fund's assets, how much will be paid to each share of preferred stock and each share of common?

QUESTIONS

1. How does the operation of an investment company differ from that of an industrial corporation?
2. What are the main differences between open-end and closed-end investment companies?
3. Why have mutual funds become so much more important than closed-end companies?
4. Why is the *net asset value* of a mutual fund share more important than the *book value* of a regular corporate stock?
5. Purchasing shares in a *regulated* investment company provides investors with certain safeguards. What are they?
6. What is the *investment advisor*, and what does this person or firm do for the investment company?
7. What is a *no-load fund*? What advantages may be had from purchasing shares of one of these companies?
8. What are the most important advantages to the purchase of investment company shares?
9. Regulated investment companies pay no income taxes on their earnings. Is this "fair" tax treatment?
10. How do *accumulation plans* differ from so-called *regular* accounts?
11. To what kind of an investor would a *withdrawal account* have the most appeal?
12. What is a *liquid asset* or *money market* fund? What advantage does it hold for small-scale investors?
13. What are *tax-exempt bond funds*? What advantage does this type fund have for investors? What persons are most likely to buy shares of these companies?
14. What does the term *risk adjusted performance* mean as it relates to investment companies?

SELECTED READINGS

Friend, Irwin; Blume, M.; and Crockett, J. *Mutual Funds and Other Institutional Investors: A New Perspective.* New York: McGraw-Hill, 1971.

Friend, Irwin, et al. *A Study of Mutual Funds.* Prepared for the SEC by the Wharton School of Finance and Commerce. Washington, D.C.: U.S. Government Printing Office, 1962.

"Forbes Mutual Fund Survey." *Forbes Magazine.* An annual performance study usually presented in the August issue of the magazine.

Investment Companies, Mutual Funds and Other Types. New York: Wiesenberger Investment Companies Services, published annually.

McDonald, John G. "Objectives and Performance of Mutual Funds,

1960–1969." *Journal of Financial and Quantitative Analysis,* IX, no. 3 (June 1974), p. 316 ff.

Mutual Fund Fact Book. Washington, D.C.: Investment Company Institute, published annually.

Potts, W. George. *Understanding Investments and Mutual Funds.* New York: Arco Publishing Co., 1973.

"Quarterly Mutual Fund Record." Published periodically in *Barron's.*

Securities and Exchange Commission. *Institutional Investors Study Report.* Washington, D.C.: U.S. Government Printing Office, 1971.

Williamson, J. Peter. "Measuring Mutual Fund Performance." *Financial Analysts Journal,* November–December 1972.

11

Speculative investments

INTRODUCTION

The preceding chapters of this book have been devoted to the description and analysis of the more common types of investments. This chapter examines several forms of investments which are somewhat lesser known and therefore held by fewer investors. Justification for including them in a basic book comes from the fact that these investments are finding ever wider usage by all investors, large as well as small.

Several of the special investments included in this chapter are *options* of one type or another. An option is simply a contract to purchase or sell something for a known value over a known period of time, at a price agreed upon when the option contract was originated. Rights and warrants and puts and calls are this type of contract. Commodity contracts resemble options. Short sales, new issue purchases, and investment in special situations are entirely different.

RIGHTS AND WARRANTS

From the viewpoint of the investor, rights and warrants have nearly identical legal characteristics. They both give their owners the right to purchase a limited number of additional shares of common stock of the company which has issued the rights or warrants, at a fixed price, until some designated future time. Rights are designed to raise capital quickly and usually expire within 30 days after they are issued. Warrants have much longer maturities.

Valuing rights

Rights are usually issued to a company's shareholders to get them to purchase additional shares of stock in the company. Firms having a preemptive right provision in their charter or bylaws *must* offer new shares to existing shareholders. Other companies may choose to sell new securities this way. The shareholders may either exercise their rights and purchase new shares of stock, or they may sell the rights to others, who may then exercise or sell them. The issuance of rights, like the issuance of a stock dividend, cannot increase or decrease the value of the shareholder's investment. Typically, rights are issued on the basis of one right for each share of outstanding stock.

An example of a hypothetical rights offering may help to make the procedure more clear. Sunnyfuture Co. has decided to sell additional shares of common stock through a rights offering. Several weeks before the offering takes place all shareholders, the financial press, and the SEC are notified that the company intends to issue new shares. Terms of the issue are (1) all stockholders of record on July 15, 1980, will receive one right for each share of common then held, (2) rights will be issued on August 1, 1980, and will be exercisable at any time until August 31, 1980, (3) four rights and $40 enable an investor to purchase one new share of stock at any time prior to and including August 31, 1980, (4) until August 15, 1980, the rights will "trade with the stock" or the stock will sell "rights on," which means that if shares are sold, the rights are sold with them. The following formula may be used to determine the *theoretical value* of a right when the stock is still selling "rights on."

Where

R = Value of a single right
P_1 = Market price of one share with its right still attached
S = Subscription price of an additional share
N = Number of rights necessary to buy an additional share

$$R = \frac{P_1 - S}{N + 1}$$

Sunnyfuture's outstanding stock was selling for $50, and additional shares cost $40 and four rights. Under these conditions each right had the following value.

$$R = \frac{\$50 - \$40}{4 + 1}$$
$$= \$2$$

After the 15th of the month, when the stock goes ex-rights, the value of a right is computed by this formula.

$$R = \frac{P_2 - S}{N}$$

P_2 is the market value of the stock *after* the stock and the rights trade separately; the other symbols stand for the same things as before. Theoretically, when the stock began trading ex-rights, each share provided security owners with a two-part investment made up of the market price of a share with no right attached to it, and the value of one right. Unless some other factor has changed the market price of the company's stock, the value of the right plus the market value of the stock can be no more or no less than it was before the stock began selling ex-rights. Since our stock had a market value of $50 with rights attached, it must have a value of

$$\$50 - \$2 = \$48$$

when the rights are sold separately. This result may be checked by using the second valuation formula.

$$R = \frac{\$48 - \$40}{4} = \frac{\$8}{4} = \$2$$

The theoretical value is the lowest value that a right should have. Because the stock price might rise before the rights must be exercised, there is the possibility that the rights could increase in value. For this reason they usually sell at a premium above the theoretical value. Rights typically have such a short life that there is not time for large price movements. Because of this their premiums are low. Warrants have much greater possibilities for price rises.

Valuing warrants

The main difference between warrants and rights, from the viewpoint of the investor, is the time each remains outstanding. Rights are designed to raise new capital quickly. When issued, their subscription price is always *below* the current market price of the common stock. Rights usually expire within a month after their issuance to insure that the company obtains this new capital by a certain date. Warrants are often issued along with bonds or preferred stock to enable the company to sell these senior securities at a lower interest or dividend cost. Warrants are also issued in mergers and to underwriters in an effort to provide equity participation in the company. The initial subscription price (also called exercise price) is usually 10 to 20 percent *above* the current stock price.

The theoretical value of a warrant is determined by a formula similar to the second one presented before.

$$\text{Theoretical warrant value} = (\text{Market price} - \text{Exercise price})$$
$$\times \text{Number of shares purchased}$$
$$\text{per warrant}$$

Warrants are almost always sold separately from the common stock, and they usually allow the holder to buy one share of common for each warrant. But there are exceptions: Penn–Dixie warrants, for example, allow holders to purchase 1.12 shares of common for each warrant.

Table 11–1 presents warrant and common stock price data for several firms having regularly traded warrants. The Modern Merchandis-

TABLE 11–1
Warrant exercise prices, market prices, and premiums for selected companies (prices as of March 6, 1979)

Company	Warrant exercise price	Common stock price	Theo-retical warrant price	Actual warrant price	Percent premium
Alleghany Corp.	1 common @ $3.75	21¾	18	17¾	−.013
American Airlines	1 common @ $14	11¾	0	4¾	∞
First Pennsylvania Corp.	1 common @ $20	13½	0	2⅛	∞
Frontier Airlines	1 common @ $11.71	11¾	0	4⅞	∞
Modern Merchandising	1 common @ $4.20	12¼	8.05	8⅝	7.14
Zondervan Corp.	1 common @ $9.25	18¾	9.50	9½	0

Source: Standard & Poor's *Stock Reports* and *The Wall Street Journal*, March 7, 1979.

ing warrant allows holders to buy one share of common for one warrant and $4.20. The common stock of this company closed at $12¼ and the warrant was priced at $8⅝ on March 6, 1979. Using the previous formula one can calculate that the theoretical value of the warrant was $8.05.

$$(\$12.25 - \$4.20) \times 1 = \$8.05$$

The difference between the actual price and the theoretical price is known as the *premium*. It may be calculated as a dollar value (57½ cents in this example), but it is usually stated as a percent of theoretical value. In this case the premium is just over 7 percent.

$$\text{Percent premium} = \text{Dollar premium/Theoretical value}$$
$$= \$0.575/\$8.05$$
$$= .0714 \text{ or } 7.1\%$$

As Table 11–1 indicates, warrant premiums vary greatly. The highest premiums, when they are calculated in percents of theoretical value, are on warrants whose theoretical value is zero or near to zero.

Speculative characteristics of rights and warrants

To account more fully for the warrant premiums it is necessary to look to the speculative value they offer investors. The following example pertains equally well to rights, but as rights do not remain outstanding very long, there is less chance for the market price of the stock to move upward. With less chance of a market price rise, the rights have less speculative value.

Assume a situation where a company has common stock selling for $20 a share and warrants entitling owners to buy one share of common at $18. The warrant has a theoretical value of $2. Now assume that the common doubles in price, to $40 per share—a 100 percent increase. The warrant should be worth $22.

$$\$40 - \$18 = \$22$$

The percentage increase of the warrant is

$$\$20/\$2 = 10 \text{ or } 1,000\%.$$

This sort of potential leverage has great attraction for investors and speculators. To obtain it they bid up prices of warrants on stocks selling near to the warrant exercise value. Leverage potential is reduced as

FIGURE 11-1
Theoretical value and market value relationships of a typical warrant

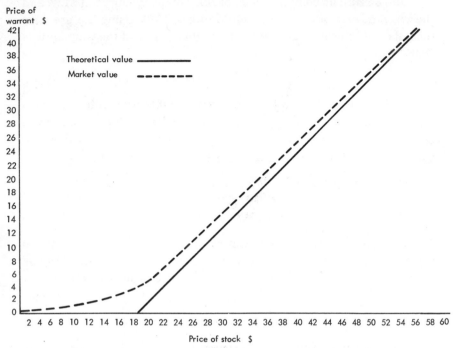

the stock price exceeds the warrant exercise price. If the price of the above stock were $60, the warrant would have a theoretical value of $42. A rise in the stock price to $80 (a 33 percent rise) would cause a rise in the theoretical value of the warrant to $62 (a 48 percent rise). Leverage from holding the warrant still exists, but it is greatly reduced.

Figure 11–1 presents a graphic representation of theoretical and market (actual) values of this warrant. When the stock price is far above the warrant exercise price the premium diminishes greatly, going to zero (see Zondervan Corporation, Table 11–1) or even becoming slightly negative (Alleghany Corporation).[1]

Warrants continue to have value even when stock prices are below warrant exercise prices. This value is due entirely to the possibility of

---

[1] A negative premium indicates that a profit could be obtained by purchasing the warrant and immediately trading it for the stock. However, trading commissions would not allow this to be done profitably in the case of Alleghany. Market forces act to keep warrant and stock prices closely aligned.

great gains if the stock price rises to or exceeds the exercise price. The American Airlines common (Table 11-1) must rise by $2.25 ($11.75 to $14) before the warrants begin to have any theoretical value. But they were priced at $4.75 because of their speculative value. The same situation prevailed for First Pennsylvania and Frontier Airlines. Figure 11-1 shows this relationship clearly: The warrant always has some value even though the stock price is far below the warrant exercise price.

Premiums also depend greatly upon the amount of time remaining before the warrant expires. In general, the longer the period, the higher the premium because there is more time during which stock prices might rise. Some warrants have exercise prices which rise as time passes. This feature usually acts to diminish premiums because potential profitability is reduced each time that the exercise price is increased. Most, but not all, warrants are protected against dilution caused by stock splits and dividends. Investors should check to make certain that any warrants purchased are so protected. Warrants themselves may cause dilution of earnings if the amount of cash received by the company for each exercised warrant cannot generate earnings high enough to maintain current earnings per share levels. Lowered EPS is a common result when large numbers of warrants are exercised.

Warrants may be used as part of an investor's total investment program. However, these securities are usually classified as speculative because of their potential for large price fluctuations. Furthermore, the warrant holder receives no dividends, nor can the warrants be voted since they do not constitute ownership in the company. A warrant is a certificate closely resembling a common stock share. Between 30 and 40 different warrants are traded on the American and New York Stock Exchanges; many more are traded OTC. Rights are listed on exchanges and also traded OTC. Information about warrants and rights can be obtained from either the company issuing them or Moody's, Standard & Poor's, or other firms providing financial information services.

Puts and calls

A *put* is a contract that allows its owner to sell a specified number of securities, to a specified buyer, at a specified price, within a specified time period. A *call* allows its holder to purchase securities under the above conditions. Both contracts are called *options*.

Prior to the opening of the Chicago Board Options Exchange (CBOE) in April 1973, all options were bought and sold in the OTC securities markets. These contracts were privately negotiated between brokers acting for the buyer and seller or between individuals. Since the contracts had no standard expiration date or exercise price, they were difficult to transfer to a third party.

The CBOE was designed to overcome the problems associated with option trading, thereby making these contracts more widely used. The CBOE and the other listed options markets that have followed are all *auction markets*. Prices in these markets are set through supply and demand by having all buy and sell orders funneled through a single trading post. This is the same system used to trade other listed securities. Price and volume information is accurate and available to all on a continuous basis. Standardization of contracts was accomplished by setting requirements which forced option contracts to be for 100 shares of the underlying stock. All options are written so that they mature on specific dates, which are three months apart. The new uniformity in the listed option contracts made their conditions more easily understood and therefore more popular with investors. It was absolutely necessary for the creation of a large-scale options market.

Marketability and safety were often a problem in earlier option contracts because these were contracts drawn up between two persons. If either party to the contract failed to perform, the dispute ended in a legal suit. This was often an expensive and time consuming procedure. Cancellation of a contract was usually through direct negotiation with the writer, or by demanding performance of the terms of the contract.

Listed options are guaranteed by the Options Clearing Corporation (OCC), a company jointly owned by the CBOE and other members of the securities industry. All contracts are written so that the OCC is responsible for their performance. If a call contract is exercised, the OCC delivers the stock, which in turn is obtained from the writer of a call contract. All option positions may be closed out (canceled) by the purchase or sale of an offsetting contract. These innovations induced thousands of investors to take part in what is now known as the "hottest game in town." Until recently only call options were traded. A limited number of put options are now being written and listed. It is expected that in the future more put contracts will become available. OTC put and call options continue to be written, but at lowered volume.

FIGURE 11–2
Listed options quotations

Tuesday, January 2, 1979

Closing prices of all options. Sales unit usually is 100 shares. Security description includes exercise price. Stock close is New York or American exchange final price. p-Put option. o-Old shares.

Chicago Board

Option &	price	— Jan — Vol.	— Jan — Last	— Apr — Vol.	— Apr — Last	— Jul — Vol.	— Jul — Last	N.Y. Close
Alcoa	...45	1	2¾	18	4⅝	2	6	47
Alcoa	...50	22	⅜	43	1⅞	6	3½	47
Am Exp	30	25	¼	53	1⅜	a	a	28⅜
Am Exp	35	3	1-16	5	⅜	a	a	28⅜
Am Exp	40	2	1-16	a	a	b	b	28⅜
Am Tel	.60	74	1 3-16	30	2¼	36	3	60¾
Am Tel	.65	176	1-16	31	⅜	21	⅞	60¾
Atl R	.. 45	1	12	a	a	b	b	56⅜
Atl R	...50	5	6¾	5	7⅝	20	9	56⅜
Atl R	...60	40	⅜	92	2¼	32	3⅜	56⅜
Avon	45	8	6	b	b	b	b	51
Avon p	... 45	50	1-16	b	b	b	b	51
Avon	... 50	329	2⅛	140	3¾	38	5⅛	51
Avon p	.. 50	597	¾	399	2¼	127	3¼	51
Avon	... 60	20	1-16	217	⅞	13	1⅝	51
Avon p	.. 60	215	9¼	106	9	2	10⅜	51
BankAm	25	18	1	67	2⅛	3	3	25⅝
BankAm	30	a	a	a	a	4	⅞	25⅝
Beth S	. 20	267	¾	53	1¾	49	2¼	19⅞
Beth S	. 25	35	1-16	10	⅜	30	13-16	19⅞
Bruns	...10	118	3	1	3	b	b	13⅛
Bruns	...15	397	1-16	186	¾	b	b	13⅛
Bruns	...20	13	1-16	a	a	b	b	13⅛
Burl N	. 35	5	1⅛	19	3¾	6	4⅝	36½
Burl N	. 40	26	⅛	1	1	8	2 7-16	36½
Burl N	. 45	5	1-16	6	½	3	⅞	36½
Burrgh	..70	1	4	a	a	a	a	73⅜
Burrgh	. 80	16	¼	21	3	a	a	73⅜
Citicp	...20	2	3⅛	8	4	b	b	23⅜
Citicp	.. 25	140	3-16	145	1 3-16	44	1 15-16	23⅜
Citicp	.. 30	5	1-16	14	¼	40	⅝	23⅜
Delta	.. 40	29	2⅝	10	4⅝	a	a	42
Delta	.. 45	5	⅜	43	2⅜	a	a	42
Delta	.. 50	a	a	60	13-16	10	1¾	42
Delta	... 60	4	1-16	a	a	b	b	42
Dig Eq	40	130	13½	100	14¼	b	b	53½
Dig Eq	. 45	13	8⅝	a	a	a	a	53½
Dig Eq	50	108	3¾	17	6⅝	2	7	53½
Disney	..35	3	5	2	6	a	a	40¼
Disney	..40	59	1	a	a	a	a	40¼
Disney	..45	40	⅛	2	1⅛	a	a	40¼
Dow Ch	.20	a	a	10	5½	b	b	25¼
Dow Ch	25	251	⅞	131	2 1-16	b	b	25¼
Dow Ch	30	22	1-16	223	7-16	b	b	25¼
du Pnt	.110	71	17¼	a	a	b	b	127
du Pnt	120	481	8¼	278	12½	17	15¼	127
du Pnt	130	248	2⅛	117	6⅞	7	10¼	127
du Pnt	.140	82	3-16	12	2⅝	a	a	127
Eas Kd	45	178	14¾	b	b	b	b	61½
Eas Kd	.50	383	11½	70	13	9	13	61½
Eas Kd p	50	212	1-16	379	⅝	49	1 5-16	61½
Eas Kd	.60	1922	2 9-16	1000	5½	222	7⅜	61½
Eas Kd p	60	1620	1⅛	422	3⅛	17	4⅜	61½
Eas Kd	.70	263	1-16	868	1 9-16	140	3¼	61½
Eas Kd p	.70	56	8¾	44	9¾	a	a	61½

a–Not traded. b–No option offered.

Source: Reprinted by permission *The Wall Street Journal.*

How put and call options are listed and sold

Learning all the important investment characteristics of rights and warrants requires interested persons to consult various sources of information: Moody's, Standard & Poor's, company prospectuses, and other publications for investors. Because listed option contracts are uniform, complete information about each option can be printed in the financial press as shown in Figure 11–2. The first column identifies the firm whose common stock is optioned. The second column lists the price at which the security may be put or called. Note that for all companies listed there are several of these *striking prices,* as they are called. The headings of "—Jan—, —Apr—, and —Jul—" designate the months in which the options expire. Options in these securities are also written to expire in October. But October options will not be written until after the January options have expired. For this reason, they were not listed in Figure 11–2.

Options on the stocks expire during different months. But all exchange-traded options are presently written with quarterly expiration dates. Options are written to expire either in January, April, July, or October; February, May, August, or November; or in a March, June, September or December cycle. Expiration takes place at 5:00 PM Eastern time on the Saturday following the third Friday of each expiration month. Trading in the option is stopped at 3:00 PM Eastern time on the business day preceding the expiration date. Time between the two dates is used to process the last minute transactions.

Returning to Figure 11–2, "Vol." indicates the number, in hundreds, of option contracts traded. "Last" refers to the price per share at which an option was sold. The final column lists the closing price of the common stock of the company against which the call options were written. Deciphering the first line of price information from Figure 11–2 tells us this: Alcoa call contracts maturing in January, April, and July were purchased in various amounts on January 2, 1979. Investors were willing to pay $2¾ per share, or $275, for a 100-share January call option. They paid $4⅝ per share for the April 100-share call and $6 per share for the July call. Since far fewer OTC options are traded, information on these securities is much harder to obtain. The financial press carries an occasional advertisement of offers to sell OTC options, but the best source of information is the brokers who write the contracts.

Investing in put and call options

Warrants and rights have investor appeal largely because of the financial leverage that they offer. Options provide exactly the same advantages and disadvantages. The owner of an average call option will make a larger rate of return on an option than on an equal dollar investment in the stock, if the stock price rises by enough to compensate for brokerage charges and the premium associated with the call option.

As an example of leverage, suppose the stock of a company sells at $25 per share. A nine-month call option on this stock is available for a premium of 14 percent of the option exercise price, which is also $25 per share. The option is for 100 shares so the total premium is

$$100 \text{ shares} \times \$25 \text{ per share} \times .14 = \$350.$$

Had the stock been purchased, the amount invested would have been $2,500 for the stock itself plus about $60 in brokerage commissions, a charge which is again made when the stock is sold. Assume now that the stock rises to $30 per share during the life of the option. When this happens the option will be worth at least $500. A profit will have been realized by owning either the stock or the call option, but the profit on the option is much greater when calculated as a percent of the dollar amount invested.

	Call	Stock
Amount invested	$350	$2,560
Amount realized	500	2,940
Gross profit	$150	$ 380
Percent return	$\frac{\$150}{\$350} = 43$ percent	$\frac{\$ 380}{\$2,560} = 15$ percent

The above illustration clearly identifies the leverage inherent in all options. It is this potential for large gain on a limited investment which provides the speculative appeal. However, had the stock not risen the option would have expired valueless—a loss of $350. In this event the purchase of shares might have been wiser because they would still be owned.

Put options provide the same leverage as call options, but the price of the underlying stock must *decline* to cause a profit from purchasing a put. Returning to the above illustration, let us assume that the investor had purchased a put at $25, rather than a call. Assuming the same premium, the price would have had to decline to $21.50 per share to allow the put owner to break even. At this price the put contract should be worth about the same amount as it cost. Lower prices would generate profits.

Strategies for options

The speculative opportunities offered by options are well understood by most investors, but options are also useful for other more conservative purposes. Imagine that someone has a large paper profit in a stock and that the investor does not wish to sell the stock at this time, even though it is feared that a price decline is coming. Purchase of a put contract on the same stock will "lock in" the stock profit, because if the stock price declines the put will increase in value. The put contract can be sold for enough to cover any loss that the stock might have. If instead the stock price rises, the put contract becomes worthless. The cost of the contract is simply "insurance" against a loss of value in the stock. This type of trade is known as *hedging*.

Protection of paper profits could have been accomplished, partially at least, by writing a call option against the stock. Such a contract can be written by anyone, given that they either own the underlying stock or can establish a margin account with a broker. The writer of an option receives a premium of several dollars per share when the contract is sold. In fact, the majority of the amount paid by the option purchaser goes to the option writer; only small amounts go for brokerage commissions. In the above example, the premium received from writing a call contract would offset a reduction in the stock price. If the price of the stock rose, the call contract would become valuable to its owner. The writer would suffer a loss on the contract, but the loss would be offset by the gain in the price of the stock. The premium for writing the call contract may be seen as extra income in this situation.

More complete protection against price fluctuations could have been obtained by writing a put and a call contract at the same exercise price on the same stock. This is known as a *straddle*. The writer receives a premium for each contract. If the underlying stock decreases in price, the loss on the put contract is at least partially offset by the fact that the call becomes valueless. If the stock rises, the loss from the call is offset by the premium from the put contract, which will now be valueless. What the straddle option writer hopes for, of course, is that the stock's price fluctuates very little from the exercise price during the life of the contracts. If this occurs, the writer obtains both writing premiums and has no losses since neither the put nor the call ever became profitable to their owners.

An investor may purchase a straddle by buying a put and a call on the same security. When pursuing this strategy, the hope is that the underlying stock will rise or fall by more than the combined premiums involved in purchasing the options. Some numbers may make this investment more easily understood. Assume that put and call options are available on a single stock for a $4 premium per share for each contract. The exercise price for each option is $50 per share. If the stock's price rises above $58 or falls below $42, the "straddler" will have a profit because the loss on one contract will be more than offset by the gain on the other.

Most call options are written on stock that is owned by the writer. These are known as *covered options*. An option written on stock not owned by the writer is called a *naked option*. Naked or uncovered options are more speculative because if the contracts are exercised the writer must actually purchase securities to meet the option contract. When stock prices do what the uncovered option writer hopes they will, the profits are large. Very little money is invested, and the entire premium is retained because the contract becomes valueless. Options are identified as being either *out-of-the-money, in-the-money,* or *at-the-money.* These terms refer to the relationship of the exercise price and the stock's current market price. An option is at-the-money if the stock's market price is the same as the option's exercise price. It is in-the-money if the stock price exceeds the exercise price. Out-of-the-money describes the opposite situation.

There are literally hundreds of ways that options may be used by speculators and investors alike. This book has attempted to identify the most common of these. For more advanced discussions of options consult the list of readings at the end of the chapter.

Risk characteristics of rights, warrants, and other options

Rights, warrants, puts, and calls are speculative investments. Their market prices can be expected to fluctuate greatly, so these investments require constant attention. Option holders never receive dividends; therefore any profit on these investments must come entirely from changes in the price of the security that the option is written against. Marketability and liquidity depend upon the issue. Rights and warrants of large, well-known corporations may have excellent marketability and liquidity while similar securities of smaller or less well-known companies may score poorly so far as these characteristics are concerned. Options traded upon listed exchanges have good marketability and liquidity characteristics. Option contracts have no interest rate risk because their prices are not related to interest rates. Their ability to protect against inflation depends entirely upon whether they increase in value.

COMMODITIES

Each year thousands of individuals undertake a type of activity known as *trading commodity futures.* This term refers to the buying and selling of mainly foodstuffs, metals, and financial futures. Beginning with apples and ending with zinc, the list includes frozen pork bellies and foreign exchange, mercury and molasses, platinum and plywood, oats and orange juice, and soybeans and Swiss francs—less than 100 types in total. This compares with many thousands of common stocks. Several criteria must be met by any commodity if it is to be traded. First of all, there has to be a substantial supply and demand. Second, the item must be definable in terms of quality and grade. A third criterion, and perhaps the most important qualification for trading interest, is a history of fluctuating prices. This acts as the encouragement for participants.

How to trade commodities

Most assets are delivered when they are purchased or soon after. For example, you can walk onto a used-car lot, buy a car, and drive it away. Commodities can be handled similarly. This is known as a *cash* or *spot* transaction. Commodities can also be bought and sold for delivery at a later time. This is known as a *futures contract*. It involves the purchase or sale of a certain number of units of a commodity at a price agreed upon when the contract is made. Contracts are written for a specific minimum number of units of whatever commodity is traded—5,000 bushels of wheat, 22,500 dozen eggs, 40,000 board feet of lumber, 100 troy ounces of gold, 100,000 Canadian dollars, and so on. Actual delivery or acceptance of the commodity will take place at a future time and place, both of which are identified when the contract is created.

Futures contracts are traded on ten major exchanges in the United States and on several international exchanges. The Chicago Board of Trade (grain contracts mainly) and the Chicago Mercantile Exchange (predominately cattle, hogs, and other foodstuffs) are the largest exchanges in the United States. Figure 11–3 is a partial listing of the various futures contracts that are actively traded, their prices, where they are traded, the number of units in a contract, and the open interest. The term *open interest* refers to the number of contracts of a certain type that are outstanding at a given time.

Commodity exchanges perform the same important clearing of contracts function as is performed by the Option Clearing Corporation. There is no direct relationship between buyers and sellers. All futures contracts are written in such a manner that the exchange is responsible for their performance. To the casual observer commodity future contracts may appear to be option contracts. They are not. An option is a contract that gives the holder the *right* to buy or sell the underlying

FIGURE 11–3
Commodity price quotations

Futures Prices

Tuesday, January 2, 1979

Open Interest Reflects Previous Trading Day.

Columns: Open | High | Low | Settle | Change | Lifetime High | Low | Open Interest

```
                                    Lifetime       Open
      Open  High  Low  Settle Change High  Low   Interest
Mar  55.80 57.25 55.80 57.25 + 2.00  72.65 49.70  2,399
May  57.25 58.27 56.90 58.27 + 2.00  72.50 50.30  2,111
July 57.15 58.85 57.15 58.85 + 1.95  72.25 50.55  1,189
Aug  57.35 57.67 56.35 57.65 + 1.97  68.90 48.40    190
Est vol 3,891; vol Fri 2,253; open int 13,087, +3.
```

—FOOD AND FIBER—

```
EGGS (CME)—22,500 doz.; cents per doz.
Jan79 56.40 58.00 56.15 57.15 + 1.05 61.85 54.60  257
Feb   54.10 55.10 54.10 54.45 + .75  57.20 51.40  281
Mar   54.00 54.60 54.00 54.20 + .30  55.50 53.00   78
Apr   50.00 50.25 49.90 49.90 + .65  52.85 49.00   80
May   49.70 49.80 49.40 49.80 + .80  52.60 48.70   69
Sept  56.90 56.90 56.90 56.90 + .50  58.65 56.90   15
Est vol 184; vol Fri 118; open int 780, −78.

COCOA (CEX)—30,000 lbs.; cents per lb.
Mr79 174.75 175.50 173.10 173.35 − 3.40 189.25 111.50  2,421
May  174.75 175.75 173.75 174.05 − 3.25 188.70 110.50  2,209
July 174.80 175.00 174.50 174.10 − 3.00 187.25 118.30  1,532
Sept 175.25 175.50 174.20 174.10 − 3.00 183.00 116.60    931
Dec  173.50 173.50 173.00 172.85 − 2.65 179.50 121.50    891
Mr80  ...    ...   171.85 − 2.40 167.85 165.00     80
Est vol 638; vol Fri 1,096; open int 8,064, −67.

COFFEE (CSE)—37,500 lbs.; cents per lb.
Mr79 135.00 135.00 133.25 134.97 + 2.09 167.50 93.75  2,956
May  131.00 132.30 130.00 132.12 + 1.64 163.50 94.00  1,477
July 129.25 130.75 129.25 130.45 + 1.12 163.13 92.00  1,105
Sept 129.40 130.45 129.25 130.20 + 1.90 158.75 90.00    704
Dec  128.50 130.00 128.25 129.90 + .90  137.00 92.50    259
Mr80 128.50 129.50 129.00 129.17 + .67  129.50 111.50    55
May  128.00 129.75 128.00 129.17 + 1.38 129.75 122.00    25
Est vol 770; vol Fri 578; open int +100.

COTTON (CTN)—50,000 lbs.; cents per lb.
Mar   67.50 67.50 67.20 67.38 − .19 73.80 54.90  18,455
May   69.60 69.60 69.25 69.44 − .22 75.70 58.35   7,207
July  71.10 71.10 70.85 70.95 − .31 75.85 61.75   4,491
Oct   66.50 66.50 66.40 66.50 − .25 69.15 64.00   1,537
Dec   64.45 64.50 64.35 64.38 − .22 67.85 64.20   5,477
Mar 80  ...   ...  65.20 − .20 68.70 65.40    107
May    ...  65.90 − .30 67.30 66.00      9
Est vol 2,450; vol Fri 1,842; open int 37,284, +40.

ORANGE JUICE (CTN)—15,000 lbs.; cents per lb.
Jan  117.00 119.00 116.55 117.50 + 2.45 131.10 81.00  2,500
Mar  121.20 122.00 119.60 120.85 + 2.60 129.50 80.15  2,974
May  125.00 125.00 121.90 122.55 + 1.75 129.00 80.15  1,287
July 127.00 127.20 124.00 124.50 + 2.30 128.80 80.00    665
Sept 127.50 127.80 124.25 125.25 + 2.25 128.50 95.00    659
Nov  121.50 121.50 118.75 119.00 + 2.50 123.00 113.50   357
Jn80 113.00 114.00 112.00 113.00 + 2.50 115.00 89.50    444
Mar  111.75 112.60 111.75 113.00 + 2.50 112.60 93.50    287
Est vol 2,000; vol Fri 864; open int 9,073, −214.

POTATOES (NYM)—50,000 lbs.; cents per lb.
Mar 79 5.57 5.63 5.55 5.63 + .08 6.77 4.86  2,066
Apr    5.88 5.88 5.83 5.88 + .03 7.19 5.14    315
May    6.73 6.88 6.72 6.87 + .18 8.59 5.62  9,192
Nov     ...  5.65 + .01 5.57 5.35     36
Mar     ...  6.40  ...  6.30 6.30      2
May    7.99 7.99 7.99 7.99 + .04 8.10 7.50      6
Est vol 1,406; vol Fri 870; open int 11,617, −100.

SUGAR—WORLD (CSE)—112,000 lbs.; cents per lb.
Mar  8.39 8.40 8.33 8.38 − .05 11.03 6.55  14,272
May  8.55 8.60 8.54 8.59 − .04 11.23 6.70   6,968
July 8.79 8.82 8.77 8.83  ...  10.90 6.87   3,960
Sept 9.01 9.07 8.98 9.07 + .01 10.30 7.05   2,376
Oct  9.11 9.17 9.10 9.16 − .02 10.38 7.15   2,992
Jan 80  ... 9.60 − .02 9.90 9.83      3
Mar  9.79 9.80 9.76 9.80 − .06 10.95 9.75    827
May   ... 10.00 − .06 9.96 9.96    100
Est vol 1,575; vol Fri 1,597; open int 31,498, +46.
```

```
                                       Lifetime      Open
      Open  High  Low  Settle Change   High  Low   Interest
SILVER (CMX)—5,000 troy oz.; cents per troy oz.
Jan79 607.00 607.90 600.50 600.00 − 6.00 644.40 487.50   4,314
Feb    ...   602.60 − 7.20 604.50 594.00     17
Mar  615.00 615.30 606.00 606.50 − 7.20 653.00 491.60  36,915
May  622.80 623.00 614.00 614.30 − 7.30 661.60 497.70  31,663
July 631.00 632.00 622.50 622.80 − 6.90 670.50 501.50  30,558
Sept 639.40 640.00 630.20 631.30 − 6.80 679.60 523.70  41,900
Dec  653.50 653.50 644.00 644.80 − 6.90 694.00 558.50  39,419
Jan80 656.50 656.50 650.00 649.50 − 6.50 698.80 569.00  39,118
Mar  667.00 667.00 658.20 659.00 − 6.50 708.50 582.00  41,124
May  676.30 676.30 669.70 668.60 − 6.40 718.30 610.50   2,379
July 682.00 683.50 681.80 678.20 − 6.40 728.20 642.40  15,196
Sept 691.50 691.50 691.50 687.90 − 6.40 738.20 666.80   9,144
Est vol 22,000; vol Fri 16,729; open int 309,797 −2,026.

SILVER (CBT)—5,000 troy oz.; cents per troy oz.
Jan79 600.00 600.00 597.00 595.30 − 10.40 624.00 578.00      1
Feb  601.30 611.90 600.00 601.30 − 8.90 648.50 475.50  23,322
Apr  619.50 619.50 608.50 610.30 − 8.30 658.00 493.50  47,740
June 627.00 627.50 618.00 619.40 − 7.70 667.70 499.00  39,057
Aug  636.50 636.50 628.00 628.50 − 7.10 676.30 504.50  39,564
Oct  644.00 644.00 637.50 637.70 − 6.40 686.50 527.00  22,944
Dec  653.50 653.50 644.00 647.00 − 5.80 695.00 534.00  15,974
Fb80 662.50 662.50 653.00 656.40 − 5.30 705.50 541.00  13,477
Apr  671.50 671.50 663.00 666.00 − 4.80 714.80 573.50  15,431
June 680.50 680.50 673.00 675.80 − 4.30 724.30 588.00  13,357
Aug  690.00 690.00 683.00 685.80 − 3.80 735.70 600.00  12,015
Oct  695.00 695.00 690.00 696.00 − 3.30 746.50 637.00   9,892
Dec  705.00 705.50 700.00 706.40 − 2.80 757.50 656.00   7,258
Fb81 719.50 719.50 711.00 717.00 − 2.30 768.50 670.20   5,059
Apr  725.60 726.50 725.60 727.80 − 1.80 779.50 698.00   2,561
June 736.30 737.50 736.00 738.80 − 1.30 746.00 713.00   1,117
Aug   ...   750.00 − .80 755.00 744.00      2
Est vol 31,138; vol Fri 11,352; open int 268,771 +2,993.
```

—WOOD—

```
LUMBER (CME)—100,000 bd. ft.; $ per 1000 bd. ft.
Jan79 234.50 235.00 233.10 234.80 − .50 235.70 177.20  1,953
Mar  222.70 222.70 220.80 222.50 − 1.10 223.90 180.10  2,897
May  209.50 209.50 207.30 208.60 − 1.30 211.00 181.60  1,298
July 200.50 200.50 199.00 200.50 − 1.10 208.50 182.00  1,133
Sept 194.60 195.00 194.10 194.50 − .50 205.50 179.20    456
Nov  188.50 188.50 188.00 188.00 − .60 189.00 179.30    385
Est vol 1,643; vol Fri 3,504; open int 8,122 +146.

PLYWOOD (CBT)—76,032 sq. ft.; $ per 1000 sq. ft.
Jan79 215.80 218.90 214.80 218.90 + 1.40 219.50 191.00    963
Mar  214.00 215.50 212.50 213.50 + .60 216.90 192.50  11,388
May  209.50 210.80 208.30 210.50 + 1.00 213.30 192.50    963
July 206.00 207.60 205.80 207.50 − .30 213.00 192.50    698
Sept 203.00 204.00 202.50 204.00 + 1.00 215.70 193.00    315
Nov  201.00 201.00 200.50 200.50  ...  212.00 192.30    152
Jan80 201.50 201.50 201.50 201.50 + 1.00 201.50 199.00      5
Est vol 651; vol Fri 857; open int 4,484 −79.
```

—FINANCIAL—

```
BRITISH POUND (IMM)—25,000 pounds; $ per pound
Mar  2.0440 2.0445 2.0270 2.0310 − .0100 2.0985 1.7530  1,839
June 2.0425 2.0425 2.0255 2.0270 − .0095 2.0880 1.7500    300
Sept  ...   2.0200 − .0095 2.1800 1.8800    257
Est vol 555; vol Fri 302; open int 2,396 −25.

CANADIAN DOLLAR (IMM)—100,000 dlrs.; $ per Can$
Mar  .8430 .8445 .8407 .8409 − .0028 .9030 .8354  2,672
June .8480 .8488 .8450 .8452 − .0031 .8765 .8390  1,216
Sept .8501 .8505 .8480 .8480 − .0030 .8775 .8500    744
Est vol 1,116; vol Fri 294; open int 4,632, −19.

JAPANESE YEN (IMM)—12.5 million yen; cents per yen
Mar  .5286 .5306 .5260 .5272 − .0002 .5850 .4485  2,240
June .5430 .5432 .5393 .5408 − .0002 .5971 .6185    521
Sept .5543 .5543 .5500 .5514 − .0001 .6060 .5295    143
Dec   ...  .5645  ...  .6180 .5705      1
Est vol 627; vol Fri 487; open int 2,905, −165.

SWISS FRANC (IMM)—125,000 francs; $ per franc
Mar  .6380 .6386 .6309 .6311 − .0036 .7113 .4625  2,645
June .6586 .6594 .6526 .6528 − .0027 .7286 .5345  1,273
Sept .6740 .6752 .6698 .6730 − .0012 .7460 .4910    656
Dec  .6920 .6930 .6888 .6888 − .0014 .7610 .6370    339
Est vol 858; vol Fri 931; open int 4,913, +103.
```

(CBT) Chicago Board of Trade; (KC) Kansas City Board of Trade; (MPLS) Minneapolis Grain Exchange; (WPG) Winnipeg Commodity Exchange; (CME) Chicago Mercantile Exchange; (NYM) New York Mercantile Exchange; (CSE) New York Coffee and Sugar Exchange; (CEX) New York Cocoa Exchange; (CTN) New York Cotton Exchange; (CMX) Commodity Exchange Inc. in New York; (IMM) International Monetary Market of CME.

Source: Reprinted by permission The Wall Street Journal.

stock. Futures contracts constitute *actual* sale or purchase of the commodity. Contract terms are met by either buying or selling the commodity under the original terms of the contract. However, this does not mean that all contracts result in final delivery. Few—about 2 to 3 percent of the total written—are ever exercised. Positions are instead closed out by either buying back or selling the same number of units of the commodity. Commodity trading is not nearly so well understood as trading in securities, and much of the trading is done by professional traders employed by companies which use commodities in their businesses. Nevertheless, all of the larger brokerage houses have commodities departments and will accept commodity trading accounts. Several other firms handle commodities contracts exclusively. In contrast to the normal brokerage account, practically all commodity trading accounts are margin accounts.

A typical futures transaction is illustrated by the following example: Suppose in September someone is interested in eggs. Production and consumption patterns have been studied. The price of eggs for delivery six months hence, for example March, is 50 cents a dozen.[2] Now suppose the prospective egg trader feels that eggs should sell for less in March. The next step would be to *sell* a futures contract. This would mean the trader is obliged to deliver eggs in six months for the price prevailing when this contract was sold, which was 50 cents a dozen. If the investor were correct, the March futures contracts that are written at a later time would be for less than 50 cents a dozen. Suppose in December this quote were 45 cents a dozen, which the investor believes is as low as eggs will drop. The trader would back this judgment with the *purchase* of a March egg futures contract in December. This would result in a profit before commissions and taxes of 50 − 45, or 5 cents a dozen.

Notice what has happened. The commodity was bought at 45 cents a dozen and sold at 50 cents a dozen, only the sequence was reversed. Gains are made by buying low and selling high but not necessarily in that order. In this case the sale preceded the purchase but the profits were the same as if the opposite timing had occurred. Short selling, discussed later, employs the same reversed sequence of transactions.

For many years futures contracts were mostly written on agricultural commodities and some metals. Recently several commodity exchanges have begun to trade what they call *financial futures* contracts. Such contracts include U.S. Treasury bills, most international currencies, Government National Mortgage Association pass-through securities, and even the Dow Jones Average. These contracts are somewhat more difficult to understand than those on standard commodities, but they provide market participants with the same opportunities for gain and loss. End of chapter references are presented for interested readers.

---

[2] This is the March futures price. It may be higher, lower, or the same as the quote in the cash market.

Reasons for trading commodities

Much commodity trading is done by producers, manufacturers, and merchandisers who may engage in hedging. Here the objective is to minimize risk. The egg illustration resulted in a profit, but an opposite price movement would have caused a loss. Hedging is designed to prevent either from occurring. For example, a grain elevator operator buys wheat when it is harvested in June. This grain will be sold later during the year, but at unknown prices. To prevent losses on the wheat which has been purchased, the operator might sell futures contracts and actually deliver the grain from storage when the contract so stipulates. There are many other methods and degrees of hedging, but the general purpose is the same. The objective is to know in advance what the purchase or sale price of a commodity will be in the future and to thereby minimize potential losses due to unforeseen market declines. The existence of futures markets has without any question made a positive contribution toward the efficient distribution of commodities into channels of use.

The "trading in tomorrows" appeals to people for various reasons. The basic attraction is the allure of quick and substantial profits. This in turn is made possible by two circumstances. The first is that price swings are often rapid. A freeze, strike, or East-West crisis can upset supply and demand and send prices plummeting or skyrocketing. Crop failures are almost regular even though unpredictable. The second circumstance is the fact that the price movements, even if small, can be greatly magnified by *leverage*. This involves using one's own funds *plus* credit to enlarge commitments in much the same manner as a house or car is bought with a small down payment. This amplification of resources is accomplished by *margin* trading. For common stocks in early 1979, the margin requirement (the proportion of the total cost that must be paid in cash) was 50 percent. For commodities it has ranged between 5 and 15 percent, depending on the particular type. With a 10 percent margin, the commodities trader will realize a gross return of 50 percent if the futures profits are 5 percent.[3] The multiplication results in fast action which entices many persons. The leverage

---

[3] If a contract was bought for $10,000 with a 10 percent margin, the investment would be $1,000 and the remaining $9,000 would be borrowed. A 5 percent price rise would result if this contract could be sold for $10,500. The gross return to the individual would be $10,500−$9,000, or $1,500, which is $500 more than the original investment. The relative gross profit would be $500/$1,000, or 50 percent. Commission and other fees would lower this figure somewhat.

also means total losses of funds can occur with equal rapidity if prices move the wrong way.

Investing in gold and silver

Gold and silver—like wheat, copper, and eggs—are commodities. But they differ from other commodities because they are also a form of money. And this is a great difference indeed!

For nearly 40 years prior to 1975, U.S. citizens were prohibited from owning gold—except as coins, jewelry, or other artifacts. Prices of gold were strictly regulated by international agreement, and gold was priced at $35 per ounce. For many years most international currencies were valued in terms of the U.S. dollar because this currency was felt to be "solid" and because the United States had suffered relatively little inflation. Rapid price inflation and continuing deficits in our balance of international payments during the late 1960s and early 1970s caused the U.S. dollar to be devalued twice in terms of other currencies. The first devaluation occurred in 1971; the second in 1973. These devaluations were accompanied by changing the official price of gold from $35 to $38, and then to $42.22 per ounce.

Because of the rapid worldwide inflation of the 1960s and 1970s and for other reasons, many persons, including U.S. citizens, strongly desired to own gold. Gold is very valuable relative to its size and weight. It can easily be stored and transported. It can always be used to purchase necessities in times of economic chaos, and in inflationary times it has maintained or increased its purchasing power. Residents of wartorn or politically unstable nations have always held gold, silver, diamonds, or other precious objects for these reasons. Americans and Europeans were attracted to gold mainly because it provided a way of storing value with no loss of purchasing power.

By the 1960s the demand for gold was so great that it sold everywhere but in "official" markets for much more than its government mandated price. In March 1968 a free market in gold was created in which prices were set by supply and demand. There has always been a free market in silver. For many years the U.S. Treasury issued a silver dollar. When the silver content of these coins became worth more than their $1 face value, the coins dropped out of circulation. The Treasury then issued a new "silver dollar," which was predominately copper and which was worth less than $1 as a commodity. The commodity value of all U.S. coins is very low. But other nations (Canada, Mexico,

FIGURE 11–4
Gold and silver prices

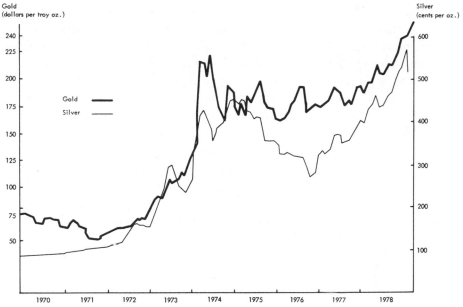

Source: *Commodity Yearbook*, New York: Commodity Research Bureau, Inc., various issues.

South Africa, Austria) have increased their issuance of commodity money as demand for gold and silver coins has grown.

Figure 11–4 presents the recent price history of gold and silver. They have both risen greatly in price, and yearly price fluctuations have often been large. The U.S. Treasury and the International Monetary Fund have been selling off portions of their inventories of precious metals. These sales have doubtlessly caused some of the price fluctuations. Inflation, political events, and varying yearly supplies have probably done more. The supply of newly mined gold has diminished from nearly 45 million ounces in 1972 to less than 39 million in recent years. The Republic of South Africa produces around 60 percent of the world total of newly mined gold; Russia is next in importance, supplying from 15 to 20 percent of the total. Russia's output has gradually increased while South Africa's has declined. Gold supplies from these countries could be stopped immediately or increased for a variety of political or economic reasons. About 70 percent of the supply of new silver is produced by Western Hemisphere nations. Little social or political risk is associated with these supplies, but production costs are increasing as lower grade ores are processed.

Persons may own gold or silver in several ways. These metals may be purchased in the form of bullion (bars, ingots, or plates), coins, jewelry, or artifacts. The typical bar or ingot of gold is too valuable for most investors. A 100-ounce bar would have a value of over $35,000 at the present time for example. Gold coins from several nations, mainly South Africa (the Krugerrand) and Austria (the Schilling), are often purchased by small-scale investors. The coins sell at a premium over their commodity value, but there is an active market in them.

Speculators generally prefer to trade silver and gold futures contracts, since they never have to take possession of the commodity and more leverage is available. Five-thousand-ounce silver contracts and 100-ounce gold contracts are widely traded as are contracts in bags of silver dollars. The main gold markets are in London and Zurich. Firms in these countries also offer both futures and option contracts.

Investors often prefer to buy common stock of companies that mine gold or silver. It is fairly easy to identify gold mining companies, but much silver is produced as a byproduct of other mining activities. Kennecott Copper, for example, produces silver, but income from this source is a very small part of total profits. Companies whose primary business is silver mining are usually small and relatively unknown. Investment in gold mining stocks is normally done by purchasing ADRs (American Depository Receipts) since most of these are foreign companies. Gold stock price indexes have risen and declined much in concert with gold prices. Prices of individual shares have, of course, been much more variable. Whether to buy gold directly or buy gold mining shares always requires consideration. Shares may provide dividends, some of which are quite high, and lower buy-and-sell commissions. But the larger mines are located in politically unstable areas, and the possibility of closure or nationalization cannot be overlooked. By owning gold directly one obtains possession of a high-value commodity that is easily transported and stored. But unless the gold is kept in a safe deposit box, it may be lost or stolen.

Many people buy gold and silver to protect against a devastating future price inflation. Gold is more likely to provide such protection because it is more of a monetary unit than silver. Silver most nearly resembles copper, lead, zinc and other metals which have value because of their industrial uses. This is not to say that the prices of these metals may not rise. They certainly have in recent times. But in periods of severe economic dislocation, production of goods and services may be at a very low level. Demand for all metals, including silver, may be low indeed.

Risk characteristics of commodities

Speaking in general terms, it is probably accurate to say that the average nonprofessional investor does not have the ability to successfully trade commodities. Many of the market participants are professional traders who can devote full time and energy to the study of commodities. They are in constant touch with the commodity markets and have the financial backing to recover from mistakes. They often receive important information before it reaches the general public, and they are usually located in a city or market center where they can act on this information immediately. Because they are usually dealing in large numbers of contracts, they are able to employ trading strategies which limit their risks. They may also pay smaller commissions and have lower-cost financing. For every writer of a profitable futures contract there is someone else who loses. This is usually the nonprofessional investor.

Market risk is especially great for all commodities. Financial commodities are greatly affected by interest rate changes. Social and political risks may be high for commodities produced in foreign lands. It is difficult to classify commodity futures contracts as anything but speculations, except perhaps when they are used in hedging.

SHORT SELLING

People can make money in the stock market when it is rising or falling. Both opportunities are shown in Figure 11–5. The conventional way of making a profit is by buying at point *A* and selling at point *B*. Short sellers simply reverse this pattern, selling at point *B* and buying later at point *C*. The transaction is simple, relatively inexpensive, and may be performed with round- or odd-lots, or with bonds.

Short sellers sell stock which they normally do not own. Persons wishing to do this instruct their brokers to sell short a certain number of shares of a particular stock. The shares are borrowed from those which the broker holds in margin accounts. A person who has a margin account agrees to this arrangement so the borrowing procedure is perfectly legal. When the sale is made, the amount of the transaction is

FIGURE 11–5
Short selling illustrated

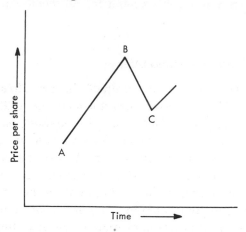

held by the broker along with a like amount of money from the short seller. Thus, if an investor sold short $10,000 of stock, the broker would credit this account with $10,000 from the sale of these securities plus $10,000 deposited by the short seller. In accordance with prevailing margin requirements, the short seller could borrow part of the $10,000 deposit.

The short position is *covered* by later buying the stock in the market. The broker uses the newly purchased shares to replenish the account from which they were borrowed. If the stock price had declined, the investor would make a profit. If the price had advanced, the result would be a loss.

Short sellers are likely to be somewhat nervous persons. A person who is *long* on a $20 stock can only lose $20 per share since the value of the stock cannot become less than zero. The person who *shorts* at $20 may buy back the stock at $40, $50, $80, or more. There is no upward limit on how high the price can go. Other disadvantages are that the short seller must pay any dividends declared to the person from whom the shorted shares were borrowed. Interest must also be paid on any money borrowed in a margin account.

SEC regulations forbid short sales at a price *below* the last preceding sale. The intent of this rule is to keep people from selling short a stock that is already moving downward, thereby increasing selling pressure and causing a further price decline. This was a common tactic of the "bear raiders" of the pre-SEC days. Several people would secretly agree to sell shares of a certain company short, forcing the price to extremely low levels. At a prearranged signal they would cover their short positions, making large profits on the transaction.

Most short sales are made by professionals, but there is certainly no reason why the individual investor who can accept the inherent risk should not use this type of investment. Securities may be shorted in anticipation of an economic recession. Specific stocks may appear to be "too high" and due for a price drop. Shorting is often used as part of an investment strategy using options. The rules often stated by professional investors, while quite general, are nevertheless relevant: (1) never short the stock of a strong company, (2) never short stock in a rising market.

Short selling against the box

The "box" in this phrase refers to a safe deposit box which holds the same shares that were sold short. In other words, in this transaction investors sell short shares of stock that they own. By doing this they are able to protect a profit that they already have in a stock. If the market price declines, the profit on the short sale offsets the loss on the long position. If prices rise, the gain from being long is offset by the loss on the short contract. The purpose of this transaction is usually to carry forward into the next tax year a gain on a security transaction.

Risk characteristics of short selling

This type of investment is probably more speculative than warrants but less speculative than puts and calls or futures contracts. Because of the potential for high losses, these investments require constant attention. Interest rate risk and purchasing power risk have little meaning for short selling.

NEW ISSUES

Corporations have an almost continuous need for external financial assistance. Some funds are provided by bank loans. Other monies are acquired by selling securities. Bonds and stocks offered for the first time are known as *new issues*. From Chapter 3 it will be recalled that these original offerings make up the *primary market*. Once these securities are outstanding they are traded in *secondary* or *after markets*. This section focuses on new issues of common stock offered to the public for the first time.

Most of these "going public" offerings are made by relatively unknown or even newly formed companies. Shortly after World War II a man named Henry Land perfected a device which he felt would find a ready market. His early investors and many others who followed them realized astronomical returns because in a relatively short time period Land's invention was successfully developed and marketed as the Polaroid camera. In 1966 the public was offered a chance to participate in a promising venture to sell cooked poultry. Phenomenal gains were realized by those who did invest since this emerging company was the Kentucky Fried Chicken Corporation.

Thousands of other innovations have followed this pattern. Indeed this is an essential element of the free enterprise system and has played a very important role in America's growth. Someone discovers a new way of doing things and proceeds to exploit this breakthrough. In countless instances these innovators do not themselves have sufficient financial resources. They turn to the public for aid, usually by selling new issues of common stock. The incentive to buy these original offerings is somewhat akin to a desire to "get in on the ground floor."

Origination

Before any securities may be legally offered to the general public, applications must be filed with federal and/or state authorities. It should be recalled from the discussion in Chapter 3 that security laws provide three main methods for the "birth" of the new issue: (1) national offerings, which are usually in excess of $2 million and are offered by well-established firms, and some new ventures, (2) Regulation A offerings, which are for $1.5 million or less and as such are normally made by newer companies, (3) intrastate offerings, most of which are between $0.5 million and $5 million. A few securities in the first category and the majority of those in the other two are offered by small firms or newly organized ventures.

Price performance

The opportunity to be in or near the start of a venture provides intuitive appeal for the new stock offerings. There is ample statistical evidence to substantiate this attraction. Studies of price patterns occurring during the first year of life for new issues show consistently larger increases compared to outstanding stocks—either listed or OTC. The superior performance is basically due to relatively small losses coupled with substantial gains.

Investment results do not always require considerable patience. It has been possible to realize substantial gains in a fev months, weeks, or, in many instances, in a matter of hours. Before the brokers closed shop on the day which Friendly Ice Cream Corporation sold shares in July 1968, the price rose 80 percent. The stock of Beef and Bison (no pun intended) went from $1.50 per share at its June 1978 offering price to $4.50 one year later. There have been hundreds of other instances of spectacular gains *and losses*. Price performance of some of 1978's new issues is presented in Table 11–2.

TABLE 11–2
Performance of selected new issues in 1978

Company	Date offered	Price per share ($)	
		Offer	October 23
American Clipper	5/12	9.00	7.25
American Pacemaker	5/4	1.50	7.75
Beef & Bison	6/4	1.50	7.00
Broughan Industries	1/27	7.50	3.00
Buckingham Motors	5/3	4.50	.75
Clark Copy International	4/28	2.75	13.50
Fremont General	1/18	14.50	11.00
Jenn-Air	4/14	14.25	24.50
Jhirmack Enterprises	3/24	12.00	24.50
MacPherson Vit.	2/2	5.00	.12
Modern Energy	7/22	1.25	.25
Omega Optical	1/25	5.33	10.00
St. Jude Medical	2/9	0.50	15.50
Sun-Heet	9/15	.50	.32
TPC Communications	7/27	4.24	12.50
Tesdata	4/27	13.00	9.50

Source: Information derived from a table in an article by John C. Boland, "Avantek to Xidex: New Issues Have Abruptly Become a Two-Way Street," *Barron's*, October 30, 1978, pp. 4 ff.

It is often difficult to purchase new issues. This is because of the method by which they are marketed and also because of the relatively small number of shares that are usually issued. There are several thousand brokerage offices scattered widely throughout the country. These businesses buy and sell virtually any stock in which secondary trading occurs. Primary markets are a different matter. A particular new issue is sold only by a small proportion of the brokerage firms. Their efforts are directed first toward their own existing clients. In many cases the new shares must be rationed. Investors usually do business with one or, at most, several brokerage firms. This means that only a few new issues will be available. For the majority of cases, the investor must wait until an after market begins. At this point anyone can buy.

It has been emphasized throughout this book that risk and return go hand in hand. New issues are no exception. There are several flags of caution. First of all the after markets for many of the new issues are extremely thin. This means that orders for a few hundred shares or more can cause a significant price change. There is a story about an investor who bought a substantial block of a new offering at $10 per share. One week later the price has risen to $20. More shares were bought. At the end of the first month the quote was $35. Not wishing to be greedy, the investor decided to sell. The broker's reply in sickening conciseness was "sell to whom?" The registered representative was telling this client that getting out of the stock was not such a simple matter. Large buy and sell orders for the newly issued or "unseasoned" stock may take time for execution. If speed is of critical importance, the price realized may vary considerably from the current quote. This problem will be recognized as *marketability*, a concept which was discussed in Chapter 2.

The search for companies offering new ideas is extremely demanding. There is no doubt that in the future many innovations will be developed by new firms that offer their stock to the public. Identifying the "acorns that will sprout" is not an easy task because the odds for success are quite low. However, the potential of spectacular returns will attract the investor.

Risk characteristics of new issues

For the most part new issues are low grade with respect to financial and market risks. They are typically highly speculative investments, although some issues may be purchased for their long-run potential provided that periodic reviews are made of each situation. Marketability depends heavily on the size of the issue and whether or not it can be traded interstate. Interest rate and purchasing power risks are not critical considerations in new issues.

TURNAROUND SITUATIONS

"Many shall be restored that now are fallen and many shall fall that now are in honor."[4] This quotation is especially applicable to corporate activity. Most firms have ups and downs. Relatively few companies enjoy continuous prosperity. This fluctuating behavior presents an opportunity for investors.

Examples of a turnaround

The term *turnaround* is applied to corporations which have done poorly in the recent past but are now expected to reverse the trend and "turnaround" and do better. Several developments might cause this recovery. The most common reasons are improvement in general economic conditions, development of a new product, discovery of a mineral deposit, receipt of a new contract, and new management. Examples of these changes in company fortunes are legion. Most manufacturers of cars, major appliances, and other durable goods realize improvements as the economy picks up after a period of slowdown. Texas Gulf Sulfur shares rose substantially when the company discovered a vast ore body. A similar price movement was triggered when Natomas struck oil in Indonesia. Ups and downs by major government contractors such as Boeing, General Dynamics, and Lockheed are "normal" patterns. Most of the above situations are difficult to predict reliably. The stock prices of these firms may soar when the developments are proclaimed, but it is usually not possible for the general public to anticipate these announcements. Timing is critical, and when the individual investor decides to purchase the stock, much, if not most, of the price rise may have occurred.

Management as a factor

In the examples just cited, the new developments were rather dramatic. The stock market reactions tended to coincide with the news. Another cause of turnaround—a change in top management—often results in a delayed price rise. Firms often shuffle their leaders in an effort to turn red ink operations into the black. The purpose is to breathe new life into the company. Improvements in these cases do not occur overnight, and stock price movements generally lag the

---

[4] Horace, *Ars Poetica* and cited in the introduction of Graham, Dodd, and Cottle, *Security Analysis.*

management changes. This allows investors time to analyze the situation.

A basic pattern occurs over and over—a declining business, new executives, sweeping changes, and subsequent improvements. The 110-year-old American-Standard Co. began the 1970s attempting to scrap its dowdy image by installing new leadership. Twentieth Century–Fox was saved from financial disaster by a new chairman who replaced the father-son dynasty that had run the film company for 38 years. Some firms stress this action in announcements. For example, Allis-Chalmers, since the hiring of a new president advertised repeatedly of a "Turnaround at Allis-Chalmers." The new officers usually have held responsible jobs in other firms. Litton Industries has the distinction of training several dozen men who have been responsible for turnaround situations, for example, Boise-Cascade, City Investing, and Walter Kidde.

It must be emphasized, however, that new management is by no means an assurance of *subsequent and continued improvement* in company performance. In some instances, it would be difficult for even a Deity to accomplish the change. Studebaker Corporation and Montgomery Ward tried numerous chieftains to no avail. Boise-Cascade, after a promising start, faltered badly and another new leader was installed before success was achieved. Nonetheless, there have been so many cases of turnaround caused by new management that the investor is well advised to take notice of companies that select new heads. Excellent sources of this information are found in the Management section of *Business Week* and the Who's News column in *The Wall Street Journal*. Once a list of potential investments has been compiled, the investor may carefully analyze the prospects of success for the corporation's recovery and then make selections.

The preceding discussion can be readily summarized by paraphrasing Horace's quotation, "Many firms shall be restored by new management."

Risk characteristics of turnaround situations

It is difficult to assign risk grades to turnaround situations because they vary so widely with respect to potential gains and losses and time periods which must pass before improvement occurs. In general, they are quite speculative and offer considerable exposure to market and financial risks. As with the other investments discussed in this chapter, the importance of interest rate and purchasing power risk is not great.

TREND BUCKERS

The 1960s were unique in U.S. history in that this period encompassed the longest sustained economic growth on record. The next decade began with a slowdown in business activity. Sessions of expansion and contraction, called business cycles, have been characteristic of the past. The duration and frequency of these ups and downs has varied widely. Another depression of the magnitude that occurred in the 1930s is a remote possiblity according to most economists. Since that disaster the economy has progressed with more moderate declines, called recessions. Economic growth rates will undoubtedly continue to fluctuate in the future. These changes present an opportunity for the investor.

"It is always a good time to buy." This advice is often given by brokers because at *any* point in time the prospects for certain industries and individual companies are very favorable. Even when most firms' activities are declining there are those who are setting record highs. These companies that continue growing in periods of economic slowdown are known as *trend buckers*.

The reasons for these "exceptional" industries can be largely attributed to two factors. Some types of economic activity are given timely boosts by developments such as new products, cost reductions, or changes in consumer buying habits. These developments are irregular and not limited to expansion periods. In a dynamic economy, invention and innovation are continuous. Because of this, breakthroughs will occur in slack as well as in boom periods. The exceptional industry in one cycle may not perform similarly in the next.

The second major reason for counter-trend behavior is that some lines of business just react differently to economic declines. Consumers will cancel or at least postpone purchases of durable goods such as new cars and appliances. Other products remain in demand regardless of the economic circumstances of the buying public. Industries offering these items are said to be recession resistant.

Examples of trend buckers

A recession resistant industry is typified by food chain stores. Many purchases can be delayed, but not food. Furthermore as people reduce expenditures they do more entertaining and dining at home. The food retailing business is thus one of the least affected by economic downturns.

Some industries do not feel the effects of a slowdown for some time. For example when overtime is cut and layoffs begin many people undertake do-it-yourself home projects. Thus the portable power tool industry does well in the early stages of a recession. If the downturn persists, this line of business will eventually be hurt, but when general declines are modest, these firms should prosper.

Several industries produce items that are almost considered as necessities by their consumers. Both the brewing and soft drink businesses are in this category. They represent habit patterns that are relatively inexpensive and are hard to alter. Traditionally they have been among the last to feel the pinch of a slowdown.

Shakespeare wrote, "Ill blows the wind that profits nobody." This is another way of expressing the effect of moving counter to the crowd. The downward trend need not be in the general economy. Things happen that create problems in some industries while benefitting others. An example is the oil crisis that began in 1973. This situation caused trouble for such industries as the automobile manufacturers, tourism, some oil firms, and chemical companies. On the other hand, the event aided coal companies, insulation manufacturers, airlines when gasoline shortages occurred, and a part of the oil industry—especially those firms connected with well drilling and secondary recovery operations. Pollution control device manufacturers have benefitted by new air quality standards. Opportunities for profit are available to investors who can discover the *silver lining* in the clouds of change and trouble.

There are several points of caution that should be made with respect to the trend buckers. First, it is difficult to imagine that any industry is truly recession-proof. If bad times continue, the decline will eventually be felt by virtually all companies. Secondly, the fact that certain lines of business can run counter to downturns does not mean that all firms in that industry will enjoy this experience. The investor must be careful to select only the most promising ventures. Finally, and perhaps most importantly, investors need to remember that growth in earnings of a company does not mean that the stock will necessarily rise. Recall from Chapter 2 that the overall market movement has a substantial effect on the price behavior of any individual stock. When the price averages are declining this will have a restraining influence on the share prices of firms that are performing well. This requires investors to remain patient and realize that the market will eventually reflect superior earning power.

It is always appropriate to look for new trends, products, and companies—even in periods of general gloom—because some trend
buckers are present.

Risk characteristics of trend buckers

Investments in these situations are usually short term and hence
speculative in nature. The potential gains and losses are less than the
other special types of investing discussed earlier in this chapter. Because of their relative price stability, in most cases trend buckers are
high grade with respect to market risk. Financial risk is usually low
and other investment risks are not of crucial importance.

SUMMARY

Rights and warrants

Rights and *warrants* are options to purchase securities for a known
price over a stated time period. The value of these investments depends upon the difference between the subscription price (the price at
which the owner of a right or warrant is entitled to purchase a security) and the security's market price. Rights are usually short term in
nature, seldom remaining outstanding longer than 30 days, while warrants may have any maturity.

These securities have speculative value because if the market price
of the underlying security rises, the price of the option contract rises
relatively more. Rights and warrants do not receive dividends or interest and do not entitle their owners to vote on corporate matters.

Puts and calls

A *put* contract allows its owner to *sell* a certain number of securities, at a specified price, to a specified buyer, at any time during a
specified time period. This contract has a market price which is dependent upon the market price of the security, the put price, and the
time remaining before the contract expires.

A *call* contract is the opposite option. It allows its owner to *purchase* shares under the above conditions. In each case losses are limited to the cost of the option contract, while profits are theoretically
unlimited. However, many of these contracts do not prove profitable

because security prices often do not fluctuate enough over the option period to offset the option's cost. Trading activity in these securities has increased greatly since options were first listed on exchanges.

A *straddle* contract is one where an investor has a put and a call contract on the same securities. If prices increase or decrease *enough*, a profit is made. The gain on one contract is greater than the loss experienced on the other.

Commodities

Thousands of investors trade in *commodity futures*. This involves buying and selling foodstuffs, raw materials, and financial contracts. Prices are established today for delivery in the future. Profits are realized if prices have changed in the appropriate direction when the deliveries are to be made. Commodity investors usually employ a high degree of leverage; so small price changes can result in large gains or *losses*. Risk is present due to the constant threat of hard-to-predict events such as floods, droughts, freezes, strikes, diseases, expropriations, and wars. Considerable effort is also required to stay abreast of other influences of supply and demand.

Investment in gold may take the form of futures contracts, holding the metal, or buying shares in companies which produce gold. Holding gold directly is relatively expensive because of storage and transportation costs, and because gold provides no returns except those from price rises. The price of free-market gold is controlled entirely by supply and demand conditions. Supply is limited in that the most easily accessible ore has already been mined and few new mines are being discovered.

Investment in silver may take the same forms as those involving gold. Silver prices are also controlled by supply and demand.

Short selling

Short selling is the name given to sales of borrowed securities made in anticipation of a price decline. The "shorted" securities are borrowed from a broker, to be repaid at a later time. If the market price of the shorted stock declines, the transaction will be profitable because the investor will repay the stock loan with lower priced securities than were borrowed. If prices rise instead, the investor will suffer a loss when the short contract is repaid.

New issues

The primary market for securities presents a special opportunity for investors. *New issues* of common stock are offered by a wide range of corporations—from billion dollar firms down to companies which are just beginning. The smaller and newly formed ventures are of particular interest because they offer an opportunity to "get in on the ground floor." Many investors have realized substantial gains by purchasing these new issues. In some periods few new offerings are made due to adverse stock market conditions.

The risk-return relationship is verified by price action in new issues. While many stocks increase substantially in value in relatively short time periods, many others decline or even become valueless. The high degree of price volatility should serve as both an incentive and caution to investors.

Turnaround situations

Many corporations that have done poorly in past times reverse the trend, *turnaround,* and do better. Early recognition of forthcoming improvements in seemingly unattractive situations can provide investors with very favorable results. A major factor in creating the turnaround is a change in management. A pattern has been established in a considerable number of firms—a declining business, new executives, sweeping changes, and subsequent improvements. Considerable judgment is required to identify which situations can be reversed and which are hopeless. Risks of not being successful in distinguishing the differences are commensurate with the potential rewards for correct analysis.

Trend buckers

Trend buckers are companies whose growth does not decline when the general economy enters a slowdown period. They provide special opportunities for investors to buy securities when stock prices in general are falling. Firms in the food industry are quite recession-resistant. Companies that supply "do-it-yourself" products may actually prosper in the early stages of a downturn. Trend bucker companies can be identified in the likely industries, but very few of them can continue to grow if a recession persists or becomes severe.

PROBLEMS

1. A company just offered its shareholders the opportunity to purchase additional shares of stock on the basis of one new share for each four old shares held. The price of the new shares is $35 each; the outstanding common stock currently sells for $50.
    a. Assume that the rights sell with the stock for 14 days. What is the value of each right during this period?
    b. When the 14-day period expires and the rights begin selling separately from the stock, how much should the market price of the stock drop? (Assume no economic or other forces cause a price change.)
    c. If the market price of the stock increased to $60 after the stock began selling ex-rights, how much would each right be worth?
2. Look in a recent newspaper for price quotes on the selected stocks and warrants included in Table 11-1. The subscription price of these warrants may change over time, so check Moody's Industrial Manual to see whether this has happened.
    a. Compute new theoretical values for the warrants of the companies you have selected.
    b. Explain the logic of the premium.
3. From information contained in Figure 11-2 outline the conditions which must prevail (timing, stock price, and so on) in the market for Alcoa common in order for the person purchasing an Alcoa $45 April call option to have a profit from this speculation.
4. Shirley sold General Electric stock short at $40 per share. If she covers her short (buys the stock later) at $36 per share, what would be her gross profit on a 100-share transaction?
5. Test the stock price performance of trend buckers by comparing the average price change for three drug industry stocks with the change in the Dow Jones Industrial Average. (Select a period during which stock prices fell substantially, such as 1966, 1969, 1973, 1974, or 1977.)
6. Trace the stock price performance of a new issue by plotting month-end prices for one year. Select the new issue by looking in the "new issues" section of the Commercial and Financial Chronicle or ask a local broker.
7. Look up commodity futures prices for frozen pork bellies (bacon) in The Wall Street Journal. Based on the quotations, do you think bacon will cost more or less six months from now? State your reasoning.

QUESTIONS

1. What is a put contract? What must happen to stock prices to make it profitable?

2. What is a *call* contract? What must happen to stock prices to make it profitable?
3. What is a *short sale*? What must happen to stock prices to make it profitable?
4. If a company wanted to raise money quickly, would it be likely to use *warrants* or *rights*? Why?
5. Why do warrants usually set at a premium over their theoretical value?
6. Why are short sales more speculative than a regular purchase of an equal number of shares?
7. Define the term *trend bucker*. Why are trend buckers of interest to investors?
8. What is a *commodity futures contract*? In what ways are these contracts similar to puts and calls?
9. What are *new issues*? Describe three different methods by which they are offered.
10. What is appealing about new issues to investors?
11. What are some problems associated with buying new issues?
12. What is a *turnaround situation*? How can potential turnarounds be discovered?
13. Define the term *financial leverage* as it relates to option and commodity future contracts.
14. When it is first rumored or announced that one company intends to acquire or merge with another firm, an opportunity for the speculator exists. Why do you suppose this may be true?

SELECTED READINGS

Appel, G. *The Stock Option Scalpers Manual*. New York: Windsor, 1979.

Browne, Harry. *New Profits from the Monetary Crisis*. West Caldwell, N.J.: Morrow, 1978.

Clasing, Henry. *The Dow Jones-Irwin Guide to Put and Call Options*. Homewood, Ill.: Dow Jones-Irwin, 1975.

Commodity Trading Manual. Chicago: Chicago Board of Trade, 1977.

Commodity Year Book. New York: Commodity Research Bureau, published annually.

Ferguson, Hugh. *Superstocks*. New York: Windsor, 1979.

Flumianai, C. S. *The Subtle Operative Techniques on How to Make a Fortune in a Bear Market when Prices Decline Sharply & May Prepare the Ground for a Robust Advance*. Albuquerque: American Classical College Press, 1977.

Kassouf, Sheen T., and Thorpe, E. O. *Beat the Market*. New York: Random House, 1967.

Powers, Mark J. *Getting Started in Commodity Futures Trading.* Cedar Falls, Iowa: Investor Publications, 1977.

Roberts, Newton. *The Cyclical Theories of Stock Market Action.* Albuquerque: Institute for Economic & Financial Research, 1978.

Rosen, Lawrence R. *When and How to Profit from Buying and Selling Gold.* Homewood, Ill.: Dow Jones-Irwin, 1973.

Smyth, David, and Stuntz, Laurence F. *Unusual Investments That Could Make You Rich.* Chicago: Contemporary Books, 1978.

Spencer, Robert L. *The Performance of the Best Investment Advisory Services.* New York: Odd John, 1977.

Teweles, Richard J.; Harlow, Charles V.; and Stone, Herbert L. *The Commodity Futures Games: Who Wins? Who Loses? Why?* New York: McGraw-Hill, 1977.

Winfield, Basil. *How to Capture the Profit Potential of Option Trading & the Magical Device of Stock Market Leverage.* Albuquerque: American Classical College Press, 1978.

Wyckoff, Richard D. *How Specialists in Panics Build Their Success in the Stock Market.* Albuquerque: Institute for Economic & Financial Research, 1979.

12

Investing in real estate

INTRODUCTION

Real property ownership represents the largest single type of investment made by Americans. It far exceeds the market value of bonds, common stocks, mutual fund shares, pension benefits, or the cash value of life insurance policies owned by individuals. Real estate investment takes many forms. The most common type is that of the owner-occupied home, but many persons own commercial real property, raw land, shares in real estate investment trusts, and other indirect real property investments. This chapter examines each of these investments with particular attention to analytical techniques used to measure their profit potential.

HOME OWNERSHIP

Ownership of one's home is part of the American dream. And it is a part of the dream that has been realized for many persons: In 1978 over 60 percent of all American families owned their own homes, while home ownership remained an unobtainable goal for the average citizen of most other countries. The market value of all single-family houses in the U.S. is extremely large, exceeding two trillion dollars in 1978 (See Figure 12-1). Even after reducing this amount by the debt outstanding against it, equity ownership in this type asset was greater than for any other asset owned by individuals.

FIGURE 12–1
Value of the single-family housing stock

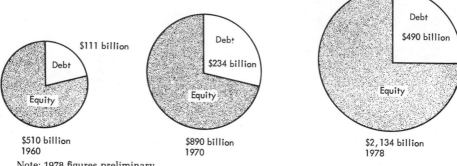

Note: 1978 figures preliminary.
Source: National Association of Realtors, Chicago, Illinois.

The home as an investment

Until recent years few people looked at a home as an investment. Over a long period, from 1880 to 1945, the price of single-family houses rose far less than the consumer price index.[1] Since that time, the increase in housing prices has greatly exceeded the rise in the consumer price index. Because of this the family home has become identified as one asset that can be counted on to maintain its purchasing power during inflation.

For the past ten years this has certainly been true. Figure 12–2 shows percentage increases in the consumer price index, the Standard & Poor's 500-Stock Index, and an index of the average price of existing homes. Calculations were made to convert 1968 to the base year. Later-year index numbers are compared to the 1968 index levels. For example, in 1968 the average CPI level was 104.2. In 1969 the CPI averaged 109.8. The percentage change was

$$\frac{109.8 - 104.2}{104.2} = .0537 \text{ or } 5.37\%.$$

It is obvious from Figure 12–2 that existing homes, on average, increased in value more rapidly than did the CPI. Therefore, home ownership may be said to have protected against inflation. During the same

---

[1] Charles D. Kirkpatrick, II, "No Place to Hide? Residential Real Estate Looks Alarmingly Over-Extended," *Barron's*, April 3, 1978, p. 11.

FIGURE 12–2

Comparison of price index changes of existing homes, the Consumer Price Index, and Standard & Poor's 500-Stock Index (base year—1968)

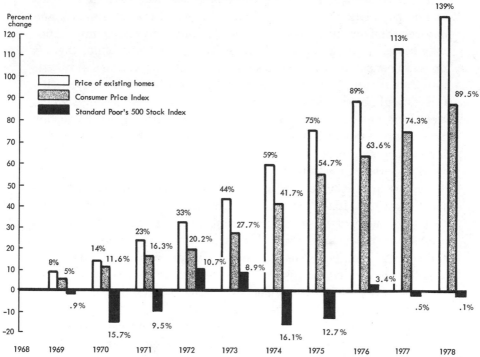

Source: *Federal Home Loan Bank Board Bulletin*, Standard & Poor's, Inc., and U.S. Bureau of Labor Statistics.

period the stock market averages performed poorly relative to either the housing price index or the CPI.[2]

But Figure 12–2 covers only a recent period of history. Over many years, common stock returns (price increases plus dividends) have increased slightly more rapidly than either single-family house prices or the consumer price index. Housing prices have risen largely because of inflation, which is widely believed to be responsible for lowered stock prices. When inflationary pressures diminish, housing prices should flatten and stock prices should recover.

---

[2] Average stock prices do not include dividends received. These would have increased stock profits somewhat, but not greatly.

An analysis of home ownership costs and returns

Financial returns from home ownership may be measured in terms of rent payments that no longer must be made, tax advantages, and any returns from price appreciation. Of equal or greater importance may be the "psychic income" from owning one's home. Since there is no widely accepted way to measure returns of a psychological nature, they do not enter into any of the calculations which follow. Nonetheless it should be recognized that the pride of home ownership is an extremely strong force, one which would cause many persons to buy homes even though such an investment could not be justified in dollar-and-cents terms.

Most persons live in rented houses, apartments, or other dwellings when they first leave home. Eventually they marry and settle in one location, at least for a few years. At this time the question of whether to buy housing or to continue to rent becomes important. Persons wishing to be scientific about this decision must accurately calculate the costs of renting versus the costs of home ownership. Renting is usually cheaper and the costs of renting are accurately known, at least over the period of a lease. Ownership brings additional costs and inconveniences, but it also provides benefits.

The most obvious home ownership costs are mortgage payments, property taxes, insurance, and maintenance. Persons who are handy with a hammer, saw, and paintbrush can reduce maintenance costs to practically nothing. They can often increase the value of a property through "sweat equity," a not-so-elegant phrase which refers to the additional value created by landscaping, adding a fence or patio, painting, and other improvements. It is not difficult to create a comparison of rental and home ownership costs. To be thorough, one must make allowance for future increases in rents, tax advantages from home ownership, the probable increase in the home's value, the cost of having funds "tied up" in the purchased property, and the difference in size between a rented and an owned property. (Most persons buy larger dwellings than they rent.)

Table 12-1 presents an analysis of a rent versus own decision. Assumptions are: The rental unit is a 900 square-foot apartment. The current rent is $325 per month, but the lease is about to expire and the rent is expected to be $350 per month for the first year of the comparison. Rents are assumed to increase at an annual rate of 7 percent thereafter. All maintenance, utility, and parking expenses are included in the rent.

TABLE 12-1
Yearly after tax costs of renting versus buying a home (dollars)

Years	1	2	3	4	5
Mortgage interest	3140	3116	3090	3062	3032
Principal repayment	259	282	308	336	367
= Financing payment	3399	3399	3399	3399	3399
+ House expenses	550	583	618	655	694
+ Real estate taxes	1350	1458	1575	1701	1837
+ Interest lost on down payment and closing costs, after taxes	480	504	528	554	581
− Income tax savings	1347	1372	1400	1429	1461
= After-tax cash cost	4432	4572	4720	4880	5050
Rental expenses	4200	4494	4809	5145	5505
Yearly after-tax cash cost of house per 100 sq. ft.	369	381	393	407	421
Yearly after-tax cash cost of renting per 100 sq. ft.	467	499	534	572	612
Ratio: house costs/rental costs per 100 sq. ft.	.791	.764	.737	.711	.688

A 1,200 square-foot house is offered for sale on the following terms: The price is $45,000. A $9,000 down payment is required; the remainder of the cost, $36,000, is financed with a 30-year 8¾ percent fully amortized mortgage.

The down payment is available and is currently invested in a savings account which yields 7 percent interest. Closing costs and legal fees will be $800. Property values are expected to increase 8 percent each year. Heat, electricity and other expenses total $550 during the first year; they will increase 6 percent each year thereafter. Property taxes will continue to be 3 percent of the property's beginning-year market value. The purchaser is expected to continue to be taxed at a rate of 30 percent of taxable income. Itemized federal and state income tax deductions are assumed.

Table 12-1 presents a five-year simulation of future after-tax costs of buying a house versus renting an apartment. The *financing payment* is the sum of yearly mortgage interest and principal payments on the house. This payment remains constant over the life of the loan at $3,399 per year, but each year the proportion of the loan that goes to interest and principal changes.

House expenses are $550 the first year, increasing to $694 by the fifth year. *Real estate taxes* are 3 percent of the market value of the house. Since the market value is assumed to increase by 8 percent each year, property taxes are also assumed to increase at this rate, from

$1,350 in the first year to $1,837 in the fifth. The money that paid for the down payment and closing costs was formerly invested in a savings account yielding 7 percent per year. *Interest lost on down payment and closing costs* represents the yearly after-tax loss of income from having drawn out $9,800 to provide the down payment and closing costs. *Income tax savings* represent the tax advantages from owning property. Interest payments and property taxes are allowable deductions from adjusted gross income, if deductions are itemized. In 1979 the federal standard deduction was $3,400 for married persons filing joint returns. Property taxes, interest payments, and other deductions associated with home ownership usually exceed this amount, making it advantageous to itemize deductions. Interest payments and property taxes can then be said to provide income tax savings equal to the amount by which they lower federal taxes. Property taxes and interest payments totaled $4,490 in the first year. Since federal taxes were 30 percent of taxable income, the amount of income taxes saved was

$$.30 \times \$4,490 = \$1,347.$$

Interest and property taxes are usually deductible expenses so far as state income taxes are concerned. Because state tax rates vary greatly from state to state no attempt was made to include tax reduction benefits from this source in this analysis. The *after-tax cash cost* is merely the sum of all cash expenses associated with owning the home less income tax savings.

Rental expenses are the total expenses of renting; if utilities, parking, or other expenses related to housing are not included in the basic rent payment they should be added in at this point. The cash costs of buying versus renting can be compared directly year by year to determine when, if ever, the cash costs of home ownership become lower. In our example this would occur just prior to the third year, when the cash costs of home ownership become $4,720 and cash rental expenses are $4,809.

The house, however, has 1,200 square feet of living area while the apartment has only 900 square feet. To take these size differences into account the cash costs of owning the house and renting are divided by the square footage of each dwelling. This figure is multiplied by 100 to provide a cash cost for each alternative per 100 square feet of living space. Finally, the cash cost per 100 square feet of house ownership is divided by the same cost for renting. A ratio greater than one indicates that the cash costs per 100 square feet are lower for renting; a ratio of less than one means the opposite.

Calculated on a square-foot basis, purchasing a house is less expensive in each year studied. The format of Table 12–1 can be followed by anyone wishing to analyze the yearly cash costs associated with any rent versus buy situation. At the very least, the cash cost comparisons should be made. Buying a house may be economically more attractive, but the cash costs of buying may be so great as to make home purchase impossible or impractical. Many people are unable to buy homes because they cannot meet the down payment requirements.

Of additional importance are the gains which come from increased house prices. In this example, house prices were assumed to increase by 8 percent each year. Such increases cannot be realized until a property is sold, but as prices rise so does the owner's equity. Owner's equity is defined as the owner's interest in the value of a property. It is usually calculated by subtracting loans outstanding from the sale price after commissions and other sales expenses. At the end of the second year, the owner's equity in the house used in this example would be $13,880, calculated as follows:

Market price at end of second year	$52,488
Less sale commission of 6 percent	3,149
Less loans outstanding	35,459
Equals owner's equity	$13,880

The return from this investment may be seen as the difference between the cash obtained if the home were sold and the cash amount invested. At the end of the second year $13,880 could be received from sale of the investment. By this time $10,110 would have been invested, calculated as follows:

Cash invested in down payment and closing costs	$ 9,800
Plus difference in cash costs of owning and renting	310
Equals total cash costs	$10,110

The home purchase, in this example, has been very profitable even if it is held for only two years. The owner could expect to have a cash return of $13,880 on $10,110 of cash invested. These amounts are often stated in the form of a *cash-on-cash ratio*, which is merely the cash returns divided by cash invested as of some point in time. At the end of the second year this ratio is 1.37, which means that $1.37 of cash is returned for each $1.00 invested.[3] This profitability was produced by the increase in house prices, by the fact that the buyer was able to obtain high financial leverage, and by the tax advantages associated with home ownership. These conditions have prevailed in the housing markets in most areas of the country for at least a decade, and have acted to make home ownership a desirable investment for most people.

Home financing

Home loans are usually the longest-term, lowest-cost loans obtained by individuals. At the beginning of 1979, the average new home sold for $68,100. It was financed by a 28.1-year mortgage of $49,600 which carried an effective interest rate of 10.02 percent. The average loan was 75.1 percent of the sale price, but nearly 30 percent of the homes were sold at loan-to-price ratios of greater than 80 percent.[4]

Primary or *first-mortgage* loans are almost always fully amortized. A *fully amortized* loan is one which has constant, usually monthly, payments due over its life. Each payment is of an amount sufficient to pay interest on the outstanding loan and to repay a portion of the loan principal. While the payment amount remains the same, the proportion of each payment that goes to interest and principal changes. Early payments are nearly all interest. Later payments are nearly all principal. On a correctly calculated fully amortized loan, the last payment completes repayment of the loan.

A *balloon loan* is one which has a larger than normal final payment. *Second-mortgage loans* are loans which are secured by a mortgage which is legally inferior to a first mortgage. In the event of financial problems, the first mortgage must be completely repaid before the second-mortgage holder can receive anything. Second mortgages are typi-

---

[3] This cash-on-cash ratio does not take all taxes into consideration. In the above transaction capital gain taxes would be levied on the difference between the purchase price and the sale price. If the property is held for more than one year, the gain is classified as a long-term capital gain and is taxed at a lower than normal rate. If the property sold was the primary residence of the seller, no taxes will be levied on the sale so long as another house of at least the same value is purchased within 18 months from the date of the sale. Beginning in 1978 homeowners are allowed a once-in-a-lifetime reduction of up to $100,000 in capital gains from the sale of a personal residence.

[4] These data and others pertaining to home financing are published monthly in *The Federal Home Loan Bank Board Journal, The Federal Reserve Bulletin*, and many other magazines and newspapers. The above figures represent national averages. Regional averages are also available.

cally of short maturity (five years is a common term) and are seldom fully amortized. In home financing these mortgages are often used to finance part or all of the down payment. Rates on this type financing are usually two to five percentage points higher than on a first-mortgage loan. The first mortgage might be at 9 percent, the second at 12. Often only interest is paid until the loan is due. Increasingly, second or even third mortgages are issued against property which has either appreciated in value, or which has a first mortage that has been nearly repaid. The owner's equity in the property is the collateral for such loans. Most first-mortgage loans are made by savings and loans, mutual savings banks, or commercial banks. Most second-mortage financing is supplied by individuals, although credit unions and small loan companies provide some of this credit.

In an inflationary period incomes rise and mortgage payments stay constant, if conventional mortgage financing has been obtained. In this situation each mortgage payment becomes less and less of a burden to its payer. At the same time house prices probably increase, and so may interest rates. Lenders who made long-term home loans at low rates find that they must now pay more to borrow funds than these old loans return. To protect against this condition some mortgage lenders are writing *variable-rate mortgages*. Under these contracts the mortgage rate rises and falls in response to changes in an interest rate index. Only a small proportion of house mortgages now carry these terms, but if market interest rates continue to fluctuate as they have in the past, variable-rate mortgages will become much more common.

Variable-payment mortgages are designed so that during the early years of a mortgage, payments are lower than the amount necessary to amortize the loan. This type loan is sought by persons whose incomes are too low to meet lenders' credit requirements. In theory, after a few years of low payments, the borrowers' income will have risen to the point where larger payments can be made.

A *wrap-around mortgage* is used to purchase a property which already has a mortgage loan outstanding against it. The lender creates a new mortgage which assumes (takes over) payments to retire the old mortgage as well as to create additional financing. In this sense the newly created mortgage "wraps around" the existing financing. This type mortgage has its greatest use in financing commercial properties, except in states having usury laws which place a ceiling on the rate of interest on mortgage loans. When new mortgage financing rates exceed the ceiling rates, wrap-around mortgages can provide lower financing charges by incorporating the old financing, which is usually at a lower rate, in the financing package.

Conventional, FHA, and VA loans

Commercial banks, savings and loans, and mutual savings banks make most of the first-mortgage home loans. Conventional loans comprise the bulk of these loans. The term *conventional loan* refers to a standard first-mortgage home loan which usually requires a down payment of at least 20 percent of the price of the home, which has an original maturity of 30 years or less, which is fully amortized, and which is uninsured.[5] Rates on these loans are set by supply and demand conditions in the lending markets.

In an effort to lower costs of home financing and to upgrade and standardize housing construction, the Federal Housing Administration was created. This agency guarantees payment of a house loan in the event that the owner defaults, if the loan meets certain specific tests. To obtain an FHA insured loan the borrower must have income which is sufficient to support the mortgage payments. The value of the property must be determined by an FHA approved appraisal, and the construction of the house must meet FHA standards. In 1979, only 3 percent of the first $25,000 of appraised house value was required as a down payment. Ten percent was required on the next $10,000 of appraised value, and 20 percent down was required on loans of over $35,-000. The maximum insured value was $45,000. Because lenders judge these loans as safer than conventional loans, the average term of an FHA insured loan is longer. The FHA sets maximum lending rates on loans that they insure, which often causes these rates to be lower than those on conventional mortgage loans.

The federal Veterans Administration loan program insures home and farm loans in much the same manner as the FHA. The main difference between the programs is the requirement of prior military service to participate in all VA loan programs. These programs enable eligible borrowers to obtain lower down payments and usually lower interest rates than on conventional mortgages. When interest rates are very

---

[5] Most institutions make loans of more than 80 percent of the sale price. When such loans are made, regulating authorities require that they be insured to minimize the risk of nonpayment. Such insurance is provided by private insurers and is paid for by the borrower.

high they may exceed the ceiling rates imposed by the FHA and the VA. In this situation lenders add charges or "points" (one point equals one percent of the mortgage loan amount) to the loan contract to increase its effective yield to approximately that obtainable on a conventional loan.

Many states have veterans' loan programs. These programs seek to make house, farm, or business loans to qualified veterans on better terms than could otherwise be obtained. Residency in the state while engaged in military service is the typical qualification for these programs, but there is wide variation from state to state in how residency is determined as well as in the types of benefits to be obtained. Some programs guarantee loans made by financial institutions. Others grant loans directly from the state veterans agency. Most of these programs were begun shortly after the Second World War. Their importance will continue to decline as veterans use up their loan eligibility or as they die.

RAW LAND

An often stated rule of appraisal theory is that land will have its maximum value when it is put to its "highest and best use." This phrase implies that for every piece of property there is a use which will generate more profits than can be produced by any other. Wheat could be grown in the center of any city. But because of demands for housing or commercial buildings, the highest and best use for land so located is usually as housing or commercial buildings. The highest and best use for a wooded lot located on the edge of a city might be as a golf course, or as farmland, or as the site of an apartment complex. To profit from ownership of raw land, one need only to identify property that is not being put to its highest and best use, buy it or otherwise gain control over it, and change its use to one that is more profitable.

The theory is simple enough, but there are several special problems associated with raw land speculation.[6] One is financing. It is usually easy to obtain 80 percent or higher financing for a house or small

---

[6] The nature of raw land ownership and development is such that it cannot be identified as anything but a speculation under the definitions presented in this text. Unfortunately, many persons do not recognize the difference between investment and speculation, so far as purchase of land is concerned. They buy such property as an investment without recognizing the many risks associated with this type of asset, and then are often disappointed when their hopes are not realized.

apartment, but many banks and savings and loans do not provide financing for purchase of raw land. They see such property as too speculative to warrant the usual high ratio of financing to market value that is offered to purchasers of more conventional real property. If such loans are made, they usually require premium interest rates and additional collateral.

Much of the financing for raw land purchases is provided by the seller. A typical arrangement is to sell property on contract with the seller retaining title to the property until it is completely paid for. Terms may or may not be generous. The owner may be elderly and may not allow the buyer a long period over which to pay off the contract. The interest rate may be high because the purchaser cannot obtain financing elsewhere.[7]

Much raw land is purchased with the intention of subdividing it. This is truly a speculative activity because of the many risks involved. One must be certain that water, sewage, and other utility services will be available. The most common and least expensive way of providing water and sewage service is by hooking onto existing facilities provided by an adjoining city or town. This is usually accomplished by having the subdivided property annexed and made part of the existing municipality. Many towns and cities now refuse to annex property or provide utility services without an affirmative vote of the citizens. This adds another element of uncertainty to what is usually an already risky proposition. Wells and septic tanks might provide the same services, but they are typically more expensive. In many parts of the country well water is not easily found. County land-zoning ordinances may rule against septic tanks, or may allow them only on one-half acre or larger-sized lots. Unless the area is remote, telephone and electric service is seldom a problem because of the ease with which electric lines can be installed.

Much acreage that is properly located for eventual subdivision is zoned as agricultural land. This zoning must be changed to residential, industrial, or whatever the highest and best use is assumed to be. It is impossible to predict with certainty that a zoning change can be obtained. Many zoning decisions are made on other than economic

---

[7] Because interest income is taxed at ordinary income tax rates, much land sold on contract is sold at what *appear* to be modest or even low interest rates. The sale price is adjusted upward to reflect the lowered interest charges. This provides a tax advantage for the seller because the price increase results in larger capital gain income, which is taxed at less than one-half the rate on ordinary income. Chapter 15 goes into this in additional detail.

grounds, and there is often no judicial or other form of review of an adverse zoning decision.

Timing and location

Timing and *location* play extremely important roles in all raw land purchases. While it is true that land values nationwide are increasing each year, it is equally true that there are great variations in the increases. The most important single determinant of how rapidly property values will rise is location. Land located adjacent to existing roads or highways is usually developed first. Land that is flat, or which is easily or inexpensively developed, usually receives early consideration. Land that is located next to existing industrial sites is often a prime candidate for this use. Property that is not so advantageously situated may eventually be developed, but many years may pass before this happens.

Timing refers to how rapidly property will be converted to its highest and best use. You may be convinced that the highest and best use for a particular property is as the site for a supermarket. But if you can't develop the property and build the supermarket yourself, you must convince someone with more resources to do so. If there are competing sites that are better located or in some other way superior, they will probably be developed first. In this event, development of your property may be postponed, perhaps for many years. During this period the land may produce little if any income. Taxes and interest costs will continue, however, until the property is sold or developed. By the time this happens the costs of holding the property may have made the project unprofitable.

Even though purchase of raw land is usually risky, it can be one of the most profitable of speculations. In its favor is the fact that the population is increasing, and the supply of usable land is not.[8] As one farmer put it when talking to a prospective buyer of his property, "Sure the price is high, but just remember, they ain't making this stuff any more!" Land will continue to become relatively more scarce. And as it does, its value should increase. The secret to success in raw land speculations is to buy land at a low price, or at very low

---

[8] This statement is not completely true, of course; some land can be created by filling in lakes, swamps, or rivers. Buildings can be constructed on air rights above existing highways or railroads. But for most purposes the amount of land is limited to that which already exists.

financing charges, and then have its potential for development quickly realized.

COMMERCIAL PROPERTY

The term *commercial property* refers to land and buildings which produce lease or rental income. Such properties include duplexes, apartments, hotels, office buildings, stores, and all sorts of other commercial establishments. Not included in this term are industrial or agricultural properties, or owner-occupied residential structures. Aside from a home, the real property investment most widely favored by the small investor is the duplex, four-plex, or small apartment building. Many persons have been able to acquire sizable commercial properties by first investing in a duplex and then "trading up" to larger units as equity in the original property increased.

The investment potential of commercial property, unlike raw land or a personal residence, can be fairly accurately measured. There are several ways of doing this but all methods compare expected future income from a property to its cost. Figure 12–3 is a form which may be used to calculate the expected profitability of commercial properties. It is far from the most sophisticated type of analysis practiced, but it covers most areas of investigation. Its greatest weaknesses are that the future expected market or sale price of the property plays no role in the analysis, and the analysis covers a maximum of three years.[9]

Figure 12–3 contains information about a six-year-old ten-plex apartment assumed to be for sale. When such properties are placed on the market, the real estate broker listing the property prepares information of the type contained in the form. If the property is not listed, the seller does this. Typically, only current year information is supplied.

It goes without saying that a potential buyer must examine such information as carefully as possible, paying particular attention to the expense and income items. The information describing the Outflow Apartments was created by using expense, income, and other ratios obtained from The National Institute of Real Estate Brokers. This

---

[9] Several computer based programs for real property analysis are available. These programs allow the introduction of changing growth rates of property values, rental income, expenses, taxes, etc. They generally provide an estimate of the net present value of the project and its internal rate of return for various holding periods.

FIGURE 12-3
Income analysis

Property name __Outflow Apartments__ Type ___Ten Pley___

Location _____ _____ List price __$200,000__

Assessed value: ___$151,500___ __100__ % Less loans __$140,000__

Land ___30,000___ __20__ %=List price equity __$60,000__

Improvements ___120,000___ __79__ %

Personal property ___1,500___ __1__ %

	Year 1	%	Year 2	%	Year 3	%
Gross income	$22,200	100				
Less vacancy and credit losses	1,110	5				
=Gross operating income	21,090	95				
Less operating expenses						
Taxes	4,200	19				
Utilities	920	4				
Insurance	300	1				
Management	1,687	8				
Services	200	1				
Supplies						
Maintenance	1,158	5				
Other	175	1				
Total expense	8,640	39				
= Net operating income	12,450	56				
Less loan payments	14,405					
= Gross spendable income	(1,955)					
Plus principal repayment	3,268					
= Gross equity income	1,313					
Less depreciation	5,456					
= Taxable income	(4,143)					

group collects cost, revenue, and other information on real property investments on a nationwide basis. The ratios are classified by size, type, and location of property and provide a rough guide of what the costs and revenues of different types of commercial properties should be. Other trade groups and companies provide similar information. The filled-in form describes an "average" ten-unit apartment building located in a small West Coast city in early 1979. Ratios and other values can be expected to vary widely among different properties and locations.

The upper section of the form identifies the property, tells what type of property it is and its assessed value. The accuracy of the assessed value can usually be checked by examining city or county property tax records. During a time of rapid increase in property values, it is to be expected that the appraised value of the property will be lower, perhaps much lower, than its current market value. The term *land* refers to the real estate upon which the commercial building is built. *Improvements* identifies the structures and other real property that are considered to be attached to the land. *Personal property* includes refrigerators, free-standing stoves, furniture, drapes, and other appliances that are not considered to be real property.

Income and expenses

Gross income refers to the total amount of income that would be obtained if the apartments were completely rented and all rents were paid. But commercial properties are seldom fully rented, and rents sometimes cannot be collected. *Gross operating income* is what remains after these losses.

Operating expenses are the nonfinancial expenses of operating the apartments. They should be self-explanatory. By convention each expense category of this income statement is divided by gross income to provide a relative measure of each cost. Estimates of income and expenses must be made for new properties. Owners of existing properties typically provide the most recent year's income statement to prospective buyers. Taxes and utility expenses can usually be verified by examining receipts. It is much more difficult to check the accuracy of most other expense and income items. Audited income statements may be obtained, or if the property is owned by an individual, a copy of this person's federal income tax records may be requested. Schedule E, Part II of the 1040 tax form provides information on total rent and current depreciation expenses. Other rental property expenses are itemized in Part III of this schedule. The purchaser must be willing to expend some effort in determining the accuracy and reasonableness of the information presented by the seller. Comparing income and expense percentages against those derived from similar properties is a good procedure. Hiring an independent appraiser or accountant to examine such information is also useful. Lending officers of financial institutions which specialize in financing real property investments may also be consulted.

The need for accurate data is obvious: *Net operating income* represents the income from the investment before financing payments and depreciation. Net operating income (NOI) when compared to the cost of the property, provides a widely used measure of the gross profitability of the investment. In this example the rate of operating income on list price is

$$\frac{\text{NOI}}{\text{List price}} = \text{Rate of return}$$

$$\frac{\$12,450}{\$200,000} = .062 \text{ or } 6.2\%.$$

A similar ratio of *gross operating income* to market price is also calculated. These ratios are often used by appraisers and lenders. This is dealt with more fully when appraisal of real property is discussed.

Financing and depreciation charges

Financing and depreciation are of so much importance to most real estate investments that by convention they are handled separately from operating expenses. To simplify this example straight-line depreciation is assumed, but in many situations investors take the most rapid depreciation possible to lower profits during early years of ownership. A three-year loan repayment schedule is presented as Figure 12–4. It assumes that the balance of the original 25-year, 7.5 percent loan can be assumed by the purchaser ($89,675), and that an additional loan may be obtained at 9 percent to provide total financing of $140,-000. The original loan has 19 more years to run before it is paid off; the second loan will also have a 19-year maturity. Since straight-line de-

FIGURE 12–4
Financing schedule for the Outflow Apartments

Existing financing:	Principal amount	Term	Annual payment	Interest rate	Final payment
1st loan	$100,000	25 years	$8,868	7½%	—
Proposed financing:					
1st loan	$ 89,675	19 years	$8,868	7½%	—
2nd loan	50,325	19 years	5,537	9	—

Repayment schedule, all loans:				
Year	Interest paid	Principal paid	Total payment	Principal remaining
1	$11,137	$3,268	$14,405	$136,732
2	10,866	3,539	14,405	133,193
3	10,573	3,832	14,405	129,361

preciation is assumed, no separate schedule is necessary. This charge will remain constant at $5,456 over the next three years.

Returning to the income analysis form one sees how financing costs are deducted from net operating income to produce the *gross spendable income* measure. Adding the yearly principal repayment on loans to gross spendable income produces *gross equity income*. Subtracting yearly depreciation costs from this figure indicates a loss of $4,143 for the first year this investment is held. Gross spendable and gross equity income are often divided by the amount of investor's equity to compare returns of each type to the equity investment.

In this example both gross spendable income and taxable income are negative. This is not an unusual situation, as many commercial properties of this type currently produce losses on a current year basis. However, if tax advantages and market price appreciation are great enough, the investments may be profitable in the long run.

Outflow Apartments' loss acts to reduce the owner's taxable income by $4,143. If the owner were in the marginal 40 percent income tax bracket, taxes would be lowered by

$$.40 \times \$4,143 = \$1,657.$$

This amount is often called a *tax saving*. Deducting this amount from the book loss shown on the income analysis form results in an after-tax cost of only $2,485.

$$\$4,143 - \$1,657 = \$2,486$$

The investment still produces a loss to be sure, but it is lower when calculated this way.

Many real property investors are primarily interested in the yearly after-tax *cash* returns (or losses) from their investments. These are traditionally calculated by using the format below. Amounts from Figure 12–3 have been rearranged to show the *after-tax cash cost* of holding Outflow Apartments.

Net operating income	$12,450
Less: Financing payments	14,405
= Gross spendable income	− 1,955
Less: Income tax	1,657
= Net spendable (cash)	−$ 298

The net spendable amount is usually divided by the equity invested to produce a ratio known in real estate as the *cash on cash return*. It is, of course, negative in this example.

So far Outflow Apartments appears to be a poorer investment than almost anything one could imagine. But this is because we have not considered market price appreciation. In recent years practically all real property prices have risen dramatically. Many persons expect price rises to continue, at least so long as inflation rates are high. These people look to increasing market prices for their profits. They are quite willing to hold property that just breaks even on a cash basis or even runs a cash loss, hoping to take their profits all at once when the property is sold.

The appendix to this chapter contains a more detailed analysis of real property investment using internal rate of return. This analysis takes price rises into consideration and shows that Outflow Apartments may be a profitable investment indeed—under the assumption of rising market prices.

However, with little resort to analytical techniques we can see that Outflow Apartments would be a quite profitable investment if its value were to increase by 10 percent per year. It would then be worth $220,-000 in one year, $242,000 in two, $266,200 in three, and $322,102 in five. Since the investor has never had much more than $60,000 of equity in the apartment, very large profits on equity invested would be created if prices rose at this rate. It is the hope of continued market price increases that causes much real property to be sold at what seem to be unjustifiably high prices. If market prices do not rise, of course, a great many investors will find that the purchase of commercial real estate can be hazardous to their financial health.

APPRAISAL OF REAL PROPERTY

Appraisal may be defined as the act of creating an estimate or opinion of the value of a property as of a specific date. The logic and procedure of a property appraisal closely follows that of assigning an intrinsic value to a security. Anyone can make an appraisal, and of course each buyer and seller does just this when deciding how much to charge or pay for a property.

Appraisal of real property is often a very formalized procedure, performed by an independent party—usually a real estate broker or professional appraiser. A third-party appraisal is often required by lenders or insurers before they will loan against property or insure it. All real property is appraised periodically by the taxing authority which levies taxes against it. A thorough appraisal will be in writing and will normally follow a format set by the American Institute of Real Estate Appraisers. For most properties this type appraisal uses three different methods of arriving at an estimate of value: the income approach, the cost approach, and the market data approach. They seldom ever produce identical results, although each is a logical method of appraising value.

Appraisal techniques

The *income approach to value* most closely resembles the valuation techniques used earlier to determine the intrinsic values of securities. This technique usually involves two steps. First one calculates future expected net income from the property and the timing, by years, of this income. Next, these income flows are discounted at a rate of interest to produce a present value estimate of the expected income flows. The difficulties of this type analysis are obvious: Neither the future income flows nor the true discount rate can be known with accuracy. In practice, the discount rate is the rate that could be earned on investments having similar characteristics—risk, liquidity, taxability, and so on. Simply divide net operating income by this rate to provide a capitalized value of the operating income. By using a 10 percent rate (a widely used figure) and the NOI of $12,450 from Figure 12–3 we could value Outflow Apartments as follows:

$$\text{Value based upon capitalized NOI} = \frac{\text{NOI}}{\text{Capitalization rate}}$$

$$= \frac{\$12,450}{.10}$$

$$= \$124,500.$$

Another valuation method which follows a similar logic is the *net income multiplier* (NIM). To use this rule-of-thumb technique it is necessary to know recent prices and net incomes of properties similar to the one being appraised. Net income is defined as gross rents less operating expenses; financing costs and taxes are not calculated. The market price of a property is divided by its annual net income, producing the NIM for that particular property, or for a group of similar properties. Multiplying the yearly net income by an appropriate NIM produces an amount which should approximate the market value of the property. A NIM of 10 would produce a value of $124,500 for Outflow Apartments. A NIM of 10 is equivalent to a capitalization rate of .10.

Another common valuation technique uses the *gross income multiplier* (GIM). It is used in precisely the same way as the NIM. However, the GIM is always smaller than the NIM to reflect the fact that a larger amount, gross operating income, is being multiplied to arrive at an estimate of value.

Other more detailed methods of income analysis estimate income on a year-by-year basis over the expected life or ownership period of a property. The sale price of the property is included as income in the final year of ownership. Income may be calculated on an after-tax basis. In this case yearly after-tax inflows and outflows would be discounted at the capitalization rate to arrive at a present value for the future income from the property. This value is seen as the maximum amount that can be paid for the property and have it yield the capitalization (discount) rate. From a theoretical standpoint this is by far the best method. It is not so widely used as either of those described above because the mechanics of the discounting process are somewhat difficult and many persons just do not understand the logic of this method. An example of this approach appears in the appendix at the end of this chapter. The income approach to value finds widest use when appraising commercial properties.

The *cost approach to value* attempts to value property on the basis of what it would cost to recreate the property in its present state. The usual method is to calculate the cost of a new structure of equal size, style, construction, and so on, and to then deduct from this cost the proportion of the existing property that has been depreciated or used up. The current market value of the land is added to this amount. This appraisal technique is widely used to value properties that have no measurable income—churches, lodges, public buildings, and single-family residences to a lesser extent.

The *market data approach* uses recent sale prices of properties of similar location, size, construction, and other features to provide an estimated value of the property being appraised. In an area where there are many similar properties that are actively traded, this method provides excellent results. Its widest use is in the appraisal of single-family homes, but it is also used to value building lots, raw land, duplexes, and other small-sized commercial properties. Returning to our earlier example, if apartment houses of similar size, age, location, and construction were selling for about $17,000 per rental unit, the market value of Outflow Apartments could be determined by multiplying this amount by the 10 units in the property. In this case the market data approach would indicate an appraised value of $170,000.

In a standard property appraisal each type appraisal would be performed, if data were available to do so. The appraiser would then identify one of the methods as being more relevant or important. For income property, the income approach is the most widely followed appraisal method by far.

Appraisal is an art, not a science. Different appraisers may use the same information and appraisal techniques and arrive at different values. Buyers and sellers do the same thing: An asking price of $200,-000 for Outflow Apartments might seem extremely high to one potential buyer who looks only at the current financial figures. Another investor might believe that rents could be increased and costs lowered with good management, or that property prices will rise rapidly. Under these assumptions $200,000 may be a realistic price.

INDIRECT REAL ESTATE INVESTMENTS

Many real estate investments are of such size and complexity that few investors would have the talents necessary to manage or develop these properties even if they had the capital to buy them. This is particularly true of large-scale developments such as shopping centers, industrial parks, marinas, large apartment houses, and recreation areas. For most persons investment in such enterprises must be through one of the following means.

Real estate syndicates

A *syndicate* is a group of two or more persons formed for some specific purpose. Syndication of real estate investment projects achieved popularity in the 1950s and has remained popular through the years. The syndicate may be organized as a corporation or trust, or more commonly as a limited partnership. Members of the syndicate buy shares in the organization and participate on a proportional basis in the profits, if any, from the syndicate. Capital losses are generally limited to the purchase price of the shares.

Syndication provides professional management and limited liability for its members. If the syndicate owns several different properties, some diversification may also be obtained. But the main reason for the formation of most real estate syndicates has been the considerable tax advantages offered. A common arrangement is for a syndicate to be formed to develop and/or manage a large-scale real estate investment. High financial leverage is used to maximize the return to equity owners; accelerated depreciation methods are then used to shelter this income. In many cases the syndicate generates no taxable income or a tax loss until the property is sold. At this time the gains are classified as long-term capital gains and are taxed at lower than ordinary rates. Recent changes in the tax law have lowered the syndicate's potential to shelter income from taxation, but many such ventures are formed each year. Although there are exceptions to every statement, most real estate syndications are too risky for the average small investor. For this person, the potential tax advantages are not great enough to overcome the potential risks.

Real estate investment trusts

REITs, as they have come to be called, are companies formed to invest in the real estate industry. Some of these companies specialize in the financing of short-term construction contracts. Others emphasize the purchase of long-term mortgages, and still others take equity positions in real estate projects. The intent of all these companies is the same. They seek to obtain funds from shareholders and lenders at rates that are lower than the returns from their real estate investments. Profits, often very high profits, may result from this arrangement. During the credit crunch of 1969–70 the number of REITs grew rapidly because these companies were able to obtain financing for the rapidly expanding real estate construction industry at rates which provided large profits.

Times have changed, however. Extremely tight credit, overbuilding, lowered construction activity, and the failure of several large construction and development companies caused many of the REITs to experience extreme financial difficulties. This and the general stock market declines of 1973–74 and 1977 brought share prices of practically all REITs to very low levels. Some REITs have been reorganized as business trusts—a legal form of organization which allows greater management flexibility—in an effort to attain financial solvency. Table 12–2 presents pertinent investment data for 14 of the largest real estate investment companies. All of these stocks are selling below their all-time highs—as are most of the other 200 or so smaller companies of this type. The REIT concept is a logical one. If construction activity increases and mortgage funds are available on reasonable terms, many REITs can be expected to resume their profitability and investor appeal. At this time, however, all but the most sound companies must be considered speculations.

TABLE 12–2
Real estate investment trusts and business trusts

Name	Market	1977 assets in millions ($)	All-time high price ($)	Closing price ($) 2/16/79
Equitable Life Mtge............	NYSE	394	35¼	17¾
Connecticut Genl. Mtge.	NYSE	324	36¼	18¼
Chase Manhattan Mtge.......	NYSE	299	70	⅞
B. F. Saul	NYSE	291	28⅞	7½
General Growth Properties..	NYSE	275	27¾	27⅜
Northwestern Mutual Life Mtge............................	NYSE	245	29½	9⅞
Loomis and Nettleton Mtge..	NYSE	224	53¼	16⅞
Wells Fargo Mtge. and Equity	NYSE	212	26	12⅛
Bank America Realty Investments	OTC	210	32⅞	12⅜
Diversified Mtge.	NYSE	207	32¾	3¾
Continental Ill. Realty	NYSE	204	40⅝	3¾
Continental Ill. Properties ...	NYSE	197	28⅝	16¼
Massachusetts Mutual Mtge.	NYSE	197	33¼	13¾
Bay Colony Prop.	NYSE	187	30⅝	3¾

Source: Howard Rudnitsky, "Speculating in White Elephants, " *Forbes,* vol. 120, no. 11, Dec. 1, 1977, pp. 84–86, and various issues of *The Wall Street Journal.*

Investing in mortgages

Mortgages and other debt contracts are commonly purchased by the more well-to-do members of most communities. Often the purchaser of a mortgage (this person may originate the contract or purchase an outstanding one) takes on some sort of risk that the financial institutions which ordinarily provide mortgage financing refuse to accept. Perhaps the mortgage is on a property for which there is no ready market. Maybe the property's title is not completely legally clear. Possibly the title is not insurable. At any rate, many persons purchase these mortgages. Such investments may provide relatively high rates of return because of their special risk characteristics.[10]

Most financial institutions will not make loans that are secured by junior mortgages. Lending against second and third mortgages is therefore left mainly to individuals. Such debt contracts are more risky than first mortgages because of their junior legal status, but they pay higher interest yields. Many junior mortgages have very low financial risk. Rising property values have in many cases increased the collateral value of the pledged property to the point where sale of the property would provide funds to repay all debt contracts issued against it. Figure 12-1 shows the amount of equity in single-family homes that might provide collateral. Increased earnings of commercial property may easily cover additional mortgage payments. Each situation must be evaluated on its own merits, but junior mortgages are often fairly safe, high-yield investments.

Participation certificates

One type of mortgage investment is nearly free from financial risk. This investment is the *participation certificates* (PCs) sold by the Government National Mortgage Association (GNMA), the Federal Home Loan Mortgage Corporation (FHLMC), and several private organizations. Participation certificates are equity investments in pools of mortgages that have been purchased by these groups. The mortgages are all of the same maturity and coupon interest rate. As interest and principal payments are made, they are collected by the pool manager and passed through to PC holders. The GNMA purchases only VA or FHA insured mortgages. The FHLMC and private groups usually purchase conventional mortgages; these too are insured, but by private insurers. In any event, holders of mortgage PCs are assured that they will receive monthly checks representing their proportionate share of interest and principal repayments even if the underlying mortgages go into default.

Mortgage-backed PCs are traded much like other securities. Prices

---

[10] Yield on mortgages are measured in the same general way that yield to maturity is calculated for bonds in that the cost of the mortgage is related to yearly interest and principal payments. This calculation can be made by modifying the present value formula presented in the appendix to Chapter 7. A simpler but slightly less accurate way is through the use of tables prepared especially to measure mortgage yields. All real estate offices and financial institutions have such tables.

are set by supply and demand but fluctuate in response to changes in long-term interest rates. Purchase amounts for GNMA and FHLMC PCs begin at $25,000, which may appear to be a large amount of money to invest in a single type of investment. However, the investment provides diversification in the sense that it is in a pool of many different mortgages. Yields are based upon the portfolio of mortgages having an assumed average life of 12 years. Experience indicates that the average repayment period is shorter. To the extent that this is true, PC holders will receive a higher than stated return on their investments if they hold them to maturity. An options market in PCs is in operation which provides PC owners with the possibility of hedging, speculating, or otherwise investing in these contracts.

CHARACTERISTICS OF REAL ESTATE INVESTMENTS

There are so many kinds of real estate investments that blanket statements about investment characteristics are not possible. Financial risk varies greatly among these investments and is one of the most important things for potential investors to investigate. Real property equity investments usually provide protection against purchasing power risk. Real property debt investments, with the possible exception of those carrying variable interest rates, provide no protection against purchasing power risk.

Most real property equity investments are long term. Profits from these investments often come in the form of long-term capital gains. Because of this and because of special tax treatment granted to real property owners, there are often tax advantages from holding real property. Real property investments commonly suffer from illiquidity and poor marketability. Because of the difficulties of obtaining financing and the legal requirements associated with sale and ownership of real property, many months may pass before a fairly-priced parcel of property can be sold. Most commercial real property investments make heavy use of financial leverage. This is an advantage when property values and incomes are rising, but it does add additional risk to these investments. Diversification of real property investments is difficult because of the large size of most real estate projects. Real estate investment trusts, GNMA, FHLMC, and private pass-through certificates, and some syndicates offer various levels of diversification.

SUMMARY

Home ownership is the most common real property investment. Over 60 percent of all American families own their homes. The home is the largest investment that most persons ever make. In recent years it has been one of the most profitable.

Home ownership costs may be compared to costs of renting a dwelling to quantify the decision of whether to rent or buy. However, many people will prefer to own property even when it appears to be more costly than renting.

Most homes are financed through long-term mortgages which are *fully amortized. Second mortgages, balloon mortgages, variable rate mortgages, variable payment mortgages,* and *wrap around mortgages* are finding ever wider use as house financing rates increase.

Conventional loans are offered by savings and loan companies, mutual savings banks, and commercial banks. Loans meeting certain tests may be insured by the Federal Housing Administration, the U.S. Veterans Administration, or through certain state veteran loan programs.

Investments in *undeveloped land* are generally speculative in nature. However, they may also be very profitable. Financing of raw land is often difficult because financial institutions typically do not see such property as good loan collateral. Sellers typically provide at least some of the financing for this property. Zoning is often a problem when developing raw land. Proper *timing* and *location* are necessary for the profitable development of this property.

Commercial property is income producing property: office buildings, apartments, and duplexes are examples of such investments. The value of these properties can be determined by several methods. *Net operating income* and *gross operating income multipliers* are commonly used. More sophisticated techniques are based upon present value calculations.

Appraisal is the act of creating an estimate of the value of a property. The most widely used types of appraisal are the *income approach,* the *cost approach,* and the *market data approach.* They seldom produce identical appraisal values.

Many properties are too large for individual investors to own or to manage. Such investments may be owned by *syndicates* or *real estate trusts.* Individual investors may purchase an interest in these organizations. Investors may obtain indirect real property investments through *mortgage* or *participation certificate securities.* These debt security investments are generally safe, but provide little protection against purchasing power risk.

APPENDIX

The present value and internal rate of return approach to real property valuation

Many real estate investors use present value and internal rate of return calculations to value commercial property investments. These analyses vary greatly in their complexity. Short-run calculations may be made by hand. More complicated analyses which measure after-tax cash flows and which cover several years usually require a powerful calculator and an understanding of the mathematics of discounting. Computer programs have been created which allow their users to simulate different investment conditions—vacancy rates, rental income, income tax rates, accelerated depreciation schedules, borrowing costs, and so forth. These are complicated analyses indeed.

Central to all levels of analysis is the measurement of the amount of before or after-tax income generated by an investment. These returns are usually calculated on a yearly basis and compared to the amount of equity that has been invested. If present value analysis is being performed, assumed yearly after-tax cash profits and losses are discounted at a known rate to derive an expected present value of the returns from the investment. The discount rate is set by the investor in that it is the annual rate of return that is "expected" or "necessary" to induce the investor to commit funds to the project being analyzed. When the *internal rate of return* approach is followed, the same yearly after-tax profits and/or losses are analyzed. However, they are equated to the cash outlay for the investment in a manner which produces a rate known as the internal rate of return, usually abbreviated IRR.

Analysis of real property is more difficult than for most other investments because tax considerations play such an important role. Noncash expenses, such as depreciation, provide noncash losses which in turn lower income tax liabilities. High financial leverage is used in most real property investments so borrowing costs are extremely important. Most gains are long term, thus qualifying for special income tax treatment. A complete treatment of the tax effects of real property investments is well beyond the scope of this book. A discussion of how present value and internal rate of return analysis may be used to analyze real property investments is not.

Let us return to Outflow Apartments and add several assumptions to the information we already have. These are: the property is to be purchased for $200,000 under the financing terms listed in Figure 12-3. The apartment will be held until the end of the third year when it will be sold through a broker who will receive a commission of 6 percent of the sale price. The value of Outflow Apartments will increase 10 percent per year. Revenue and costs (except for interest payments) will remain constant over the three-year holding period. The owner requires a 12 percent return on the investment. And finally, the owner pays income taxes at a 40 percent rate.

By using the above assumptions and other information on Outflow Apartments, one can calculate that the cash amount received from the sale of the apartment in three years will be about $107,500—this is after the sales commission, after outstanding loans are paid off, and after capital gain taxes. Because the yearly taxable loss from Outflow Apartments acts to lower the owner's total income tax burden, and because one large expense item (depreciation) is not a cash expense, this investment actually produces only a small after-tax loss to the owner each year. These losses are $298 in the first year, $337 in the second, and $449 in the third.

Present value analysis

This technique was first used in the appendix to Chapter 9 to calculate the intrinsic or present value of a common stock. In the Outflow Apartments example, each yearly cash cost and the final after-tax cash amount received are discounted at a 12 percent rate to see how this discounted stream of income compares with the cash cost of the investment. The equation is familiar:

$$\text{Present value} = \frac{-\$298}{(1+.12)^1} + \frac{-\$337}{(1+.12)^2} + \frac{-\$449 + \$107,500}{(1+.12)^3}$$
$$= -\$266 + -\$269 + \$76,197$$
$$= \$75,662.$$

Since the cash investment was only $60,000 (the list price equity from Figure 12-3) and since the expected returns are more than this amount even after being discounted at a 12 percent rate, this investment meets and exceeds the owner's requirements of a 12 percent annual return.

Internal rate of return analysis

This technique is used to calculate the rate of return obtained from the investment. This calculation uses the same information as was used to obtain the net present value, but instead of setting or assuming a discount rate, the following equation is *solved* for this rate.

$$\text{Cash investment} = \frac{\text{Year 1 return}}{(1+r)^1} + \frac{\text{Year 2 return}}{(1+r)^2} + \cdots + \frac{\text{Year n return}}{(1+r)^n}$$

Using data from Outflow Apartments

$$\$60,000 = \frac{-\$298}{(1+r)^1} + \frac{-\$337}{(1+r)^2} + \frac{-\$449 + \$107,500}{(1+r)^3}$$

$$r = .2097 \text{ or about } 21\%.$$

This is the rate of return that would be generated from this investment if one assumed that all income from the project could be immediately reinvested in the project or in another one having the same yield. Calculating this rate is not easy when one does not have access to a calculator which provides the solution directly. To obtain a solution "the hard way," a rate r must be assumed and the yearly cash flows discounted by this rate. The rate is changed until the discounted cash flows are about equal to the cash outlay.

PROBLEMS

1. A piece of commercial property has gross rentals of $50,000, and operating expenses of $18,000 per year. Depreciation charges are $9,000 per year and financing charges are $22,000. What is the net operating income capitalization rate if the property is purchased for $420,000?

2. Assume the same conditions as prevail in the first problem. What should the property value be if one uses a net income multiplier of 14? What would be the value if a gross income multiplier of 8 were used?

3. An apartment building is being considered for investment. Its gross operating income is $75,000, its net operating income is $50,000, depreciation charges are $22,000, yearly mortgage interest payments are $19,-500, and yearly mortgage principal repayments are $8,600. The owner calculates that $5,400 of taxes on the profits from this investment must be paid. What is the after-tax *cash benefit* or *cost* from this investment?

4. Obtain the conventional home mortgage rates in effect in your area from a commercial bank, a savings and loan company, and a savings bank (if these institutions operate in your vicinity). Compare these rates and terms (down payment, length of financing, maximum amount available, etc.) with the national averages presented in a recent copy of the *Federal Home Loan Bank Board Journal*, the *Federal Reserve Bulletin*, or any other appropriate source. Are there differences in the financing terms? If so why?

QUESTIONS

1. What is a Government National Mortgage Association "PC." What are the investment characteristics—financial risk, marketability, purchasing power risk, and so on—of this form of investment?
2. What is a Real Estate Investment Trust? What are the investment characteristics of this type investment?
3. "Ownership of a home is one of the best investments that one can make." Comment on this statement paying particular attention to the investment characteristics of the average home.
4. What are the investment characteristics associated with purchase and sale of raw land?
5. What is the "cash return" from a commercial real property investment? How is it calculated?
6. What are second mortgages? What are their usual investment and legal characteristics?
7. When comparing renting versus buying a dwelling, what are the most important considerations? What factor would be most important to someone attempting to logically analyze the merits of both courses of action?
8. What is a *fully amortized* loan? A *balloon* loan?
9. What is a *variable-rate mortgage*? What advantages and disadvantages might such a contract offer borrowers?
10. What is the Federal Home Administration? What services does this organization perform for homeowners?
11. In appraisal theory one often hears the term, "highest and best use." What does this term mean, and what is its significance for real property investors?

SELECTED READINGS

Beaton, William R. and Robertson, Terry. *Real Estate Investment*. 2nd ed. Englewood Cliffs, N.J.: Prentice-Hall, 1975.

Hoagland, Henry E.; Stone, Leo D.; and Brueggeman, William B. *Real Estate Finance*. 7th ed. Homewood, Ill.: Richard D. Irwin, 1977.

Levine, Mark L. *Real Estate Fundamentals*. St. Paul, Minn.: West Publishing Co., 1976.

Mader, Chris. *The Dow Jones-Irwin Guide to Real Estate Investing.* Homewood, Ill.: Dow Jones-Irwin, Inc., 1975.

Maisel, Sherman J., and Roulac, Stephen E. *Real Estate Investment and Finance*. New York: McGraw-Hill, 1976.

Ring, Alfred A.; Dasso, Jerome; McFall, Douglas. *Fundamentals of Real Estate*. Englewood Cliffs, N.J.: Prentice-Hall, 1977.

The Appraisal of Real Estate. 7th ed. Chicago: American Institute of Real Estate Appraisors, 1978.

Thomas, Danah. "Ginnie Mae's Kid Sister: Private Insured Mortgage Pass-Throughs Score on Wall Street," *Barron's*, November 14, 1977, p. 3ff.

part four

INVESTMENT TIMING

13

Economic analysis and relative value analysis

This chapter presents several methods of using economic data to predict the direction of stock and bond price movements. Such analysis is based upon the assumption that security prices of all types are closely related to economic events. This is certainly logical in the case of common stocks: Rising economic activity makes business more profitable; larger earnings may be reflected in higher stock prices. Reduced economic activity has the opposite effect. For the average company these statements hold true, but changes in economic activity affect different industries and companies within industries in different ways. For example, during the period from the last recession through early 1979 industrial production rose nearly every year. Most industries fared well over this period, but prices of basic metals rose little and some agricultural products posted price declines. During recessions, some industries suffer great losses while others may continue to profit or even to increase profits. These are known as "recession-proof" industries.

Bond prices are controlled almost completely by market interest rates. Increasing rates mean declining bond prices and vice versa. Interest rates are set by a combination of economic conditions and actions of the Federal Reserve System. There is a more consistent relationship between economic activity and bond prices than there is between economic activity and stock prices. Several types of economic analysis are examined in the first part of this chapter.

The second part of the chapter is given to a discussion of *relative value*. The underlying assumption here is that there is some normal or average value around which stock prices and interest rates fluctuate. Higher than normal values will correct downward, and lower than normal values will eventually correct upward. This sort of analysis is valuable because it allows investors to examine current prices in historical terms, thus providing perspective to overcome a natural tendency toward overpessimism and overoptimism.

BUSINESS CYCLE ANALYSIS

The term *business cycle* refers to the periodic major swings in the level of business activity. This topic is studied intensely by many public and private economic research organizations. Thousands of pages of economic data relating to the business cycle are generated each month by these groups.[1]

The Federal Reserve Board's Index of Industrial Production measures the relative level of the total volume of physical production in the United States. The index is divided into several subindexes of production, any of which might be used in certain situations, but the composite index is usually used as the measure of total economic activity. Figure 13–1 compares the Standard & Poor's Industrial Index to the FRB Index of Industrial Production. The dotted lines identify times when the industrial production index began a decline which lasted for an extended period. It is obvious that there is a strong relationship between declines in economic activity and declines in stock prices. Generally, stock prices have decreased several months before a reduction in industrial production. Likewise, stock prices have started to rise before industrial production turned around.

While this sequence has not been followed throughout every business cycle, it occurs often enough that stock prices are identified as one of the more consistent of the 12 *leading economic indicators* compiled on a continuous basis by the National Bureau of Economic Research (NBER). A convenient source of data on all economic indicators—leading, coincident, and lagging—is the monthly *Business Conditions Digest* published by the U.S. Department of Commerce.

---

[1] The Federal Reserve Board of Governors provides much economic information in its monthly *Federal Reserve Bulletin*. The National Bureau of Economic Research is engaged in continuous research on the general topic of business cycles. Much information is produced by this group. Practically all large commercial banks provide monthly economic reports, as do many brokerage houses and other financial institutions. *Monetary Trends,* a monthly publication of the Federal Reserve Bank of St. Louis is an especially good source of money supply information.

FIGURE 13–1
The Standard & Poor's Industrial Index and the FRB Index of Industrial Production

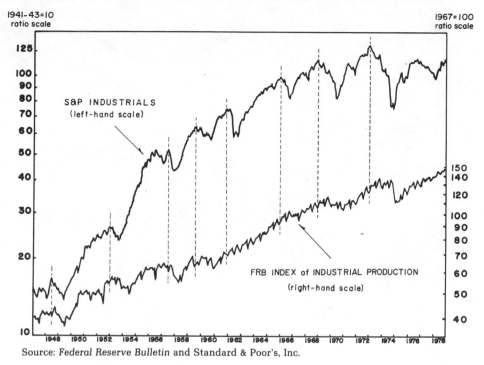

Source: *Federal Reserve Bulletin* and Standard & Poor's, Inc.

Figure 13–2 is an illustration from this publication showing six of these twelve leading indicators. Those omitted are average work week of production workers, layoff rate in manufacturing, new orders for consumer goods and materials, vendor performance, new business formations, and orders for plant and equipment. The darkened areas indicate recession periods. Two things are obvious: All the leading indicators do not decline at the same time. Some of the indicators give false readings. Because of these failings the NBER and most other economists prefer to rely upon a combination of leading indicators to predict business cycle changes. This is called a *diffusion index*. It measures what proportion of the leading indicators are predicting a business downturn or upturn at any given time. The larger the number of indicators predicting the same event the more certain and the sooner the event is expected to occur.

FIGURE 13–2
Cyclical indicators

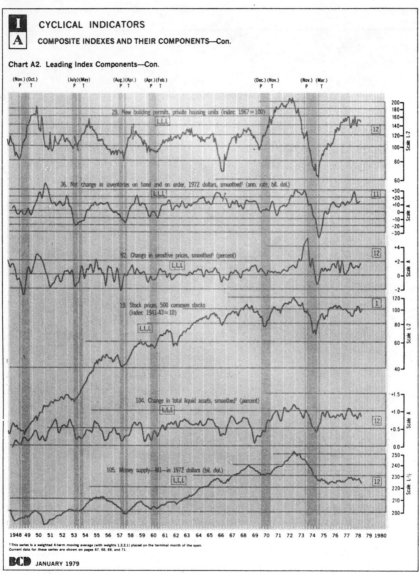

Source: *Business Conditions Digest*, Washington, D.C.: U.S. Department of Commerce, January 1979, p. 13.

At this point one might logically observe that we are not as interested in predicting business activity as in predicting stock prices. And since stock price movements usually precede changes in business activity this is clearly a case of having the cart before the horse. How can such economic data be useful to investors?

First of all, stock prices do not usually decline greatly unless a majority of the other leading indicators are declining. Sinking stock prices, with few other leading indicators declining, may be interpreted as a short-run movement. A good opportunity to buy perhaps. The same sort of logic would be applied to a situation of rising stock prices. If the other leading indicators aren't rising with stock prices, one should be cautious. Stock prices may soon falter.

Sometimes the leading indicators precede stock prices and strongly predict a rise or decline in economic activity. This creates a situation where investors may act as if stock prices will soon follow the other leading indicators. They may buy or sell securities as appropriate.

Coincident economic indicators are those which rise and fall at the same time as business activity. These four economic series are used by stock market analysts to confirm what the leading indicators predict.[2] A diffusion index of coincident indicators may be used as a gauge of the relative strength of economic activity at any point in time.

Lagging indicators do not have a great deal of value for stock market analysts. These economic series, as the name implies, follow economic activity. They confirm that the bottom and top of a business cycle were reached at a certain time, but they have little value as predictors of stock prices.

Interest rate movements

Interest rates are also related to economic conditions. Figure 13–3 graphs Aaa bond yields and industrial production from 1952 through 1978. Earlier years are not included in this study because interest rates were closely controlled by monetary authorities from the 1940s until 1952 and did not reflect economic conditions.

Historically, whenever industrial production slowed or turned down, interest rates usually turned down. The dotted lines of Figure 13–3 identify major downturns in industrial production. During 1953, 1957, 1960, 1966, and 1974 the reduction in industrial production was

---

[2] These series are employees on nonagricultural payrolls, personal income, manufacturing and trade sales, and industrial production.

FIGURE 13–3
Aaa Bond Yields and the FRB Index of Industrial Production

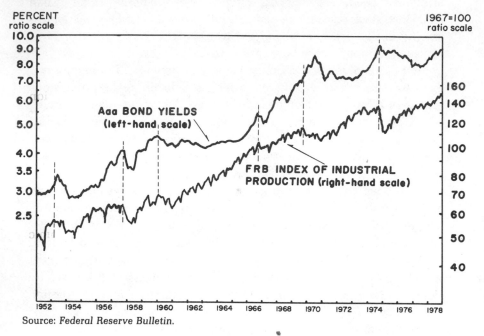

Source: *Federal Reserve Bulletin.*

accompanied by a downturn in interest rates. In 1969 the relationship didn't hold at all well since interest rates continued to climb for nearly a year before turning down. But on average, the index of industrial production was a fairly accurate predictor of interest rate movements. Persons who bought bonds when industrial production declined and sold them when industrial production increased would have had a profit. Persons who held bonds over any long period of time would have suffered losses because the general trend of interest rates has been up, which means that the general trend in bond prices has been down.

Capital market analysis

The capital markets may be defined as the markets for investment capital—bonds, stocks, mortgages, loans, and other such investments. Prices in these markets are set by supply and demand. Over any period a certain amount of capital is needed to finance economic activity.

Amounts needed are determined by the expectations of corporate managers about how much money they need to purchase plant and equipment and to meet other business expenses. Governments also borrow in this market. Their demands are set by the expected expenses of federal, state, and local programs and expected tax revenues. Individuals also require capital for mortgage and other debt contracts.

The supply of funds to meet these needs comes from a variety of sources. Savings of individuals constitute the largest source, but corporations and some government units have surpluses which they may invest in the capital market. Over any period of time, the amount of investment must equal the amount of saving. This is simply a truism which reflects the fact that investment funds can come only from someone else's savings, and savings can only go into investment.[3] If people would rather spend their money than save and invest it, then less money is available to persons wishing to obtain investment funds. The reverse is, of course, equally true.

At the beginning of any period investors have demands for a certain number of dollars of investment funds. If demands exceed the normal amount of savings for the period, investors will bid actively for the limited supply of savings. The result will be a rise in interest rates, and an increase over normal savings amounts because of the higher rates. When demand for investment funds is soft, below amounts normally saved, interest rates decline. Rewards for saving are low, so consumption is increased. Over the full period investment and saving are equal, and interest rates have increased or decreased because of supply and demand pressures.

Investors, particularly those interested in debt securities, are vitally concerned with the relationship between the supply of and demand for capital. They know that if demand for capital is high, or savings are low, that interest rates will rise. And when the opposite conditions prevail, rates will lower.   Government policymakers, businessmen,

---

[3] The assumption here is that all income not consumed somehow finds its way into the capital markets and becomes available to investors. This is perhaps most easily seen by examining what happens when John and Mary Doe earn more than they spend. Assume that they don't buy bonds, stocks, mortgages, or any of the many other investments that would put their savings directly into the capital markets. Instead, the surplus is left in John and Mary's checking account. When this happens the bank simply lends the deposit to someone or some company. The surplus has therefore been invested. Hoarding of money outside the banking system does take place. This is, of course, an example of a "leakage" in the system. However, hoarding is but a very small proportion of savings, and is unimportant to this type of capital market analysis.

and economists also have strong interest in these relationships. They go to great lengths to prepare estimates of how much capital will be required by various sectors of the economy, and how much will be made available by others. Such information is abundant and much in the news, particularly at the beginning of each year when the federal government and most large banks and brokerage houses make their forecasts of the coming year's economy.

As an example of this type of analysis, Figure 13–4 is presented. It is the summary table from the Bankers Trust 1979 Credit and Capital Markets report.[4] Historical and projected amounts are listed for each large economic sector. Most sectors are broken down further in other tables contained in the report. For example, a later table contains more detail on the demand for and supply of mortgage funds; another does the same for bonds. For persons interested primarily in the general direction of future interest rates, the residual figure, Individuals and Others in Figure 13–4 tells the story. The table is constructed by making separate estimates of the demand for and supply of capital over a year. The amounts are never identical. However, by the end of the year the total capital invested must equal the total supplied. Supply and demand are made equal by using the residual sector, Individuals and Others, to "balance the books" so to speak. Considering that this sector is the one that provides most investment capital, this is a logical way to proceed. A large residual indicates that demand for capital exceeds supply and that interest rates will rise to induce more saving to at least partially meet the demand. A decreasing or low absolute residual value indicates that savers will not be under pressure to save; interest rates should decline.

Since the result of this analysis is an estimate of the future direction (up or down) of interest rates and their absolute level, debt security investors make heavy use of this information. But it is also useful to equity investors because of the strong historical relationship between interest rates and stock prices. Interest rates are usually high when economic activity is high, and stock prices are high at the same time for the same reason. Therefore, throughout the typical historical business cycle, when stock prices were high, bond prices were low. Investors could buy equities or debt securities, depending upon what part of

---

[4] Copies of this report are widely available. Most libraries receive the publication as do many brokers and financial institutions. A similar type report is prepared annually by Salomon Brothers, a large investment firm. Federal Reserve flow of funds data may be used for the same purpose.

FIGURE 13–4
Demand and supply of investment funds

SUMMARY OF FINANCING – TOTAL FUNDS							
(In billions of dollars)							
	1973	1974	1975	1976	1977	1978 (est.)	1979 (proj.)
FUNDS RAISED							
Investment funds	121.5	115.8	120.8	151.0	198.8	205.5	209.3
Short-term funds	61.3	57.2	4.6	55.8	86.3	102.3	87.3
U.S. Government and budget agency securities, privately held	−.4	10.2	78.1	59.4	51.5	46.8	47.7
Total uses	182.4	183.2	203.5	266.2	336.6	354.6	344.3
FUNDS SUPPLIED							
Insurance companies and pension funds							
Life insurance companies	15.9	15.2	19.0	26.7	29.4	33.7	36.4
Private noninsured pension funds	9.2	7.9	14.1	12.5	16.5	11.7	19.2
State and local retirement funds	6.7	8.0	10.5	11.7	13.3	15.3	17.7
Fire and casualty insurance companies	5.8	4.4	6.0	12.4	19.3	19.8	21.0
Total	37.6	35.5	49.6	63.4	78.5	80.5	94.3
Thrift institutions							
Savings and loan associations	26.5	19.6	36.4	51.9	65.0	59.5	56.8
Mutual savings banks	4.7	3.4	10.9	12.5	11.7	8.7	8.2
Credit unions	3.6	3.0	5.0	6.3	8.0	10.2	8.2
Total	34.8	26.0	52.3	70.8	84.7	78.4	73.2
Investment companies	1.4	2.0	3.1	1.4	2.9	5.8	3.5
Other financial intermediaries							
Finance companies	8.5	5.5	2.0	8.3	16.2	16.4	13.8
Real estate investment trusts	5.6	.2	−4.9	−3.7	−2.4	−1.3	−.6
Mortgage brokers	2.2	−1.4	1.2	2.7	4.0	−1.0	2.0
Total	16.3	4.3	−1.7	7.3	17.8	14.1	15.2
Commercial banks	78.3	59.3	30.0	64.8	85.4	100.7	85.4
Business							
Business corporations	−2.2	13.4	18.1	17.5	7.3	12.2	11.5
Noncorporate business	1.0	.7	1.0	1.2	1.6	1.7	1.5
Total	−1.2	14.1	19.1	18.7	8.9	13.9	13.0
Government							
U.S. Government	−.3	4.6	6.4	1.2	2.2	1.1	2.5
Nonbudget agencies	7.7	12.8	6.6	6.9	2.8	13.7	11.4
State and local general funds	4.1	3.1	9.2	9.7	14.3	14.9	8.0
Total	11.5	20.5	22.2	17.8	19.3	29.7	21.9
Foreign investors	4.0	12.2	10.4	17.9	42.2	40.2	38.3
Individuals and others	31.4	32.9	23.7	19.9	24.0	38.1	42.5
Total gross sources	214.1	206.8	208.7	282.0	363.7	401.4	387.3
Less: Funds raised by financial intermediaries							
Investment funds	5.7	5.5	4.4	8.2	10.9	8.5	8.6
Short-term funds	10.1	4.5	−.9	5.6	10.2	13.8	13.4
Nonbudget agency securities, privately held	15.9	13.6	1.8	2.0	6.0	24.5	21.0
Total	31.7	23.6	5.2	15.8	27.1	46.8	43.0
Total net sources	182.4	183.2	203.5	266.2	336.6	354.6	344.3

Source: *Credit and Capital Markets, 1979*, New York: Bankers Trust Company, February 1, 1979, Table T1.

the business cycle the economy was in, and obtain "guaranteed" capital gain profits!

Unfortunately, this historical relationship has not held in recent years. We have seen high interest rates and low stock prices at the same time, and in economic downturns interest rates have not declined to their former levels. Some people blame the recent high levels of inflation for these changed relationships. Others claim the Federal Reserve System and its money management policies are responsible. At any rate, the historical reverse relationship between stock and bond prices can no longer be trusted. Some market analysts have abandoned the relationship entirely and see stock prices as being controlled more by Federal Reserve monetary policy than other factors. These theories are examined in the next section.

The analysis of capital flows remains a useful tool for forecasting interest rates and economic activity. Such information may be used along with that obtained from business cycle analysis to refine the projections.

MONETARY THEORIES OF STOCK PRICES

In recent years there has been an increasing acceptance of the general theory that monetary policy has a great deal of influence upon stock prices. *Monetary policy* may be defined as the policy of the Federal Reserve System as it relates to the supply of money. This organization has the responsibility for regulating the money supply so that sound banking conditions are maintained and excessive use of credit is prevented. Purposes also include encouragement of full employment and maintenance of stable prices.

The "Fed" has much control over the commercial banking system, and it is through the banks that it implements monetary policy. Commercial banks must keep a certain percent of their deposits as reserves in a Federal Reserve bank.[5] Increasing this percent reduces the banking system's ability to create credit; reducing it has the opposite effect. The Fed may obtain the same result through buying or selling Treasury securities which it owns in huge quantities. Selling these bonds to

---

[5] The Fed has direct control only over banks which are members of the Federal Reserve System. However, nonmember banks are controlled by state banking authorities who generally follow Fed policy so far as reserves are concerned. A very few banks may be totally free of Fed influence, but these are invariably small banks whose actions are unimportant to the enactment of Fed policy.

banks and others uses up money that banks might otherwise have lent out. Buying bonds puts more money into the economy. The Fed may lend money to its member banks who are unable to maintain the required dollar amount of reserves. The *discount rate* charged on these loans determines the cost and amount of loans that are made, and serves to publicly state whether the Fed's policy is toward easier or tighter credit.

The Fed has direct control over margin requirements. When the stock market exhibits an undesirable level of speculative activity, margin requirements are raised to reduce this type of credit. Table 13–1 shows margin requirements in effect for various securities at various times. Some securities are exempt from margin requirements (Treasury and municipal bonds for example). However, when the Fed signals its concern about high speculative activity by raising margin requirements, many lenders demand tougher terms (higher interest or larger collateral) on loans used to buy all types of securities. Margin requirements are thus widely felt throughout the investment community.

TABLE 13–1
Margin requirements
Per cent of market value; effective dates shown.

Type of security on sale	Mar. 11, 1968	June 8, 1968	May 6, 1970	Dec. 6, 1971	Nov. 24, 1972	Jan. 3, 1974
Margin stocks	70	80	65	55	65	50
Convertible bonds	50	60	50	50	50	50
Short sales	70	80	65	55	65	50

Note.—Regulations G, T, and U of the Federal Reserve Board of Governors, prescribed in accordance with the Securities Exchange Act of 1934, limit the amount of credit to purchase and carry margin stocks that may be extended on securities as collateral by prescribing a maximum loan value, which is a specified percentage of the market value of the collateral at the time the credit is extended. Margin requirements are the difference between the market value (100 per cent) and the maximum loan value. The term "margin stocks" is defined in the corresponding regulation.

Regulation G and special margin requirements for bonds convertible into stocks were adopted by the Board of Governors effective Mar. 11, 1968.

Source: *Federal Reserve Bulletin*, Table 1.161, January 1979, p. A 10.

Monetary policy also makes its impact by increasing or decreasing the money supply. The effect is most easily seen in the level of interest rates. When monetary policy is "tight," interest rates are relatively high. A less restrictive policy results in lower rates. Short-term rates are most affected by monetary policy. Because many short-term loans are used to finance stock market activity, it is widely believed that high short-term interest rates act to depress the markets for common stocks.[6]

There are a wide variety of monetary stock market theories, but common to them all is the thought that a tight money supply (high interest rates) reduces stock prices, and a rising money supply is conducive to increasing prices.[7]

As one might imagine, monetary theorists use many more variables than the money supply in making their forecasts of stock prices. Many writers of stock market advisory letters and other market analysts quote money supply figures, amounts of banking reserves, and other measures of credit availability as the basis for their forecasts. They are not uniform in their use of these data, and their predictions are not always accurate. One stock market and business forecasting firm employs ten different measures of credit use and availability to construct what it calls a "monetary thermometer."

> The ten underlying indicators making up the Thermometer fall in four main categories of policy, transactions, liquidity, banking liquidity, and combinations of each. The basic idea is that each of the ten indicators is potentially capable of obtaining 0, 1, 2 or 3 points (demerits) depending on the degree of deterioration in the particular series. The consensus reading can therefore lie between 0 and 30, but in practice has never been above +27. When the reading has moved up to +8 or higher, the Thermometer has consistently given major warning signals of impending trouble in the stock market and business.[8]

Figure 13-5 is a 59-year history of the Monetary Thermometer plotted against the Dow Jones Industrial Average. Whenever the Thermometer registered +8 or above, it indicated worsening stock market and business conditions. As a reading of Figure 13-5 indicates, the prediction has often, but not always, been correct.[9]

---

[6] Buying on margin and selling short both require the creation of short-term loans. Many people borrow against other assets to obtain money to purchase stock. Rising interest rates lower the potential for profits, and reduce people's desire to invest.

[7] The monetarist view of economic activity and stock prices is well-presented and documented in Beryl W. Sprinkel, *Money and Markets: A Monetarist View,* (Homewood, Ill.: Richard D. Irwin, 1971).

[8] *The Bank Credit Analyst,* 21, no. 12 (June 1970), p. 10.

[9] See A. Hamilton Bolton, *Money and Investment Profits* (Homewood, Ill.: Dow Jones-Irwin, 1967) for a fuller explanation of the Thermometer.

FIGURE 13-5
The monetary thermometer and the market

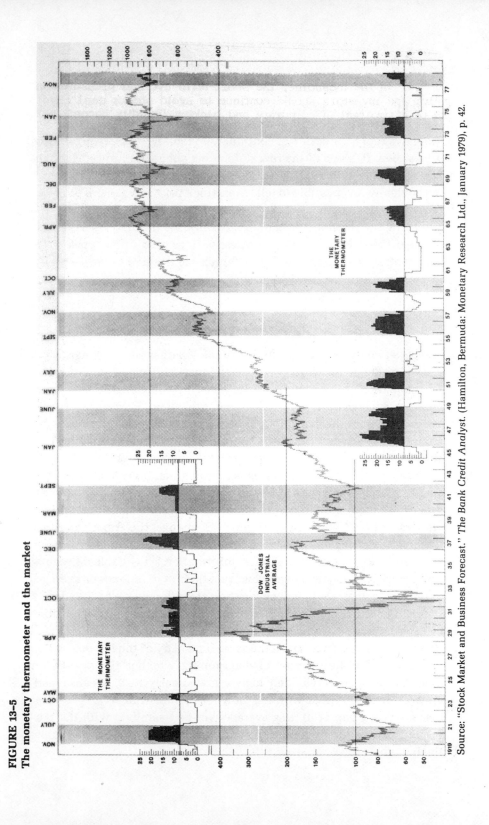

Source: "Stock Market and Business Forecast." *The Bank Credit Analyst.* (Hamilton, Bermuda: Monetary Research Ltd., January 1979), p. 42.

RELATIVE VALUE ANALYSIS

Many years ago a reporter asked the eminent financier J. Pierpont Morgan to predict what the stock market would do in the future. Mr. Morgan's reply, "Stocks will continue to fluctuate," is as true today as it was then. It is one of the few statements about the future which always seems to be true. The following sections of this chapter attempt to show how it is possible to tell when stock prices in general or prices of stocks of companies in specific industries have fluctuated "too much" in one direction or another. Techniques of analysis which are directed toward individual securities, options, and other types of investments appear in later chapters which are devoted to these specific investments.

Market analysis

Market analysis attempts to determine whether security markets in general are relatively high or relatively low. This type of study focuses on the markets for common stocks, bonds, preferred stocks, or commodities such as coal, plywood, wheat, and so on. Different variables are examined in the evaluation of each market, but the question to be answered is always the same: Is the current market for common stocks, bonds, or other securities relatively high or low?

Because this book emphasizes common stock investments, discussion of market analysis will be centered around the markets for these securities. From earlier chapters we know that there are several securities markets: The New York Stock Exchange, the American Stock Exchange, the regional exchanges, and the over-the-counter-market. We also know that much statistical information is available on each of these markets. The exchanges construct their own indexes or averages of security prices, as do independent organizations such as Standard & Poor's, Moody's, Value Line, NASDAQ, and others. The composition of each index is slightly different, but with minor variations they all move in the same direction at the same time. Any of the indexes would be suitable for the purpose of determining whether the market for common stocks was relatively high or low in early 1979. Because readers are already familiar with the Dow Jones Industrial Average (it was discussed in Chapter 4), this average will be examined with the purpose of determining whether the current level of stock prices is relatively high or low.

FIGURE 13–6

Price, earnings, and dividends per share of the Dow Jones Industrial Average

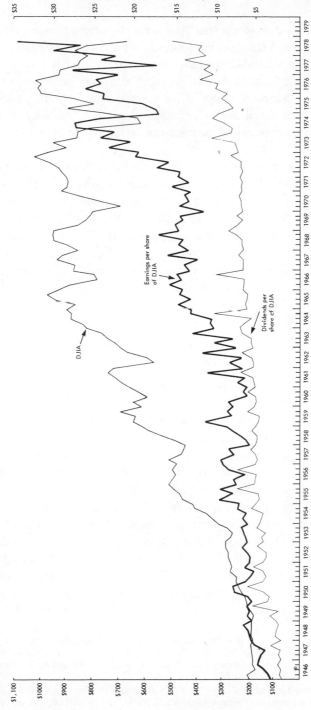

Source: *The Dow Jones Investor's Handbook—1979* (Chicopee, Mass.: Dow Jones Books, 1979), pp. 16–20.

Figure 13-6 presents the DJIA over the past 33 years. One can tell from this graph that market prices were higher in 1978 than they were in 1962. One can also see that prices varied greatly over this period. While this information is interesting and may provide the observer with a rough idea of when this market is relatively high and low, our preference is to not use this or any other stock index by itself to analyze relative conditions because the index only reveals current security prices.[10]

The prices of investments—a single security or a market average—are meaningless figures unless they can be equated to the current and expected returns from owning the investment. For example, at one time a security may sell at $10 and have a current and future expected return of $2 per year. At another time it may sell at $20 and have a current and future expected return of $5 per year. Without making use of the earnings information the investment at $10 appears to be a better buy because its price is lower; in reality it is not. It is a better buy at $20 because earnings, when related to price, are relatively greater.

Security earnings and their effect on security market prices

Chapter 9 emphasized the fact that it is earnings and dividends which provide value for stocks. (Interest payments have the same relationship to bond prices.) There is no question but that over the long run, prices of individual stocks are related to the earnings and dividends expected to accrue to the owners of the securities. The same logical relationship holds for stock indexes and the dividends and earnings of the firms making up the index.

While one might expect the amount of dividends to have the stronger influence upon security prices, a brief examination of Figure 13-6 shows that this is not the case. Of the two earnings-associated measures presented in this illustration, annual dividends are the least closely related to security prices. The graph of quarterly earnings more closely resembles changes in market prices in that when earnings decreased so did the market price index.[11] But even this relationship is

---

[10] Several types of market analysis attempt to use indexes and individual stock prices directly to determine future stock market prices. These methods are commonly grouped together under the heading of Technical Analysis, a topic which is examined in Chapter 14.

[11] In constructing the DJIA and the averages of dividends and earnings, adjustments have been made which attempt to take into account the stock splits

FIGURE 13-7
Dow Jones Industrial Average price–earnings ratios (quarterly data)

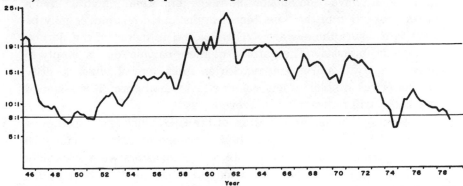

Source: *The Dow Jones Investor's Handbook—1978* (Chicopee, Mass.: Dow Jones Books, 1978), pp. 16–20.

not a very reliable one. Very minor reductions of EPS are often associated with very large declines in security prices.

Figure 13-7 presents the price-earnings (P/E) ratio of the DJIA. This ratio is computed in much the same way as it was for individual securities—by dividing the average price by the annual earnings per share of the securities making up the average. For example, if the average were at $800 and annual earnings were $40, the P/E ratio at that time would be 20:1. These ratios tell us how much investors were willing to pay for the earnings of securities making up the DJIA at different points in time. In the first quarter of 1961 investors paid $676.63 (the price of the average) for annual earnings of $29.54. In the last quarter of 1978 they paid $805 for $112.79 of earnings. In the first example the P/E ratio was 23:1; in the second it was about 7:1. Is it possible to identify either of these ratios as being relatively high or low?

Over the 33 years studied, the DJIA price-earnings ratio has varied between 6.1:1 and 24.2:1. If one assumes that the "normal" P/E ratio of the index lies within a range of values of from 8:1 to 19:1 during the period covered in Figure 13-7, the P/E ratio would have been "normal" about 80 percent of the time. Obviously, if a narrower range of values

---

and dividends which have occurred through the years. These adjustments have resulted in some difficulty in interpreting the DJIA because its price at any time cannot be determined by summing the prices of the 30 stocks making up the average. However, these same adjustments have been made in the dividends and earnings of securities in the average. These measures are directly related to the DJIA and it is logical to equate them to the price averages.

(10:1 to 17:1, for example) were defined as the normal range, the P/E ratios would have been outside the range (abnormally high or low) a larger proportion of the time. More sophisticated techniques may be used to measure the average P/E ratio, and to calculate the normal range more precisely. The purpose of these calculations is simply to provide analysts and investors with an indication of when security market prices are high or low, relative to a stated norm. It is assumed that ratios will return to normal levels.

Assuming that the normal range of the DJIA price-earnings ratio is between 8:1 and 19:1, the ratios that prevailed in 1974 and late 1978 clearly were abnormally low. At this time investors were extremely pessimistic and refused to pay what they had paid in the past for earnings.

A RELATIVE VALUE FORMULA

There are other methods of identifying whether the stock market is relatively high or low. One such technique relates stock prices to three main factors: current earnings, the historical growth rate of stock earnings, and the interest rate on high-grade bonds. This technique was used in Chapter 9 to calculate an intrinsic value for a single stock. It is of equal value when used with stock indexes or averages.[12] The important relationships are presented in the following formula:

$$\text{Value} = \text{Earnings} \times \frac{37.5 + 8.8G}{\text{Aaa bond rate}}$$

where,

Value = Expected (intrinsic) value of the DJIA
Earnings = Current or expected annual earnings of the DJIA
G = Historical growth rate of DJIA earnings
Aaa bond rate = Current interest rate on long-term Aaa rated corporate bonds.

---

[12] Variations of this formula are in common use by securities analysis. A discussion of this particular formula in Benjamin Graham, "The Decade 1965–1974: Its Significance for Financial Analysts," from *The Renaissance of Value* (Charlottesville, Va.: Financial Analysts Research Foundation, 1974), pp. 1–2. A much more detailed discussion of the analysis of security market prices is presented in Benjamin Graham, David L. Dodd, and Sidney Cottle, *Security Analysis: Principles and Techniques,* 4th ed. (New York: McGraw-Hill, 1962).

The numbers 37.5 and 8.8 are constants that were derived through statistical techniques. Their values will not change unless the relationships between value, earnings, growth in earnings, and the Aaa bond interest rate change.

In the first quarter of 1979 annual earnings of the DJIA were $124.43. Growth in earnings over a ten-year period were at a rate of about 6.9 percent. The Aaa bond rate was about 9.5 percent. These figures are entered into the valuation equation, which is solved as follows:

$$\text{Value} = \$124.43 \times \frac{37.5 + 8.8\,(6.9)}{9.5}$$

$$= \$124.43 \times 10.34$$

$$= \$1,286.60$$

The DJIA should have been valued at $1,286.60, based upon this formula, but its actual value was $821. Analysts basing their estimates of intrinsic value either upon the formula presented above or upon the P/E analysis presented earlier would have concluded that in early 1979 stock price averages were well below their intrinsic values and offered investors the chance to buy securities at relatively low prices.

There are many variations of this and the previous type of analysis. Different averages, more sophisticated mathematical techniques, and longer or shorter periods of analysis, are all used for the purpose of measuring relative value. The strength of this type of analysis lies in the ease with which it is understood and performed and the fact that it has given reasonably good answers in the past. The main weakness is that the analysis deals with past relationships. A primary assumption in the P/E analysis, for example, is that if the "normal" P/E ratio in the past were 16:1, this ratio will continue to be normal in the future. The formula type valuation is also based entirely upon historical relationships. It is assumed that the mathematical constants 37.5 and 8.8 will continue to cause the formula to produce correct answers, and that earnings, the growth rate, and the Aaa bond rate continue to be as important in the calculation as they once were. The relationships of all these variables are historical. If some underlying condition changes these relationships, the formula must be altered to record this change or it will produce faulty answers. The analyst really needs to know what P/E ratio will be normal in the future, what the future growth rate will be, and how the variables of the relative value formula will interact in the future. Obviously none of this information is available.

Another weakness is one that is common to the use of indexes and averages. At any time, some stocks in the DJIA will be increasing in price while others are decreasing. The use of an average hides the performance characteristics of the individual stocks that make up the average. It should be remembered that whenever averages such as the Dow Jones, the Standard & Poor's, or others are used as tools of analysis, that they only show very broad trends and relationships.

INDUSTRY ANALYSIS

Investors who call their brokers for information often begin the discussion by asking, "What did the market do today?" Attention may then focus on the price action of industry groups and finally on individual stocks of interest. Such a sequence is quite logical—it begins with the general and moves to the specific. A number of studies have supported this approach.[13] One in particular has found that, on average, price change of market and industry or similar groupings explained about four-fifths of the price changes in common stocks.[14] The belief of a strong industry price influence is shared by most securities research departments. They typically have their analysts become specialists in one or two groups such as chemicals, airlines, paper, and so on.

Industry relative value analysis

A technique used by industry analysts that is identical to the one discussed in the market analysis section involves the P/E ratio of an industry or group of similar companies. The historical pattern of this ratio identifies periods when investors placed high or low values on earnings per share. Subject to the cautions mentioned previously, the P/E ratio is most helpful in gaining a perspective of relative values. Figure 13–8 illustrates this point.

Data plotted are the high and low P/E ratios of the S&P industrials and a sample of firms in the electronics industry, those manufacturing semiconductors and electronic components. Included in this group of companies are AMP, American Micro Systems, Fairchild Camera,

---

[13] Many are summarized in Richard A, Brealey, *An Introduction to Risk and Return from Common Stock* (Cambridge, Mass.: The M.I.T. Press, 1969).

[14] Ibid., pp. 59–61. More recent studies at the brokerage firm of Paine, Webber, Inc. have confirmed this result.

FIGURE 13-8
Range of annual P/E ratios of electronics companies (semiconductors and components) and the Standard & Poor's Industrial Index

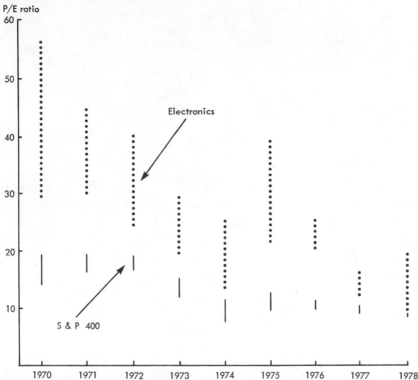

Note: 1978 data for electronics companies is based upon the last 12-months' earnings.
Source: Standard & Poor's *Industry Reports* and Standard & Poor's *Statistical Series*, various issues.

M/A Com, Mostek, Motorola, National Semiconductor, and Texas Instruments.

Notice the wide swings in yearly P/E ratios for this group of young, rapidly growing companies. Investors have been willing to pay more for a dollar of earnings of this group than of the average industrial company. But recent years have seen lower swings in P/E ratios of the group, the effect of a market less given to speculation.

Having the past record available helps an investor to decide whether or not the industry is overpriced or underpriced, relative to the average security. As previously mentioned, P/E data must be carefully interpreted. A low P/E ratio does not always indicate an undervalued situation; it simply calls attention to a possible opportunity.

FIGURE 13–9
Relative strength index of the soft drink industry

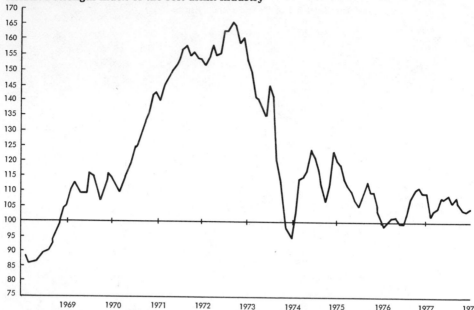

Note: Relative strength index constructed by dividing the S&P Soft Drink Index by the S&P Industrial Index and multiplying by 100.
Source: Standard & Poor's, Inc.

Another measure of relative value may be constructed by relating prices of a given industry to those of the market as a whole. Prices of Standard & Poor's Soft Drink Index are compared to the S & P Industrial Index in Figure 13–9. To do this the soft drink index is divided by the industrial index and the result is multiplied by 100. For example, in January 1969 the soft drink stock index stood at 90.36 and the industrials were 102.0.

$$\frac{90.36}{102.0} \times 100 = 88.6$$

This calculation tells us that at this time beverage stock prices were about 88.6 percent of the industrial index value.

During the years 1971, 1972, and 1973 the soft drink industry was much in favor with investors. High sugar prices in 1973 acted to reduce investor confidence, resulting in a much lower relative value for shares of these companies. Studying these ebbs and flows in investor expectations over time can help give the analyst an idea about the industry's investor appeal. A substantial rise in the ratio should make one cautious about the prospects for continuing relative strength of the industry under examination. A long period of decline in the measure serves to call attention to the industry as perhaps being in an attractive position.

One weakness of the relative strength ratio is that the indicator may be misinterpreted. Suppose the ratio points to an improving industry position relative to the market. This performance could occur during a falling stock market. Relative strength would be shown if the industry fell at a slower rate compared to the market. This would offer little consolation to investors using the relative strength measure, unless one could say they are only *relatively* unhappy.

Another method of determining relative value involves a *cause and effect analysis*. In this activity, factors which create value are identified. The research includes a careful examination of what makes an industry "tick." For example, the financial prospects for a furniture manufacturer can be appraised by studying influences on the demand for home furnishings. These are population by age groups, consumer spending patterns, housing starts, credit usage and availability, and so on. Table 13–2 and Figure 13–10 illustrate the principle of relating value to its basic causes. This type of activity can be highly refined. It constitutes the essence of *fundamental analysis* which has been described previously.

SUMMARY

This chapter showed how security market prices, and to a lesser extent the prices of individual securities, were related to economic events. It also showed how to determine when markets and individual security prices were relatively high or low.

Economic analysis assumes that there is a strong relationship between economic activity and security prices. Historically this has been true: Rising economic activity has often been associated with rising stock prices and vice versa. Most analysts use the Federal Reserve Index of Industrial Production as the measure of economic activity and relate this economic measure to a stock price index.

Interest rates and bond prices are also related to economic activity. Interest rates tend to rise as economic activity increases, and to decline as it falters. But monetary policy plays a large role in the determination of interest rate levels. Most analysts base interest rate forecasts on

TABLE 13-2
Factors influencing demand for home furnishings

| Year | Consumer expenditures | | | | | New residential dwelling units started (thous.) | Sales of existing single-family home (thous.) | End of Period | | | | Consumer confidence index (1969–70 =100) |
| | Total (bil. $) | Durables (mil. $) | % of total expend. | Furn. & hsehld. equip. (mil. $) | % of total expend. | | | *Total installment credit outstanding | | Personal savings | | |
								Total (mil. $)	% of disp. inc.	Total (mil. $)	% of disp. inc.	
P1978	1,340.4	197,500	14.7	77,600	5.8	2,019	3,905	275,640	19.0	76,200	5.3	95.6
1977	1,206.5	178,400	14.8	71,300	5.9	1,987	3,572	230,829	17.7	66,910	5.1	89.7
1976	1,090.2	156,600	14.5	63,900	5.9	1,538	3,002	193,977	16.4	68,042	5.7	86.8
1975	979.1	132,600	13.6	58,000	5.9	1,160	2,450	172,353	15.9	83,648	7.7	69.6
1974	889.6	122,000	13.7	54,900	6.2	1,338	2,272	164,594	16.7	71,653	7.3	63.9
1973	809.9	123,700	15.3	50,700	6.3	2,045	2,334	155,108	17.2	70,324	7.8	87.7
1972	733.0	111,200	15.2	44,800	6.1	2,357	2,252	133,173	17.9	49,370	6.2	94.4
1971	668.2	97,100	14.5	39,400	5.9	2,052	2,018	118,255	17.2	57,336	7.7	75.1
1970	618.8	84,900	13.7	36,700	5.9	1,469	1,612	105,528	16.7	50,574	7.4	81.7
1969	579.7	85,500	14.7	35,000	6.0	1,500	1,594	N.A.	...	35,109	5.6	118.3

* Series has been revised from 1943, effective Dec. 7, 1978. P—Preliminary. N.A.—Not available.
Sources: Department of Commerce, Federal Reserve Board, National Association of Realtors, and The Conference Board. These statistics were tabulated in
The Outlook, "Slower Demand in View" (Standard & Poor's, Inc., 1979), p. H53.

FIGURE 13–10
U.S. population trends

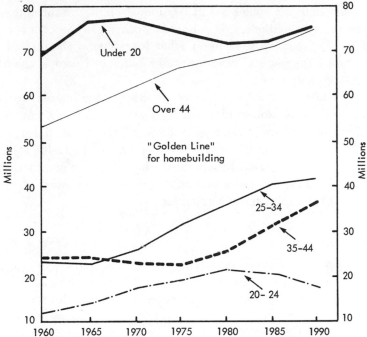

Source: Bureau of the Census and shown in "Building Industry", *Value Line*, May 11, 1979, p. 852.

supply and demand relationships in the capital markets and upon monetary policy actions.

Some persons believe that monetary policy, as much as any other force, controls stock and bond prices. These *monetarists* perform little fundamental or economic analysis, basing investment decisions instead on predicted changes in the money supply and other measures of financial liquidity.

Relative value analysis attempts to identify when the market price for securities, commodities, or other investments is too high or too low. The central concept in this type of analysis is that there is some *normal* (intrinsic) *value* at which an investment should sell. The normal value is based upon many factors—historical investment prices, relationship of stock prices to bond yields, and the relationship of earnings to investment prices, to mention but the most obvious. Market analysis consists of using these relationships to answer the question of whether current prices are relatively high or low, based upon the factors studied.

Industry analysis makes use of techniques similar to those used to analyze security markets and individual securities. The concept of a *normal value* that is based upon what investments should sell for, given certain market and other considerations, is a central theme in this type of analysis.

Cause and effect analysis attempts to identify the factors most important to the profitability of a company and/or industry. For example, there is a strong relationship between the demand for home furnishings and population, consumer spending, and housing starts. If housing starts are predicted to increase, then furniture manufacturers can be expected to sell more products. Profits should increase and so should stock prices of those companies.

PROBLEMS

1. Consult the *Business Conditions Digest* or another source of economic indicator information. On the basis of what you read, forecast common stock prices (direction and level) for the next six months. State all assumptions used.
2. Assume that DJIA earnings are growing at an 8 percent annual rate, that yearly DJIA earnings are $110, that the money supply is growing at a 6 percent rate, and that Aaa corporate bonds yield 8.5 percent. Use this information to calculate a probable intrinsic value for the DJIA.
3. Examine a recent copy of the Bankers Trust study titled *Credit and Capital Markets*. From information contained in this publication determine,
   a. Whether interest rates in general should rise or fall in the next year.
   b. Whether mortgage loan rates should rise or fall in the next year.
   Defend your answer.
4. From *Barron's, The Wall Street Journal,* or other sources, obtain current information about the DJIA (earnings, price, growth in earnings) which will enable you to make an estimate of the current intrinsic value of the DJIA. Is it overvalued or undervalued?

QUESTIONS

1. Historically, common stock prices have led economic upturns and downturns by from three to six months. Is this a logical relationship? Defend your answer.
2. Why do interest rates move more in concert with economic activity than do stock prices?

3. What are the main ways that *monetary policy* is carried out by the Federal Reserve System?
4. What are *margin requirements*? What organization sets them? What purpose do they have?
5. What is the central theme to *monetary theories* of stock prices?
6. What is *relative value* analysis?
7. The relative value formula presented in this chapter bases stock average values upon earnings and growth in earnings of the DJIA and the Aaa bond rate. List and defend your choices of two other variables which you believe are also related to stock prices.
8. What is the difference between *industry* and *market* analysis? When would you use one or the other?
9. What is the *relative strength ratio*? What does it tell the investor?
10. What is *cause and effect analysis*? How does one perform such analysis?

SELECTED READINGS

Amling, Frederick. *Investments: An Introduction to Analysis and Management.* 4th ed. Englewood Cliffs, N.J.: Prentice-Hall, 1978.

Cohen, Jerome B.; Zinbarg, Edward D.; and Zeikel, Arthur. *Investment Analysis and Portfolio Management.* 3rd ed. Homewood, Ill.: Richard D. Irwin, 1977.

Graham, Benjamin. "The Decade 1965–1974; Its Significance for Financial Analysts," *The Renaissance of Value.* Charlottesville, Va.: Financial Analysts Research Foundation, 1974.

Graham, Benjamin; Dodd, David L.; and Cottle, Sidney. *Security Analysis: Principles and Techniques.* 4th ed. New York: McGraw-Hill, 1962.

Hayes, Michael. *The Dow Jones-Irwin Guide to Stock Market Cycles.* Homewood, Ill.: Dow Jones-Irwin, 1977.

Levine, Sumner N., ed. *Financial Analysts Handbook.* Vols. 1 and 2. Homewood, Ill.: Dow Jones-Irwin, 1975.

Sharpe, William F. *Investments.* Englewood Cliffs, N.J.: Prentice-Hall, 1978.

Sprinkel, Beryl W., and Genetski, Robert J. *Winning with Money.* Homewood, Ill.: Dow Jones-Irwin, 1977.

14

Timing of investment decisions

INTRODUCTION

Fundamental analysis uses corporate financial statements and other accounting information to arrive at an intrinsic value for a security. This type of analysis is logical and readily accepted as such by most investors. Most of the earlier chapters have emphasized fundamental analysis in one way or another. However, it is a well-known fact that security markets are irrational: They overreact to good and bad news, and in so doing cause security prices to become temporarily out of line with historical norms. The preceding chapter showed ways to measure how far out of line security prices are at any given time. This chapter moves one step further away from fundamental analysis by taking up the broad topics of technical analysis and formula investment plans.

These topics all relate to the *timing* of security purchases and sales. Since almost all securities are affected by market upturns and downturns, if market turning points could be predicted, one could profit handsomely through correct timing of investment decisions. Buy when prices are low and sell when they are high! Nothing could be simpler—or more profitable. Potential rewards from correct timing decisions are so great that there is a never-ending attempt on the part of the investment community to discover an accurate way of predicting security price changes.

It must be admitted that a completely reliable way of predicting price movements has yet to be devised. No theory or method gives correct answers every time. Nevertheless, all investors should be aware of the most popular theories and their strengths and weaknesses. With some modifications most of the theories and plans are applicable to bond, preferred stock, and common stock investments. Emphasis is placed upon common stocks because it is here that most investor interest is centered.

TECHNICAL ANALYSIS OF MARKET DATA

Technical analysis is a broad general term which refers to practically any sort of analysis that uses information *internal* to the securities markets. Included are security prices, sales volume, trading activities of certain groups of market participants, and many other things. Excluded from the tool kits of most technical analysts are such things as earnings per share, sales data, gross national product levels or practically any information that would be used by the fundamental analyst.

Chart patterns as predictive devices

Basing investment decisions on stock chart patterns is not new. Most of the present theories are modifications of the work of Charles Dow, the creator of the Dow Jones Stock Averages and the organizer of the Dow Jones financial news service. Other investors probably used methods similar to his, but because he wrote down his theories in editorials which appeared in *The Wall Street Journal* during the late 1800s he is usually identified as the father of stock charting.

Dow Theory attempts to identify *trends* in stock prices and changes in these trends. The theory uses market statistics of stock averages and individual stocks. All data used in the analysis are internal to the market—the volume and price changes of securities. In their strictest form, none of the chart-based theories pays any attention whatsoever to the intrinsic value of a share or share price averages. Justification for this approach is that all the data that go into intrinsic value calculations— earnings, dividends, growth, and so on—are taken from historical accounting records which are meaningless so far as current decisions are concerned. The market looks ahead and discounts all future events.

> In brief, the going price as established by the market itself comprehends all the fundamental information which the statistical analyst can hope to learn (plus some which is perhaps secret from him, known

FIGURE 14–1
Dow Theory primary and secondary trends

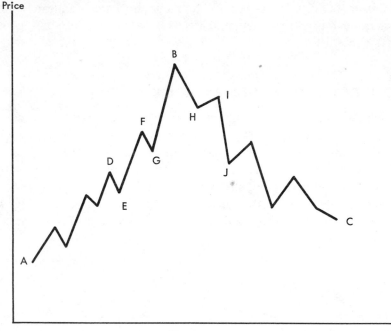

to only a few insiders) and much else besides of equal or even greater importance.[1]

The theory further states that stock prices—individual companies and stock indexes—move in trends which continue until something happens which changes the supply and demand relationships which determine prices. *Major* or *primary* trends are the extensive market movements of long duration which are usually called bull or bear markets.

From A to B and B to C represent primary trends in Figure 14–1. *Secondary trends* are movements in the opposite direction of the primary trend. These are pictured as the reversals that took place from D to E, F to G, H to I, and all others. They have shorter duration and amplitude than the primary trend but are larger and longer than *minor*

[1] Robert D. Edwards and John Magee, *Technical Analysis of Stock Trends,* 5th ed. (Springfield, Mass.: John Magee, 1966), p. 6.

trends, which closely resemble weekly or daily price fluctuations. No minor trends are pictured in Figure 14-1.

Dow theorists do not consider that a primary trend has ended until a secondary trend has exceeded the last secondary movement of a primary trend. From Figure 14-1 it is obvious that the primary trend reversed at B. However, until J was reached the price trend was still considered upward. Point H did not signal a reversal because the price level at H did not "penetrate" (go below) the price set at G, the last secondary reaction that took place prior to point B. Further confirmation of a trend reversal is sought in the Dow Jones Transportation Averages. These and the industrials must move in the same direction at the same time. Without this confirmation no change can occur in a major trend—so states the theory.

This basic theory has been modified by different analysts to make it more modern and/or reliable. Emphasis now seems placed upon the charting of individual stocks rather than averages, and several charting systems have extended the original Dow Theory goal of *identifying trends* to that of *predicting changes* in trends and *predicting future prices* of individual stocks and stock averages. The fact that major turning points are not identified until prices have moved strongly in the opposite direction is a weakness of this type analysis.

The purpose of this book is not to make readers into chart analysts. In fact, any seeming endorsement of charting is highly qualified because the chart patterns are difficult to interpret and sometimes give misleading information. Nevertheless, a significant proportion of the investment community follows the charts and reacts to signals of "trendline breakthroughs," "head and shoulders patterns," "support and resistance areas," and other formations (real or imagined) that the charts trace. All investors should be familiar enough with stock charts to understand how they will affect the investment decisions of those who follow them.

Constructing a bar chart.   *Bar charts* all resemble the graphs of the Dow Jones averages—the industrials, rails, and utilities—which are published daily in *The Wall Street Journal.* Such stock averages were, in fact, some of the earliest bar charts, the ones prepared by Charles Dow. Prices may be entered into a bar chart on a daily, weekly, monthly, hourly, or practically any other regular time period. Data usually plotted are the high, low, and closing price for the period as well as the volume of shares traded. These charts may record prices of stock averages, industry averages, groups of stocks, or individual companies. Price is usually plotted on the "Y" axis (the one that is vertical); time and volume are usually plotted on the horizontal "X" axis. A chart, Figure 14–2, has been prepared from the trading data for a single stock listed in Table 14–1.

TABLE 14–1
Hypothetical trading data

Date	High	Low	Close	Daily volume
May 1	$37	$36	$36¼	1,000
2	36⅞	36	36¼	1,200
3	36¾	35⅝	36	800
4	36¼	35⅜	35½	1,500
5	36⅞	36	36¾	600

The vertical line at the top left of Figure 14–2 indicates that the stock of this company on May 1 was sold as high as $37 and as low as $36; it closed at $36¼. The closing price is indicated by the "tic" on the vertical line. The lower portion of the graph records the daily volume.

This chart cannot be used to predict any event because it covers only a short time period. After a stock has been plotted for a longer duration it may begin to trace patterns which are interpreted to mean certain things by the chart analysts. As can probably be imagined, the patterns traced by an individual company or a stock average may take many different shapes. Furthermore, the same data may generate different chart patterns, depending upon whether the chart is plotted on a daily, weekly, monthly, or other time basis. Charts may be kept for a long period of time before they indicate anything of importance. Interpretation of some of the more common bar chart patterns can wait until the other leading method of constructing stock price charts has been examined.

Constructing a point and figure chart.   *Point and figure charts* are based upon the same price data as the bar chart, but time and trading volume are not used. Stock price indexes may be plotted, but individual securities are more commonly analyzed this way. These charts are made on paper that is marked off into square blocks. The left-hand side of the paper contains a scale which indicates the closing prices of a single stock or stock index. Each square has a given dollar value which varies according to the market price of whatever is being plotted. The squares are usually valued at $2 each for stocks trading at over $100 and $1 each for those trading below $100 and above $20.

FIGURE 14–2
Bar chart of price and volume data

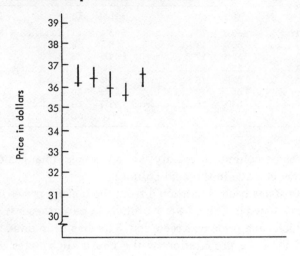

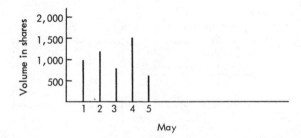

Units are valued at ½ or ¼ of a point for stocks having values of $20 or less.

Technical analysts (often called chartists because of their dependence upon this technique) hope to identify supply and demand forces from the chart patterns. To chart a stock under the point and figure method, a mark or symbol is placed in a square on the chart to indicate that the stock has closed at a certain price or has attained a certain price during the trading period. Fractions of dollars are usually ignored. No mark is placed on the chart until the closing price has moved at least one complete unit up or down.

By convention analysts usually use "O" to indicate declining prices and "X" to record the opposite event. This makes the charts easier to read. So long as prices move in the same direction all recording marks

TABLE 14–2
Hypothetical closing prices

Date	*Price*	*Date*	*Price*	*Date*	*Price*
May 1	$56½	10	$55¼	19	$53¼
2	56¼	11	55	22	52⅛
3	55½	12	54⅞	23	52⅜
4	55¾	15	54¼	24	52⅝
5	55⅞	16	54½	25	51⅝
8	55	17	53⅞	26	51¼
9	54⅞	18	53⅝	29	51¾
				30	52½

are in the same column. It is only when a stock "changes direction" that an entry is made in the next column.

Figure 14–3 has been constructed from the closing prices of a hypothetical stock listed in Table 14–2. Numbers in parentheses indicate the date on which each price was recorded. This has been done to make it easier to follow the preparation of the chart; such dates would not normally be recorded.

FIGURE 14–3
Construction of a one-point point and figure chart

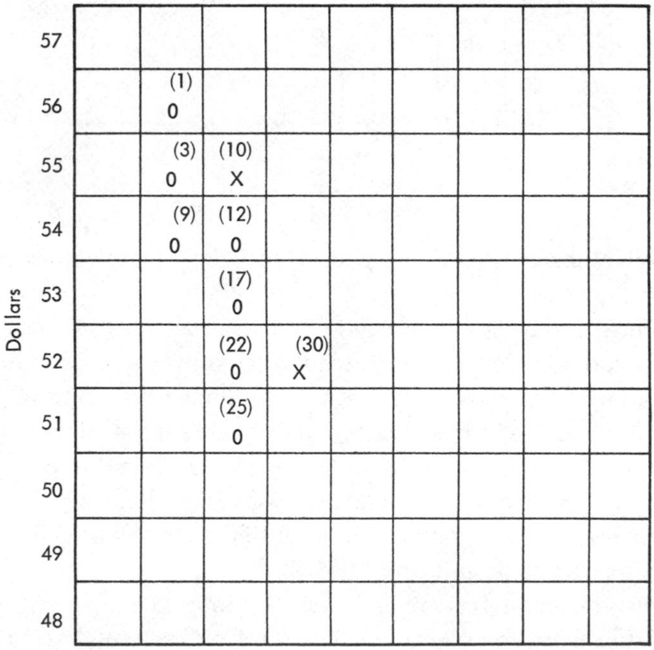

Most chartists record the dates of major turning points or other events simply to give them an idea of when something took place. Volume data are not usually recorded on the charts, nor is this measure used in the interpretation of chart patterns. These charts are as easy to prepare, and easier to maintain, than bar charts. If stock prices have fluctuated little or if all price movements are in the same direction, a month or more of trading activity may be recorded in very few horizontal spaces. Obviously, the value of the basic unit ($2, $1, $0.50, and so on) is critical because if it is "too small" the chart will record price reversals every few days. If the value is "too large," the chart will record practically no activity.

The chart was begun on May 1, so an "O" was placed in one of the squares next to $56. No record of the May 2 price was made because it was the same as May 1 since all fractions are ignored. On May 3, the price dropped to $55, and on the 9th it dropped to $54; these changes are recorded because they are a full dollar lower than the previous price. If the price had dropped from $56 to $54 in one day, an "O" would still have been placed in the $55 square. The other entries should be easy to follow by comparing the dates at which they occurred to the market prices.

Reading the charts.   The Dow Theory, which underlies all chart analysis, attempts to identify stock market trends shortly *after* they occur. At this time the vast majority of investors will still be unaware that security markets in general, or the market for a particular security, have changed. The astute chart reader supposedly has time in which to benefit from the information revealed by the charts. Reading the charts consists of interpreting various patterns that are developed by the price changes of security price indexes or individual securities. There are many ways of preparing and interpreting charts. The following examples are provided to illustrate some of the more common patterns and types of charts.

Figure 14-4 is a classic example of the "head and shoulders" pattern. This pattern is identified by rising stock prices which develop the beginning of the "left shoulder." Prices fall back and then rise to form the "head." They again retreat and begin their buildup which creates the right shoulder. The two "valleys" of the shoulders may be connected with a "neck line." According to the theory, when the neck line is "penetrated" after the right shoulder has been formed, the stock will decline in price and should be sold and/or shorted. If the neck line is not penetrated, the price is expected to continue rising. In this example

FIGURE 14–4
Bar chart of Dart Industries, Inc.

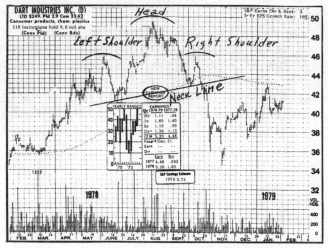

Courtesy of Trendline, New York

FIGURE 14–5
Bar chart of Gannett Co., Inc.

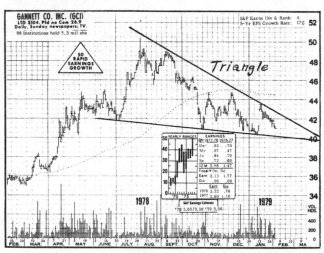

Courtesy of Trendline, New York

everything worked out according to theory. As soon as the neck line was penetrated the stock plummeted.

Figure 14–5 pictures a triangle formation. These are relatively common since the triangle need not be symmetrical. Theory states that when prices break out of the triangle, they will continue in the direction of the breakout. This formation often appears at the end of a fairly large advance or decline. The reader is encouraged to examine more recent charts to learn whether the triangle formation prediction was borne out.

Figure 14–6 presents point and figure charts for four corporations: General Instrument, General Medica, General Motors, and General Portland. These charts are prepared and printed by a computer for a

FIGURE 14–6
Point and figure charts of four companies

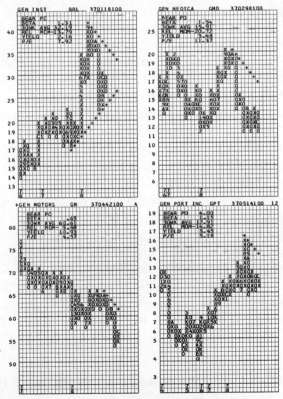

Source: *The Chartcraft Point and Figure Chart Book* (Larchmont, N.Y.: Chartcraft, Inc., January 1979), p. NYSE–91.

company which sells the completed charts by subscription to investors. The computer is programmed so that it enters price changes on the charts and creates trendlines which slope upward or downward. The downward sloping line (the + marks) is called the *bearish resistance line*. This line indicates the price level at which resistance to further price increases is expected. The upward sloping line is called the *bullish support line*. This line indicates price levels at which the security is expected to find price support. Many charts contain both support and resistance lines. Numbers and letters indicate months: 1 is January, 2 is February, A is October, B is November, and so on. Dates are unimportant to the interpretation of chart patterns but are listed to provide readers with an indication of how long a pattern took to develop.

The Chartcraft Company includes several additional pieces of information along with their charts. In the General Instrument example, the ticker symbol for the common stock, GRL, and the nine-digit number used by the securities industry to identify the stock are shown. The top right-hand number of the General Motors chart refers to the Standard & Poor's group index to which this stock is assigned, if it is so assigned. In January 1979 the Chartcraft price prediction for all four stocks was bearish. A price objective (PO) was stated only for General Portland ($4.00 per share). The beta, yield, and P/E figures should be self-explanatory. The 30-week moving average figure lists the current value of this average. Relative momentum is the percent that current stock prices are above or below the moving average. Moving averages are discussed later in this chapter.

These charts may be used to identify certain patterns—double tops and bottoms, triangles, and others—which many persons believe will predict the direction of future price movements. A word of caution is in order. Identification of the patterns is difficult. There are no universally accepted rules for determining either when a chart pattern has been begun or completed or exactly what the patterns indicate. The entire process relies upon "history repeating itself"—a principle which stock price movements often violate.

RATIOS, AVERAGES, AND INDEXES AS PREDICTIVE DEVICES

Many investors closely follow the timing devices presented in this section. Although they are not based upon charts, the goal of these diverse market strategies is the same as that of charting: Identification of market turning points soon after they occur.

The odd-lot trading index

The logic behind the use of odd-lot trading statistics as market predictors can be stated simply: (1) Small investors generally do the "wrong thing" at important turning points of the stock markets; (2) The action of the average small investor is revealed in the odd-lot statistics. It will be remembered that odd-lot purchases and sales are those of less than 100 shares. Such trades are widely believed to be those of the man in the street, the small-scale investor.

Figure 14–7 pictures what historical odd-lot data indicate the small investor typically does at various times in a stock market cycle. As prices rise, this person is cautious, a seller on balance. When prices near their peak, greed overcomes reason and securities are purchased aggressively. The small investor remains hopeful as prices decline, buying more shares than are sold. But as the bottom of the market approaches, fear sets in and large amounts of securities are sold. The small investor does the correct thing to generate profits *some of the*

FIGURE 14–7
Odd-lot investor syndrome

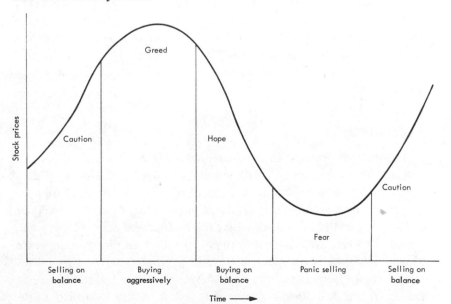

time by selling as prices increase and buying as they decrease. The errors are mainly made at *turning points*.

Data on daily and weekly odd-lot sales and purchases are widely available in most newspapers having a financial section. The SEC publishes statistics of odd-lot trading monthly in its *Statistical Bulletin*. The most popular use of odd-lot information is through a ratio of selling to purchasing volume. This tells whether, and in what proportion, the small investor is a *net* seller or buyer.

Some analysts relate total odd-lot to total round-lot purchases and sales in an attempt to measure whether the small buyer is relatively *more* or *less active* than the round-lot purchaser.

Odd-lot data are usually used to verify that a turning point has occurred in the security markets, rather than as a leading indicator. For example, some persons believe that a declining market has not reached bottom until there is evidence of panic selling on the part of the odd-lotters.

Historically, odd-lot data have done a good job of indicating market turning points. But in several recent periods the ratio has not performed well at all. Some market observers believe that many small investors have left the market entirely (odd-lot trading volume statistics bear them out) and that those remaining are smarter. Others maintain that this isn't the case at all, and that recent odd-lotters have just been lucky. At any rate, in recent years the ratio has not been the accurate predictor that it once was. It has indicated that in several periods— contrary to theory—small investors *sold* on balance at market peaks and *bought* on balance at bottoms. This ratio has a large number of followers, but until it produces more accurate results one should use it only with caution.

Insider trading

Odd-lot trading statistics are examined to learn what the "little guy" is doing. The behavior of another group, known as insiders, is also closely watched. *Insiders* are officers, directors, or principal owners (10 percent or more of a corporation's outstanding common stock) or exchange specialists (brokers who execute buy and sell orders in the company's stock). It is logical to presume that if anyone has accurate information about a company it is these persons. The U.S. Securities and Exchange Commission, in an attempt to provide full disclosure of insider trading activities, requires all persons legally identified as insiders to file periodic reports of their purchases and sales of stock in companies where they hold an insider position. This information is made available to the public by the SEC in its monthly publication *Summary of Stock Transactions and Holdings of Officers, Directors, and Principal Stockholders.*

Many people have examined insider trading data to determine whether and how it can be used to indicate future stock price movements. These studies have generally produced inconsistent results. Insiders buy and sell securities for a wide variety of reasons, many of which are not related to future corporate prospects. And yet it is logical to assume that insiders do have special knowledge about their firms, and that they will not buy securities if prices are expected to decline, and vice versa.

Several investment advising firms use insider trading data in formulating their recommendations. One company uses trading information on corporate insiders, specialists, and fund managers (although fund managers are not technically insiders) to create a single measure of expected stock market performance. The *risk exposure ratio,* as this measure is called, is pictured as a pendulum which swings from bullish to bearish and back in advance of market movements. Figure 14–8 shows that in early December of 1978 the risk exposure ratio was exceptionally bullish, indicating a market upturn.

Various risk exposure ratios and Dow Jones Industrial Average levels are detailed as part of Figure 14–8. These data indicate that the risk exposure ratio has often predicted market movements. Whether it will continue to be accurate is of course open to question.

Index of short to regular sales

Investors make short sales when they expect prices to decline. Since these short sales will someday be covered by repurchased securities, they constitute a future demand for the stock.[2] Decreased *short interest* (a term used to indicate the amount of securities sold short) forecasts a lower future demand. These data are usually analyzed by constructing a ratio of the short interest outstanding on various dates to the average daily stock trading volume. An increasing ratio indicates that future demand for the stock will strengthen. As short sales

---

[2] See Chapter 11 for a discussion of the mechanics of short selling. Not all short sales result in future purchases as some investors short securities they own. This is thought to be a small proportion of total short selling.

FIGURE 14–8

Consensus of Insiders

Since 1962

P.O. BOX 10247 • FORT LAUDERDALE, FLORIDA 33305

December 1, 1978   No. 48

The Advance Risk Exposure Ratio registers a duplicate BULLISH reading of 49% this week as the Dow Jones slipped below the 800 level. We are guessing that foreign buying is sopping up enough of the forced margin selling to keep the market in equilibrium so far. Odds favor the "tug-o-war" will be resolved on the upside eventually. Note that in the actual, rather than predicted action, two of the three Index of Market Professionals' parts have turned positive. Only the Funds line keeps us from a <u>confirmation</u>. The shaded RER-Advanced "shadow" on the yellow IMP sheet shows good times ahead so we are moving slowly towards a 68% equity position in our managed FUNDS. No guarantees that we won't have one more downward plunge but we will predict that Insider stocks bought when the Dow is under 800 will work out profitably.

RECORD OF ACCURACY
RISK EXPOSURE RATIO.

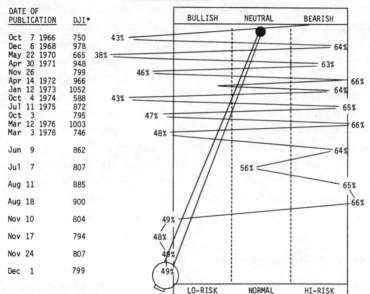

DATE OF PUBLICATION	DJI*
Oct 7 1966	750
Dec 6 1968	978
May 22 1970	665
Apr 30 1971	948
Nov 26	799
Apr 14 1972	966
Jan 12 1973	1052
Oct 4 1974	588
Jul 11 1975	872
Oct 3	795
Mar 12 1976	1003
Mar 3 1978	746
Jun 9	862
Jul 7	807
Aug 11	885
Aug 18	900
Nov 10	804
Nov 17	794
Nov 24	807
Dec 1	799

No assignment of this subscription may be made without consent of subscriber

*Close of previous day.

Registered with the SEC as an investment advisor. We may buy and sell stocks mentioned in these reports. While data used in these reports is obtained from sources believed to be reliable, we cannot guarantee its accuracy or completeness. Pursuant to Rule 206(4)-1 of the SEC we advise that readers should not assume that recommendations made in the future will be profitable or will equal the performance of past recommendations. It is not our intention to state, indicate, or imply in any manner whatsoever that any charts, formulas, theories or methods can guarantee profitable results and/or equal past performance. Consensus of Insiders is not an official publication of the New York or American Stock Exchanges or of the S.E.C.

Source: Reprinted with permission of *Consensus of Insiders*, Fort Lauderdale, Florida.

FIGURE 14–9
NYSE short interest
information

	1/15/79	12/15/78	Avg. Daily Volume
ASA Ltd	30,145	35,045	23,305
Abbott Laboratories	127,465	130,365	43,257
tAetna Life Casualty	120,587	108,053	58,426
Ahmanson H.F.	26,200	None	7,047
Akzona Inc	1,000	12,280	4,610
AM International	81,042	99,662	22,946
Alaska Interstate	26,850	26,445	14,089
Allegheny Airlines	28,106	34,586	34,852
Allen Group	21,840	21,550	4,684
Allergan Pharmac	20,425	20,875	4,452
Allied Chemical	28,128	16,453	39,000
Allis-Chalmers	34,554	63,570	9,157
Aluminum Co America	82,208	86,402	24,873
Amerada Hess Corp	56,121	56,335	32,852
Amer Airlines	27,158	36,688	55,452
Amer Airlines wts	92,200	207,400	27,926
Amcord Inc	20,231	17,508	3,026
tAmer Broadcasting	251,903	248,546	39,410
Amer Can	21,930	12,732	7,815
Amer Cyanamid	9,752	20,885	41,910
Amer Electric Power	5,400	79,614	58,315
American Express	90,665	93,627	75,126
Amer Family Corp	4,000	19,300	21,621
Amer General Ins	8,587	19,705	23,578
Amer Home Products	49,758	55,182	107,242
Amer Hospital Supply	21,717	24,206	34,700
Amer Investment	1,500	13,800	9,894
Amer Medical Int	26,103	29,765	83,800
Amer Motors Corp	34,500	49,575	39,073
American Standard	26,824	25,216	13,557
tAmer Telephone & Tel	176,539	125,444	110,384
Amer Tel & Tel 3.74 Pr	None	10,892	10,700
Amic Corp	16,549	32,349	10,447
AMP Inc	43,215	52,337	28,936
Ampex Corp	31,300	22,900	21,089
Ansul Co	47,804	44,546	16,226
Applied Dig Data Sys	66,100	64,300	39,247
Aristar Inc	2,944	13,826	5,905
tAshland Oil	115,201	132,592	25,673
Athlone Ind	25,666	28,200	3,026
tAtlantic Richfield	128,414	136,711	72,289
Auto Data Processing	48,190	47,270	23,805
tAvco Corp	140,385	174,148	78,505
Avery Intl	25,530	27,791	6,621
Avon Products	323,923	336,747	45,410
Baker Intl	44,165	70,091	31,410
tBally Mfg	282,323	511,067	87,605

Note: The figure "t" indicates
that the security is possibly involved in arbitrage, depending on
prices of the securities involved.
Source: *Barron's* January 22,
1979, p. 85.

are covered, the price of the stock should rise. A declining ratio indicates that short contracts are being covered and that the demand for
the stock from this source is being reduced.

A dramatic shift in short interest of a single firm may indicate that
this corporation has impressed the investment community—favorably
or unfavorably—with its future prospects. If short interest increases
(or decreases) greatly, it is wise to try to find out why this has happened before purchasing (or selling) this stock.

The New York and American stock exchanges release short interest
reports near the middle of each month. Figure 14–9 is a portion of a
short interest report prepared for the trading month ended January 15,
1979. This report only lists securities having short positions of at least
5,000 shares and securities in which there was a short position change
of at least 2,000 shares over the month.

Short interest data may be used to analyze the markets as a whole
by constructing a ratio of total short interest to the daily average stock
volume. NYSE data are usually used to make this calculation, although

the AMEX provides similar information on the companies it lists. Those who follow this method of prediction expect a general market downturn soon after the ratio of short interest to average share volume declines to a predetermined figure. When this ratio rises to another predetermined level, a market upturn is expected. Different analysts use different ratios, of course, but the usual sell signal has been at a ratio of short interest to average daily trading volume of 0.75:1; the buy signal has come when the ratio reached 1.75:1.

On January 15, 1979, NYSE short interest was 37,135,473 shares, down 5,481,115 shares from the previous month. During the period studied NYSE stock trading volume averaged 25.4 million shares per day. The ratio of short interest to average market volume was therefore about 1.46:1, a neutral ratio under the above guidelines.

$$\frac{37.1 \text{ million shares shorted}}{25.4 \text{ million shares traded}} = 1.46:1$$

Short ratios of individual securities are more difficult to interpret because there is a pattern of higher average short sales in some securities than in others. Persons using short interest ratios to predict individual stock price movements usually prepare a chart of historical company ratios to create a basis for determining when the current short interest ratio is relatively high or low. After creating this information, the individual company short interest ratios are interpreted the same way as those for the general markets.

Odd-lot short sales

As its name implies, this forecasting technique attempts to use data on these trades to indicate turning points in the markets. The interpretation of the action of small investors is the same as in the previous example. Under this theory, odd-lotters are not only wrong in that they sell securities at the bottom of a market downturn, but they are doubly wrong in that they short securities in great numbers at this critical time. The ratio used in this analysis is that of odd-lot short sales volume to that of total odd-lot market activity. The ratio usually averages about 2 percent, but at certain past stock market turnaround dates, it has risen to as high as 7 percent. The index appears to be a better predictor of upturns than downturns.

Advance decline index

Many market analysts believe that the end of a *bull market* can be identified by a progressive weakening of security prices. While the stock prices of the larger and better known companies remain strong, and perhaps even rise, prices of securities of weaker firms decline. Eventually the market collapse spreads to practically all securities and a *bear market* begins. Because most stock market price indexes are made up of or at least dominated by securities of larger, stronger, and better known companies, the indexes do not reveal the beginning price weaknesses that foretell of a major market downturn. The Dow Jones Industrial Average, because it is composed of a small number of blue chip securities, is particularly misleading in this respect.

The advance decline index is simply the number of securities that advanced compared to the number that declined in a given period of time. The most common way of arranging this information is by subtracting the number of gainers from losers at any given time. Most persons use a continuous sequence of weekly calculations. These computations can easily be made from data provided by the stock exchanges. Figure 14–10 is the Market Diary section taken from a *Wall Street Journal* published early in 1979. Over the six trading days listed there were on balance ten more stocks which declined than advanced.

The absolute level of the index has no meaning because it depends entirely upon when the series of calculations was begun. What is meaningful (in theory) is whether the net gains and losses move roughly in concert with the security averages. Logically, as security prices in general increase there should be a steady net increase in gains over losses, and vice versa. What users of the advance decline index look for is a situation where market measures—the Dow Jones Industrial Average for example—are increasing, while on balance more stock prices are declining than advancing.

FIGURE 14–10
Market diary information

MARKET DIARY						
	Tue.	Mon.	Fri.	Thu.	Wed.	Tue.
Issues traded	1,878	1,871	1,859	1,852	1,854	1,902
Advances	957	664	792	921	595	433
Declines	515	773	606	520	857	1,101
Unchanged	406	434	461	411	402	368
New highs	36	14	20	22	17	22
New lows	10	8	4	8	16	17

Source: Reprinted by permission *The Wall Street Journal*, January 24, 1979, p. 39.

This excess of declines over advances is interpreted to mean that a market downturn may have begun, but that the downturn is not yet revealed because the weakening of stock prices is currently limited to the shares of smaller, lesser known companies. Since these "second tier" companies are not included or have less significance in security price indexes, the indexes often do not identify the market downturn until it is well underway.

Advance decline statistics are also used by some persons to identify the "bottom" of a bear market. Followers of the Dow Theory believe that bear markets end with a major selloff of securities. Extraordinary increases in declines over advances are looked for by some analysts as the signal that a bear market has bottomed out and that the stage is set for a recovery in stock prices.

Confidence indexes

It has been established beyond argument that the psychology of the market place strongly influences stock prices. Confidence indexes attempt to measure the degree of optimism and pessimism held by investors, and from this information to determine whether stock prices are likely to increase (caused by continued high optimism or increasing optimism) or decline (decreasing optimism).

The Survey Research Center of the University of Michigan, the Conference Board, and several other market research organizations use questionnaire surveys in an attempt to predict consumers' purchasing intentions. These findings are often interpreted as indicating confidence or lack of confidence in the total economy. These surveys relate only in a general way to security prices, however, and have not been very useful in predicting stock price movements.

Another way to gauge security market optimism is by measuring the degree of *risk* that investors are willing to accept. This may be done by comparing the trading volume and prices of OTC stocks to the DJIA. The OTC stocks are seen as more risky; the 30 blue chip DJIA stocks are less risky stocks. Rising volume and rising OTC prices indicate that investors are confident because they are willing to accept the risk of price fluctuations inherent in these securities. Confidence implies higher equity prices in general, so the followers of this theory buy stocks when investor confidence is apparent. When prices of newer and less familiar issues are rising rapidly and are *greatly* outperforming the DJIA, conservative investors become cautious. Historically, overconfidence has brought speculation in low-priced issues, an activity which eventually ends with a great reduction in stock prices—particularly the lesser known and more risky issues.

Barron's publishes several indicators of investor confidence. One is a price index of 20 low-priced stocks. Another is a ratio of the trading volume of 20 low-priced stocks to the trading volume of the DJIA. An increasing ratio identifies rising interest in low-priced (more speculative) common stocks. This in turn indicates investor confidence. The ratio also identifies periods of high speculative activity. The same sort of ratio may be constructed by using NYSE volume and AMEX volume.

Confidence may also be measured with bond yields. High-grade bonds always have lower yields than low-grade issues. Investor sentiment is indicated by the *relative premium required* for taking on the risk associated with lower-graded bonds. In times of high investor confidence there is minimal difference between yields on high- and low-graded bonds—so states the theory. Large yield spreads identify investor reluctance to take on risk, a sign of low confidence.

The *Barron's Confidence Index* is published each week as part of its *Market Laboratory*. The index is created by dividing Barron's weekly best-grade bond yield index by Barron's weekly intermediate-grade bond yield index and multiplying the answer by 100. An increasing ratio indicates that yields are narrowing and that investors are becoming more optimistic.

Moving averages

A moving average is an average which uses the same number of observations (stock prices) each time it is calculated. A new observation value is added and the oldest is deducted each time the calculation is made. Table 14–3 lists the data for constructing a three-period moving average of the S&P Industrial Index.

TABLE 14–3
Moving average data

Week ending	S&P Industrial Index
4/13	101
4/20	103
4/27	106
5/4	110
5/11	115

The first three-period average would use S&P price levels for weeks ending on 4/13, 4/20, and 4/27.

$$\frac{101 + 103 + 106}{3} = 103.3$$

The next would use data from periods 4/20, 4/27, and 5/4; the oldest value from 4/13 is dropped out, and the next period value is added.

$$\frac{103 + 106 + 110}{3} = 106.3$$

The most recent average would be constructed from data recorded on 4/27, 5/4, and 5/11.

$$\frac{106 + 110 + 115}{3} = 110.3$$

Moving averages as short as these are not useful to stock market technicians, but they do show how such averages are constructed. They also explain the logic of moving average theories of stock behavior. In the previous example the S&P index moved upward in each of five weekly periods. The moving average also moved upward, but it *followed* the index. The most recent stock index value is 115; the most recent moving average is 110.3. So long as the index continues to rise, the moving average figure will be *below* this measure. When stock prices turn down, the moving average might remain below the index, depending upon how rapidly prices fall off. This would signal no alarm of a reversing price trend. But when the latest-period index price closes *lower* than the moving average, persons following this type analysis would conclude that the price trend had changed; a bear market had set in.

One need not be much of a mathematician to see that the shorter the moving average (the fewer the number of periods of data averaged) the closer it will follow recent price changes. Short-term moving averages—10 to 25 trading days—are used to indicate short-term price trends. Longer term moving averages—30 to 60 trading days—are used to measure intermediate trends. Still longer term averages—100 to 200 days—would identify long-term price trends. A stock or market index that had risen above its short- and intermediate-term moving averages but which remained below its long-term moving average would be judged to be in an upward short- and intermediate-term trend, but in a declining long-term trend.

FIGURE 14–11
Moving averages

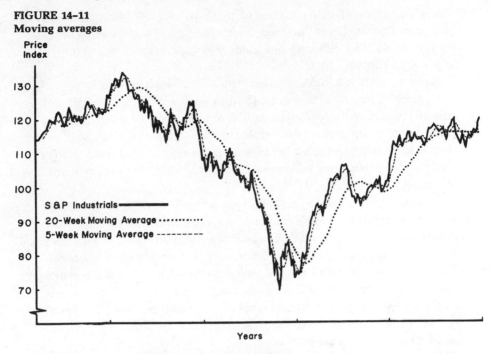

Moving averages are often plotted along with bar charts (as in Figures 14–4 and 14–5). Many people rely heavily upon moving averages for indications of changes in the direction of prices of individual securities or security averages. However, moving averages may give false signals. Prices often penetrate through the trend lines and signal a buy or sell condition, only to quickly reverse. Investors who have acted upon these signals are "whipsawed" and lose money on their trades. Moving averages are usually most helpful with stocks having a history of wide price swings. In these situations the moving average dampens the volatile patterns created by the price changes and in so doing makes it easier to interpret the movements.

Figure 14–11 is a line graph of nearly five years of S&P Industrial Index weekly prices. Also graphed are a five- and a twenty-week moving average of these prices. Note how the moving averages have reacted relative to absolute price levels through this up-down-up cycle.

Random walk and efficient markets

No discussion of technical analysis would be complete without a brief mention of two theories, which if true greatly discredit the technician's practice of using historical price patterns to predict future price movements. These two theories are interrelated and can be fairly simply stated. The difficulty has come when persons have attempted to prove or disprove them.

Random walk is a mathematical term which describes the behavior of a series of numbers or events. If stock prices were independent of one another, past observations could not be used to predict future prices. This group of numbers would then be called a random walk series. A long and impressive list of studies has convinced most academicians that stock price movements, certainly short-term movements, are indeed random.

The *efficient markets hypothesis* may be used to explain the source of this randomness. This hypothesis states that security prices fully reflect all available information about the company whose securities are being examined. New information is seen as being quickly and efficiently passed on to all market participants who use it in their buy and sell decisions. There is no pattern to when information becomes available, what it is, or how investors and others react to it. The result is that prices fluctuate randomly; the pattern of these fluctuations being described as a random walk.

If security markets are efficient and stock price changes are indeed random, then no form of technical analysis which makes use of past price data can be expected to produce better than average results. In general the academic community is convinced that stock market prices are random; all types of technical analysis which make use of past security prices are therefore useless.

Technicians consider the many studies of the academic community to be inconclusive, and certainly of not enough merit to discredit technical analysis. Technicians reply that their form of analysis is an art, not a science, and therefore it cannot be judged on a scientific basis. This debate, like those involving religion, politics, art, and other such topics is likely to go on for years. What is the individual investor to do in the meantime, ignore technical analysis or accept it completely? A middle ground approach is suggested; one that is used by many brokers and analysts.

First, accept the fact that there are many persons who believe in technical analysis and who base investment decisions on it. For example, the financial newspapers all report when the Dow has approached a support level, or penetrated a resistance level, and so on. Many people buy or sell because of these reported events. If enough persons believe that the stock market is about to rise, and because of this belief buy stocks, the market will probably rise. Such an event is called a self-fulfilling prophecy. Regardless of the reason for the price rise, a chart pattern will have predicted it. Wise investors pay attention to developing chart patterns of markets and individual securities even though they do not "believe in" technical analysis. If enough other people are believers, they help cause events to happen.

A combination of technical and fundamental analysis is often used. When examining individual stocks some persons look for patterns of increasing or decreasing volume or certain of the stock price patterns. When an interesting pattern is discovered, fundamental analysis is employed to identify changes in profitability, dividend policy, market penetration, type of product, or other fundamental events that could be causing the price or volume changes to occur. It is much easier to scan one hundred stock charts in a chart book looking for a developing price formation than it is to perform or to read one hundred fundamental analyses.

Indexes of breadth of market, odd-lot trading, short sales, and other such technical market measures have merit too. These are often used along with economic analysis since they all pertain to the market rather than to individual securities. Keep in mind that technical analysis is definitely an art. Interpretation of technical signals is difficult. And the signals, even when they clearly forecast an event, are sometimes wrong. Many technicians claim their techniques are accurate well over half of the time; fundamental analysis typically does no better.

FORMULA INVESTMENT PLANS

These strategies attempt to keep the investor from making poor *timing* decisions by setting down a formula which tells when to buy and sell. The usual tendencies toward over-pessimism and over-optimism are controlled because actions are taken according to a predetermined plan which was set with full awareness that prices are going to move down as well as up. These plans do not solve the problem of *selecting* the best security or securities. They have most appeal for investors who have little faith in economic analysis, fundamental analysis, or technical analysis.

Dollar cost averaging

Dollar cost averaging is a technique which allows an investor to realize profits so long as market prices fluctuate and so long as a constant dollar amount of investments can be periodically purchased. It is the simplest of formula plans, and it works.

As an illustration, assume that someone has $1,000 to invest in each of five periods. This money will be used to purchase the stock of a single company, regardless of its current market price. To simplify the example further, dividends and commission charges are ignored and it is presumed that fractional shares may be purchased. Table 14–4 presents a "no growth" situation in which the market price begins and ends at $100 per share while fluctuating an even amount above and below this figure. One thousand dollars is invested each period at the current market price, and all purchases are held until the fifth period is completed. Note that while the market price has fluctuated an equal amount above and below $100, the investor has realized a small profit of $83 over the period. Five thousand dollars were paid for securities worth $5,083. This profit resulted from the fact that when stock prices were high at $120, the investor could only buy 8.33 shares for $1,000; when prices were low, 12.5 shares could be acquired. At the average market price of $100, more low-priced than high-priced shares were obtained. Under these conditions dollar averaging will always result in profits. But to realize gains the investor must first be willing to purchase securities of an equal dollar amount when prices are low as well as high. Many persons simply will not buy stocks after their prices have fallen. Pessimism overrules logical actions.

TABLE 14–4
Hypothetical prices and purchases of stock shares over a five-year period

Period	Market price	Number purchased	Total owned	Total invested	Cumulative value
1	$100	10.00	10.00	$1,000	$1,000.00
2	120	8.33	18.33	2,000	2,199.60
3	100	10.00	28.33	3,000	2,833.00
4	80	12.50	40.83	4,000	3,266.40
5	100	10.00	50.83	5,000	5,083.00

Also, security prices must be volatile, and they should be trending upward, or at least not be trending downward, over a period of time. Free markets produce volatile prices, so this characteristic can be expected to continue. As long as our nation's productivity continues to increase, stock prices should rise. Next, the investor must be prepared to purchase securities over a period of time long enough that purchases are made at both high and low prices. Ten years is probably a minimum amount of time for one of these plans to become effective, although if security prices are very volatile, a shorter time period would provide the required high and low prices. Purchases should be made often enough—semiannually, quarterly, or monthly—so that price fluctuations are not missed because no purchases were made. Lastly, investors should not be under pressure—financial or psychological— to sell out quickly when prices are low. Most people advise liquidating a dollar cost averaging plan portfolio gradually so that all securities will not be sold at relatively low prices. Such a plan makes it impossible to sell out at relatively high prices either, but to attempt to do this would result in making timing decisions, the very thing one hopes to avoid through dollar cost averaging.

Is dollar cost averaging the answer?   The above conditions do not seem very difficult to attain, and success seems guaranteed. People ask, "If dollar averaging is so good, why don't professional investment managers use it?" Many of them do! However, the professionals are equipped by their training to make decisions on timing. Most of them believe they can do better than the averages, and some of them do.

Dollar cost averaging does not solve the problem of which securities to purchase. Obviously, a dollar cost averaging plan which was made up of securities that rose in price will produce superior results to one which acquired securities which did not perform as well. Identifying the best possible securities—given certain risk and return characteristics—is the task of security analysis, however.

Dollar cost averaging is used by millions of investors, many of whom do not recognize that they are using this technique. Buying securities under a monthly investment plan is really dollar averaging. Periodic contributions to a pension fund which invests its receipts in common stocks does essentially the same thing. Regular purchase of mutual fund shares may also be classified as a type of dollar cost averaging program.

More complex formula plans

Dollar cost averaging allows a person to pursue an investment program unburdened by the need to make timing decisions. Other formula plans make timing signals on the basis of predetermined rules (the formula) which attempt to cause the investor to buy stocks when prices are relatively low and sell them when they are relatively high. There are two general categories of these formula devices: *constant* and *variable ratio plans*. Many subcategories exist but they all have two common characteristics: (1) the investment portfolio is divided into an aggressive and defensive portion, and (2) timing decisions are made automatically.

Constant ratio plans. These resemble dollar cost averaging in that once the plan has been started, the only decision required is that of selecting securities to be bought and sold. All decisions on timing are determined by the "formula." Under such a plan, an investor decides to place a certain proportion of an investment portfolio in aggressive and the remainder in defensive securities. If the requirement is that this ratio be maintained at 50–50, and it becomes greater or less than this due to changes in market prices, the portfolio is brought back into balance by selling the appropriate securities from the portion of the portfolio which is too large and replacing them with securities having the opposite investment characteristic. Prices change daily, so the portfolio is almost never exactly in balance. To keep from constantly making adjustments, most formula plan users allow the ratio to become out of balance by as much as 5 or 10 percent before making adjustments.

Aggressive investments are usually defined as common shares or senior securities convertible into common. Defensive investments are either straight debt or preferred stock of fairly high grade, savings accounts, or money-market mutual funds. Historically, when stock prices are high, interest rates are high and bond prices are therefore low, and vice versa. But as was mentioned earlier, this relationship has not held in some recent periods.

During the market slump of 1973–74 and again in 1977–78, bond and stock prices were both low at the same time. This relationship between these securities doesn't make the constant ratio plan unworkable. It just makes it less profitable because bond investments do not yield the anticipated profits. In such a situation the defensive portion of the portfolio should be invested in a savings account. Doing so protects one from a loss on the defensive holdings. But it makes it impossible to profit from rising bond prices—the hoped-for event. Many of the balanced mutual funds follow investment policies which are similar to fixed ratio formula plans.

Variable ratio plans. These are extensions of the constant ratio plan which allow the investor to follow a more aggressive investment policy while still being controlled by a predetermined set of decision rules which tell when to buy and sell. As the name implies, in the variable ratio plans, the aggressive-defensive ratio is altered as security market conditions change. When common stock prices rise, the investor *reduces* the proportion of the portfolio held in aggressive securities; at the same time *increasing* the defensive proportion. This is a significant departure from the fixed ratio plan. Under a fixed ratio plan the investor in effect says, "Regardless of what happens to the market, I want to have 50 percent (or 60 or 80 or whatever) of my investments in aggressive securities and the remainder in defensive ones." An investor choosing a variable ratio plan might say this: "As stock prices rise, I want to own fewer and fewer aggressive securities; as stock prices become relatively low, I want to hold a high proportion of my investments in this form. By acting in this manner, I will increase the profit potential of my portfolio." The logic of the statement is correct, but for this kind of plan to be successful several difficult conditions must be met. Before examining these conditions, let us organize and set in operation a simple variable ratio investment plan.

These are the decision rules:

1. The portfolio will be invested 50–50 in aggressive and defensive securities when the stock market is "normal."
2. As the market proceeds above normal, for every 10 percent increase, the basic ratio will be changed by a like percentage.
3. As stock prices decline, the ratio of defensive and aggressive securities will be substituted in the reverse of rule No. 2.

Table 14–5 lists the proportions of an investment portfolio that

TABLE 14–5
Operation of a hypothetical variable ratio plan

Percent market is above or below normal	S&P 400 index	Percentage invested in	
		Aggressive securities	Defensive securities
+50	97.5	0	100
+40	91.0	10	90
+30	84.5	20	80
+20	78.0	30	70
+10	71.5	40	60
Normal level	65.0	50	50
−10	58.5	60	40
−20	52.0	70	30
−30	45.5	80	20
−40	39.0	90	10
−50	32.5	100	0

FIGURE 14-12
Standard & Poor's industrial stock indexes and trend lines

1941-43=10
ratio scale

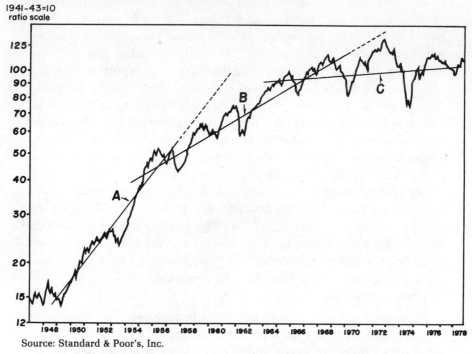

Source: Standard & Poor's, Inc.

would be invested in aggressive and defensive securities under various market conditions. When the stock market is 40 percent above normal (S&P 400 = 91.0), the portfolio would be only 10 percent aggressive and 90 percent defensive. When the market is 50 percent below its norm (S&P 400 = 32.5), the entire portfolio is invested aggressively.

On paper, this appears to be an almost infallible method of assuring one of high investment returns. It also appears to solve the problem of timing. Unfortunately, the recent history of the stock market is such that none of these variable ratio plans would have worked well without a great many changes in the rules—after the plan was in operation.

The plan should be started with a ratio of aggressive to defensive investments which is based upon how far the market is above or below normal. But what is normal? A trend line fitted to several years of prices can be used to estimate this value. However, the choice of years makes a substantial difference in this calculation. Figure 14-12 is a graph of the Standard & Poor's Industrial Index. If the period of 1949 through 1956 had been chosen as the normal period, line "A" would estimate anticipated future stock prices and would provide the basis for a variable ratio formula investment plan. But soon after 1956 the rise in prices slowed. Persons basing a formula plan on prices predicted by line "A" would have sold out of stocks in 1956 and never bought back in. They would have missed many opportunities for stock profits.

A formula plan based upon 1956–68 prices (line "B") would have worked well for a longer time. But after 1968 the investor would again have been sold out of common stocks. A plan based upon years 1964 through 1974 (line "C") would have produced good results, at least through 1978.

But in order for variable ratio formula plans to operate successfully, the stock market must rise and fall with some regularity and within predictable limits. And to maximize profits, bond prices should be low when stock prices are high. We have not had these conditions in recent years. Consequently variable ratio plans have not produced particularly high profits. The plans are certainly logical enough, and if conditions are right they should produce better than average profits. But the entire success of the plan depends upon a correct determination of normal price levels.

Dollar cost averaging does work. It is especially suitable for persons accumulating investments since it requires regular purchases of new securities to make it operate. Formula plans also work, under certain market conditions. They are used mainly to manage existing portfolios, but they too can accommodate new investment funds. Formula plans promise more profitability, but they are more difficult to manage successfully. Their weakness is that they lock investors into rigid programs over fairly long periods of time. Several years may pass before it becomes obvious that conditions have changed and that investment opportunities are being missed.

SUMMARY

This chapter outlined several methods of *timing* investment purchases and sales. *When* securities are purchased and sold is important because markets for most investments—particularly equities—fluctuate more than they logically should. At one time prices are abnormally and unrealistically high; at another they are equally unrealistically low. If a person were able to always buy when prices were "low" and sell when they were "high," profitable investments could be made most of the time no matter which individual securities were purchased. Conversely, another investor might purchase the very "best" investments—on the basis of intrinsic value calculations—and lose money because the purchases were at abnormally high prices. Successful timing minimizes the problem of individual security selection.

Technical analysis encompasses a large number of theories which attempt to predict future security price changes on the basis of events *internal* to the security markets. These theories are complex and sometimes not completely logical, but large numbers of investors follow them. Stock charts record the history of prices of individual stocks or stock indexes. The patterns graphed by these prices are used, often along with other data, to predict future price movements.

Odd-lot statistics are used by many analysts to indicate turning points of stock markets. The theory is that the odd-lotter—the small investor—is usually *wrong* at major market turning points. If it can be determined that most small investors are selling, then the "smart investor" should be buying, and vice versa. Data on *short sales* are used to predict market turning points. The *advance decline index* also attempts to identify major turning points in stock markets.

Insider trading statistics tell whether corporate insiders were on balance buyers or sellers of stock. Insiders are believed to be most knowledgeable about corporate prospects. If they are buying, prices are expected to rise; if they are selling, especially if they are shorting securities, a price decline is anticipated. *Moving averages* indicate how current security prices have changed relative to historical prices. Analysts use this information in an attempt to identify turning points in price indexes and in prices of individual securities. *Confidence indexes* attempt to measure investor confidence. Broadly speaking, high levels of confidence are believed to cause high stock prices; low confidence has the opposite effect.

Formula investment plans are plans for making investment timing decisions automatically. The simplest of these is *dollar cost averaging*, a plan under which an investor periodically purchases a specified dollar amount of a given security or securities. If the market prices of these securities move up and down, as they are expected to do, the plan will result in profits. Ratio and other formula plans attempt to improve on dollar averaging by holding larger or smaller amounts of "aggressive" and "defensive" securities, depending upon whether security prices are relatively high or low. Such plans do increase profits, if they are successful, but this requires that investors be able to make accurate predictions of future security prices.

No timing devices have been 100 percent accurate, nor could one reasonably expect them to be. However, they are useful tools for the investor.

PROBLEMS

1. Examine *Barron's Confidence Index* over the past several months. What does this index indicate for stock prices?
2. Prepare a point and figure chart or a bar chart for a given security over a yearly period. What does this chart indicate to you? (We suggest using weekly data on this exercise since a great number of plots must otherwise be made. *Barron's* presents weekly stock prices, or end-of-week prices can be obtained from any newspaper having a financial section.)
3. Design a dollar cost averaging program which operates over a five-year period with purchases at six-month intervals. Choose a security and obtain historical security price data which indicate how well the plan would have done if it had been followed over the past five years.
4. From data contained in *The Wall Street Journal* or other sources construct a ratio of total short interest to daily average stock volume. Interpret the meaning of the ratio.
5. Create a weekly advance-decline index of NYSE stock prices for a three-month period. Interpret the results of your index in light of changes in the DJIA over the same period.
6. Check the stock price indexes to determine whether the predictions contained in Figure 14–3 were borne out.

QUESTIONS

1. What is the *random walk* theory? What is the *efficient markets* theory? How do they relate to technical analysis?
2. What is *technical analysis?*
3. What is the logic of using data on odd-lot trading to predict market turning points?
4. Explain how an increase in short interest of a security might indicate future increases in the price of this security.
5. What is *dollar cost averaging?* Explain how such a program operates. What are its strong and weak points?
6. All formula plans are supposed to remove the burden of making investment timing decisions and forecasting from the investor. To what extent do they do this?

7. How do variable ratio plans differ from constant ratio plans?
8. Define *aggressive* and *defensive* investments.
9. What is a *moving average*? How can such averages be used to identify turning points in security prices?
10. How does *technical analysis* differ from *fundamental analysis*?

SELECTED READINGS

Bishop, George W., Jr. *Charles H. Dow and the Dow Theory.* New York: Appleton-Century-Crofts, 1960.

Cohen, A. W. *Technical Indicator Analysis by Point and Figure Technique.* Larchmont, N.Y.: Chartcraft, Inc., 1975.

Cohen, Jerome B.; Zinbarg, Edward D.; and Zeikel, Arthur. *Investment Analysis and Portfolio Management.* 3rd ed. Homewood, Ill.: Richard D. Irwin, 1977.

Edwards, Robert D., and Magee, John. *Technical Analysis of Stock Trends.* 5th ed. Springfield, Mass.: John Magee, 1966.

Fogler, H. Russell. *Analyzing the Stock Market.* 2d ed. Columbus, Ohio: Grid, 1978.

George, Wilfred R. *The Profit Box System of Forecasting Stock Prices.* Homewood, Ill.: Dow Jones-Irwin, 1977.

Granville, Joseph E. *Granville's New Strategy of Daily Stock Market Timing for Maximum Profit.* Englewood Cliffs, N.J.: Prentice-Hall, 1976.

Hayes, Michael. *The Dow Jones-Irwin Guide to Stock Market Cycles.* Homewood, Ill.: Dow Jones-Irwin, 1978.

Kerrigan, Thomas J. "Behavior of the Short Interest Ratio," *Financial Analysts Journal,* November–December 1974.

Levy, Robert A. "Conceptual Foundations of Technical Analysis," *Financial Analysts Journal,* July–August 1966.

Lorie, James H., and Hamilton, Mary T. *The Stock Market: Theories and Evidence.* Homewood, Ill.: Richard D. Irwin, 1973.

Malkiel, Burton G. *A Random Walk Down Wall Street.* College ed., rev. New York: Norton & Co., 1975.

Tomlinson, Lucile. *Practical Formulas for Successful Investing.* New York: Wilfred Funk, 1953.

Zweig, Martin E. *Understanding Technical Forecasting: How to Use Barron's Market Laboratory Pages.* New York: Dow Jones & Company, 1978. (Free copies are available through the Dow Jones Educational Service Bureau, P.O. Box 300, Princeton, N.J. 08540.)

part five

MANAGING YOUR INVESTMENTS

15

Tax aspects of investments

INTRODUCTION

Income taxes concern everyone except the very poor and the very rich. The poor are not concerned because they have little or no income to tax; taxes are low and preparing the tax forms is easy. The wealthy may pay more taxes, but because they have large incomes, it almost always pays them to hire tax consultants to compute and minimize their taxes. For the large group of middle-income persons, income taxes are a terrible bother. The incomes of this group are not high enough to justify the use of expensive tax consultants, so the burden of tax record keeping and tax form preparation usually falls upon the head of the household.

The United States government, like most modern governments, attempts to tax its citizens on their ability to pay. This philosophy of taxation results in a *progressive income tax structure*. Simply stated, as taxable income increases, each addition to income is taxed at a progressively higher rate. These rates currently begin at 14 percent and continue to a maximum of 70 percent. This does not mean that individuals in the "70 percent bracket" pay 70 percent of their income in taxes. It does mean that a single person earning over $102,200, or married individuals filing joint accounts and earning over $203,200, will pay taxes at a rate of 70 percent on taxable income over these amounts. The *marginal rate of taxes* is the rate at which each dollar of additional income is taxed. A single person earning taxable income of

461

$12,000 will be taxed at a marginal rate of 27 percent on the next $2,000 of income.[1]

If our tax laws had no exceptions, and if all types of income were taxed at the same marginal rates, all citizens would be taxed proportionately on the basis of their income. However, there are several classes of income—each taxed at a different rate or not at all—and there are many ways to avoid taxes. Tax *evasion* is illegal, but tax *avoidance* is practiced by most people to the extent possible.

The purpose of this chapter is to identify the most important methods of minimizing the income tax bite and to outline a record keeping system that will simplify the unavoidable paperwork that accompanies investing. These are important aspects of all investment programs. It is self-defeating to invest wisely and profitably only to pay the highest possible taxes on profits. Adequate records of investment transactions must be kept for tax purposes; they should also be kept to provide important investment information.

First a word of caution: This chapter contains the most up to date information that was available when the book was published, but the laws of taxation change as courts reinterpret existing statutes and Congress passes new ones. The investor must always be alert for changes in the tax law. Furthermore, the tax aspects of investments which will be examined are those which are expected to be of most importance and interest to the largest number of persons. Many special features of the tax laws are not covered. These may be valuable to certain investors, but the scope of this book does not allow examination of them.

Tax law is extremely complex, and any person having a modestly large income is probably well advised to obtain competent advice in setting up a program which will minimize taxes. Possible advisors are attorneys, bank trust officers, accountants, brokers, financial planners, and investment advisors. The examples and illustrations to follow are general in nature and are routinely hedged with the statement "this is usually true," "normally this is the case," or something similar. This must be done because there is hardly a portion of the tax code to which there is not somewhere an exception.

CAPITAL GAINS VERSUS ORDINARY INCOME

Ordinary income refers to the income received as salary, wages, interest payments, sales commissions, rent, and other normal sources of

---

[1] See Table 15–1 for the 1978 tax rate schedules. Effective with the 1979 tax year, tax rates for all persons will be lowered somewhat.

TABLE 15-1
Federal income tax schedules

1978 Tax Rate Schedules

If you cannot use one of the Tax Tables, figure your tax on the amount on Schedule TC, Part I, line 3, by using the appropriate Tax Rate Schedule on this page. Enter the tax on Schedule TC, Part I, line 4.
Note: Your zero bracket amount has been built into these Tax Rate Schedules.

SCHEDULE X—Single Taxpayers

Use this schedule if you checked Filing Status Box 1 on Form 1040—

If the amount on Schedule TC, Part I, line 3, is:

Not over $2,200.......... 0

Over—	But not over—	Enter on Schedule TC, Part I, line 4:	of the amount over—
$2,200	$2,700	14%	$2,200
$2,700	$3,200	$70+15%	$2,700
$3,200	$3,700	$145+16%	$3,200
$3,700	$4,200	$225+17%	$3,700
$4,200	$6,200	$310+19%	$4,200
$6,200	$8,200	$690+21%	$6,200
$8,200	$10,200	$1,110+24%	$8,200
$10,200	$12,200	$1,590+25%	$10,200
$12,200	$14,200	$2,090+27%	$12,200
$14,200	$16,200	$2,630+29%	$14,200
$16,200	$18,200	$3,210+31%	$16,200
$18,200	$20,200	$3,830+34%	$18,200
$20,200	$22,200	$4,510+36%	$20,200
$22,200	$24,200	$5,230+38%	$22,200
$24,200	$28,200	$5,990+40%	$24,200
$28,200	$34,200	$7,590+45%	$28,200
$34,200	$40,200	$10,290+50%	$34,200
$40,200	$46,200	$13,290+55%	$40,200
$46,200	$52,200	$16,590+60%	$46,200
$52,200	$62,200	$20,190+62%	$52,200
$62,200	$72,200	$26,390+64%	$62,200
$72,200	$82,200	$32,790+66%	$72,200
$82,200	$92,200	$39,390+68%	$82,200
$92,200	$102,200	$46,190+69%	$92,200
$102,200	....	$53,090+70%	$102,200

SCHEDULE Y—Married Taxpayers and Qualifying Widows and Widowers

Married Filing Joint Returns and Qualifying Widows and Widowers

Use this schedule if you checked Filing Status Box 2 or 5 on Form 1040—

If the amount on Schedule TC, Part I, line 3, is:

Not over $3,200.......... 0

Over—	But not over—	Enter on Schedule TC, Part I, line 4:	of the amount over—
$3,200	$4,200	14%	$3,200
$4,200	$5,200	$140+15%	$4,200
$5,200	$6,200	$290+16%	$5,200
$6,200	$7,200	$450+17%	$6,200
$7,200	$11,200	$620+19%	$7,200
$11,200	$15,200	$1,380+22%	$11,200
$15,200	$19,200	$2,260+25%	$15,200
$19,200	$23,200	$3,260+28%	$19,200
$23,200	$27,200	$4,380+32%	$23,200
$27,200	$31,200	$5,660+36%	$27,200
$31,200	$35,200	$7,100+39%	$31,200
$35,200	$39,200	$8,660+42%	$35,200
$39,200	$43,200	$10,340+45%	$39,200
$43,200	$47,200	$12,140+48%	$43,200
$47,200	$55,200	$14,060+50%	$47,200
$55,200	$67,200	$18,060+53%	$55,200
$67,200	$79,200	$24,420+55%	$67,200
$79,200	$91,200	$31,020+58%	$79,200
$91,200	$103,200	$37,980+60%	$91,200
$103,200	$123,200	$45,180+62%	$103,200
$123,200	$143,200	$57,580+64%	$123,200
$143,200	$163,200	$70,380+66%	$143,200
$163,200	$183,200	$83,580+68%	$163,200
$183,200	$203,200	$97,180+69%	$183,200
$203,200	....	$110,980+70%	$203,200

Married Filing Separate Returns

Use this schedule if you checked Filing Status Box 3 on Form 1040—

If the amount on Schedule TC, Part I, line 3, is:

Not over $1,600.......... 0

Over—	But not over—	Enter on Schedule TC, Part I, line 4:	of the amount over—
$1,600	$2,100	14%	$1,600
$2,100	$2,600	$70+15%	$2,100
$2,600	$3,100	$145+16%	$2,600
$3,100	$3,600	$225+17%	$3,100
$3,600	$5,600	$310+19%	$3,600
$5,600	$7,600	$690+22%	$5,600
$7,600	$9,600	$1,130+25%	$7,600
$9,600	$11,600	$1,630+28%	$9,600
$11,600	$13,600	$2,190+32%	$11,600
$13,600	$15,600	$2,830+36%	$13,600
$15,600	$17,600	$3,550+39%	$15,600
$17,600	$19,600	$4,330+42%	$17,600
$19,600	$21,600	$5,170+45%	$19,600
$21,600	$23,600	$6,070+48%	$21,600
$23,600	$27,600	$7,030+50%	$23,600
$27,600	$33,600	$9,030+53%	$27,600
$33,600	$39,600	$12,210+55%	$33,600
$39,600	$45,600	$15,510+58%	$39,600
$45,600	$51,600	$18,990+60%	$45,600
$51,600	$61,600	$22,590+62%	$51,600
$61,600	$71,600	$28,790+64%	$61,600
$71,600	$81,600	$35,190+66%	$71,600
$81,600	$91,600	$41,790+68%	$81,600
$91,600	$101,600	$48,590+69%	$91,600
$101,600	....	$55,490+70%	$101,600

SCHEDULE Z—Unmarried Heads of Household (including certain married persons who live apart (and abandoned spouses)—see page 6 of the Instructions)

Use this schedule if you checked Filing Status Box 4 on Form 1040—

If the amount on Schedule TC, Part I, line 3, is:

Not over $2,200.......... 0

Over—	But not over—	Enter on Schedule TC, Part I, line 4:	of the amount over—
$2,200	$3,200	14%	$2,200
$3,200	$4,200	$140+16%	$3,200
$4,200	$6,200	$300+18%	$4,200
$6,200	$8,200	$660+19%	$6,200
$8,200	$10,200	$1,040+22%	$8,200
$10,200	$12,200	$1,480+23%	$10,200
$12,200	$14,200	$1,940+25%	$12,200
$14,200	$16,200	$2,440+27%	$14,200
$16,200	$18,200	$2,980+28%	$16,200
$18,200	$20,200	$3,540+31%	$18,200
$20,200	$22,200	$4,160+32%	$20,200
$22,200	$24,200	$4,800+35%	$22,200
$24,200	$26,200	$5,500+36%	$24,200
$26,200	$28,200	$6,220+38%	$26,200
$28,200	$30,200	$6,980+41%	$28,200
$30,200	$34,200	$7,800+42%	$30,200
$34,200	$38,200	$9,480+45%	$34,200
$38,200	$40,200	$11,280+48%	$38,200
$40,200	$42,200	$12,240+51%	$40,200
$42,200	$46,200	$13,260+52%	$42,200
$46,200	$52,200	$15,340+55%	$46,200
$52,200	$54,200	$18,640+56%	$52,200
$54,200	$66,200	$19,760+58%	$54,200
$66,200	$72,200	$26,720+59%	$66,200
$72,200	$78,200	$30,260+61%	$72,200
$78,200	$82,200	$33,920+62%	$78,200
$82,200	$90,200	$36,400+63%	$82,200
$90,200	$102,200	$41,440+64%	$90,200
$102,200	$122,200	$49,120+66%	$102,200
$122,200	$142,200	$62,320+67%	$122,200
$142,200	$162,200	$75,720+68%	$142,200
$162,200	$182,200	$89,320+69%	$162,200
$182,200	....	$103,120+70%	$182,200

Source: U.S. Internal Revenue Service, 1978 Income Tax Schedule.

income. This type of income is taxed at the rates listed in Table 15–1. *Capital gain* income is defined as income resulting from the sale or exchange of a *capital asset*. Capital assets are those which are held for the production of income rather than for consumption or resale. In the United States, securities are classified as capital assets. The gain or loss from their sale is classified as a *long-term capital gain* or *loss* if the security has been owned for over 12 months.[2] This is an important distinction because long-term capital gains are taxed at 40 percent of the rate at which short-term gains and other ordinary income is taxed.[3] Table 15–2 presents an example of how ordinary taxes and long-term capital gain taxes would be levied on $1,000 of income. Other assumptions are that the $1,000 gain is net of any commission or other investment expense and that the recipient files jointly with his or her spouse who together earned $20,500 of fully taxable income. From Schedule Y (Table 15–1) it can be seen that $1,000 of short-term capital gains would be taxed at a 28 percent rate—the same as ordinary income. Only 40 percent of the long-term gain would be taxed, so the effective tax rate would be 11.2 percent. This lowered rate provides a tax saving of $168, a substantial amount. Note that the saving would have been even greater, $204, if the income belonged to a single tax payer filing under Schedule X.

TABLE 15–2
One thousand dollars of income taxed as ordinary versus long-term capital gain income

Tax on short-term capital gain	$1,000 × .28 = $280
Tax on long-term capital gain	$1,000 × .40 × .28 = $112
Difference in taxes	$168

---

[2] A definition of what assets, other than securities, are classified as capital assets may be obtained from several sources. The Internal Revenue Service *Tax Code* is the most authoritative source and the most difficult to read. The current edition of *Your Income Tax* (Washington, D.C.: Internal Revenue Service) is a readable, condensed version of the *Code*. Other sources are the *U.S. Master Tax Guide* (Chicago: Commerce Clearing House) and J. K. Lasser's, *Your Income Tax* (New York: Simon & Schuster).

[3] Accelerated depreciation, depletion allowances, income from stock options, and several other forms of income or methods of reducing income are known as *tax preferences*. When tax preferences total over $5,000 for a single person, or $10,000 for two persons filing jointly (after various adjustments), an additional tax in an amount of 15 percent may be levied against tax preference income in excess of these amounts. These are annual publications.

COMPUTATION OF CAPITAL GAIN AND ORDINARY INCOME FROM SECURITY TRANSACTIONS

Almost all residents of the United States must file a federal income tax return.[4] All persons now filing income tax returns use IRS Form 1040, and if they have gains or losses from the sale of securities, these transactions must be recorded on Schedule D, Form 1040 (see Figure 15–1).

This schedule is used to record the sale of all types of capital assets—real property, livestock, and so on—but our discussion includes security transactions only. Schedule D has been designed so that the Internal Revenue Service can identify the assets sold, their period of ownership, and the amount of taxable loss or gain from their ownership. The form also makes it easy to separate short-term and long-term gains and losses.

Recording capital gains and losses

In the normal process of filling out the form, short-term gains are first merged with short-term losses and long-term gains are merged with long-term losses. The purpose is to determine the two types of *net* gains and losses. Lines 2, 8, and 9 of Schedule D are not used when recording security transactions. The use of lines 4, 7, 10, and 12 will be explained later.

Figure 15–1 contains an example of net short-term and long-term capital gains. Investments in companies "W" and "X" were entered as short-term transactions because the securities were not held for *more than 12* months. The gain on "X" was $400 and the loss on "W" was $1,000.

The holding time of "Z" is only one day longer than "X," but this is enough to qualify this gain as being long-term. Transactions in both "Y" and "Z" were profitable. The total long-term gain is $2,500; this amount is recorded on line 13 after combining this gain with those from any other sources. Line 14 is used to record the net gain or loss on all security transactions.

Directions for filling out lines 14 through 23 are self-explanatory, but the form is constructed in such a way that is is difficult to see ex-

---

[4] There are exceptions to this rule. See the *Federal Income Tax Forms* (U.S. Treasury Department, Internal Revenue Service), or any of the many tax guides for these exceptions.

FIGURE 15-1
Schedule D (sales or exchanges of property)

SCHEDULE D (Form 1040) Department of the Treasury Internal Revenue Service	**Capital Gains and Losses** (Examples of property to be reported on this Schedule are gains and losses on stocks, bonds, and similar investments, and gains (but not losses) on personal assets such as a home or jewelry.) ▶ Attach to Form 1040. ▶ See Instructions for Schedule D (Form 1040.)	**1978**

Name(s) as shown on Form 1040	Your social security number

Part I Short-term Capital Gains and Losses—Assets Held One Year or Less **D**

a. Kind of property and description (Example, 100 shares of "Z" Co.)	b. Date acquired (Mo., day, yr.)	c. Date sold (Mo., day, yr.)	d. Gross sales price less expense of sale	e. Cost or other basis, as adjusted (see instructions page 19)	f. Gain or (loss) from all sales during entire tax year (d less e)	g. Enter gain or (loss) from sales after 10/31/78
1 100 shares of "W" Co.	2/6/78	4/11/78	2,000	3,000	(1,000)	
100 shares of "X" Co.	2/9/77	2/9/78	2,000	1,600	400	

2 Enter your share of net short-term gain or (loss) from partnerships and fiduciaries	2	-0-
3 Enter net gain or (loss), combine lines 1 and 2	3	(600)
4 Short-term capital loss carryover attributable to years beginning after 1969 (see Instructions page 19)	4 (-0-)	
5 Net short-term gain or (loss), combine lines 3 and 4, column (f)	5	(600)

Part II Long-term Capital Gains and Losses—Assets Held More Than One Year

6 200 shares of "Y" Co.	2/22/76	1/5/78	5,000	3,000	2,000	
$1M bonds of "Z" Co.	7/9/77	7/10/78	1,000	500	500	

7 Capital gain distributions	7	100
8 Enter gain, if applicable, from Form 4797, line 6(a)(1) (see Instructions page 19)	8	-0-
9 Enter your share of net long-term gain or (loss) from partnerships and fiduciaries	9	-0-
10 Enter your share of net long-term gain from small business corporations (Subchapter S)	10	-0-
11 Net gain or (loss), combine lines 6 through 10	11	2,600
12 Long-term capital loss carryover attributable to years beginning after 1969 (see Instructions page 19)	12 ( )	
13 Net long-term gain or (loss), combine lines 11 and 12, column (f)	13	2,600

NOTE: If you have capital loss carryovers from years beginning before 1970, do not complete Parts III, IV, or VI. See Form 4798 instead.

Part III Computation of Capital Gain Deduction
(Complete this part only if line 14 shows a gain)

14 Combine lines 5 and 13, column (f), and enter here. If result is zero or a loss, do not complete the rest of this part. Instead skip to Part IV, line 24 on page 2	14	2,000
15 Enter line 13, column (f) or line 14, whichever is smaller. If zero or a loss, enter zero and skip to line 23 .	15	2,000
16 If line 11, column (g) is a gain, combine lines 3 and 11, column (g), and enter here. If this line or line 11, column (g) shows a loss or zero, enter a zero and skip to line 20	16	2,000
17 Enter line 11, column (g) or line 16, whichever is smaller	17	2,000
18 Enter line 15 or line 17, whichever is smaller	18	2,000
19 Enter 60% of amount on line 18	19	1,200
20 Subtract line 18 from line 15	20	-0-
21 Enter 50% of amount on line 20	21	-0-
22 Add line 19 and line 21. This is your capital gain deduction	22	1,200
23 Subtract line 22 from line 14. Enter this amount on Form 1040, line 14	23	800

Source: U.S. Internal Revenue Service, 1978 Income Tax Schedule D.

actly what is being done. The 1978 Schedule D is particularly troublesome in this regard because the Revenue Act of 1978 lowered tax rates
on capital gains obtained after October 31, 1978. Transactions occurring before this date are recorded in column f; column g records later
sales. The 1978 schedule takes these changes into account in its construction; 1979 and later schedules will be simpler, unless further tax
legislation is passed. The Tax Reform Act of 1969 closed several tax
"loopholes" and limited the amount of capital losses that could be
taken in any given year. Pre-1969 losses receive different treatment
and are recorded on a separate form.

But with all its complications, the goal of Schedule D is simply to
identify and record short-term and long-term capital gains and losses,
and to integrate these transactions with others experienced by the taxpayer during the year of record. Total capital gains, after merging
short- and long-term gains, appear as an addition to regular income on
line 23 of Schedule D, and line 14 of Form 1040. The computational
process has reduced the amount of long-term capital gain income to be
taxed so that regular tax rates are applicable. Short-term gains are
taxed at regular rates.

Capital losses are handled similarly except that losses are used to
offset (reduce) ordinary income. Yearly loss deductions are limited to a
maximum of $3,000 for persons filing jointly. Since 1969 only 50 per-
cent of net long-term capital losses can be used to reduce other income.
Losses not used because of limitations may be carried forward into future years until they are used up. Carryovers are recorded on lines 4
and 12 of Schedule D. Yearly capital losses appear as a loss on line 14
of Form 1040.

Capital gains distributions, recorded on line 7 of Schedule D, are the
capital gains dividends paid by an investment company in which the
investor owns shares. Investment companies are required to inform all
shareholders of the amounts of long-term capital gains credited to
their accounts each year. Dividend income and short-term capital
gains of investment companies are taxed as ordinary income. Line 10
of Schedule D is used to record the taxpayer's prorata share of certain
income generated by Subchapter S corporations.[5]

---

[5] Subchapter S corporations are domestic corporations which are eligible for
special income tax treatment. Information about these corporations is available
in all of the tax guides.

468

FIGURE 15-2
Form 1040, Schedule B

Schedules A&B (Form 1040) 1978   **Schedule B—Interest and Dividend Income**   Page **2**

Name(s) as shown on Form 1040 (Do not enter name and social security number if shown on other side) | Your social security number

Part I   Interest Income

1 If you received more than $400 in interest, Complete Part I. Please see page 8 of the instructions to find out what interest to report. Then answer the questions in Part III, below. If you received interest as a nominee for another, or you received or paid accrued interest on securities transferred between interest payment dates, please see page 18 of the instructions.

Name of payer	Amount
Cloverleaf Bldg. and Loan	$ 16.75
State Savings Bank	574.28
U. S. Series E Bond ($100 bond) redeemed	25.00
Reynolds Tobacco Co. 8 1/8% Bonds (2M)	162.50

2 Total interest income. Enter here and on Form 1040, line 9 . . . .   **$778.53**

Part II   Dividend Income

3 If you received more than $400 in gross dividends (including capital gain distributions) and other distributions on stock, complete Part II. Please see page 9 of the instructions. Write (H), (W), (J), for stock held by husband, wife, or jointly. Then answer the questions in Part III, below. If you received dividends as a nominee for another, please see page 18 of the instructions.

Name of payer	Amount
H Share of Smith Bros. Partnership	$175.00
H XYZ Mutual Fund	200.00
H R. D. Budge, Inc.	60.00
W Ford Motor Co.	55.00
W General Motors Co.	30.00

Part III   Foreign Accounts and Foreign Trusts

If you are required to list interest in Part I or dividends in Part II, OR if you had a foreign account or were a grantor of, or a transferor to a foreign trust, you must answer both questions in Part III. Please see page 18 of the instructions.

	Yes	No
A Did you, at any time during the taxable year, have an interest in or signature or other authority over a bank, securities, or other financial account in a foreign country (see page 18 of instructions)? . . .		
B Were you the grantor of, or transferor to, a foreign trust during any taxable year, which foreign trust was in being during the current taxable year, whether or not you have any beneficial interest in such trust? . If "Yes," you may be required to file Forms 3520, 3520-A, or 926.		

4 Total of line 3 . . . .   **$520.00**

5 Capital gain distributions. Enter here and on Schedule D, line 7. See Note below . .   100.00

6 Nontaxable distributions . . . . . .   -0-

7 Total (add lines 5 and 6) 100.00

8 Dividends before exclusion (subtract line 7 from line 4). Enter here and on Form 1040, line 10a **$420.00**

Note: If you received capital gain distributions and do not need Schedule D to report any other gains or losses or to compute the alternative tax, do not file that schedule. Instead, enter the taxable part of capital gain distributions on Form 1040, line 15.

☆ U.S. GOVERNMENT PRINTING OFFICE : 1978— 0-263-269-E.I. (#95-238446

Source: U.S. Internal Revenue Service, 1978 Income Tax Schedule.

Recording dividend and interest income

Income in the form of dividends and interest is *ordinary income* and must be recorded as such on lines 9, 10a, 10b, and 10c of Form 1040; it may also be reported on Schedule B of Form 1040. Figure 15-2 is a "filled in" Schedule B, and Figure 15-3 is a partially completed Form 1040.

Part I of Schedule B is used to report taxable interest income. All interest payments received throughout the year are recorded here and identified by their source if they amount to $400 or more. Part II of Schedule B lists dividend income; it must be filled out only if gross dividends are $400 or more. Regular dividends are listed on line 3 and totaled on line 4. On line 5 are listed capital gain distributions. Companies paying such dividends (mutual funds mostly) will identify which portion of their dividend is considered to be a capital gain. (See Chapter 10 for a review of how mutual funds report dividends.) On line 6 are recorded additional nontaxable distributions. Dividends listed on lines 5 and 6 are summed on line 7 and deducted from total dividends listed on line 4. The amount remaining on line 8 is entered on line 10a of Form 1040.

Each taxpayer may exclude up to $100 of qualified dividend income from taxation. However, married persons filing joint returns are not automatically allowed to exclude $200 of dividend income. The exclusion applies to $100 of dividends *for each person*. In the example presented in Figure 15-2, the husband had total dividend income of $435, of which only $100 was excluded. The wife had only $85 of dividends. The total exclusion (line 10b, Form 1040) was $185. One hundred dollars of the XYZ Mutual Fund dividend of $200 was a capital gain dividend and is listed on line 5 of Schedule B; it was also listed on line 7 of Schedule D (shown in Figure 15-1).

Persons receiving over $400 of interest or dividends or who had foreign accounts or foreign trusts are required to complete Part III of Schedule B.

A strategy for capital gains

The tax savings on long-term capital gains are so large and so obvious that many investors seek this kind of income to the exclusion of short-term gains. These investors reason that they can increase the

470

FIGURE 15–3
Form 1040

Form **1040** Department of the Treasury—Internal Revenue Service
U.S. Individual Income Tax Return 19**78**

For Privacy Act Notice, see page 3 of Instructions | For the year January 1–December 31, 1978, or other tax year beginning ___ , 1978, ending ___ , 19 ___ .

Use IRS label. Other-wise, please print or type.	Your first name and initial (if joint return, also give spouse's name and initial)	Last name	Your social security number
	Present home address (Number and street, including apartment number, or rural route)		Spouse's social security no.
	City, town or post office, State and ZIP code		Your occupation

Do you want $1 to go to the Presidential Election Campaign Fund? Yes ▨ No | **Note:** Checking Yes will | Spouse's occupation
If joint return, does your spouse want $1 to go to this fund? . . Yes ▨ No | not increase your tax or reduce your refund.

Filing Status
Check only one box.

1 ☐ Single
2 ☐ Married filing joint return (even if only one had income)
3 ☐ Married filing separate return. If spouse is also filing, give spouse's social security number in the space above and enter full name here ▶
4 ☐ Unmarried head of household. Enter qualifying name ▶ .... See page 6 of Instructions.
5 ☐ Qualifying widow(er) with dependent child (Year spouse died ▶ 19 ___). See page 6 of Instructions.

Exemptions
Always check the box labeled Yourself.
Check other boxes if they apply.

6a ☐ Yourself ☐ 65 or over ☐ Blind | Enter number of boxes checked on 6a and b ▶ ☐
b ☐ Spouse ☐ 65 or over ☐ Blind
c First names of your dependent children who lived with you ▶ .... | Enter number of children listed ▶ ☐

d Other dependents:

(1) Name	(2) Relationship	(3) Number of months lived in your home	(4) Did dependent have income of $750 or more?	(5) Did you provide more than one-half of dependent's support?

Enter number of other dependents ▶ ☐

Add numbers entered in boxes above ▶ ☐

7 Total number of exemptions claimed . . . .

Income
Please attach Copy B of your Forms W–2 here.
If you do not have a W–2, see page 5 of Instructions.

8	Wages, salaries, tips, and other employee compensation	8	$778.53
9	Interest income (If over $400, attach Schedule B)	9	
10a	Dividends (If over $400, attach Schedule B) 420.00 , 10b Exclusion 185.00		
10c	Subtract line 10b from line 10a	10c	235.00
11	State and local income tax refunds (does not apply unless refund is for year you itemized deductions)	11	
12	Alimony received	12	
13	Business income or (loss) (attach Schedule C)	13	
14	Capital gain or (loss) (attach Schedule D)	14	800.00
15	Taxable part of capital gain distributions not reported on Schedule D (see page 9 of Instructions) . .	15	
16	Net gain or (loss) from Supplemental Schedule of Gains and Losses (attach Form 4797)	16	
17	Fully taxable pensions and annuities not reported on Schedule E	17	
18	Pensions, annuities, rents, royalties, partnerships, estates or trusts, etc. (attach Schedule E)	18	
19	Farm income or (loss) (attach Schedule F)	19	
20	Other income (state nature and source—see page 10 of Instructions) ▶	20	

Please attach check or money order here.

21 Total income. Add lines 8, 9, and 10c through 20 . . . . ▶ | 21 |

Adjustments to Income

22	Moving expense (attach Form 3903)	22	
23	Employee business expenses (attach Form 2106) . .	23	
24	Payments to an IRA (see page 10 of Instructions)	24	
25	Payments to a Keogh (H.R. 10) retirement plan . . .	25	
26	Interest penalty due to early withdrawal of savings	26	
27	Alimony paid (see page 10 of Instructions)	27	
28	Total adjustments. Add lines 22 through 27 . . . . ▶	28	

Adjusted Gross Income

29 Subtract line 28 from line 21 . . . . | 29 |
30 Disability income exclusion (attach Form 2440) . . . . | 30 |
31 **Adjusted gross income.** Subtract line 30 from line 29. If this line is less than $8,000, see page 2 of Instructions. If you want IRS to figure your tax, see page 4 of Instructions . . . . ▶ | 31 |

☆ U.S. GOVERNMENT PRINTING OFFICE : 1978— O-263-261-E.I. (P5-228444)   Form 1040 (1978)

Source: U.S. Internal Revenue Service, 1978 Income Tax Schedule.

after-tax return from their stock transactions by simply holding all investments until they qualify as long-term gains or losses. This policy is believed to be illogical and one that may actually *cause* losses.

Important factors in the decision to hold out for long-term treatment are (1) the time which remains to complete the 12-month-and-one-day holding period, (2) the possible market price loss of the security over this period, (3) the marginal income tax rate paid by the investor, (4) already realized capital gains and losses, (5) the available investment alternatives. An example will illustrate how these factors are interrelated.

Assume that an investor has owned stock for one month and one day, and that it could be sold for a profit of $1,000. Further assume that the investor has no other capital gains or losses for this year and that taxes are levied at the marginal rate of 28 percent on additional income. To analyze this situation logically, the investor should compute the after-tax profit from this investment that could be realized through immediate sale. The following formula may be used to do this. As with most examples in this book, brokerage fees and other selling costs are omitted to simplify the calculations, and state income taxes are not included.

Let

I_a = Income after taxes
I_b = Income before taxes
T = Investor's marginal tax rate
t = Investor's long-term capital gain tax rate.

Then

$$I_a = I_b(1 - T)$$
$$= \$1,000(1 - 0.28)$$
$$= \$1,000(0.72)$$
$$I_a = \$720.$$

If the investor sells now, the after-tax profits will be $720. If the securities are held for 11 more months, the gain (if any) will be *long-term* and taxed at 40 percent of the regular rate—11.2 percent. The important question is how much of this present $1,000 gain could be lost over the next 11 months and still provide the investor with $720 of after-tax income. By substituting the long-term capital gains tax rate of $t = 11.2$ percent into the above formula and solving it for I_b, one can determine the lowest price to which the investment can drop and still give the investor $720 of after-tax profit.

$$I_b = I_a/(1 - t)$$
$$= \$720/(1 - 0.112)$$
$$= \$720/0.888$$
$$I_b = \$810.81$$

If the value of the investment did not drop to less than $810.81, the after-tax profit on the investment would remain the same. The investor should base the decision of whether to hold or sell partially on whether it is likely that the profit on the investment will be reduced by no more than this amount over the next 11 months. If it is unlikely that the market price will dip this low, after-tax profits can be increased by holding for the 12-month period.

Of further consideration are the available alternative investment opportunities and the gains and losses on other capital investment transactions which already have taken place or which might take place. For example, if this person has available another investment which appears very profitable, it may be logical to sell this one to provide funds to buy it. In this case lowered taxes through long-term capital gains may not be an important consideration. If this investor already has a substantial amount of losses it may be prudent to establish this gain immediately, without regard to whether it is long-term or short-term. The already realized losses can be used to offset the gain from this investment regardless of its holding time.

Each investor should consider his or her own situation when making investment decisions. Long-term gains are usually preferable to short-term gains, but as it has often been said, "You cannot go broke taking a profit."[6]

The example of security trades in Figure 15–1 shows that if the investment in "X" company had been held one more day it would have qualified as a long-term capital gain. The natural reaction is to say it should have been held one day longer. However, had this been done, the taxes paid by this investor in the current year would not have been altered because total merged gains would still be $2,000. It is unlikely

---

[6] While this statement is completely true, taking a profit *too soon* may lower the potential return from the investment. Studies indicate that many small investors are unsuccessful because they sell profitable investments too soon and hold losing investments too long. The old stock market adage "cut your losses short and let your profits run" is as true today as it ever was.

that an investment would suffer much loss in value in one day. However, if the additional period necessary to qualify the investment for long-term gains had been a week, a month, or longer, substantial price decline could have occurred. In the above example there was no tax-associated reason for accepting this risk. Investors should not blindly seek long-term capital gains. They should analyze each investment decision in light of its effect on their total tax burden and the likelihood of losing profits once achieved while waiting for short-term gains to become long-term gains.

TIMING OF INVESTMENT INCOME

Gains and losses on investments affect the income tax position of the person receiving them during the year in which these gains or losses are realized, except to the extent that they can be carried forward. It is often desirable to shift investment profits or losses from one tax period to another to lower income taxes. Several of the more common methods of doing this are presented. It also should be recognized that there are other, more complex, ways of obtaining the same results.

Taking losses or gains in a particular year

The tax year for almost all individuals begins January 1 and ends December 31. To establish a *loss* during a given tax year an investment may be sold at any time during the year *up to and including* December 31. To establish a gain the proceeds from the transaction must be available by December 31. This usually means that an investor can take a gain in a given year only if securities are sold at least five business days before the end of the year. This rule is based on the current five-day delivery period allowed brokerage houses. Exceptions to it may be made for persons using an accrual accounting system and for securities sold for next-day delivery. *Paper profits* and *losses* are profits and losses that an investor has or has had from investment but which have not been realized through sale. A paper profit or loss has no meaning for tax purposes until it is realized through sale of the security.

Taxpayers should begin preparation of their personal income tax statements in December, if not earlier. Although all information necessary to complete the return will probably not yet be available, it can easily be determined whether to attempt to shift gains or losses into or out of the current tax year. If one waits until February, when all pertinent information is available, it will be too late to make any shifts.

The simplest kind of tax timing problem is one of determining whether to take gains or losses in the current tax year or in a later one. As a general statement, if current year income is higher than the expected income of next year, losses should be taken in the current year and gains postponed until later. If future income is expected to increase, the reverse strategy should be used. Since personal income tax rates increase as income increases, total taxes may be minimized by keeping any single year's income from becoming "too large."[7]

It is possible to take investment *gains* in a given year and continue to own the investments. An investor having a large gain in a security that was expected to rise in price might wish to do this. This security could be sold and repurchased immediately at the same price, plus brokerage charges of course. The sale would establish a profit in the year in which the investor wanted to take it, and the "new" securities that were purchased would provide a higher base from which to compute future capital gains.

However, an investor is not allowed to take a *loss* in a given year and still own the investment. One may not repurchase the identical securities sold or "substantially identical securities," or an option to purchase substantially identical securities, within 30 days before or after the sale of the security in question.[8] A transaction which violates this rule is called a *wash sale*. Losses from wash sales are not deductible losses.

There are several ways around this law. First, identical securities can be purchased 31 days before the "old" securities are sold. Investors may take losses this way, but they must own double the original number of shares for 31 days. Second, the investor can sell the securities and wait 31 days to repurchase them. But in the interim the price may

---

[7] The tax effects of very large year-to-year changes in income may be reduced by *income averaging*. This procedure allows current-year income to be averaged with income from the four preceding years and may reduce taxes in a year of very high income. Contributions to tax deferred retirement plans (discussed later) may be increased to maximum amounts in a year of very high income to lower taxable income.

[8] The courts have defined "substantially identical securities" in various ways. Nonconvertible bonds and preferred stock are usually not identical to the common of the same company, but convertible bonds, preferred stock, or warrants of the same firm generally are. Persons contemplating this sort of switch should seek competent professional advice *before* beginning the switch.

go up or down, and this is exactly the risk that the investor wishes to protect against. Third, this investment can be exchanged for one having similar, but not identical, characteristics. This is easy to do if the securities are bonds, because bonds of like grade and maturity are very similar securities indeed. Finding a suitable exchange for common stock is more difficult; one always runs the risk that the new securities will not perform identically to those originally owned. Most of the large brokerage houses compile lists of securities which they believe would be good "tax exchanges." Figure 15–4 is an example of such a list. Advanced Micro Devices is seen as a good exchange for Spectra Physics and vice versa, Air Products & Chemicals for Big Three Industries, and so on down the list. If the exchange is into securities of a different company, there is no question that the loss will be allowed, but if the exchange is into another class of securities of the same company, the Internal Revenue Service may not allow the loss.

Gains can be protected by complicated transactions involving put and call options, warrants, and/or convertible securities. It is suggested that investors obtain professional advice on these types of trades.

Tax treatment of debt securities sold at a discount

Certain debt securities, most notably Treasury bills and Series EE savings bonds, do not pay periodic interest. The yield on these securities is the difference between the current value and the maturity value. Owners of these securities have the option of either paying taxes on the interest income each year as it accumulates or all at once when the security matures.

The longest Treasury bill maturities are one year. Consequently, the maximum amount of time that the taxes on these investments can be deferred is from one year to the next. For example, the income from bills purchased during one year can be taxed in the next if the bills mature during the next year. Series EE savings bonds offer investors better income tax deferral characteristics than most discount securities because these investments have longer maturities.

Some persons choose to hold Series EE bonds until retirement. At this time their incomes are usually lower, and as a consequence income from the securities is taxed at a lower rate. Of further advantage is the ability to exchange Series EE for Series HH bonds. So long as the entire accrued value of the Series EE bonds is converted into the other

FIGURE 15-4
Tax exchanges

Merrill Lynch
Pierce
Fenner & Smith Inc.

Tax
Exchanges

Securities Research Division   November 28, 1978

Tax exchange considerations may be especially important this year, because of the recently passed Revenue Act of 1978. Of special significance to investors is that, as of November 1, 1978, 60%, instead of half of an individual's long-term capital gain, will be exempt from regular income taxes. Beginning in 1979, the top rate on capital gains for individual taxpayers has been cut from 49% to 28%, and the lowest rate on such gains has been reduced from 7% to 5.6%. The current alternative 25% rate on the first $50,000 of gains is to be repealed on January 1. But the excluded 60% of gains—as well as one other preference item—excess itemized deductions—are to be subjected to a new alternative minimum tax, starting in 1979.

For those investors who may wish to establish capital gains or losses for tax purposes, we have prepared two lists of suggested changes.

I. SUGGESTED TWO-WAY EXCHANGES FOR TAX PURPOSES

We consider the exchanges in this first list to be satisfactory in either direction; that is, exchanges may be made from stocks in the left-hand column into stocks in the right-hand column and vice-versa, as appropriate. We have included in the list, only those issues that our specialists have rated "Buy" or "OK to Buy" for the intermediate term. Essentially, the suggestions are made to enable investors to take a profit or loss and to reinvest the proceeds in another issue that, in our opinion, offers comparable attraction in terms of appreciation prospects, quality, and yield; where possible, we have listed alternatives that trade in a comparable price range.

Company	Price 11/28/78	Dividend	% Yield	Company	Price 11/28/78	Dividend	% Yield
• Advanced Micro Devices (AMDV)	21	Nil	—	Spectra Physics (SPY)	20	Nil	—
Air Products & Chemicals (APD)	25	$0.60	2.4	+ Big Three Inds. (BIG)	30	$0.72	2.4
Airborne Freight (ABF)	20	1.00	5.0	Emery Air Freight (EAF)	20	0.92	4.6
Alcan Aluminium Ltd. (AL)	33	2.00ª	6.1	Aluminum Co. of Amer. (AA)(L)	46	2.00	4.3
Allen Group (ALN)	15	1.00	6.7	• Simpson Inds. (SMPS)	16	1.08	6.7
American Airlines (AMR)	12	0.40	3.3	Braniff Intl. (BNF)	13	0.36	2.8
Amer. Home Products (AHP) (M)	28	1.40	5.0	Bristol Myers (BMY)	31	1.22	3.9
Apache Corp. (APA)	19	0.50	2.6	Mesa Petroleum (MSA)	31	0.48	1.5
Armco Inc. (AS)	19	1.36	7.2	National Steel (NS)	29	2.50	8.6
Atlantic Richfield (ARC)	56	2.40	4.3	Marathon Oil (MRO)	54	2.20	4.1
Avon Products (AVP)	52	2.60	5.0	Revlon Inc. (REV)	52	1.30	2.5
Bangor Punta (BNK)	20	0.60	3.0	Lear Siegler (LSI)	17	0.80	4.7
Borden Inc. (BN)	27	1.72	6.4	Consolidated Foods (CFD)	22	1.60	7.3
Bristol Myers (BMY)	31	1.22	3.9	Warner Lambert (WLA)	25	1.20	4.8
CPC International (CPC)	48	2.70	5.6	Kraft Corp. (KRA)	45	2.80	6.2

Source: Merrill Lynch, Pierce, Fenner, and Smith, Inc.

series no taxes are levied on the accrued income. Series HH bonds pay semiannual interest to their holders and therefore have much appeal to retired persons living partially or wholly on income from savings. The periodic interest payments are taxed as ordinary income in the year they are received. When the Series HH bonds mature, taxes must be paid on the amount of income on the Series EE bonds which was converted into Series HH bonds. Series HH bonds currently have a maturity of ten years. Investors may, through purchase of Series EE and later conversion to HH bonds, defer taxes on the Series EE income for over 20 years.[9]

INVESTMENTS PROVIDING TAX-FREE OR REDUCED-TAX INCOME

Municipal securities

Interest on debt obligations of all states and political subdivisions of states are wholly exempt from federal income taxes. This broad class of securities includes the debt of toll road commissions, port and utility service authorities, and other bodies created to further public functions. The investment characteristics of these securities, which are all called municipals, have been examined in Chapter 7. At this time the tax treatment given these securities is of concern.

Municipals have the greatest value for persons in the high income tax brackets. This can easily be seen by using a formula which tells how much a taxable security would have to yield on a *before-tax basis* in order to provide an after-tax yield equivalent to that of a municipal bond of a given grade and maturity. This formula is nearly identical to that derived in the previous section of this chapter. The formula works equally well using the yearly dollar amount of interest paid as *I* or by using the current yield as *I*. For reasons explained later, it is incorrect to use the yield to maturity rate.

Let

I_b = Interest payment before taxes
I_a = Interest payment after taxes, or tax-free interest
t = Marginal income tax rate of person receiving interest.

---

[9] See Chapter 7 for a discussion of the earlier Series E and H savings bonds and the new EE and HH series. The older series bonds have not been sold since December 1979. Those which are outstanding may be held long past their stated maturities, thus providing an opportunity to postpone taxes for many years on Series E bond interest.

Then

$$I_a = I_b(1 - t).$$

Assume that you are offered a municipal bond which has a current yield of 5 percent. How much yield would you have to receive on a corporate bond having the same grade and maturity in order to be indifferent to which security you purchased? Assume taxes are 36 percent of all taxable income, and that both bonds sell at par.

$$\begin{aligned} I_b &= I_a/(1 - t) \\ &= 0.05/(1 - 0.36) \\ &= 0.05/0.64 \\ I_b &= 0.078 \text{ or } 7.8\% \end{aligned}$$

If you were taxed at a rate of 36 percent, a 7.8 percent current yield before taxes would just equal 5 percent after taxes. It should be obvious that as the tax rate increases, the tax advantage of municipal securities increases, and vice versa. At an income tax rate of 60 percent, a nontaxable current yield of 5 percent is equivalent to a taxable yield of 12.5 percent. At the lowest personal income tax rate of 14 percent the equivalent before tax yield is only 5.8 percent. Because of this, municipals are owned mainly by businesses and persons in the very high income tax brackets.

Investors can use the above formula to determine whether they would be better off to invest in tax free or taxable bonds. This is done by comparing the current yield of a municipal bond to the current yield of a taxable bond having similar grade and maturity characteristics to see which provides the greater *after-tax* yield. Brokerage houses routinely prepare computations which equate taxable and nontaxable bond yields at various tax rates. Figure 15–5 is one of these tables.

Capital gain taxes on municipals. Capital gain income from the sales of municipals—long-term as well as short-term—is *taxable,* and capital losses are *deductible.* A municipal purchased for $900 and held to maturity would cause its owner to pay taxes on the capital gain of $100. Such losses and gains must be recorded along with other capital losses and gains on Schedule D of Form 1040.

The yield to maturity calculation includes the capital gain or loss on bond investments as part of the yield.[10] Such yields are often presented by financial reporting services for both taxable and nontaxable securities. While these yields may be used for comparative purposes,

---

[10] This computation was explained in the appendix to Chapter 7.

FIGURE 15-5
Table equating nontaxable municipal bond yields to taxable yields

Tax-exempt yields	Individual federal income tax brackets					
	34%	40%	45%	50%	60%	70%
3.75%	5.68%	6.25%	6.82%	7.50%	9.38%	12.50%
4.00	6.06	6.67	7.27	8.00	10.00	13.33
4.25	6.44	7.08	7.73	8.50	10.63	14.17
4.50	6.82	7.50	8.18	9.00	11.25	15.00
4.75	7.20	7.92	8.64	9.50	11.88	15.83
5.00	7.58	8.33	9.09	10.00	12.50	16.67
5.25	7.95	8.75	9.55	10.50	13.13	17.50
5.50	8.33	9.17	10.00	11.00	13.75	18.33
5.75	8.71	9.58	10.45	11.50	14.38	19.17
6.00	9.09	10.00	10.91	12.00	15.00	20.00
6.25	9.47	10.42	11.36	12.50	15.63	20.83
6.50	9.85	10.83	11.82	13.00	16.25	21.67
6.75	10.23	11.25	12.27	13.50	16.88	22.50
7.00	10.61	11.67	12.73	14.00	17.50	23.33
7.25	10.98	12.08	13.18	14.50	18.13	24.17

the investor should realize that the portion of the yield to maturity that is due to the capital gain obtained from holding the security to maturity is taxable. The after-tax yield to maturity is therefore different than indicated by the formula.

INVESTMENT IN ASSETS WHICH RECEIVE PREFERENTIAL TAX TREATMENT

Tax shelters

In its broadest form a *tax shelter* is an investment which in some manner acts to lower current taxes by sheltering income. Tax liabilities may be postponed, as they are when a tax deferred retirement program is created, or taxes may be reduced. This would occur if a short-term capital gain were turned into a long-term gain and taxed at the lower capital gains rate. Given the high marginal personal income tax rates many investors pay, it is understandable that they will seek to postpone or reduce taxes. In general we recommend this practice.

However, there are many examples of investment programs that appear to have as their main recommendation the promise of sheltering income. These take several different forms. Real estate investment, where small equity positions and large accelerated depreciation and finance charges are used to generate large tax losses, is a prime example of such a shelter. For others the attraction has been investment in oil well or natural gas drilling programs, coal mining ventures, or other investments centered around natural resource exploitation. Here the generous depletion allowance (discussed in Chapter 5) which greatly reduces taxable income, or the intangible drilling costs that reduce income, provide the shelter. Other programs involve the production of movies or television shows where the investor receives tax benefits from the investment tax credit and early-year losses. Highly leveraged equipment leasing programs may provide the same advantages. Many investors who didn't know "which end of the cow to feed" have entered the cattle feeding business—because of the promised tax advantages.

Most of these investments are "created" by investment firms specializing in the promotion and sale of such programs. The investment vehicle usually takes the form of a *limited partnership*. The organizers are the general partners, and the investors are the limited partners. The general partners may obtain their share of the deal as compensation for their organizational efforts; they also obtain a management fee and a portion of any profits. Investments take the form of units of the program, which are usually priced at $5,000 and up. They are seldom highly marketable, but they are usually highly risky.

Such investments have their greatest appeal to persons earning exceptionally large incomes, historically a small proportion of the population. Inflation, however, has advanced many U.S. families, especially households where both spouses work, into the 40 or 50 percent marginal income tax bracket. These persons may not have large disposable incomes (inflation sees to this) but because they are being taxed at high rates, tax shelter investments may seem to offer advantages. It must be emphasized that many shelter-type investments are exceptionally risky and illiquid, and because unit prices are often high they reduce the possibility of diversification. All too often these investments emphasize tax postponement or reduction, with little emphasis upon profits. All such investments must be examined with great care, and when promised tax advantages are great, with some skepticism. The goal is to invest money where it will produce profits with some reliability. Any investment that does not meet this test should be avoided, no matter how good the tax sheltering aspects may seem.

Retirement plans which defer taxes

For many years employees have received the benefit of deferred taxes from retirement plans which were paid for by employers. More recently, employees in specified lines of work have been allowed to make contributions from their salaries into retirement plans which grant them tax advantages. Tax advantages of the employer-financed plans derive from the fact that the employee is not taxed upon the amounts of money the employer contributes to the employee's benefit plan. Retirement benefits are taxed as income as they are received, but when this happens most persons have lowered incomes and are therefore taxed at a lower marginal rate. If they have reached the age of 65 they receive additional tax concessions which act to decrease the amount of taxes paid. Employees normally do not have any control over the amount of employer contributions to these plans or the benefits attained because the plans must by law provide equal treatment for all classes of employees.

Employee contribution plans provide eligible persons with the ability to purchase additional retirement benefits by making the contributions themselves. Such plans, known as *qualified retirement plans* by tax authorities, are available to many government employees and others working for nonprofit organizations. Persons not covered by an employer-sponsored retirement plan may create one of two types of tax deferred retirement programs. *Keogh plans* (also known as HR–10 plans) are available to self-employed persons. Those qualified to create a Keogh retirement plan may contribute 15 percent of their annual taxable income to a maximum of $7,500 per year into this plan. These contributions are *tax deferred;* yearly taxable income is reduced by the amount of the contribution. Returns to the fund are not taxed until removed.

Individual Retirement Accounts (popularly known as IRAs) are available to persons who do not qualify for an employer-sponsored retirement plan or a Keogh plan. Such persons may contribute 15 percent of their earned income (as reported on line 8 of Form 1040) to a maximum of $1,750 per year. Funds may be invested in an IRA account at a bank, savings and loan, federally insured credit union, or other financial institution that may act as a trustee or custodian. Funds may also be used to purchase endowment contracts or retirement annuities, or placed in trust accounts. Individual retirement bonds, issued by the U.S. Treasury, may be purchased. These investment alternatives are also available to Keogh plan users.

IRA and Keogh plans must be approved by the U.S. Treasury to qualify for tax deferral privileges. Each year the amounts placed in either program must be reported to the IRS. Contributions to the plans and earnings from the investments first become available when the beneficiary reaches the age of 59½ years or becomes disabled. In any event, distribution must begin before the end of the tax year during which the beneficiary reaches the age of 70½ years. Distribution amounts are set at a level designed to exhaust the fund at about the same time that the original beneficiary is expected to die. Money remaining in the fund after the death of the beneficiary escapes income taxation. However, these funds become part of the beneficiary's estate and may be subject to federal estate taxes. Money may be removed from either fund before the individual reaches 59½, but it then is taxed as ordinary income and assessed a 10 percent additional tax penalty.

Advantages of the employee contribution plans are straightforward and for the most part obvious: Contributions made into a qualified retirement plan reduce current-year income by the amount of the contribution. The amount of tax savings from retirement plan contributions can be computed by using a formula similar to the one derived earlier in this chapter.

Let

S = Tax saving
C = Contribution to a retirement program which is tax deferred
t = Marginal income tax rate of person making contribution.

A person in the 40 percent income tax bracket who makes a contribution of $5,000 into a qualified retirement program will have a tax saving of $2,000, calculated as follows:

$$S = Ct$$
$$S = \$5,000 \ (.40)$$
$$= \$2,000.$$

Stated another way, the $5,000 contribution to the retirement fund only "cost" the taxpayer $3,000 in lowered current-year income because the contribution "saved" the taxpayer $2,000 in the form of reduced income taxes. True, when payments from the retirement fund are received by the taxpayer they will be taxed. But taxes will probably then be at a lower marginal rate. Even if tax rates remained the same it would still be beneficial to postpone payment of taxes, because the money not paid in taxes can be invested.

For example, tax deferred contributions allow a person to invest more money in a retirement account than could be invested if the contributions were not tax deductible. The ability to do this increases the total value of the account when the owner wishes to make use of it. Let us return to the above example, where the person making the contribution earned $5,000 which was put directly into a retirement plan. Had this contribution not been tax deductible, $2,000 of the $5,000 would have gone to taxes; only $3,000 could have been put into the retirement fund without lowering the person's after-tax income. A fund receiving annual contributions of $5,000 will obviously accumulate to a larger amount than one receiving $3,000 contributions. Table 15–3 shows how great this difference can amount to over three different time periods.

TABLE 15–3
Value of a retirement fund after various periods of time* (yearly contribution is $5,000)

Annual rate of return	After 10 years		After 20 years		After 30 years	
	Tax free account	Taxable account	Tax free account	Taxable account	Tax free account	Taxable account
5%	$62,890	$37,734	$165,330	$ 99,198	$302,195	$199,317
6%	65,905	39,543	183,930	110,358	395,290	237,174
7%	69,080	41,448	204,975	122,985	472,305	283,383

* This example assumes that the contributor pays taxes at a rate of 40 percent while the fund accumulates, that the full $5,000 contribution was placed in the tax-free account but that only the after-tax amount of $3,000 was placed in the taxable account, and that lump sum payments of these amounts were made to each fund at the end of the year.

Income from tax deferred retirement funds is not taxed until it is received by the beneficiary. But when disbursements from such a fund are made—whether they be from principal or income of the fund— they are taxed as ordinary income to the recipient. Only *income* from a fund created from after-tax monies is taxed. Since taxes have already been paid on the principal, this amount is not taxed again. Except in cases where the taxpayer will obtain more income after retiring than before, the ability to reduce current taxes through deductible retirement contributions is advantageous. Such programs should be considered by all persons who wish to build a retirement program in excess of that provided by their employer and Social Security. Of all areas of investment, this is probably the most complex and difficult for the average person to understand. An error in the preparation of a retirement program can have enormous long-run adverse effects. Competent advice should be obtained before embarking on any such program.

Investments exempt from state income taxes

Most states levy their income taxes against the same income as does the federal government. The single most important exception is interest on certain bonds issued by the federal government. Most states exempt all or a portion of interest income on federal securities from their income taxes. They almost universally exempt the interest on debt issued by municipals located in the state. Interest income on the debt of municipals located in other states is sometimes taxed. Since state income taxes are always levied at a far lower rate than federal income taxes, the ability to avoid these taxes may seem unimportant. However, the alert investor can often increase after-tax investment returns by choosing securities that have tax benefits. When this can be accomplished without sacrificing yield or some other desirable investment characteristic it should be done even though the gain seems small.

KEEPING RECORDS

Some people purchase investments, lock them away in a safe deposit box, and forget them. This practice minimizes the time spent in managing investments, but it also may minimize their profits. Investments should be followed closely, and records should be kept of price performance, dividend and interest income, and any other important changes in the conditions of the issuer. Records may be kept in many different ways, depending upon the purpose of the record.

Keeping records for income taxes

By law, U.S. taxpayers must keep records which will enable them to prepare an accurate tax return. Furthermore, these records and supporting documents—canceled checks, brokerage tickets, or other receipts—must be kept for as long as they may be material in administering any internal revenue law. This does not mean they must be kept forever. Rather, they must be kept until the *statute of limitations* has expired. Normally, this means that records supporting a given income tax return must be kept for three years from the date the return was filed, or two years from when the tax was paid. If securities were purchased and held for ten years, then sold, the records of that

FIGURE 15-6
Form for recording capital gains and losses on securities

No. of shares or bonds	Company	Date acquired	Date sold	Purchase price	Sale price	Short-term Losses	Short-term Gains	Long-term Losses	Long-term Gains

particular transaction would have been held by the investor for a total of 13 years to comply with the legal requirements for reporting taxes.

Because the holding period for an investment may span several income tax periods, it is usually desirable to keep investment records separate from other tax records. For purposes of recording capital gains and losses, the record form should identify the amount and type of investment, the date acquired and sold, the cost price and sale price, and a column to record whether the transaction was a long-term or short-term gain or loss. A form which would record this information is presented as Figure 15-6. Most brokerage houses have such forms available for the asking.

This sort of form is usually maintained throughout the year and examined closely while it is still possible to sell securities to take gains and losses within the current tax year.

Keeping records for investment purposes

For recording data on the prices, dividends or interest, and other characteristics of various security investments, a form like the one presented in Figure 15-7 may be used. This form provides data of as much detail as the investor may wish to prepare, while the form presented as Figure 15-6 is used mainly for income tax purposes.

Figure 15-7 allows the investor to anticipate dividend and interest payments. Such information is useful for persons who are obtaining a substantial portion of their income from interest and/or dividends. It allows them to plan for their arrival; and it also helps the investor to make certain that dividends or interest that are owed have in fact been received. This is less of a problem when securities are held by the investor; dividends and interest are then mailed directly to this person.

FIGURE 15–7
Investment record form for a single security

Name of company _____

Type of security _____ Number of shares or bonds _____

Purchase date and price _____

Sale date and price _____

Gain or loss on transaction _____

Dividend or interest payment dates:

	1st quarter			2d quarter			3d quarter			4th quarter		
Year	Declaration date	Amt. recd.	Date recd.	Declaration date	Amt. recd.	Date recd.	Declaration date	Amt. recd.	Date recd.	Declaration date	Amt. recd.	Date recd.

Price history of security:

Year	Jan	Feb	Mar	Apr	May	June	July	Aug	Sept	Oct	Nov	Dec

Other important information:

When securities are held in a nominee's name or a street name at a brokerage house, dividends and interest payments are made to the brokerage house which then credits these amounts to the account of the owner. It is a wise precaution to keep track of these payments as they arrive even though the brokerage house provides you with a monthly statement. Mistakes are made, and without some sort of procedure for recording dividends and interest payments as they are received, it is difficult to detect when a payment has been missed. By February 15, all shareholders are supposed to be notified of the amounts of dividends and interest they have been paid during the preceding year. This information is usually accurate, but it arrives too late to be useful in preparing an "early" tax estimation.

Many investors like to record the price history of their investments on a monthly, weekly, or even daily basis. Figure 15–7 is arranged for monthly compilations, but it would not be difficult to alter the form for weekly use. Several companies sell prepared charts for the recording of this type of information.

The record keeping suggested above is probably the *minimum amount* that an investor should undertake. Obtaining profits from investments is a difficult and somewhat time-consuming task. The intelligent investor constantly examines all securities owned to see how they are performing and whether individual investments continue to live up to the expectations that prompted their purchase. This need not be a full-time occupation, except for persons having exceptionally large amounts of investments, but each investor must spend some time at this task. Investments do not take care of themselves.

SUMMARY

Taxes are the burden of modern man. Not only are they costly to pay and bothersome to compute, but under our *progressive* income tax structure, the more you earn, the larger the fraction of taxable income that is taxed away. Or so goes the theory of progressive taxation. In actuality it is possible to reduce and minimize taxes by perfectly legal means. This chapter explains some of the simplest ways of minimizing taxes on investment income and how to keep the necessary records of investment transactions.

Ordinary income is income received as salary, wages, interest payments, rent, and so on. This income is taxed at regular income tax rates. *Capital gain* income is that received from the sale of a capital asset. *Short-term capital gains* are taxed as ordinary income; *long-term capital gains* are taxed at 40 percent of these rates. The procedure for recording income received as capital gains is to offset short-term losses against short-term gains, and long-term gains against long-term losses. In this way, *net* short-term and long-term gains are computed and taxed at the appropriate rates. With few exceptions, the gain or loss from the sale of an asset owned over 12 months is classified as a long-term gain or loss; the transaction is short-term if the asset is held less than 12 months. It is usually, but not always, desirable to hold securities long enough to qualify them for long-term capital gain treatment since taxes are thereby appreciably lowered.

Capital gains and losses from security transactions are currently recorded on Schedule D of the Internal Revenue Service Form 1040. Dividend and interest income—if over $400 in amount—is recorded on Schedule B of Form 1040. Dividends on stocks are of three main types—regular, capital gain, and nontaxable distributions. Regular dividends are taxed as ordinary income, but each taxpayer is allowed to exclude up to $100 of dividend income from taxation. Nontaxable distributions are not taxed, but capital gain dividends are taxed at the lower capital gain rate if they qualify for such treatment.

Timing of investment income refers to when (in which tax year) a given gain or loss is taxed. The rule is that a transaction is completed and taxed in the year in which it is sold. It is sometimes desirable to take a loss in a given year while continuing to own the security. This can be accomplished by purchasing an identical number of the same securities 31 days before or 31 days after selling the securities in question. The gain or loss from the "old" securities is taken in the current tax year, but the same number of identical securities continue to be owned. Losses from security sales are not allowed if identical securities are purchased within 30 days of the sale. Another way of taking a loss, while continuing to effectively own a security, is to exchange the security sold for that of a different company having identical investment characteristics.

Tax shelters are investments which promise to either reduce or postpone taxes. In general it is desirable to pursue such goals. But many shelter investments are designed more to reduce current-year taxes than to produce profits. They are often risky and illiquid and should be avoided by the average investor.

Securities sold at a discount which pay no periodic interest provide investors with the ability to defer payment of taxes on the income from these securities until the security matures. This feature is espe-

cially valuable for owners of Series EE bonds because of their relatively long maturity feature.

Interest payments from municipal bonds are tax free to the recipient. This feature is very valuable to persons in the high income tax
brackets or corporations because their income is taxed at high rates.
Yields on municipal bonds are lower than those of taxable bonds of
equal grade because of the feature of nontaxability. The capital gain
from buying a municipal at a discount is taxable income. Some states
exempt Treasury bond interest from state income taxes. Retirement
plans which meet certain federal guidelines allow persons to deduct
contributions to these plans from their taxable income. This ability is
valuable for most persons.

Record keeping is an important part of investing. Records are necessary for reporting income for taxation and for determining how profitable investments have been.

PROBLEMS

1. Tom Jones is tired of paying income taxes on his investments. He states
   to a friend that he is going to sell all his corporate bonds and invest the
   money in municipals. Currently, municipals yield 6 percent and corporates yield 9 percent.
   a. Tom pays taxes at a marginal rate of 30 percent. Is this exchange to
      his advantage?
   b. At what income tax rate would Tom be indifferent to whether he
      owned the corporates or the municipals?
2. Ann Parsons is computing her security transactions for the current year.
   She sold the following securities during the year of 1978:

Company	Number of shares or bonds	Purchase price	Purchase date	Sale price	Sale date
Excell	$2,000 par	$2,000	3/15/76	$1,950	1/11/78
Ajax	100 shares	4,600	7/12/77	5,200	6/1/78
Quick...................	200 shares	2,010	4/15/78	1,800	7/3/78
Bilco	500 shares	6,400	4/15/74	7,020	10/14/78

   a. Construct a form resembling Part I and II of Schedule D (Figure
      15–1), and determine Ann's taxable income from these security
      transactions.
   b. If Ann's other income is $16,000, how much tax will she pay on these
      investments? (Ann is unmarried and uses Schedule X tax rates.)

3. Three months ago you purchased 200 shares of stock in the New Process Data Processing Company. The stock cost $25 per share and is now priced at $55. The investment community is divided on the outlook for NPDP; some brokers recommend selling the stock while others say hold for long-term capital gains. You are in the 30 percent marginal income tax bracket. Outline the most important considerations in your decision to hold for long-term gains or to sell now.

4. In the current tax year your income has been unusually low. However, you hold several hundred shares of stock that have appreciated 100 percent in value over what you paid for them just 14 months ago. You are convinced that the price of this stock will go higher, but you would like to pay taxes on this gain in the current tax year. How can you do this and continue to own the securities in anticipation of a higher gain?

5. Construct a chart like the data recording portion of Figure 15-7. Consult Moody's, Standard & Poor's, or any other financial reporting service to obtain interest and dividend payment dates, declaration dates of dividends, and a one-year price history for a selected bond and common stock. Record this information on the form.

6. Select several of the suggested two-way exchanges from Figure 15-4 and determine whether they were in fact good exchanges.

7. A self-employed person may contribute up to $7,500 per year into a Keogh retirement plan. Other income places this individual in the 40 percent marginal income tax bracket. How much is this person out-of-pocket because of this contribution; or, stated another way, how much current spending power is lost through this contribution?

8. If you and your spouse owned 300 shares of stock that paid dividends of $1.50 per share per year, and neither of you owned any other securities, how much of this income would be taxable if, (a) The securities were owned jointly by you and your spouse or (b) If the securities were held in your spouse's name only?

QUESTIONS

1. Why have the tax courts defined convertible bonds or preferred stock in a given company as "substantially identical securities" to the common stock of that company, while not defining straight (nonconvertible) bonds or preferred stock as substantially identical?

2. Why do most investors try to defer the payment of taxes on investments as long as possible?

3. What is meant by the term *marginal income tax rate*?

4. Why is long-term capital gain income more desirable than ordinary income?

5. What are *paper profits* and *paper losses*? Do they alter income tax liabilities?

6. What is a *wash sale?*
7. When is the interest on Series EE savings bonds taxed? Do these securities offer investors any particular tax advantages?
8. Why are most municipal bonds owned by corporations, commercial banks, and wealthy individuals?
9. What special tax advantages do "in state" municipals have for their owners?
10. What is an *Individual Retirement Account?* What are its main features?

SELECTED READINGS

Christy, George A. and Clendenin, John C. *Introduction to Investments.* 7th ed. New York: McGraw-Hill, 1978.

Investors' Tax Kit. New York: Data Digests. This publication is distributed by many brokerage houses.

J. K. *Lasser's: Your Income Tax.* New York: Simon & Schuster, published annually.

1980 United States Master Tax Guide. Chicago: Commerce Clearing House, published annually.

Sharpe, William F. *Investments.* Englewood Cliffs, N.J.: Prentice-Hall, 1978.

Sommerfeld, Ray M. *The Dow Jones-Irwin Guide to Tax Planning.* Rev. ed. Homewood, Ill.: Dow Jones-Irwin, 1978.

Your Federal Income Tax, 1980 Edition for Individuals. Washington, D.C.: U.S. Internal Revenue Service, published annually.

16

Managing your investments

INTRODUCTION

Managing investments is a difficult and often frustrating job, but one that cannot be delegated entirely to others. The purpose of this book so far has been to provide the basic information necessary to select various types of investments and to time their purchase and sale. This chapter outlines a procedure for constructing and maintaining a personal investment program. Before taking up this topic, however, we shall briefly summarize the preceding chapters of this book, and thereby emphasize the main points that were made. All are important to the development of a sound investment program.

Chapter 1 was concerned with basic definitions of investing and speculating, risk and return, and the concept of wealth. Chapter 2 carried these concepts further. From the viewpoint of an individual seeking to increase or conserve wealth through investments, the most important concepts were those of risk and return. All investments have some sort of risk attached to them. High-grade debt securities have little financial risk, but they usually make the investor liable to loss of purchasing power due to inflation. Market prices of these issues are controlled by changes in the market rates of interest, and price changes due to this source may be large. Equity investments have substantial amounts of financial risk, but because the returns from these investments can increase in value, they may provide the investor some long-run protection against loss of purchasing power.

Chapter 3 and 4 examined the securities markets, sources of investor information, the broker-customer relationship, and the regulation of various aspects of investing. These chapters should have great value for the beginning investor because they describe the environments in which investments are made. Chapter 5 explained the use and meaning of financial statements.

Chapters 6 through 10 described the risk, return, and other investment characteristics of the more usual forms of investments. Chapter 11 did the same thing for less common, but still important, types of investments. Chapter 12 analyzed the particular field of real estate investments with specific attention to techniques used to measure profit potential.

Chapter 13, on economic and relative analysis, and Chapter 14 on investment timing, outlined ways to measure market performance and to time investment purchases. Taxes are important, even to small-scale investors, because one can only spend what remains after taxes are paid. Minimizing taxes—by legal means, of course—should be an important goal of every investor. Chapter 15 examined this topic.

Constructing a successful investment program consists of balancing the bad or negative characteristics of investments—purchasing power risk, financial risk, or interest rate risk, for example—against the positive points—yield, growth, marketability, tax status—in such a way that the "best" mixture of risk and return is obtained. But what is best? A given mix of risk and return may be 100 percent suitable for investor A and completely unsuitable for investor B. Another type of investment program might be highly desirable for A at one time and be totally inappropriate at another.

Designing an investment program is much like designing a house. The homeowner decides what the house must provide in terms of number of rooms required, room sizes, home location, and so on. The architect then plans a home around these basic needs and attempts to fit the cost of the house into the owner's budget. For persons of limited financial means, the compromise is usually in the direction of fewer or smaller rooms because their budget is less flexible than their desires. The compromise in designing an investment program is usually in deciding which risks to accept, and which to attempt to avoid, given certain goals of the program.

A further analogy between homes and investment programs is that the requirements of both change as persons move through their life cycles. When the children are still living at home, more bedrooms and recreation areas are necessary. At a later time a smaller home is often more suitable. Investment programs must be tailored to fit changing lifestyles. When a person's earnings—and taxes—are high, returns in the form of capital gains will probably be preferred. Upon retirement, regular cash dividends and interest become more desirable.

DESIGNING AN INVESTMENT PROGRAM

As F. Scott Fitzgerald once said to Ernest Hemingway, "You see, Ernest, the very rich are different from you and me." And so they are, especially in how they administer their investments. Wealthy persons usually have available excellent legal, tax, and investment advice because (1) they can afford to pay for it, and (2) their accounts are of such size that the commissions generated provide a handsome income to investment advisors. Small-scale investors can obtain the same services and advice, of course, but at a price. As a result, most small investors must rely more on their own devices than their wealthy counterparts do. This chapter is not written for the Rockefellers, Du Ponts, Mellons, or others having vast wealth and much investment counsel, but rather to persons who must invest largely on their own.

Before beginning the actual design of an investment program some very basic questions must be answered. The first deals with the financial ability to invest.

A total financial plan

An investment program cannot and should not be separated from the other financial dealings of the family.[1] It should be an integrated part of an overall financial plan which covers the complete life cycle of the family. While it is always uncomfortable to think of such matters, the plan should anticipate death and make arrangements for the settling and passing of the estate. Insurance needs should be satisfied. Planning is difficult because of the many uncertainties of the future. Questions such as the following must be answered: What will future earnings be? Will we have additional children? Are large unexpected

---

[1] This chapter is directed toward *family* financial planning for the following two reasons. First of all, most people are married before they are 23 years old. Marriage and attendant responsibilities seem distant to the college sophomore or junior, but they will arrive, perhaps sooner than anticipated. Next, the single person is not really omitted from the discussion. In most cases the only difference between this person's financial plan and that of a family is that the single person has more money to invest and may be willing and able to take on more risk.

expenses likely? These questions require careful analysis and decisions.

At this point many persons are tempted to throw up their hands in dismay and give up, citing the uncertainty of the future as making it impossible to plan effectively. However, even a plan which eventually proves to be inaccurate may have current value. It forces persons to think about the future in a way that they probably have never done before, and it indicates some of the basic constraints on their investment program.

Determining net worth. The first step toward a financial plan is to make up a current statement of family (or personal) net worth. This is accomplished by adding up the value of all the things owned and subtracting all debt. The remainder is net worth. This is intended as a rough-and-ready calculation. Do not try to include everything. Table 16–1 illustrates how this calculation might be made. Naturally, different families have different types of assets and liabilities, but this general format can be used with minor changes.

TABLE 16–1
Simplified statement of net worth

	Assets	
Cash	$ 1,000	
Investments	4,000	
Savings deposits	3,000	
Cash value of life insurance	500	
Home and furnishings	55,000	
Automobile	3,000	
Other assets	6,000	
Total assets		$72,500
	Liabilities	
Consumer debt*	$ 300	
Home mortgage loan	36,000	
Total liabilities		36,300
Net Worth		$36,200

* Unpaid bills, credit card debt, department store credit, and so on. This amount should be the average of this type of debt.

This calculation often reveals that the person has more net worth than was imagined, and it allows one to see where cash might be obtained if it is needed. By comparing current income to certain of the asset categories, persons can tell whether they are "living within their means," at least in an average sense.

The cash reserve. A historical rule of thumb is that a person's home should cost no more than two or two-and-a-half times the family's yearly take-home pay. Twenty thousand dollars of after-tax income would "support" a house valued at between $40,000 and $50,000. However, in light of recent rises in housing prices, a more realistic ratio is probably two-and-a-half to three times take-home pay. One would expect a family of nine to spend substantially more of their income on housing, while a family of two or three would spend less.

Many financial counselors advise having six months of after-tax income in a *liquidity reserve,* in anticipation of unexpected expenses. This money is usually held in a savings account or money-market fund—to earn interest—rather than in cash. However, it is doubtful that all persons need to hold this proportion of their earnings in a ready cash reserve. Many people now have unemployment insurance, insurance to continue salary in case of sickness or disability, medical and dental insurance, auto and home insurance, and life insurance. The well-insured family can probably get along with a rainy day reserve of three months' salary. An uninsured or underinsured family needs a larger cash reserve, as would one which had an erratic income pattern. Single persons also need a cash reserve, but it is usually small.

Life insurance as an investment. The question of how life insurance relates to an investment program is of great importance. First of all, *pure insurance* is not an investment. Pure insurance simply allows a policyholder to obtain financial compensation if some statistically predictable event occurs, for example, the cash benefit received upon death. There is no compensation unless the event occurs, and there cannot be a profit to the beneficiary.[2]

Term life insurance is pure insurance. This type of policy compensates the beneficiary only if the insured event—death of the policyholder—occurs. Such insurance provides the maximum amount of coverage per dollar of premium because the policy includes no element of saving or investment. Term policies may be purchased which are automatically renewable at the option of the insured. Unless it is definitely known that insurance will not be needed after a certain time—when all children have graduated from high school for exam-

---

[2] It might be argued that when old uncle Gottbucks dies and his nephew Frivolous becomes the beneficiary of his life insurance policy, that the nephew shows a profit on the transaction. It is true that he has more cash, but this is to compensate him for the death of his uncle. In theory there is no profit to him.

ple—renewable term insurance should be purchased even though its premium is slightly higher than nonrenewable.

Term insurance is practically a necessity for young married couples. It is often the only way that an estate of sufficient size can be built to provide financial support for the family if the breadwinner dies. Premiums increase with the age of the insured to the point where term insurance is seldom purchased by people over 50. By that time, however, few need this kind of protection.

Straight life, ordinary life, and *whole life* insurance policies contain elements of saving. Part of the premium goes for term insurance, and another part accumulates as reserves. Premiums for these policies are "level" in that they remain constant over the life of the policy. Many of these policies prepay premiums so that the policyholder stops making premium payments at a fixed time—often age 65—but remains insured until death. The element of saving is small; it is merely the amount of premiums accumulated in excess of the protection part of the contract. This savings amount is known as *cash surrender value* and may be borrowed from the insurance company by the policyholder.

Endowment insurance resembles the above three types except that in this policy the element of saving is even larger. Most of these policies are written so that the insured can receive the face value of the policy after paying premiums for a specific time period. If the insured dies before this time the face value of the policy goes to the beneficiaries. Because the element of saving is such a large part of this policy, $1 of premium will buy less protection in this form than in either straight life or term insurance.

Before embarking on an investment program, an individual should make certain that family insurance coverage is adequate. This usually means that in the event of the death of the head of the household, insurance will support the spouse and family until the children are either out of school or until they are old enough so that the remaining parent can go to work. Term insurance provides this sort of protection best, but many people purchase policies having a saving feature because they feel that they will then be *forced* to save something. Savings accumulate at a slower rate in insurance policies than in bank time deposits or in practically any other savings investment. For this reason most people are well advised to purchase term insurance to cover insurance needs and to place savings in the appropriate financial institution.

The cash budget. Assuming that insurance coverage and cash reserves are adequate, it is now time to attempt to answer the question of how much money can be invested. A cash budget is most useful in arriving at this amount.

The cash budget somewhat resembles the net worth calculation except that net worth is a value that exists *at a certain point in time,* while the cash budget lists income and expenses received and paid *over a period of time.* Begin this computation by estimating after-tax cash income from all sources for the coming year. From this amount deduct all anticipated cash expenses.[3] The difference between the two is the amount that is *surplus;* it is not necessarily the amount that should be invested (see Table 16–2).

TABLE 16–2
Family cash budget

	1980	1981	1982
Revenue (after taxes)			
Take home pay	$16,000	$17,500	$19,000
Interest and dividends	400	450	500
Other income	500	600	700
Total income	$16,900	$18,550	$20,200
Expenses			
Ordinary living expenses	$ 7,000	$ 7,500	$ 7,900
Home mortgage and taxes	3,900	3,900	3,900
Insurance premiums	500	500	500
Retirement contribution (paid separately)	750	750	750
Large capital outlays			
Sailboat	2,550	0	0
Refurnish bedroom	0	2,450	0
College expense of child	0	0	4,550
Total expenses	$14,700	$15,100	$17,600
Revenue less expenses equals surplus	$ 2,200	$ 3,450	$ 2,600

Revenues, expenses, and surplus will become less predictable the further into the future the cash budget is projected. And yet, on a year-to-year basis the budget will probably be fairly accurate because budget figures are periodically reviewed as better information becomes available. Stated another way: in 1980, the 1985 projection is probably way off, but by 1984—due to constant revision of data—the

---

[3] The emphasis is on cash although persons may receive a part of their compensation in retirement benefits, stock options, profit sharing plans, housing, use of an automobile, or other service. These all have value and may indirectly affect investment decisions, but at this point our concern is only with cash revenues and expenses.

anticipated 1985 revenues and expenses may be right on target. Preparing a budget such as this has definite advantages, whether or not there is any surplus. It allows one to identify major expenses.

Living costs can be subdivided into such classifications as food, clothing, and so on, which more precisely identify where the revenue is going. Separate unlisted classifications—entertainment for example—can be set up. Perhaps more importantly, it allows the family to ready itself for large capital outlays like sailboats and college expenses. Whether or not the budget is very accurate, it forces one to think in terms of future expenses and revenues, a distinct advantage in itself.

The cash budget and the net worth statement can and should be projected into retirement years. If this date is far into the future the figures may not be very accurate, but they will indicate in a general way what normal expenses are anticipated upon retirement and, from that, what revenues are necessary to cover them. The face value of insurance policies, and retirement income from Social Security and other plans, become important when these retirement calculations are made. Even though retirement is too far away to plan toward, the focus should be on specific events which will cause large financial outlays. A family having three children under five years of age can project some rather heavy expenses beginning in 12 years and continuing on for perhaps nine more—if the children are expected to attend college.

Setting investment program goals

Goals refer to what the investment program is supposed to do for the investor. A statement of these goals should be prepared at the time an investment program is begun. The statement should be in writing and should be specific enough that it is possible to determine whether the investment plan is actually accomplishing its goal or goals. Such a procedure may seem somewhat rigid and formal, but by proceeding in this fashion the investor is forced to do several things that might not ordinarily be done.

First of all, preparation of a goal statement causes in-depth thought about what the investment program seeks to do. When the investor attempts to balance program goals against whatever restrictions the program has, a more realistic view develops of what can be expected from the program. Preparation of goals usually cannot—and certainly should not—be done without reference to a total family financial plan.

It is important that the investment program be integrated into this plan, and this is one way to guarantee that this is done.

Writing down the goal statement is desirable because it allows the investor to periodically review the investment program to see how well it is doing. But measuring the performance of a given program is impossible if the goal is not stated in terms which allow measurement. For example, a goal statement of "maximum long-term capital gains" may initially seem very specific and clear, but how could one tell whether maximum capital gains had in fact been attained? The goal is not related to a performance standard which provides the basis for appraising attainment of the goal. A more specific way of stating the goal would be in terms of capital gains appreciation relative to one of the common stock indexes. For example, one might revise the "maximum" statement to that of "obtaining long-term capital gains at least 10 percent greater than the increases of the Dow Jones Industrial Average over a ten-year period." A simple statement might define the goal as, "at least $2,000 (or 7 percent) per year in interest and dividends." These statements are precise enough to provide the basis for determining whether the goal was attained or how far below or above it the investment program performed.

Constraints on investment policy. It is unusual when the goals of an investment program can be stated in a single sentence, because most programs have goals which are constrained by factors unique to the investor. For instance, to attain the previously stated goal of capital gains performance at least 10 percent better than the Dow Jones Industrial Average, an investor would almost certainly have to invest in a limited number of common stocks that offered a potential for exceptional performance over the next ten years. Shares chosen to implement this investment program may very well increase in value by the required amount over ten years, but during this period they may decrease in value at some time by as much as 20 percent, 30 percent, or even more.[4] This action should be expected since this is the way common stock prices fluctuate. The question is, can the investor accept this much price variation?

There are some constraints on practically every investment pro-

---

[4] During 1968 the low of the DJIA was 18 percent below the high. In 1969 it was 22 percent below. During 1974 the low was more than 50 percent below the high. It should be remembered that many of the individual stocks that make up this average showed *greater* changes—60 percent or more—in market price. Higher grade stocks will usually experience less market price fluctuation than those of lower grade.

gram which, if realistically considered, act to make the initial goal statement less aggressive. Constraints, as the word is used here, refer to conditions which keep the investor from maximizing the primary goal of an investment program—whatever that may be.

Constraints may take many forms. In the example of a goal of capital gains 10 percent greater than the Dow Jones industrials, the investor who set this objective may have done so because this amount of capital appreciation was *needed* to provide a given sum of money for retirement which was to take place in ten years. In other words, the goal of the investment program was integrated perfectly with this person's long-run financial plan and was in this sense "correct." However, to realize this goal the entire portfolio should probably be invested in fairly risky common stocks. Possible constraints to this investment program might be the following:

1. To provide liquidity, securities should always be marketable at no less than 80 percent of their purchase price. Obviously, securities which can be expected to decline in value by as much as 30 percent could not be used in an investment program so constrained.

2. Cash income (dividend income in this case) must be a minimum dollar amount per year. This may or may not be an important restriction depending upon the relationship of the minimum income necessary to the total securities purchased. However, if the minimum dollar amount is high relative to the amount of principal, the investor may be forced to purchase only very high-grade, dividend-paying stocks. These securities will probably not perform better than the Dow Jones Industrial Average.

The list of constraints could be extended almost indefinitely. The important point is that nearly every investment program contains limitations. An investment program should be constructed so that these restrictions are honored, because if they are not, the program simply will not meet the investor's needs. Constraints usually cause investors to act less aggressively than they might prefer and may be seen as "standing in the way of profits." This is often true, because constraints almost always cause revision of the original investment program so that it is more prudent. Since risk and return are directly related, as risk declines so does the expected return from the investment portfolio.

Attempting to get too much return from too little principal. This often happens when people are planning for retirement. They first decide how much income they need to live, then they decide how to get it. For example, next year Mr. Jones is retiring. He will receive a pension and Social Security of $5,000 per year, and he calculates his minimum yearly expenses at $8,000. Obviously an additional $3,000 of income is needed. Suppose he has $20,000 for investment. The most direct solution is to invest the $20,000 so that it returns 15 percent ($3,000) per year.

If this course of action is taken, disappointment is the likely outcome. A 15 percent per annum return on investment is difficult to obtain; it is impossible to obtain without accepting a rather great risk of loss of principal. Mr. Jones should realize that this goal is probably unattainable if any constraints whatever are set on the investment program, and that he had better look to reducing his living expenses.[5] This is an undesirable solution perhaps, but in the long run probably the wisest one.

Most investment programs that are carefully and realistically planned contain several constraints. These should be listed in writing along with the goal or goals of the investment program. If possible, priorities should be assigned to each limitation. If liquidity is more important than protection of purchasing power, this fact should be noted. A way of approaching the problem of measuring the importance of various restrictions is to specify them and assign to each a measure of its importance. Table 16–3 is not an exhaustive list, but it identifies some of the more common constraints on investment programs. This list is no more than a formalization of what an investor should be considering when designing an investment program. Certain of these restrictions will possibly be relaxed as time passes, while others may become more important. The conditions should be revised periodically as the performance of the portfolio is appraised.

TABLE 16–3
Listing of investment program constraints

Need for	High	Medium	Low
Liquidity	X		
Constant income		X	
Constant purchasing power			X
Constant market prices			X
Tax exemption	X		

[5] Actually, there are several possible ways that Mr. Jones might make ends meet. He could purchase an annuity that would pay a certain amount per year until death. The return from this annuity would be constant and would be at a fairly high rate. He might also use part of the principal each year to make up the difference between what he can earn with the required amount of safety and what he needs.

Psychological constraints. Most constraints are set in an attempt to make an investment program more responsive to the needs of the investor, and most of them result from logical, dollars-and-cents analysis of the present and future financial situation of the family. It is difficult to bring the psychological attitudes of the investor or investors into this analytical decision-making process because numbers cannot readily be assigned to attitudes. But somehow it must be done.

All investments contain a certain amount of risk, and one purpose of the investment program is to identify the types and degrees of risk that must be accepted by the investor in order for certain investment returns to be realized. The risk-return relationship is derived on the basis of what would be the most profitable course of action under given circumstances; it does not necessarily attempt to deal with the *preferences* of the parties involved. As an example of this type of logic, historical evidence indicates that an investor who purchased common stocks and held them for a period of time would have earned between 9 and 10 percent per annum after taking into consideration losses and costs of buying and selling the securities.[6] Savings deposits would have yielded something less than half this rate. Based upon these historical data, investors should forego the safety of savings deposits for the profit of common shares whenever they have a choice of investment media.

The argument is logical because purchasing common stocks would enable the investor to make more profit. But from a purely psychological viewpoint, investment in common stocks may be very undesirable. Stock prices will fluctuate on a daily basis, while savings deposits will not. Fluctuating prices make some persons so nervous that they simply cannot endure the price uncertainty of investing in equity securities, even though they realize that in the long run this is probably the most profitable course of action. Others continue to invest in equities because it is "logical" in dollars-and-cents terms for them to do so, but they too might be better served by investments having more constant market prices. If an investor is the type of person who must check the stock quotes before breakfast and if the stomach muscles tighten and the heart pounds every time stocks are off a point, caution may be in order. Such a person may not be psychologically equipped to invest in common stocks, or any other investment which has great market price

---

[6] Laurence Fisher and James H. Lorie, "Rates of Return on Investments in Common Stock, the Year by Year Record, 1926–1965," *Journal of Business,* July 1968, pp. 291–316, and ———, "Some Studies of Variability of Returns on Investments in Common Stocks," *Journal of Business,* April 1970, pp. 99–134.

fluctuations, even though the investor's financial situation is such that these investments should logically be purchased. If this characteristic exists, it should be honored as a strong constraint in the investment program.

Tenure of ownership. Psychological constraints are an overriding consideration which often restrict investment programs to less risky investments. Tenure of ownership is a consideration that may affect an investment program in two different ways. If tenure of ownership is weak—meaning there is a strong possibility that all or a portion of a security portfolio will have to be sold quickly—it limits an investment program to liquid securities. If tenure of ownership is strong—meaning there is little possibility that securities will have to be sold quickly—an investment program can be made up of less liquid securities having a wide range of price fluctuations. Such investors can "wait it out"; they will not be forced to sell securities at the wrong time.

Weak tenure of ownership may be caused by several things. If an investor has much personal debt, repayment of this debt may cause liquidation of a portion of the investment portfolio. This sort of expense can usually but not always be anticipated in the cash budget. Personal debts may come due at unexpected times and in unexpected amounts. When securities have been purchased on margin, tenure of ownership may become exceptionally weak during market downturns. Securities may have to be sold to meet margin requirements—just when security prices are low. Persons having fluctuating or uncertain incomes usually have weak tenure of ownership unless they have a large cash reserve.

Estate planning often identifies conditions of weak tenure of ownership. Death of even a modestly wealthy person causes formidable taxes to be levied against the person's estate. Unless plans have been laid carefully beforehand to have these taxes paid from a cash reserve or from insurance, securities may have to be sold unexpectedly. There is an element of probability in measuring strength or weakness of tenure of ownership from this cause. It is unlikely that a young person will soon die. Tenure of ownership of such individuals is therefore stronger than it would be for individuals of advanced age, all other considerations remaining the same.

Estate planning

Estate planning is personal financial planning carried to the ultimate point of making arrangements for the complete settlement and passing on of the estate of the person or persons involved. Most people can plan their own investment programs, at least in general terms, but estate planning, because of its legal, tax, and liquidity problems, is the domain of the expert.[7] The purpose of including this topic in this book is *not* to tell how to plan for the settlement of an estate, but rather to indicate the need for such planning and to show some of the benefits to be derived from it.

A person who dies *intestate* is a person who has left no valid will. In such circumstances the person's estate will be passed on in a legal procedure set down by the state in which the person resides. If the estate is small or held in joint tenancy by husband and wife, it may pass to the remaining party quickly, and with a minimum of cost. But even in this situation, the property may pass through the courts—a time-consuming and sometimes costly procedure. If the wife and husband die at the same time and there is no will, the property will pass to the legal heirs in accordance with state legal procedures. In either event, the law of the state "plans" for the disposition of the estate, even though the owner of the estate had no written or otherwise stated plan. How property is held—in joint tenancy, as tenants in common, singly, or in some other form—helps determine how rapidly an estate can be settled.

People who wish to speed up the process of estate settlement, and make certain that their property is disposed of according to their wishes must either make a *will*, place property in a *trust*, or *give it away* before death. Under a will property is controlled by the owner until death, when the terms of the will take effect. Under a trust arrangement another person, the *trustee*, is granted control over the property. The trustee must manage the property in accordance with the wishes of the person who created the trust and in accordance with the state laws which control the actions of trustees.

Trusts can be used to control the disposition of property over many years (but not indefinitely). They are particularly useful when one wishes to grant the proceeds from an estate to a person, persons, or an institution without allowing control over the estate itself to pass into their hands. The most common example of this is when property is left in trust for a minor child. A trustee manages the property and holds title to it but pays out income from the property to the child. Often

---

[7] Several books are listed at the end of this chapter for those who wish to read about this subject in more detail. Most banks which have active trust departments prepare literature written to the layperson which explains the purpose of estate planning and how one can begin a plan.

when the child becomes of legal age, the principal of the trust passes to the child's control.

People increasingly choose to give away part of their estate prior to death. Gifts can often be used to reduce federal and state estate taxes, and they allow givers to see what is done with their gifts. A parent's gift of securities to a minor child may be particularly desirable because interest or dividends from the securities are taxed as income received by the child. Taxes will usually be levied at a rate substantially below that of the parent. Control over the gift may be maintained by the parent until the child reaches 18½ years of age, at which time the child obtains control over the gift. Gifts of a limited amount are completely tax free to the persons receiving them. All gifts are taxed at rates lower than estate tax rates.

One of the greatest advantages of estate planning for individuals of substantial means is that it enables them to plan for the minimizing of federal and state estate taxes. Individuals can often lower their income taxes by making gifts of property to nonprofit institutions such as museums, colleges and universities, and even trusts. If these gifts are to be made anyway upon death, there is often a substantial tax advantage to making them early, while the person still has taxable income.

CONSTRUCTING AND ADMINISTERING AN INVESTMENT PORTFOLIO

At some point, a person will begin accumulating a portfolio of investments. Hopefully this is after enough financial planning has taken place to insure that the investor has a good idea of what the investment program should accomplish. After the investment program is begun, it should be administered so that the goals of the program, as well as the individual investments, come under the investor's regular scrutiny.

Constructing the portfolio

Constructing any portfolio involves purchasing securities which have investment characteristics consistent with the goals of the investment program. Through the use of tools described earlier the investor will be able to create investment program guidelines. At the same time one will also develop a reasonably good idea of the total amount of funds which can be devoted to investments, both now and in the future. Most portfolios contain a cash reserve and securities which are aggressive or defensive so far as certain risks are concerned.

The cash reserve. Investing for liquidity is not difficult. The primary consideration is how rapidly the investments can be turned into cash without loss of principal; a secondary consideration is yield. For the small-scale investor, savings accounts at commercial banks or other financial institutions meet these requirements almost perfectly, as do most money market funds. U.S. savings bonds do about as well, except that they are not as quickly turned into cash. For the large-scale investor, Treasury bills provide a good liquidity reserve and usually the highest short-term yields available. Long-term government, corporate, or municipal bonds are unsuitable for use as a liquidity reserve. They are safe as far as financial risk is concerned, and they are marketable, but their prices fluctuate greatly with changes in interest rates. Turning these securities into cash quickly can result in large capital losses.

Defensive investments. Ideal defensive investments are difficult to list because there are several things that an investor might wish to defend against. For example, one could seek to defend against loss of principal, loss of purchasing power, or loss of current income, or all three, in the defensive section of a portfolio. Unfortunately, securities which provide maximum protection of principal, and which promise to pay predictable interest or dividends for the foreseeable future, are those securities which provide least protection against loss of purchasing power from price inflation. There is always an element of conflict in the defensive portion of an investment portfolio as long as there is inflation.

The investor usually resolves this conflict by redefining "defensive" to mean defense against financial risk. When this is done, the obvious choice of defensive investments is debt securities of high grade. These would ordinarily be government bonds, corporate bonds or municipals of A grade or better, or possibly high-grade mortgages. These investments are secure so far as principal and interest income are concerned. Prices of high-grade long-term bonds fluctuate because of changes in interest rates. But these securities are purchased because they provide constant interest income; they will probably be held for a long period of time. Staggering maturities so that some bonds mature every year or so guarantees the investor the ability to redeem some of these securities at par, thereby allowing a certain amount of cash to be obtained with no loss of principal. Buying the bonds of companies in several different industries—utilities, industrials, communications, and so on—provides additional diversification in this part of the portfolio. The same diversification, and probably more, could be obtained through purchase of shares of a mutual fund which invests in bonds exclusively.

Investors often attempt to protect themselves against loss of purchasing power in the defensive portion of their portfolio by purchasing securities which they hope will increase in price over the long run. High-grade convertible bonds and convertible preferred stocks offer the potential of price appreciation sufficient to overcome losses from price inflation. The investor can also follow a policy of purchasing lower grade bonds at discounts and holding them to maturity. In the spring of 1979 many highly rated, low-coupon bonds were selling at fairly large discounts and at yields greater than 10 percent. The current yield and potential price appreciation made these securities good hedges against moderate rates of inflation. Commercial and residential real estate rental revenues usually rise with inflation. These kinds of investments may provide defense against loss of purchasing power, but this protection is obtained at a price. Investors must not delude themselves into believing that this last-mentioned group of investments is "just as safe" as the first group. They are not. Compromise is always involved in attempts to obtain protection against financial and purchasing power risk with the same securities.

Aggressive investments. These may be defined as investments which have rather high potential for loss or gain. They are usually characterized by great market price fluctuation and a yield which may vary from year to year. Common stocks are the most obvious of these investments, but any investment having the above characteristics would qualify as "aggressive." For example, low-grade bonds, "risky" mortgages, raw land, mutual fund shares in performance funds, warrants and options, low-grade preferred stock, and certain convertible securities are all aggressive investments.

These investments are aggressive about financial, purchasing power, and market risk. They are usually of such low grade that interest rate risk is not much of a factor in determining their price. If the financial situation improves, prices will climb. This is most clearly seen when a company having bonds rated at B or Ccc, or a company having preferred stock that has passed dividends, becomes more financially able. Grades of these fixed income securities increase, and so do their prices. A buoyant market, with the majority of investors in an optimistic mood, may cause an even more rapid increase in prices.

Diversification is the most important single thing to emphasize when constructing the aggressive portion of an investment portfolio. Over the long run, average returns can consistently be obtained from risky investments only if enough different securities are held so that portfolio gains exceed losses. How many securities are enough to do this? There is no hard and fast rule, but the absolute number of different securities increases as the risk factor increases because risky securities imply widely fluctuating returns. Less risky securities, because returns are more constant, produce an average experience with less diversification.

Shares in a single mutual fund might provide adequate diversity of risk, if the investments of the fund are truly diversified. Industry funds, real estate funds, and other funds which stress concentration of investments will not normally meet the requirements for diversification. Shares of funds having broader investment policies might.

Directly held common stocks are usually diversified by purchasing securities of companies in several industries. It is not necessary to buy securities in all or most industries simply to obtain diversification. Adequate diversification is obtained when investments are made in enough different companies that economic downturns in one or two industries will not affect all securities. A general downturn will affect them all, unfortunately, but some less than others. So many different securities can be purchased in the attainment of diversification that they cannot be conveniently managed. As a rule of thumb, from 9 to 15 carefully chosen stocks are believed adequate to provide sufficient diversification for most investors. Diversification does not allow the investor to sit back and wait for profits; the portfolio still requires regular attention.

There is a school of thought which advocates purchases of just a few securities which are carefully chosen for excellent future performance. "Put your eggs in one basket and watch that basket" is the way one writer describes this strategy. We have no quarrel with this policy, but we do wish to correctly identify it as being *speculation* rather than *investment*. Concentration of investments has no place in the average investment portfolio because it introduces more risks than are usually acceptable. If the basket drops, *all* the eggs may break.

Security analysis and portfolio construction

Security analysis may be defined as the art (it is not a science) of examining individual securities, industries, and securities markets and assigning them probable future values. The professional security analyst is a person knowledgeable in accounting, finance, and economics. In addition, this person may also be trained in specific areas—geology, engineering, or chemistry, for example—if the investigation of companies using these types of technology is the analyst's primary assignment. Most professional analysts are not brokers. They work in the research departments of large brokerage houses, investment companies, financial institutions, or financial news services. Their efforts produce research reports and recommendations on the future prospects for various companies.

Analysts make use of both fundamental and technical analysis in their work, but most of their effort is of a fundamental nature. This usually means that the researcher thoroughly examines the history of the companies under study and is completely familiar with the way company earnings react to, changes in various economic conditions. The analyst usually follows the management of the company carefully and attempts to measure this important variable. Many analysts attend corporate annual meetings and often visit with the top management of companies in which they have an interest. Good researchers may know as much about a given company as some of the company's directors.

Many investors prefer to make investment decisions on their own, and there is much information available to aid them in their selections.[8] To make these choices intelligently, the investor does not need to be a security analyst. But one should be able to read the analysts' reports with understanding and with discrimination. One of the goals of this book has been to provide enough background information so that the average investor is prepared to make such decisions.

Most investors do not have to make these decisions completely on their own, however. They will be purchasing security investments through a broker, and most brokers are willing and able to help with the selection of securities. It is important to specify what the securities are supposed to do. This can be done by providing the broker with an outline of the entire investment program. The broker should not ordinarily be concerned with setting the goals of the program—this is the individual's responsibility.

Investors can delegate complete management of their investment portfolios to others. This service is not free. It varies in price with the

---

[8] Chapter 4 lists these sources of information and how to use them.

size of the portfolio and the amount of attention required, but for larger portfolios it is relatively inexpensive. The same service can be purchased by smaller investors, although the cost may be higher in relation to the value of the portfolio. A large number of banks and other financial institutions as well as firms and individuals offer financial management advice for a fee. In all but exceptional circumstances (a minor child or a senile person for example) the investor should have control over the setting and review of investment program goals.

Managing an investment portfolio

The job is not completed when an investment program has been set and investments purchased. Investors must periodically review their programs to see (1) if the stated goals of the program are still the most desirable ones, and (2) if presently held investments are the best ones to realize these goals. At a minimum the investor should review an investment program once a year, ideally more often.

First, one should consult with other affected persons and answer this question: Are the goals of this program as currently stated still desirable? Conditions may have changed over time, causing investment goals to be altered. Investors commonly go through three clearly identified phases in their investment programs, phases which coincide roughly with their age and earning power.

The average under-40 investor has many family responsibilities. Life insurance premiums use a large amount of money that might otherwise go for security investments. Buying, furnishing, and maintaining a house is expensive, as are children. The need for liquidity is likely to be great. It is often said that young people are most able to take large investment risks because they have so much time to make up their losses. "Buy risky common stocks and wait for them to rise." This simply is not true! The beginning investor usually has little money to invest, and this money may well be needed for emergencies. Furthermore, such persons may have limited time to spend managing investments. Young people are often *willing* to take great risks in their investment programs; such is the optimistic nature of youth. Cash budget and net worth calculations should help to temper this optimism by providing a realistic appraisal of the kinds and amounts of risk that can be accepted.

From roughly age 45 to retirement, the investor is usually more settled in a job, business, or profession. The children have either flown the nest or their departure is imminent. The house may well be paid for and all other foreseeable financial obligations covered. This person's cash budget may show large amounts available for investment. When these conditions prevail, and if the investor is willing to accept rather high risk, investment program goals will likely become much more aggressive, to build up resources for retirement. By this time the person may be more "savvy" about investments, and may have a broker or financial advisor whose past recommendations have proved sound and profitable.

This investor may seek very rapid portfolio growth through high-risk investments. Peformance mutual funds, options, convertible securities, and other risky investments may make up the bulk of this person's portfolio. Income property or part ownership in small businesses may be acquired. After all, such a person can afford to take investment risks. Since current income is probably high, it may be desirable to seek to lower income taxes by investing in municipal bonds, or to make contributions into a tax deferred retirement plan.

The third phase in an investment program occurs when retirement becomes imminent. At this point—hopefully before—the investor should begin some sort of estate planning. Investment program goals will probably shift back to a more conservative policy, and constant income from the portfolio will usually be important. It may become desirable to sell investments which require managerial effort—for example, rental properties and small businesses. But this differs with the individual. Some people do not want to retire completely, and proprietary investments may provide a desirable outlet for such a person's energy and time. Others do not want to be bothered about anything that smacks of business. They want to be completely retired. Retirement age investment plans are often stated contingently: As long as Ms. Smith lives, the program is of one type. In the event of her death or disability, the program changes to another. Regardless of what the personal preferences are, the goals of these programs should be stated just as specifically and as formally as before.

Reviewing individual investments. It is unlikely that the goals of an intelligently conceived investment program will be changed very often. The annual, semiannual, or quarterly review of the investment portfolio will normally concern itself with the question of whether the goals of the investment program are being realized. Is the defensive section of the portfolio really defensive? Are aggressive investments doing what they were acquired to do? Is the cash reserve producing as much return as possible under the circumstances?

This type of analysis must at one stage or another examine individual investments. Such examination usually requires that the performance of each stock, bond, savings account, or other investment be compared to similar investments having like grade and risk characteristics. The important question is always, "Can I replace any currently held investments with others that will make the total investment portfolio more efficient?" Efficiency in portfolio construction occurs when the goals of a program are met and return from the portfolio is maximized, given certain constraints.

Theoretically, this search for maximum portfolio yield is a continuing one which consists of comparing the historical and expected future yields of all investments one against another, after classifying them by their most important risk characteristics. In practice, complete comparison is impossible because of the large number of different investments involved. There has been a great deal of research on the construction of efficient portfolios, with computers used to make the many comparisons. But most of this work cannot yet be practically applied to the individual investor's problems of portfolio planning and evaluation.[9]

The individual investor can simplify the problem of investment program maintenance by identifying the poorest investments in the portfolio and replacing them with better ones. This does not maximize the efficiency of the portfolio, but it acts to constantly improve efficiency, and this may be the best that can be hoped for under the circumstances. Under this approach, the worst investments are periodically exchanged for others which better meet the requirements of the portfolio.

Two things to look for when seeking the "worst" investments are risk characteristics and returns. As an example, assume a portfolio which requires that $10,000 be invested in grade A or better corporate bonds. Several of the bonds have dropped in grade to Baa or lower. Although there will probably be a capital loss on the transaction, these bonds should be sold and replaced with securities of the required

---

[9] See William F. Sharpe, *Portfolio Theory and Capital Markets* (New York: McGraw-Hill, 1970) or Keith V. Smith, *Portfolio Management: Theoretical and Empirical Studies of Portfolio Decision-Making* (New York: Holt, Rinehart and Winston, 1971) for a detailed discussion of the theory of portfolio construction.

FIGURE 16–1
Recommended security selections

⮡⮡Hutton Portfolio Ideas

Investment Research Department

PORTFOLIO   IDEAS

APRIL   1979

I. PRESERVATION OF CAPITAL, HIGH CURRENT INCOME AND MODERATE GROWTH

Stocks in this category are most suitable for conservative investors to whom safety of principal, generous current income, and moderate capital appreciation potential are primary goals. All of these stocks on this list are rated "Fundamentally Undervalued" by our industry specialists. In addition, all are large, high quality issues of relatively low market volatility: common stock market capitalizations are over $500 million (except for utilities); S & P quality grades are A- or better (except for financial companies which are not rated); and beta coefficients (measures of historic market volatility) do not exceed 1.0 with the exception of Woolworth and Chase Manhattan. Finally, dividend yields are 5% or better, price-earnings multiples are less than 10 times, latest year's returns on invested capital are over 5%, and projected growth rates in earnings per share over the next five years are at least 5% on annual average.

This month we have raised our earnings estimates for Woolworth.

Company	4/6 Price	Div. $	Yield %	Mkt Value ($Mill)	S&P Qual[1]	Beta	Earnings Per Share($)[10] 1977A	1978E	1979E	Price/ 1979E	Return on Cap(%)[2]	Proj. % Growth[3]	Fund Value[4]	Tech Opin[5]	Rec
Chase Man. Corp.	32	2.40	7.5	926	NR	1.1	3.71	5.59	6.30	5.1	5.2	7	Und	Unfa	Buy
Exxon Corp.	54	3.60	6.7	21,924	A+	0.9	5.45	6.19	6.50	8.3	11.0	9	Und	Fav	Buy
Florida Pwr.&Lt.	27	2.08	7.7	1,122	A	0.9	3.81	4.54	4.65	5.8	7.6	6	Und	Neut	Buy
Gen. Telephone[12]	28	2.48	8.9	3,944	A	0.9	3.78	4.26	4.50	6.2	7.5	6	Und	Neut	Buy
Houston Inds.[11]	30	2.36	7.9	929	A	0.9	4.41	4.21	4.60	6.5	7.9	6	Und	Neut	Buy
Mobil Oil	76	4.80	6.3	7,657	A+	0.9	9.44	10.61	11.50	6.6	10.2	8	Und	Fav	Buy
Nabisco Inc.	24	1.50	6.3	763	A-	0.9	2.43	3.16	3.60	6.7	12.3	8	Und	Neut	Buy
Santa Fe Ind.	38	2.40†	6.3	923	A-	1.0	5.39	5.59	6.00	6.3	7.3	5	Und	Neut	Buy
Timken	58	3.50	6.0	563	A-	0.9	6.65	8.00	8.25	7.0	12.4	11	Und	Neut	Buy
United Telecomm.	19	1.44	7.6	1,130	A-	0.8	2.34	2.59	2.75	6.9	8.5	6	Und	Neut	Buy
Western Bancorp.	27	1.36	5.0	882	NR	0.9	3.34	4.55	5.10	5.3	9.0	8	Und	Neut	Buy
Woolworth	25	1.40	5.6	565	A-	1.1	3.03	4.00	4.60†	5.4	6.9	7	Und	Neut	Buy

The information above has been obtained from sources believed reliable but is not necessarily complete and cannot be guaranteed. Any opinions expressed are subject to change without notice. Neither the information presented nor any opinion expressed, constitutes a representation by us or a solicitation of the purchase or sale of any securities. From time to time, this corporation, its officers, stockholders, or members of their families may have a position in the securities mentioned. Copyright © E. F. Hutton & Company Inc. 1977.

FIGURE 16-1 (continued)

II. LONG-TERM GROWTH

Issues on this list are especially suited to investors to whom long-term capital appreciation potential is of paramount concern with current income of less importance.

All of these stocks are currently rated "Fundamentally Undervalued" by our industry specialists. All are high quality issues of at least reasonable size: S & P quality grades are A- or better (except for financial companies which are not rated). While in several cases dividend yields are modest and price-earnings multiples are higher than those on list I, in all instances at least some dividend is being paid, and in no cases do price earnings multiples exceed 15 times. Most important, however, latest year's return on invested capital all exceed 10%, and projected growth rates in earnings per share over the next five years are at least 10% on annual average in 10 out of 11 cases.

Sperry Rand and Time, Inc., still rated a "Hold", have been deleted from this list and now appear on Table IV. In addition, we have increased our earnings estimate for Melville Corp. and USLIFE.

Company	4/6 Price	Div. $	Yield %	Mkt Value ($Mill)	S&P Qual[1]	Beta	Earnings Per Share($)[10]			Price/ 1979E	Return on Cap(%)[2]	Proj. % Growth[3]	Fund Value[4]	Tech Opin[5]	Rec
							1977A	1978E	1979E						
Atlantic Richfield	64	2.80	4.4	6,546	A	0.9	5.76	6.60	7.50	8.5	10.4	12	Und	Fav	Buy
Boeing Company	66	2.00	3.0	2,674	A-	1.1	4.24	7.57	10.50	6.3	13.8	11	Und	Neut	Buy
Burroughs	72	2.00	2.8	2,652	A+	1.3	5.31	6.21	7.20	10.0	11.8	12	Und	Unfa	Buy
IBM	319	13.76	4.3	43,743	A+	1.0	18.30	21.20	26.00	12.76	21.2	12	Und	Neut	Buy
Melville Corp.	30	1.40	4.7	691	A	1.3	2.95	3.52	3.80↑	7.9	21.5	10	Und	Unfa	Buy
Missouri Pacific	53	2.80	5.3	724	A	1.0	8.01	8.83	9.25	5.7	10.8	9	Und	Unfa	Buy
Phillips Petroleum	36	1.20	3.3	5,066	A	1.1	3.37	4.61	4.40	8.2	13.8	12	Und	Neut	Buy
Rollins	18	0.60	3.3	223	A	1.4	1.86	2.00	2.30	7.8	16.8	15	Und	Fav	Buy
SmithKline	96	2.40	2.5	2,640	A	0.9	2.98	5.45	8.00	12.0	17.7	13	Und	Neut	Buy
Southern Nat. Res.	39	1.25	3.2	687	A	0.9	4.34	5.14	5.35	7.3	10.8	8	Und	Neut	Buy
USLIFE	24	0.64	2.7	465	NR	1.4	2.88	3.36	3.75↑	6.4	10.9	12	Und	Fav	Buy

---

MELVILLE CORP.'s (MES) — fourth quarter and full year 1978 results exceeded our expectations. Aided by the excellent retailing climate in the December quarter, Melville's profits rose by better than 21% to $1.53 per share from $1.26. Sales rose by approximately 20% in the same period. This strong quarter brought full year results to $3.52, a 20% gain over the $2.94 of the previous year. Our estimate had been $3.40 or better. Melville opened 382 new stores in 1978 and closed 104 units. As a result there were 3,812 stores in operation at year-end.

We look for continued good gains in the current year. Volume progress should be aided by an aggressive new store opening program with 405 new units planned and only 44 closings. The year has begun on a firm note with January volume ahead by better than 20%. We are increasing our 1979 projection and now estimate earnings at $3.75-$3.85 per share. This compares with our former projection of $3.70. The dividend was recently increased to $0.35 per share quarterly from the former rate of $0.29. The stock which sells at about 7 times our new 1979 earnings projection and which yields approximately 5% at current levels is again recommended as an attractive purchase for capital gains and for increasing income.

Source: E. F. Hutton & Co. Inc.

grade. If this is not done, the effect is to alter the risk characteristics of the portfolio.

Another example might be of a corporation whose stock had been purchased because of its anticipated growth in market price. Over the years the growth has taken place, and in every respect the shares have met the investment characteristics of the portfolio. It has recently become apparent that the rapid growth of the company has ended, management is now expected to concentrate upon paying large dividends (which had not been paid when the company was growing) and increasing earnings per share. These shares may continue to be excellent investments, especially from the yield standpoint, but their investment characteristics have changed. The shares may be held, but they should be reevaluated on the basis of their new investment characteristics. If there is no place in the portfolio for securities of their type, they too should be sold.

An easier type of replacement decision occurs when an investment has a poor performance record. Risk characteristics have remained constant as anticipated, but earnings have been lower than expected. The natural tendency is to continue to hold these securities in the hope that they will eventually justify their expectations and thereby prove that the investor's choice was correct. People generally do not like to admit that they have made a mistake, but these securities should be sold—and the losses taken—just as rapidly as securities whose investment characteristics have changed. Some investors overcome the psychological barrier to selling securities at a loss by requiring that the two, three, or four, worst performing securities be sold each time their portfolio is examined. By making this procedure a regular part of the management of the portfolio, it becomes less difficult to take losses.

Brokers and other financial advisors are helpful in identifying "poor performers" and securities to replace them. They have more time to examine investment data, and they may have better sources of information than the average investor. Figure 16–1 is an example of securities of several different types recommended by E. F. Hutton & Co. Each group is made up of securities which promise to provide the investor with different types of risks and returns. Many brokerage houses provide similar information. Obtaining investment advice is no problem; evaluating the worth of this advice is.

Advice from Bernard Baruch. This book has been written to answer the questions of *who, what, why, when, where,* and *how,* as they relate to personal investments. It is our hope that these topics have been covered well enough so that the reader can construct and intelligently manage an investment program. We further hope that the reader's curiosity has been whetted to the point where additional reading will be done in areas of interest. The Selected Readings at the end of each chapter identify books and other publications which we have found interesting and informative.

It seems entirely fitting to close by paraphrasing and expanding upon several rules of investing that were given by Bernard M. Baruch, a man who was a far more successful investor and speculator than your authors ever hope to be. Mr. Baruch was a self-made man, a person of rather modest origin who made a large fortune in the securities markets. He was a financier, businessman, diplomat, and presidential advisor. His advice is worth repeating and following.[10]

1. *Speculation.* Normally, this type of investing should be done by professionals or persons who can devote their full time and energy to it.

2. *Tips.* Be cautious of free "inside information" of all types; it is usually worth exactly what it costs.

3. *Obtaining information.* Before investing, examine the company as thoroughly as possible. Seek information on management, competition, and earnings possibilities.

4. *Timing of purchases and sales.* It is nearly impossible to buy at the bottom and sell at the top, so don't waste a lot of effort attempting to do so.

5. *Taking losses.* If you have made an error and purchased the wrong investment, take your loss as quickly as possible. No one is right all the time.

6. *Diversification.* Don't buy so many securities that you cannot watch them all carefully. Invest only in areas you know best, even at a sacrifice of diversification.

7. *Portfolio examination.* Periodically examine all investments to see that they are living up to your expectations. If they are not, sell them.

8. *Taxes.* Examine your income tax position so that you know when it is advantageous to take profits and losses.

9. *Cash reserve.* Don't invest all your funds. Keep some cash in reserve for safety and to take advantage of unforeseen opportunities.

---

[10] From Bernard M. Baruch, *My Own Story*, p. 254.

SUMMARY

Persons owning investments must manage them, at least to the extent of setting investment program goals. Designing an investment program is much like designing a house. In both cases, the end product should satisfy the needs of the owner in an efficient manner. The most important limitations on home building are usually the amount of money available, preferred location, style, and number of persons in the family. While these limitations—or constraints—are fixed at one point in time, they change as the life cycle of the family changes. Limitations on investment programs are often more subtle. The amount available for investment is of obvious importance. Need for insurance protection is also a key factor. Program goals may change several times during an investor's life. Other constraints deal with the ability and willingness of a person to accept risk and the need for certain levels of investment return.

An investment program is but one part of a *total financial plan* which should encompass all present and future financial aspects of an individual's or a family's existence. A good way to begin the formulation of this plan is by taking stock of how many assets the individual or family owns. This computation is the same as that for measuring the net worth of a business,

Assets less liabilities = Net worth

To determine how much money can be invested it is necessary to construct a *cash budget*. This budget closely resembles a business income statement.

Total income less total expenses = Surplus

It is this surplus amount that may be invested, after setting aside funds for a cash reserve and for insurance. Projecting net worth statements and cash budgets into the future provides an indication of future uses for and sources of cash. These schedules provide the basic data for constructing investment program goals.

Goals are statements of what a given investment program is supposed to do for an investor. Goals should be presented in writing and in a form specific enough to allow measurement of attainment. Constraints almost always act to reduce the potential profitability of a given investment program because they usually reduce the investor's ability to accept risk. Stating goals and constraints in writing makes it easier to identify possible areas of conflict between them.

One of the more important, and less obvious, constraints is the psychological one. Some people are ill-suited to investments which have high financial risk, even though their financial position and the goals of their investment program indicate that they should be able to accept such risks. Investments should not cause anxiety and frustration; if they do, they should be replaced with ones that are more suitable.

Estate planning is financial planning carried to the point of arranging for the passing on of the estate of the person or persons involved. Legal advice is usually needed for this type of financial planning because trusts and wills are involved.

Managing an investment program need not be a full-time job, but it requires some effort. Programs must be monitored to make certain they are "on track." Securities which no longer meet the requirements of the portfolio (financial risk, maturity, yield) must be replaced by others which do.

Brokers and other investment counsel are helpful sources of information on which securities to purchase, but the investor should remain responsible for the overall management of the program. At the very least the program's goals should be set by the investor.

PROBLEMS

1. *a.* Construct a personal net worth statement.
   b. Construct a personal cash budget for a period of either several months or several quarters.
   c. Identify amounts for a "rainy day" and insurance.
   d. How much do you have available to invest?
2. Construct an investment program for you or your family.
   a. State the goals of the program in specific terms.
   b. State any investment program contraints that would act to alter the above goals.
   c. How would you expect this program to be changed in five years? Ten years?

QUESTIONS

1. Why is it desirable to state investment program goals and constraints in writing?
2. Of what value is a *net worth statement?* How is such a statement prepared?
3. What is a family cash budget? How is it prepared?

4. What contribution should a broker make to the setting of a person's investment goals?
5. How does life insurance relate to the setting of investment goals?
6. "Building an investment program is much like building a house." What are the similarities and dissimilarities of these two tasks?
7. What are *psychological constraints*, and how do they affect investment program goals?
8. What is *estate planning*?
9. What are *aggressive investments*? *Defensive investments*?
10. What is a *security analyst*? How can this person's services help the investor?

SELECTED READINGS

Barnes, Leo, and Feldman, Stephen. *Handbook of Wealth Maximization.* New York: McGraw Hill, 1977.

Clay, William C. *The Dow Jones-Irwin Guide to Estate Planning.* Rev. ed. Homewood, Ill.: Dow Jones-Irwin, 1978.

Dixon, Lawrence W. *Wills, Death and Taxes.* Rev. ed. Totowa, N.J.: Littlefield, Adams, 1977.

Engel, Louis, and Wyckoff, Peter. *How to Buy Stocks.* 6th rev. ed. New York: Bantam Books, 1977.

Fisher, Lawrence, and Lorie, James H. "Rates of Return on Investments in Common Stocks." *Journal of Business,* July 1968, pp. 291–316.

Graham, Benjamin. *The Intelligent Investor: A Book of Practical Counsel.* Rev. 4th ed. New York: Harper & Row, 1973.

Stillman, Richard J. *Guide to Personal Finance.* 2nd ed. Englewood Cliffs, N.J.: Prentice-Hall, 1975.

Glossary of investment terms

Most terms have been entered in alphabetical sequence except those under the general headings of Bonds, Investment Companies, Preferred Stock, Risk, Savings Accounts, and Yield. Terms pertaining exclusively to these headings have been entered there as an aid to locating them.

The definitions in this glossary are as brief as it was possible to make them. Most terms are defined in greater detail and explained in the context of the investment environment in the chapters. Look to the index for a listing of pages containing references to each term.

Advisory service An organization offering information for sale to investors. This information may be financial data only, or it may consist mainly of buy and sell recommendations.

After market The market which develops after a security issue has been sold. Trading in an after market occurs on exchanges and over-the-counter. Also called secondary market.

Agency securities Securities sold by federal agencies such as the Federal Home Loan Bank, The Federal National Mortgage Association, and so on.

American depository receipt A negotiable security evidencing ownership in a block of foreign securities held in an American financial institution.

Amortization The payment of a debt through scheduled installments.

Arbitrage The act of buying securities in one market and immediately selling them, or equivalent securities, in a different market.

Asked price In security trading, the price at which a seller offers to sell securities.

Assets An accounting term which refers to something that is owned.

Auction market The trading procedure on the NYSE whereby specialists and brokers call out their bid and asked prices for stocks.

Authorized stock The number of shares of stock that are authorized in the company's charter. Seldom are all authorized shares outstanding.

Balance sheet An accounting statement which shows the amount of a company's assets, liabilities, and capital as of a given date.

Bar chart A type of graph commonly used in the securities industry to show the high, low, and closing prices of securities over a given time period, usually one day. Technical analysts often use such charts.

Bear market A declining market. A bull market is a rising market.

Best efforts An arrangement in which an investment banking firm agrees to sell an issue using its best effort. Any unsold securities will be returned to the issuer. See underwriting.

Bid price The price currently offered for a security.

Blue sky laws A general term which refers to all state laws which regulate the sale of investment securities.

Boiler room operation High pressure selling of stocks by telephone. Stocks sold are often of dubious value.

Bonds

Assessment bonds Bonds issued by municipalities which are to be repaid through assessments made against property, usually that which has benefited from the improvements financed by the bond issue.

Collateral trust bonds A debt issue secured by collateral such as other securities which are deposited with a trustee.

Convertible bond A debt security which is convertible at the option of the owner into a certain number of shares of common stock, usually of the company which issued the bond.

Coupon bonds Bonds which have interest coupons physically attached to the bond. As interest payments come due, coupons are presented to the issuer for redemption.

Debenture bond A debt security which has no specific collateral pledged as security.

Estate tax bonds Certain issues of long-term Treasury bonds which may be redeemed at their par value for payment of federal estate taxes.

Full faith and credit bonds A type of municipal debt security which has no specific collateral. The issuer promises to use its "full faith and credit," to obtain funds to pay interest and redeem this security.

Guaranteed bond A debt security whose payment of interest and principal is guaranteed by another company.

Indenture The agreement between the bond issuer and the owners of the bond which sets forth conditions of repayment and other legal obligations of the company.

Industrial development bond A bond issued by a city, state, or other unit to finance the building of industrial facilities. Interest on this security is normally not taxed.

Joint bond A debt security which is issued and guaranteed by two or more companies.

Mortgage bond A debt security which has a mortgage on a piece of real property as its collateral.

Municipal bond The name given to debt securities which are issued by states, local governments, or other nonfederal taxing agencies.

Revenue bonds Municipal bonds whose interest payments and the repayment of principal are to come from income generated by the facility which was financed through the issuance of these bonds. Common examples are bonds used to finance toll roads, sewers, bridges, transit systems, and so on.

Savings bonds Debt securities sold by the U.S. Treasury to individual investors. These are fully registered securities, usually sold in small amounts.

Serial bond A debt security issue which matures in relatively small amounts at periodic pre-stated intervals.

Yankee bonds Debt securities issued by international organizations and foreign governments or corporations. Interest payments and principal are paid in U.S. dollars.

Book value Accounting term which in general means the value of an asset as it is listed on the company's balance sheet. A stock's book value is determined by deducting all liabilities from a company's assets and dividing this amount by the number of common shares outstanding.

Broker An agent who handles buy and sell orders for securities or commodities for a commission charge. This person is often referred to as a registered representative, customers' representative, or account executive.

Bull market A rising market. A bear market is a declining market.

Call option A contract which gives its owner the right to buy a certain number of shares of stock, at a specific price, within a specified time period.

Call premium Compensation paid when a security is called.

Call protection A clause specifying the amount of time during which a company cannot call a security.

Callable A term which indicates that an issuer may repurchase, or call back, a bond or preferred stock which it has issued before the indicated maturity date.

Capital gain The profit obtained from selling a capital asset. Short-term capital gains result from the sale of assets held less than six months. Long-term capital gains result from assets held six months or longer.

Capital gain dividends Dividends paid by investment companies from the long-term capital gains they have realized from the sale of portfolio securities.

Capitalization Total amount of securities (bonds, preferred and common stock) issued by a corporation plus its retained earnings.

Capital stock Preferred and common shares which represent the ownership of a business.

Cash flow The amount of money available for reinvestment by a company over a given period of time. Cash flow is retained earnings plus noncash expenses such as amortization, depreciation, and depletion charges occurring during a given period of time.

Chartered Financial Analyst (CFA) Designation given to someone who has met rigid criteria establishing knowledge and experience in the field of security analysis.

Chicago Board Options Exchange (CBOE) An auction market located in Chicago on which call options of selected securities are sold. Such contracts are also sold on the AMEX and OTC.

Commercial paper Short-term, highly liquid, unsecured promissory notes of large financially secure companies.

Commission The amount paid to a broker or other agent to buy or sell securities.

Commission broker A member of the New York Stock Exchange whose function is to execute orders to buy and sell securities for the firm's customers.

Commodities Items having useful value. Active trading occurs mainly in foodstuffs and metals. See futures market.

Commodity trading The buying and selling of contracts which provide for future delivery of certain numbers of units of commodities at a certain time in the future.

Common stock Securities which represent the primary ownership interest of a corporation. The owners of these securities vote for the directors of the company.

Common stock dividends The amounts paid to the owners of common shares. Dividends are usually in cash, but they may be in stock, merchandise, or practically any other thing.

Common trust funds An arrangement to combine and invest funds which have been placed in trust for a bank to manage.

Competitive bidding A procedure in which investment bankers submit written bids to purchase new securities. This arrangement is used mainly for municipals and public utility issues.

Consolidated accounting statements Accounting statements which record the combined financial condition of a corporation and its subsidiaries.

Consolidated quotation system An electronic display of bid and asked prices and the number of shares wanted or available for listed and major OTC stocks.

Consolidated tape The integrated reporting of trades in listed stocks that occurred in all markets.

Constant ratio plans A formula investment plan under which an investor purchases and sells securities so that the investment portfolio contains a constant ratio of two or more types of securities.

Corporation charter The federal or state authority under which a company does business.

Cumulative voting A type of voting for directors of a corporation which enables minority shareholders to elect one or more directors.

Dealer Anyone who makes a market in a security by offering to buy or sell that security for his or her own account.

Deflation An economic condition in which the purchasing power of the dollar increases.

Depreciation A noncash accounting charge against earnings used to spread the cost of an asset over its useful life. Depletion and amortization are related terms.

Dilution A term which refers to the actual or potential reduction in earnings per share, asset coverage, and so on, that has occurred or may occur because of the issuance of new shares of stock or stock options.

Discount the amount that a bond or preferred stock sells below its par value.

Diversification The act of purchasing securities having different risk characteristics.

Dividend The amount paid to owners of common and preferred stock. It is usually paid in cash but may be paid in securities, in products, or practically any other thing.

Dividend reinvestment programs Plans whereby existing shareholders may automatically use dividends to purchase additional shares of stock in the company.

Dollar cost averaging A type of formula investment plan under which an investor purchases an equal dollar amount of the same security periodically.

Dow Jones Averages Measures of the average prices for groups of stocks—industrials, transportation, utilities, and a composite group.

Dow Theory A stock market theory which attempts to identify stock price trends shortly after they occur. Market price movements are divided into major or primary trends, secondary trends, and minor trends.

Dual listing The practice of listing a security on more than one stock exchange.

Earnings per share The amount of earnings obtained by a company over a given period of time for each share of common stock outstanding.

Economic analysis The examination of fundamental economic conditions (industrial production, gross national product increase, and so on) to determine the direction of stock prices.

Equipment trust certificate A debt security issued to purchase equipment, usually railroad rolling stock. The certificate is usually secured by a first lien on the piece of equipment which it was issued to purchase.

Equity security The common and preferred stock which evidences ownership of a corporation.

Ex-dividend A term which means "without dividend." A person buying stock which is selling ex-dividend will not receive the most recently declared dividend. Later dividends will be received if the stock continues to be held.

Ex-rights A term meaning "without rights." A person buying a security which is ex-rights does not receive the rights.

Flat quote A bond price quote which includes both interest and principal. (Bonds are often sold on the basis of a market price plus accrued interest.)

Floating rate notes Debt securities whose interest rate is not fixed but instead is adjusted over time in relation to the prevailing level of interest rates.

Floor broker A member of the New York Stock Exchange who executes orders to buy or sell securities. These individuals assist commission brokers by helping handle their orders during periods of heavy trading activity.

Formula investment plan An investment technique which makes timing of investment decisions automatically.

Fundamental analysis A type of security analysis which emphasizes the study of accounting information, management, market position, and other "basic" data to determine the value that a security should have. Also referred to as basic analysis.

Futures market The market for trading contracts to deliver foodstuffs and metals. Often called commodity futures market.

Government bonds The title usually used to identify debt securities issued by the federal government. Often called "governments."

Grading securities The activity of assigning a relative ranking to securities based on their exposure to a particular risk.

Holding company A corporaton which owns controlling interest in at least one but usually several other companies.

Housing condominiums An arrangement in which housing units are sold with an accompanying agreement for someone to manage the units and support facilities. They are considered to be security offerings.

Income statement An accounting statement which shows total revenues, costs, and profits of a firm realized over a certain period of time.

Inflation An economic condition in which the purchasing power of the dollar decreases.

Insider Someone who is closely connected with a publicly held corporation. Usually this means company officers, directors, and owners of 10 percent or more of the common stock, although the definition has been broadened in recent court actions.

Interest The amount paid for the use of debt capital. The "rent" on money.

Intermarket Trading System An electronic linkage of the six major U.S. stock exchanges' trades and quotations.

Intrastate offering The offering of new issues of securities which are registered in only one state and may only be sold to those residents.

Intrinsic value The value that a security "should have" based upon the company's assets, earning power, dividends, future prospects, and its management.

Investing The committing of money for the purchase of assets, primarily in the form of securities, based on careful analysis of risks and rewards anticipated over a period of one year or more.

Investment banking The business of assisting organizations in raising funds, usually by helping to sell new security issues.

Investment clubs Groups of individuals who invest small sums that have been contributed by each member. A major purpose of the organization is to educate the membership about investing.

Investment companies

Accumulation plans An arrangement under which a purchaser of mutual fund shares agrees to acquire more shares over a given period of time. There are two types of these plans, voluntary and contractual.

Automatic dividend reinvestment plan An agreement between a mutual fund shareholder and the fund, whereby dividends are automatically used to purchase additional shares of stock in the fund.

Balanced funds A mutual fund which has an investment policy of balancing its portfolio, usually between bonds and common stocks.

Bond and preferred stock funds Mutual funds whose investment policy is to invest in bonds and preferred stock.

Capital gains funds Investment companies which have the investment policy of seeking profits primarily through capital gains.

Closed-end investment company An investment company which has a fixed number of shares of stock outstanding. These shares are traded like other shares of common stock and are not redeemed by the investment company

Common stock funds Investment companies whose investment policy is to seek profits by investing in common stocks.

Dual purpose funds Closed-end investment companies which sell income shares and capital shares. Owners of income shares receive all the income that the company obtains through dividend and interest payments. Owners of capital shares receive the profit that the company obtains from capital gains.

Funding companies The name given to a new type of financial company which offers investors a package of mutual fund shares and life insurance.

Hedge fund A type of mutual fund which has an investment policy which seeks profits through purchase of risky investments, often using borrowed funds to increase profit potential.

Income funds A type of investment company which has as its main investment goal the obtaining of liberal current income for shareholers of the fund.

Investment company A generic term which includes mutual funds, closed-end funds, and the several other types of companies engaged in the business of investing the money of their shareholders in securities of other organizations.

Money-market funds Investment companies which invest in short-term, high yield, high grade, debt securities. These mutual funds offer investors the promise of high dividends and are seen as an alternative to savings accounts.

Mutual fund The popular name given to open end investment companies.

No-load mutual funds A type of mutual fund which does not

charge sales commissions. These funds may be readily identified in the lists of mutual fund quotations presented in the press because bid and asked prices are identical.

Open-end investment company An investment company which can increase its size through regular sale of additional stock.

Regulated investment company An investment company which has met the terms of the Investment Company Act of 1940 and has chosen to be regulated under this act.

Withdrawal accounts A type of mutual fund account which pays a certain amount of money periodically to the owner of the account. Most commonly used by retired persons as a source of income.

Legal investments A list of investments which may be purchased by insurance companies, banks, and other financial institutions which are regulated by state and federal governments. They are often called "Legal List Securities" and are invariably of the highest quality.

Leverage In finance, a term used to indicate a condition whereby earnings per share of common stock is either increased or decreased because of the use of senior securities in the capital structure of the company. A nonleveraged company would have only common stock in its capital structure.

Liabilities An accounting term which refers to the amounts that a company owes to others.

Lien A form of encumbrance which usually makes property security for the payment of a debt or discharge of an obligation.

Limit order An order to buy or sell a security at a stated price or better.

Liquidating value The value of a company if it ceased operations, sold its assets, and paid off all creditors.

Liquidity The ability to convert assets into cash with little money loss in relation to the original purchase price.

Listing A procedure which involves meeting certain requirements for having a security traded on a stock exchange.

Margin Involves the use of borrowed funds in security transactions. It is the down payment or owner's equity.

Marketability The ability to buy or sell a security quickly without driving the price up or down.

Market averages Measures of price levels for groups of securities.

Market letter A brief publication issued by brokerage firms and investment advisory services to provide investors with recommendations to buy or sell securities and other investment information.

Market order An order to buy or sell securities at the most advantageous price obtainable at the moment.

Market value The price at which a security can be sold.

Merger A form of consolidation under which two or more firms create a third company which is made up of the liabilities, assets, and capital of the original companies.

Monetary policy The policy of the Federal Reserve System as it pertains to the supply of money and interest rates.

Money market certificates Six month certificate savings accounts having variable rates which are tied to rates on U.S. Treasury securities and a minimum face value of $10,000.

Monthly investment plan A plan under which investors may purchase stock in small periodic amounts.

Moody's Investors Service A company which provides information for investors. It assembles financial data, assigns ratings to securities, and offers buy and sell recommendations.

Mortgage A lien against real property used to secure a debt.

NASDAQ Automated system developed by the NASD for reporting OTC trading information. System uses a central computer to tie dealers around the country together for instantaneous price quotes.

National Association of Securities Dealers (NASD) A self-regulatory body of broker dealer firms organized to develop, promote, and enforce standard procedures and ethical practices in the securities industry.

National Market System The newly developed electronic techniques for linking major U.S. securities markets for price quotations and transaction reporting.

National Quotation Bureau A company which publishes daily quotations on over-the-counter securities.

Negotiable The property of a security which allows it to be sold to another investor.

Negotiable order of withdrawal account An account at a savings institution which resembles a checking account except that instead of having funds transferred from the fund by check, a negotiable order of withdrawal (NOW) is used for the same purpose. It is legal to pay interest on NOW accounts.

Negotiated sale A procedure in which an investment banker and an organization seeking funds establish terms of a security issue which the investment banker will sell. See competitive bidding.

Net asset value A term commonly used to define the value of shares in investment companies. To determine net asset value, the market values of all outstanding securities are totaled. From this amount, all liabilities are deducted. Dividing the remaining amount by the number of outstanding shares provides net asset value per share.

Net worth An accounting term which defines net worth as assets minus liabilities. The net worth is the capital of the business.

New issue Securities being offered by an organization for the first time.

Notes Debt securities which are of shorter maturity than bonds.

Odd lot An amount of stock less than the standard trading unit of 100 or 10 units. A round lot of stock is usually 100 shares.

Offering price The price at which a person is willing to sell securities. Often referred to as the asked price.

Opportunity cost The rate of return from the best alternative investment. Stated another way, it is the highest rate of return that will not be earned if funds are invested in a specific investment. If one purchased bonds, and the next best investment were a savings account which yielded 5 percent, the opportunity cost of investing in the bonds would be the 5 percent foregone by not investing in the savings account.

Over-the-counter market Involves the buying or selling of securities without the use of stock exchange facilities. A vast communications network ties together security dealers in hundreds of cities for their OTC trading activities.

Paper profits and losses These are profits or losses which an investor has had because of fluctuating market prices in his or her investments, but which have not yet been realized by actually selling the securities.

Par value The dollar amount assigned to each share of stock by the corporate charter. This value has practically nothing to do with the market value of common shares; preferred shares may eventually be redeemed on the basis of their par value. In the case of bonds, par value is the amount the company pays upon maturity to redeem the security.

Point and figure charts A charting device used by technical analysts which records security price changes only.

Portfolio Securities which are held by an individual, trust, or institution.

Preemptive right The right enjoyed under common law by all shareholders to maintain their proportional share in the ownership of the company.

Preferred Stock

Convertible preferred stock Preferred stock which is convertible at the option of the owner into a certain number of shares of common stock, usually of the same company.

Cumulative preferred stock A preferred stock which has the feature of having unpaid dividends accumulate. These dividends must be paid in full before common stockholders can be paid any dividends.

Participating preferred stock A type of preferred stock which may receive higher than regular dividends if the company's earnings are high enough to warrant additional payment.

Preferred stock An equity security whose dividends must be paid before any dividend may be paid on the company's common stock. Preferred shareholders usually receive preferential treatment over common shareholders in case the company is liquidated. Preferred dividends are usually paid at a specified rate.

Premium The amount that a bond or a preferred stock sells above its par value. Also the amount by which the market value of a convertible security exceeds its conversion value.

Primary market The original sale of securities.

Private placement An arrangement in which an organization's securities are sold to a small number of investors as opposed to a public offering.

Prospectus A document issued to prospective purchasers of new securities. It describes the purpose and terms of the issue and the business and management of the issuer.

Proxy A legal document which gives one person the power to act for another. A proxy is also the name given to the person who acts for another. In investments the most common use of the proxy is when a company's management asks shareholders for their proxies to vote at the annual meeting.

Proxy statement Required information which is sent to stockholders along with a request for their voting proxy.

Public offering An arrangement in which securities are offered for sale to the investing public. This requires filing a registration statement with a regulatory body, whereas a private placement avoids this requirement.

Put option A contract which gives its owner the right to sell a certain number of shares of stock, at a specific price, within a specified time period.

Ratio analysis A method of analyzing the performance and financial position of a company through ratios of balance sheet and income statement data.

Real Estate Investment Trusts (REITs) Companies formed to invest in real estate. These companies usually use high financial leverage to increase shareholder profits. "Mortgage trusts" are so named because they invest mainly in mortgages. "Equity trusts" are those which specialize in the purchase and management of real property.

Real property Land and whatever is erected upon or growing on the land and all rights pertaining to the land.

Record date The date at which one must be registered as a shareholder on the books of a corporation to receive dividends or rights, or to vote on company matters.

Red herring A preliminary prospectus. Prepared when information about a proposed security offering is filed with the Securities and Exchange Commission.

Regional stock exchanges A name used for all the stock exchanges except the New York and American Stock Exchanges.

Registered security Any security which is registered in the name of the owner by the issuing company. These securities can be transferred only if they are endorsed by the registered owner. The opposite type is a "bearer" security: ownership is not registered and the bearer is presumed to be the owner.

Registered competitive market maker A member of the NYSE who trades for his or her account. This member does not deal with the public.

Registrar (of securities) A bank or trust company which countersigns securities to indicate their validity.

Registration A procedure required by various security laws for publicly held corporations, stock exchanges, and security firms which causes them to file data with regulatory bodies.

Regulation A The Securities and Exchange Commission regulation that exempts corporations from a full registration procedure in the case of a public offering of securities. The maximum amount that can be raised under this exemption is $1,500,000.

Regulation Q The Federal Reserve Board regulation which sets the maximum rates member banks may pay on savings deposits.

Regulation T The Federal Reserve Board regulation which sets the maximum amount of credit which may be granted by brokers and dealers for the purpose of purchasing securities.

Regulation U The Federal Reserve Board regulation which sets the maximum amount of credit which may be granted by a bank to customers for the purpose of purchasing securities.

Relative strength ratio A measure obtained by dividing an industry stock price index by the market stock price index. The ratio indicates relative price performance.

Reorganization A procedure under which the courts create a successor corporation from a bankrupt corporation.

Retained earnings The amount of capital that has been reinvested in the company.

Right An option to purchase a specified number of shares of a new issue of securities at a de-signed price. This option is usually of short duration.

Rights offering An offering of new securities which is made to existing stockholders. The number of new securities which may be purchased is usually proportional to the number of old securities that were held on the date of record of the rights offering.

Risk

Financial risk The uncertainty of future returns from a security because of changes in the financial capacity of the organization that issued the security. Sometimes called business risk.

Interest rate risk The uncertainty of future returns or security prices due to changes in market rates of interest.

Market risk The uncertainty of future prices because of changes in investor attitudes.

Political risk Uncertainty of future returns from a security because of political developments such as revolution, currency devaluation, nationalization of facilities, and so on.

Purchasing power risk The uncertainty of the purchasing power of future returns due to changes in the price level.

Social risk Uncertainty of future returns from a security because of shifts in public attitudes. This may involve changing consumption patterns, pollution, population control, and so on.

Round Lot A unit of trading securities on exchanges. In most cases, it involves 100 shares or one $1,000 par value bond.

Savings Accounts

Bonus accounts Savings accounts paying a higher than normal rate of interest.

Insured deposits Deposits in banks and other financial institutions which are insured by the FDIC, FSLIC, or any other federal-sponsored or state-sponsored insuring agency. If the institution fails, deposits are insured against loss.

Multiple maturity time deposits A type of savings deposit which has limited withdrawal privileges and pays a higher than normal rate of interest.

Mutual savings bank A financial institution which accepts deposits from savers and reinvests most of these deposits in mortgages. These institutions differ from commercial banks mainly in the fact that they cannot offer checking accounts to depositors and that they make relatively few personal and business loans.

Notice account A type of savings account which requires the depositor to give notice of intent to withdraw funds. These accounts usually receive a premium rate of interest.

Saving and loan company A financial institution which sells saving shares to investors, paying interest or dividends on each saving share.

Time certificates of deposit Also called Certificate of Deposit, or abbreviated CD. A time deposit which is evidenced by a certificate rather than a passbook or any other device. These accounts are not redeemable until the certificate matures. Certificates may be negotiable.

Time deposits—open account A type of savings account into which a depositor may place funds at any time. A written request is necessary to withdraw money from this type of account.

Secondary market The trading of securities after they have been originally sold in the primary market. This includes both stock exchange and OTC transactions.

Securities Act of 1933 Its main provision requires issuers of securities to disclose relevant information about the organization and its offering to the investing public.

Securities and Exchange Commission (SEC) The federal agency which administers various federal acts and regulates the securities industry.

Securities Exchange Act of 1934 Its main provision regulates activities for trading securities in secondary markets.

Securities Investor Protection Corporation (SIPC) A nonprofit company organized to insure investors against loss of up to $100,000 per account when their brokerage firm fails.

Security A certificate evidencing ownership or debt.

Selling group A group of brokerage firms who assist underwriters of an issue by helping to sell it.

Short interest A term used to indicate the number of futures contracts or lots of stock that have been shorted.

Short sale A way that investors may profit from declining security prices. In expectation of lower prices, securities are borrowed and sold, and the loan is to be later repaid by reimbursing the lender with the same number of securities as were borrowed.

Sinking fund Required payments may by a company to retire a bond or preferred stock issue gradually before maturity, or to provide money to retire the issue at maturity.

Specialist A member of a stock exchange who is responsible for maintaining a fair and orderly market in one or more securities. Specialists sometimes act as dealers by buying and selling for their own accounts. At other times they act as agents or brokers' brokers.

Speculation The act of investing so as to assume relatively high short-term financial and other risks in the hope of better than average gains.

Standard & Poor's Corporation (S&P) A company which publishes financial data on organizations which have issued securities. It also rates securities and offers advisory services.

Stock dividend A dividend which is paid in securities rather than in cash. A dividend is usually in additional shares of the issuing company, but it may be in shares of another company.

Stock split Increasing the number of outstanding shares of a corporation by granting existing shareholders more shares of the company in proportion to their original holdings. A person owning 10 shares of stock which were split 3 for 1 would own 30 shares after the split.

Stockholders' equity An accounting term which refers to the amount of capital that has been invested in a firm by the equity shareholders.

Stop order An order to buy or sell a security after the price reaches a certain stated level.

Straddle The action of combining a put and a call option on the same security.

Street name A term for recording the ownership of securities in the name of a brokerage company rather than in the name of the legal owner.

Striking price The price at which an option contract holder may purchase or sell the optioned security.

Subchapter S corporation A domestic corporation which has only one class of stock and no more than 10 shareholders. If all shareholders agree, the corporation's income may be taxed as income of the individual shareholders rather than as income of the corporation.

Subordinated debentures A debt security whose legal claim for payment of interest and repayment of principal is subordinated to that of another security.

Syndicate A temporary association of two or more persons formed to carry out some specific business venture. Examples are syndicates formed by underwriters to sell an issue of securities and those formed to develop large-scale real estate projects.

Tax avoidance Managing of financial matters so as to lower taxes as much as is legally possible.

Tax evasion Not paying taxes owed. This is illegal.

Tax exempt bond Debt securities of states, cities, and other public authorities, the interest of which is exempt from federal income tax.

Tax free dividend income Dividend income which is partially or wholly free from federal income taxes.

Technical analysis The analyzing of supply and demand factors in security markets to determine the direction of security prices.

Third market Over-the-counter trading of listed securities. Involves large orders.

Trading posts Locations on the floor of an exchange where stocks are bought and sold.

Transfer agent The person or firm who accounts for the changes of ownership in a company's shares and makes certain that shares redeemed and issued are genuine.

Treasury bills Debt securities having maturities of one year or less. These securities are sold at a discount by the U.S. Treasury.

Treasury stock Stock issued by a company and then later reacquired and held by the company. No dividends are paid to treasury stock nor may it be voted.

Trend bucker A company whose sales and earnings do not decline when the general economy recedes.

Trustee Someone who holds the security for a bond issue and who carries out other duties specified by the indenture. Also someone who undertakes administrative obligations under a trust agreement.

Turnaround A situation in which a company's declining sales and/or earnings are reversed.

Underwriting An arrangement in which an investment banker buys securities from an issuing organization in the hope of later selling them to investors.

Unit trust A trust which is constructed in such a way that portions (units) may be held by different persons. Some investment companies are organized as unit trusts.

Variable ratio plans A formula investment plan under which an investor changes the ratio of certain types of securities in a portfolio depending upon whether the stock market is relatively high or relatively low.

Warrant An option to purchase a certain number of securities at a certain price over a period of time which is usually longer than that allowed for exercise of rights.

Wash sale The sale and repurchase of substantially identical securities within a 30-day period. Losses from such transactions are not legal deductions from income when reporting federal income taxes.

Yield

Coupon yield The yield in percentage terms that is stated on the face of a bond. It can be determined by dividing the annual interest payment in dollars by the par value of the security and converting this figure into percentage terms.

Current yield The yield of a security determined by dividing its annual interest or dividend payment by the current market price and converting this figure into percentage terms.

Yield   Dividends or interest paid on a security expressed as a percentage of either the current price, the purchase price, or the par value of the security.

Yield to maturity   A yield calculation which takes into account the relationship between the security's maturity value, time to maturity, current price, and coupon yield. This calculation allocates bond premium or discount over the life of the security and is the most accurate type of yield calculation.

Index

This book has been set in 10 and 9 point Melior, leaded 3 points. Part numbers are 27 point Melior bold and part titles are 20 point Melior. Chapter numbers are 52 point Melior and chapter titles are 18 point Melior bold. The size of the type page is 26 by 44 picas.

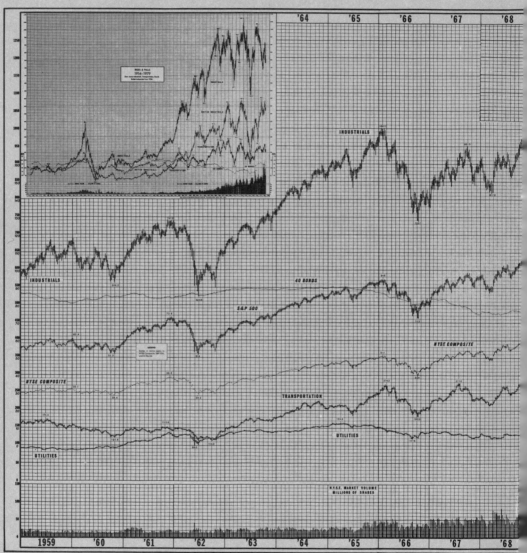

Courtesy of Securities Research Company, 208 Newbury St., Boston, Mass. 02116